Popular Alienation:

A Steamshovel Press Reader

Popular Alienation:

A Steamshovel Press Reader

Edited by Kenn Thomas

EX LIBRES
N D LAMB

1995

IllumiNet Press

Library of Congress Cataloging in Publication Data

Popular alienation : a Steamshovel press reader / edited by Kenn Thomas.
        p.   cm.
    Includes bibliographical references.
    ISBN 1-881532-07-0
    1. United States—Politics and government—1945-1989.
    2. United States—Politics and government—1989.
    3. Conspiracies—United States. I. Thomas, Kenn, 1958- II. Steamshovel press.

E839.5.P67 1995
973.92—dc20   95-34668

Cover art by Martin Cannon

IllumiNet Press
P.O. Box 2808
Lilburn, Georgia 30226

10 9 8 7 6 5 4 3 2 1

Printed in the United States of America

Acknowledgements

Steamshovel Press owes its greatest debt to the patience of Beth, Sara and Simon, the editor's wife and two children. Trips to the post office, time on the phone, face-to-face and radio interviews, writing, production and distribution of the magazine all inevitably make cuts into quality time with the family, time already intruded upon by the day job as well—but the catching up is always fun.

Steamshovel's second greatest debt is to Jim Martin, CEO of *Flatland* Books and *Flatland* Magazine. Jim not only does the graphic design for *Steamshovel,* but he has provided it with much sage wisdom and guidance through the tangled web of zine production and distribution. He also came up with the title of this book. Jim has been a gracious host during my visits to San Francisco and his shop in Mendocino. He deserves large credit for encouraging many writers and researchers to pursue their work, giving honest assessments of the available *ouevre*, and providing a means to pursue research—all with a money-back guarantee.

The third nod goes to Ron Bonds, the proprietor at IllumiNet, for making this volume possible in the first place. Ron is the logical successor to such alternative journalists as Richard Shaver, Penn Jones or, perhaps more appropriately, Harold Weisberg, in that his wares primarily come in the form of quite remarkable books. This includes not only what IllumiNet offers through its book catalog, but the line of obscure titles it publishes utilizing the ufological public record and research more completely than virtually any other publisher. *Steamshovel* has received no shortage of good business advice from Ron as well.

Particular computer problems posed by the production of *Popular Alienation* were resolved by Joe Rottman. *Steamshovel Press* also needs to thank Joyce Bauer at Missourian Publishing for her great help in getting the magazine printed.

A long list of correspondents and acquaintances deserve much credit for allowing me to bounce ideas off them, supplying research and leads and discussing the broader implications of what gets printed in *Steamshovel*. These include Len Bracken, Tom Brown, David Hatcher Childress, Tom Christopher, Loren Coleman, Jim Cregan, Dr. James DeMeo, X. Sharks DeSpot, Roy Dripps III, Dave Emory, Happe, Wayne Henderson, Bob Heyer, Al Hidell, Alex Horvat, John Judge, Jim Keith, John Kimsey, David K.M. Klaus, Louis Krasser, G.J. Krupey, Jenny Ledeen, Roy Lisker, Sean Mansfield, Judy Miller, Ray Nelke, Mark Oakes, Preston Page, Adam Parfrey, Keith Preston, Brian Redman, Steve Richardet, Duncan Roads, Sherman Skolnick, C.D. Stelzer, Jonathan Vankin, David Vincent, Alfred Vitale, Wendy Wallace and Robert Anton Wilson. Time, space and a poor memory makes this list extremely abbreviated and I apologize in embarrassment for the names that inevitably got left off. Everyone who writes to or for or otherwise interacts with *Steamshovel* contributes to what Jim Martin might call a synergistic whole greater than the sum of its parts and deserves great credit and appreciation. I admire each of these people individually and marvel at their collective work-democratic spirit.

"Recent history is the record of a vast conspiracy to impose one level of mechanical consciousness on mankind..."

—Allen Ginsberg

What's Inside

Introduction

Allen Ginsberg predicted the Kennedy assassination. Readers can find this in *Journals Early Fifties Early Sixties,* a volume of Ginsberg's personal writings produced by Grove Press in 1977 and edited by Gordon Ball. The prediction appears in an entry entitled "Dream, Oct. 31, 1959":

"Depression, couldn't get to typewriter after running round town on Burroughs business—contract maybe to transfer from Wyn Co. to Avon to get him money—sat & read *Look* mag at Dr's office, 14 St. accompanying my brother to his checkup—all about 1960 presidential races, Kennedy's politicianings & shiftiness—He has a hole in his back. Thru which Death will enter." (p. 111)

According to the magic bullet theory, the back wound traveled up and out JFK's throat, despite being shot from the elevated position of the sixth floor of the book depository. *Steamshovel Press* readers know that JFK's death, indeed, may have also entered through the back, but it did not exit through the throat. Arlen Specter, who authored the convoluted and contradictory magic bullet theory, at this writing has begun his own campaign for the White House.

Ginsberg's weirdly precise premonition gets mentioned in the introduction to this anthology in part to deflect criticism that the disparate elements comprising *Steamshovel Press*—political assassinations, the Beats, UFOs, plagues, plots and conspiracies—have no relationship. It also appears because the earliest inspiration for *Steamshovel* began during a week-long party Allen Ginsberg threw at the University of Colorado in Boulder in 1982. In observance of the 25th anniversary of the publication of Kerouac's *On The Road,* Ginsberg and his colleagues at the Naropa Institute organized a conference of lectures, workshops and debates by the likes of Tim Leary, Abbie Hoffman, William Burroughs, Gregory Corso, Diane DiPrima, Peter Orlovsky, Anne Waldman and the rest of the familiar crew at the Jack Kerouac School of Disembodied Poetics.

I met long-time *SP* correspondent and contributor Roy Lisker at that conference, had to rescue him, in fact, from the Denver Greyhound Bus security office. The Greyhound gendarmes hauled Lisker off after he demonstrated his unusual form of chanting poetry to people in the terminal awaiting their ride into Boulder. The gendarmes could not have paid a greater compliment, especially considering that for many years they had no doubt become accustomed to the creative and unusual behavior of those attracted to the Kerouac school. The bust served as enough of a credential for me to offer Lisker crash space at the U. of C. dorm building where I stayed for the week.

We spent some of the week comparing notes. At the time, I did free-lance writing for local and regional papers and also worked as the rock critic for St. Louis' old *Globe-Democrat* newspaper. Lisker published, and still publishes, a photocopied 8x10, folded-over newsletter of commentary, poems and essays entitled *Ferment!* While I dutifully attended beatnik workshops, he spent much of the conference trying out his chants on the masses, which had assembled more to see the counter-culture celebrities and partake of the beach acid and other inebriants. The conference participants did put on quite a show. Abbie Hoffman and Tim Leary had perhaps their greatest showdown; Gregory Corso publicly razzed several fellow Beat icons; panels plucked the memories of honored Beat veterans to verify rumors about their lives and examine their legal history; Robert Franke screened his movies, *Pull My Daisy* and *Cocksucker Blues*; David Amram did a remarkable concert; a falling-down drunk Chogyam Trungpa nevertheless let loose with a wise Buddhist homily and hand-signal; and Ginsberg introduced a new song entitled "Birdbrain" with a new-wavish band called the Gluons.

Identifying the conference participants as "heros of the 60s", or even as Beats, hippies, hipsters or "the counter-culture" is useful only to a media that needs a cubbyhole or an intelligence agency looking for something to infiltrate. In fact, Abbie Hoffman made the point there that the word "beatnik" originally served as a Red smear, from the Soviet Sputnik satellite. The suffix "nik" actually helped non-Beat America to reduce the whole generation to a *Mad Magazine*-type lampoon, with a parade of peaceniks, no-goodniks, etc. Although some of the personalities that participated in the Kerouac conference have since died—Abbie chief among them—Ginsberg and company still provide a powerful voice of opposition to crushing corporatism, mindless consumerism, over-industrialization—the culture at large. I make this observation despite the fat book contracts enjoyed by some of the Beat elite, the rock'n'roll retinues and rumors of their own links to the CIA. There is conspiracy fodder here yet to explore, but a deconstruction of the Beats as sell-outs to the status quo seems as fruitless as boxing them in as relics of a particular decade. The *On The Road* week served as an inspiration, a gift of manic energy that kept on giving for many in attendance for quite some time. With me, it later re-surfaced in the form of *Steamshovel Press*.

The enormity of celebrity did seem to stand between the Beats and their progeny that week, however. The conference gave ample opportunity for unknown poets and non-poets to vent their spleen at open mikes, and the Beat celebrities made themselves available after workshops and inter-mingled often with their students. They were up on a pedestal, however, and even Lisker's chants could not find a spot on the roster of the poetry competition made up entirely of known Beat celebs. Alienated even from this group, only the small-group open mikes—and maybe a future issue of *Ferment!*—remained for the creative expression of others. I attended a few of these, regarding a well-conceived rant as a thing of beauty as I do, and discovered some but surprisingly few people ranting about conspiracies. Of all the sub-cultures that *Steamshovel* taps into—at UFO conferences, JFK symposia, militia gatherings, New Age bazaars—I have re-discovered many times that literary gatherings, poetry readings, are the poorest opportunities to sell copies of the magazine. Although interested, poets lean toward self-absorption—and usually have their own book to push.

I did little with the lessons learned at the Kerouac conference until an interview with Ram Dass in 1988 failed to find publication in the St. Louis press, where the philosopher/psychologist even had an appearance it could help promote. The interview took the form of a *Ferment!*-sized newsletter circulated among the handful of people in town who would have an interest. Although it was a small, photocopied zinelet, it had enough substance to send to book publishers to entreaty them for books to review in future issues. The first three issues of *Steamshovel Press* served that function, in addition to finding a home for the conversation with Ram Dass, as well as a later one with Imamu Amiri Baraka that also did not seem to hold the interest of the local media. Baraka's connection to the Fair Play for Cuba Committee in New York (Oswald was the only member of the New Orleans chapter) provided *Steamshovel*'s first push away from literary themes to conspiracy theory.

As the magazine's mission evolved and production values improved, *Steamshovel* no longer made these available as back issues and their content is not included in this volume.

Popular Alienation begins with *Steamshovel Press #4*. By the time of the third issue of the "old" *Steamshovel*, energies were waning in the conspiracy research community. Mae Brussell died in 1988 and her heirs embroiled themselves in combat over the disposition of her legacy, which included a vast library that still has no public access. Bob Banner, who had long published a journal/magazine named *Critique*, the only regular newsstand outlet for conspiracy research and scrubbed-up rants, abandoned the effort in favor of joining an interpersonal self-development group. When a friend with access to printing equipment offered free printing allowing *Steamshovel* a larger format and print-run, it seemed like a good opportunity to shift its focus from literary angst to alienation central, another nebulous underground sometimes cubbyholed by the media as "conspiracy theorists."

In fact, the media often pairs the word "conspiracy" with the word "theory" in much the same way as the word "Beat" was wedded to the suffix "nik," as a means to diminish the assertions of certain writers and researchers. Readers will discover, however, that while *Steamshovel* contributors do offer theories, they carefully document them with verifiable facts and references when possible, while not shying away from logical conclusions where smoking guns have long been buried. *Steamshovel* also includes ample doses of satire, lampoon and self-lampoon (particularly in *SP4*) and critiques of political, religious, scientific and computer cultures. The magazine makes no attempt to reconcile the multiple points of view, to make the research community speak in a single voice, or to fit what it prints into a particular left-right political mold. If I had to select a favorite among particular philosophical paradigms discussed in *Steamshovel Press*, I would choose Vladimir Terziski's bulletin board model from chapter 6. The magazine, however, keeps its editorial voice as silent as it can, attempting to give an unfiltered voice to the contributors—a commitment to individual insight and expression that it picked up from the Kerouac conference. *Steamshovel Press* contains rants, to be sure, but rants of erudition and documentation, not "theories" that have no basis in reality.

Enough copies of *Steamshovel #4* sold to raise money for *SP5*, a full-size, 60-64 page newsprint, newsstand magazine that prints the gamut of conspiracy-related material, and each issue has sold enough copies to produce the next issue and allow some room for growth. Since *SP10*, the magazine has included a glossy cover; the current issue includes the Mark of the Beast, the UPC code; circulation figures have improved by ten times since *SP4*—although by a definition that would include *Time* and *Newsweek,* "popular" may not be the best word to describe interest in the magazine, save *among* the alienated (it did make the first of *Factsheet Five*'s Top Ten zine lists). Although attention has been paid to it by such mainstream sources as *The Smithsonian*, the *Washington Post* and *USA Today, Steamshovel Press* remains a part of the marginal press, not available in bookstores where the Conspiracy prevails.

Steamshovel Press does have seventeen distributors in seven different countries, however, in lieu of the magazine wholesalers that prefer to shove such sham corporate journalism as *Time* and *Newsweek* down the throats of the discerning newsstand reader. *Steamshovel* also deals directly with bookstores interested in stocking more than fifteen copies on consignment. If readers of *Popular Alienation* have had trouble finding *Steamshovel,* please complain to bookstore management. They can pick up *Steamshovel* from the following partial list of distribution services: AK Distribution (Scotland and San Francisco); Arcturus Books; Armadillo and Company; Counter Productions (England); Daybreak Distributors; Desert Moon (505-474-6317; xines@nets.com); Fine Print (512-452-8709; mags@bga.com); Marginal (Canada; 705-745-2326); Network Distributors Limited (New Zealand); New Leaf (404-699-7213); News Agents Direct (Australia); Don Olson Distribution; Tower Records and Magazines; Ubiquity (718-875-8047); Zed Distribution (Canada; 519-570-2196).

I initially made the mistake of telling some of the writers that *Steamshovel* intended eventually to pay its contributors with coin of the realm. As the complications of zine economics interfered with that goal, only two contributors gave up in frustration. One of them actually sued me and was laughed out of court. The contributions of both have been left out of the current volume. Otherwise, *Popular Alienation* contains the complete content of issues 4-11 of *Steamshovel Press* (sans the letters pages, which were cut for space reasons), plus a virtual issue, #13 (Chapter 9). *Steamshovel* subscribers should note that their subscriptions have been bumped up a number and the delivery of issue #14 will arrive at the time #13 would have otherwise.

Paying money to contributors remains one of *Steamshovel*'s great ambitions, and it even has paid small sums for research and one contribution. For the most part, however, readers will find here research and writing that has been done only for the sake of revealing hidden truths, regaling others with satire or enlightening them with explorations of the intellectual and spiritual dimensions of conspiracies, or just bringing a new perspective to a larger community. The only guaranteed recompense for the work is three contributor copies. Circumstances might change by the time potential contributors read this volume, but this is the bottom line that all such contributors should understand. They should also know that contributions work best when limited to 3500-5000 words and have been submitted in IBM format. These technical requirements should not discourage writers, however. Scribble a rant on a banana peel, and *Steamshovel* will at least consider it for publication—as long as the sources check out.

Another connection between the Beats and JFK: someone named Bill Burroughs ran the concession stand at the Texas Theater when Oswald walked in. That qualifies only as a coincidence. When the police followed, this Burroughs directed them—perhaps inadvertently—to the balcony, although Oswald had gone in on the ground floor. That would qualify as a synchronicity, if one thinks that this is what *the* Burroughs might have done, give a little breathing space to the hapless patsy in his deadly encounter with a Nova-like mob. Arthur Koestler explains synchronicity as serial coincidences that have meaning, an acausal principle that presents a real challenge to the study of physics. Koestler's 1971 book, *The Case of the Midwife Toad*, which documents the story of how biologist Paul Kammerer (who counted Wilhelm Reich among his students) articulated the concept, which Kammerer called seriality, before a conspiracy to sabotage his work drove him to suicide. Jacques Vallee has gone on at length in his 1979 book, *Messengers of Deception*, about the notion that personal computer technology, through things like boolean searches, utilizes synchronicity as a functioning principle. Vannevar Bush, a scientific advisor to Truman, predicted the rise of personal computers in 1947 in an essay entitled "As We May Think". Bush is also one of the alleged signers of the infamous MJ12 documents. Like any good conspiracy theory, these connections require some participation and judgement from the reader (maybe the real Burroughs would have sent the police right to Oswald), allow little room for closure (unless the reader is prepared to confess to a full understanding of Jacques Vallee) and, hopefully, like much of the present volume, stretch boundaries of understanding.

Kenn Thomas
Editor/Publisher
Steamshovel Press
April 18, 1995
St. Louis, MO

1

Steamshovel Press #4, 1992

Tales of Abbie Hoffman: Jack Hoffman Interviewed

"We were young, we were reckless, arrogant, silly, headstrong...and we were right! I regret nothing."
—Abbie Hoffman's last public words
Vanderbilt University, April 4, 1989

The publication of *Live This Book* by Theodore Becker and Anthony L. Dodson (The Noble Press, 1991, $8.95) occasioned the following interview with Jack Hoffman, brother of the late Yippie, Abbie Hoffman. *Live This Book* is the first book since Abbie Hoffman's death to deal with the legacy of his life. It's a slim volume that restates the obvious about Abbie, that he was an engaged and gregarious political critic with a tremendously insightful sense of humor and a flair for guerilla theater. But the book also characterizes Abbie Hoffman as someone who "matured" into an ecological outlook similar to that of the Green Party in Europe, hence the subtitle, "Abbie Hoffman's Philosophy for a Free and Green America."

That approach covers the two most successful aspects of Abbie's last years, cleaning up the riverways in the Hudson Valley and stopping the CIA from recruiting on college campuses in western Massachusetts. Becker and Dodson fall short of calling these successes Abbie's crowning achievements, but the book is revisionist enough to relegate guerilla theater to the dustbin of Abbie's baby days and gives short shrift to his essence, the style and substance of which is certainly not limited to courtroom battles. Abbie Hoffman inspired a generation to say what it felt and do what it wanted and not to be bullied by oppressive social and political constraints.

Live This Book also inaccurately depicts Abbie's lack of repentance in his final years and ignores the plans he had when he died, including reprinting of his '60s works, like *Steal This Book,* and his research involving the 1980 October Surprise of the Reagan-Bush campaign. Although the authors rightly admit that it would have been impossible for Abbie himself to easily summarize his own political philosophy, there was nothing enigmatic about the fact that, to the end, he was a fuck-the-system hell-raiser. Since *Live This Book* seems intended for undergraduate political science classes, it is perhaps small wonder that it transforms that philosophy to one of "changing the system from within."

Jack Hoffman wrote the introduction to *Live This Book,* and although flattered by the portrait it paints of his brother, he shares some misgivings about it. Questions still surround Abbie Hoffman's death and part of brother Jack's crusade in promoting this book has been to assuage suspicions that it was a murder and to convey the conviction that manic depression caused Abbie Hoffman's suicide. But Abbie was no stranger to conspiracy theories, and neither is Jack: both had researched the secret machinations of the October Surprise long before it became political fodder. Veteran peace activist Dave Dellinger believes Abbie Hoffman was killed, and real questions remain: is it possible to lift another hundred phenobarbitals after swallowing a handful or so? Was Huey Newton's death in the same month as Abbie's merely a coincidence? Are ex-CIA agents Philip Agee and John Stockwell just being cranky when they talk about U.S. government pogroms of domestic assassination?

Jack Hoffman has answered these questions to his satisfaction, although he's not so sure if Abbie's October Surprise article is an important posthumous salvo from Abbie aimed at the Bush administration or a simple rifling through of information that was already public. The questions about Abbie's death still get asked, however, partly because Abbie might have asked them himself. But perhaps it is presumptuous to expect Jack Hoffman to have his brother's sense of confronting conventional wisdom as it is to expect anyone's textbook to recapture the living Abbie.

Q: Do you think that the CIA killed Abbie?
A: No.
Q: You don't?
A: It's interesting. I'm asked that question quite a

bit and I can understand that because from a lot of us who have been on the left side of the fence you can understand our cynicism about that and our distrust of the CIA. So from people maybe like yourself, or people like Dave Dellinger who feels that the CIA might have been behind the killing of Abbie, I can understand the cynicism.

I can tell you this, and it doesn't go over big with a lot of people. Abbie was a manic depressive and if people understand a lot about manic depression they'll understand his death. That's why I came public with it, for which I received a lot of criticism within the family itself.

There is no doubt about it, there were two hundred phenobarbitals in his system and boom. And I don't see any reason why the CIA would want to put Abbie out at this point in time. There were other times (laughs) when they might have wanted to put Abbie out. And I think giving them credit is wrong. I don't think that they're as good as people think they are. That's my personal opinion of the CIA.

Q: If Abbie did commit suicide then, how do we see that in terms of evaluating what his life is all about? I don't think that diminishes anything that he did, but do you? Do you think it puts some kind of...

A: What, the suicide? No. Not at all.

Q: Yeah, a suicide. Does it tarnish anything that he stood for?

A: No, not at all. It just manifests the pain he lived with all these years. And he tried to cover over for that pain and the pain became so great that eventually...

This is an individual that loved life and wanted to live. He just in the end couldn't live any longer. Serious depression is a very serious problem, obviously, and if you understand it then you understand his death. I don't believe that it should have any reflection upon on his life and the things that he accomplished and the battles that he fought, not in the least bit. I mean there's a lot of great leaders that were manic depressives and a lot of great people that died, you know, killed themselves, from it.

Q: Was the suit that Abbie and Amy Carter brought against the CIA completely resolved at the time of Abbie's death?

A. Oh, sure.

Q: So Amy Carter isn't continuing that suit?

A: No. no. They didn't sue the CIA. I think that is a misunderstanding. They were brought to trial for trespassing on the University of Massachusetts campus. Instead of making it a simple trial of trespassing, they turned it into a case against the CIA where they were able to prove that they committed a crime in order to prevent another crime from happening. The

necessity defense, as it's commonly known, it's recognized in Massachusetts. For example, they committed a crime to prevent someone else from committing another crime that may be greater, that being the CIA. And they were able to prove that in court and they were found innocent. They were the defendants, they weren't the plaintiffs in the action, but there was nothing that came from that trial other than that.

Q: At one point Abbie had written an article for *Playboy* about the October Surprise thing that is so current in the news now. Abbie reported to Dave Dellinger that he got into an accident trying to deliver the manuscript and he felt that the brakes had been tampered with and then there were questions about the autopsy, that there was a delay in actually releasing the information about the phenobarbital and the alcohol and other suspicions. But there's nothing to any of this?

A: Nothing. I'm going to answer a lot of these questions. I have a book that will be out in about another year and I'm getting from you vibes that the public wants to hear more about his death. So I believe that I'm going to write a lot about it so I hope...I don't think that I'll ever put it to bed but I hope I can to some degree.

You know, that accident. I can tell you he was eating an ice cream and he rolled into a truck. It was just that: an accident. The evidence on that particular article—I was holding a duplicate copy in case something did happen to him. A lot of what he had the CIA knew. It was out there. It was public information. So he didn't have any bombshell or any smoking gun in that particular article.

I myself have picked up on that story and I'm working on it every day right now. A lot of information I've fed to Congressional aides. I'm glad you brought the subject up because there is going to be a Congressional hearing I believe in October. It will be another October surprise, I believe.

Q: So you're actually carrying on the research about the October Surprise?

A: Yeah. I worked on some of that prior, with Abbie, on that particular article, and Jonathan Silvers wrote a lot of it. So I mean, if you want to talk about that...

Q: OK, we can get back to that. I just want to cover this whole thing about how Abbie died so we can get on and discuss the book and discuss how Abbie lived. The last question that I want to ask you about how he died concerns another current theory that the drugs themselves brought on the suicide, a side effect of the drugs. Now what you're saying is that the pain and struggle that Abbie went through all his life...that this is a genuine depres-

sion, a genuine suicide, not one that was exacerbated by chemicals.

A: Chemicals can augment the depression. There's no doubt about that. If you drink or smoke or do drugs or anything, I mean, those things can contribute to depression. We know that. I recommend William Styron's book. He pretty much explains about deep depression and what happens to you. As a matter of fact, in his original article, he talked about Abbie's death.

I know what you're talking about. You're talking about the Prozac in particular. We could spend an hour on that particular subject. I've been asked to be on *Phil Donahue*. I've been asked by the Scientology group to get involved in their battle which I want nothing to do with, but I'll explain more about the Prozac issue in the book. It's tough to do it in a couple of minutes.

Q: OK.

A: There's no proof, I can tell you this, that Abbie was on Prozac at that particular time.

Q: OK. Unless there is anything else that you want to say on this topic we will leave it right now and go on.

A: No, but it is interesting that people are concerned but here we are, we've spent half the conversation on that and I mean I think that we should talk about Abbie's legacy. I think Abbie's really happy about the fact that they're going to start talking about the October Surprise. I think that he would be really excited about that.

You know, I was asked a question by a reporter several months ago about how Abbie would feel about the war, wouldn't he be excited and all this kind of thing. And I said my brother probably would have been sorry that he didn't put himself off this planet two years sooner.

Q: (laughter)

A: You know? It wasn't exactly exciting.

Q: Let's talk a little bit about this book that you've written an introduction for. It's called *Live This Book* and its authors are Theodore Becker and Anthony L. Dodson and it's published by the Noble Press. Do you agree with what they say in the book?

A: I have to tell you this: I read this book about three or four months ago. When I was approached by Teddy Becker originally about it I was a little bit skeptical. You know, concerning the fact that they were from Auburn University, and I said why don't you send me the manuscript and let me read it and see what I think and, of course, I started to read and I said, "Oh God, that's not my brother," you know, because I'm his brother. I mean, no one sees his

brother as any great political philosopher in life. I mean, it's very hard for me. I see him as just a brother and a good friend. It's interesting. The book gives Abbie... it's about time somebody gives him the credit that he justifiably deserves in life. And that's what I feel. I mean, it's hard to get in the book...they make a case for it, especially in the last part, but to say that *my brother* is in the ranks of Thoreau? I'm almost embarrassed about it, you know?

I think that this is a great book for academia to take up and discuss around the table. I think that it would be good for that.

Q: In reading the book, my concern was that they were drawing a lot of analogies to Mark Twain, to Will Rogers, to Charlie Chaplin and having seen Abbie and seen him speak, being inspired by watching him perform, my real fear was that this might be the first attempt to fossilize Abbie, to put him into some kind of category and put him on a shelf for academia. Does that agree with you at all?

A: Sure, sure.

Q: So how did you get involved with writing the introduction?

A: They approached me to write something and I told them at the time that it was kind of difficult. What can I say about the book? It's flattering to my brother, obviously. I must admit at times that I'm almost embarrassed by it, like I said. I said to them, "I don't think that I'm the right guy to be writing anything about the book."

Q: Did either of them know Abbie?

A. One of them had met Abbie. That's exactly how they felt about Abbie. I think that it's wonderful that people do think this about him. I think it's great. Abbie did dedicate his life to a lot of these causes.

There is only one individual that they left out. That's my criticism of the book. And that's Lenny Bruce.

Q: Lenny Bruce!

A: Yeah. My brother always felt that he was the reincarnation of Lenny Bruce, I felt.

Q: They didn't mention Lenny. They've got Will Rogers in there, but they didn't mention Lenny Bruce.

A: They do not mention Lenny Bruce.

Q: Yeah. That's an oversight. . .and a big one.

A: A big one—a damn big one. I mean, Lenny Bruce went the same way. Bye bye American Pie. But it's a good book to read and discuss it, but I'm no one to sit on one side or the other to be a judge of it. I should be asking you that question.

JFK Redux:
The Role of Richard Nixon and George Bush in the Assassination of President Kennedy
by Paul Kangas

A newly discovered FBI document reveals that George Bush was directly involved in the 1963 murder of President John Kennedy. The document places Bush working with the now famous CIA agent, Felix Rodriguez, recruiting right-wing Cuban exiles for the invasion of Cuba. It was Bush's CIA job to organize the Cuban community in Miami for the invasion. The Cubans were trained as marksmen by the CIA. Bush at that time lived in Texas. Hopping from Houston to Miami weekly, Bush spent 1960 and '61 recruiting Cubans in Miami for the invasion. That is how he met Felix Rodriguez.

You may remember Rodriguez as the Iran-contra CIA agent who received the first phone call telling the world the CIA plane flown by Gene Hasenfus had crashed in Nicaragua. As soon as Rodriguez heard that the plane crashed, he called his long-time CIA supervisor, who was now Vice President, George Bush. Bush denied being in the contra loop, but investigators recently obtained copies of Oliver North's diary, which documents Bush's role as a CIA supervisor of the contra supply network.

In 1988 Bush told Congress he knew nothing about the illegal supply flights until 1987, yet North's diary shows Bush at the first planning meeting Aug. 6, 1985. Bush's "official" log placed him somewhere else. Such double sets of logs are intended to hide Bush's real role in the CIA; to provide him with "plausible deniability." The problem is, it fell apart because too many people, like North and Rodriguez, have kept records that show Bush's CIA role back to the 1961 invasion of Cuba. (Source: *The Washington Post,* 7-10-90.)

That is exactly how evidence was uncovered placing George Bush working with Felix Rodriguez when JFK was killed. A memo from FBI head J. Edgar Hoover was found, stating that, "Mr George Bush of the CIA" had been briefed on November 23rd, 1963 about the reaction of anti-Castro Cuban exiles in Miami to the assassination of President Kennedy. (Source: *The Nation,* 8-13-88)

On the day of the assassination, Bush was in Texas, but he denies knowing exactly where he was. Since he had been the supervisor for the secret Cuban teams, headed by former Cuban police commander Felix Rodriguez, since 1960, it is likely Bush was also in Dallas in 1963. Several of the Cubans he was supervising as dirty-tricks teams for Nixon were photographed in the Zapruder film.

In 1959 Rodriguez was a top cop in the Cuban government under Batista. When Batista was overthrown and fled to Miami, Rodriguez went with him, along with Frank Sturgis and Rafael Quintero. Officially, Rodriguez didn't join the CIA until 1967, after the CIA invasion of Cuba, in which he participated, and the assassination of JFK. But records recently uncovered show he actually joined the CIA in 1961 for the invasion of Cuba when he was recruited by George Bush. This is how Rodriguez claims he became a "close, personal friend of Bush."

Then "officially" Rodriguez claims he quit the CIA in 1976, just after he was sent to prison for his role in the Watergate burglary. However, according to *Rolling Stone* reporters Kohn & Monks (Nov. 3, 1988), Rodriguez still goes to CIA headquarters monthly to receive assignments and have his blue 1987 bulletproof Cadillac serviced. Rodriguez was asked by a *Rolling Stone* reporter where he was the day JFK was shot, and he claims he can't remember.

George Bush claims he never worked for the CIA until he was appointed Director, by former Warren Commission director and then President Jerry Ford, in 1976. Logic suggests that is highly unlikely. Of course, Bush has a company duty to deny being in the CIA. The CIA is a secret organization. No one ever admits to being a member. The truth is that Bush has been a top CIA official since before the 1961 invasion of Cuba, working with Felix Rodriguez. Bush may deny his actual role in the CIA, but there are records in the files of Rodriguez and others involved in the Bay of Pigs invasion of Cuba that expose Bush's role. The corporations would not put somebody in charge of all state secrets held by the CIA unless he was experienced and well trained in the CIA. (Source: *Project Censored Report,* Feb. 1989, Dr. Carl Jensen, Sonoma State College)

According to the biography of Richard Nixon, his close personal and political ties with the Bush family go back to 1941, when Nixon claims he read an ad in an L.A. newspaper placed by a wealthy group of businessmen, led by Preston Bush, the father of George Bush. They wanted a young, malleable candidate to run for Congress. Nixon applied for the position and won the job. Nixon became a mouthpiece for the Bush group. (Source: *Freedom* magazine, 1986, L. F. Prouty.) In fact, Preston Bush is credited with creating the winning ticket of Eisenhower-Nixon in 1950. (Source: *George Bush,* F. Green, Hipocrene, 1988.)

Richard Nixon was Vice President from 1953 until 1961. In fact, Nixon was given credit for planning Operation 40, the secret 1961 invasion of Cuba, during his 1959 campaign for President. After Batista was kicked out by the starving people of Cuba, and Fidel Castro came to power, Castro began telling American corporations they would now have to pay Cuban employees decent wages. Even worse, Pepsi-Cola was told it would now have to pay world market prices for Cuban sugar.

Pepsi, Ford Motor Co., Standard Oil and the Mafia drug dealers decided Fidel had to be removed since his policies of requiring corporations to pay market wages were hurting their profits. So the corporations asked then-Vice President Nixon to remove Fidel. Nixon promised he would, just as soon as he won the 1960 elections against some underdog, an unknown Democrat named John Kennedy. It would be an easy victory for Nixon. All the polls had Nixon winning by a landslide. Besides, Kennedy was a Catholic, and Americans would no more elect a Catholic President than they would elect a woman, a black or a Jew. This was 1959.

Nixon told Pepsi, Standard Oil and the other corporations who lost property, given back to the farmers of Cuba, that if they would help him win, he would authorize an invasion to remove Castro. To further impress contributors to his campaign, then-Vice President Nixon asked the CIA to create Operation 40, a secret plan to invade Cuba, just as soon as he won.

The CIA put Texas oil millionaire and CIA agent George Bush in charge of recruiting Cuban exiles into the CIA's invasion army. Bush was working with another Texas oil man, Jack Crichton, to help him with the invasion. A fellow Texan, Air Force General Charles Cabel, was asked to coordinate the air cover for the invasion.

Most of the CIA leadership around the invasion of Cuba seems to have been people from Texas. A whole Texan branch of the CIA is based in the oil business. If we trace Bush's background in the Texas oil business we discover his two partners in the oil-barge leasing business: Texan Robert Mosbacher and Texan James Baker. Mosbacher is now Secretary of Commerce and Baker is Secretary of State, the same job Dulles held when JFK was killed. (Source: *Common Cause* magazine, March/April 1990.)

On the Watergate tapes, June 23, 1972, referred to in the media as the "smoking gun" conversation,

Nixon and his Chief of Staff, H. R. Haldeman, were discussing how to stop the FBI investigation into the Watergate burglary. They were worried that the investigation would expose their connection to "the Bay of Pigs thing." Haldeman, in his book *The Ends of Power,* reveals that Nixon always used code words when talking about the 1963 murder of JFK. Haldeman said Nixon would always refer to the assassination as "the Bay of Pigs."

On that transcript we find Nixon discussing the role of George Bush's partner, Robert Mosbacher, as one of the Texas fundraisers for Nixon. On the tapes Nixon keeps referring to the "Cubans" and the "Texans." The "Texans" were Bush, Mosbacher and Baker. This is another direct link between Bush and evidence linking Nixon and Bush to the Kennedy assassination.

In the same discussion Nixon links "the Cubans," "the Texans," "Helms," "Hunt," "Bernard Barker," Robert "Mosbacher" and "the Bay of Pigs." Over and over on the Watergate tapes, these names come up around the discussion of the photos from Dallas, that Nixon was trying to obtain when he ordered the CIA to burglarize the Watergate. (Source: "Three Men and a Barge," Teresa Riordan, *Common Cause* magazine, March/April 1990, and *San Francisco Chronicle,* May 7, 1977, interview with Frank Sturgis in which he stated that "the reason we burglarized the Watergate was because Nixon was interested in stopping news leaking relating to the photos of our role in the assassination of President John Kennedy.")

After Nixon's landslide victory in 1972, he knew he had to centralize all power into the White House to keep his faction in power. Not only to hold power, but to prevent the media from digging into how he secretly shot his way into the White House, just like Hitler shot his way into control of Germany. The first thing Nixon did was to demand signed resignations of his entire government. "Eliminate everyone," he told John Ehrlichman about reappointment, "except George Bush. Bush will do anything for our cause." (Source: *Pledging Allegiance,* Sidney Blumenthal.)

The reason why Bush will "do anything" is because his hands have as much of Kennedy's blood on them as do Nixon's, Hunt's, Sturgis', Felix Rodriguez' and Gerald Ford's. This White House gang fears that if the public ever realizes how they shot their way into power it could set off a spark that would destroy their fragile fraud and land them in jail.

Other famous Watergate members of the CIA invasion that Bush recruited were Frank Sturgis, E. Howard Hunt, Bernard Baker and Rafael Quintero. Quintero has said publicly that if he ever told what he knew about Dallas and the Bay of Pigs, "it would be the biggest scandal ever to rock the nation."

Meanwhile, in 1960, Preston Bush was running Nixon's campaign. Nixon was sent to South Vietnam to assure the French-connection government there that if France pulled out, the U.S. would step in to protect the drug trade from the Golden Triangle. (Source: *Frontline,* 1988, "Guns, Drugs and the CIA"; Alexander Cockburn, "Cocaine, the CIA and Air America," *San Francisco Examiner,* Feb. 2, 1991; *The Politics of Heroin in Southeast Asia,* Alfred McCoy, 1972.)

In 1959 Vice President Nixon was flying all over the world, acting just like presidential material. It was an easy race for Nixon. Congressman Jerry Ford was doing a great job fundraising for Nixon, as was George Bush. The rich loved Nixon. The media picked up every bone Nixon tossed out to them. The biggest problem was that Nixon was afraid to speak openly of his plan to invade Cuba. The plan was a secret. No sense alerting Cuba to the coming invasion. But Kennedy was taking a harder line on Cuba than Nixon, because Kennedy was not aware of the corporate/CIA planned invasion.

Nixon lost the 1960 race by the smallest margin in history. At first, Bush, Nixon, Cabel and Hunt decided to just go ahead with the invasion, without informing President Kennedy. Then, at the last second, at 4 a.m., just two hours before the invasion was set to go, General Cabel called JFK and asked permission to provide U.S. air cover for the CIA invasion. Kennedy said no.

The CIA was furious with JFK, but decided to go ahead with their private invasion anyway. Due to poor intelligence, the CIA landed at the worst possible beach. A swamp. The invasion failed. The CIA lost 115 of its best men, killed, with another 1100 in Cuban prisons. It was the worst single blow the CIA ever suffered. (Source: E. Howard Hunt, *Give Us This Day.*)

Bush, Nixon and Hunt blamed Cabel for asking Kennedy, and blamed Kennedy for saying no. They were livid with anger. Nixon's corporate sponsors ordered JFK to make any deal necessary to recover the 1100 CIA agents imprisoned in Cuba. JFK did. Once the CIA had its well-trained Cubans back, they decided to continue the invasion of Cuba just as soon as they could get rid of that S.O.B. Kennedy.

The 1964 election was fast approaching. Nixon was running against Kennedy again. Bush, Ford and Nixon knew that they had to get rid of JFK now, or else the Kennedy clan, with Robert and Ted in the wings, could control the White House until 1984. They decided not to wait until '84 to get back the White House. The Cuban teams of "shooters" began following Kennedy from city to city looking for a window of opportunity to shoot from. They came close in Chicago, but couldn't get the cooperation of Mayor Daley.

But in Dallas they had an ace. The mayor was the brother of General Cabel, whom the CIA blamed for the failure of the invasion. The general prevailed on his brother, Earl, and the motorcade was changed to pass the grassy knoll at 3 m.p.h. Hunt and Sturgis shot JFK from the grassy knoll. They were arrested, photographed and seen by 15 witnesses. But the media turned a blind eye to the photos, and for 25 years the world has been searching for the truth.

On the day JFK was murdered, Nixon, Hunt and some of the Watergate crew were photographed in Dallas, as were a group of Cubans, one holding an umbrella up, like a signal, next to the President's limo just as Kennedy was shot. The Cubans can be seen holding up the signal umbrella in the Zapruder film and dozens of stills taken during the assassination. After the murder they can be seen calmly walking away.

Nixon denied he was in Dallas that day, but new photos and stories prove he was there. Nixon claimed to the FBI he couldn't remember where he was when JFK was killed. (Source: FBI memo, Feb. 23, 1964, published in *Coup D'Etat in America,* Weberman and Canfield.) Bush, too, claims he can't remember where he was. Jack Anderson did a TV special in 1988 proving beyond any shadow of doubt that two of the tramps arrested in Dallas behind the grassy knoll were Hunt and Sturgis.

After the murder, former Vice President Nixon asked President Lyndon Johnson to appoint Nixon's friend, former FBI agent Jerry Ford, to run the Warren Commission. Nixon also asked LBJ to appoint Nixon's long-time supporter, Judge Earl Warren, to head the Commission. LBJ agreed. Ford interviewed all the witnesses and decided which ones would be heard and which ones eliminated.

It is no coincidence that Nixon selected Ford as his Vice President after Spiro Agnew was ousted. When Nixon himself got busted in the Watergate scandal, Earl Warren offered to set up another special commission if it would help get him out of trouble again. Ford, of course, pardoned Nixon for the Watergate burglary, but Nixon is still not out of the woods. There are 4000 hours of Watergate tapes. On the June 23, 1972 discussions with John Dean and Haldeman, there is clear evidence that Nixon is openly "confessing" to hiring Hunt to kill JFK. That is why the Watergate "investigation" went into secret session after Congress heard some of the tapes. That is why only 12 hours of the 4000 hours have been released to the public.

Did Congress realize that Nixon and Bush had openly discussed killing JFK for stopping the air cover of the Bay of Pigs invasion of Cuba? Remember, Nixon taped virtually every discussion he had with anyone in his inner circle, including Bush, in order to blackmail people later. There is a photo of Bush reporting to Nixon in the White House in 1968. It will be interesting to see what they were talking about on that day, when the full 4000 hours are finally released. The key to unlocking the secrets behind the 1963 murder of JFK is hidden in the 3988 hours of unreleased White House tapes.

Bush was in Dallas the day Reagan was shot. (Source: *George Bush,* F. Green, 1988.) That must have given Bush a flashback to November 22, 1963.

Black Holes and the Trilateral Commission
by Roy Lisker

There exist documents in the Pentagon with such tight security surrounding them, that they can only be retrieved by persons who possess an unbreakable cryptographic key, a so-called Shannon matrix code. In these one discovers that the Trilateral Commission has installed a hidden sperm bank in a vault below the buildings of the Rand Corporation in Santa Monica, California. The raw materials from this bank are used for research in genetic engineering, almost all of which in the United States is also funded by the Trilateral Commission. This important fact is known only to a few people. The purpose of this research is to produce human clones sensitive to magnetic fields from distant stars.

The Graham-Shockley sperm bank for Nobel Laureates has been exposed as a Maoist Communist front. The Rand Corporation's bank is the real thing; its sperms come from the fathers of Nobel laureates, who are far more likely candidates for having something special in their seed. All of the fathers of Nobel laureates, still alive and in the United States, were rounded up on June 14, 1980, by the national guard acting under direct orders from David Rockefeller, then forced at gunpoint to ejaculate into small plastic bottles. This would never have become public knowledge if I had not encountered a Nobel father last Sunday in the john of a sleazy hotel at 58th Street and 8th Avenue in New York. He was trying to puncture his throat with the opened end of a coat hanger left lying in a clogged drain by the hotel maintenance man.

David Rockefeller is not a person. He is a robotoid. The substitution was made ten years ago by creatures of atheistic and communistic practices living in the black holes of the Galaxy Cygnus X-I. Privately, one refers to them as "greigles"; they can take any shape at will. Via the Trilateral Commission, the greigles exchange human sperm like money. When all the earth's energy resources run out, each greigle-baron will be able to generate its own corral of cloned slaves.

I first discovered that David Rockefeller is a robotoid (and that Karl Marx was probably a robotoid) when after 8 months of arduous computations I broke the complex code transmitted in the high-frequency overtones of all music performed by the Da Capo Chamber Players, all of whom are witting or unwitting agents of sinister cosmic meta-forces. It may be that some of the composers whose works they regularly perform are also subject to the powerful hypnotic commands of the greigles—Elliott Carter, Mario Davidovsky, or Miriam Gideon for example. However, these messages are not transmitted in the actual notes, but in the manner in which the Da Capo Players play them. I am one of the few beings on earth able to hear these peculiar frequencies; my bulldog is another one.

Later on I discovered that similar messages were also being sent by a much larger group of musicians performing complicated contemporary music. Coded signals passed between the Trilateral Commission and the Ayatollah refer to them collectively as "the music circle." (Full details were given to me by a confidential source near 80th Street and Amsterdam Avenue last Monday night.)

After listening to recent concerts of the Da Capo Chamber Players, I am now certain of the following:

- That the Ayatollah Khomeini, himself a greigle, was responsible for the disaster at Three Mile Island.
- That all the cancer in the world is caused by a team of virologists working at the Vatican under the direction of the Pope.
- That the Reverend Sun Myung Moon has a warehouse of nuclear warheads underneath his seminary in Barrytown, NY.
- That brain cells can be cloned from LSD, in the presence of blood.
- That our world is really two-dimensional, with its third dimension created by mass hypnotic illusion. Much of what goes wrong with our lives is due to this misfortune.
- Immanuel Kant, who may also have been sensitive to high frequencies, tries to tell us as much in his *Critique of Pure Reason*.
- That nuclear power is actually a sinister plot against homosexuals, directed by the Freemasons with Pentagon support.
- That the Day of Judgement has already arrived in Cygnus X-I.
- That prolixin is highly radioactive and should not be used as a psychiatric drug.
- That the Americans, the Russians and the Japanese are presently building a huge concentration camp in the Antarctic where they intend to incarcerate all peoples of the Third World living below a pre-determined standard of living.

The greigles ultimately intend to suck the Earth out of its orbit and drag it to the Event Horizon of a black hole in Cygnus X-I, where all life can be permanently frozen into fixed modes of behavior. They are also responsible for the permanent energy crisis. This fact has already been understood by our best scientists. Stephen Hawking, the astrophysicist, through his "Cosmological Censorship Hypothesis," can explain how energy can fail to be conserved inside black holes without violating the laws of physics. We can now see why the greigles found it advantageous to replace the Ayatollah with one of themselves. By placing an energy-violating black hole creature at the head of an important oil-producing nation, Cygnus X-I maintains a controlling interest in world political economy.

Other griegles include Pinochet, Moshe Dayan, Nixon, Joan Baez and the Basques, Robotoids include the Rockefellers, Kissinger, Giscard d'Estaing, the mayors of Hazelton, Pennsylvania, Gary, Indiana, Monroes, Michigan, Fall River, Massachusetts, to name a few. If Barry Commoner is a robotoid, then David McReynolds (Citizens Party and Socialist Party presidential candidates, respectively) is a greigle; the opposite may also be true.

All white males will be sterile within three years, there being a slightly longer time limit for other races.

Roy Lisker is a mathematician, poet and musician. His newsletter, Ferment!, *is available from Broughton Place, 152 Kisor Road, Highland, NY 12528.*

The Multi-Screen Setup
by Walter Alter

Why is the multi-screen setup the intrinsic shape of the medium? Why will the number of screens you can read simultaneously become the pre-eminent measure of human intelligence?

Big screen projection and screen insets (pull downs) are an evolutionary dead end for video no matter what the resolution or price tag. A multi-screen modular add-on array will become the universal application of imaging technology as a conceptual spinoff of high velocity, high necessity TV gauge instrumentation as in airplane cockpit flight decks. You can multiply your IQ (heretofore based on print literacy) by a factor of ten simply by placing two thrift store black and white TV sets side by side, tuned to two different channels, volume up on both, and concentrating on following the information flux simultaneously. Within ten minutes of moderate concentration you will have eclipsed 500 years of obsolete sequential print patterning. Multi-screen image literacy will position your perceptions within a flux of simultaneous info, i.e., a more accurate model of the real 3-D world of simultaneous events.

Why multi-screen array with six, eight or ten screens rather than a single screen with insets or message overlays? First of all, the same screen size creates equal domains where important info can pop up anywhere. With the peripheral visual field sharing a conscious role, the hierarchical dominance of the central visual field is lessened allowing for an awareness of field interplay rather than point objects. Point scanning is the dominant uptake mode of print literacy. The TV's electron scan already does this for us at a far greater velocity than our eyes. Instead of mimicking a pencil thin visual uptake tunnel as in reading, we can begin to apperceive in blanket areas and allow the eye to "read" the situation as the situation dictates instead of being trapped in a line by line left to right top to bottom schema. The obvious result is an increase in interpretative flexibility, tending to downplay expectations based on "subject predicate" linearity and thus allowing for true discovery rather than extrapolation. A second result is a cognitive breakout from the specialist's tunnel vision. No longer are phenomena, particularly social phenomena, allowed to exist divorced from relationship, as existential isolates. A third result is the repatterning of thought from words into pictures. If a picture is worth a thousand words, thinking in pictures is a three orders of magnitude increase in efficiency.

The eyes, jumping from screen to screen, look for important data at a rapid rate. This makes the domain boundaries (screen borders) become more and more permeable and is diametrically opposed to the single screen (theater/cinema) limitation of having the viewer captive to a single bounded area (and thus be a single bounded area!). Societies are not single bounded areas, and any singular oriented media of communication which attempts to overlay itself upon plural fields is an unfaithful model of the real 3-D world and does not prepare us to act effectively in the 3-D world.

Breakthroughs in human invention are characterized by the translation of concepts across boundaries, usually by the synthesis of several extant processes into a new process. To perform such an inventive synthesis requires a breakdown of conceptual boundaries and a reintegration of the contents. The nice thing about using boundary crashing activity within a defined array of monitors is that the array itself is less able to be conceived of as an isolated single domain, ie., a single tool for a single problem, and the processes occurring within it are encouraged to breakout and be applied synthetically to the real 3-D world. The "activity," then, becomes the organizing frame of reference. Moreover, that activity consists of more than shifting attention from screen to screen. It also consists of zooming in and out on a single screen to pick up detail. The zoom in/out action of attention focus is as important as domain jumping in the breakdown of conceptual boundaries, possibly even more so since it essentially turns any visual field boundary into an elastic one. Conceptual synthesis and conceptual elasticity work hand in hand.

When both operate in concert, a powerful amplification of information throughput and analysis can come into play for the first time in human affairs. A great deal of human misery is caused by the inability to reintegrate new information with old information in a way that reflects adequate problem solving within a new situation. The simple tyranny of word categories wherein a single entity word is used to describe impossibly complex ideas as in the case of the word "life" attempting to convey anything close to the concept; does more to keep humanity from discovering its potential than any other single impediment. A single picture can provide far more info on the subject, a motion picture even more, and an array of video screens with real time programming can begin to approach the kind of modeling we need in order to act in a problem solving manner. This schematic also holds for inner visual imagination processes as well, although our ability to inner visualize with full memory and in color, stereo with synthetic freedom is almost totally inhibited by our endocrinal dampening system which has been genetically developed for far more hostile circumstances and overexercised by physical and emotional trauma. Insofar as vision is the one human perception capable of the most information flux density, then inner imaging exercises a corresponding proportional ideational mix on the inside. Over half the brain's neurons are used to process and understand visual input. Its visual input data channel has a bandwidth estimated to be about two gigabits (billion bits) per second. Total memory recall is probably more than half visual and obviously the key factor of photographic memory in human genius. Any effort we make to undampen human visual perception, both inner and outer, will pay off by increasing human intelligence.

To recap: the concept of unitariness (as opposed to a flux of necessity-based emphases, ie., an emphasis field) is the single most intelligence inhibiting factor in human affairs. Unitariness has the irritating capability to make "A" visual field and turn it into "the" visual field, a dangerous game when the game board of perception consists of an infinity of internal and external visual fields belonging to each of our fellow cohabitants of dimension number three. Singularity is thus, paradoxically, chaotic because it inhibits meaning formation. Again, this can be best illustrated in the verbal domain where unitary word symbol packages come to stand for pictures. This is obviously quicksand when you add the difficulty of synonyms and inflection. It is easy to see how a unitary word symbol can mean a range of things not intended. Imagine if humans spoke a single word, waited for a single word reply, spoke a single word again, etc. The essence of the problem is apparent. With sentences the problem of accuracy remains although the setup is workable in a one on one situation, even a one on several situation but begins to break down in a one on many situation and absolutely does not operate in reverse, not to mention a many to many situation. Verbal communication is sequential and slow, 700 mph. Visual communication is simultaneous and fast, 186,000 mps. The creation of a new visual language capable of communicating within an electrical social matrix is the one key invention that will unlock the future in a more unlimited sense than ever imagined. A high definition mathematical hieroglyphics able to model a complex unfolding of realtime subject matter will propel our imaginations at ultra warp speed, yet at ultra applicability topologies.

The application of boundary crunching concepts to organize data dynamically into temporary clumps of greater specific utility is an impulse towards efficiency. Of course a dimension with no time would be the most efficient of all, everything simultaneous. Our dimension contains/is contained by time, but since all dimensions connect, overlay and superimpose to varying degrees, our closest perceptual approximation of trans-dimensionality is the visual field in which a picture consisting of many elements is perceived at once. Continuity, any continuity, whether conceptual or visual, is easily seen as being sort of timelessness. So if we overlay visual meaning upon data fields, and make the process dynamic by relating them into greater efficiencies, we are participating more and more in timeless dimension, and if that ain't cosmic, kids, I don't know what is.

So find two TVs and clump them together into a field and engage the clump with your significance amplifier engines. It doesn't matter what the programs are since the meaning of the exercise is not "what's on" the screen, but what's on in the head, ie., what cognitive tools are fashioned irrespective of program content. The overriding consideration is the formal arrangement of 2+ screens and the cognitive rearranging it instigates to cause simultaneous mini-continuities to occur within the maxi-continuity of consciousness. My bet is that anyone seriously experimenting with this setup will necessarily find themselves eventually filling the screens with whatever program material best serves the primary function of gauge. This is because the multi-screen setup not only encourages domain jumping but also makes it very easy to exercise comparative judgement in field free of constants. The yardsticks are relative, no inches, pounds or BTUs. Constants are replaced with threshold awareness which would indicate subsequent efficient actions. This is to say that problem solving actions would be more likely to solve the problem than be an exercise in role playing or intellectual whacking off. The only universal constants are those which are the intersection of all dimensions. Life is such an intersection. Potential is such an intersection. It's hard to use real constants for a yardstick since they are so big, like having an inch be one ten flamillionth of the universe. So we use inches that are the average length of a thumb to the first knuckle because we can build apparatuses that with that constant which allow us to approach the next threshold of instrumentation, etc., etc., until we find ourselves living a very long time and knowing a very great deal. There is a workable point of view (projection) in which the pi relation between the radius and the circumference of a circle is a whole number.

Walter Alter publishes Little Wally's Anathema, A Repair Manual for the 21st Century. *He can be reached at Renaissance 2000, Studio 26, 40001 San Leandro Street, Oakland, CA 94601.*

The Kabbalah Papers

Found in a folder in a box in the attic of the residence occupied by the late Professor Luther X. Frankenfurter:

On Smythe College at San Patattoh letterhead:
January 17, 1978

Mrs. Gwendelphia Buffo
1 Crustant Woods
Fontendue, Tuscany
Italy 897 6G4 Y

Dear Mrs. Buffo:

Thank you for your generous donation from the papers of the late Sir Huckleberry-Bixby. Your attention to and generosity for Smythe College at San Patattoh continues unabated. Speaking for the College in toto, I cannot express sufficient gratitude for this most valuable gift and the others preceding it.

The Huckleberry-Bixby manuscript attracted immediate interest upon its arrival. Distinguished faculty members in our Center for the Propagation of Culture have received it so enthusiastically that outstanding scholars in our mathematics, philosophy, and literature departments are complaining the CPC boys are hogging the action! The Library has even received queries from our scientists in the Department of Materials. The name of Mrs. Buffo is on almost every pair of lips in the halls of Smythe-Patattoh, as it is upon my own.

We all look forward to your visit next month for the dedication of the Elmer F. Creameree Building, for which you have been its greatest patron. Until then, Smythe College at San Patattoh continues to bask in the munificent sunshine of your intelligence.

Sincerely yours,
Luther X. Frankenfurter, Ph.D.
Director of Libraries (sic)

Handwritten on 5x7" 28-lb. canary yellow card-stock:
January 2, 1978
My Dearest Temitia,
I'm sure Smythe-P will care for and study these papers from the late Sir Hubert Y.J. Huckleberry-Bixby. I know Hubie would be very happy to know that some of his work was being carried forward at the P.

Looking forward to seeing you next month, President Crackenworster. Tell Luther I'm also looking forward to his own naughty little monkey.

Fondly, Gwed

handwritten on yellow, lined 10"x14" paper:
The attached book review—though report may be the more correct term—comprises the only evidence I have, besides that of my own senses, of the existence of Vistavius, a small Pacific island of some 1000 square miles with a plentiful fresh water supply, an abundance of shade, a seemingly inexhaustible variety and supply of wild fruits and vegetables, and a small colony (987 souls) of multi-lingual and exceedingly sophisticated chimpanzees.

My personal story of more than 170 days spent on Vistavius has been widely reported in the popular periodicals and electronic information services, and will appear in book form in my forthcoming work from *Steamshovel Press*. It thus becomes unnecessary for me to say little more than that I arrived on Vistavius on 3 July 1975 with two books in my possession: *Gravity's Rainbow* by Thomas Pynchon, and *Sabbatai Sevi: The Mystical Messiah, 1626-1676* by Gershom Scholem. By the morning of 5 July, Ugasu, the leader—if that is at all the word to choose—of the chimpanzees—with whom I communicated freely since they were all literate in English (the result, I later learned, of the shipwreck during the late 1860s of a group of American nuns on a South Sea vacation)—Ugasu had finished reading *Gravity's Rainbow* and begged me to leave "this remarkable book," as she phrased it, in the chimpanzees' library. By the end of the month, the apes had all listened to the complete text of *Gravity's Rainbow* because of a series of readings organized by Ugasu. Now the library had a waiting list hundreds of names long of patrons wanting to borrow *Gravity's Rainbow*.

Soon thereafter, Ugasu read *Sabbatai Sevi* and wrote the attached review for her community, in the language of the book being reviewed as has been the custom among the chimpanzees for apparently thousands of years.

On standard duplication paper:
Gershom Scholem, *Sabbatai Sevi, The Mystical Messiah, 1626-1676*. Princeton: Princeton UP, 1973.

Apocalyptic Jewish thought sees the process or redemption not as a result of historical forces but rather that which "arises on the ruins of history, which collapses amid the 'birth pangs' of the messianic age" (9). Such an outlook, combined with a history of exile and oppression, has provided Jewish history with several messianic claimants. The Sabbatian movement was different from any previous and subsequent messianic movement because it occupied the attention of

Jews all over the world. Sabbatai Sevi had a strong following in countries that persecuted their Jews and in countries that were less repressive; in communities that were economically prosperous and those that were not.

The Sabbatian movement is also interesting because it is a sect of *kabbalah* the mystical method of interpreting Scripture to penetrate sacred mysteries and foretell the future. According to those who practice *kabbalah,* the physical world is only a symbol or intimation of an inner reality that controls the external world we perceive. The purpose of the kabbalist's activity and meditation is to come into contact with that inner reality, or *En-sof.*

Popular notions concerning *kabbalah,* things like magic and numerology, are not what this religion is all about. These misconceptions influence the ideas that many of Pynchon's characters have about *kabbalah,* though Pynchon himself demonstrates a good grasp of kabbalistic concepts. The precepts of *kabbalah* can be explained with the definition of various key terms:

En-sof (the Infinite)-"The hidden God...far removed from everything created; he is unrevealed, non-manifest, and unknown." (115).

sefiroth-An emanation from the *En-sof;* there are ten individual *sefirah.* "The first three *sefroth*...do not manifest themselves by direct activity in the world below. But the lower seven...are the forces that build the manifest and visible universe . . ." (120).

qelippoth-The left side, the impure side, the female side of the cosmos; evil. "...the soft meaty slug of a soul that smiles and loves, that feels its mortality, either rotted away or been picked at...a process by which living souls unwillingly become the demons..." (*Gravity's Rainbow* 176)

tiqqun-The effort to reunite the male and female sides of the cosmos.

Shekhinah-The Talmud defines this as the presence of God. To the kabbalists the term serves as a technical term for the tenth and last sefrah

maggidim-Angels or holy souls who would supposedly visit kabbalists and convey heavenly wisdom.

Mystery of the Jubilee-"...kabbalistic view that at the time of redemption the supernal lights of the hidden *sefiroth* and configurations would become manifest on earth" (275).

gematria-Numerology; the invention of mystical allusions by way of the numerical value in words. (Sabbatai Sevi delighted in their use, especially references to himself as messiah. He played with it like a writer might play with puns.)

Sabbatai Sevi was born in Smyrna, August, 1626, on the Ninth of Ab (Hebrew calendar)-the day commemorating the destruction of the First and Second Temples. Since he was born on the Sabbath he was named "Sabbatai," this being the practice of the time. Sevi received a thorough religious and Talmudic training. He became an ascetic as a young man and this turned him to the works of *kabbalah.*

While most of his contemporaries were becoming involved in Lurianic *kabbalah,* Sabbatai read no Lurianic literature, only the Zohar, the great mystical work of *kabbalah,* and the two volumes of the *Qanah,* a voluminous work on the meaning of the commandments. Sevi's special outlook was also influenced by his particular mental health. He suffered from "a Manic-depressive psychosis" (126) that left his faculties intact but could plunge him into despair or exaltation on an irregular basis. There were also "normal" periods.

When Sabbatai was in a state of illumination, the excitement phases, he would perform strange or paradoxical acts, and outright blasphemy, such as uttering the Ineffable Name of God. Doing this kind of thing once too often led to Sevi's being expelled from Smyrna in 1651. This was before he had made any public claims to being the messiah. This breaking of taboos became an important part of Sabbatai's personal philosophy. He argued that the arrival of the messianic age meant a new law, and the new law was symbolized by doing that which was forbidden. One such act which thoroughly shocked the Jewish establishment was Sabbatai's consumption of strictly forbidden animal fat, punishable by "excision"—"that soul shall be cut off from among his people. Of the thirty-six transgressions listed in the Talmud as incurring this punishment, the majority are sexual offenses . . ." (242). Thus, the symbolic meaning of Sevi's acts were even more important, and it was this behavior that got him in trouble, not claiming to be the messiah.

Sabbatai Sevi would never have made it alone, however. "Devoid of will power and without a program of action, he was a victim of his illness and his illusions" (208). The man was able to carry out the role of messiah only because of his prophet, Nathan of Gaza, renowned as a man of God.

In late 1664, or early 1665, Nathan had been imposing particularly heavy penance and fasting upon his congregation. He was beginning to develop prophecy about the coming messianic age. When Sabbatai on a journey to Jerusalem stopped to visit Nathan, the prophet told him he was the messiah. Not in a state of illumination, Sevi declined. Later, when Sabbatai was no longer depressed, he visited Nathan again. The two became close friends. In May 1665, Sabbatai Sevi revealed himself as the messiah.

Nathan explained how the messianic struggle would occur: "His real war will be against the demonic powers of the *qelippah,* and it will be waged essentially on the 'inner,' spiritual levels of the cosmos, although it might eventually manifest itself on the material level as well" (227).

Nathan was indispensable to the movement. His presence outweighed any rabbinic threat of excommunication. Nathan helped explain the strange behavior of the messiah and the repellent aspects of his personality. He helped shape a movement that was characterized by a combination of severe penitence and great rejoicing.

Sabbatian theology differed from Lurianic kabbalism because of the central role played by the messiah. The underlying assumption is that during the messianic age, life will return to uncorrupted spirituality. Sabbatai and his followers were working to hasten the coming of such a world. Nathan explains that the defeat of the demonic powers of the *qelippoth* is also related to any tyranny on earth. The destruction of the gentile rule was also necessary.

The purpose of prayer for the Sabbatian was "to lift the *Shekhinah* from her low position . . . to her rightful and exalted place...rise not only to the level of *Tif'ereth* (the 'husband of the *Shekhinah*') but even to the highest *sefirah*...raised to a realm where she would be the crown of her husband" (278). Thus, when Pynchon has Greta impersonate a homicidal *Shekhinah* (*Gravity's Rainbow* 478) he is drawing on an important image and giving it ironic meaning by having Greta murder. For being faithful to their *Shekhinah,* Jews have always been persecuted.

Once Sabbatai revealed himself as the messiah, he gained control of the Jewish community in Smyrna. A reign of terror from the believers kept the opposition quiet. The city was under Turkish dominion and all of this messianism was allowed to continue because of bribes. The Cadi also took money from the unbelievers. Less than three weeks passed, however, before Sabbatai left for Constantinople, the capital of the Ottoman Empire. This was either late December 1665 or early January 1656.

On route to Constantinople, Sabbatai was arrested. Scholem states that there is good evidence to believe that Jewish opponents had a hand in this. On February 8, 1666, Sabbatai was brought to Constantinople in chains. The Turks were not upset by the boldness of the Jewish messianic thought, but rather "the disruption of normal life and the cessation of business activities in the Jewish community which controlled so much of Turkey's commerce" (449). Pragmatic economics seem to have dictated much of the behavior of the Turkish authorities throughout the history of the Sabbatian movement. It is analogous to the apparent motivation of "Them" in *Gravity's Rainbow.*

Sabbatai appeared before the Sultan's Divan, presided over by the Grand Vizier, and through "intelligent and sensible deportment" (430) he was not executed but sent to Jail. This was considered quite a miracle by most of his fellow Jews. Analogies were drawn with the suffering of captivity in the hands of the demons of the *qelippoth.* "It was only natural that [the messiah's] fate express itself ...in external, material reality" (453). Bribes from his followers to the authorities allowed him a comfortable life and visitors.

When the Grand Visier had to leave to conquer Crete, he ordered Sabbatai to the fortress of Gallipoli, on the European side of the straits of the Dardanelles. Sevi arrived on April 19, 1666. At Gallipoli, Sabbatai was also allowed visitors thanks to the Turkish custom that allowed people to come in by paying an appropriate "entrance fee" (603). Regular pilgrimages to the new messiah began.

One of the guests who came to see Sabbatai at Gallipoli was a mysterious R. Nehemiah Kohen, from Poland. He arrived in Gallipoli September 3 or 4, and remained for only two or three days, speaking to Sabbatai. There are two versions of what took place. The Jewish account states that Nehemiah told Sabbatai that messianic prophecies had to be fulfilled in a literal manner, or else it was not an act of the messiah. This idea, of course, implied that Sabbatai was *not* the messiah. The Christian version says that Nehemiah argued that he was the martyr messiah of the house of Joseph, and that Sabbatai had no right to be the Davidic messiah when he had yet to begin his ministry, which, according to prophecy, had to come first. Sabbatai had argued that one of his early disciples, killed in the Polish massacres of 1648, had been the messiah from the House of Joseph.

After the argument with Sabbatai, Nehemiah apostatized, that is, became a Moslem, and denounced Sevi for "fomenting sedition" (666). From then on, Nehemiah wandered about, changing his name to hide his identity, avoiding places where he might be recognized.

On September 12, or 13, 1666, four messengers arrived to take Sabbatai back to the capital. He was brought before the Sultan's Privy Council on September 16. The Jewish community expected Sabbatai to take the Sultan's crown and place it on his own head. This did not happen. Instead, the Turks gave Sevi a choice: "to be tortured to death, or to apostatize" (677). Sabbatai opted for the latter, taking the name Asiz Mehemed Effendi, after the sultan. He was appointed to the honorary office of *kapici bashi* (keeper of the palace gates) and given a royal pension of a little less than two lion's dollars (ecus) per day.

Sabbatai went to live in Adrianople and from his home remained in touch with his chief adherents. The mass of the people who were his followers still believed in him. Nathan explained the apostasy as a "logical, albeit unexpected, sequel to earlier 'strange actions' which had played such a central role in the elaboration of his doctrine and ministry of the messiah" (709). Sevi was able to maintain contact with Jews after the apostasy because the Turks believed he was trying to gain converts for Islam. In fact, several of his followers did apostatize in his wake.

Since December of 1666 the rabbis of Constantinople had been threatening excommunication to all Sabbatian believers. Nathan of Gaza was persecuted extensively until 1668, when it stopped mysteriously, although he continued to be a powerful influence in the movement.

The earlier prophecies concerning when the messianic age would begin now had to be revised. Nathan had to make revisions in his original theological arguments. Nathan's "earliest letters had stated quite clearly that the unbeliever could neither disturb nor delay the inexorable progress of the messianic consummation. . . Now, under the pressure of events, Nathan had to revise his earlier opinions and ponder where he had misinterpreted his original vision" (775). The view developed by the Sabbatian circle in

Adrianople was that there was a "holy seed," which the gentiles were part of, and to garner it the messiah had to convert the gentiles to Sabbatian Judaism. This was the secret meaning of the apostasy.

On September 12, 1672, Sabbatai and some of his followers were arrested for conducting Jewish prayers. Evidence suggests that the head of the palace guard was bribed to have Sevi arrested. Witnesses were produced against Sabbatai who swore that he uttered blasphemies on other occasions. The punishment for being found guilty of reviling or denying Islam was death. Sabbatai got off with banishment because of his friendship with the Sultan. Sevi was sent to the fortress of Dulcigno.

Sabbatai Sevi died in Dulcigno on the Day of Atonement (the most holy day in the Jewish year), 5437 (September 17, 1676). The general reaction of the believers was not to talk about it but only to wait and see if it was a "real death," or an occultation, merely an illusion. The prophet Nathan died four years later.

—Ugasu

A Gemstone Darkly
by Jim Keith

At a certain point, while researching my book on the Gemstone File, I changed my mind about it. Initially I had been very skeptical, but in something short of minor satori I became less skeptical and realized that virtually everything of importance that Bruce Roberts had said lo these 18-and-more years ago could be true. That is, the Mafia really could have been the ones behind the JFK, RFK and MLK hits, and Aristotle Onassis, while there's not a hint of it in the standard biographies of the guy, could have been the Mr. Big ordering the hits.

That's the thesis of Gemstone, in a nutshell, but it's embroidered with any number of other different strange and unsavory events with the 24 pages of this samizdat classic, this Secret Letters of Chicken Little—dark mini-history of the twentieth century that has circulated hand-to-hand since 1974 or so.

Why hadn't I believed Gemstone to begin with? To be blunt, the thing reeks of paranoia and the spy biz of a man with no apparent connections to the intelligence (or less than intelligent) agencies.

Bruce Roberts, before his death (all deaths are mysterious in the world of conspiracy research, and Bruce Roberts' death was at least as mysterious as the rest of the guys on the San Francisco obituary page the same day) wrote something on the order of 1000 pages of letters, purporting to expose the inner workings of the Mafia and the US government, and sent those letters to his mother and sundry other figures like Marshall Tito and Anwar Sadat. The letters existed and some exist; we have the word of Mae Brussell, Stephanie Caruana, and Paul Krassner on that. For my own part, I have yet to see a single page of the original Roberts' letters.

All I have to go on is what the rest of us (aside from the above mentioned) have seen, namely *The Skeleton Key to the Gemstone File,* and a continuing bramble-laden correspondence with Stephanie Caruana, the woman who edited the Gemstone letters down from 1000 pages to a 24 page synopsis.

Caruana is a study in herself. I'd spent some time trying to locate her while working on the book, and had had no luck. And then, by accident, if there are such things, and this instance certainly strained credulity, I ran across her name and address. Caruana is very concerned that her address doesn't leak out (she's survived 18 years since she did the Skeleton Key, but since some of the principals of the Gemstone Files live, she'd just as soon remain anonymous) so I won't give you any clues on this one; suffice it to say that she's been doing other things since the Skeleton Key.

Caruana believes utterly in the truth of the Gemstone File and believes Roberts to have been the bravest man she ever met. She thinks that I'm a dilettante who only indulges in conspiracy theory because I'm certain that it couldn't be true—but she has taken the time to answer any question I've had about the File. She also has 8 pages of Roberts' original letters and an expanded 60 page *Skeleton Key* (with photos) that no one that I know has ever seen. When my book comes out from IllumiNet, those things may or may not be in it; probably not, she wants $4500 for photocopies of those items.

In putting the book together, I began researching the individual events depicted in the Skeleton Key, and at a certain point things seemed to at least partially crystallize. The Skeleton Key, for instance, maintains that Howard Hughes was kidnapped by the Mafia and replaced by a lookalike. It turns out that everyone and his brother has speculated on the same thing at one time or another; Charles Colson, the IRS, Carl Oglesby, lots of people. It's at least as plausible as the other theories about what happened to Hughes.

Onassis was more difficult. I read half-a-dozen bios of the Greek tycoon looking for something, anything that would suggest that he was anything more than wily, and found nothing. But then connections finally started to fall in place and I found out that Onassis, while I can't prove any wrongdoing on his part, hung out with Nazis, Mafia, and men who were identifiable links to the JFK assassination. You might even say that I felt I glimpsed a tentacle of the Danny Casaloro "Octopus." These associates don't absolutely prove that Onassis was up to dirty work that he's portrayed as doing in the Gemstone File, but it did make the whole conception...quite plausible.

And then W. Scott Walker called me from Tahoe and tried to threaten me off from the book. He's the publisher of a book (and I use the term loosely, since I've had a chance to peruse the thing) by Peter Renzo, called *Beyond The Gemstone Files*. It's basically a crappy rip-off of the Caruana *Skeleton Key* that Renzo claims are the files that G. Gordon Liddy thought he had burned. Walker maintains that Renzo is ex-CIA and an ex-member of the "Fighting Tigers Assassination Squad." He also implied that if I went ahead with my plans for doing a book on the Gemstone File that the Fighting Tigers just might have a reunion and use me for target practice.

I think the guy is loony, but who knows? That

didn't keep Liddy out of the Company. Greg Krupey tells me that he's run into a reference to a "Fighting Tigers," supposedly the hit squad who took out Kennedy witnesses after the assassination. Whatever; I've spent the advance and I have to do the book.

The problem, as I see it, was that Bruce Roberts was paranoid, which tended to cause him to interconnect and view everything as part of the Web. Although I've not seen his original letters, I've heard them described, and they sound...well, Caruana compares them to Joyce's *Finnegan's Wake*. That's only a shade of difference from calling them crazy. Brilliant, but crazy, let's say. In addition to the letters being rambling and manic, they were synopsized for posterity by Stephanie Caruana, and she turned out a *Gemstone* that is flawed—unsubstantiated at best.

The odd thing, though, is that I have the suspicion that Gemstone could be true. Roberts may have walked a thin line as he followed the thread of Mafia influence in international politics, but at the same time it is possible that he knew what was going on in the big conspiratorial picture.

That's where I stand. I'm dickering with Caruana for some Roberts letters, and I'm putting the final touches on the book. And I ain't (if you're familiar with the *Skeleton Key*) eating any apple pie.

Jim Keith's book on the Gemstone File is available from IllumiNet Press, POB 2808, Lilburn, GA 30226.

Mysterium Coniunctionis:
On the Hidden and Oppository Parallels Between Anti-Esotericist Conspiratology and Traditional Esoteric Teachings
by Tim O'Neill

There is an inherent human desire for a sense of order, centrality and certainty, in a universe which seems to move in mysterious, vibrant and perhaps chaotic patterns. With this deeply-seeded constellation of mental patterns revolving around the need for a centralized source, the tendency is usually to seek out a unified and highly artificial world-view when the truth is far more likely to be closer to the labyrinthine, weblike and multi-valent network of monadic "events" existing somewhere outside the framework of time and space. In Illuminist terms, it is only when the eye is "single" that it can even begin to discern the hidden conjunctive unity behind polar opposites of historical movement. The single eye of Horus, one of the greatest symbols of the true esoteric tradition, is often pointed out by conspiratologists as damning proof of "fascistic" intent of the Illuminist tradition. The idea behind this assertion is that the single eye really represents the autocratic, theocratic and dictatorial aspects of the personage or cabal employing it. This old symbol really suggests a strange similarity between the world-view of conspiratology and the doctrine, taught in traditional metaphysics, of the Pythagorean principle of the "many out of the one"...the cosmological principle of the Emanation of Being. Just as esotericists seek to trace the existence of unity behind the mask of apparent complexity, so conspiratologists seek to discover the "One"; the unified source of historical movement in all-encompassing cabals, individuals, or metaphysical forces. On this model, virtually all conspiracy theories revolve around:

1. A human-based cabal, such as Speculative Freemasonry, the various groups of Illuminati, or an intelligence agency, such as the CIA.

2. An exceptional human individual, such as Adam Weishaupt or Adolf Hitler, who is, again often the leader of a cabal.

3. Non-human beings or forces, such as extraterrestrials, demons, angels, Satan and other spiritual, metaphysical or quasi-physical entities.

As a practicing esotericist and initiated Illuminist, I would certainly be the first to admit that there does, in fact, exist some unified guiding energy or force which lies behind the patterns of human evolution as designer. This "figure" is often codified into such symbolic complexes as the "Great Architect of the Universe" or "The Lord of the World," which are essentially deist conceptions that transcend the more anthropomorphic figure "Yahweh," warrior god of the desert nomads. Having admitted that traditional esoteric teaching does hold a centralized force of Being and Wisdom extended throughout the length and breadth of space and time through a mysterious process called "Emanation," we have opened the door to the prime directive of conspiracy theory...to discover "who" is ultimately in charge!

In point of fact, the ultimate conspiracy theory would involve the mysterious "Lord of the World," also known as the "Fisher King," "Prestor John," "Melchisadek," or "The King of the Grail" in Arthurian legend. Every one of our three potential categories of conspiracy theory can be easily seen to reside beneath the figure of the all-wise, omnipotent and all-seeing World-King. His Being is a trans-human and trans-non-human essentia, which melds extraterrestrial, spiritual and human into a powerful matrix.

The cores of both conspiracy theory and traditional metaphysics thus contain a strikingly similar proposition: "That there is a 'one' at the core of history." The separation of viewpoints, or "Primal Scission," of these two world-views, occurs as soon as the problem of "Evil" enters consideration. "Evil" is, of course, the fuel which fires conspiracy theory in its essence. The need at the root of conspiracy questing is to find the source for human pain and suffering...our primal existence of disharmony and disunity...which is held to flow out of some central fountain, running in rivulets throughout the world. In most conspiracy theory, evil exists as an absolute metaphysical reality, nigh as a substance, which can poison life through viral contamination. For traditional metaphysics, evil is seen as an abstract tool for the ultimate universal attainment of harmony. Under this theory, light would have no meaning without shadow and the two will always coexist as aspects of the transcendent. There is a very old Gnostic myth that Shaitan, Lord of the Shadows, is actually the twin brother of Christos, acting with him in hidden harmony, in order to further the evolution of Humankind into more open fields of awareness and wisdom.

Thus, we find a subtle morphological mirroring between metaphysical teaching and conspiratology which resides in a common desire to find the ultimate source for history. The usual structural model for conspiratologists involves a cabal or secret society which actively seeks to exert universal dominion and evil through invidious infiltration (or "emanation") into the lifestream of history. The purpose of meta-physical teaching is also to discover the "one," however the "one" who is sought transcends the oppositions of slavery and freedom, light and dark, good and evil. As hard as conspiratologists seek, they will never find an earthly group either capable of or responsible for ruling the World. What they will eventually find at the Center, if they press forth hard enough, is an ultimately benevolent force of universal evolution with its own Wisdom and Being, which seeks only to open the "Single Eye" that it might see again! This force, for all of its purely impersonal and transcendent benevolence, is also capable of using what we have cognized as "evil" or pain to further the work of evolving awareness...a force which presses forward, whether we as individuals are ready to move forward or not.

The paradox remains, that while conspiracy theory tends to provide us with panoramic and "mind-blowing" vistas onto aspects of hidden history, what it is really doing is focusing upon the shadow side of the Great Temple. It is this higher level of transcendence, along with its rich and multivalent complexity which conspiratology simply misses in its quest for the One. The conspiratological world-view has tremendous value for the discernment of certain difficult-to-identify aspects of historical trends within the transcendent system, however it mistakes the part of the whole and the shadow for the light. That there is a great universal "conspiracy"...a hidden force moving history into certain guided arenas, I will not doubt. However, it is clearly toward the ultimate goal of universal sentience and Illumination that we must look. This is a conspir-acy hidden out in the open for all to see, since the best way to preserve a secret is to reveal it! The golden dreams of Illuminists and the pitch-black nightmares of conspiratology do both have tremendous reality to them. It is our task to rise above both to discover the hidden third term in the dialectic and to discover what actually might lie beyond good and evil...in a place where the true metaphysical foundations of Conspiracy originate...at the end of Time and Space.

Bibliography and Notes:

On the Teaching of Schwaller de Lubiscz, on the "Primal Scission," see: *Serpent in the Sky: The High Wisdom of Ancient Egypt* by John Anthony West, published by The Julian Press, New York, 1987.

For more information on my theories of Conspiracy, see:

"The Christian Theory of Occult Conspiracy," in *Apocalypse Culture,* edited by Adam Parfrey, Amok Press, New York, 1987.

"A Dark Storm Rising: Right-Wing Christianity and its Paranoid Worldview of Occult Conspiracies," in *The Fenris Wolf,* issue number 1, available from Psychick Release PCP, POP 26067, S-10041 Stockholm, Sweden.

"Under the Sign of Gemini," in *The Fenris Wolf,* issue number 2.

"Who Rules Over The Earth? The Archetype of the World Ruler and the Work of Universal Regeneration" and "A History of Vengeance and Assassination in Secret Societies" in *Apocalypse Culture,* expanded and revised edition, edited by Adam Parfrey, Feral House Books, Los Angeles, 1990.

Hotel Kalifornia
by Wayne Henderson

The stock-in-trade stands at approximately one million units, requiring minimal upkeep. A minimum of $30,000 changes hands on each unit, per annum; and supply of new units, handled by a string of related companies, is constant.

Welcome to one of the most profitable growth industries in the state of California.

Welcome to the California Department of Corrections (CDC).

The tens of billions of dollars that change hands each year in the normal, day-to-day operations of the CDC represent only the largest segment of this industry; one must also factor in the $20,000 per annum that changes hands for each occupied unit in the extensive network of county jails that peppers the state from the forested north to the Mexican border. Accurate figures for this network are hard to come by. The county jails feed the burgeoning "stock" of the CDC warehouses at an alarming rate. As prisoners are released back into the community, a high rate of recidivism is maintained by likely the most unbalanced parole system in existence, one that guarantees that, for all intents and purposes, anyone arrested, at any time, in the state of California will indeed be returned for several one-year stays as "parole violators," even if the parole violation occurs in the absence of any crime.

With such a high amount of guaranteed income generated each year, and protected (if not expanded) by governmental mandate, one might assume that those employed by the CDC as guards (or in one of the related capacities in the prisons) would be among the highest paid civil service employees in the state, if not the entire country, but such is not the case. The majority of correctional officers are low-paid scut-workers, glorified stockboys, their paycheck annually equalling roughly the amount allocated for upkeep of one prisoner. As the correctional workers are outnumbered by the prisoners, at a ratio in the neighborhood of 20:1, this is actually minimal cash output for the higher-ups.

The average CDC guard is undereducated, from a position of disadvantage in the community, poorly-trained (but heavily indoctrinated in the "US vs. THEM" ideology held by police departments) and encouraged, by CDC policy, to consider the prisoners somewhat less than human. The real money is pocketed by the higher-ups, as in any industry, a private "Old Boys" network of inexperienced but well-connected wardens such as the warden at Folsom State Prison, Robert Borg. Borg received his post, recently vacated by the corrupt Camp and his family, from friends in the CDC administrative offices in Sacramento due to his legendary abilities on the handball court, rather than any discernable ability, let alone experience, in wardening a Level 4 (high security) prison.

A brief trip through the system that feeds the CDC—a close-up look at the "criminal justice" process in California—would likely be the best illustration of the problem.

First comes the arrest. Police in the state of California, from the lowest traffic cop on the California Highway Patrol to the much better-connected inspectors in the various departments of the larger city police forces, are expected to fill a monthly quota. To fall below this quota incurs penalties, hence every officer, no matter what his relative position in the pecking order, makes certain to fill, if not exceed, his or her quota before the end of the month.

So you've helped a nice police officer make quota. You've entered the system. First up, there is the intake procedure; a brief medical exam (generally a medical technical assistant, or MTA, asking a list of questions regarding previous infections); followed by an intake officer who checks you for gang-oriented tattoos. Recently, an AIDS test has been added to the procedure, years too late. Once intake is completed, one is ungently escorted to the holding cells, only a few county facilities boast individual cells anymore, the overwhelming majority use "tanks," large 8, 12, 24 or higher capacity cages, dorm style, in which you will reside from time of arrest until - ? For many incarcerees, the stay is brief; they've been arrested before, done time before, and whether they've been detained for a simple parole violation (something as minor as having a roommate move in with them without first clearing it with a parole officer), or for a serious crime such as rape or murder, the parole violator will be offered the chance, in most cases, to plead guilty to the parole violation, take a year's stay in prison, and all other charges are dropped.

For the first-time arrestee, however, the process differs: being in this category myself, I speak from experience. Prosecutors and police departments fear the first-time arrestee. He or she is an unknown quantity. Worse yet is the first-time arrestee who might well, judging from the evidence in the case, be innocent of the charges, someone whose guilt, though assumed by the prosecution, is questionable. Convicts, whether in prison or on parole, have a lower life expectancy than the run of the general population, hence replacements are needed periodically to keep CDC stocked and provide the various cities and counties with fresh blood, need to be brought into the system. But who knows what connections the new faces have or what to expect from them? County jail and the trial by ordeal process generally pigeonhole the newcomer quite handily. A willingness to implicate others, especially those that the investigators mention during questioning, or a willingness to take a deal without putting the county courts through a lengthy trial fraught with work and expense for all involved, is generally taken as an indication that this arrestee qualifies for a lower custody-level prison, a shorter prison term, perhaps even to have some of the charges dropped. The uncooperative demand a jury trial and can generally expect to have charges enhanced or added (I saw the charges against me rise from four to seven, and the severity of the charges increase tenfold, after preliminary hearing because I refused to take a deal), will receive the maximum penalty if at all possible, and can generally count on confinement in the worst and highest security prisons.

Prosecutors, no less than police, have quotas. To lose one case is an embarrassment; to fall below conviction quota brings penalties. If it is necessary to "Fudge" the facts a bit, to have investigators make return trips to "counsel" the witnesses, then that's the price a prosecutor must pay to keep filling quota. Normally, however, the county jail itself is enough to pressure a detainee into taking a deal. In Los Angeles, the staff of the county jail relies on brutality; in San Francisco, the main tool is unhealthy conditions. Each county has its specialty. Each county jail administrator expects the detainee to show the good sense to take a deal and leave quickly for a more comfortable cage in prison. My own stay in the San Francisco county jail, at four and one-half years, is one of the five longest stays in that facility, a stay that brought down on me the wrath of Captain Frank Cook, the facility commandant, who couldn't understand why anyone, no matter how much they protested their non-complicity in the charged crimes, wouldn't just be a good boy and plead guilty to something, freeing up another bed in his facility.

The majority of defendants are provided with overworked, underpaid, and thoroughly apathetic public defenders, most of whom aspire for a better-paying job in the office of the District Attorney, and jockey for the few available positions in that office by cooperating as much as possible with the prosecutors against whom they're paired in court. Trade on cases is rampant. "You let me get a criminal trespass on this robbery and I'll get the rape to plead grievous assault by the end of the week." The lives of defendants are oft sold out for as little as a "power lunch" that will advance the defense attorney's career. Worse yet are the attorneys in private practice who specialize in handling court-appointed cases, especially when two or more defendants are charged in the same cases. Handling divorces and other such cases to keep their private practices valid, the court-appointed attorneys do even less work than the public defenders. Attorneys in the public defenders' office are required to prepare and file all their own motions, generating a massive amount of court paperwork. All that is required of a court-appointed attorney is to put in an appearance at the court dates and "join" in the motion presented by the public defender - no paperwork, indeed no work at all, required - and the court appointed attorney takes home a sizeable paycheck for no more than putting in a brief appearance and mumbling a sentence or two.

In four and a half years at the San Francisco county jail, I only rarely saw a defendant win a case. Judge's careers are built on rates of conviction and sentencing.

Intake into the CDC is essentially a repeat of the county jail process. The bored MTA asks the same old questions in monotone; the AIDS test; the ensconcement in a cell: then comes the committee. Classification committees are those CDC employees who decide on the placement in one of the myriad state prison facilities based upon the paperwork generated by the county authorities as well as their own mood at the time. Be a prisoner who refused to take a deal seated before them on a bad day and you'll likely wind up at the worst possible facility. I currently rest at 33 security points, qualifying me for a Level Three prison (such as the California Men's Colony or the Vacaville Medical Facility and Intake Center), but am maintained at Level Four Folsom because I had the audacity to turn down a deal for twenty years.

Once within the CDC system, you become, for all practical purposes, the property of the state. Your mail and "Care" packages are opened and anything that appeals to the guards employed in the mailroom or in the receiving area is confiscated as contraband. You are eligible to be pressed into service in the Prison Industries Authority shops at your prison, virtual slave labor that pays a maximum of 90 cents an hour to the prisoner and reaps major profits for the hierarchy in Sacramento. Most prison jobs don't quite pay that well. The average is actually closer to $30 a month, but there are plans to move a major number of prisoners south to the new, ultramodern, all industrial facility in Imperial Valley, scheduled to open by early next year. While the inmate pay won't increase, the profits will. Prisoners are also subject to covert medical experimentation. Recently, the AIDS confinement unit at Vacaville was made "Voluntary" and "Overflow" from the AIDS unit has been transferred here to Folsom, where they are free on the mainline, unidentified, and interspersed among the uninfected population. A friend spoke briefly with a Lt,'s clerk who had actually seen a copy of the list of AIDS cases on mainline here and was able to report that there are approximately 250 such people; between 70 and 80 in cell block #2 and an equal number in cell block #3 alone. Exchange of bodily fluids, via a shared cigarette, or joint, or cup of coffee, is endemic in prison. The majority of prisoners here will be released into the community well before any symptoms appear. Most prisoners, on release, make it their first priority to acquire sexual gratification and a dose of the drug of their choice, in no particular order, thereby serving to spread this designer virus even further in the population. Further, on October 22, 1991, the entire CDC system underwent "Tuberculosis testing," involving the injection, subcutaneously, of an unidentified fluid, mandatory for all incarcerees. While it might be the height of paranoia to assume that the CDC would forcibly infect all prisoners with some designed virus, one with an extended gestation period that would permit the CDC perhaps another ten years useful work out of each of the recipients, one should remember that the AIDS virus was spread in a very similar way, via smallpox and "experimental" hepatitis vaccines, and that charges have been made against clinics presently introducing other "vaccines" into the population. It is hardly beyond plausibility that the CDC would sentence all incarcerees to a slow, lingering, and yet productive death.

The current governor of the state of California, Pete Wilson, seems to oppose the construction of new prisons, unlike his predecessor, George Dukemeijian, under whom new facilities sprouted up like mushrooms after a thunderstorm, so it is possible that the CDC found itself at the tail end of a long line of contributors and friends in the new governor's retinue. Nonetheless, those numerous prisons built under the previous regime yet stand and are being opened only slightly past their original deadlines. Older prisons are not being decommissioned and the populations remain stable. The only logical assumption must be that more people will be fed, with or without cause, into the gaping maw of the ever hungry CDC system. California presently has incarcerated more prisoners than any country on earth, let alone more than any other state in the union. According to a report of the ACLU, at least one quarter of all prisoners in California are imprisoned wrongly, worse than even the 16 percent rate of wrongful conviction in the backward states of the deep south. Abuse of police power in California is legendary. The celebrated Rodney King incident is but a tip of the iceberg.

What does all this mean? It points unswervingly to a massive increase in arrests, more convictions, more enslavement of innocent people or people of questionable guilt, to serve the moneymaking machine of the CDC. In the absence of outside regulatory oversight, with no input from the electorate (save the investment of 30,000,000,000 tax dollars per year), it is not inconceivable that the CDC could, within the next ten years, have perhaps one in ten residents of the state (the total is now in the neighborhood of one in twenty) incarcerated, producing further profits for the CDC administrators in Sacramento.

Wayne Henderson currently resides at California State Prison at Folsom.

Wilhelm Reich Died for Einstein's Sins
by Jim Martin

The editor has asked me to answer the question: what, in the final analysis, brought the wrath of the government down upon Wilhelm Reich, M.D., and was he murdered, and if so, how? From my perspective, I think the most dangerous work that Reich was involved in wasn't advocating children's sexual rights, or his penetrating analysis of the patriarchal family and fascism, nor even his invention of the orgone accumulator: the single most important therapeutic technique ever discovered, bar none. The real reason Wilhelm Reich, M.D., was imprisoned was because he stumbled onto some scary facts about nuclear radiation during a critical point in that newly developed industry during the early 1950s.

Simply put, Reich found that there is no shielding possible against the biological effects of nuclear radiation. In 1952, in what was called *The Oranur Experiment,* Reich placed a small sample of a radioisotope inside a powerful orgone accumulator. Reich's shocking report, which can be found in the now out-of-print *Selected Writings*, details how radiation sickness is a function of the organism's response to invasive radiation, and not a direct result of the radiation poisoning itself. Thus different people may be more susceptible to very minute doses, while others may feel no noticeable effects; each person's reaction is different according to their own character structure.

It must be recalled that at that time there was little understanding of the biological effects of small doses of radiation. Many people remember that soldiers were sent directly into test sights, shortly after the dust cleared from nuclear explosions. They wore no shielding, and were merely dusted off afterwards. Today, thanks in large part to the antinuclear movement of the eighties, as well as the Ban the Bomb movement of the late fifties and early sixties, there is a greater awareness of the issue. But there is little understanding, even today, of the true nature of Reich's research.

Space does not allow a full discussion of Reich biography, but those interested won't find a better place to start than with Myron Sharaf's *Fury on Earth*. When Reich first discover the specifically biological energy he called orgone, he waited a long time before publishing anything about it. He knew how crazy it all sounded, and was unsure himself until he verified the phenomena under a variety of experimental protocols. One such experiment, TO-T, measured the temperature difference between an orgone box (constructed with alternating layers of metal and wood), and a similarly constructed box that lacked the metal lining, but had the same capacity for insulation. An orgone box is generally warmer than the outside temperature. I have verified this phenomena myself. Moreover, the temperature difference varies as a result of changes in the atmosphere. A change in the weather can increase or decrease the temperature differential.

Think about it: if you had two boxes, and left them inside your garage, wouldn't you expect them to be pretty close to the room temperature over time? If I could construct a box such that it remained warmer by four or more degrees for extended periods of time, wouldn't you want to know where that heat came from? I've had many scientifically trained people scoff at me at the very possibility, or say there must be some very simple explanation for this phenomena, but no one has offered me a satisfying reason for why this is so.

Albert Einstein was one person who found the question intriguing enough to invite Reich to his home to demonstrate the effect. Reich had written him a cautious letter in the hopes that this "Father of the Atom Bomb" would recognize the experiment's results violated the Second Law of Thermodynamics, the law of entropy, which states that equal volumes tend to equalize in temperature.

Reich traveled to Princeton with several devices with which to demonstrate the orgone. He described his long session with Einstein as a meeting of minds. Einstein observed the phenomena, and said, "If this is true, it would be a bombshell for Physics." Indeed, because it was at a fundamental variance with Einstein's theory of relativity. Einstein's biographers have painted this meeting in a ridiculous light, saying it was an example of Einstein's eccentricity. Perhaps, but the exchange of letters, which Reich published later, belies this assumption.

Einstein met once again with Reich and then dropped the matter. An assistant offered a simplistic and contrived explanation, that the effect was due to "convection" between the air above and below the table upon which the accumulator had been placed. Reich responded with a long letter which described the protocols under which he answered this objection. He buried the accumulator underground, removing the possibility of such convection. The temperature differential increased under these conditions. He concluded the letter with an agonizing and heart rending appeal for respect and consideration. Reich did not receive it. Einstein discontinued the correspondence.

When rumors circulated that Einstein had tested the device and found it worthless, Reich published the full correspondence including Einstein's statement that the temperature differential had been clearly observed.

A decade later, the Oranur experiment revealed the folly in casual use of nuclear radiation. A scandal stirred up by leftist magazines talking about Reich's "sex-cult" alongside right-wing attacks from ministers and schoolmarms brought the crisis to a head.

The FDA launched a multi-million dollar investigation of the orgone accumulator, declared it a fraud, and set about bringing criminal proceedings against Reich. Reich's FBI files reveal a blistering blizzard of letters directed towards getting rid of Reich, from doctors in the AMA threatened by such a simply constructed device threatening their practices, from the Atomic Energy Commission advising the FDA what "a thorn in the side" Reich had been.

Conspiracy theories abound as to the nature of Reich's death, and his own daughter, Eva Reich, M.D., believes that he was murdered. Reich died only two months from his parole date. The official cause of death was a heart attack, and the autopsy showed enough formaldehyde in Reich's system to interfere with testing for other compounds. In the final analysis, the real tragedy in Reich's life and death was the silence and obscurity that greeted his fantastic discoveries. These discoveries are being used today under different names and guises. As replication after replication of Reich's experimental findings pile in today, there is still a conspiracy of silence around the issues. Those who know, don't say. I am constantly surprised how many people know about Reich.

Why was Reich murdered? Those who can understand what he says at the end of the book *The Einstein Affair* will know: "Einstein succeeded in fascinating the first half of the twentieth century just because he had emptied space. Emptying space, reducing the whole universe to a static nothing, was the only theory that could satisfy the desert-like character structure of man of this age. Empty, immobile space and a desert character structure fit well together. It was a last attempt on the part of armored men to withstand and withhold knowledge of a universe full of life energy, pulsating in many rhythms, always in a state of development and change; in one word, functional and not mechanistic, mystical or relativistic. It was the last barrier, in scientific terms, to the final break-down of the human armoring."

Jim Martin runs Flatland, *a mail-order newsstand that offers unusual lore and literature, including much on Wilhelm Reich. POB 2420, Fort Bragg, CA 95437-2420.*

Or Was it the Sins of the Air Force?
by Kenn Thomas

Indeed, Reich suggested in *The Einstein Affair* that Modju (l)—Reich's acronym for conspirators from Moscow—"had done a job" on Albert Einstein's interest in the orgone. A *New York Times* article from March 17, 1950 cited at the end of the book reports the return to Communist Poland of an Einstein associate, Dr. Leopold Infield, to organize educational programs for the country's "progressive" government (2). *The Einstein Affair* does not give an indication as to whether or not Reich had reason to believe Dr. Infield to be the assistant who explained away the accumulator's temperature difference. He certainly had reason to believe European Communists were hostile to his work, as it earned him only enmity and rejection from the German and Dutch CPs.

The threads of conspiracy surrounding Reich were difficult enough to follow during his life; thirty years later the task has become impossible. Consider the Mata Hari scenario for his death as an instance: Reich moved to Washington, DC at the behest of his last paramour, a former HEW employee who "would sometimes disappear for days on end without warning," (3) according to the memoirs of Reich's last wife, and who had contact with the FBI after his death, as reflected in its files. Elsewhere, of course, the relationship is portrayed as a loving one; Reich deepest passion, in fact, during his most troubled time.

Certainly the visibility of *The Oranur Experiment* (it had been reported upon widely by the news media in Maine and Arizona) and the implications it had on the use of nuclear energy made him an apt candidate for subterfuge by the government and the nuclear power industry. And they *were* paying attention: it is ironic and revealing (and sad) that Eisenhower used Reich's phrase, "Atoms For Peace," to help promote nuclear power.

Reich had developed another device, the cloudbuster, which harnessed orgone energy to help deal with the threat of nuclear radiation. However, he discovered a second and third use for the machine: weather modification and as a defense against unidentified flying objects. In his last book, *Contact With Space Oranur Second Report, 1951-1956* (4), and to his associates toward the end of his life, Reich insisted that the Air Force had a keen interest in his UFO work. Reich claimed as his own a report that Edward Ruppelt, author of the popular paperback on the Air Force's Project Blue Book, *The Report On Unidentified Flying Objects* (5), asserted "had circulated around high command levels of intelligence." (Reich and Ruppelt both also discuss UFO films that were included in a 1956 movie, *Unidentified Flying Objects.*)

Even Reich's defenders tread warily on his UFO theories, some seeing his protestations that the Air Force took him seriously as eccentricity or stress related paranoia, some viewing them simply as a decline in his reasoning faculty. Considering the zeal with which the Air Force no doubt coveted "death ray" research as part of its Cold War arsenal, however, and particularly in light of recent revelations about the extent of government interest in flying saucers, it is not unreasonable and requires no belief in UFOs to take Reich at his word. Another clue: Reich's last manuscript, *Creation,* purportedly detailing an anti-gravity theory, disappeared at his death, although copies may have been smuggled out of the Lewisberg prison by its librarian or Reich's attorney. (6)

"One must live things to judge them," Reich notes in *Contact With Space.* That he was killed in prison as surely as was Jack Ruby seems certain, but the fading trail of history leaves only questions as to why.

Notes:

1. From Mocenigo, who turned Giordano Bruno over to the Inquisition- and Djugashvili, the real name of Joseph Stalin.

2. *The Einstein Affair,* Orgone Institute Press, Rangeley, Maine, 1953.

3. Reich, Ilse Ollendorf, *Wilhelm Reich A Personal Biography,* Avon Books, New York, 1969, p. 166.

4. Reich, Wilhelm, *Contact With Space Oranur Second Report 1951-1956,* CORE Pilot Press, New York, 1957.

5. Ruppelt, Edward J., *The Report On Unidentified Flying Objects,* Ace Books, 1956.

6. Eden, Jerome, *Sincerely, Elsworth Baker,* Eden Press, 1988, pp. 107-108.

Book Reviews

Apocalypse Culture
edited by Adam Parfrey
Feral House, 362 pp., $12.95

Did anyone notice that George Bush's forty day jihad in the Persian Gulf was precipitated by a series of United Nations resolutions hovering frighteningly around the number 666? Few news sources reported which resolution actually used the magic number—inlaid on the rubber stamp of the Great Beast according to the cosmology of St. John—and the silence was suspicious. Was it being reserved for a special purpose? The media certainly didn't restrict End Times rants to the superstitious Iraqis; it did make large mention of the $666 million Germany plans to send to Israel in foreign aid. In the Reagan days of Armageddonism and the Evil Empire, this would have been big news.

But Apocalypse rarely goes out of fashion in America. This book, in fact, seems to take as its premise that the irrationalism and paranoia of apocalyptic thinking have become a dominant mode of national expression. *Apocalypse Culture* provides more of a sampling than a survey of the phenomenon, but it also offers some discussion of its roots and purpose. "It was my recurring childhood game to believe that I could avert disaster (car crashes, atomic bombs, etc.) by imagining the calamity while holding my breath," editor Adam Parfey confesses in underscoring the universality of the impulse. "It is entirely possible that *Apocalypse Culture* is the outgrowth of this kind of superstition."

Parfrey contributes the opening overview of historic werewolfism and its modern manifestations, replete with an illustration of a fanged and hairy Charles Manson. Parfrey argues for the re-emergence of the wolf archetype as "some measure [of] psychic preparation for the millenial calamities that are thought to lie ahead." The chapter heads a section on "Apocalypse Theologies" that includes interviews with several notorious weirdos: Karen Greenlea, a necrophiliac arrested in 1979 for having sex with a corpse after abducting it from the mortuary that employed her; "Frank," a psychopath who publishes "handy hints for messier massacres" newsletters from prison and promises only to control his lust for mass murder for a few years after his release; G. G. Allin, whose masturbatory gesticulations and fecal feeding on the rock'n'roll stage got him incarcerated; and child pornographer Peter Sotos ("Humanitarians [are] very enjoyable indeed. Often their tears and wails and pain over molested children and slaughtered co-eds can be

very exciting.") The section also contains the prison writings of schizophrenics; the flesh-piercing practices of Fakir Musafar; additive and subtractive surgical practices; and an argument for self-castration.

Apocalypse Culture would read like the print version of the *Faces of Death* video series were it not for the book's insights on the meaning and tenor of cultural trends. In an essay on the case against art, John Zerzan argues that "we see in art ever more fitting parables of its end...'serious' music is long dead and popular music deteriorates; poetry nears collapse...and the novel is eclipsed by non-fiction as the only way to write seriously." To this, David Peel adds a report on the millenial/apocalyptic dimensions of nano technology: "we'll probably reach a stage at which every subtle nuance of imagination and consciousness can be realized, stored and displayed through machinery." With these and other arguments, the view that emerges from *Apocalypse Culture* is not one of a culture collapsing back on religious superstitions, but one pushed to the documented extremes by an exhaustive modernism.

The book's last half, "The Invisible War," deals more directly with apocalypticism and its more organized and perforcely paranoid dimensions. It includes essays by Anton LaVey warning against microwave radiation, ultrasonic and subsonic targetting, and even three day weekends as "catechisms of demoralization." Parfrey contributes both a historical survey of eugenics and a report on Ron J. Steele, a prophetic author who makes it plain that Michael Jackson is Lucifer and the UPC code is the devil's own rubber stamp. The section also reprints part of Wilhelm Reich's *Contact With Space,* documenting his bouts with UFOs. Nothing here is presented as a lampoon or as an exposure of human embarrassments, but as serious ideological undercurrents of the mainstream.

Apocalypse Culture concludes with an attempt by Dennis Stillings to define war imagery in the post-atomic era. "This time around we are not confronted with 'babe wrapped in swaddling clothes,' which is easy enough to accept, but with a 'rough beast, its hour come 'round at last,' that's slouched toward Almagordo to be born.'' Well, maybe. Since Stallings wrote those words, of course, the Persian Gulf War has come and gone and it wasn't the end of the world for apocalypticists. The Big One is always just ahead, even if the empire looks less evil these days and even less like an empire. The terms of the apocalypse debate have changed just a bit since the publication of this book. George Bush, of course, is supported by the same lunatic religious rightists who would like to end it all in one big blow out for the Lord, so *Apocalypse Culture* has not lost much of its relevance. It's just that the Bush style, the New World Order, has been one of smaller, more manageable mini-apocalypses providing signposts to that calamitous end.

The Idle Warriors
by Kerry Thornley
IllumiNet, 265 pp., $10.95

Kerry Thornley's novel about malaise among soldiers stationed in post-war Japan has more to recommend it than its stature as a historic curiosity. IllumiNet Press' edition *is* the first complete publication of Thornley's novel about his Marine chum, Lee Harvey Oswald, written a full year before the Kennedy assassination. But it includes interesting new introductions by the author and David S. Lifton, whose compulsive commitment to applied physics lifted the JFK debate to new levels of macabre speculation. With Oliver Stone poised to deify Jim Garrison in a soon to be released flick (that Lifton has called *Mr. Garrison Goes To Washington)* reading Lifton's retelling of the Garrison-Thornley legal entanglements should be sobering to assassination buffs. For his part, Thornley suggests in his preface a deeper involvement with the events of November 22 while apologizing for the macho-Marine style and the conclusions of *The Idle Warriors,* that Oswald defected to the Soviet Union because of the aforementioned malaise. Was Thornley brainwashed to concoct this cover story?

Thornley is probably best known as one of the pair that half-perceived, half-created the Discordian Society, a lampoon chaos-worshipping cult popular among Robert Anton Wilson's readers, at a bowling alley in Richard Nixon's hometown. The product of the meeting, *Principia Discordia,* also has been reprinted by IllumiNet with a new introduction and a new book by Thornley, *Zenarchy,* is available too. *Zenarchy* imparts wisdom gleaned from a variety of humorous and hippy-esque sources, Alan Watts, Wilson, Leary and Camden Benares among them, and gets truly weird only when Thornley discusses government pogroms to create "transistorized untouchables."

Unfortunately, *The Idle Warriors,* holds out promise of more details concerning the Thornley-Oswald link for an as yet unpublished effort. Thornley's speculation that he and Oswald were both part of a Nazi breeding experiment are left documented elsewhere. Until that one surfaces, IllumiNet has presented here enough mondo fodder to keep the ball rolling. One other detail: Oswald's character, named Johnny Shellburn in the book, has a look-alike friend often mistaken as his twin!

Open Magazine Pamphlet Series
Open Media, $3.50

"Media Control, The Spectacular Achievements of Propaganda" by linguist Noam Chomsky is the best of these. In explaining the horrific spectacle of Americans treating the Persian Gulf War as some kind of video entertainment, Chomsky reviews the history of public relations in the U.S. His study begins with the earliest use of PR to subvert labor organizing and continues to the mindless sloganeering of "supporting the troops" used even by otherwise peaceful Americans during the Gulf conflict.

Such sentiments are manufactured, argues Chomsky, by propagandists who hold a classist conception of democracy: that a responsible, specialized class makes the decisions and it pushes a stupid mob around to carry them out. Chomsky outlines the usual means by which this accomplished: distorting history; demonizing an enemy; ignoring sensible alternatives, etc. (To date, what makes the Bush administration's intentions in Iraq so obvious is the absence of contact with any form of Iraqi opposition.) What's lacking in the essay, however, is any sense that the "bewildered herd" has any control over these manipulations and therefore shares little of the blame. Warfare culture seems like a much more difficult thing to accomplish than possible with mere condescension.

Chomsky certainly identifies the public relations tactics used by the government to support unsupportable policies, but he doesn't address why people fall for it. Otherwise enlightened minds on the UC-Berkeley campus recently denounced Bay Area bookstores for sponsoring one of Chomsky's foreign policy talks. Chomsky's own linguistics research has been funded by the Army and the Air Force. While ostensibly arguing for a conception of democracy truer to the common sense meaning of the word, the important issue of what to do about a citizenry that actually *prefers* to be marginalized (or terrified, or whatever) is left to be dealt with by others. Remaining are not only reverberations of Walt Kelly's admonition that we have met the enemy and he is us but of the question "why create a fascist state when you don't need one?"

A wartime interview with John Stockwell and essays by Howard Zinn and Michael Emory are also available in this back-pocket format series.

The COINTELPRO Papers
by Ward Churchill and Jim Vander Wall
South End Press, 467 pp., $16.00

Authors of *The COINTELPRO Papers* previously produced *Agents of Repression: The FBI's Secret Wars Against the Black Panther Party and the American Indian Movement,* and this effort purports to let FOIPA documents support their earlier conclusions by reprinting many of the actual artifacts. Reproduced in total are revealing FBI memoranda that reflect COINTEL-PRO's expansion from a counter-intelligence program directed against the Communist Party to one of "extra-legal" harassment against civil rights leaders, the leaders of Puerto Rican and Black independence movements, AIM, the New Left and others. The book begins with a letter by J. Edgar Hoover from as early as 1919 illegally planning to make a legal case against Marcus Garvey, and ends with a 1976 FBI memo arguing that its right to suppress dissent is superior to the free speech and privacy rights of citizens. AIM leader and poet/musician John Trudell contributes a poem fragment as the book's forward.

One chapter also does a lot to explain all the magic marker strokes and deletions on the FOIPA documents; what kinds of things were left out and why, and the legal authority for such censorship. Even with that caveat, however, the paper trail only goes so far in documenting COINTELPRO crimes—hate mail harassment that in some cases was no doubt easy to ignore, and dopy plans to bully Martin Luther King into killing himself, etc. While *The COINTELPRO Papers* also provides a narrative describing FBI support of the Klan and many other murderous activities, questions about on-going operations involving the assassination of domestic political dissidents, brainwashing programs and links between the intelligence community and affairs/experiments like the Jonestown massacre and the spread of AIDS, are left wanting answers. Despite the book's many revelations, the notion remains that many more of the secret government's behaviors go undocumented, certainly well beyond the feeble reach of the Freedom of Information Act.

Positively Bob Dylan
by Michael Krogsgaard
Popular Culture Ink, 498 pp., $55

In 1986 Bob Dylan helped publicize a recorded effort by John Trudell and another musician, the late Jesse Ed Davis, entitled *AKA Graffiti Man,* probably the only rock recording to mention John Lennon as a possible victim of a Manchurian Candidate-type plot. Dylan played the tape as pre-show music for many of his concerts that year and spoke highly of it in *Rolling Stone.* In addition to giving the premise more than usual national exposure, it reminded Dylan's audience that, now at age 50, America's premiere singer-songwriter can claim great success as a survivor. In the course of his long and varied life, much speculation has surrounded many public events in Dylan's life: was it LSD or the JFK assassination that transformed his Woody Guthriesque folk tunes into the surrealist

visions of *Highway 61 Revisited?* Did he fall victim to a Christian cabal during his conversion in the late 70s, was he brainwashed like Tim Leary suggested, or did it have something to do with Jonestown?

This book does not ask, answer or document these questions except in the most oblique way. Krogsgaard lists every Dylan tape available to the international network of Dylan collectors and aficionados, replete with song lists and the names of musicians in every band. It is a formidable effort, one that began with its first publication in Denmark in 1981 and a second in 1988. This volume is part of Popular Culture Ink's *Rock & Roll Reference* series. Its enormous size and price tag puts it out of the range of those with just a general interest in Dylan, but to enthusiasts of his music as well as students of the popular music industry and its history, it is an extraordinary work and a model for as yet undocumented and under-documented musical careers.

Such readers can imagine improvements: *Positively Bob Dylan* does not contain transcriptions of Dylan's on-stage banter, as wild and weird in 1966 as it was during the preachy period of the early '80s; lyric variations are unmentioned; even annotations like the first electric concert or the first acoustic version of "Desolation Row" are missing; and new information about the extant recordings surfaces all the time among Dylan fans, notorious for relishing every nuance. The wealth of secondary sources recounting Dylan's backstage and off-stage life, perhaps included as marginalia to the tape lists, might actually yield some new information about conspiracies in Dylan's life. A massive bibliography of the Dylan-book cottage industry included as an appendix would also be a valuable addition.

Alas, Krogsgaard's efforts are Herculean enough, and he does an admirable job of explaining his intentions and methods in the preface. Short of expandable, updatable and relational databases, this is as thorough a book as can be produced.

One plot that Krogsgaard should have included concerns the earliest known Dylan tape, a May 1960 tape made in St. Paul, Minnesota. Although it appeared in earlier editions, Krogsgaard no longer includes it because the consensus among one group of fans is that it's fake. Like the Zapruder film, an "official" version—or omission—should be looked at askance and some discussion of the tape at least would have been in order here. In any event, this is an argument for specialists and detracts little from an otherwise spectacular accomplishment in reference research.

Conspiracies, Cover-Ups and Crimes
by Jonathan Vankin
Paragon House, 319 pp., $24.95

Jonathan Vankin seems to have written a book about conspiracies for the uninitiated. *Conspiracies, Cover-Ups and Crimes* touches a lot of bases and goes into just enough detail with each to leave the reader impressed that he or she has some comprehensive view of undercurrents in the vast realm of conspiracy speculation. Of course, this is precisely why the book cannot be trusted. Vankin takes great care not to lampoon the subjects of his study and, in fact, comes away as somewhat a believer himself. "He never strays far from the perspective outlined in the book's introduction, however: I've steeped my mind in conspiracy theories, figuring the only way to truly understand them is to see the world from their point of view...I've emerged with my sanity in tact...coming back to port with a new understanding..." Despite his good intentions, Vankin allows his readers an unshaken assumption that some common sense plateau out there puts all this nonsensical conspiracy stuff in perspective. Anyone with familiarity in these waters realizes that Vankin hasn't gone as deep as it gets.

Tidbits like Lyndon LaRouche's belief that the Grateful Dead actually work for British intelligence proliferate in the book. Also, Vankin's treatment of Kerry Thornley in the first chapter spells out Thornley's theory that a Nazi breeding experiment produced him and Lee Harvey Oswald in more detail here than elsewhere. (Thornley says that Vankin is thinking about writing a Thornley biography.) But the UFO chapter fails to even mention Zechariah Sitchin's scholarship on the possible extraterrestrial origins of the ancient Sumerians. Sitchin's work supplants that of the pseudonymous William Bradley (*The Gods of Eden*), discussed at length by Vankin, and includes interesting ruminations about the UFO encounters of a Soviet probe of the Martian moon Phobos that would have added much to the chapter. Vankin does everything but mention the name of John Lear, leaving this figure a shadowy one when some investigation and commentary would have given much even to UFO conspiracy specialists. Topics from Reich to the Gemstone File go slighted or ignored.

Still, this is the book to give to skeptics, not to convert them but to provide an overview without souring them with too much detail. One chapter title makes a good point: *there is no word for rational fear.*

2

Steamshovel Press #5, Summer 1992

JFK Redux:
Interviews with Mark Lane, Kerry Thornley
Jim Marrs, and Dick Gregory

Introduction

A week prior to the release of Oliver Stone's *JFK* movie last winter, *Newsweek* ran the cover headline: "The Twisted Truth of JFK: Why Oliver Stone's New Movie Can't Be Trusted." In addition to echoing the sentiments of the rest of the media blitz bent on discrediting the film, the article called the stories of Marita Lorenz, a key player in Mark Lane's *Plausible Denial* (Thunder's Mouth, $22.95), "wacky" and attributed the quote to a "well-respected researcher" named Gus Russo. Lane had this to say about Gus Russo: I called two people who wrote the article for *Newsweek*. The first was Howard Manley. I said, "Who's Gus Russo?" He said, "I don't know." I said, "But you quote him as a respectable researcher. It's a little odd to me because I've been looking into these matters for twenty eight years. I never heard of him. Who is he?" And he said, "I haven't the faintest idea. You have to talk to David Gates, he wrote that part of it." So I talked to Mr. Gates and I said, "Who is Gus Russo?" And he said, "He's a researcher." And I said, "OK, has he ever written a book?" And he said, "No." "Ever given a speech?" "No." "Ever written a paper?" "No." "Well, who respects him?" And he said, "I could give you the names of a couple of people but they gave me that information with the promise that it wouldn't be attributed to them." I said, "Oh, I see, in other words these people said to you [whisper] 'Listen, Gates, I can give you some information: Gus Russo is respected, but never use my name about it.' Is that what you're saying? Are you all crazy at *Newsweek*?" And he said, "Well, I can tell you this: you know this woman Jane? Well, there's this woman down in Dallas at the conference on the Kennedy assassination a couple of months ago, named Jane, and she was selling t-shirts for Stone's movie. She said he was respectable."

I said, "So that's your source?" Now it turns out that he lives in Baltimore. I've never heard of anyone who's heard of him. But they spelled his name wrong. It's not Russo, it's Ruso. In other words, he is so well-known to *Newsweek* that they don't know how to spell his name. And what he did say according to the article is that the statements made by Marita Lorenz were totally unverifiable. And then I said to Mr. Gates, "I faxed your partner, Mr. Manley, sixteen pages of FBI documents which verified major portions of Marita Lorenz. Isn't that true?" He said, "Well, yes." And I said, "This is what she said: they went from Miami to Dallas, they took automatic weapons, they drove across state lines. Didn't I give you FBI documents which confirm the fact that she was allowed to drive stolen vehicles across state lines, allowed to carry illegal weapons and transport bombs illegally? They were giving her a license to do that. Don't you have those documents, for example? Then how do you publish a story in which it says it's totally unverifiable when a good portion of her story is verified?" He said, "Well, I think you ought to write a letter to *Newsweek*." And I said, "Well, I'll do that at the very least." So much for the testimony of *Newsweek*'s experts on the question.

Among the revelations in the following interviews with authors connected to the JFK assassination is Lane's report that Fletcher Prouty, the redoubtable "X" played by Donald Sutherland in Stone's movie, planned to sue *Esquire* for an article written by Robert Sam Anson that misrepresented his (Prouty's) relationship with the filmmaker. After the release of *JFK*, *Steamshovel Press* went back to the *Esquire* article to prepare for a possible interview with Prouty and discovered that, indeed, Gus Russo had been mentioned by Robert Sam Anson as a "well-regarded researcher," a description strangely similar to the one in *Newsweek*. According to Anson, Russo tried to get Stone to pare down the wilder aspects of conspiracy theorizing and lost a consulting contract for the effort.

Steamshovel Press also checked its library of JFK assassination books, certainly not a comprehensive one but one that includes Harold Weisberg's first two *Whitewash* books, Jim Marrs' *Crossfire*, Anthony Summers' *Conspiracy, Reasonable Doubt* by Henry Hurt, *Best Evidence* by David Lifton, many other books and a considerable stack of magazines and privately published materials. Russo had not been well-regarded enough to warrant a mention anywhere in the collection.

Someone named Philip Russo was instrumental in putting under Jim Garrison's case against Clay Shaw. Although he testified to being at a meeting where Shaw, David Ferrie and Lee Harvey Oswald planned the assassination, the testimony was discredited when Russo revealed that he only recalled the event after hypnosis. In the labyrinthine machinations of JFK assassination studies, where there are no coincidences, certainly the similarity of names here is one. Unless, of course, whoever attempted to tone down Stone's movie and discredit Lane chose the Gus Russo pseudonym to add some panache to his disinformation scheme.

The other linchpin in Garrison's original investigation concerns a police officer named Aloysius Habighorst, who would have testified that Clay Shaw told him he used the name "Clay Bertrand" as an alias when he filled out his fingerprint card after his arrest. Garrison based much of his case on Clay Shaw and Clay Bertrand being the same person. The judge ruled Habighorst's testimony as inadmissible because he failed to inform Shaw of his right to silence before asking him for aliases. These events comprise two key scenes in *JFK* but Mark Lane believes it never happened. He did not make it clear whether his opinion stems from personal knowledge or his belief in the justice system.

These interviews should reach *Steamshovel Press* readers shortly after *JFK* arrives at the video stores. All of them were broadcast on radio during the movie's theatrical release and hopefully they contributed to the media climate that mainly consisted of predictably hostile opinions about the film from TV pundits and newspaper columnists. Among the more interesting of television's revelations during the first wave of reaction to Stone's movie:

David Belin and Gerald Ford were quite visible attempting to exonerate Jack Ruby from any conspiracy because a delay in Oswald's release—caused by the unexpected arrival of a postmaster in the Dallas sheriff's office—made the timing impossible. Oliver Stone challenged this by commenting on the *New York Times* letters page that "the plotters would have wanted to get Jack Ruby into place before bringing Oswald down, regardless of the surprise visit." Another letter writer pointed out the obvious possibility of the postmaster's involvement in the plot. But CBS newsman Ike Pappas, whose voice says "Oswald's been shot" on the old video footage, inadvertently contradicted both sides on CNBC. Pappas said that Oswald arrived right on time.

Although Belin ostensibly supports the Warren Commission view, he nevertheless nervously noted on *Nightline* that proof exists of Oswald's visit to the Soviet embassy in Mexico City. Said Belin: "There was one photograph that I identified that was not a photograph of Lee Harvey Oswald but there is other information that I identified that did indeed show that Oswald, Lee Harvey Oswald, was at the embassy." As Mark Lane reports in *Plausible Denial,* CIA western hemisphere ops chief David Atlee Phillips admitted "Lee Harvey Oswald never visited...that is a categorical statement...there is no proof of that." Apparently this was not enough to convince Stone, who asked Bryant Gumbel on *Today,* "what was Oswald doing in Mexico City?"

The Mexico City scenario figures prominently in developments concerning the sealed House Assassination Committee files that Louis Stokes has been working to get released. On the *Nightline* program with Belin, British author Anthony Summers (*Conspiracy*) discussed a possible relationship between Oswald and Phillips. According to the program, the head of the anti-Castro group Alpha 66 saw the men together (he knew Phillips as "Maurice Bishop" and this cover name was verified by another CIA official) two months prior to the assassination. *Inside Edition* also reported that the sealed files reveal much about the Phillips/Oswald connection, plus much about FBI infiltration of Garrison's investigation.

On *Primetime Live* Sam Donaldson insisted to Stone that there was no phone blackout of Washington after the assassination, that he (Donaldson) made many calls from "Washington to the Capitol." Stone promised to check his facts on that one. Neither were apparently cognizant of the possibility that the blackout was of phone service between cities. On the same program, Donaldson seemed to suggest that Garrison and Fletcher Prouty never met or exchanged ideas, at least in the way Stone depicts in the film. Stone used only "artistic license" as his defense and has been curiously quiet about Prouty throughout his talk-show circuit travels.

Government agencies certainly seem to be monitoring some of these programs. Within hours after James Earl Ray called his ex-wife on *Donahue* and repeated charges he makes in his new book, *Who Killed Martin Luther King?* (National Press Books,

$21.95), that the FBI was involved, US marshals were dispatched to the home of his brother John, a diabetic with two feet amputated, to enforce a two-year-old arrest warrant for probation violation. After a pool hall attendant named Harold Doyle told *A Current Affair* that he was one of the men arrested in the railroad yard behind the grassy knoll, the FBI came to question him. Living in Klamuth Falls, Oregon, Doyle made an uncharacteristic Amtrak trip to Portland after the program aired, where he encountered the agents. Were they making sure Doyle told *A Current Affair* producers only what he had been told to tell them or was it, as the show would have it in a follow-up program, proof positive that the railroad yard hoboes were not Watergate figures E. Howard Hunt and Frank Sturgis? For his part, Hunt dismissed the topic with a quip on *Larry King Live* that "nobody rational" believes he was involved, making no mention of the trial discussed in Lane's *Plausible Denial*.

A final surprise: NBC ended its *Today* show series on various JFK conspiracy theories by rolling credits of people connected to the assassination who died violently. A television first found its way onto the list: rare acknowledgement of Mary Pinchot Meyer, JFK's LSD paramour. It was no surprise, of course, that Dan Rather, who initially reported that the Zapruder film showed a *forward* head snap, spent another hour on CBS' *48 Hours* supporting the Warren Commission.

Mark Lane, author of *Plausible Denial*

Q: You were the campaign manager for Kennedy in 1960 in New York?

A: In New York City. There were two campaign managers. I was one of the two and I worked closely with Bobby and with John and the campaign. That same year I was a candidate for the New York State Legislature and John Kennedy came to my district and campaigned with me and for me and I was elected to the state legislature and, of course, he was elected to the presidency.

Q: How do you think your life and career would have developed had Kennedy not been killed?

A: Oh, very differently, I guess. When I heard that he'd been killed and read about it the next day in the *New York Times,* because I knew him, because we shared an agenda on a number of questions, I was really at least as concerned as most Americans and perhaps a bit more. I called up a woman named Jean Hill. I didn't know who she was. Her name appeared in the *New York Times* as a witness who was perhaps closest to the president. She was a spectator watching the motorcade go by. She was perhaps closest to him of those standing around when the bullets were fired at him, struck him and killed him. And I just called her up. I got her number from directory assistance and asked her if she would describe the scene to me. I told her that I knew Kennedy and that I was concerned about his death and she said, "Have you been to Dealey Plaza?" And I said I had never been to Dallas, actually. She said, "Let me describe the scene for you." And she said that in front of his car to the right front was a grassy knoll. It had a wooden fence on it and it was from that area behind the fence on the grassy knoll that the shots came. I said, "Can I repeat this to the news media later?" and she said yes. At that point the official story was that the shots had all come from the book depository building, which had been behind the President when he was shot. And I did and the words "grassy knoll" became part of the American experience and I never talked to Jean Hill again, although I have said on numerous occasions Jean Hill named it the grassy knoll. I'm not sure that she knows that. And just a few days ago I was in Dallas twenty eight years after we'd originally talked one time on the phone and we were at a seminar together and we met, embraced each other and I said, "Did you know that you named it the grassy knoll?" And she said, "Well, I read your book, *A Citizen's Dissent* in 1969 and you said that was the first time, that I had named it." In any event, she gave me a lot of information, as other witnesses did, and then my investigation began.

Q: Has the situation changed enough now so that we can get closer to the truth?

A: I think we know the truth. *Plausible Denial* is the book I've written now and it's so different from *Rush To Judgement,* not contradictory to it but complementary, but very different in that when I wrote *Rush To Judgement* all I had before me was the conclusions of the Warren Commission, the committee appointed by President Johnson to look into the facts surrounding the death of President Kennedy. I compared those conclusions with the evidence the Warren Commission had amassed by interviewing key witnesses the Warren Commission refused to interview. Basically, all *Rush To Judgement* said was that the conclusions of the Warren Commission were not true. And that book was written, as I said—some five thousand citations and references and footnotes—and I was quite surprised when it became the number one best-selling book in America. And that was basically my commitment to it, to try to remove the Warren Commission as an obstacle.

Later, I came to Washington, DC and I formed the Citizens Commission of Inquiry and I worked for the Congress to investigate the assassination of Dr. King and President Kennedy. I drafted the original legislation. I personally briefed more than one hundred members of Congress and more than one thousand congressional aides and we formed over one hundred eighty chapters of the Citizens Commission of Inquiry all around the United States. When the legislation was finally reported out of the Rules Committee of the House of Representatives, we were able to organize more than one million letters, telegrams, signatures on petitions and the legislation passed and then, of course, the Congress investigated. So the House Select Committee on Assassinations concluded that in all probability, to a ninety five percent certainty, there had been a conspiracy to kill President Kennedy and they asked the Department of Justice to investigate it and they declined to do so.

That's basically where the matter rested until a newspaper article was published by an organization called the Liberty Lobby. The newspaper was called *The Spotlight,* a national publication in Washington, DC, and it was an article written by Victor Marchetti, at that time perhaps the highest ranking officer of the CIA to leave that organization and write a book exposing their misconduct. And the article basically said that there's a memorandum floating around signed by Richard Helms and James Jesus Angleton, two of the leaders of the CIA, which implicated both the CIA and E. Howard Hunt, who'd been an officer in the CIA and who, of course, was involved in Watergate and spent some time in prison.

The newspaper published the article, Hunt sued and the newspaper got a local lawyer in Florida, where the case was brought by Hunt—the United States District Court for the Seventh District in Miami. And the newspaper said in essence, "We're sorry we published it, but certainly there was no actual malice."

Hunt got up on the witness stand and said to those jurors, "When my children came to see me with this newspaper that implied I killed President Kennedy, was involved in the conspiracy, they said, 'Dad, did you kill the president?' I said no, of course not. And then the children said, 'How could they put it in the newspaper if you didn't?'" And he described the worst day of his life, when his own children believed this newspaper rather than him.

In any event, the jury awarded a verdict of $650,000 for Hunt, and that was taken on appeal. And the U.S. Court of Appeals for the Eleventh Circuit concluded that in reality the judge had given an incorrect instruction for the jury and they sent it back for a new trial. At that point Marchetti and the publisher came to me and said, "Will you represent us? We

know this is serious. If there's a judgement like that we'll be bankrupt." And I said, "Oh, yes, but I'm not going to defend it on the basis of lack of actual malice. I will try to prove to the satisfaction of a jury that the CIA killed President Kennedy." And I devoted the next year of my life to taking sworn statements under oath which were compelled by the federal rules of civil procedure. From everyone who in my view has made our lives a delight for the past two decades, and that includes G. Gordon Liddy, E. Howard Hunt, Richard Helms, David Phillips, who ran the western hemisphere for the CIA, Stansfield Turner, who was also director of the CIA as Richard Helms had been, and many, many others.

And above all I took the testimony of a woman named Marita Lorenz, and the jury then heard the whole thing. We picked a jury, both sides participated in picking a jury, both sides were satisfied that we had picked a jury made up of men and women who were impartial, who had no fixed opinions, and the evidence was then developed. I think probably the first turning point came when E. Howard Hunt himself testified and under cross examination, when I asked him what he had done on November 22, 1963, he gave what I believe is now his ninth version under oath. (chuckle) Oh, somewhat different. This one is contradictory from the seventh and eighth.

First, he started by saying he had earlier said that he was with his wife in Chinatown in Washington, DC at about lunch time and they went to a Chinese grocery store named Wah-Lin and his wife purchased some food. But when we checked the records we discovered that Wah-Lin, while in existence at the time of that testimony, didn't exist in November 1963. Therefore, Hunt came up with his next, probably his last, version as far as what he recalls of where he was that day. The rest of us don't have a problem. Everyone who I know as an adult on November 22, 1963 knows exactly where he was or she was or what he or she was doing.

Q: Not Richard Nixon or George Bush.

A: Well, that's true. Those are the two. (laughter)

Q: And wasn't part of Hunt's testimony that he was with his family and these are the same children then who he previously said had come to him and said "can this be true"?

A: Exactly. What he said when he gave the details was that he waited until his wife came out of this new grocery store, Chuck Chun, and they drove and they heard over the radio that the president had been killed. They picked up their children, all of whom were teenagers, went home and they stayed in their room, the family room, which he described in great detail. "We were there forty eight hours without ever leaving the room." "Maybe," he said, "maybe, it was seventy two hours. It was a very long time. We were huddled together." I said, "You never left?" "Well, we went to the bathroom." "How about eating?" "We would send out for fried chicken or pizza or something. But we were all together the whole time." And he gave all these details.

When he finished, I said, "Do you remember testifying at the first trial?" He said, "Yes." I said, "Remember what you said?" He said, "Well, exactly what?" I said, "You said your children came to see you later. When the newspaper," I held up the newspaper, "when the newspaper was published, he came to you and said, 'Dad, did you kill the president?'" And the family almost broke up because they didn't believe your denial. And by then the blood drained out of his face because he then realized that this was a very different story that he was telling now under oath from the last one he told under oath.

And I said, "Tell me, if your children had been with you for forty eight or seventy two hours, why didn't they say instead of 'Dad, did you kill the president? Were you down there?' why didn't they say, 'Dad, we know it's a lie. We're your alibi witnesses. We want to go on TV and nail these liars. Why didn't they say something like that?" Well, there was a pause. I know it wasn't really five hours long, as all the people in the courtroom believed later. It probably was a minute. Hunt was stunned. He was looking at his shoes. Then he looked up at me and said, "May I answer?" And I said, "Please. There's a question pending. I'd like an answer." He said, "I had to remind my alibi witnesses that they were with me." Which was not a terrific answer (laughter) but probably there was not really a good answer at that point.

At that point I thought we'd won the case. We had a recess and I said to my client, "I think that this case is won. Let's try to prove that the CIA killed Kennedy and let's forget about defending the defamation case now." And he said to me, "You know, there's a $650,000 potential here against us. Have you ever been this sure that you'd won a case then lost it?" I said, "Oh, sure. (laughter) No." "Do whatever you want." I abandoned everything else about actual malice and all that stuff. I was just then on the offensive.

We put on the testimony of Marita Lorenz. Now she's a very interesting character in history. Her father was the commander of a German luxury liner which was anchored in Havana Bay during the end of 1958 and during the first days of 1959. The first day of 1959, January 1, is when Fidel Castro's revolution succeeded. And they were under Batista and all of a sudden they were there with Castro in charge. And

Castro went to the Havana Hilton a couple of weeks later, looked out into the beautiful Havana Harbor Bay, and he saw this wonderful boat. And he left and he went down and he got on board to talk to these folks. And everybody asked him for his autograph and he met with the commander of the boat, Commander Lorenz, and the commander had a very, very beautiful eighteen year old daughter. I have a picture of Marita Lorenz when she was eighteen on the boat with Fidel Castro. They're sitting together in the captain's quarters there. And he was taken with her. She was just remarkably beautiful.

And he said, "How about coming back into town with me and spending a few days?" She said, "I'd like to Fidel (chuckling) but the problem is my parents want me to go to school in New York City and I have to do that." And he said, "Well, alright, Marita, give me your telephone number." She said, "OK" and gave him the telephone number and a couple of weeks later he called her in New York. The head of state of Cuba called her in New York and said, "Marita, would you like to come down here?" She said, "Well, I don't know if I have a way." He said, "I'll send a plane for you." You know heads of state have certain prerogatives that the rest of us don't have. He sent a plane for her.

She went down and she lived with him for almost a year and had a child. And one day a man named Francis Fiorini, this is her testimony now, Francis Fiorini was really a man named Frank Sturgis, a contract employee for the CIA and he was apparently then working for the CIA and at the same time he was the head of security for Castro's air force, and Fiorini went to her and said, "Marita, Fidel has decided that you are an embarrassment with a child and he's ordered that you both be killed. But I can smuggle you out of here." She smuggled herself and the child into the American Embassy and started to arrange for her to get back to Miami and there she was recruited by the CIA. There they said to her, "Listen, this man wanted to kill you and the baby. You're very close to him. You could poison him. We can arrange for you to poison him."

She says now that she found out some time after she made that poisoning attempt, which was unsuccessful, that it was not true that Castro planned to kill her or the baby. The CIA had lied to her because they knew number one, that she was not a Cuban and, number two, that she was a young woman with a child and, number three, that she was close to Castro. She was the one person they knew who they could convince that Castro was a monster that might have the ability to kill him. And so they recruited her.

But before she learned all of that, she was back in

Miami again and there she was used as a decoy in various operations run by—this is her testimony—run by Frank Sturgis, who was the military operator in charge. And E. Howard Hunt, the other Watergate burglar, whose code name was Eduardo, basically acted as paymaster for the operation. Her testimony is that she had done that for a long time, worked at a way to get guns, navigate the guns into anti-Castro forces in Cuba to overthrow Fidel Castro. After all of that was done, she was told by Sturgis one day, "We have something which is really tremendous, a real tremendous opportunity. It's going to take place this month in Dallas." This was in November, toward the end of November 1963. She was recruited and went on a two-car caravan from Miami into Dallas. And in the cars were Sturgis, the CIA operator who was the general of the operation; Marita, who had a job as a decoy but was never told, not at this time or any other time, what the specific job was going to be. And a car filled with sharpshooters who were anti-Castro Cubans working for the CIA with their rifles in the trunks, they had rifles, some automatic weapons—all the telescopic sites—arrived in Dallas on November 20, 1963, two days before the assassination. That night, she said, Eduardo, E. Howard Hunt, entered the hotel room with the envelope with a large sum of money and gave it to Sturgis for the operating expenses.

She said she later saw Jack Ruby there in the room. She didn't know who Ruby was then. He wasn't going to be famous for three more days, when he killed Oswald. But she realized it was very, very big. And she was nervous. They were nervous. She was nervous. She left. And they drove her to Love Field and from there she flew to Miami, picked up her child and flew to what was then Idlewild. Ironically, of course, it is now JFK Airport in New York City. She went to New Jersey to be with her mother, she said later, because the day she arrived Kennedy had been killed. Sturgis came to her to recruit her for another CIA operation. And she said, "Tell me exactly what you did that day." And he said that, "You know, we killed Kennedy. It was perfect. The local police, everything was covered. There will be no investigation. You missed the big one, Marita. The fact is that no one will ever be able to prove that we are the ones who did it."

Q: Now you were on the air recently with Sturgis, right?

A: I wasn't on exactly with him. It was *A Current Affair* and they recorded an interview with me and I had recorded an interview with Marita Lorenz and they utilized that on the air and then they had Sturgis on after that. But I never did meet the gentleman. I guess everybody else has seen it except me. I understand that he used a lot of vulgarity, was furious, threw my book on the floor, called me all kinds of names.

Q: He threatened to sue, right?

A: If he sues, we're ready. Let me say that it appears that Frank Sturgis can't take a joke. [laughter]. No, that's not serious. It appears to me that he doesn't understand what the law is and obviously what Marita was describing was a violent man given to outbursts who was very vulgar. That's the man she described. I guess Sturgis proved he's not that kind of guy at all [laughter] on the television show.

But what I did in *Plausible Denial* is quote the record of the testimony. Not only the testimony that Marita Lorenz gave to this jury but the testimony that Frank Sturgis gave in other cases. And it is not acceptable. First of all, it's all true and truth is an absolute defense. It's true that *that's* what was said. And secondly, it's immune from suit because it's part of a court record. In any event, it's been passed upon by a jury.

The jury heard Marita Lorenz and heard E. Howard Hunt and heard all of the evidence for a period of two weeks. They retired and they came out, they retired late into the afternoon just to reorganize themselves to decide who the foreperson should be. It was a woman named Leslie Armstrong and the next morning they met and, as I recall, there was a little over one hour, which I thought was a remarkably short period of time. They came out and they found for us, for the newspaper, for the author, for the writer, unanimously. And then the foreman of the jury, who was a very attractive woman, left the building, all the media surrounded her because the television cameras are not allowed inside the courthouse in the federal court system in Florida, and they saw her on the steps and they said, "Please talk to us." And all the news media was there. And I was off to the side listening to her. And this is what she said, it's on the jacket of the book: "Why did you reach the conclusion you did?" And she said, "Mr. Lane was asking us to do something very difficult. He was asking us to believe that John Kennedy had been killed by our own government. Yet, when we examined the evidence, we were compelled to conclude that the CIA had indeed killed President Kennedy."

This is the first jury verdict in the history of America on the question of the assassination and they have concluded that the CIA killed President Kennedy.

Q: This is something a little bit short of convicting Hunt of the assassination.

A: Oh, sure.

Q: You won a libel case.

A: Oh, sure.

Q: I understand that Hunt is in Mexico now and he sends five hundred dollar checks each month to Liberty Lobby?

A: The court also imposed costs upon Hunt for having troubled the Liberty Lobby with a law suit. I think it was something like twenty thousand dollars. And he then moved from Miami. His lawyer told me that he and his wife sold the house and moved to Mexico and every month I get a five hundred dollar check toward paying this off. I just endorse it over to the organization. That's correct.

The amazing thing to me is that it hasn't been published. For example, the *Washington Post,* when Hunt won the first case, which was not a terribly important case—it was a defamation case where the facts were not at issue because the newspaper said "we're sorry we published them", it was just a question whether there was actual malice. They ran a big story on the front page of the style section, as I recall it was almost a full page.

Q: *That* was news, but when your verdict was delivered, it wasn't news.

A: I haven't read it in the *Washington Post.* I actually rushed down to see if it's there now after six years.

But I'll tell you what the *Washington Post* did do in this case. Not the *Post,* but the same folks. Channel Ten was there. Channel Ten in Miami is the *Post-Newsweek* station. It's owned by *Newsweek* and the *Washington Post.* And the reporter for Channel Ten was very upset with Leslie Armstrong, the forewoman of the jury when she said we'd convinced her the CIA did it. He said, "How about actual malice? Wasn't that a factor?" She said, "No we didn't consider actual malice to be a factor. I was convinced that the article was true and if it's true you don't get to the next question of actual malice." He said, "Are you saying actual malice is not a factor in a defamation case?" She said, "No, no. I'm not saying that. The judge explained to us carefully about actual malice and it *is* a factor in a defamation case, if you consider that the article is untrue. But here it was true."

That evening, the anchor person on the early news on Channel Ten in Miami said, "E. Howard Hunt has lost a defamation case. Here's what the forewoman of the jury says is the reason..." And she came on, this is what you heard: "Actual malice is always a factor in a defamation case." Period. And that was all.

She was furious. She called everybody at the station and they said, "Sorry if we made a mistake but the other things you said had been erased on the tape and we don't have them." She said, "Come to my house and do it over again." She was quite insistent.

They did and on the late-night news in Miami on Channel Ten they ran about thirty seconds or a minute of an actual statement by Leslie Armstrong. But it took a juror who was the forewoman of the jury who was an activist to insist and finally that word got out. But it got out almost nowhere else.

Q: I've seen you on shows in the last week where sometimes you're cut off and in other cases they put you on with the someone who still thinks Oswald acted alone and somebody else who thinks the mob did it.

A: The worst show I was on I thought was this thing, *Sonya Live* on CNN. I don't know if you saw that, with Robert Sam Anson. I really loved it that she was in the studio with him and I'm in another city. So they're sitting there together. I don't know if they're sharing a cigarette or what.

I'm out here some place and she asked me my "theories," as she puts it. I'm trying to explain that this is not a theory and I think it's irresponsible to guess, as one of the authors did, that the FBI or that Hoover did it because he hated Kennedy. A lot of people didn't like Kennedy. But in any case, in any crime in any state or federal court in the United States, *motive* is not an element. You have to prove certain elements. I go through this in *Plausible Denial.* To show what the elements of a crime are, and the person who wrote the book about about the FBI doing it is a lawyer too—he's a young lawyer, but he's a lawyer—and he should know that motive is not an element. You have to have evidence. And we have evidence. We presented it to a jury and the jury has ruled.

In any event, I tried to explain that to Sonya and she listened and she turned to Anson and said, "Is Mark Lane a crackpot?" He's not my psychiatrist. I actually don't have one. If I chose one, it wouldn't be him!

Later, when he gave his position, I said, "Let's talk about Mr. Anson now." Because he wrote the cover story in *Esquire.* Now the cover story in *Esquire* was on the *JFK* movie. "Oliver Stone Reshoots History," by Robert Sam Anson. It's a long article and it's very important what is happening to Oliver Stone right now.

I can write a book and they can try to stop it. They can influence book reviews and I have CIA documents which say to have "our assets" in the news media—they're referring to propaganda assets who belong to the CIA in the news media throughout the United States—destroy Mark Lane. Of course, everybody denies that they are one, but *somebody* is an asset. They've got many. That's what they say in their own documents.

What's happening to Oliver Stone is instead of writing a book, something I have done, he has access to a fifteen million dollar budget for a film that every star in Hollywood appears in. Ed Asner, Walter Matthau, Jack Lemmon, Kevin Coster—everybody's in it. It's going to have an impact like nothing else has ever had. And they know that. It's a thirty five million dollar budget for prints and publicity. We're now at the figure where they must have a two hundred million dollar gross in order to break even. They have to make it. If they have to, they do it. They just pour money into publicity. They have to do it and they will do it. That means that something like thirty five million Americans *must* see the film if the economy is not going to go under. [chuckle]

That film's going to be seen. It's going to have an impact greater than anything that has happened since the shots were fired in Dealey Plaza. Good or bad, it's going to put the matter on the discussion table. Thirty five million people see a film about the Kennedy assassination raising questions. It's on the agenda as it has never been before.

So there has been, in my view, an intelligence effort to destroy the film. I'm afraid they've been somewhat successful already. For example, you have Robert Sam Anson writing this cover story in *Esquire* magazine. What's wrong with that? First of all, Anson is not a film reviewer. Secondly, nobody reviews a film until it is on the screen. There also has been a similar effort by George Lardner, Jr., the intelligence writer for the *Washington Post* who has declined every opportunity to debate with me on radio and TV in Washington which has been offered to him. He won't debate.

One day a member of Congress gave me a hearing room and said come over and talk to his aides. I went over and there were a number of members of Congress present. It was a room that held about three hundred and it was filled with Congressional aides and some members of Congress and some reporters and Lardner was there. I called Jim Garrison and said to him, "Listen, I'm going over there. I know Lardner will be there. What time did David Ferrie die?" I think he said something like two o'clock in the morning. That's what the coroner fixed it at. I'm not sure of the hours but they're relatively unimportant. So it was two o'clock in the morning. Then I went over and I finished my presentation and Lardner's hand went up to ask a question. I said, "Oh, Mr. Lardner, before you ask a question let me ask you a question. You were with David Ferrie when he died that night. Same morning, right?" He said, "Yes." I said, "What hours were you there?" He said, "I was talking to him, interviewing him from midnight until 4AM."

And I said, "Let me ask you this one question, Mr. Lardner. Did you notice that toward the second part of the interview he was less responsive than he had been during the first half? Because he apparently died two hours before you left." there was a scream by him and he said, "Are you charging me with murdering David Ferrie?" I said, "No, no, Mr. Lardner. I'm just doing what you reporters do all the time. I'm just asking questions."

Kerry Thornley
columnist and author of *The Idle Warriors*

Q: **Would you explain a little about the origins of your book,** *The Idle Warriors* **(IllumiNet, $10.98) and your acquaintance with Oswald?**

A: I was in the Marines at a Marine base in California. He had just been overseas. He had just been to Japan and I wound up going overseas and wound up stationed in the same outfit that he'd been in when he was over there. I arrived in July and that autumn I read in the papers that he had gone into the American embassy in Moscow and plopped down his passport and had attempted to renounce his American citizenship. That came as a surprise to me because even though he claimed that he was a communist, it seemed tongue-in-cheek to me. It didn't seem to me like he was very serious about it. So I got to thinking about it and I decided I was getting disillusioned with the United States myself at the time. Not very long afterwards, the next spring, the U2 incident occurred and Dwight David Eisenhower was actually caught lying about something, which seemed inconceivable to me until then.

Q: **This was 1959?**

A: It was 1959 that Oswald attempted to defect or defected or whatever it is that he actually was doing. I believe the U2 incident was in May of 1960, if I'm not mistaken.

As my tour of duty over there continued, more and more I began to feel I understood why he defected to the Soviet Union. Everything I've read since then has convinced me that I didn't know what I was talking about, that I was projecting my own feelings and experiences on to him. So I decided I was going to write a novel about being in the Marines anyway because I'd wanted to be a novelist and being in the Marines was the first exciting thing that ever happened to me. So I decided to make my main character defect to the Soviet Union in the last chapter.

I made a lot of notes for the novel when I was overseas but none of them ever found their way in the final draft. I started working on it when I got back to California. I wrote the first five chapters in California and then my friend Greg Hill and I went down to New Orleans and lived in the French Quarter and that's when I wrote the rest of it. We arrived there in February 1961 and I got a part-time job and spent much of that summer working on the book. Finally, I wrote the last chapter, I think, probably late in 1961.

I had no idea that Oswald had ever been in New Orleans. He'd been there that summer of '63 a few years later, when I was out in California. There had been an overlap of a couple of weeks when we'd both been in there together. District Attorney Jim Garrison has always been convinced that Oswald and I met with one another in New Orleans, but that's a hypothesis very wide of the facts.

Q: Why were you suspicious that Oswald's announced intention to defect was not the real reason?

A: I didn't become suspicious until many years later when I began reading the material about Oswald and the writings of the Warren report critics. I have become convinced since then that he was military intelligence and that he was probably working for the CIA when he went to Russia. I think Carl Oglesby makes the most interesting and compelling case for that, also Anthony Summers in *Conspiracy* makes a very good case for the same thing. Among other things, Oswald wrote a letter to the Soviet Union at one point that Sylvia Meagre quotes in her work where he says he's done intelligence work before and he's offering his services to them or something.

Q: The premise of *The Idle Warriors* is that Oswald defected because of this malaise in post-war Japan?

A: Just because of the lousy morale situation overseas. Actually, it was a very rebellious outfit, Marine Air Control Squadron 1. They finally broke it up and sent it back to the states on paper and divided us up and sent us in to a bunch of other outfits over there because we were so hard to handle. It had been the same outfit with a few guys leaving it every month since World War 2 when it still had a very salty wartime personality. We didn't salute officers and enlisted men pretty much ran the outfit. It was like PFC Wintergreen in *Catch 22*, when he didn't like an order he changed it because he was in charge of the mimeograph machine. It was almost like that.

Oswald behaved the same way that most people behaved in Marine Air Control Squadron 1. When he came back to the states there just wasn't all that support for it among the other enlisted men. They weren't that organized or that capable of resisting authority in the states. So he got himself into a lot of trouble for that reason alone, just because he maintained the same attitude that he had overseas and it was very accept-

able overseas. We could get away with it there but for some reason we couldn't in the states.

Q: So this view that you put forth in *Idle Warriors* is one that you maintained even after the assassination. It was only in the period after that when you started reading the critics that your view changed?

A: I didn't become a critic of the Warren Report myself until 1965, and I wrote a book, *Oswald,* about Oswald after the assassination, a nonfiction book, or one that I imagined was nonfiction at the time. It had pretty much the same view as I had in the novel, that basically it was a psychological matter that caused him to defect and I assumed to kill the president at the time. I think I was just all wet on that entirely. I think he was probably a CIA agent spying on the FBI for Kennedy by the time of the assassination. I think that's probably why they set him up.

I hate to talk about this because it causes a lot of people to think I'm crazy, but when I was in service with him at the same time I began to experience audio hallucinations in the borderline area between sleeping and waking as I was going to sleep at night. I'm absolutely certain that it was mind control. There's no doubt in my mind that it was mind control, that they had planted an electrode in the base of my skull and were mind-controlling me.

Q: One of the interesting things about your novel is that you have a character in there named Mike, who is a close friend of Johnny Shellburn, the Oswald character, but who is also regarded as a twin.

A: That's an unfortunate coincidence. I'd forgotten all about that until I read the novel again recently. That may have given rise to theories that I'm the second Oswald and so on. Actually, it is my understanding that Gordon Novel's wife told Jim Garrison's grand jury that Gordon Novel and William Seymour were the second Oswalds. Whoever it was, in my opinion, was planting proof of conspiracy because after Oswald became famous, these impersonations made it obvious that there was a conspiracy. So I think it's a compliment that Garrison and some other critics should assume that I was one of the second Oswalds. However, it isn't true. I think that whoever it was was trying to leave evidence rather than trying to cover something up.

Q: Jim Garrison charged you with perjury over the novel?

A: Not over the novel. There was a woman in New Orleans who swore up and down she saw me and Oswald sitting together in the Bourbon House in New Orleans one afternoon. I remembered the incident. I remembered the afternoon. I remembered everything except who I was sitting with. I could not for the life of me remember who it was. I have remembered since then. It was a man named Glen. He was a country-western singer type. He was from Texas. He was talking about going back to Texas. Barbara Reed, this woman, was sitting at the bar and she overheard that snatch of conversation when Oswald appeared on television and they were talking about how he was from Texas and all that. She decided that *that* had been Oswald that I'd been sitting with. So that was what I denied and was charged with perjury, denying that I had seen Oswald in New Orleans in 1963. As I say, I wasn't even aware that he was there until after the assassination. Even though he had been in the newspapers, I had been in California at that time, when he was passing out the leaflets on Canal Street and all that.

Q: But Garrison didn't believe in the authenticity of your book, either, right? Or did he?

A: I don't know if he ever even read the book. David Lifton's theory is that he read the book and on the basis of the book decided I was guilty. I don't believe he read my Warren Commission testimony much less the book as he misquotes it and misrepresents it constantly in his writings.

Q: What do you think about this Oliver Stone movie and all the attention it gets?

A: I went over to see Oliver Stone. They paid my way to California, put me up in a Holiday Inn for a couple of days, spent a couple of hours talking me. I think Stone's going off on a tangent myself. He was very skeptical about what I had to say about not seeing Oswald in 1963. His mind is very much up the same tree as Garrison's, in my opinion. John Stockwell was there also, former CIA, renegade CIA agent. He believed me. He understood. When I got in to all the weird stuff, and there are such weird things going on in the intelligence community , a professional realizes that stuff like that goes on. But Stone himself was very skeptical and I felt like I couldn't get through to him.

Q: Oliver Stone flew you and John Stockwell in together?

A: Yeah. We were both there at the same time. Stockwell and I went out and had a couple of drinks together after the interview and Stockwell believed me. He had no problem at all with credibility as far as he was concerned. But Stone was skeptical. Stone was convinced that I must have seen Oswald in 1963. I can see why people would think that I had. I told him at one point I wish that I had so that I could say that I had so they'd believe everything else I was telling them. That was the stumbling block.

I think that there was an implant I developed on a boil on the back of my neck, right at the center of my neck, right at the base of my skull. I spent a lot of time in New Orleans talking to a guy who I realize in retrospect was connected to the intelligence community and who probably was involved in the assassination. It wasn't Oswald, however. It was another guy. I think he may have been Howard Hunt. That guy mentioned the business about the implants in the base of the skull.

I talked with a man about assassinating Kennedy for about three years in New Orleans, right after the Bay of Pigs invasion until two weeks before the assassination. In fact, he was talking about who to frame for it and I said, "Why don't you frame some Communist?" He smirked. I didn't realize why he was smirking at the time.

Basically, I don't think they were pumping me for ideas about the assassination. I think they were setting me up to frame somebody because he was using somebody else's name other than his own. The idea was that I would go up before the Warren Commission and that I would say that I talked with this guy about assassinating Kennedy in New Orleans. The reason that didn't work was because I didn't believe in conspiracies in those days. I didn't realize that I had been part of a conspiracy. To me, conspiracies just didn't exist. That was just something John Birchers believed in as far as I was concerned at the time.

Q: What was the name that this person was going by at the time?

A: Gary Kirsten was the name he was using. He left trails of evidence that he might be somebody else, two or three mutually exclusive trails of evidence. One of them that he might be a mad scientist who had been one of Hitler's scientists. Another one that he might be Mortimer Bloomfield of the Permindex corporation. I don't think he was any of the above at all. I think he was probably Howard Hunt. Watergate is what convinced me of the relevance of these conversations with this man. Up until then I didn't even think they were relevant.

Q: Jonathan Vankin's book, *Conspiracies, Cover-Ups and Crimes,* mentions a little about this idea that both you and Oswald might have been part of a Nazi breeding experiment.

A: That's my theory. That's the theory I came up with in the last few years. I thought it all started when I knew Oswald in the Marines and the more I investigated it, the more I tried to piece it together, the more I realized that it had to have started earlier than that.

There are numerous reasons why I think I'm the product of a breeding experiment. My mother's family is Switzer and that's a name that goes clear back to the Crusades, as does the name Oswald. They weed people out of the breeding experiments. They pick two of them and they observe them for a number of years and they get rid of one of them. That's what I think they were doing with me and Oswald.

Q: What do you think is our best defense against things like mind control and government conspiracies?

A: I don't think there is a defense, in my opinion, against mind control. This is something that everybody thinks I'm a nut about. I think the best defense is to abolish the absentee control of property. It's the absentee control of production that makes mind control a profitable thing to research and finance. If it was, say, a Proudhonian economic system or an anarchist society or whatever, I don't think there would be much profit in mind control. There wouldn't be much reason for one person to control another person. However, I don't think there is any direct defense against it whatsoever. I think there's a brighter side to it, in a way of looking at it, anyway. Some day there might not be any more violence because mind control might replace violence entirely.

Q: Some option.

A: However, I've given up on the idea of absolutely abolishing mind control. I think it can be made less profitable and I think it can be reduced, but I don't think it can be eradicated any more than nuclear weaponry can be eradicated. I think it's an equally hopeless task.

Q: Obviously you feel that major portions of your life have resulted from mind control, but at the same time it's not as if your whole life has been being led around blindfolded. You have done writing, you've published things.

A: I harbored the conceit, up until I discovered I was a mind control subject, that I was a particularly independent thinker. So it came to me rather hard to realize that I owed much of my thinking and much of my independence, what looked to me like my independence, to mind control. However, I probably would have become an elder in the Mormon church if I hadn't become a mind-control subject. It probably would have been the most perfectly boring life you could imagine.

Jim Marrs
author of *Crossfire* and consultant to *JFK*

Q: How did you get involved in Oliver Stone's movie? From the outset, was Oliver Stone doing a movie about both books or did your book come in after he had Garrison's?

A: I'm not real clear on that. I know that just shortly after my book, *Crossfire* (Carroll and Grof,

13.95) was published, his people contacted my agent and wanted to know if the movie rights were available. They were and we worked out a deal. It's my understanding that somewhere after that he was trying to put the thing together and he wanted specifically to do a movie on the Kennedy assassination. Of course, it is a movie and as such needs a story and a protagonist and at some point he settled on Jim Garrison. In other words, present the assassination material through the eyes of Jim Garrison. I think the reason he added my book, *Crossfire,* was because I deal with almost all aspects of the assassination, including the Jim Garrison investigation, whereas the other book involved, *On The Trail of the Assassins,* is Jim Garrison's account of his investigation there in New Orleans in the late 60s.

Q: Does your book give more particular credence to Garrison's theories over any others? It's really a compendium, isn't it?

A: I have a chapter called "Conclusions" and I try to put all the information I have presented into some sort of framework. I don't think it's fair to present someone with a massive amount of information and then not try to put it into some kind of framework. In other words, "What does all this mean?" But in *Crossfire,* for the most part, up until that last chapter, I pretty well try to avoid theories and theorizing and conclusions. I simply tried to present the massive amount of information in a lucid forum.

I will say this about Jim Garrison's investigation: in the late 60s, when he put New Orleans businessman Clay Shaw on trial as a member of the conspiracy, he was vilified in the national media as being on a witch hunt, as not having anything, as persecuting Clay Shaw and of trying to just grandstand for himself. A lot of people bought this. And there were a lot of problems with the investigation. But let me say this: he did come up with a plot centered in New Orleans and he did come up with David Ferrie, a strange character who was associated with Lee Harvey Oswald even back to the time when he was fifteen years old. Garrison did come up with Guy Bannister, a former FBI man and a virulent anti-Communist who was also connected to Oswald in the summer of 1963. He came up with a variety of anti-Castro Cubans that he said were connected with Oswald, and he said that the plot was a plot that involved people within the federal government of the United States and particularly the Central Intelligence Agency.

Of course, he was blasted at the time for saying these things. Most people thought that he was absolutely nuts for even saying this stuff. But I've got to point out that in the late 1970s, when the House Select Committee on Assassinations went back and studied it, they came to the conclusion that most of the stuff Garrison had been saying was correct. They verified the presence of David Ferrie and Guy Bannister and of the Cubans, there in New Orleans, and Oswald's connection to them. In the light of history, looking back of course with better perspective, we now see that Garrison wasn't as far off as we were told.

Q: Hasn't it been one of the criticisms of Garrison, though, that he soft-pedaled the mob?

A: Yes, that has been one of the criticisms and that is a criticism I take very seriously and I'll have to admit that it's caused me some problems. Garrison has steadfastly refused to even name Carlos Marcello, the reputed New Orleans mob boss and the object of a very good book by John Davis, *Mafia Kingfish*. Davis, of course, makes the argument that Marcello may have personally been the key man who ordered the assassination of President Kennedy.

When I had the opportunity to sit down and talk with Jim Garrison, I broached this to him. I was very forthright about my concern that he had more or less downplayed the role of the Mafia in the assassination. His response, paraphrased, was something like, and it makes sense to me, "Look, I have no problem with the idea that there were Mafia people involved in the plot to kill Kennedy. But I know that they did not initiate it nor did they cover it up. That could only have happened at the highest levels of federal government. Once I understood that there was a conspiracy involved, I lost all interest in the low-level players. I wanted to know who was behind the whole thing." Now that makes some sense to me, although I'm sure there are those who will say yes, but he's still soft-pedaling the role of the Mafia.

Q: The official view of the assassination now is no longer the Warren Commission view, right? The official view is that there was some kind of conspiracy. Or no?

A: It's kind of funny. I'm really not quite sure what the official view is since there's nobody who can or will speak officially for the United States government. I think the official version of the federal government is still the Warren Commission, that it was the work of one, lone individual. Congress, on the other hand, which is a branch of the federal government, says that there was at least two people shooting at Kennedy. So, unfortunately though, there's nobody to turn to so it's up to researchers, the private citizens of this country, to start using their heads and start figuring out for themselves what really happened to Kennedy.

Q: What do you think about the George Bush who got debriefed by the CIA after Kennedy's assassination?

A: In 1988, prior to the election, an FBI document surfaced, written by an FBI person to the Central Intelligence Agency the day after President Kennedy was killed in Dallas, that said, "Please check with George Bush of the CIA to see what the reaction of the anti-Castro Cubans is to the assassination." Now a lot of people said, "A ha!" George Bush was more closely connected to the CIA a lot earlier than he led us to believe.

Q: He denies that. He says he didn't work for the CIA until he became its director.

A: That's true. The CIA never responded to this but some of his campaign people said there's another George Bush within the CIA and that's who they were referring to and it was not the George Herbert Walker Bush who is now our president. So the issue died down a little bit. He was elected in 1988, of course. After the election, however, researchers located George Bush of the CIA and he said, "Hey, I was a low-level analyst and I had no contact with the anti-Castro Cubans and I've never seen this memo before and never heard anything about this, so obviously they were not referring to me." So we're back again with the questions of, were they referring to George H.W. Bush. Bush's Zapata Oil Company may have been one of the oil companies used as cover for movement of supplies and arms and ammunition for the anti-Castro Cubans at the Bay of Pigs, which of course was two years prior to the Kennedy assassination. We have to remember that two ships that were struck by Castro's forces in the Bay of Pigs were the Barbara and the Houston.

Q: Kennedy was killed by the CIA and now we have the CIA basically running the country, the former director, the same actual people.

A: That's very true. They're still talking about confirming Robert Gates as the new director of the CIA. This was the right hand man to Bill Casey, the man that everybody's now pointing the finger at since he's dead saying that he did all this dirty stuff. He met with Ayatollah Khomeini's people in 1980 and arranged to hold the hostages longer than necessary so that Reagan could get elected; he's the one who created the Iran-Contra network and set it all up against the will of the Congress. He's the one that did all that and Robert Gates was his right-hand man. They're trying to put Gates in to take over and become the new Bill Casey. My point is that they can argue back and forth that he didn't know anything. Hey, if he didn't know what was going on, he's incompetent. If he did know what's going on, then he's a crook. Either way, why are they pushing him for head of the Central Intelligence Agency? Why don't they simply go out and find some nice police chief or mayor or anybody who has a clean, unblemished record and put him in there and stop all this stuff? They don't want somebody who's clean heading the CIA because they might stumble across all this wrongdoing that's been going on for thirty years.

Q: Let's talk about Fletcher Prouty. He is connected to the Liberty Lobby and the Liberty Lobby is a right-wing group that, among other things, is into Holocaust revisionism and Prouty has failed to really distance himself from that. What do you think about all that?

A: I have to admit that it bothers me some too. Now I will admit that I also subscribe to the Liberty Lobby newspaper for some twenty years now. I don't necessarily subscribe to everything they say or what they conclude. Their position on the Holocaust is totally indefensible. I think that what they have is a grain of truth. Any balanced, objective historian will tell you that the six million figure that's always bantered around is probably inflated and cannot be substantiated. But the fact is that there were people murdered as part of official German government policy. I don't care if it's six million or two million or six hundred thousand or even six. If people are murdered as the conscious result of government policy, then that's wrong.

The point, though, is that just because they're wrong or I don't believe some of the things they say, it doesn't make all of their information invalid. They have come out with some really good pieces of information. Any good journalist or news person will tell you that you have to take your information where you can get it. What we know about the Mafia largely has come from Mafia turncoats, people who have turned state's evidence, like Joe Valachi. Are we going to say that we don't believe anything Joe Valachi says simply because he's a criminal? It's stupid. You can't say that.

Now Prouty is apparently arguing that he has written articles for these people because they'll publish his articles. Other publications will not. They term themselves as populists and they certainly espouse some very populist ideals. One thing that impressed me about the Liberty Lobby is that there are people who call in on their talk shows and write letters lambasting them for their positions and they print these letters. They give the other side a chance to rebut some of their positions. So the main thing is that I don't think that you can hold one person up for ridicule or lambast his ideas or his statements simply because he's connected one way or another to the Liberty Lobby, particularly when he's simply writing articles for a publication or group that you don't necessarily agree with.

Dick Gregory, activist and comedian

Q: Were you an investigator for Jim Garrison?
A: No. At one time I was probably the most visible of all the people that had information. Back in those days I did about two hundred and fifty dates every year. Now I wasn't booked on the colleges to talk about the JFK assassination or assassinations or the CIA. I was booked mainly because I was in civil rights, in human rights. I was a celebrity and had come through a time when African Americans were exploding on white college campuses for the first time. So they had to bring speakers in that would reflect that new part of society. And the fact that I was one of the most visible, I was brought in. I could draw a crowd. In other words, people were coming to see the celebrity.

In the process of that many of the colleges would air what I said over the radio. You would have press conferences. I could say things about the assassination that a lot of other people couldn't say because of my peers. Remember, I'm not a lawyer, so I don't have to answer to no legal board. I'm not a doctor, so I don't have to answer to the medical profession. I'm an entertainer and who cares what entertainers think? And, too, I'm a human rights fighter and they just go along a line of integrity. So I was able to put stuff out there and in the process I was able to...like, right now, with Mark Lane's new book out on the assassination and the movie out, who benefits more by this more than anybody? I would say *me* because all of those young minds that I talked to back then sit up and say, "God, Dick Gregory said that twenty years ago!" So you just open up that crack.

I was able to do that because five minutes after that I was telling you a joke, saying something else socially, so it wasn't a Dick Gregory coming and doing an assassination bit where it could be challenged and the CIA could send counter-people in to react.

Before this movie was even made seventy three percent of the America people said they thought it was a conspiracy, they thought we didn't get all of the truth. The interesting thing is that when I look at Oliver Stone, you know first that the CIA would be stupid if they hadn't infiltrated the American press. You'd have to be silly. Now the American people have to be stupid to be so naive to believe in a free, democratic society, the CIA wouldn't infiltrate the American press. Then how is it that all at once this man gets trashed? You can do *Jesus Christ Superstar* and show God as a hippy, show Jesus as a hippy and everybody says that's artistic freedom. I can go to a movie and see Victor Mature playing Hannibal and everybody knows Hannibal was a black man. I see

Elizabeth Taylor playing Nefertiti and we all knew *that* was a black woman. And nobody questions artistic freedom. But now all at once they pull the stoppers out on this man.

Did you see the president faint in Tokyo? Did you see where one of the networks had to run the whole piece last night? They had to run the whole part because too many people were saying, "How come Mrs. Bush didn't run to his aid?" When you saw the whole part, she did. I'm sure there was so much flak because I questioned that and I still question that. As many poor folks as I know in the ghetto that don't even know how to spell "Medicare" I've never known one to pass out from the flu! So this man has to tell me how you faint from the flu.

The other thing that somebody needs to tell me is that, look, I'm sixty years old this year. I've been in show business thirty five years. I've been a celebrity for thirty years, which means that when I come I sit at the head table, right? In thirty years of sitting at head tables I've never seen nobody throw up in their plate! And if they did throw up in their plate, I hope the people would have enough sense to cancel the meal!

Q: (laughter)

A: Now they're talking about Japanese bashing. You can't bash them no more than to say here's a cat that threw up at their table and nobody stopped eating. Now, at that point, all he had had was the smoked salmon. Are you aware of that?

Q: Uh huh.

A: Do you know where the smoked salmon came from?

Q: Where?

A: The United States! Alaska! We finally jump on them about they don't import enough stuff and they said, "OK, we'll import your smoked salmon" and the president eats it and...Now, the reason I'm laughing is that I don't believe it. Did you see the black guy who jumped up on the table?

Q: Yeah.

A: Once I noticed that I said, "My God, a black guy? Jumping up on the table?" I mean, he's got to be important, right? You know who he is? He's the guy that carries the black box.

Q: Is that right?

A: He's the one that carries the black box for the president with the buttons in it for the nuclear bomb, OK? So meanwhile, when the president got up and we saw that horrible picture where he looked dead, right?

Q: Right. Ashen. Totally ashen.

A: Now, use your own human experience. How many poor folks do you know, black and white, that go to work every day with the flu? Right? They don't pass out.

Now the other thing is, if I came to St. Louis I would be very angry with you if you put me up in a hotel and while we was out to dinner I fainted, right, and you carried me back to the hotel. Please carry me to the hospital! How can you take the president of the United States back to his room and not take him to the hospital? Here's a man who had a known heart murmur, see.

Now the reason I'm spending this much time on that is that I look at this as part of that whole Kennedy mis-use of the American blah, blah, blah...I think it was a trick and let me tell what I think the trick is. I think it was a trick to get Quayle off the ballot. Six days before this happened, the *Washington Post* started running these series of interviews about Quayle, right?

Q: Yes, a very favorable series of articles on Quayle.

A: Until today. Until Sunday the twelfth. You know what it said? That some of his closest friends say that we're afraid to see him as being president.

Q: So the series turned ugly on him.

A: But now remember the series started *before* the president collapsed and we didn't see the president with the flu. We saw somebody who looked dead. Now that's in everybody's psyche, OK? So now we're going to see the opinion polls now come up and say that eighty percent of the American people say that if Bush kept Quayle on the ticket he would be defeated. And that's a reason to get rid of Quayle because now Quayle has to be the same type of nice guy that Sununu was, right? If me being around will hurt your election, then I will step down, right? And if he stepped own, who do you think they would pick? Who do you think? Colin Powell. Have you seen the promos for *Sixty Minutes*? "If you think you liked Powell last year, wait until you see him on Sunday night?" Have you ever known *Sixty Minutes* to be this nice in a promo?

When you look at what is said now about the JFK conspiracy and when you look at what's said now about Robert Kennedy, when you look at what is said now about King. All together now there's a new awareness because of new information that the government can't control. There are so many different ways out here now to get information other than the press. The press doesn't even ask certain questions. For instance, when Robert Kennedy was shot we happened to see that on television, remember? And we saw Rosey Greer grab Sirhan Sirhan. Sirhan Sirhan wasn't even within three feet of Robert Kennedy and he was in front of Robert Kennedy. And yet Kennedy had three bullets, two in the back and one in the back of the head at a point-blank range of a quarter of an inch. How come somebody hasn't said how those bullets got in the back? He never turned around. Sirhan Sirhan never got within a quarter of an inch of his head.

I went out and bought two *New York Post*s and I'm going to take them home and put them up in the kitchen: "Ted Kennedy Says Movie Is Too Painful. It Is Time To Open JFK Files." You have to see that in the *New York Post,* in the headline. Because what that movie did because of the information era, it said to people who were going to see it, "Wait a minute. Yeah, he did take some liberties but this is a bit too much."

Q: Have you seen the movie *JFK*?

A: Yes. I came out of the movie and you know who I called? I called Donald Sutherland. His performance was so brilliant in just that little short span. Now there's certain things that I don't agree with, but, hey, I'll take it up. I don't agree that Kennedy was going to get out of Vietnam. Kennedy killed the Diem family. My God, this man. This wasn't no nice, clean saint. I don't think he was going to extend it with a whole a lot of people. I think he found a nice, secret way to go in and set-up little assassination teams.

Now let me just tell you my feeling, I don't have evidence. I think that if you want to know what happened to the Kennedy family you have to go back to Joseph Kennedy and look at the book about him, *Of Captains and Kings.* Here's old Joe that stole the money from the Chicago bank and by the time they almost caught him he had the money put back in. He was into the whole Scotch whiskey bit. And he got him some big bucks, so he left Chicago and he went to Boston and he found out when he got to Boston he was an Irish Catholic and you cannot live in this neighborhood. And, man, to find out that you're a nigger and didn't know it is a heck of a thing. And he said, "I'm going to get you all one day." So he started grooming boys to become president the same way you would groom an organic garden. And one day the forces looked around and said, "Oh my God, he's about to pull it off." Then they looked around and they saw Jack on his way in and they said, "Oh my God, Jack will be in eight years, Bobby will be in eight and Ted will be in eight. The American people are fascinated with this family." And I think that's what got him wiped out.

Q: Are you aware of the information that Garrison came up with about Jules Ricco Kimble, who knew David Ferrie and Clay Shaw and flew James Earl Ray into Canada after Martin Luther King's assassination?

A: Yeah. One of the things that we found out was that one of the three tramps was called Raoul. Once they really check it they might find out that he was the one that hit King. You know he ran through a flophouse, remember?

Q: This is Ray's Raoul?

A: Yeah. When he ran through the flophouse, this woman looked him in the face and it was kind of interesting. In order to expedite James Earl Ray from England they had to almost prove to the British government that he really did it because they have one of the stiffest extradition laws and they had to go and get this woman and they kept showing her James Earl Ray's picture and she'd say, "That's not him." And they'd say, "Wait a minute, lady. Do you know there's like a reward, almost three million dollars and you'd get all of that?" "That's not him!" So finally she was committed to a mental hospital. Do you know the story?

A: This was Grace Stephens.

Q: She was committed to a mental hospital and those poor folks there at the mental hospital never knew this government would do things like that. When they showed up with her and the doctors would say that she had high/low depression, she thinks she witnessed the murder of Dr. Martin Luther King, Jr. They put her there for ten years. When Mark Lane and some folks went into the hospital to get her out—and this is so beautiful and I never will forget: imagine me, a black man, an African American, married to a black woman for thirty two years, have ten black children, and this woman they got her out on the Saturday before Mother's Day and when they crawled along the side of the wall and shined the flashlight in her face, ten years they've had this woman locked in this mental hospital because she wouldn't lie, and do you know what she said to them thinking they were coming to kill her? "I tell you now what I told you then. That's not the man."

Be black for a minute and have ten children. Here's a woman that never had a child in her life. I flew to California at Mother's Day so I could be with this snaggle-toothed white woman who's been living in a flophouse for twenty years who really exemplifies what God means motherhood should be about. Are you willing to die? I died to make people holy, are you willing to die to set people free? And it is that type of courage that all the CIAs, all the FBIs in the world can not stop.

Shortly after this interview was conducted, Dick Gregory joined a fast begun by choreographer Katharine Dunham to protest the plight of refugees repatriated to Haiti as a matter of Bush administration policy. Gregory and poet/playwright Amiri Baraka have both suggested that the Haitian crisis is a prelude to a new American invasion of Cuba. Katharine Dunham later endorsed George Bush's re-election.

Presidency-as-Theater
by John Robert Martin

Was the "assassination attempt" on President Ronald Reagan on March 30, 1981 a fake? Was it staged? Chances are the answer is yes. That it was Theater, intended for a particular purpose. That it was a calculated move to force a radical change in our nation's history that we never would have accepted otherwise. And it worked.

Consider: Reagan the movie actor, only a couple of months into his presidency, has begun his term of office with a country badly divided and relatively low public credibility. He and his "handlers" and supporters among the power elite are aware of the malaise that has divided the nation for the nearly 18 years since John Kennedy was assassinated in Dallas. The catastrophic loss in national prestige over Vietnam has only exacerbated the problem. If he, Ronald Reagan, can reenact the tragedy and *walk away* he will at one stroke heal the country's most grievous wound and make himself a hero such as America has never known.

A certain delicacy is required. The public must believe the President has actually been shot, or the effect will not be maximal. How best to do this? Should he actually be hit by a low velocity dummy slug? No. Too dangerous; what if it hit him in the face? Instead a spent bullet is planted in his bulletproof vest. The "assassin" will have no live ammo; the shooting will be done carefully, surgically, by someone else—perhaps an off-duty Secret Service man.

The tableau is set up, with or without Reagan's foreknowledge (it works either way). The moment is at hand. Shots ring out. Reagan is down beneath his Secret Service agents. He is spirited away. One of Reagan's underlings is hit and horribly injured, but these are minor costs when Presidential Theater is being played out.

The gun is "found" to have been fired by a young man perhaps under some form of mind control, perhaps a knowing conspirator. John Hinckley is taken quickly into custody before he can utter a possibly injudicious word. In case the population should be tempted to sympathize with him, he is quickly discredited by his supposed obsessive pursuit of a young movie actress (what else), Jodie Foster, whose peculiar sensuality has branded her image in the public mind.

Reagan is taken to the hospital. He walks in. He says he didn't even realize he was hit. Simple. He wasn't. His medical examination is a farce, or doesn't take place at all; if Kennedy's autopsy can be falsified, so can Reagan's mere checkup. He walks out.

The transfigured President *walks away*. It cannot escape his actor's mind, with its queasy mixture of vanity and fantasy, how much like Jesus Christ he is, miraculously resurrected. (How appealing, how coincidental, that this is the Easter season!) He is Kennedy risen. He goes on to forge an eerie popularity, smelling of decay and death, yet buoyed by his miraculous escape.

The public feeling has been successfully coopted. An entirely new national mood takes center stage, a mood that is used for an unprecedented elite grab of power and money, and corresponding impoverishment of the nation. All stage-managed so that the public can be duped into cheering it on. With modern media, this is easy. Barnum was born too soon.

And John Hinckley? We hear little more of him. Like Sirhan Sirhan, he will never emerge, never be available for questioning. The remainder of his life will be carefully managed. Probably by now his mind, like Sirhan's, is no longer amenable to examination, having been destroyed and rebuilt. There is never a trial. Never will be.

Reagan is not the first to play the role of the rescued martyr. Recall those two curiously inconclusive "assassination attempts" on President Gerald Ford. One was by (or blamed on) a more or less anonymous disturbed middle-aged woman, the other by former Charles Manson associate Lynette "Squeaky" Fromme, conveniently free (if she had been you or I, they would have thrown the key away) and in the right place at the right time. Did Fromme get a sweet deal for playing the role?

Who remembers all this today? Forgetfulness is our besetting sin. Yet Ford was the covert power boys' patsy—sat on the Warren Commission, pardoned Nixon. Few can have been so well placed to appreciate the value of Presidential Theater. Except it didn't work for Ford. He lacked even the elementary vertebrate charisma to take advantage of his gift-even after it was tried out twice.

Never mind: Ford's Republican successor, Reagan, was chosen specifically for his mastery of Theater. Nor did he have to wait until he took office to try it out. After Carter's 1976 election victory over a hapless Ford, Reagan was given carte blanche by the "Party Out of Power," the Republicans who, even though they lacked the White House, actually controlled nearly all the levers of American society, especially the covert ones, and could work behind the scenes with impunity.

That they did so, there seems little doubt. The Reagan-Bush campaign of 1980 probably did perpetrate an October Surprise, persuading the Iranians to hold the U.S. hostages until after Reagan was sworn in, and denying Jimmy Carter the reelection that would likely have been his had he gotten the hostages out before Election Day. What could be more theatrical, or more useful? If ever proved against them (and the trail is very cold now), the October Surprise amounts to treason on the part of both Reagan and Bush, and they would be the first Presidents ever to be so charged.

But we must go further, and ask whether a Reagan-Bush campaign capable of an October Surprise could also have seen to it that the captured Americans were used as hostages in the first place. In November 1979, with a Democratic administration in the White House, how valuable would it have been to the Republican Right-Wing power elite, then lining up its guns for the campaign, to make a deal with the Khomeini regime to hold, rather than releasing, the American hostages after the American Embassy was taken? Those hostages were an embarrassment, not an asset, to Iran. But a deal with the forces behind America's unelected President, Reagan — a deal, let us say, that put Iran on a better footing against its enemies in the region — would clearly make it well worth Iran's while to hang them around Jimmy Carter's neck, to the Republican power elite's great advantage.

Once embarked on wholesale sabotage of the American political process (not to mention the laws of the land), it would have been no trouble for the Reagan and Bush backers to see to it that the subsequent attempt to rescue the hostages from Iran suffered shipwreck and turned into a propaganda defeat for Carter. This is not something Reagan could do for himself, but his future running mate, with his ties to the intelligence community, could easily arrange it for him.

But why would Bush agree to help Reagan? Weren't the two men rivals for the Presidency?

Maybe not really. It may not have mattered, to those who turn them both on and off like faucets, which man won. And so we must ask whether the rivalry between Reagan and Bush in the primary campaign was more apparent than real. Whether it was, like so much else, staged.

Who is George Herbert Walker Bush? We really don't know. It is widely suspected that he was, and is, lifelong CIA. But we don't know how deep he goes;

Bush's life, apart from the little he has chosen to reveal, is poorly documented. He is the one President, out of the host of politicians eager to thrust their lives before us, who is a mystery man.

Where there is a mystery, there is usually a good reason. In some way it is advantageous to Bush not to permit detailed knowledge of what he was doing in those years when he was just making money in Texas with the oil company named after Mexican bandit hero Emiliano Zapata. If he was CIA, he could hardly have been better placed, in that bastion of American Right-Wing power.

It is tempting to ask whether Bush could be the real key figure in the lengthy right wing takeover that began with Kennedy's assassination in 1963 and culminated with Reagan's election in November 1980 — or perhaps, more accurately, with his pretended shooting in March 1981. Could Reagan, with all his popularity, have been merely the shoehorn for the relatively unpopular Bush? That would make sense if Bush is the Secret Government's first President.

The whole procession of events that has indelibly marked the United States and turned it toward "friendly (read consumerist) fascism" since Kennedy's assassination nearly 30 years ago seems to have been pointed toward one crowning event: putting the clandestine power of the Right — the Secret Government nobody wanted to talk about when it came up in the Iran-Contra hearings — in overt power and keeping it there.

Remember the worldwide consternation when Yuri Andropov, head of the KGB came to power in the Soviet Union? Yet here in the United States the takeover of the White House by the intelligence services took place without a murmur.

Reagan, in that context, is a cipher; but the deceptively mild Bush would seem to be the spook par excellence. Is he, then, the American Secret Government's first wholly owned avatar?

Whatever or whoever Bush is, Presidency-as-Theater continues under him today. Learning from the show-and-tell antics of his predecessor, Bush has taken us through a make believe war in which his Ambassador, April Glaspie (perhaps acting in good faith but Trojan-horsed by her President), entrapped Saddam Hussein into believing that the U.S. would wink at his assertion of Iraq's claims in Kuwait.

As an old CIA hand, perhaps Saddam should have known better, but he took the bait. Or he may have gone in with open eyes and a guarantee that, while the U.S. would relieve him of onerous responsibility for the troublesome civilian economy of his country after the long Iranian war, Saddam himself, and the core of his military hierarchy, would be preserved. But he shouldn't have believed it. Lately, just in time for the 1992 election campaign, Bush is floating trial balloons about getting rid of him. Saddam should realize that nothing, and no one, stands in the way of the Republican Right's murderous electoral politics.

Bush is now poised to do whatever is necessary to ensure that no Democrat captures the White House this year — maybe any year. The dirty tricks against Bill Clinton are a replay of the string of Republican Right-Wing sabotage operations against viable Democrats stretching back through Gary Hart and Ed Muskie to Chappaquiddick, which looks more and more like a covert-operations setup with every passing year.

JFK, RFK and MLK were killed; Teddy Kennedy was set up for a plane crash, but miraculously survived. The perpetrators have since realized, however, that you don't have to kill a Democrat to neutralize him. Indeed it is better to discredit him, leave him hanging around like a corpse at a wedding, nullifying those who come after. Lest he forget the Mary Jo Kopechne collar, Ted Kennedy was recently handed a Patricia Bowman sandwich. Clinton is proving surprisingly resistant against the Gennifer Flowers allegations, and may require a double dose.

But even the best conspiracy may not be proof forever against cracks in the woodwork. Flowers almost blew it when she began sounding like she'd been pressured. "I didn't choose this, it chose me," she said at her news conference, "and I'm dealing with it as effectively as I can...I want to be set free." Free of what? What chose her? A few more ill-chosen words like those, and people may start to read between the lines. Don't be surprised if Flowers has an unfortunate accident, or goes into seclusion only to reemerge months later sounding like a completely different person.

And look for more "surprises." Paul Tsongas, till now scarcely a credible candidate, at this writing is rising in the polls in New Hampshire. Ripples of sabotage are surfacing against him, too. (What a remarkable coincidence!)

Depend on it, *any* credible Democratic front-runner will be discredited. And the news media will fail to seek a source for the problem, will even fail to suspect there could be anything rotten in Denmark.

Once he has secured the White House for himself and his cabal in '92-96, what can we expect of George Bush? The scary thing is, we have no way of finding out. More of the same, of course: enriching the rich, scuttling the poor, throwing America "of by and for the people" out the door. But his core agenda, which may be much worse than that, is hidden from US. Are you worried? I am.

And beyond '96? Will Bush make an illegal third term possible for himself, perhaps pleading a National Security emergency? Or is Dan Quayle really the heir apparent, despite his lack of everything but Right-Wing credentials? Who and what is Quayle, really? I don't think we can assume we know. And what is the Secret Government's long-term agenda for what used to be the Land of the Free?

You can depend on one thing: there will never be another Democratic liberal President—never. All measures necessary, from vote fraud and the hole card, assassination, to National Emergency are ready for use to prevent it. And day in and day out, the chief means of swaying the American public (so that we will not even want a Democratic president) will be plentiful use of that sovereign mode of the video age, Presidency-as-Theater.

It's never failed yet.

Mail addressed to John Robert Martin, a writer in Massachusetts, returns stamped "No Such Address." He is urged to recontact Steamshovel Press *if he would like to have his contributor copies forwarded.*

KKK, GOP and CIA
by Tim Wheeler

David Duke, it is said, idolized his father, an engineer for Shell Oil Company, who, like his son, was a white supremacist. The father, David Hedger Duke, volunteered for service in Southeast Asia during the Vietnam War. He was sent to Laos as an agent of the State Department's Agency for International Development (AID.)

Young David, meanwhile, completed high school and enrolled at Louisiana State University, where he became notorious on "Free Speech Alley" for his racist and anti-Semitic harangues. Just before he dropped out of LSU, on March 4, 1971, Duke was ordered to report for active duty. Selective Service records show that he was classified 1-A. But in a "highly unusual move," reports Tyler Bridges of the *Times-Picayune* of New Orleans, "Duke was given a student deferment, March 18, even though he soon left school and didn't return for eighteen months...None of the members of his draft board contacted said they knew why the injunction notice was rescinded." When Bridges asked Duke why he hadn't been drafted, Duke responded, "Well, I was in Laos during the war."

And indeed he was. He boasted that he spent nine months in Laos beginning in May 1971, flying twenty missions "behind enemy lines aboard CIA Air America transport planes, dropping supplies to CIA mercenary troops in the mountains. In attempting to debunk details of Duke's story, critics only confirm the main point. Charles Green, for example, head of the Agency for International Development (AID) language school in Laos, said Duke served only six weeks as an English language instructor of Laotian army officers. Green claims he fired Duke when he walked into his classroom and saw that Duke had drawn a Molotov cocktail on the blackboard."

It is well known that the CIA used AID as a cover for covert warfare in Southeast Asia. It is entirely plausible that David Duke was recruited as a covert agent of the CIA. That would explain why his induction into the military was mysteriously rescinded.

It would also explain Duke's strange immunity in other criminal and terrorist activities. In September 1976 Duke was the sponsor of a conference of neo-Nazis and Klansmen at a hotel near his home in Metairies, an all-white suburb of New Orleans. When police arrived, Duke and his followers surrounded the squad car. Duke led the mob in chanting, "White Power." Duke screamed at the officers, "You are a Jew. You work for the FBI. They are commie traitors and you are too." The police radioed for help and Duke was among those arrested. He was tried but received a suspended sentence. Why?

On December 31, 1980, Duke sat on a French quarter balcony in New Orleans with a convicted felon named Michael Perdue. According to Gwen Udell, a close friend of Duke's who was there, the two men "hashed over Perdue's plan to invade the Caribbean island of Dominica." " A small band of mercenaries would sail to the tiny black populated country, overthrow the government and set up a white supremacist junta," reports the *Times-Picayune*. Perdue "dreamed of making millions by running a casino and exporting lumber." Others say the real "export" was to be cocaine and other narcotics.

Duke reportedly helped Perdue find a charter boat to transport his mercenary commandos and put Perdue in touch with people who would finance the bizarre expedition, codenamed Operation Red Dog.

On April 27, 1981, officers of the federal Bureau of Alcohol, Tobacco and Firearms arrested them just before they boarded the yacht in Lake Ponchartrain. Despite his ringleader role, Duke was not arrested. He was subpoenaed to appear before a grand jury, where he pleaded the Fifth Amendment, refusing to testify. Nine of the ten other conspirators, including Duke's co-hort Klanman Don Black, were found guilty and served time in prison. Why was Duke let off?

The above is reprinted from People's Weekly World, *Long View Publishing Company, 235 West 23rd Street, New York, NY 10011.*

An American Nazi and Ozark Tourism
by Kenn Thomas

While many people in St. Louis, Missouri have made great contributions to racial harmony and the civil rights struggle, charges of racism against the town's citizenry have deep historic roots. The life of one St. Louisan, Gerald L.K. Smith, serves as a reminder of one citizen who wrote a dark chapter in local race relations. Gerald L.K. Smith was a nationally prominent right-wing evangelist headquartered in St. Louis who promoted racism and anti-Semitism throughout the country. He retired as a tourist site promoter in Eureka Springs, Arkansas, and made a fortune.

In the 1940s, Smith toured the Midwest and the South making inflammatory speeches denouncing blacks, Jews and Communists and organizing racists. He formed a Nazi-like political party called the Christian Nationalist Crusade and propagated his bigotry through a regularly published and widely distributed magazine, *The Cross and the Flag*. During the peak of its popularity Smith's magazine reached over 20,000 American households. Without ever holding political office, Gerald Smith exerted a powerful influence on the racial attitudes of ordinary citizens, and contributed greatly to the philosophy of a vocal minority that continues to blemish the public debate on race issues.

The only extant biography of Smith is *Gerald L. K. Smith, Minister of Hate* (1), written by Glen Jeansonne and published by Yale University Press in 1988. It tells the chilling tale of an Ozark Nazi, but it reads more like an adventure in research than an examination of the darker side of Midwestern racial politics. As one might expect of a book from an academic press, *Minister of Hate* takes on an academic tone that might discourage the general reader. Author Glen Jeansonne has researched his work thoroughly and has provided copious documentation. He also utilizes previously untapped primary sources, mostly from the Bentley Historical Library at the University of Michigan, and conducted several interviews with Smith himself prior to Smith's death in April 1976.

Jeansonne's reportage is fairly comprehensive. He traces the evangelist's rise to prominence as part of the political organization of Huey P. Long, the King-fish of Louisiana politics in the 1930s. Long had become the dominant force in that state campaigning as an enemy of its corporate establishment, a populist style that Smith coveted. Like Long, Gerald Smith became notorious: for his spell-binding oratory. Gesticulating wildly and drenched in sweat, Smith's tirades against wealthy bankers, FDR, the New Deal and whatever else was handy, often worked crowds into a frenzy.

After Huey Long's assassination in 1935, Smith used his charismatic talent to the advantage of a number of political movements. During the Depression, he served as one of the chief lieutenants of the Townsend Plan, an outline for government-supported pensions that foreshadowed the Social Security. As a part of this movement, Smith formed an alliance with Father Charles Coughlin, the priest and right-wing radio commentator from Detroit. Coughlin later denounced Smith for his extremism.

In January 1943 Smith formed the America First Party in Detroit. Like the America First Committee started by Charles Lindbergh, to which it was not formally connected, the party served as an early precursor to the xenophobia politics of Patrick Buchanan. It advocated creating jobs by the deporting of foreign-born laborers; raising the U.S. living standard before aiding other nations; and protecting white citizens from minorities and Communism. At an America First Party rally in St. Louis in February 1944, Smith nominated Lindbergh for president.

Gerald L.K. Smith traveled throughout the Midwest and the South in the mid-1940s exhorting crowded auditoriums to oppose his litany of public enemies. In addition to FDR, Smith spoke against the Red and Jewish menaces; celebrity conspirators such as Charlie Chaplin and Drew Pearson; Jewish Wall Street bankers; and labor radicals.

In his Detroit hometown, Smith attracted smaller crowds, mostly hecklers, had difficulty renting halls, and had his property vandalized. Smith decided to move to St. Louis, Missouri in December 1947 for these reasons and because of the city's central location. The political atmosphere in St. Louis might also have been a factor contributing to his decision: in the previous year seven men, one of them a World War II veteran and former chairman of the local Communist party, were fined heavily for peace disturbance after street brawls broke out in protest over an America First rally in St. Louis. (2)

Many St. Louisans resisted the move. A Jewish landlady evicted Smith from the first building he leased and other realtors turned him down flat. One detractor told the *St. Louis Post-Dispatch* that "any appearance Smith makes in St. Louis should not be in the auditorium, or even in the city Jail, but in a cage at the zoo." (3) Yet four-hundred people attended the two-day convention at Kiel Auditorium which accompanied the move.

Smith fanned the flames of racism and resentment against St. Louis's large black population. Smith's group ran candidates for state and national offices that fared poorly but attracted media attention for their racism. It also started a petition drive to make segregation compulsory in St. Louis, but did not come up with enough signatures to put a referendum on the ballot.

In 1949 Smith organized the Racial Purity Committee to counteract a new city charter that would eliminate Jim Crow buses. The Committee's countermeasure would have required separate building entrances for blacks and segregated restaurants, night clubs and athletic events. The measure also failed to get the required signatures.

Founded in 1942, *The Cross And The Flag* became the official organ of the America First Party (which was renamed the Christian Nationalist Crusade in 1947). Jeansonne notes that although the magazine operated at a loss from its inception to its discontinuation in 1977, *The Cross and the Flag* had the largest circulation of any extreme rightist periodical and a larger circulation than either *The Nation* or *The New Republic*. Jeansonne also points out that Smith rarely intended to convert people to his style of bigotry. Smith told one distributor, "please do not hand the magazines to people who need conversion. Our problem in America is rather to crystallize the people who already feel like we do."

According to Jeansonne, Smith's popularity declined over the years for several reasons. In 1947 the American Jewish Committee organized an effort to convince newspaper publishers to ignore Smith, and subsequently his press coverage dropped dramatically. Jeansonne argues that as times changed, Smith refused to move on to different issues and his inflammatory oratory became so archaic even his supporters became bored. The style and substance of *The Cross and the Flag*, however, re-emerged in the tracts of such hate groups as the Minutemen and the American Nazi Party in the 1960s.

No longer in demand as a speaker, Gerald L.K. Smith retired in 1964 to a town called Eureka Springs in the Ozark Mountains of northern Arkansas. He soon announced plans to build a giant statue of Christ there as a tourist attraction. Using a front man to promote the project, and later promising not to bring the Christian Nationalist Crusade to town, Smith received the cooperation of civic leaders to construct the potentially lucrative tourist attraction. The statue, called the Christ of the Ozarks, was formally dedicated in June 1966 and continues to draw tourists.

The Christ of the Ozarks is the site for a summer Passion Play at an amphitheater carved in the mountains surrounding the statue. While some critics praised the professionalism of the production, others decried it as anti-Semitic. In letters to local newspapers, Smith attacked his critics as enemies of Christ. In 1969 Smith opened another of his Sacred Projects attractions, the Christ Only Art Museum. In 1971 he opened a Bible Museum in Eureka Springs. Until his death in April 1976, Smith had plans to construct an amusement park in the image of the middle eastern Holy Land, almost two decades before similar aspirations helped land evangelist Jim Bakker in prison.

The Cross and the Flag continued until December 1977, leaving only the Christ in the Ozarks statue, the Passion Play, and a continuing influence on American racist groups as monuments to Smith's blending of fascism and evangelical Christianity.

Jeansonne spares few details in covering the life of Gerald L.K. Smith, but his conclusions say little about why figures like Smith recur with such frequency on the political and social landscape and why they are so greatly rewarded. "Perhaps they are always present but gain power in times of privation and turmoil," he concludes, "We can never rest assured that, should troubled times persist, it can't happen here." In the city where it did happen local racists announced plans to patrol the suburbs as recently as spring 1991.

One other conspiratorial footnote to Gerald L.K. Smith: in a book entitled *The Assassination of Robert F. Kennedy,* authors William Turner and John G. Christian, note that a long-time associate of Smith's, a fellow evangelist named Jerry Owen, who was known as the Walking Bible, waited at the Ambassador Hotel the night of RFK's murder to help Sirhan Sirhan make a getaway. (4)

Notes:

1. Jeansonne, Glen. *Gerald L.K. Smith Minister of Hate,* Yale University Press, New Haven and London, 1988, 283pp.

2. "Seven Gerald Smith Rioters Fined $100 to $1100," *St. Louis Globe-Democrat,* August 14, 1946.

3. *St. Louis Post-Dispatch,* May 15, 1946.

4. Turner, William and Christian, John G., *The Assassination of Robert F. Kennedy,* New York, Random House, 1978, 397pp.

A Modest Enquiry: Some Possible Problems with a New Santa Cruz Anti-Discrimination Law
by Robert Anton Wilson

I fear that a new law banning discrimination in renting or hiring on the basis of "personal appearance" or "sexual orientation" creates certain intractable logical problems which may lead to protracted legal struggles. In the following note I attempted to explain my misgivings to the Hon. Neal Coonerty, author of the law.

1. To avoid expensive and unnecessary litigation (one of the primary goals of any landlord or business operator) all of us should have a clear and unambiguous idea of what actions can potentially lead to litigation. Except as a last resort in collecting bad debts, litigation always seems a cure worse than the problem. Thus, in most matters, the *avoidance of litigation* and the *comprehension of the guidelines to avoid litigation* always remain paramount concerns.

But in matters relating to *intangible* and *subjective* inner processes of choice and decision, one simply cannot formulate clear and unambiguous guidelines to avoid litigation.

Nobody, not even the Hon. Councilperson Coonerty, ever really "knows" why you choose A over B. (According to the Freudians, even *you* don't know.) Thus, you can never *prove* that your motive qualifies as "legally pure." Any attempt to find such "proof" leads inevitably to Kafka-like abysses.

Historically, in societies aiming at freedom, legislators do not even attempt such control over the citizens' invisible and unknowable states of mind, realizing that this leads to what Burke once called "that great Serbonian bog where armies whole have sunk."

In other words, when accused of "thought crime," you face the sort of no-win problem confronting Joseph K. in *The Trial*: you can never find a Court metaphysically capable of judging your inner "state of grace" (or lack of it) or attorneys who can find any sort of legal evidence that will "prove" innocence or guilt. I doubt that Constitutional scholars can even form a coherent idea of what might constitute either *evidence* or *proof* in this matter.

Pragmatically, the only rule most businesspeople have for dealing with our current herd of "politically correct" lawmakers (those who do increasingly try to control our invisible, unknowable mental states) consists of "When in doubt, play it safe."

In the present context, considering the matter of appearance first, this means that if two candidates apply for the same job, or the same domicile, the "pragmatically safe" choice will award the job or domicile to whoever of the two (in ordinary language) "looks funnier" or "looks weirder" or "looks uglier," etc., because if one chooses the candidate who looks less "funny," "weird," or "ugly," an expensive lawsuit *might* result.

Thus, under the "when in doubt, play it safe" rule, I suspect that in only one year after the Coonerty law comes into effect, tenants and employees in Santa Cruz will begin to look slightly strange and a bit bizarre, considered as a group, compared to the present year.

2. Now, assume conservatively that only 1/20 of all jobs become available in a year's time, due to deaths, retirements, the founding of new enterprises, people moving elsewhere (to find better jobs, to live closer to parents or children, etc.). This means that the Santa Cruz Strangeness Quotient (SCSQ) will increase 1/20 in one year.

It then follows that in, say, five years the SCSQ will reach 5/20 or 25%; in 10 years, SCSQ will = 50% etc.

In 20 years then, the SCSQ will change 20 x 1/20 or 100% and all employees here will look decidedly "weird" compared to people elsewhere.

Tourists will then come from nearby towns, or some not so nearby, to gape and ogle at Santa Cruz natives, for the same reason people have always gone to circuses, carnivals, freak shows or horror movies. We should carefully consider if we really want a town that looks like that. Maybe "we" (or a loud minority of us) do—I certainly stipulate that it would boost tourism—but we need to debate and carefully consider this issue fully before plunging ahead.

(And let us at least pray that the debate and consideration can occur thoughtfully, without the herds of the politically correct howling, chanting and otherwise drowning out all voices not entirely consistent with their Dogma.)

3. In the above calculus, I have considered only a single generation. The results of Coonerty's Law over a period of a few generations appear even more dramatic. In brief, the law can only produce *a breeding population of very "strange"-looking men mating with equally "strange"-looking women.* In several generations, *the statistical definition of 'human' will perforce change,* and businesspeople wishing to play it safe will hire only the strangest of the strange, the weirdest of

the weird. Ergo, Santa Cruz must eventually, by anti-Darwinian selection, take on the look of one of those "sinister and ill-regarded" hamlets in the terror fiction of H.P. Lovecraft, where everybody looks vaguely ape-like, frog-like, fish-like or somehow inhuman (see e.g. "The Dunwich Horror" or "The Shadow Over Innsmouth.")

4. If you have jobs to offer or rooms to rent, the probability of a lawsuit against you will *decrease* as the number of "odd-looking" tenants or employees *increases*. Thus, under the "play it safe" rule, the more truly amazing-looking or nearly unbelievable tenants or employees you can find, the safer your legal position becomes.

Thus, within a generation, to attend to business, seek a profit and avoid interminable legal expenses and court appearances, you will do well to fill your premises not just with the somewhat "ugly" or mildly "unattractive," but with the truly, hideously *loathsome,* and especially the *"terrifying"* and *"eldritch"*—i.e. with those who look as if they had in fact escaped from Lovecraft's fantasy, or from *Tales From The Crypt.*

5. *A paradox then arises.* At the precise point when Santa Cruz does look like Horror Comix, the Coonerty law will encourage legal actions by those who appear (or *think* they appear) conspicuously gorgeous and/or handsome.

In simple logic, if everybody in Santa Cruz looks like a member of the Juke or Kallikak families, or the Addams family, or a relative of Gill Man, a few Venuses and Adonises can argue plausibly that *good-looking people have defacto become excluded from dwellings and jobs.* These "movie star" types will have suffered "discrimination," and they can sue. As we have seen, the Coonerty law (enacted) and the "play it safe" rule (un-enacted but omnipresent) will indeed discriminate against the comely, and the lawyers will gladly encourage them in fighting this "injustice."

The increasingly subtle art of avoiding litigation under this law, it then seems, will consist of an initial strategy of hiring or renting to people who look creepy or crawly by ordinary standards, but to reverse this strategy and again hire some "normals" shortly before all Santa Cruz residents actually look like Godzilla and his sisters and his cousins and his aunts.

This requires extremely delicate judgement, and in any choice that requires extreme delicacy, lawyers will happily sue you for not having had *quite enough delicacy* to meet the "intent" of the law. You will never know if you have enough "Aliens" in your office to hire one "Sigourney Weaver"—or you will only find out when a lawsuit against you begins, and the lawyer

for the plaintiff asks not only civil damages but $23,000,000 in punitive damages as well.

6. I have used extreme examples to illustrate one possibly defective aspect of this law, *but average examples create even worse potential legal disputes.* Thus:

"Beauty," as we have all heard, "resides in the eye of the beholder."

Two seemingly ordinary-looking people arrive to apply for a job you have advertised. Under the "when in doubt, play it safe" rule (always prudent and usually *necessary for survival* when dealing with *politically correct* governments), you try to decide which of the two might qualify as a little less attractive. The more unlike my previous grotesque examples these people seem to you, the harder your legal problem becomes. If candidate #1 seems fairly comely but 20 pounds overweight, does that outrank a huge hairy wart on the nose of otherwise-comely candidate #2? How many warts out-rank 30 pounds of weight?

Since the safest choice consists in always choosing the less appealing candidate, and since beauty, as noted, appears relative, the optimum solution, as Game Theory would call it, consists in obtaining a consensus. In other words, install a one-way glass wall in your office and hire a few random citizens to sit behind it and vote on which candidate appears a bit more unattractive. (These citizens could also testify for you, if litigation nonetheless results, to show that you at least made a *sincere effort to avoid hiring good-looking people.*)

The Coonerty law does not propose to pay business people for installing these walls of one-way glass and hiring independent "citizen judges." This does not seem fair. Should not the city appropriate funds to pay for this, as an incentive to those who truly wish to follow the intent of the law, either out of altruism or just to avoid endless litigation, and as a partial compensation for the Judicial and other burdens this law will place on businesspersons?

7. The law does not specifically include *smell* as part of "personal appearance," but most people do, in fact, notice odor and consider it in forming a judgement of job applicants or possible tenants. Lawyers will certainly insist that the intent of the law should include smell—it certainly seems that the law would have included smell if Coonerty had thought of that—and, as I understand the legal mind, honest judges will have to agree with this viewpoint.

Once again, the change in Santa Cruz yields to mathematical analysis. Under the "when in doubt, play it safe" guideline to avoid litigation, businesspeople will tend to hire whoever smells less pleasing. Thus in one year, Santa Cruz will smell 1/20 less pleasant than at present, and in 20 years 100% worse than at present, etc.

This can only "level off" when the town takes on a general aroma of an open cesspool and businesses feel "safe" in now and then hiring one or two less malodorous employees. Meanwhile, it would appear prudent to buy a gas-mask.

8. When we turn to the matter of "sexual orientation," the logical and legal problems multiply like microbes.

Contrary to folk-lore, nobody can judge another's sexual preference by their appearance or "body language." The most experienced interviewers from the Kinsey Institute, studying sexual behavior for decades, still find that they cannot guess, in advance, whether a subject's life history will reveal an all-homosexual lifestyle, an all heterosexual lifestyle, or a mixture, which may run from 90% gay/10% straight to 10% gay/90% straight, or even to 99%/1% either way.

"When in doubt, play it safe" simply does not apply here. The employer will have to *guess,* and will guess wrong around half the time (as Kinsey interviewers do). The endless litigation can prove satisfying only to the Hon. Mr. Coonerty—and to the lawyers.

9. A way out exists if employers had the right to *ask* the sexual orientation of candidates, *and prudently hire only those with unpopular or minority preferences,* but this violates numerous State and Federal ordinances. In this area of law nobody has the right to *ask,* but under the Coonerty Ordinance all employers will have to guess (with penalties for guessing wrong).

We seem to have surpassed Kafka and arrived at the portals of George Orwell's Ministry of Love. This does not appear at all like a Constitutional legal system but like a cruelly labyrinthine trap.

10. No rational person can seriously fear an increase in the number of masochists in Santa Cruz; masochists hurt nobody but themselves. But a law banning all forms of "discrimination" will also attract an influx of sadists, will it not?

How many new sadists does Mr. Coonerty wish to lure to our community?

How many sadists do the majority of us want?

Some may claim that the Coonerty Law does not mention sadists and "really intends" only to increase the number of gainfully employed homosexuals here. *But the law does not single out homosexuals as some specially blessed group among all the sexual minorities, because if it did, it would conflict with State and Federal ordinances against such special group bias.* Lawyers will quickly find it profitable to insist on *what the law does exactly say.*

(Meanwhile, we can expect some spectacular demonstrations, with signs like "A LITTLE DISCIPLINE NEVER HURT ANYBODY," "NO GAIN WITHOUT PAIN" etc. and the inevitable chant, "Hey Hey Ho Ho Sadophobia Has To Go.")

11. How many necrophiles do we really want? The Coonerty law opens the floodgates to them also.

12. I have no personal bias against people who want to have sex with toy poodles or dobermans, but what will the toy poodles and dobermans think about this?

Have the Animal Rights people had a chance to comment on this perplexing issue? Has the Hon. Coonerty given any effort to deciding the age of consent for dogs? For cats? For swine? For other animals?

In summary, the Coonerty law does not advantage ugly homosexuals only but *all unpleasant-looking people with sexual "orientations" different from the majority.* It will benefit, not just the groups already mentioned, but hunchbacked child molesters, dwarfish rapists, obese foot fetishists, pock-marked leather fetishists, etc. along with generally ugly suideaphiliacs, deformed iguanaphiliacs, foul-smelling ichthyophiliacs etc. (See R Kraft-Ebing, *Psychopathia Sexualis.*)

13. Considering these *possible* consequences of the Coonerty Law—all of them highly *probable* eventually, due to well-known propensities of the legal profession—we should perhaps take steps to make the image of Santa Cruz (although a weird one) appear more fey and whimsical (like St. Olaf's on the TV comedy *Golden Girls*) than downright *monstrous and nefarious* (like Lovecraft's demoniac towns, already mentioned).

(In other words, we will find it easier, in the long run, if nearby towns—and the nation as a whole—only regard Santa Cruz as ridiculous, rather than sinister. People laugh at the absurd, but often attack what they fear.)

To start with, we might order our police to abandon their present uniforms and dress in clown suits. We could also require that teachers in our schools, male and female, must wear those Groucho Marx comedy spectacles which give the wearer huge eyebrows, an astounding false nose of gigantic proportions and a *banditto* mustache. Statues of Salvadore Dali, say, and/or The Mad Hatter, Pooh Bear, Wile E. Coyote, The Three Stooges (in scuba diving suits) etc., outside each government building would also help create a ludicrous rather than a frightening ambience.

Removing the dull ruminations by DWPS (dead white politicians) from these buildings might also help our Comic, not sinister image, if we replace them with bits of bizarre or inscrutable humor—e.g. *Keep the Lasagna Flying Proudly Over Capitola Mall, The Mome Rath Doesn't Exist That Can Outgrabe Me, When Laws Are Outlawed Only Outlaws Will Have Laws, I Always Believe Three Impossible Things Before Breakfast,* etc.

Most helpful of all, perhaps, the Township should consider the propriety of buying some adult standing a regal 8 feet high and allow them to mingle with the City Council during all important public hearings, bringing to our urgent municipal proceedings the absurd and pathetic dignity that only these giant wingless birds embody. The mad surrealist poetry of this legislative innovation should appeal to both Mr. Coonerty and Ms. Atkins, even if they prefer not to meditate too deeply on its possible symbolism.

14. Assuming that Jeffrey Dahmer's lawyers somehow win him a parole, he would appear the ideal future Santa Cruz renter and employee. Once he announces, casually, "'Oh, by the way, I like to sodomize little black boys and then cook them and eat them," everybody will see him as Ideal Tenant and Ideal Worker, since his presence will in itself serve as a truly *spectacular legal, logical and Public Relations argument against any charges of homophobia, sadophobia, necrophobia or miscellaneous "discrimination"* that might later arise.

Other of Dahmer's orientations will think of this and we expect them to arrive here soon. The politically correct may rejoice in this triumph of their odd logic, but how many others, who have not yet achieved full correctness, can sincerely share the rejoicing?

In none of the above have I considered the emigration of businesses away from Santa Cruz and the rising unemployment that will result. Nobody knows how many businesses will just move elsewhere, and I do not attempt to estimate. Perhaps many will stay, because of the lovely scenery and the climate in these parts. *Let us hope so.* Many, however, will prefer to leave rather than attempting to do business in this Kafka-like context, and we should also ask, even if we cannot answer immediately, how much more unemployment do we really want?

I can only conclude with words attributed to Henry David Thoreau: If you scan the horizon and see a politician approaching with the intent to improve your morals, run for your life.

POSTSCRIPT: Nobody on the Santa Cruz City Council, except the Hon. Coonerty himself, saw fit to answer this communique. Public law prevents me from quoting Mr. Coonerty's letter to me, but since paraphrase does not violate said law, I can say that Coonerty made no effort to win me to his position but merely suggested that I should bloody well go to hell and take my book on logic with me.

Robert Anton Wilson is most recently the author of Reality Is What You Can Get Away With *from Dell. He lists the* Illuminatus! *trilogy and* Cosmic Trigger *among his most renown works.* Cosmic Trigger II *and other RAW titles can be ordered from New Falcon Publications, 7025 East First Avenue, Scottsdale, Arizona 85251. Wilson's newsletter,* Trajectories, *is available (four issues, $20) from The Permanent Press, POB 700305, San Jose, CA 95170.*

Is Language a "Language" Language?
On the Analytic Systems of Noam Chomsky and Heinrich Schenker
by Roy Lisker

"All dull sentences are ungrammical." —Panini

Few things are more characteristic of 20th century thought than the promulgation of highly dogmatic abstract systems of analysis which explain to us when our thinking, speaking, writing, drawing, composing, performing, or even humming, are kosher. Rarely does one find a modern day homo sapiens who dares express any confidence anymore in his/her ability to invent ideas, or to communicate them to others. How else explain the present tendency, planetary in its dimensions, for people to turn to experts, to reassure them that what they say continues to make sense to anybody else?

The instinct to take recourse in the scripture of venerated Authority is eternally active in Mankind. Moses is his eternal archetype with his tally sheet of Thou Shalt Nots! In many ways things have changed little since the Middle Ages: economics has its Marx, psychology its Freud, anthropology its Levi-Strauss, literature its Derrida, while religion has, and always has had of course, its popes, gurus, prophets, Messiahs, etc., etc...

Yet a major difference between the law-givers of antiquity and their resurgent contemporary descendants remains. For whereas the ancient prophets restricted the domain of their chastisement to our bad conduct, the modern day usurpations of their role widen their scope to include our languages, our grammatical constructions, our thought patterns, our habits, our slips of the tongue, our brain waves, our musical phrases, our games, our tastes in vegetables and ice cream, our private reveries. All these are pungently offensive to the nostrils of the gods, all must be eviscerated from our living tissues and incinerated at the town landfill!

Two of our modern ArchPopes are Noam Chomsky and Heinrich Schenker, the former in language, the latter in music. Beginning in the 1920s, when Heinrich Schenker began publishing his analyses of classical music, and again in the 1960s, when Zellig Harris and then Noam Chomsky astonished us with their boasts—with remarkably little to show for it in the decades that followed—that they knew of a mathematics that could describe the intricacies of language, the universities, teaching colleges, high schools, conservatories and little one-room schoolhouses around the world have throbbed with the denunciatory harangues of professors and their subaltern telling us all what is good and what is evil in musical form and sentence structure.

For many people this may come as no surprise, but I have always found it strange. It is far less surprising to me that the Marxists and the Freudians should have tightened their ideological garrote over economics and psychology, traditionally murky areas bound up with anger, envy, power, righteousness and ignorance. Almost any claim made in these areas is bound to have some partial validity; the presence of a Church Father even serves the valuable function of channeling the discourse.

It strikes me as extremely peculiar that the dogmatic malaria has surfaced in two areas in which for hundreds, even thousands of years people have known perfectly well what they are doing, and written much beautiful prose, poetry and music besides.

Why not blame automation? The celebrated radical activist Noam Chomsky initially obtained his research monies (and for all I know still does) from the U.S. Army Signal Corps, the Air Force Office of Scientific Research, and the Office of Naval Research. These enormous humanitarian foundations were interested in uncovering grammatical laws applicable to all languages because this might save time and effort in the design of computer software for language translation. That might help them to know what our enemies were up to so we could murder them first.

That similar application might be made of Heinrich Schenker's hallucinations was evidently discovered by tonaural ideogogue Milton Babbitt, who manages a thriving laboratory of musical vivisectionists of Princeton University, whirling the flail of Schenkerian Bible to the beat of Radetzky March, Babbitt claims that all classical compositions can be reduced to computer programs, that such programs can be designed to "generate" classical music, that the music of Schoenberg's 12-tone school can be reduced to group theory, and that music which would not be generated by these purely hypothetical programs (which noone has ever thought of trying to write down) would just not be music. It is difficult on the face of it to see what interest the Air Force or the Navy might find in these ideas, but there may be some application to the brainwashing research of the Pentagon and the CIA.

Roy Lisker is a mathematician, poet and musician. His newsletter, Ferment!, *is available from POB 441, New Palz, NY 12561.*

Book Reviews

John Keel first documented his experiences at Point Pleasant, West Virginia in 1975 and now IllumiNet Press has re-issued *The Mothman Prophecies* (IllumiNet, $16.95) during a ufological climate that includes rumblings about a fifteen mile long UFO orbiting the Martian moon Phobos, new information on the Roswell crash, and rumors linking Danny Casolaro and MJ12. Despite that, this seventeen year old recounting of flying saucer adventures loses none of its resilience or immediacy. This is primarily due to Keel's stridency in refusing to simplify (and in some cases even classify) the peculiar events surrounding happenings in Point Pleasant. This was more than just the observation of aerial light phenomenon and airborne discs; it included chats between the locals and the grey aliens; much furtive espionage on contactees by the Men In Black; flybys of the winged devil Mothman him/herself; weird telephone harassment that rivalled the treatment Wilhelm Reich received from the Air Force; and the final culmination in a destructive bridge collapse that took the lives of forty six people in Point Pleasant.

"The UFO phenomenon itself is a trivial fragment of a much larger phenomenon," writes Keel, "Somebody somewhere does not want us to understand the phenomenon and its true purpose...It is the foundation of all religious and occult beliefs, of our philosophies and our cultures." Although Keel notes that JFK investigators received the same kind of telephone harassment, he states that he "cannot accuse the CIA as the source of the weird incidents outlined here. Rather, *the phenomenon is imitative.*" Presuming that this means the non-human things in the saucers imitate the CIA (although the CIA must have learned something about humanity from somewhere), Keel nevertheless also provides an interesting historical aside about terrestrial paranoia: his observations regarding the CIA in Tibet support what researcher Loren Coleman has written about the Yeti expeditions as fronts for secret operations.

Keel's style combines elements of Charles Forte and Raymond Chandler, but the mix might put some readers off, particularly those with vested interests in the topic. Keel claims some credit for encouraging New Age interest in the new physics, for instance; elsewhere he takes ufologists to task for scaring away government interest in the phenomenon, and he handily dismisses the work of other researchers, most notably those involved with the Roswell crash (which Keel believes was a Japanese balloon bomb). Keel's is certainly an intelligent look at the varieties of ufological experience, and any arrogance one might perceive in his writing is well-earned from the field work documented here, but his is certainly not the last word on this topic.

It would be a shame, for instance, if the Japanese balloon bomb theory kept readers away from *Final Report On Operation Majestic 12* by Stanton Friedman ($15 from 79 Pembroke Crescent; Fredericton, New Brunswick E3B 2V1, Canada). The report looks at the MJ12 documents, secret government memoranda discussing recovered alien bodies from the 1947 flying saucer crash in New Mexico. Researchers calling the documents a hoax claim that the 1952 memos were typed on a post-1963 Smith Corona. Friedman assured *Steamshovel Press* that other researchers have contradicted that claim with a "much higher level of scholarship." Hopefully, this will all be looked at in-depth in *Cosmic Collision,* Friedman's new book on the Roswell crash due in the spring from Paragon House, the Moonie (Korean CIA?) publishers. Suspicions that the secret MJ12 group still exists (along with MKULTRA, the 1950s LSD operation said also to be responsible for Jonestown) and somehow involved with the murder of researcher Danny Casolaro near Keel's stomping ground in West Virginia could help explain the motivations behind the sustained attacks on the documents.

True or no, the MJ12 documents comprise only a small part of Stanton Friedman's contribution to research in this area. The most important thing about *Final Report* is the material on Donald Menzel, a UFO debunker whose name appears on the documents. Friedman has essentially exposed Menzel as an NSA operative with top secret clearance who had the ear of JFK. "Menzel knew Kennedy," reports Friedman, because Kennedy was a member of the Board of Overseers at Harvard and had chosen astronomy as his particular area of interest. Was Menzel back channeling information about MJ12? Will Oliver Stone team up with Steven Spielberg?

Menzel also had an association with Vannevar Bush, a top scientific advisor to the government whose name also appears on the MJ12 list. Bush's name has some currency among technophiles: he wrote a strange essay called "As We May Think" for *The Atlantic* two years prior to the Roswell crash. The essay is prescient in envisioning the personal computer revolution, particularly hypertext programs, but Bush casts it in terms of microfiche and photograph film, like a Rube Goldberg machine.

John Keel's assertion that UFOs represent a small

manifestation of an ages-old phenomenon in human culture gets a sustained examination in William Bradley's *The Gods of Eden* (Dahlin Family Press, $23.95.) Bradley finds it best for his personal injury practice to remain psuedononymous. *The Gods of Eden* is nevertheless a very credible exercise in paranoid scholarship. Its premise: an extrapolation of the Fortean admonition that "we are property," humans have been bred by aliens as slaves. Bradley claims that his interest in the sociological and historical origins of human suffering led him to UFOs, The saucers have had a direct impact on human history according to Bradley, responsible for the Black Death in the Middle Ages among many other things. Secret Societies developed as human reaction to the alien slave masters, were later coopted by the otherworldly elite and the consequent dialectic resulted in man's sad history. Side roads to the thesis include examinations of the Freemasons (R.A. Wilson's satire that Adam Weishaupt killed and replaced George Washington appears here as a rumor and is dismissed); to that Nazi cosmology that we're inside a globe, not on one: to the Bush family connections to the family of wannabe Reagan assassin John Hinckley.

A caveat should govern any consideration of Frederic Seaman's account of his life with John Lennon (*The Last Days of John Lennon*, Carol Publishing Group, $19.95) just prior to the singer/songwriter's mysterious murder in December 1980: a jury convicted the author of grand larceny for the theft of Lennon's diaries. David and Victoria Sheff report in the March 1984 issue of *Playboy* that Seaman, a trusted aid to Lennon and Yoko Ono, conspired to remove the diaries and other materials in a shopping bag and give them to a writer named Bob Rosen, who planned to have them published as part of a project called *Operation Walrus*. A third person, Norman Schonfeld, transformed the project into a campaign to discredit Yoko Ono, "so the world can receive what John Lennon left behind through his anointed messenger, Fred Seaman," according to the Scheffs. Seaman does admit culpability in the theft of the diaries, but he explains that his conviction was due more to pressure from the lawyers of a wronged Yoko. It was irresponsible to take John's journals...[it was a] misguided attempt to carry out what I understood to be John's wishes, confesses Seaman. The confession is at odds with Seaman's earlier description of the older Lennon's relationship with son Julian, the ostensible recipient of the stolen journals. Even those sympathetic to Seaman can see that he not only second guessed Yoko but John as well.

Incongruities must have been standard operating procedure in the life of a gopher and confidant to John Lennon during his last days. Elsewhere in the book, for instance, Lennon alternately has premonitions of the violence of his death and visions of living to a ripe old age in the image of a Hungarian mystic named Beinsa Duono, whose photograph he found by happenstance at an occult bookstore in Florida. Anecdotes of this sort give the book some value. In many ways, it is a thoughtful book, not lurid, but Seaman is certainly self deceptive about his own motives.

Nevertheless, *The Last Days of John Lennon* is an anti-Yoko diatribe, the slim remnants of *Operation Walrus,* intended to wrest away Lennon's legacy. It is, in fact, written as a jail-bunk memoir, starting after Seaman gets beat by thugs at Yoko's behest. Seaman stops short of accusing Yoko of involvement in Lennon's murder, but is vitriolic in his condemnation of what he regards as her callousness in its wake, an assessment that can be as trusted as his self analysis. Fenton Bresler remains as the only author to deal seriously with the real questions surrounding the crime: why was the same psychiatrist (Bernard Diamond) used to evaluate Sirhan Sirhan and Mark David Chapman? Why was the behavior of the assassins identical, with "voices" compelling each to commit their horrible crimes? Were they Manchurian candidate killers? Fred Seaman's suspicions pale in comparison to the real ones surrounding the last days of John Lennon.

It's encouraging to find another pop culture creator, Steve Ditko, not only still plying the trade but pushing it to visual and intellectual excess. *The Ditko Public Service Package* (Steve Ditko and Robin Snyder: 255 N. Forest, #405, Bellingham, WA 98225-5833; $12.95) looks like scraps from a comic book artist's studio floor brought to life in an acid vision. The book is a visual gem, filled with the graceful style that first energized *Spiderman* and *Dr. Strange* for Marvel Comics in the 1960s. The message is, well, complicated. Ditko has championed an Ayn Randian philosophy and uses it here to skewer an industry that has no arguments with its basic assumptions. Anthropomorphized cartoonist tools (ink brushes, pages and personified idea bulbs) float around in an assault on small minded editors and practices that help keep comics banal. The authoritarian style philosophy seems as much at odds with the wonderfully chaotic visual style as it did when it illustrated superhero adventures. *The History of the Comics,* newsletter revering comics past, is also available from the publisher.

David Ross has taken up one of Abbie Hoffman's last great causes, protest against mandatory drug testing, and produced *Pissing Away The American Dream* (Digit Press, $8.95), an eye-opening look at the assault that drug testing represents on the first, fourth and fifth amendment constitutional guarantees. Simply put, the government's "war on drugs" hysteria is a thinly disguised campaign to invade private homes, steal property and assert control over ordinary citizens. The relationship between the war on drugs and the police state is as obvious as that of Dan Quayle's recent efforts to de-regulate the FDA and his financial interests in the Eli Lilly company. In that sense, *Pissing Away The American Dream* serves mostly to fill in the details about a government program whose broad strokes are already keenly felt.

Ross comes to the battle not as a celebrant of smoke but as a pipeline controller suddenly hit with a Department of Transportation decree mandating random drug tests. His efforts here will no doubt lead him to discover just how random the tests are. Ross details not only his appeals to the likes of the Secretary of Transportation and Georgian senator Sam Nunn, but to the ACLU, which doesn't make legal appeals because it fails to understand that the mandatory tests originate with the government, not private employers. Ross has certainly identified the depth of confusion and indifference over this plain violation of the Constitution.

There is much here for the conspiracy minded as well. Lewis Lapham contributes a reminder of George Bush's frame-up of a petty pusher in Lafayette Park "to make the rhetorical point about the dark and terrible sea of drugs washing up on the sun-dappled lawns of the White House." Oliver Steinberg notes that Lyndon LaRouche revived drug-baiting with a magazine, *War On Drugs,* a year before Reagan took office, virtually setting the tone for the administration's entire anti-drug propaganda style thereafter. (For his part in the 1992 presidential campaign, LaRouche has been underscoring the link between George Bush and the H. Smith Richardson Foundation, which financed MKULTRA, the CIA acid experiments of the 1950s.) Ross' view on paranoia is well put: "if they don't trust me, I certainly don't trust them." For updates on drug testing, Ross offers a newsletter, *Urine Nation News,* for $ 1 an issue from POB 920066, Norcross,

GA 30092. Digit Press also offers a THC neutralizer and powdered urine to help beat the tests.

William S. Burroughs makes the point again in the forward to *The Drug Abuser Documents 1840-1960* (Blast Books, $10.95) one of the thankfully perennial anthologies of great writings inspired by drug experiences: "It is disquieting to speculate what may lurk behind this colossal red herring of the War Against Drugs–a war neither likely to, nor designed to succeed. One thing is obvious: old, clean money and new, dirty money are shaking hands under the table." The collection also includes selections from Albert Hofmann, Freud, Antonin Artaud, Aldous Huxley, R. Gordon Wasson and Fitz Hugh Ludlow. No Leary, though.

Three other important books have surfaced on the Beat writers: *Hank* by Neeli Cherkovski (Random House, $21.95), a biography of Charles Bukowski in many ways as entertaining as Ted Morgan's take on the life of Burroughs, although less distanced since Cherkovski is a longtime acquaintance of Bukowski's (released by Black Sparrow virtually in tandem: *Hot Water Music,* a new collection of Bukowskian observations); *What's This* Cat's *Story?* (Paragon House, $21.95), a collection of essays by the late Seymour Krim, who coined the term "radical chic" and thereby set the current agenda of most urban weeklies, and who also spells out great insights into Kerouac and the Beats and *The Bohemian Register* (The Scarecrow Press, $32.50), a brave attempt to annotate over two hundred writers and seven hundred titles of Beat literature. After all that research, it's a small wonder that author Morgen Hickey is a Ph. D. candidate in clinical psychology at the University of Missouri-Columbia. Finally, other book news of note includes Jonathan Vankin's *Conspiracy, Cover-Ups and Crimes* due in paperback some time this year from Dell. The author calls it "somewhat updated." Vankin also will be interviewed in the next issue of *Mondo 2000.*

Saucer Section:
Whose Saucers Are They?
by Jim Keith

There is no question in my mind that there is a "conspiracy" at the top running things, or at least attempting to run them. As to the nature of the conspiracy; that is another question. I had always assumed that it was big money rubbing shoulders and making secret deals in cabals like the Bilderbergers, the Council of Foreign Relations and the Trilateral Commission, but lately I haven't been so sure. I've begun to take seriously the thought that there really might be a secret centuries-old agenda among the Illuminati not mention the Templars, the Freemasons, the Rosicrucians, the Knights of Malta or the Priory of Sion. No, I haven't completely bought into the Lear-Cooper-Hamilton-English-Lazar-et. al. scenario, that the "boys" behind this age-old conspiracy really run things from outer space, or even the inner earth, but I'm no longer dismissing it out of hand, either.

George Bush knew the connotations of the term "New World Order" when he used it. As a 33rd degree Mason and a member of Skull and Bones and the CIA and God knows what other groups of kameraden, how could he not? He would also be aware that using that phrase would be calculated to set every right-wing conspiratologist in the country spinning. The question was: what is he getting at? Was it a phrase used as a code to alert other members of the Masons or other in-group of something, of some culmination or mobilization or battle plan? Right about the same time that Bush uttered that phrase, I noticed that CBS started using an abstract geometrical station ID that metamorphosizes from an Eye in a Triangle and, perhaps, with the turning of the pyramidal forms, coalesces into an inverted five pointed star. I also notice that now they have replaced it with an immobile version that does not call up the same connotations. Perhaps a coincidence, but I'm certain that the bigwigs at CBS were quite aware of those symbolisms, too.

Jerry Smith made the statement to me, "the United States is a Masonic conspiracy," and that seems like a succinct statement of something that is pretty obvious, yet admitted by few. Many of the founders of the United States were Masons and occultists, and the dollar bill looks like one of those hodgepodge Masonic aprons that you see George Washington depicted wearing in Masonic literature; it is crawling with Masonic symbols, slogans and numerology.

Tim O'Neill's "Who Rules Over The Earth?" in *Apocalypse Culture* goes into the existence of a single archetypical world ruler, linking that personage to the symbolism of the Great Seal and the Great Invisible Government and says that, "...the political doctrines of Illuminism, the blueprints for the government of the Ruler, tend toward Universalism, Theocratism, Republicanism, in the original Platonic sense. The 'New Secular Order' of the Seal is a pure, theocratic republic. Direct rule by the Monarch implies no necessity for church, state, or even family structure."

When you think about various other fairly recent innovations like the UPC code and Electronic Fund Transfer, the United States of Europe and the laser tatooing handscan tested on 3000 recruits at Fort Benjamin, it's not hard to start thinking in paranoid lines.

Now, here's where a clear cut connection to UFOlogy emerges. Many, if not most, students of the phenomenon of UFOs have long suspected that there might be a terrestrial origin to the saucers. Conspiratologist John Judge, in his tape, "Unidentified Fascist Observatories," makes a strong case for the saucers being a hidden and higher echelon of government research project, utilizing the secrets of disk craft that we inherited from the Nazis at the end of World War II. The time-line certainly fits.

Another possibility is that saucers are a "suppressed technology," reminiscent of the stories one hears about engines that run on water, light bulbs that last forever. Tesla's secret plans, etc., being bought off or shot off by agents of the government or big business to protect the investment and profits in internal combustion engines and an oil-based world economy. I wouldn't doubt it. There is no doubt in my mind that at the more rarefied strata of control and the more concentrated levels of dough that the welfare of everyman is strictly a tertiary consideration. "Evidence" to support this is, of course, is nearly impossible to locate (or live through the attempt) and yet...

Futurists, like Robert Anton Wilson and Alvin Toffler, point out that there has been a geometrical progression of the doubling of the knowledge of Mankind in shorter and shorter periods of time. Currently by projections, we should be doubling the total knowledge of the human race every nine years or so...So where is the technology that should be coming out of this? Look around, nothing much has changed in oil based technology (airplanes, automobiles, etc.) since the late fifties, early sixties. Or, as Claude Steiner put it: "The future sure ain't what it used to be."

Jacques Vallee, in *Messengers of Deception,* suggests that he does not believe that abductees have actually been taken aboard technological craft. He says, "It is more likely that they have taken a non-physical trip, controlled and guided by a system that acts on human consciousness (the Soviets use the term 'psychotronic' to designate such devices), rather than one that is purely physical. The symbols it uses are engineered to have certain effects."

Granting that it is possible that there is a level of technology, or at least technological experimentation, that our government isn't telling us about—and perhaps doesn't know about—it would seem likely that the control of this hypothetical technology would reside at the top, where the money is.

While I don't really expect to see the Beast 666 tromping like Godzilla down Madison Avenue (maybe I should, or maybe the people of Iraq just did), there is a gradual evolution to "One World" themes going on and a worldwide technological control and meshing that is very sinister...even divorced from any occult or 'otherworldly' significance, and even if it isn't ordained from On High by a World Monarch.

Jacques Vallee also says, "I believe there is a very real UFO problem. I have also come to believe that it is being manipulated for political ends. And the data suggest that the manipulators may be human beings with a plan of social control."

John Keel has reported that during the flurry of UFO reports in West Virginia in 1967 there were also reports of unidentified trucks and vans moving around on back roads. If there was 'psychotronic' tomfoolery going on, then this might have been the way that it would have been done. Considering the rampant excesses of the CIA, tossing LSD and disinformation at everything that moved during the MKULTRA phase, it is not in the least difficult to believe that they would have been capable of this kind of populace manipulation.

Who knows? Maybe the U.S. is, at the top, a Masonic or other occult conspiracy after all, and maybe Bush has fired the starting gun for its next evolutionary transformation with his talk of the New World Order. Whatever the case, the logic is inescapable. If the saucers, even some of them, do have a terrestrial origin, then there is a good chance that they are owned by the group that some have called the Illuminati.

Supermarket Tabloids and UFOs
by X. Sharks DeSpot

The supermarket tabloids comprise a strange part of the American popular culture and ideology. They sell many millions yet are universally decried as lies. They have an army of readers but are treated always with contempt. They are not kept by libraries and not indexed by the *Reader's Guide To Periodical Literature*. These tabloids, however, reflect the view of the majority and are about as "sensationalistic" as the *New York Times*. To prove this, examine as an example a tabloid favorite: Unidentified Flying Objects. First, an Unidentified Flying Object is just that: an object sighted in the sky which has not been identified. Problems arise when UFOs are thought of as "flying saucers." A flying saucer, obviously, is a space ship from another world. From the outset, this prejudice makes the situation regarding UFO reports tricky.

A medical student reports seeing an unidentified flying object and the Air Force left it "unsolved" in its study. The authors of a "debunking" book solemnly say the witness was under stress and probably hallucinated the UFO. If the same student had reported a World War 2 fighter plane had swept down and buzzed his car on the same road, how would the report have been received? First, it would have been handed over to the Federal Aeronautics Board, who would have dispatched an investigator to nearby airfields in search of an antique airplane that flew too low. The pilot would have been fined and his license revoked. If, after having failed to find a World War 2 fighter plane, the worst that might have happened is that the witness would be accused of lying, or at best, having panicked and misidentified a modern piper cub aircraft.

The medical student was attacked because he saw the "wrong" thing. If he had seen an airplane, even an improbable one, no one would have given it a second thought. If one day you look up and see an object shooting through the sky that you cannot identify, consider the wide variety of possibilities. It could be an airplane seen from the wrong angle. It could be a hoax. It could be an angel from God. It could even be a living creature of some sort, floating around in the atmosphere. But all these interesting ideas are not usually even considered. Unfortunately, in the popular mind, there exist only three points of view. These points of view include: 1. There are no such things as UFOs; 2. There may be UFOs; 3. There are UFOs. What people actually mean, however, is: 1. There are no alien beings in space ships; 2. There may be alien beings in space ships; 3. The aliens are here, now, spying on us from the sky above.

The first point of view, of course, is almost an official one. It is generally accepted that anyone who believes this has no business working for the Air Force or have any other responsible position. This is the sincere belief of the people who run the country on a daily basis. Newspaper editors obviously believe this. They accept the view of the U.S. Air Force, which concluded in 1949 that it's all nonsense and has since produced such boring studies as Projects Blue Book and the Condon Report to protect the "official" point of view.

For some supermarket tabloids, however, this point of view does not exist. Sure the cool-headed editors and clever businessmen who print trash about UFOs "know better." But how often does anyone want to read about that? It doesn't sell magazines to report that "we are alone." Does the Committee For The Scientific Investigation of the Paranormal ever say anything sexy? Of course not. Dull men who say they represent "science" already proved their point back in 1947. That date, 1947, is significant. In 1947, when the era of UFOs began, the *Reader's Guide* listed "flying saucers" under "hallucinations" in its pages. The common point of view was restricted really to just that. The scientific community has never really moved beyond that. The issue never became "there may be UFOs, what's out there?" but "don't go feeding the public's head with a lot of nonsense." Although two groups emerged that held the other points of view: people curious in the subject; and those like George Adamski who held regular conversations with people from Venus, the "hallucination" definition. Contrary to popular belief, it reflects the view of the *National Enquirer* and of every single newspaper and news magazine in the country right now.

If someone sees a glowing object in the night sky, he can usually report it to a sympathetic editor who will take him seriously and send a reporter to check out the story. An exciting UFO story! Just the thing to fill up pages between the shoe and car ads! Of course, part of the game is to refuse to do any background research, regard it as a "silly season" item, and yield to the "official" point of view that there is nothing there.

Supermarket tabloids, however, come in two varieties. One is the group of nearly identical tabloids that focus on celebrities like Cher, Elizabeth Taylor and the Kennedy clan. *The National Enquirer*, *Star*, *News Extra*, *Globe*, and *National Examiner* appear in the wire racks near the cash register each week and often sell out completely. The second group focuses on obviously false stories about people with eyes in the back of their heads, or babies born with tattoos of the solar system on their backs. These include the black-and-white *Weekly World News* and the color-covered *Sun* tabloid. The difference between these and the other five is obvious. None of the articles deal with living celebrities, aside from a centerfold of trivia. Men in South Africa using barbed-wire hula hoops, for example. Or man undergoes sex operation to get a higher pension check in Ghana. Or a child is born with a pacemaker already installed in its chest somewhere in England.

It would seem that this is where the point of view that aliens have landed has found a home. One would think that here, at least, someone would interview people who have met "them," present photographs of evidence, express some interesting opinions. But here, alas, things are strange.

The front page of the *Weekly World News* for August 6, 1991 reads: "Horse Born With Human Face!" It's a dull article about some scientists in Amsterdam having done gene splicing to create a human faced horse. Aside from the headline, the story might as well be about a new form of corn starch or a diabetes treatment.

Now, allegedly beneath Dulce, New Mexico a massive underground base exists run jointly by the U.S. government and alien beings. Here, nightmarish experiments have created half-man, half-lizard crea-tures begging for help, or apparently many people believe this. According to author John Keel, a community of about 2000 UFO buffs fully believe that the U.S. government has such a base. That is a major portion of the *Sun* and *Weekly World News* audience. To people who have never heard of this underground base, it's just a silly, fake story. For those who believe in the base and its monstrous creations, an article in the supermarket tabloids provides more evidence.

The writers write articles meant to appeal to both audiences. The "Horse Born With Human face" article will please both, as will the August 6, 1991 *Sun* article, "First Photo Ever of America's Captured UFO." To quote it: "Arrangement was made to trade the UFO for alien rights to land in certain locations of Earth." In it, General Norman Schwarzkopf is glorified between hints of the nightmare. It also provides more evidence to believers that aliens are landing near Dulce, New Mexico.

The editors of the *Sun* and the *Weekly World News* specifically ask that its articles about UFOs be written this way. They have two audiences to please: one amused by "fake" stories that nevertheless re-affirm ideas like General Schwarzkopf being an admirable figure, and another to have their worst fears confirmed by the "true" stories. Those tabloids which should break out of the mold set in 1947, of focussing on the question of Unidentified Flying Objects as alien space ships, instead perpetuate the "official" point of view by exploiting the other two for the sake of making money. Serious discussion about the issue, of course, is subsumed in the general lack of credibility. It is time for that to change.

3

Steamshovel Press #6, Winter 1992

An Interview with Deborah Davis
author of *Katharine the Great, Katharine Graham* and *Her Washington Post Empire*

Q: Tim Leary suggested that your book was originally censored and pulped because of references to Mary Pinchot Meyer. Do you feel that way and can you tell us a little bit about Mary Meyer?

A: Mary Pinchot Meyer was the sister of Ben Bradlee's second wife, Tony Pinchot. She was a very beautiful, talented artist who was living in Washington in the early 60s and she was the lover, I would say the principal lover, of John Kennedy, who was President of the United States. He was supposedly very much in love with her and wanted to divorce Jackie and marry her.

The Timothy Leary connection is interesting because at that time in the early sixties there was a group of society-type women in Washington who thought that if they could get men in power involved in mind-altering drugs they could see the world in a different way and this would end the Cold War and end all warfare. It was a very ambitious plan and a lot of them got their marijuana and LSD from Timothy Leary, who at that time was a professor of psychology at Harvard and had access to these drugs. At that time they were very experimental and they were going around in a lot of the elite circles. It didn't have the same connotation that it has today of the hard stuff, of the cocaine and the heroin. This was all very beautiful and mind-expanding type stuff. So she was involved with Kennedy and they used to supposedly smoke marijuana together in Kennedy's bedroom and I think Leary said that she also gave him LSD, although I couldn't swear to that.

Anyway, she got murdered. She was murdered a year after Kennedy died. Kennedy was killed in November '63 and Mary Meyer was killed in 1964. She was walking her dog in Georgetown through a wooded area and she was stabbed to death. And they never found the killer. Some young black man was put in jail for ten months, held over until his trial and then he was acquitted because there was no evidence. And they've never found the killer but people who have investigated the case say that it had all the earmarks of a professional assassination.

Q: She was, of course, married to Cord Meyer, who was an intelligence agent.

A: She had been. She was divorced from him at the time she was with Kennedy. She had been with Cord Meyer in Europe when they were living. He was involved in a lot of counter-espionage over in Europe and she was supposedly a security risk because she tended to fall in love and have affairs with handsome men. She had an affair with one Italian count who was supposedly an intelligence agent and this constituted a security risk. And I suppose that their divorce was partly caused by the gulf between them because he really just couldn't talk about his work. Anyway, she was a very talented painter and very charming and beautiful and Kennedy was in love with her.

Q: Let's talk a bit about what exactly happened to your book. The first edition came out in the late 70s, right?

A: 1979. November '79.

What happened was all part of one great big, giant society that these people in Washington have created for themselves where the most important thing to them is putting forward this myth about themselves that they are supremely moral, supremely powerful, all-knowing, all-caring. They'll take care of the rest of us and anything that they do that is questionable they try to cover it up. You might ask why they're so afraid of having these things found about them because after all nothing that anyone knows about them is going to take away their money, their power, their friends, their influence or anything else. It's a sense that they want to maintain this myth about themselves, because that's the only way that people will buy into everything else that they do. You know, the newspaper that they put out, the whole aura that they create, that they are the ones who are in charge—not only *in charge* of things, but *should be* in charge, and it's because they're morally and intellectually superior to the rest of us.

Q: The book was pulped before it was distributed?

A: No, it was distributed and they recalled it from the bookstores and shredded the entire print run of twenty five thousand copies. A few copies that had been sold out of the bookstores and had gotten into private hands in the six week period before it was recalled, those books are still around and they are very valuable. The last I heard they were going for sixty dollars in used bookstores.

But the book came out in November '79 and right away there was an orchestrated attack on it by the people that have reason to try to make common cause with the *Post*. The *Post* itself didn't attack me. They didn't need to. They had people do it for them. David Ignatius, who is now the foreign editor of the *Washington Post,* was a young, ambitious reporter at the *Wall Street Journal* at that time. He did a very, very nasty, damaging piece about my book.

If any of your audience have read the new paperback edition of *Silent Coup,* it describes the same process going on for that book. In the back there's an appendix that talks about the campaign against that book. And they're so much alike, so much the same what happened to me. Because they start this thing about "errors" in the book. This is like the worst thing you can say about a book, right?

Q: Right.

A: "Errors" in the book. And then the authors: who are they? How do they know these things? They're outsiders. They weren't there the way we were. They're just speculating. *Silent Coup* is about a 400 page book. They named four errors. One of them is that it got somebody's name wrong. Of course, the people doing the accusing are lying, so they're not really errors to begin with. This is the same thing that happened with me. Errors in the book. Errors in the book. This was like a flag that was being waved. David Ignatius did it in the *Wall Street Journal* piece and then Alexander Cockburn did it in the *Village Voice.* So they were attacking me from the left and the right, right?

Q: You were right in the middle.

A: It was a non-partisan attack on me because the attack came from two people that were in different places in the political spectrum. This was supposed to be an objective evaluation now.

Q: So we can assume that the authors of *Silent Coup* were on to something then, if the powers that be want to do away with the book. Am I mistaken in calling *Silent Coup* a pro-Nixon book? Isn't the issue here, what they're afraid of, is the story of Nixon's real fall from power as opposed to the way it was played in the media?

A: I don't think that characterizing it as a pro-Nixon book is very useful. It's like the rationale Alexander Cockburn used for attacking the movie *JFK* because it's trying to bring back Camelot. I mean, that is sort of irrelevant. There is some merit to wanting to know the truth without having to say that it's furthering another agenda.

Q: Right. That's why I'm saying that isn't the real story, the thing that some people are afraid to get out, is the real reason that Nixon was run out of office, from whatever perspective?

A: Different people have different motives. The motive of the *Washington Post* in attacking *Silent Coup* was to protect the reputation of Bob Woodward because his reputation is what has earned the *Post,* and Woodward, and a number of people associated with him, many millions of dollars since then in book and movies and inflated salaries. I don't think the *Post* cares why Nixon was brought down. I don't think that *that's* what their interest is. Their interest is in closing ranks around Woodward and saying you can't question our golden boy because if you do the greatness of the *Washington Post* is all a lie.

Q: Let's question the golden boy a bit. Can you tell us what you know about Woodward?

A: Bob Woodward has consistently lied about his background ever since the first time anybody started asking who this person is. He came from Wheaton, Illinois. His father was a judge. He joined the Navy and became a communications officer, which is not Naval Intelligence *per se.* Naval intelligence is a separate organization. Communications officers are at the very highest level of receiving coded and top secret information from around the world and they get it before anybody else does. It's up to them to relay this information to the people in power.

In Woodward's case, first he was in the Navy serving somewhere in California for four years. At the end of his term he was in California, before that he was on a ship I believe. He's never said what he was doing in California. He just won't talk about it. But you remember that this was the time of the height of the anti-war movement and there was a domestic counter-intelligence operation going on called Operation Chaos, which was coordinating Army, Navy and FBI and CIA intelligence on the anti-war movement, spying on leaders and so on, trying to find foreign influence. And I believe that this is what Woodward was involved in at that time.

So after his four years were up he was eligible to leave the Navy, having completed his service. Instead he re-enlisted for another year and he came to Washington and he started working in a top secret Naval unit inside the Pentagon. Actually, they went between the Pentagon and the White House. This was during the first years of Nixon's presidency. And I believe that at this time he started working directly with Richard Ober, who was the deputy chief of counter-intelligence under James Angleton. He was the one who was running Operation Chaos and I believe that he was the one who was Deep Throat. I disagree with those people in *Silent Coup,* although it hardly matters who exactly it was because I know Woodward had many sources.

But the point is that at this time he was getting top secret information. He was briefing the Joint Chiefs of Staff, he was briefing the National Security Council and he was briefing Alexander Haig, who was Nixon's chief of staff. He was right in the very, very center of the Nixon White House in terms of the information that was being conveyed and the people he knew. After that, he decided for some mysterious reason that he wanted to be a reporter and he went to the *Post* and the *Post* has thousands of applications a year of experienced reporters, most of whom never get in. But instead they took this guy who couldn't write, who had never been a reporter in his life and they said, "You have to learn how to write better so go to work on the suburban paper for a year and then we'll hire you."

Now I don't know if they decided that he was somebody they wanted to cultivate or whether somebody had the word on him ahead of time or what. But after a year he came to the *Post* and right away Ben Bradlee, the executive editor, started giving him the choice assignments. They felt a common bond between each other because Bradlee had a very similar background in the Navy himself.

Carl Bernstein was coming from a whole different place. He was a very messed up person, you know, had a lot of trouble keeping his job at the *Post.* He would always fall asleep on the job, stay up all night and miss deadlines and he was just a mess. If it weren't for the newspaper guild rules about not firing reporters, he would have been fired a long time ago. But he had a sense about politics. He still does. He had a very good sense about politics and he hated Nixon because during the McCarthy era, when Nixon was a congressman, his family, his father and mother, who were very left-wing, had experienced a lot of persecution during the McCarthy era. So he associated Nixon with this. And he had his own reasons for wanting to do a story that he thought might lead to exposing Nixon and bringing down Nixon.

It's a very strange friendship. There was a lot of tension between Woodward and Bernstein and there's a very strong bond between them because each of them owes the other one the fact that they are now

millionaires and can get book contracts for any amount of money they want.

Q: Let's get back to Ben Bradlee. I know part of what's in the book and part of what upset those forces that caused the withdrawal of its first publication is what you've said about Ben Bradlee and his connection to the Ethyl and Julius Rosenberg trial. Would you talk about that a bit?

A: In the first edition, the one that was recalled and shredded, I looked in State Department lists for '52 and '53 when Bradlee was serving as a press attache supposedly in the American embassy in Paris. This was during the Marshall Plan when the United States over in Europe had hundreds of thousands of people making an intensive effort to keep Western Europe from going Communist. Bradlee wanted to be part of that effort. So he was over in the American embassy in Paris and the embassy list had these letters after his name that said USIE. And I asked the State Department what that meant and it said United States Information Exchange. It was the forerunner of the USIA, the United States Information Agency. It was the propaganda arm of the embassy. They produced propaganda that was then disseminated by the CIA all over Europe. They planted newspaper stories. They had a lot of reporters on their payrolls. They routinely would produce stories out of the embassy and give them to these reporters and they would appear in the papers in Europe.

It's very important to understand how influential newspaper stories are to people because this is what people think of as their essential source of facts about what is going on. They don't question it, and even if they do question it they have nowhere else to go to find out anything else. So Bradlee was involved in producing this propaganda. But at that point in the story I didn't know exactly what he was doing.

I published the first book just saying that he worked for USIE and that this agency produced propaganda for the CIA. He went totally crazy after the book came out. One person who knew him told me then that he was going all up and down the East Coast having lunch with every editor he could think of saying that it was not true, he did not produce any propaganda. And he attacked me viciously and he said that I had falsely accused him of being a CIA agent. And the reaction was totally out of proportion to what I had said.

Q: You make a good point in the book that other people who have had similar kinds of—I don't even know if you want to call them accusations—but reports that they in some way cooperated with the CIA in the '50s, that the times were different and people were expected to do that kind

of thing out of a sense of patriotism and they blow it off.

A: That's right. People say, yeah, this is what I did back then, you know. But Bradlee doesn't want to be defined that way because, I don't know, somehow he thinks it's just too revealing of him, of who he is. He doesn't want to admit a true fact about his past because somehow he doesn't want it known that this is where he came from. Because this is the beginning of his journalistic career. This is how he made it big.

Subsequent to my book being shredded in 1979, early 1980, I got some documents through the Freedom of Information Act and they revealed that Bradlee had been the person who was running an entire propaganda operation against Julius and Ethyl Rosenberg that covered forty countries on four continents. He always claimed that he had been a low level press flack in the embassy in Paris, just a press flack, nothing more. Julius and Ethyl Rosenberg had already been convicted of being atomic spies and they were on death row waiting to be executed. And the purpose of Bradlee's propaganda operation was to convince the Europeans that they really were spies, they really had given the secret of the atomic bomb to the Russians and therefore they did deserve to be put to death.

The Europeans, having just a very few years before defeated Hitler, were very concerned that the United States was going fascist the way their countries had. And this was a very real fear to the Europeans. They saw the same thing happening in the United States that had happened in their own countries. And so Bradlee used the Rosenberg case to say, "No this isn't what you think it is. These people really did this bad thing and they really do deserve to die. It doesn't mean that the United States is becoming fascist." So he had a very key role in creating European public opinion and it was very, very important. This was the key issue that was going to determine how the Europeans felt about the United States.

Some of the documents that I had showed him writing letters to the prosecutors of the Rosenbergs saying "I'm working for the head of the CIA in Paris and he wants me to come and look at your files." And this kind of thing. So in the second edition, which came out in 1987, I reprinted those documents, the actual documents, the readers can see them and it's got his signature and it's very, very interesting. He subsequently has said nothing about it at all. He won't talk about it all. He won't answer any questions about it.

So I guess the point about Bradlee is that he went from this job to being European bureau chief for *Newsweek* magazine and to the executive editorship of the *Post*. So this is how he got where he is. It's a very clear line of succession. Philip Graham was Katharine Graham's husband, who ran the *Post* in the '50s and he committed suicide in 1963. That's when Katharine Graham took over. Bradlee was close friends with Allen Dulles and Phil Graham. The paper wasn't doing very well for a while and he was looking for a way to pay foreign correspondents and Allen Dulles was looking for a cover. Allen Dulles was head of the CIA back then and he was looking for a cover for some of his operatives so that they could get in and out of places without arousing suspicion. So the two of them hit on a plan: Allen Dulles would pay for the reporters and they would give the CIA the information that they found as well as give it to the *Post*. So he helped to develop this operation and it subsequently spread to other newspapers and magazines. And it was called Operation Mockingbird. This operation, I believe, was revealed for the first time in my book.

Q: To get back to Phil Graham for a minute. There are two things that I'd like to bring up about him: first, he supported Alger Hiss, first, right? And he flip-flopped on that issue? But he was at loggerheads with Nixon on that and that was the beginning of this kind of life-long enmity between Nixon and the *Post*?

A: Yes, he supported Alger Hiss largely because he had been a Supreme Court law clerk for Justice Felix Frankfurter. Frankfurter felt very strongly that Hiss was innocent. Hiss was accused of spying also. But Phil was interested in being a with-it kind of guy, very modern, up to the minute, involved in the thinking of his times. So the thinking of his times was the Cold War and was anti-Soviet and get all the domestic spies. He eventually gave in to this way of thinking, with the majority of his friends and associates thinking if Hiss wasn't a spy himself he should at least be made an example of because there were spies among us.

So he was instrumental in that, but before he did turn around on Hiss, I believe he accused Nixon of excesses in trying to prosecute Hiss. Hiss was one of the cases that Nixon made his reputation on as an anti-Communist and as an important national political figure. He was the one who was running around screaming about Hiss, so Phil Graham criticized Nixon for this.

Nixon takes things like that very personally and he never forgot it. So when he became president a number of years later, Phil Graham was dead, Katharine was the head of the *Washington Post* and she made her usual overtures to the incumbent president. You know, "Come over, get to know my editors, tell them how you want your stories covered."

And Nixon, instead of accepting it, he rejected it because he was still angry about what happened fifteen years ago. So he rejected her overtures and then for her own reasons, I guess she had nothing to lose, went after him.

You see, everybody that was involved in that Watergate investigation was doing it from their own perspective. Woodward was doing it from the Naval Intelligence perspective, Bernstein was doing it from the perspective of being a reporter who finally wanted to do a story that would get him out of his suburban courtroom beat. Katharine Graham wanted to keep Ben Bradlee happy and Bradlee had his own sources of information about, you know, Nixon is going to be brought down and you're going to be the one to do it. And she didn't care because she hated Nixon by that time.

If she had had a close friendship with Nixon, if Nixon hadn't rejected her friendship, she would have protected him the way that she had protected Reagan. Because none of those Reagan scandals ever got pursued by the *Post* the way the Nixon scandals did. In fact, one of the first things that the Reagan people did when Reagan got into office was to make friends with Katharine Graham and that was precisely for that reason. They decided that Nancy should be best friends with Katharine Graham and they did it. They got her over there, they met her, they had her invited over to the White House, they just did all these things. And nothing bad about Reagan ever got in the *Post* unless it was somewhere else first They just had to do it to show that they were still a legitimate newspaper. But they never broke any stories on Reagan that were damaging and he sailed through eight years looking as good as she could keep him looking.

Q: Before we get too far from Phil Graham, I'd like to talk a little bit more about his suicide. Getting back to the article that Leary wrote, he seemed to suggest that there was a reason to believe that it could have been something other than suicide. The "suicide" happened shortly after this public event where Graham was talking about the JFK/Mary Meyer liaison. Can you talk a little bit more about that?

A: Phil died in 1963 and it's now 1992. There's still continuing speculation, 29 years later, that he was murdered. In my book, I wrote it as a suicide because that's the way it's been represented and I didn't have any independent knowledge of anything else. If I were doing it today, or if I ever do another edition, I will probably expand on that and spend some time investigating it and finding out whether there is any evidence that it was murder.

There were a couple of reasons why it could have been murder. One is the one you mentioned. The people that were protecting Kennedy might have done it because of he was a manic depressive. He was in and out of institutions and he was very mentally unstable. A lot of that probably had to do with the fact that he married into a wealthy family. He married the boss's daughter and they gave him the newspaper, but they were watching every move he made. So he did not react well to the fact that Katharine Graham's father had owned the *Washington Post*. He may have been killed for that reason, if he was killed.

He may have been killed because he had a mistress named Robin Webb. By that time he had moved out of Katharine's house and he was living with Robin Webb in another house and he was actually behaving as if they were married. He had dinner parties over there with her and invited various members of the Washington elite over there for dinner parties and making it very clear that this was the woman he preferred to Katharine. And at the same time, he was re-writing his will. He re-wrote his will three times. Edward Bennett Williams was his attorney. Edward Bennett Williams was very well-known as a Washington power broker. He recently died, but he was very much involved in this. Each time, he willingly, at Phil's request, wrote a will that gave Katharine less and less of a share of the *Washington Post* and gave more and more of it to Robin Webb. By the third rewrite she had nothing and Robin Webb had everything. And this was at a time when Katharine had pretty much given up on the marriage and realized that in order to save the newspaper, which she thought of as her family newspaper—her father built that newspaper and she didn't want to let it go to some mistress of her husband's—and she had come to the conclusion that she either had to divorce him and win the paper in a divorce settlement, or she had to have him declared mentally incompetent. Each of these alternatives was very unattractive to her. And so there's some speculation that either she arranged for him to be killed or somebody said to her, "don't worry, we'll take care of it" and there's some speculation that it might have even been Edward Bennett Williams.

She took him out of the sanitarium one weekend and took him out to their farm in Virginia and this was where he blew his brains out with a shotgun. And the police report was never really made public. After my paperback edition was published this fall, I got a call from some woman who claims that she knew for a fact that it was murder. And if I ever do publish another edition, I intend to look into that.

This is the kind of talk that people live with in Washington, DC.

Q: Tim Leary's speculation seemed to be that if

it was a murder it was connected with this public statement that Phil Graham made, apparently at a convention of journalists in Phoenix, Arizona. Considering the flap that one hears about JFK's liaisons with Marilyn Monroe and Judith Exner, Mary Pinchot Meyer's name is not brought up a lot. You indicate in the book that she had a diary and that it may still exist, that James Angleton took it. May we explore that a little bit more?

A: Mary Pinchot Meyer, after she divorced Cord Meyer, moved to Washington and she was living in Ben Bradlee's garage, which had been made into an art studio and this is where she was living. And when she was killed on this tow path, James Angleton showed up at the garage at the studio. There's two versions of the story that I've heard. One is that he searched for the diary and found it and took it away, and the other is that Ben Bradlee handed it to him and he took it away. Supposedly he burned it, but people that knew Angleton say he never burned anything, he saved everything. So supposedly it still exists. Angleton is dead now, so if anybody has it it's probably his widow.

Q: There's no Freedom of Information way of accessing it I guess.

A: Not unless it's in official government files. It's a sketchbook. Bradlee talked about this in an interview with David Frost a couple of months ago and he said that it was just a sketch book and he's seen it and it only has sketches in it and a few pages of writing, but it wasn't a diary *per se*. Now I trust Bradlee about as far as I can throw him.

Q: NBC did a series on the JFK assassination this week and the last thing they did was roll a list of people who had been killed that were somehow connected to the JFK assassination and there Mary Meyer's name rolled by.

A: She was alive for another year. I don't know what went on in that year. Maybe she was trying to expose something. That's something that also worth looking into. There's a man right now doing a book on Mary Meyer which should be very interesting. His name is Leo Damore and I'm very much looking forward to reading that book. I'm sure it's going to have a lot of new information in it. It's not out yet but it will be soon.

Q: Let's turn the conversation back to this term that you coined in the book, *mediapolitics*, or the political uses of information. Is there a way that any average person who picks up the paper to read it and judge it against what is just a regurgitation of a government report or press release and what is actually true?

A: The way to read the *Washington Post,* and I

suppose this applies to any newspaper in any city that you live in, is to read certain reporters of certain beats. They develop certain contacts with certain politicians, and if you know that and if you know who they're talking to every day and you can just sort of know by whose by-line is on the story where their information is coming from. So you don't read it as this reporter's story, you read it as the politician using this writer to say something. In the case of the *Post,* even Katharine Graham has described it this way, that the *Post* is the internal memo system of the U.S. government. I mean, politicians try to get things in the *Post* to talk to each other. To say, "I have something on you, if you don't play something my way I'm going to leak more of this. This is just a taste of what I know about you." This kind of thing. So that goes on all the time and you have to kind of spend some time studying who your reporters are and who their sources are.

I look at the *Washington Post* and I see a Bob Woodward piece in there and I say, "Oh, OK," like when he did the series on Dan Quayle. A seven part series on this complete non-entity, all about what a decent human being he is and even though he doesn't have brains, his wife does. It took up more column inches probably than any story they've done since Watergate, and it was Bob Woodward doing it. I thought, "OK, now either he has gotten the word to push Dan Quayle or he's gotten the word that Dan Quayle is going to be it and he wants to get on the band wagon and look like he's in on the big thing." That's the only two ways you can read it with Bob Woodward. And depending on what you know about the reporter, you can understand that.

Now some people are very independent and really probe all with their sources. They'll ask hard questions and not just be a cipher for letting the politician say whatever he wants through them. But these people tend to lose their access and the sources tend to get mad at them and not talk to them anymore and start giving the good stuff to reporters who will tell it their way. They know that the reporters have a job and they've got to fill a certain number of inches everyday or they're in trouble. You just don't have time to go running around digging. That's why I personally never really wanted to be a reporter because I like to spend my time developing stories for as long as it takes. So it's just a way of looking at the newspaper where it's not facts but it's people fighting to get their points of view out to you through using the reporter as a vehicle.

And if you're interested, if you're really interested in the story, you make phone calls and ask your own questions. The publications that really want to be in the big time are the ones that are most suspect because they are the ones that are most vulnerable to blackmail or withdrawal of prestige or that kind of thing, like the *Post* and the *Times*. They are also the ones that are in a very strong position to go against the grain if they really want to because they are financially independent and don't need to be worried that they're going to lose their advertisers or lose readers if they do something courageous once in a while.

It's ironic because it's the very function of being so inside, and playing the game so well and getting so much money and so much power that they can occasionally turn against the establishment and really do something courageous if they only want to. But they don't want to do it too often because they don't want to make a habit of it and they don't want to get a reputation of being like that. After the Watergate stories, the first number of speeches Katharine Graham made were all about getting back to business. She didn't want the reporters to think that they were always going to be against the government, that they were always going to exposing politicians. That was her first concern. She didn't want to be like that ever again. That was it. That was an aberration. She wanted her reporters to understand that. And to underline this, she withheld a contract for three years, a Newspaper Guild contract. She made them work without a contract, no raises, made them very vulnerable to being fired or being moved to night assignments or out of town if they didn't do what she wanted in the way of just cooling it in terms of antagonism to the powers that be.

Q: Had your book been given the push that they originally intended to give its original edition, how do you assess what kind of impact it would have had back then, in the late 70s? I wasn't familiar with the second edition, I'm not sure who published it or how well known it is, and this third edition, the publisher is Sheridan Square Press. The editions have all been much smaller than they would have been had there not been such a reaction to its original publication.

A: The first edition was their biggest book for that season. The first printing was 25,000 and it was sold out before publication. And they were already into a second printing and it was a Literary Guild se-

lection and it had a publisher in London and it had seven paperback houses bidding on it at the time they pulled the book off the market. I think it would have had a very big impact because it was the first book about the truth underneath the myth of the *Washington Post* which had come out ever since Watergate. And these people were at the height of their power, the height of their glamour and nobody really thought twice about who these people were. I think it would have had an enormous impact.

Q: And you sued, right?

A: I sued Harcourt Brace for breach of contract for taking my book off the market.

Q: And won.

A: And won, yeah.

Q: Who published the second edition?

A: A little publisher called National Press in Bethesda, Maryland. That was out for a year or two but they didn't promote it. And the third edition is now out with Sheridan Square Press, which is small but a very good publisher. And they're the people that published the Jim Garrison book that became the *JFK* movie.

Q: *On the Trail of the Assassins.*

A: That's right. And they're very sharp politically and they're very courageous and I like them a lot.

Q: What you do now? You've got the book out. Are you a reporter?

A: I'm writing a book on Henry and Clare Booth Luce, which is going to be a further investigation of *mediapolitics*. But it's going to be a much broader scope book. It's going to be about *Time* magazine and how it transformed American culture. And it's going to be a psychological portrait of Henry Luce and Clare Booth Luce and how these people projected their own needs to be powerful on to this enormously successful, influential magazine. It is really one of the most—I want to use the word Thought Control—it really worked on people's minds in a way that nothing else had before it.

Q: If that book is any bit the eye opener that your current book is, it's certainly going to be interesting reading.

A: Thank you.

Has Carbon Dating Buried the Shroud of Turin?
by John Hayward

On October 13, 1988, it was announced to the world that carbon-dating (C-14) results from the famous Shroud of Turin, reputed to be the actual burial shroud of Jesus of Nazareth, showed that the cloth was dated between AD 1260-1390, suggesting that it could not be that of Jesus, who was crucified about AD 30. For most people, that settled the question: the Shroud was a fake, even though no one can still explain, much less duplicate the front and back, full-length images, which are photographically negative (photography wasn't even invented until the nineteenth century), superficial (only on the top several thousands of an inch of the fibers), three-dimensional (no other picture in the world contains true three-dimensional information) and physiologically/anatomically correct (poorly understood in the thirteenth-fourteenth centuries).

One could usually count on seeing many articles on the Shroud in religious periodicals, especially in Lent. Despite the fact that there have been five major symposia on the Shroud since the C-14 results (and one to come in Rome in 1993), even religious periodicals are now virtually ignoring the Shroud. But many eminent researchers and scientists, including those who actually examined the Shroud in 1978, have expressed at these symposia and elsewhere grave reservations about the C-14 test. They believe that the tests were performed in such a way as to cast severe doubts on the validity of the results. These protests have fallen on deaf ears. The media has given very little air time to the doubts expressed. Most people seem happy to put out of their mind such an important issue, which deals with no less than the meaning of life. As one author writing about the Shroud put it, "Many categorically refuse to notice any issue that is ontologically important; they refuse to think beyond beer, sex, TV, and money."

Another case associated with the death of a famous leader, albeit a secular one, has seemingly taken the place of the Shroud—ironically even in the religious media: the assassination of President John F. Kennedy. There are some fascinating similarities between the two cases. As mentioned, both deal with the death (some might use the word "execution") of a famous leader. Both cases have people in powerful or exalted positions espousing a view that is contested by groups that do not accept the discrepancies, irregularities, and suppression of evidence emanating from the "official" view. Both cases are hampered by the deci-

sion of the people in positions of power, who seem to be afraid to let all the data to come out in each case.

In the case of the Shroud, carbon-dating officials, who knew virtually nothing about the Shroud and its history (the latter being crucial for proper C-14 testing) and who had never observed the whole cloth firsthand, pronounced that the Shroud was definitely medieval, despite the fact that this data conflicted with over eighty years of other scientific data that suggested that the Shroud is authentic. The labs refused to release the raw data from their experiments, normal procedure for all scientific experiments, and only released their final report, which was not peer-reviewed (i.e., analyzed and critiqued by other scientists—another standard procedure in science) and left many unanswered questions.

In the case of JFK, the official government position is that Lee Harvey Oswald acted alone, despite the fact that there is overwhelming evidence that there was a conspiracy. Officials who were not at the scene decided that dozens of people who witnessed the assassination and had testimony that conflicted with the "official" view were simply wrong. Many documents pertaining to the assassination were to have been sealed until 2039. Although it has been reported that researchers will get access to some of these documents very soon, there has been enough abuse and tampering with previous evidence to cause concern about the integrity of the remaining documents. It has also been reported that any bill passed to release these documents will get a Presidential veto. No surprise there!

However, let us return to specific details concerning the controversy surrounding the Shroud of Turin. Much doubt has been cast upon the validity of the C-14 results by many researchers and scientists, especially by a French priest named Bruno Bonnet-Eymard, whose work appears in a periodical published by his religious order, and Italian authors Orazio Petrosillo and Emanuella Marinelli, who published a book in 1990. The evidence presented by Bonnet Eymard and Petrosillo/Marinelli is startling. It indicates that there was an enormous lack of professionalism in the testing process. Discrepancies and irregularities abound in the saga. The Cardinal of Turin's scientific adviser, Luigi Gonella, indicated after the results that he believed that an anti-Catholic conspiracy had been at work. "There are those who speak of a Jewish-masonic conspiracy," write Petrosillo and Marinelli. The Vatican Secretariat of State has reportedly opened a dossier to examine whether such allegations are true.

Why would the Masons get involved? According to French author Yves Marsaudon, "Only Masonry can resolve the vast problems imposing themselves upon man today and which despite irrefutable goodwill neither the organized Churches nor political parties are fit to tackle."

Many scholars had expressed the need for caution in interpreting C-14 results on the Shroud, which has been in several fires and exposed to many contaminants over the years. The test, which was performed on a minuscule fragment of the cloth, is extremely sensitive, and it doesn't take much for the results to be completely misleading. Michael Winter, a C-14 specialist, has written, "If a dating by Carbon-14 confirms our theories, we put the results in plain view in the main text: if it contradicts them, but not entirely, we relegate the results to footnote; and if the dating contradicts our theories completely, we hide the fact from everyone." But in reality, the errors in some C-14 cases are well publicized. The magazine *Science* in December 1988 revealed that some live shells of snails were dated to 26,000 BP (Before Present). The geographical periodical Antarctic reported recently that a newly killed seal dated to 1,300 BP. The journal *Radiocarbon* reported that the skin of a 26,000 year old mammoth was judged to be only 5,600 years old. Such errors are not rare. Not long after the Shroud C-14 results, the British Research Council gave 38 laboratories around the world objects of a known age to be tested. Only 7 laboratories achieved results deemed acceptable by the BRC.

The three labs that performed the Shroud dating have all recently had some interesting results on other objects. The director of the laboratory of Zurich, Switzerland had attempted to date the linen handkerchief of his mother-in-law. Although the handkerchief was about 50 years old, the C-14 results indicated an age of 350 years. "The fault of detergents" was the explanation. The Tucson laboratory dated a Viking horn to the year 2006 AD (that's right—we haven't reached it yet). In 1991, the Oxford lab (England) was asked to date ancient rock painting by South African bushmen. Their results estimated the rock to be 1,200 year old, but they were dumbfounded when a grandmother named Joan Ahrens said she had painted them 11 years previously.

It seemed that the C-14 test was to be only be one test, inserted into a context of multi-disciplinary examination. The Shroud had already been subjected to various tests, with results suggesting that the Shroud dated to the time of Jesus. Pollen analysis showed that the cloth had been in Palestine and Italy and including all the places in-between where tradition maintains that the cloth once was. The late Fr. Francis Filas, a professor at Loyola University in Chicago, had found evidence of the imprint of coins placed over the eyes of the man in the Shroud, a practice known to have existed at the time of Jesus. The imprints of the coins match coins minted by Pontius Pilate, who reigned in Palestine from 26-36 AD. Jesus is believed to have been crucified in 30 or 33 AD. Traces of aragonite, a rare mineral present in the grottoes of Jerusalem, has been found. There are traces of hemoglobin; the coagulating blood had been interrupted without the stains being altered and before the decaying process started. With such scientific results, the Shroud of Turin Research Project (STURP), a group of 40 American scientists, presented in 1984 to Cardinal Ballestrero of Turin a new plan of research, called Phase II. In Phase II, the STURP team proposed to see answers to 85 questions related to the formation of the image (still a complete mystery to this day), its preservation and its authenticity.

A bitter struggle began at this point. According to Bonnet-Eymard and Petrosillo/Marinelli, the scientists who eventually carbon-dated the Shroud had the objective of preventing any inter-disciplinary research and to base the verdict of authenticity on C-14 alone. The tests would be conducted with as little input as possible from the Turin archdiocese and the Pontifical Academy of Sciences, the Pope's advising body on scientific matters. Two men who were allegedly key figures in this saga were the Episcopalian priest David Sox and C-14 scientist Harry Gove.

Sox, who had been secretary of the British Society for the Turin Shroud, had for years been urging C-14 for the Shroud. Beginning in 1976 he had contacted a number of laboratories and interested them in being involved in a dating of the Shroud. In 1977 he contacted Harry Gove, one of the pioneers of C-14 dating. Gove then contacted two Oxford scientists, Robert Hedges and Edward Hall. These two would be the men who would present the results obtained by the three laboratories to a press conference on 14 October 1988. Along with them, Michael Tite, director of London's British Museum, which was the sole coordinating institution and "guarantor" of the results. On the blackboard behind them, the results were written with a large exclamation point following. According to the authors, this behavior showed a lack of impartiality and scientific neutrality.

Sox, who resigned from the British Society for the Turin Shroud in January 1981 after stating his belief that the Shroud was a painting, based on the opinions of Chicago microscopist Walter McCrone, whose work was contested by the STURP group. Although the testing was to be performed in secret, Sox managed to get in to the Zurich lab with a BBC television crew to watch and film various phases of the test. A book by Sox, *The Shroud Unmasked: Uncovering the Greatest Forgery of All Time* was ready for release long before the results of the test were even made public. Gonella, Ballestrero's adviser, would say, "I realized only at the end of the tests there was a veritable radio-carbon mafia."

Harry Gove appeared at the Radio-Carbon Congress of Dubrovnik in June 1988 and presented himself as "the principal spokesman and coordinator for the dating of the Shroud." In fact, there had been an on-going dispute between Gove and Gonella for some time. In 1986, Gove had confided to Carlos Chagas, president of the Pontifical Academy of Sciences, that Gonella did not respect him. Shortly before that, Gove had declared that if STURP, which had proposed the program of interdisciplinary research, was allowed to participate, he would pull out.

In the preparatory meetings held in June 1986, Gove had proposed that Sox be present along with the directors of the laboratories that would be chosen to do the testing. Gonella, who preferred that STURP participate in the testing, wrote a private letter to Chagas. Another official in the Pontifical Academy of Sciences saw the letter and revealed the contents to Gove; the letter was even published in Sox's book. In the letter, Gonella accused Gove trying to obtain funds from the National Science Foundation and wanted to present himself as the leader of the laboratories (which at the time was going to include Gove's Rochester lab) to increase the prestige of his lab. From that time on, there were two "camps", one led by Gove and Chagas, the other by Gonella and STURP. The former seemed to prevail, although Gonella managed to get Gove's lab removed from the testing. Not to be outdone, Gove managed to get himself invited to the Tucson lab for observation of the testing there.

Although there are two types of C-14 tests, one being older and more proven, the three laboratories chosen all use the newer and more suspect AMS method. Since the sample was also taken from only one suspect area of the cloth instead of from several places as recommended, the notion of independent tests, essential to a rigid scientific methodology, being performed is absurd. One simply has 1 sample being tested 3 times under similar conditions.

So why did Gonella, though hostile to Gove and favorable to multi-disciplinary testing and who had authority to accept or reject procedures, accept such conditions? At a Shroud symposium in May 1989, Gonella stated, "The Church found herself faced with a challenge launched by a few persons who, with their requests, did everything they could to make us say no,

in order to say that the Church as afraid of science. So, faced with this danger, it was decided to proceed to the scientific examination at all costs, even with protests." And he added: "It was a matter of blackmail. They backed us against the wall with the threat of blackmail: either we would accept the Carbon-14 dating tests under the conditions set by the laboratories or a campaign would be unleashed against the Church with accusations that the Church feared the truth, that the Church was the enemy of science...In any case, the laboratories acted very badly. I protest their absolute lack of scientific professionalism. I protest the base way they conducted their experiments. I have told them to their faces that they are mafiosi."

One can understand those who are knowledgeable about the Shroud continue to hold to their belief that the cloth is authentic. One expects a neutral and detached attitude on the part of scientists performing such an important experiment but it clearly was not the case. Edward Hall, director of the Oxford lab, said in an interview in 1989, "I certainly did not believe that the Shroud was the burial cloth of Christ" and added that he did not know whether the blood on the linen was that of a man or a pig. And although to this day, the image-formation process on the Shroud is a mystery, Hall states that it's not an important question in light of the fact that the results show it to be medieval. What kind of scientist is it that is satisfied while major questions are still unanswered?

The tests to date the Shroud were supposed to be "blind" tests; the Shroud samples along with control cloth samples (dates of which were known by the authorities but not supposed to be known by the labs) were to have been prepared in such a way to avoid tampering or exchanges and to insure the trustworthiness of the dating. But the sole overseer of the whole operation, Michael Tite of the British Museum informed the labs of the dates of the "control" samples. In addition, the representatives of the laboratories had been able to see the Shroud, which has a very unusual weave, during the cutting of the samples in Turin. "They did not trust the cardinal and a whole group of them came to Turin," Gonella would say later. They were easily able to identify the Shroud sample when it came time for the testing. The director of the Zurich lab admitted in front of Sox's television camera: "All that you need to do is look at the photographs of the Shroud's fabric published in *National Geographic*. It is not difficult for me to recognize the Shroud's material: it is the sample marked Z1."

There is more. On April 21, the three small pieces cut for the testing were packaged along with the "control" samples in steel cylinders in a private room (this part of the proceedings were not videotaped) by

Tite and Cardinal Ballestrero. At this point Gabriel Vial, an expert on ancient fabrics, introduced a piece of cloth dating from the medieval period. Vial had obtained the cloth from French C-14 scientist Jacque Evin, who had been asked by Tite to find a piece of material as similar to the Shroud as possible dating from the medieval period. Tite had asked that the fabric be brought to London, but Evin, fearing it would not arrive on time, had it brought to him in Turin.

This sample, not called for by the official protocol, requested and delivered in a strange way, when Cardinal Bellestrero, believing the procedure concluded, had left the room, was also cut into 3 pieces and given to the laboratories. This sample was put into envelopes rather than steel containers, making it easily identifiable. Almost no report, note even the semi-official one of that day, mentions this last sample, which is so close to the age eventually announced for the Shroud, has led some to claim that there was a substitution.

There are also discrepancies regarding the supposed weights of the samples. In a lecture in Paris, Giovanni Riggi, who made the actual cut, said it was 497 milligrams. But later in the talk, he gave the figure of 540 milligrams. In the film made of the cutting, the scale showed 478.1 milligrams. Another textile expert involved in the operation, Franco Testore, indicated a figure of 298 milligrams.

In short, there are many unanswered questions. This has led some to speak of an "anti-Catholic plot" designed to erasing traces of the visible presence of Christ. Although there are no immediate plans for another round of testing, it seems certain that the Vatican does not consider the case closed.

Sources:

Chambers, Roger. "War of the Shroud." *Christian Standard,* 18 April 1982, p. 13.

"Ecumenism and Masonry: As 'They' Like It". *30 Days In the Church and in the World,* No. 3, 1992, pp. 38-41.

Paci, Stefano M. "The Case Is Not Closed." *30 Days In the Church and in the World,* 3(6), June 1990, pp. 36-40.

The Vatican's Alliance with Reagan
by Tom Flynn

We note with concern recent media allegations that former President Ronald Reagan and Pope John Paul II formed a secret alliance to help topple communist rule in Poland. If true, the stories help to explain certain elements of the Solidarity saga that always seemed incredibly fortuitous. But they also mark a papal return to geopolitics on a scale unmatched in more than a century. And they raise serious questions about church-state separation: How can a secular democracy order its relations with an entity that is both a sovereign foreign power and a religious community? And what is implied when the Vatican makes United States compliance with its moral program a quid pro quo to secure the church's political cooperation?

Writing in *Time,* Carl Bernstein reported that Reagan and the pope forged a secret alliance to preserve Solidarity, whose leaders had gone underground in Poland after General Wolciech Jaruzelski imposed martial law on December 13, 1981. They acted swiftly: United States' sanctions were imposed upon Poland and the then USSR Top-security intelligence data was funneled to the pope on the authority of Reagan and then-CIA director William Casey. If the United States enjoyed superior military intelligence, the Vatican had more timely, better quality intelligence regarding social and political matters as the crisis unfolded. On at least one occasion in 1984, Reagan relaxed certain sanctions against Poland when Archbishop (now Cardinal) Pio Langhi flew to the western White House to warn that the pope felt the sanctions had grown counterproductive. At other times, Philadelphia John Cardinal Krol is said to have served as a papal intermediary to Reagan.

Within Poland, American spies and Catholic priests worked hand in hand to distribute millions of dollars worth of fax machines, video recorders, two-way radios, mimeographs, cash, and more—all the accoutrements of a propaganda "war from below" against a repressive communist regime. We read that Casey himself coordinated efforts to build the remnants of the Socialist International within Poland into a force like the Christian Democratic parties in many Western European countries.

All of this reflected a vision that Reagan and the pope shared: a vision that the post-World War II division of Europe, ceding Eastern Europe to the Soviets, could be overturned. In the fifteenth century, the Borgia pope Alexander VI had imposed a similar partition, dividing the known world between Spain and Portugal. With little less audacity a twentieth-century pope joined forces with the president of United States to dissolve the partition of Yalta. "This," said Reagan national security adviser Richard Allen without a trace of irony, "was one of the greatest secret alliances of all time."

But the alliance was not without its cost to the United States. Secularists cannot help but be concerned at the spectacle of an American spymaster laying clandestine foundations for "Christian Democratic" anything in a foreign land. Equally dubious, in our view, was the Administration decision to grant the Vatican full diplomatic recognition as a sovereign state.

Perhaps most disturbing was the quid pro quo on birth control policy that Rome is said to have extracted from Washington as the price of alliance. William Wilson, Reagan's first ambassador to the Vatican, told Time that the Vatican demanded an outright ban on the use of American funds for the promotion of birth control or abortion, whether by foreign countries or international health organizations. However reluctantly, the State department had no choice but to accede. This is the background of Reagan's 1984 bombshell that rocked the World Conference on Population in Mexico City—and led to America's defunding of the UN Fund for Population Activities and the International Planned Parenthood Federation.

During the 1980s, the unfolding drama of Polish resistance galvanized the world. To the degree that developments in Poland laid the groundwork for the collapse of Soviet communism, we must endorse them. Yet we must ask what price America paid when it allied itself with "the church that thinks it's a nation...the nation that thinks it's a church." That alliance altered American policy in the direction of Catholic dogma, to the detriment of millions in the third world. And it caused the frequent repetition of a spectacle we have long been encouraged to dismiss as an anti-Catholic delusion: namely, the spectacle of Catholic prelates like Langhi and Krol acting incontestably as agents of a sovereign foreign power while within the borders of the United States.

At the highest level, these disclosures would suggest that Vatican leaders have enjoyed broad access to Washington policymaking. At the local level, during the abortion debate numerous conservative prelates have dared to remind Catholic judges, politicians, journalists, and others that their church demands of them a loyalty higher than their oath of office, their professional code, or the duty they perceive as American citizens. Perhaps it is time to look more favorably on calls that high-ranking Catholic churchmen register officially as agents of a foreign power.

Reprinted from Free Inquiry Vol. 12, No. 2, Spring 1992. *Tom Flynn serves as an associate editor for* Free Inquiry, *published by the Council For Democratic and Secular Humanism (CODESH), 3965 Rensch Road, Buffalo, NY 14228-2713.*

When Lenny Bruce Played St. Louis
by Kenn Thomas

Bread! was the motivation behind Lenny Bruce's appearances in as unhip a place as St. Louis in 1959, he made that clear. "I honestly don't think I have a function as a comedian," he told then *St. Louis Globe-Democrat* staff writer Joe Pollack, "Except maybe to make money for the guy who books me."

Bruce made his share of money during his meteoric rise to prominence as America's premiere "sick" comic in the '50s. He died a pauper, however, in August 1966, of drugs and on a toilet, like Elvis. Like Elvis, too, Bruce became enshrined in the lexicon of pop culture heroes. He still exerts an enormous influence over what gets said and heard in 1990s America. Andrew Dice Clay only walks through doors that Lenny Bruce opened, and if the content of Bruce's stand-up pales in comparison, the style certainly does not. Joe Pollack regarded him as an "expert boxer...He keeps them off balance. He jabs them here with a quip, there with another—then hooks with a biting remark on some facet of society." Moreover, Bruce made an impression on people in St. Louis that still lingers.

"The motivation for work is bread," Bruce repeated to Jay Landesman, the proprietor of the Crystal Palace, where Lenny Bruce played. The Crystal Palace served as the central showplace of St. Louis' Gaslight Square, the bohemian district that bordered the city's West End in the '50s and '60s. Bruce regarded the club as a "church gone bad," with its ornate interiors of chandeliers and stained glass, and its beatnik reputation.

In his new book, *Rebel Without Applause* (The Permanent Press, 1990), Landesman records his disbelief at Bruce's cynical assessment that money was "all that matters," insisting that if Bruce really meant it, he would have wound up rich. And apparently Bruce did take advantage of the more than the three thousand dollar fee Landesman paid him. He propositioned Landesman's wife Fran during the first go 'round and shot Dilaudid with her in a "more intimate" dressing room setting on his return visit. Landesman holds no grudges, *Rebel Without Applause* serves as a virtual picaresque of his entrepreneurial and sexual dalliances and those of his wife.

Although Landesman clearly relishes his memories of Bruce, his book is perforcely self-serving. After patting himself on the back for taking a chance on Bruce (much less of risk in 1959 than during the public clamor around Bruce in the '60s), a significant part of the Lenny Bruce chapter concerns the club owner's admittedly over-long on-stage introduction of the comedian to his audience. Elsewhere, Landesman mistakes a rare booklet Bruce published called *Stamp Help Out!* with Bruce's autobiography, *How To Talk Dirty*. But in the overall he provides a thoughtful glimpse of Bruce's transformation from a snappy hipster to a zoned-out junkie.

Landesman's earliest impressions of Bruce match the kind of admiration that Joe Pollack heaped on the comedian as the champion against social hypocrisy. Bruce arrives at Lambert Airport in "a mohair suit and fifty dollar shoes," a kind of Don Quixote with even a Pancho Villa bodyguard in tow to help keep him off heroin. Bruce also was well-regarded by the local audience. He offended only one older couple enough for a walk-out, according to the *Globe,* which was quite good for Bruce. He played to an SRO audience the following night.

A reel-to-reel tape of a Lenny Bruce show at the Crystal Palace has long been rumored to be the possession of a local politician's son, but even the doggedness of avid Bruce collectors has never brought it to the surface. The only real documentation of those nights came in 1984 when Bruce's daughter Kitty published some of her father's papers. Bequeathed to her by long-time Bruce supporter and friend Ralph Gleason, the jazz critic for San Francisco's *Herald & Examiner,* the papers included Lenny's notes for the St. Louis and Chicago gigs of 1959.

At the show, Bruce apparently returned to his theme of money: "Why can you people afford to sit at the tables? Because *you* people have exploited the people who sit in the bars!"; and opining about some unidentified socialite with a strange haircut, "That's how his family got rich—they never spent money on haircuts." Bruce also lamented that he couldn't kill a fly anymore without thinking of Vincent Price and expressed his wish to get Kruschev "balled, juiced, loaded; forget the museum."

But the Lenny Bruce that played the Crystal Palace the second time worked for half the fee, according to Jay Landesman. Landesman gives no dates for that second show in his book, only that it occurred after a Chicago obscenity bust that cost Bruce the majority of his bookings. Landesman recounts that from the airport to the club stage, Bruce rattled off one long litany about the legal dimensions of obscenity, the constitutional protections of free speech, and his own precarious legal predicament.

Instead of money, Bruce had become enamored with how threatened the world seemed by his harmless sex and drugs humor. "His lectures on jurisprudence failed to captivate the audience," according to Landesman, "and they left feeling cheated out of the real Lenny Bruce." Bruce regarded his trials simply as stand-up bits funnier than the ones he could concoct himself. His real obsession was drugs—teaching Landesman and his wife "how to get the maximum high by jacking off the blood in the needle while it was still in his arm." Landesman did succeed in steering his St. Louis' prosecuting attorney and his two daughters from attending the show. Landesman saw Bruce only once more, in New York. According to *Rebel Without Applause,* at the show Bruce did ten minutes on the Crystal Palace and his relationship to its owner.

Today, it is difficult to get into a discussion about the '60s in St. Louis with Gaslight Square veterans without Bruce's name being dropped—by someone who knew him, or someone who hung out with him on those nights, or even someone who claims to have shot up with him. Bruce also lives on in perennial St. Louis stage productions, one at the old Union Station in 1979, and as recently as 1989 when a locally produced one man show entitled *The Return of Lenny Bruce* played the New City School. Joe Pollack termed the latter "surprisingly tame." Certainly the irony of local performers still pulling in the "bread" from his stand-up bits would not have been lost on Lenny Bruce himself.

Italian Air Space Mystery
From the Other Side of the Pond
by Jim Cregan

One night in June 1980 an Alitalia flight from Bologna to Palermo mysteriously disappeared from all radar and crashed into the sea near Ustica Island off the coast of Sicily. Early investigations revealed nothing and the aircraft was not recovered. It seemed a curious coincidence that every major radar unit in the area, from Civil Aviation in Rome and Sicily to the American sixth fleet in Naples was turned off. Each one with a convenient excuse about repairs, maintenance or the technician in the bathroom. No one saw what caused the DC9 to go down.

After years of building political pressure from families of the victims to re-open the case, with accusations of a cover-up and wild theories of midnight dogfights between American pilots and marauders from Libya, the plane was found.

Thanks to advances in diving technology and a hand from the French government, investigators brought up parts from the plane. However, the evidence was inconclusive and the case passed from the scene again.

The case has come back to public attention in recent months and new investigations are in progress. A second dive by an Italian company has finally brought up crucial parts from the damaged plane as well as the black box flight recorder. It appears that the plane was indeed hit by an air-to-air missile. There were subsequent accusations that the French had purposely left certain evidence on the sea floor, leaving questions deliberately unanswered.

In the same period, a wreckage from a Libyan Mig was found in Calabria, on the southern tip of Italy. No cause was ever determined for the crash, but official reports give the date of the crash as one month later than the date given by eyewitnesses.

After numerous and intensive interrogations of military personnel, one officer finally decided to talk. He testified that he was on duty and that every radar unit watching the Tirreno sea, including that of the sixth fleet, was on that night. Numerous Italian, French and American radar technicians saw the entire scene. No one knows to this day the nationality of the pilots involved in the pursuit of a Mig observed crossing the Mediterranean from Libya. No one knows why the Mig was there. But the flight from Bologna to Palermo was caught in a crossfire and the cover up has gone on for ten years.

We only know at this point that the planes attacking the Libyan Mig were NATO planes. The Italian Air Force has adequately demonstrated that none of its aircraft were in the region that night. The Americans and the French have been accused. The American government has officially denied all involvement, although it has given little cooperation in the investigation. It has not explained contradictions with recent testimony that the sixth fleet radar recorded the events of that evening. The French have offered no additional cooperation and have neither denied or admitted the accusations.

The latest development: the head of the Italian Joint Chiefs of Staff and the head of the Air Force at the time of the incident has been formally accused of high treason for involvement in the cover-up and will stand trial.

Jim Cregan is a free-lance writer living in Italy.

Wilhelm Reich in Hell
by Jim Martin

" *My factual position in this case as well as the world of science today does not permit me to enter the case against the Food And Drug Administration, since such action would, in my mind, imply admission of the authority of this special branch of government to pass judgement on primordial pre-atomic cosmic orgone energy.* "
—Wilhelm Reich's letter to the Court

Although they are sporadic and brief, documents revealed in a recent FOIA release to the editor, Kenn Thomas, indicate many details about the tragic final months of Dr. Wilhelm Reich, who was sentenced to two years in federal prison and died in Lewisburg, Pennsylvania Federal Penitentiary on Sunday, November 3rd, 1957. Kenn passed them on to me and asked for a report.

Dr. Reich had been ordered by the FDA and federal courts to cease distribution of his medical device, the orgone accumulator. When an assistant, Dr. Michael Silvert, transported the devices across state lines, he and Reich were charged with the violation of the court injunction. Unbelievably, the 59-year-old scientist, researcher, and teacher was sentenced to two years and, as with many people his age, this proved to be a death sentence.

Upon sentence recommendations, Reich was ordered to undergo psychiatric counseling, mostly to determine whether he knew the difference between right and wrong. At that time, there was a general agreement that Reich suffered from "paranoid schizophrenia" among professionals in the medical and psychiatric communities. They felt constrained to say that this assumption was "not based on personal observation." It is an idea that somehow found its way into early governmental assessments of Reich as a national security risk. It was repeated in subsequent documents. This diagnosis can be traced back to a rumor begun by Otto Fenichel, a co-worker of Reich's, in Europe. The diagnosis, based on a personal animosity rather than on therapeutic treatments, was confirmed by the prison psychiatrists, who reported in their evaluation: "In his discussions he unraveled a rather intricate and somewhat logical system of persecutory trends, particularly regarding the Rockefeller Foundation 'which made me a tool of its socio-economic interpersonal relations'."

By the way, in layman's terms, one of the symptoms of schizophrenia is hearing voices in your head.

Schizophrenics can be the most outwardly "crazy" people. However, the doctors claimed that "Reich gave no concrete evidence of being mentally incompetent." However, "it is felt that Reich could easily have a frank break with reality, and become psychotic, particularly if the stresses and environmental pressures become overwhelming."

Reich's parole officer commented that he had an "unusually keen interest in getting an early release." (I've been in federal prisons, and it's filled with such people, so what did the officer mean by "unusually keen?") Reich went so far as to initiate an executive clemency hearing with President Eisenhower. The parole officer, Frank Walker, Jr., reported that "Reich went on to state that he was the victim of an international conspiracy and that is why he was sent here... that his situation was unique and different because the fate of the planet was involved." Reich's appeals for early release were denied. That line of reasoning didn't get me anywhere, either, when I was involved in anti-nuclear demonstrations.

Reich openly suspected a conspiracy of "Hoodlums In Government" (Higs) had been behind the decade-long, multi-million dollar prosecution. Indeed, his own personal lawyer, Peter Mills, turned up on the prosecution team, and much of the evidence provided by the FDA failed to take into account Reich's experimental protocol.

"I have carefully observed the methods of destruction of the moral fabric of society by Stalinite murderers by proxy," Reich wrote in a letter to his third wife, Aurora Karrer. My sense is that Reich wasn't talking about a literal cabal of commies so much as a loosely organized but coordinated attack on free sexual and emotional expression. In his therapeutic work, Reich was fond of extremely concrete metaphors (such as "character armor" to describe physical attitudes of emotional withholding). To describe the bureaucratic assault upon his work he seems to have drawn on his own recent experience with the Stalinist left in Europe. Prison officials derided Reich's marital status (common law) and his views on compulsory sexual morality. "Since the defendant does not believe in marriage as an institution, he has never developed any strong home ties. Where he lives is mostly a matter of convenience to the defendant and if he has any sentimental attachments they are not connected with the home as an institution," reads Reich's "Prison Classification Study."

"Our marriage, love and oneness have already become widely known as a model of clean living as against the usual filth," Reich wrote, as if he was responding to that in a letter to Aurora from Lewisburg.

After Reich's death, Aurora requested information about a packet of unsent letters that Reich wanted published after his death. "You may one day read that (Not Sent) letter /blank line: erased/ ...large publishing house my 'Silent Observer' or 'Creation': The 3rd Volume of the History of Orgonomy. This volume is nearly completely conceived and constructed." This reference, found in Reich's letter to Aurora dated Sept. 16th, 1957, apparently refers to the mysterious book Reich mentioned having written while in jail. This manuscript has never turned up. If it exists, it would complete a trilogy with *The Oranur Experiment* and *Contact With Space*. Reich sent it to the Department of Education, to be forwarded to Aurora, where she worked.

Reich and those around him had developed an elaborate conspiracy theory involving leftists, government officials, Stalinist spies, and social moralists. He called them the Emotional Plague, signifying the contagious nature of the affliction.

Thus he was suspicious when two volumes of specially-prepared defense briefs, called "Vol IV and V of the Suppressed and Secret Evidence" was sent to him in prison with different colored binding and "handwriting that is familiar to me but which I cannot identify" on one of the covers. Reich seemed to have believed that someone pulled a switch on him.

After Reich's death, Aurora's lawyer wrote to the Warden at Lewisburg in an effort to obtain the missing manuscript, as well as to mention that on her last visit, Reich mentioned "that he had asked for aspirin and had been given two pink pills instead. ...I wondered whether you would permit us access to the prison hospital and dispensary record concerning the decedent." In the margins of the letter in the records, the Warden pencilled "NO."

The autopsy revealed damage to the heart (Reich had previously suffered a heart attack but was in good health when sent to prison). However, the stomach contents were not analyzed, because of "lack of facilities to do so." In any event, Reich's immediate family, in this case, his daughter Eva, had not even requested an autopsy, believing, as she stated to the coroner, that her father "had died of a broken heart." The prison in fact ordered the autopsy.

It might be easy to read into some of these facts explanations of a conspiratorial nature, but it seems to me to be more important to look at the wider social realities of America in the 1950s, a big Gulag where free thinkers led short and nasty lives. Reich's jailers didn't seem to have a clue about their famous charge, as evidenced by a copy of *True* magazine's expose called "The Marvelous Sex Box" filed dutifully in Reich's background papers.

The Warden himself, before he tired of Reich's numerous requests for an audience, reported about one such session, "He is difficult to follow in his statements, but generally he feels that there is a subversive group operating in our country that rail road people like himself to prison to get them out of the way. He pledges to devout [sic] his life to uncover this subversive force and he prefers to use great secrecy here in the institution and is not willing to deal with anyone but the Warden. Claims there are others here in the same position as he is in and he will confer with me from time to time if I will listen to him." To me, this account lacks some of the subtlety of Reich's conspiracy theory, but I recognize Reich's naivete when talking about "others here in the same position".

Jail must have been pure hell for Reich, who had never crossed paths with the law before and who was already pretty well isolated before his sentence. In an effort to find someone inside who could hear him out, he began speaking with the prison chaplains. He introduced himself as the author of a book called *The Murder of Christ* and began with saying, "Due to my discovery of the Cosmic Orgone Energy and its social implications, I am in deep trouble, emotionally and socially." Reich was reaching out to the only officials in the prison who dealt with emotional life, to unburden himself of an unbearable weight.

To Reverend Silber, Protestant minister, Reich wrote in a handwritten "Inmate Request to Staff Member":

"I am burdened by a conflict between the rational necessity to fight for my freedom from *unlawful imprisonment* by removing irrational obstacles in the way toward freedom here and the danger of falling prey to 'buying' my freedom by concessions to political pressure. The borders are not sharp. As a free man, I refuse to yield under pressure what I would gladly give under conditions of responsible freedom. As the central object of an international conspiracy and foreign espionage, I must succeed in tackling the *abuse of human personal relations by political highway robbers*. The case of this [wavering?] demonstrates clearly the ineffectiveness of the routine security measures. The methodology used by the Devil to deceive due, bona fide authority are unknown, therefore unchallenged. We are faced with the task of, instead of having eternally and without success to expel the devil into hell, to reconvert him—speaking in terms of

Christian Mythology—into the heavenly angel or even par of God (= Cosmic Orgone Energy) within the *bedeviled organism*. It requires far more than praying. The political devil operates in *practical* terms of *living life by perversion of all our virtues and their abuse to political, evil ends.*"

(signed) Wilhelm Reich, June 6, 1957

"I am merely fulfilling my public duties as a U.S. Citizen and worker in planetary affairs if I continue to point out where the *true* danger to our social and personal existence is placed: it is *Emotional Poisoning;* disruption through sowing distrust throughout our society, doping and drugging of our population, esp. our YOUTH; draining us financially through arms race, a camouflage of the true menace, the *Emotional Poisoning* a la Little Rock racial upheavals; keeping our high-placed officials at bay through fear of sexual scandal; railroading efficient men and women into prisons or lunatic asylums through breaking up their environments; subverting justice by whispered little lies & frightening or using judges. Doing all this destruction unnoticed as it were by all those responsible. It was clear from the very beginning that prayer, and now lyrics, were subverted by such use of *stupidities and evasions* on our part, especially by the staid reluctance to talk bluntly & take the bull by the horns. The bull is really no more than a few *slimy tapeworms* eating away at our emotional guts. It is high time to start giving social power to the established functions of Love, Work & Learning as bastions against the tapeworms."

(signed) Wilhelm Reich, Sept. 14, 1957

Ever the man for the historical moment, Reich requested that this and other letters to the Chaplain be placed in his file. This should end the conjecture that Reich "got religion" in his final days. And I find it pretty heady stuff, and can only imagine what the prison staff, especially the chaplain, thought of Reich.

In the end, I can't help comparing Reich's case with the case of the current death sentence which has been placed upon the head of contemporary British writer Salman Rushdie. In a series of public and pathetic attempts to mollify the Emotional Plague of Islamic Fundamentalism, Rushdie has shown the strain of losing his wife and family, loss of public access privileges, and simple isolation from one's best friends because of the enormous social pressure directed at him *personally*. One can only imagine the petty details and consequences of such a life. Because of one sentence issued by the Ayatollah Khomeini, hundreds, if not thousands of assassins are ready to enter heaven by killing a writer. That makes for a conspiracy of insidious proportions, as if a contagious disease had been suddenly introduced into the general population.

But the virus is extremely discriminating, selecting only specific individuals or cell clusters. The emotional plague killed Reich in jail, but most of us can take comfort that we aren't "high-risk". Or are we?

Jim Martin publishes Flatland, *a catalog of obscure and difficult to locate literature, including much on Wilhelm Reich. The new Flatland catalog is available from POB 2420, Department K2A, Fort Bragg, CA 95437-2420.*

Saucer Section:
The Octopus Conspiracy: Fictional Tale or Factional Trail?
by Kenn Thomas

The Casolaro Case

Danny Casolaro might not have been the central figure in the real story behind the media flash accompanying his death in a hotel room in Martinsburg, West Virginia on August 10, 1991. Casolaro was not an investigative reporter. He was more a novelist (*The Ice King*) and a poet, a "sensitive" type who had some experience writing for tabloids and news services. He had more credentials as the publisher of a computer industry PR organ (*Computer Age*) than as an investigator. Moreover, his sad fate may have been more the result of a factional rift in the intelligence community than of any impending fictionalized account of the Octopus story he would have written.

Police found Casolaro's body atop a razor blade in the tub with deep gashes in the wrists. His previous admonition to his brother to not believe any "accidents" that might happen to him belied a terse and ungrammatical "suicide" note. The body was mysteriously embalmed without the family's permission before the autopsy, eliminating any chance of discovering poisons. The all-too-familiar pattern, of course, brings to mind the dictum that if They control the coroner, They control the city. Two veritable MIBs even attended Casolaro's funeral, one in a light-colored overcoat and another dressed as a soldier.

Most of Casolaro's notes and his manuscript have disappeared, too, naturally. The only information available to an interested reader comes from friends, family and reporters who pieced it all together *ex post facto,* most notably James Ridgeway and Doug Vaughan of *Village Voice*. Apparently the tentacles of Casolaro's Octopus reached out from a small body of Illuminati, a half-dozen or so conspiratorial cognoscenti. They have reached out to the October Surprise, BCCI, the Savings and Loan scandals and Iran-Contra. Ridgeway and Vaughan keep the door open to the possibility that Casolaro did indeed commit suicide and they assure *Voice* readers that the Illuminati definitely do not exist.

Octopus Surprise

The central figure in the Casolaro story might be Michael Riconosciuto, the techno-wizard who first let on about Justice Department head Ed Meese giving his buddy Earl Brian a software program called Promis in exchange for Brian transporting forty million dollars to Iran as part of the October Surprise deal. Brian apparently made a fortune bootlegging and selling Promis internationally to police agencies. Promis tracks legal cases through various prosecutors' offices. This October Surprise connection brought the story to the attention of the media. October Surprise, of course, is the catch phrase for the 1980 Reagan-Bush campaign's alleged payoff to the Khomeini regime to delay the release of American hostages in Iran and thereby steal the election from Jimmy Carter. The Promis software, produced by a Washington firm called Inslaw, co-owned by St. Louisans Bill and Nancy Hamilton, was sold for six million dollars to the Justice Department for the department's exclusive use. The Hamiltons have engaged the services of Watergate attorney Eliot Richardson to continue that legal battle.

Riconosciuto now sits in a jail in Tacoma, Washington for manufacturing and selling drugs. Police busted him in April 1991 after providing testimony that he modified Promis so the Mounties could use it in Canada. Riconosciuto claims to have been in on the October Surprise funds transfer with Earl Brian while both worked for Wackenhut, a security group that had William Casey as counsel. Ridgeway and Vaughan trace Riconosciuto's misadventures with the law back to police surveillance in 1968 that led to a 1973 bust for manufacturing psychedelics. Since childhood, Riconosciuto had been adept at electronics to the extent that as a teenager he worked as a research assistant in a laser lab and with a Nobel laureate.

Riconosciuto adds to his list of accomplishments the development and manufacture of weapons technology, including see-in-the-dark goggles designed for the Contras, chemical and biological weapons, and a way to convert an ordinary explosive into an atomic bomb and air into fuel. Much of this was done, according to Riconosciuto, as joint development projects with Wackenhut, a private security firm called Coral Gables and the Cabazon tribe of Native Americans in Riverside County, California, from whose sovereign reservation this technology was created for export. That sovereignty allowed the Cabazons to open megabuck gambling facilities. Casolaro planned a visit to the reservation at the time of his death.

Quick and the Dead

Reporters for the *San Francisco Chronicle*

Jonathan Littman and Michael Taylor have written at length about Riconosciuto's link to a series of strange murders among the Cabazons. Someone named Paul Morasca, who had been in on Riconosciuto's high-tech deals with the Cabazons, was found brutally hog-tied and strangled. Riconosciuto admitted finding the body a day before the police and reporting it only to the Cabazons' non-native administrator, John Phillip Nichols. Shortly thereafter an elderly school teacher named Mary Quick was murdered in what Riconosciuto later claimed was a robbery connected to his machinations with the Cabazons: Quick's body was missing a super secret ATM card that she was to pass on to him.

According to Lippman and Taylor, the Morasca and Quick deaths were parts of a string of murders involving the Cabazons, including that of tribal council vice chairman Alfred Alvarez, who made public statements decrying the mismanagement of Cabazon funds. Pressure from higher-ups in the police bureaucracy caused one investigator working on the murders to leave California altogether. Like Casolaro, investigators have discovered "so many spokes leading out...by the time you finish going out on one lead, another crops up and drives you to distraction." Are these the throes of the Octopus?

The Saucer Spin

Riconosciuto's inability to produce tapes and photographs he says supports many of his claims undermines his most recent revelations. According to an article in *Technical Consultant,* Riconosciuto reports that the only information Casolaro had resulted from a factional split in the intelligence community. One faction, COM-12, has leaked the information to embarrass the other, called Aquarius with a sub-group leadership known as MJ12. MJ12, of course, appears on the still debated memoranda ostensibly documenting the retrieval of aliens from a 1947 flying saucer crash in Roswell, New Mexico. According to *UFO Magazine,* Wackenhut does the security work for the rumored "Area 51" flying saucer hangars.

William L. Moore and Jimmy Ward carry on the discussion about the veracity of the MJ12 documents in a newsletter entitled *Focus,* available for $6 from the Fair Witness Project, Inc., 4219 W. Olive Avenue, Suite 247, Burbank, CA 91505. *The MJ12 Documents: An Analytical Report* by Moore and Jaime Shandera, which provides the up-to-the-minute minutiae of the debate, can be ordered from the same source for $25. Without reproducing its detail, the report supports the authenticity of a series of documents connected to MJ12 and the Roswell crash, expressing doubt about only one Harry Truman signature on one document. (It's an improbable original because of its similarity to a signature on a non-related document. The report does not even entertain the possibility of a signature machine being used for secret UFO memos.) Thus far, *Focus* has not addressed Riconosciuto's claims. Stanton Friedman has done some interesting research suggesting that UFO debunker Donald Menzel back-channeled MJ12 information to John Kennedy. Jacques Vallee, who fails to credit Friedman for this information in his recent *UFO Chronicles of the Soviet Union* (Ballantine, $18.00), nevertheless speculates that Menzel had a role in discrediting an important scientific study of UFOs in the Soviet Union. At one point, a rift developed between Friedman associates Moore and Shandera after Friedman became involved with a Roswell book project that all three now seem to view as a disinformation scheme. Moore has admitted his own involvement in similar schemes. (See the interview with Stanton Friedman following this article.)

Hunt Continues

The Kennedy connection is interesting in that *Voice* reporters Ridgeway and Vaughan note that Casolaro's Gambino crime family contacts put him in touch with E. Howard Hunt, the Watergate burglar and author of fictionalized spy novels. These contacts were developed from sources close to jailed presidential candidate Lyndon LaRouche. LaRouche, of course, has a long history as a politico and intelligence gadfly. His crank status belies his power among followers and his real connections to officialdom. In his other current book, *Revelations* (Ballantine, $20) Vallee suggests a link between LaRouche's European followers and the UMMO cult of UFO hoaxers in Spain, Argentina and lately of Russia.

E. Howard Hunt lost a defamation suit he filed against a group called Liberty Lobby when it published claims of his involvement in the Kennedy assassination. In a new edition of *Coup D'Etat In America* (Quick American Archives, $12.95) by Alan Weberman and Michael Canfield, the authors describe Hunt's inability to sue them over similar claims. The first edition of *Coup D'Etat* originally produced the photograph overlays of Hunt's picture superimposed on that of one of the "railroad tramps" arrested after JFK's murder. Mark Lane describes the Liberty Lobby case, with depositions from the key players and supporting testimony from witness Marita Lorenz, in his book, *Plausible Denial* (Thunder's Mouth Press).

Ridgeway and Vaughan describe the relationship between Casolaro and Hunt as "cordial, even effusive." They also tell of an incident in Casolaro's life when friends found him in his home with a bloodied towel wrapped around his head. Casolaro blamed it on a weight-lifting accident. After his death, Casolaro's autopsy revealed a mild case of multiple sclerosis that friends and family believe Casolaro knew nothing about. In support of the suicide argument, however, the *Voice* writers note that he did discuss "slow viruses, including MS" with a nursing professor friend. Kerry Thornley, a Marine acquaintance of Lee Harvey Oswald who fictionalized Oswald's life in much the same way Casolaro planned to fictionalize the life of the Octopus, told a *Steamshovel Press* interviewer of a brain implant he felt he received after conversations with E. Howard Hunt.

Another similarity between the cases of Danny Casolaro and Lee Harvey Oswald concerns surveillance technology. Inslaw designed Promis, of course, precisely to track and control people. Thornley knew Oswald around the time of the latter's experiences at the Atsugi Air Force base in Japan, where Oswald worked in a radar tower that tracked the U2 surveillance plane missions over China and the Soviet Union. Gary Powers blamed his famous shoot-down on information supplied to the Soviets by Oswald. Before getting his job at the book depository, Oswald worked at a graphics business that contracted to work on U2 photo data. A spy camera that officials tried to pass off as a light meter was found among Oswald's belongings. The space connection is there, too: Oswald's closest co-workers at another job later got work at NASA when he went to Dallas. The last interesting comparison between Casolaro and Oswald may be how, in lieu of all the facts, the best speculation makes them look like hapless pawns in a game of control played by larger, more invisible forces.

More To Come?

Was Casolaro used by feuding intelligence factions, was he brainwashed outright or merely victimized by a talented acid head who kept up on the UFO scene? Riconosciuto needed only to have watched a 1989 TV documentary entitled *Cover-Up* for the MJ12 material he now includes in his weird tales. Casolaro is no longer able to divulge further information about the Octopus. Nightline apparently does have some of Casolaro's files. A bibliography follows for those interested in the details of the Octopus conspiracy that have emerged before and since Casolaro's death. The article by Ridgeway and Vaughan contains the most information; *UFO Magazine* is a good place to look for new developments. Developments—and corroboration—are most likely to come from Michael Riconosciuto, still awaiting trial in the Tacoma prison for manufacturing methamphetamine in a process he claims to use in refining platinum.

Please note that Edward Brian and the Royal Canadian Mounted Police deny any connection to events surrounding Danny Casolaro's death. Thanks to Kevin Belford for bibliographic research assistance.

Bibliography:

Anderson, Jack and Van Atta, Dale, "Another Casualty in the 'Octopus' Case," *Washington Post,* August 28, 1991.

Ayres, B. Drummond, Jr., "As U.S. Battles Computer Company, Writer Takes Vision of Evil To Grave," *New York Times,* September 3, 1991, p. A17.

"Barr Asks Judge To Probe Inslaw Case," *St. Louis Post Dispatch,* November 14, 1991.

Barrett, Paul, "Software Maker Finds Wheels of Justice Grind Slowly When Justice Department Is The Accused," *Wall Street Journal,* May 18, 1990, p. A12.

Barrett, Paul, "Thornburgh, Brooks Clash Over Charge Of Wrongdoing at Justice Department," *Wall Street Journal,* December 10, 1990.

Brown, Colin, "CIA Computer Genius Alleges Massive Conspiracy," *Technical Consultant,* December-January 1991.

Brown, Colin, "The Octopus Revisited," *UFO Magazine* Volume 7, Number 2, 1992, p. 12.

Ciampoli, Paul G., "Was It Murder?" Letter To The Editor, *St. Louis Post-Dispatch,* September 26, 1991

Corn, David, "The Dark World of Danny Casolaro," *The Nation,* October 28, 1991, p. 511.

"Death of Writer Called Suicide," *New York Times,* January 27, 1992, p. A9.

"Free-Lance Journalist's Death Appears To Have Been Suicide: Autopsy Consistent With Theory, But Investigation Continues," *St. Louis Post-Dispatch,* August 13, 1991.

Freivogel, William, "No Review For Inslaw Case: New Lawsuit Against Justice Department Planned," *St. Louis Post Dispatch,* January 14, 1992, p. 9A.

Freivogel, William and Koenig, Robert, "Inslaw Case Will Go To Grand Jury," *St. Louis Post-Dispatch,* January 31, 1992.

Hamilton, William A. and Nancy B., "Appoint A Special Prosecutor In Inslaw Case," *St. Louis Post-Dispatch.* September 19, 1992.

Hewitt, Bill, "Clouded In Mystery: The Death of Writer Danny Casolaro Stirs Rumors of Conspiracy," *People,* October 14, 1991, pp. 89-90.

"The Injustice Of It All," *Time,* October 12, 1987.

"Inslaw Case Moves Forward," Editorial, *St. Louis Post Dispatch,* February 9, 1992.

"Inslaw Case Needs A Special Prosecutor," Editorial, *St. Louis Post Dispatch,* November 1991.

Kilpatrick, James, "FBI Should Find Out Who Killed Casolaro," United Press Syndicate, 1991.

Lacayo, Richard, "The Man Who Knew Too Much?" *Time,* August 26, 1991

"Law: Set Back For Inslaw," *Wall Street Journal,* May 8, 1991.

Lee, Gary, "Area Writer Investigating Inslaw Case Found Dead: Freelancer Went To Meet Source, Friends Say," *Washington Post,* August 13, 1991.

Lee, Gary, "Writer's Papers Shed Little Light On His Death: Casolaro Sought to Prove 'Octopus' Theory Encompassing Hostage Delay, Inslaw, BCCI," *Washington Post,* August 19, 1991.

Linsalata, Phil, "The Octopus File," *Columbia Journalism Review,* November-December 1991, p. 76.

Littman, Jonathan and Taylor, Michael, "Bizarre Murders Puzzle Cops," *San Francisco Chronicle,* December 30, 1991, p. 1.

Mahar, Maggie, "Inslaw Charges: Government Sold Software Abroad," *Barrons,* April 22, 1991, p. 48.

Masters, Kim, "What Killed Danny Casolaro? The Reporter Had A Lot of Friends. Did He Have An Enemy?" *Washington Post,* August 31, 1991.

McGrory, Mary, "Appointee May Seek Truth About Inslaw," Universal Press Syndicate, 1991.

McGrory, Mary, "Tentacles of Octopus Overwhelm A Victim," Universal Press Syndicate, 1991.

Morgenthau, Tom (with Clara Bingham), "A Victim of The Octopus? A Reporter's Death Fuels Theories About A Conspiracy," *Newsweek,* August 26, 1991, p. 21.

O'Brien, "Conspiracy and Death," *Publisher's Weekly,* September 9, 1991, p. 15.

O'Harrow, Robert and Lee, Gary, "Frequent Drinking Marked Writer Casolaro's Final Days," *Washington Post,* August 25, 1991, p. A19.

O'Harrow, Robert and Lee, Gary, "Homicide Not Ruled Out in Death of Writer Probing Inslaw," *Washington Post,* August 14, 1991, p. A4.

"One More Reason To Press The Inslaw Case," Editorial, *St. Louis Post Dispatch,* August 1991.

Primm, Alex, "Suicide Or Murder?" Letter To The Editor, *St. Louis Post Dispatch,* August 1991.

Ridgeway, James and Vaughan, Doug, "Who Killed Danny Casolaro?" *Village Voice,* October 15, 1991, p. 31.

Sawyer, Jon, "Free-lance Journalist's Death Appear To Have Been Suicide; Autopsy Consistent With Theory, But Investigation Continues," *St. Louis Post-Dispatch,* August 12, 1992, p. 4C.

"The Unified Scandal Theory," Chart in *Newsweek,* September 23, 1991, pp. 22 and 23.

Weisberg, Jacob, "Computer Trouble," *New Republic,* September 10 & 17, 1990, pp. 24-27. (also "Correspondence" *New Republic,* October 29, 1990.)

Other Sources:

Lane, Mark, *Plausible Denial,* Thunder's Mouth, 1992.

Melanson, Philip H., "Was Lee Harvey Oswald Having An Affair With The U2 Spy Plane?" *Critique,* Volume V, Numbers 3, 4 (#19/20), Fall/Winter 1986, p. 306.

Vallee, Jacques, *Revelations,* Ballantine Books, 1992.

Vallee, Jacques, *UFO Chronicles of the Soviet Union,* Ballantine Books, 1992.

Weberman, Alan J. and Canfield, Michael, *Coup D'Etat In America,* Quick American Archives, 1992.

An Interview with Stanton Friedman
"Uncharted Areas of Space and Science"
JFK's New Frontier Speech
co-author of *Crash at Corona,* on UFOs & Disinformation

Q: I would like to alert the readers to research you did uncovering Don Menzel's role in MJ12 and in order to get that far we have to talk about MJ12.

A: I think that most people will recognize that if the government's got two crashed saucers and some dead alien bodies and a live alien, they're going to do something about it. They obviously would like to know what the technology is and so forth. That means that they probably set up some kind of a very highly classified group. And *The Roswell Incident* came out in 1980 and when Bill Moore was promoting that he met some Air Force insiders and in 1984 at the end of the year a roll of film showed up at another colleague's house, Jaime Shandera, and on the roll of film were eight pages of a top secret, eyes only, "Magic" briefing for President-elect Eisenhower dated November 18, 1952. There was a list of attachments, only one of them, attachment A, was there and I'd give my left arm for the rest of them. And this casually, well, maybe not casually, tells the story of a recovery of a crashed saucer outside Roswell and four alien bodies and the establishment of this group, Operation Majestic Twelve, accountable only to the president, Harry Truman originally in 1947. And it names the twelve members and some of them were pretty much what you'd expect: the first secretary of defense, James Forrestal; the first three directors of central intelligence; several outstanding scientists like Dr. Vannevar Bush, who was the top dog in technology development during World War II.

But there was one kicker on the list, and that was Dr. Donald Menzel, a Harvard professor of astronomy. It's hard to imagine: why would a Harvard professor of astronomy have a high-level security clearance in the first place? And much more important, I guess, was the fact that he was known as a thorough debunker of flying saucers. He was sort of the Phil Klass of his day. And he had written three anti-UFO books, so when I first heard the other names, they made sense, but Menzel's name made me think this must be a hoaxed document. Somebody's trying to get us to take the bait, you know, and they're going to say, "A Ha! Gotcha!"

I did a lot of checking and there was too much good stuff in there. There was name like General Robert Montague, who very few people had ever heard of but we had noted that he was introduced to the Secretary of War in the second week of July in 1947. And he was named the head of a special group in Sandia base in New Mexico right around this time. That's not the kind of name a hoaxter would pick up on and there were several others.

Anyway, I had to get permission from three different people to look at Menzel's files. All the members of this group were dead by the time we got the document. Interestingly, the last survivor died only two months before the document arrived. I don't know whether you can say that *that*'s convenient negatively or positively, but, anyway, I got permission. I went to the Harvard archives, discovered much to my surprise, because I didn't like Dr. Menzel when he was alive, such a debunker we don't need, I discovered that he led a double life. Oh sure, he was a Harvard professor of astronomy and he led eclipse expeditions and he served on various committees and he debunked UFOs. But, amazingly enough, he wrote John F. Kennedy in 1960 that he, Menzel, had a longer continuous association with the super-secret national security agency, the NSA, and its predecessor group, than anybody else in the country. Turned out that he had taught cryptography. Turned out he had done work for the CIA of all people and had a top-secret, ULTRA clearance, had close connections to Dr. Bush and several other people...it's a long story, but I found stuff that isn't in any of the bios of Menzel. Even people who knew him for twenty years, and I talked to some of them, didn't know, that he had learned Japanese, that he was an expert in code-breaking, that he had written some science fiction. I found his travel book and he made several trips to New Mexico in 1947 at federal government expense. It's a long, involved story and we tell part of it in the book.

But my finding, which took me totally by surprise along with everybody else in this field, certainly made it appear that Menzel belonged with those other guys. That made it much more likely that the document was genuine. I put together a big, fat report, *Final Report of Operation Majestic Twelve,* it's a hundred and eight pages long, and in it I have a list of more than thirty pieces of information, trivia if you will, that are in the documents that turn out to be true but that nobody on the outside knew at the time. Some of the dates, for instance. If you pick a date for a document and say that two people met, and one was in Berlin and one was in Tokyo, you're in trouble. So there's a lot of that kind of stuff which I found that took a lot of work for me to dig out and that nobody had dug out before that can hardly be explained away as coincidence.

Q: In his book on flying saucers in the Soviet Union, Jacques Vallee mentions Don Menzel's role in disrupting the organized efforts to form UFO study groups in the Soviet Union, although he doesn't acknowledge your research.

A: You know, one of the many interesting things about Menzel was that his 1953 book, his first book on UFOs, was translated into Russian, and because it was favorably reviewed in both the Soviet Union and the United States, in the United States by Dr. J. Allen Hynek, who was the Air Force consultant on UFOs, it effectively kept two groups of scientists, Americans and Russians, from seriously looking at UFOs. Because, after all, Menzel had spoken. How much higher can you get on the totem pole than Harvard? National Academy of Sciences and all that sort of stuff.

So those findings, I believe, are very important, totally unexpected, certainly I didn't know...some people have accused Bill Moore of faking the document, I guarantee he didn't know about Menzel's background either. Some people have suggested that, well, anybody could have just gone in to the library and found that. Well, it isn't true. The stuff is in archives, which means they bring you the boxes you ask for, but...

Q: You had to get Menzel's widow's permission, didn't you?

A: His widow's permission to read his unpublished autobiography and the head of the astronomy department, head of the Smithsonian Institution, in writing, and that took a while, before I could gain access to those papers. So the notion that anybody could have found that out...and it's the same with some of those other trivia bits that I mentioned. It took the Truman Library and the Eisenhower Library, working pretty hard, to dig out some of those pieces of information. It wasn't something that you just walk in and go rummaging around and anybody can find...it wasn't like that at all.

Q: It's interesting that you brought up J. Allen Hynek's name. Are you suggesting that he had some kind of disinformation role?

A: No, you see Hynek was many years younger, lower on the totem pole than Menzel was. And Hynek was a kind of skeptic for a long time. It was only after he left his Air Force project Blue Book role as a consultant that he started to speak up a bit, in the late 60s. Anyone who might have gotten interested in

UFOs would have turned to the two experts at that time, two astronomers. I don't know why people want to link astronomy and UFOs. Certainly astronomers aren't competent to talk about interstellar travel, technology and motivation...areas in which they are always sounding off. But any scientist who was interested would have noted the favorable review by Hynek of this negative book by Menzel. And if they read Menzel's book, they would think that there were no sightings that couldn't be explained by a smart astronomer, as long as you allowed him to change the data to match his explanation, which is what he did.

It would have taken an awful lot of courage, in other words, to go against the current, so to speak, in the field. And remember this was before the space age. Hynek once told me that in a real extreme case there might be a year in which seven satellites were launched. Astronomers know from nothing about space stuff. No, I'm not implying that Allen was part of disinformation, only that he was sticking to the party line. His excuse later on was that, well, he wanted to keep his foot in the door. Allen, I should mention...Menzel is noted in this MJ12 document as pushing for an interstellar origin for flying saucers. Not another planet in our own solar system, in other words, but other solar systems. Hynek had never done his homework about the technology of interstellar travel.

Q: I would guess that some of the incompetent assessments of interstellar travel from official sources are not intended to explain anything but to explain things away and confuse the issue.

A: I'm sure there has been some disinformation put out about flying saucers. Frankly my feeling often with some of the pro-UFO types is that with friends like this, who needs enemies? The government doesn't have to do anything.

Q: So you don't think that someone like Phil Klass is actually working officially to discredit your work?

A: I don't know. It may be a *quid pro quo* thing. Certainly as somebody who wasn't married until he was age sixty and with training in electrical engineering and working in Washington, he would have been approached by intelligence agencies. So whether he's doing *quid pro quo,* "hey, Phil, we'll give you all kinds of information but you've got to help us keep this on the back burner," or whether he honestly believes that he's protecting Americans against this nonsense, the zealot, you know, the PSICOP types.

Q: The people who know everything.

A: Yes.

Q: What do you think about the Paul Bennewitz affair and Bill Moore's confession to his role

in disinformation?

A: Well, he passed some disinformation on to Paul. He tried to convince Paul that it really wasn't worth paying a lot of attention to. Paul fell for it. It's unfortunate. Paul was determined that he was going to...I mean he looked at pictures and he saw stuff that nobody else saw on those pictures. He fell for it. But I don't consider Bill a disinformation specialist.

Q: But you do say that he does have the contacts to do this sort of thing.

A: People approached him after his book, *The Roswell Incident,* came out and said they liked his style and they'd try to help him and certainly on occasion had pieces of information they could only get from inside. Stuff about me that the outside world wouldn't have known about. So they had established their bonafides, alright. That doesn't mean you believe anything they say.

Q: Apparently there was some kind of split between you and Moore and Shandera over your cooperation with Kevin Randle and Donald Schmitt's book *UFO Crash At Roswell?*

A: That was a whole involved mess but I have also written a quite negative review of the book in the *MUFON Journal* last year because although we had all cooperated together, Don Berliner, my co-author, and Randle and Schmitt, especially for conferences sponsored by the Fund for UFO Research, we seriously disagreed over things. I know they worked darn hard, they found a lot of new witnesses, they pursued it. I suppose the difference is simple. I'm a nuclear physicist who has had to please his bosses for a lot of years and Kevin has written more than sixty seven books of fiction. I keep running across instances where he confuses what might have been with what must have been. Those aren't the same thing.

Q: Does he have a military intelligence background?

A: Yes and no. You have to be little careful about that. Kevin was a helicopter pilot in Vietnam. He went to school and joined the Reserve and in the Reserve he was an intelligence captain. I am not suggesting he therefore must be working for the government or anything like that. There's a couple of UFO encyclopedias and one of them has several articles by Kevin and his approach is close to Phil Klass' in the reasoning than it is a scientist's. That's unfortunate but I must give them credit. They found the witnesses, they worked hard at it.

I was cooperating with them but there were other reasons for the rift. Bill Moore was very upset that I didn't let him know about the *Unsolved Mysteries* program. My reason was pretty straightforward: I live in eastern Canada, Bill lives near Hollywood. I didn't figure that they would go for using me if they used him. Also, I felt that he had two shots at the whole Roswell story, first with the book, and second with what I look at as a terrible UFO show, *UFO Cover Up Live.*

We patched up our quarrels and we got together and shouted at each other for a while and agreed, what the heck, let's get on with it. It's kind of a shame. Bill shot himself in the foot at the MUFON conference in Vegas in 1989 by talking twice as long as he was supposed to, he didn't submit his paper, and he wouldn't take any questions, and he admitted that he had been involved with Bennewitz but he never said that he was sorry if there had been any problems with Bennewitz, which he should.

Q: Do you think that his admission about Bennewitz has any bearing on the credibility of the MJ12 documents?

A: No. No, I don't. I think they are completely separate matters. Bill can be a darn good researcher when he puts his mind to it. He can be very persistent, travel a lot and do a lot of digging. So you have to look at everything on its own merits. Guilt by association is not a scientific technique.

Stanton Friedman's book, Crash At Corona, *co-authored with aviation/science writer Don Berliner, is available from Paragon House (1-800-PARAGON). Friedman can be reached directly by sending a large SASE to POB 958, Houlton, ME 04730.*

Book Reviews

Committee for An Open Archives co-founder John Judge perhaps said it best to *Steamshovel* editors at the JFK assassination symposium in Chicago last June: "When you have a state based on secrecy, on covert operations and criminal activity and on manipulation and control, it's those people who don't want to use violence, who want to break free from the control, to improve human relations and rely on human trust who really are threatening to that system. And so we find that the people they spend the most time surveying and going after are those that aren't doing any violence or terrorism or illegal activity of any sort but are in fact trying to figure out a way to improve basic human values of trust and integrity, normal human relations. Because this system is designed to alienate us from each other." Presumably this spirit inspired the organization of the Chicago symposium as well as a similar event, the ASK conference in Dallas in October, and is the guiding force behind the recent successes of the improved visibility of the "conspiracy research community," for lack of a better term, more so than the recent attention foisted upon it by Hollywood. Chicago conference organizer Doug Carlson also told *Steamshovel Press* that he hopes some kind of consensus can develop within that community by the time of another conference planned for April. Next year may indeed be in a banner year for assassination research: it observes the twenty-fifth anniversaries of the deaths of Robert Kennedy and Martin Luther King, the thirtieth anniversary of JFK, and the possible advent of a Democratic administration (the last one led to the formation of the House Select Committee on Assassinations), as well as the continued momentum proffered by the efforts of Oliver Stone.

Would that the various researchers, advocates and activists spoke in one voice, however. Experience teaches that the complexity of the topic and the egos, rivalries, misunderstandings and accusations among various factions in this community make it unlikely. Mark Lane, for instance, complained to *Newsweek* editors that they attempted to discredit his work by reporting Gus Russo's doubt about testimony from Marita Lorenz he used in his book, *Plausible Denial*. *Steamshovel* reported this last issue with the note that the two extant references to the "well-respected researcher" bore a strange resemblance. Russo's name has since emerged as a consultant to Oliver Stone, *Frontline* and other documentary efforts. He introduced himself to *Steamshovel* editor Kenn Thomas in Chicago, insisting that Lane knew very well who he was. Russo also insisted on his mistrust of Lorenz, even when questioned about Frank Sturgis' break-in of her apartment during the time of her testimony to the House Select Committee.

At this weird point in the Kennedy labyrinth, *Steamshovel Press* would like to apologize to Mr. Russo for any suggestion that he doesn't exist. (It also apologizes to Perry Russo for calling him "Phillip.") Lane's point, that *Newsweek* editors used second-hand sources to discredit testimony that Lane verified with FBI documents, still needs to be made, however, and new suspicions that the mainstream media might be pitting the burgeoning "research community" against itself need to be considered. If this is a community that values communication and interaction, it also has been one tolerant of conflicting and contradictory views: questions about Lane's intelligence background have long been asked, as have those pertaining to Jim Garrison's mob connections; A. J. Weberman and Michael Canfield have made good research efforts supporting the view that E. Howard Hunt and Frank Sturgis were the railroad tramps, but Weberman does not believe in the grassy knoll gunman and others who support that view don't believe the Hunt/Sturgis scenario, and on and on. The media previously had hoped to confuse the average reader by reporting on the cacophony of conflicting views. The only consensus conspiracy researchers have ever reached seems to have been that truth will emerge from the cacophony. This is a view that can be disrupted and manipulated by the mis- and disinformation ploys in the mainstream, hence the need for the trust, integrity and communication that Judge spoke about.

In the interest of fostering communication and interaction links among various elements of the research community, *Steamshovel Press* offers the following list as the most recently visible, making no claims to being comprehensive:

John Judge's Committee for an Open Archives continues to press for the release of documents from the Warren Commission and the House Select Committee on Assassinations, despite the emasculation of legislative efforts to get this done. A twenty five dollar contribution gets updates on the work, as well as new research and transcript of media events that flashed by too fast on TV. POB 6006, Washington, DC 20005. An interview with Judge will appear in the next issue of *Steamshovel*.

Fifteen dollars will get twelve monthly issues of *Conspiracy Update,* a newsletter produced by Jon Arnold and SSG Publishing, 5715 S. Harper, Chicago,

IL 60637. According to Arnold, "unlike the American left, *Conspiracy Update* is serious about putting the CIA out of business." If this can be done by exposing a wealth of information on a variety of topics, the obvious JFK/RFK/MLK material but also including less examined issues such as the Israeli A-Bomb link to the USS Liberty and the October Surprise, readers can look forward to some success in this area.

Prevailing Winds Research offers a catalog of such, like collections from the works of John Judge, Mae Brussell, Barbara Honnegger, Daniel Sheehan, John Stockwell, etc, in affordable, accessible formats, for a one or two dollar contribution in the form of money or stamps, from POB 23511, Santa Barbara, CA 93121.

Kennedy-focused researchers would do well to send $7 plus $2 postage to Bob Harris, another Oliver Stone consultant and Gus Russo compatriot, who has pulled together an enormous amount of material into a photocopy-cum-lecture he tours with and makes available through the mail. Box 4-18, New York, NY 11215.

Steamshovel Press looks forward to hearing more from Dave Emory's *Archives on Audio,* available from POB 170023, San Francisco, CA 94117-0023.

Two recommended sources for the JFK books reviewed here: Tom Davis Books, POB 1107, Aptos, CA 95001-1107; and the Last Hurrah Bookshop, 937 Memorial Avenue, Williamsport, PA 17701. The latter carries copies of the previous issue of *Steamshovel* as well as an impressive array of JFK materials and research.

(Caution: Some publications identifying themselves as vanguards of the left, most notably *The Progressive,* consider many of the sources above "unreliable." And Alexander Cockburn still believes the findings of the Warren Commission.)

What to make of Howard Donahue's assertion, as reported by Bonar Menninger in *Mortal Error, The Shot That Killed JFK* (St. Martin's Press, $23.95), that Secret Service agent George Hickey accidentally shot JFK when he picked up an AR-15 rifle in response to gunfire from the Book Depository? Donahue does have credentials as a ballistics expert. For one thing, he remains the only marksman to perform the Warren Commission's fantasy firing feat by hitting a moving target three times with a rigged Manlicher in under 5.6 seconds. Donahue now admits the scenario is demonstrably false, but for reasons widely at variance with other critics. His thesis "explains" much evidence that others easily dismiss as faked, but he does not make a convincing argument that Hickey's actions were *accidental*—Oswald's shot could just as well have been a signal for a *coup de grace* from

inside the motorcade.

Harry Edward Livingstone's *High Treason 2, The Great Cover Up: The Assassination of President John F. Kennedy* (Carrol and Graf, $25.95), has become the latest best source for good, many and color reproductions of photographic evidence, as well as the arguments that much of it has been doctored, including that "blob" of brain matter seen on the Zapruder film. Excessive and confusing in some respects, Livingstone's book nevertheless makes passionate arguments not only indignant about the cover-up but with a view that connects JFK's death to other political murders, including those of sixteen anti-Vietnam rock stars, John Lennon among them. Livingstone also deserves credit as the only visible critic at the *Journal of the American Medical Association* press conference.

Photographs abound too in *Destiny Betrayed, JFK, Cuba and the Garrison Case* by James DiEugenio (Sheridan Square Press, $19.95), including a photo-within-a-photo of David Ferrie's brain. If Livingstone waxes almost too eloquently in his enthusiasm for Kennedy, DiEugenio does the same for Jim Garrison here. It is enthusiasm well-deserved and long overdue and a study that complements the Stone movie in many ways better than the book version of the film, but it lacks a sustained critical look at the Garrison-as-mafioso proposition, making only one reference to Carlos Marcello in the text and four in the endnotes. Any reader wondering if much of what has been revealed about the JFK assassination has surfaced because of Mark Lane's intelligence agenda or Garrison's mob connections will leave this book wanting. *Destiny Betrayed* is also distinguished, however, by an appendix containing the Shaw trial testimony of Dr. Pierre Finck, the only Bethesda autopsy doctor to resist the misdirection and falsification of the *JAMA* article. It clearly indicates military manipulation of the autopsy proceedings.

Vigorously argued theses have served to emphasize and amplify aspects of the JFK assassination in two books: *Act of Treason* by Mark North (Carroll and Graf, $26.95) and Craig Zirbel's *The Texas Connection* (Texas Connection Company, $21.95). In addition to copious documentation that J. Edgar Hoover's only response to assassination plans he learned about in September 1962 was to position himself to best take advantage of the act, North presents an old photograph in a new light. Hoover's countenance shines out from behind the hearse as JFK's casket is lowered with RFK and Jackie O. in the background. David Lifton might argue that Hoover is making sure the casket is empty.

Zirbel's book spells out the case against Lyndon Johnson. It draws together much information and renews suspicions everyone has had about Johnson since the event, but needlessly dismisses every countervailing theory at the very beginning. This is conspiracy macho, with Zirbel presenting the Johnson-did-it theory as the bully on the playground. What could the author, a co-panelist at the opening press conference in Chicago, have made of co-panelist Dick Gregory's suggestion that Johnson's death, coming weeks after his statement of belief in a conspiracy to CBS, may have been connected to JFK's, like RFK's and many eyewitnesses?

By now, Dr. Charles Crenshaw's admission in *Conspiracy of Silence* (written with Jens Hansen and J. Gary Shaw, Signet, $4.99), that at Parkland he observed a head wound inflicted from the front, has been entered into the annals. Crenshaw's soft-spoken manner belies the anguish he must feel over his thirty year silence, although he mentions this repeatedly from the lectern. One aspect of his book also deserves more attention, however: he reports that Ted Kennedy told Evelyn Lincoln, JFK's personal secretary, that autopsy materials collected by Robert Kennedy, whose public statements indicated that he would have used the power of the presidency to re-open the investigation of his brother's murder, were "under control." Here we find the suggestion of privately held materials—undoctored autopsy records—that potentially could yield more information than the recent efforts to unlock government files.

Another inexpensive Signet paperback, *The JFK Assassination: The Facts and Theories* (Signet, $4.99), is a tremendously useful overview by Carl Oglesby that includes—hallelujah—a chapter on Inslaw. Professor Oglesby mentioned to *Steamshovel* editors an "information burden" on this topic that underscores the need for this kind of handy but encapsulating short view. To this end, Oglesby (whose *Steamshovel* interview will also appear next issue) has produced a second, even slimmer and still quite comprehensive, volume for the smaller Odonian Press entitled *Who Killed JFK?* (Odonian Press, $5). Odonian specializes in affordable paperbacks examining important issues. It recently released *Burma: The Next Killing Fields* by Alan Clement, with a forward by the Dalai Lama. Contrast both with John Newman's *JFK and Vietnam* (Warner Books, $22.95) a large study continuing decades-old pioneering research begun by researchers like Peter Dale Scott. The emphasis is less the assassination than the likelihood that the trauma of the Vietnam War was not as much the product of Kennedy's sensibilities as is often assumed. Newman has made a good case that this issue should not be looked at in terms of "would Kennedy have pulled the US out of the war", but would he have instituted the same policy reversal

that cost Johnson the presidency.

—**reviewed by Kenn Thomas**

Salvador Freixedo's *Visionaries, Mystics and Contactees* (IllumiNet, $12.95) is the latest entry into the "we are chattel" school of ufological thinking, that an alien presence manipulates mankind for its own dimly perceived purposes. Freixedo served as a Jesuit priest for thirty years, wrote a book that got him kicked out of Batista's Cuba and another one that got him kicked out of the church. Church authorities apparently became nervous over some of Freixedo's theological arguments, that "miracles"—including stigmata and various paranormal gifts—are best understood as interaction with alien intelligence, not interaction with God and/or Satan.

Visionaries, Mystics and Contactees contains an intelligent critique of religion and ends with a renewal of an "immortal faith" that recognizes the spent mission of Christianity and points to the application of scientific intelligence to transcendental affairs. One could quibble with Freixedo's particulars and construct alternate theological arguments. His assertion, for instance, that various revisions of the Bible, from the Dead Sea Scrolls to the 1611 King James Bible, belie any notion of holy inspiration and infallibility. Other theologians might suggest that constant revision reveals the hand of an intelligent, ever-changing Almighty. In other places, Freixedo admonishes against the "short cut of drugs," offers a terse dismissal of homosexuality in the church, and refers to one woman contactee as "a little impressionable," indicating that he has not strayed entirely from many orthodoxies.

But Freixedo concerns himself mostly with the paranormal and the Fortean, in some instances adopting Charles Forte's laundry list approach to detailing unusual happenings. He shares that basic Fortean outlook: "something unknown uses us the same way we use animals" and while perforcely not very forthcoming about the identity the alien presence, he nevertheless reports lucidly on attempts at getting to know it. One anecdote tells of a brave woman who unsuccessfully attempts to bed one of the buggers in the name of research. Freixedo's arguments center on the notion that UFOs are "semi-real," extra-dimensional and malignant.

John Keel contributes the introduction, again deriding the majority of ufologists as porn-obsessed illiterates. Strangely, in addition to disagreeing with Keel's assessment about the size of the UFO community, Freixedo accepts as credible much of what one assumes Keel would reject: Uri Geller, Billy Meier, UMMO and even the Shaver mystery. He also mentions Jim Jones as a possible contactee, a suggestion that bears more discussion and research.

Jacques Vallee, of course, has contributed two good additions to the UFO literature: *UFO Chronicles of the Soviet Union, A Cosmic Samizdat* (Ballantine, $18.00) and *Revelations* (Ballantine, $20.00), and readers should be looking forward to the rumored publication of Vallee's journals from the 1960s as well as the film version of his 1979 book, *Messengers of Deception.* In *Cosmic Samizdat*, Vallee notes an unusual resemblance between the belt symbols on sketches of aliens made in Voronezh and the symbol found on photographs of the obviously hoaxed UMMO spacecraft. He fails to note, however, the similarity between that symbol and the company icon of his publisher. The significance of this connection will no doubt be left to that long overdue study of the relationship between synchronicity and UFOs, by Vallee or anyone who cares to undertake it.

Was it Terence McKenna who first noted the similarity between the titles *Messengers of Deception* and J. Edgar Hoover's *Masters of Deceit*? Like the UMMO/Ballantine symbol and the concession worker named Bill Burroughs who misdirected the police searching for Oswald and the Texas Theatre, it's hard to know what to make out of that as well, but McKenna's *Food of the Gods* (Bantam, $21.50) certainly contributes greatly to the understanding of psychedelic plants in history and modern culture. It is philosophically a bit quiescent, however, and maybe a bit macrobiotic for some tastes, particularly those who hold views that regard overpopulation, pollution, alienation, etc, as space migration signals. Eco-awareness, after all, is one trip among many. But McKenna makes a good study of an old conundrum: that tobacco, sugar, alcohol (and McKenna adds television to the list), which enslave and alienate people, seem favored over psychedelics, which encourage thought and natural harmony. Further proof of the veracity of the latter can be found in Wavy Gravy's *Something Good For A Change, Random Notes on Peace Through Living* (St. Martin's Press, $18.95), a memoir of the 56 year old psychedelicized personality who has harmonized rather gracefully over the years. Mr. Gravy co-founded the charitable group Seva Foundation, became director of Camp Winnarainbow, a performing arts summer camp, and enjoyed life with a number of notables, including Bob Dylan, Janis Joplin, Abbie Hoffman, Bill Graham and Ram Dass, all of whom he reminisces about here.

The varieties of psychedelic experience can also be found in two important books by independent publishers: *PIHKAL* by Ann and Alexander Shulgin (Transform Press, POB 13675, Berkeley, CA 94701; $18.95) and *Freeplay* by Len Bracken (Backbone Books, 1142 North Stuart St., Arlington, VA 22201; $8.95). *PIHKAL* presents an elaborately detailed account of love and drugs, with much "conception, synthesis, [and] definition" of the former and even the chemical structures of the latter. *Freeplay* details the fictional adventures of a group called the Players in a cross-cutting, info-bite style that almost outdoes the *JFK* movie. It would make a great hypertext, in fact, if it was available in some kind of software format. The Players traverse settings that include the Soviet Union and Yugoslavia, made even more interesting by the recent geo-political transformations, and are as familiar as the Hawaiian surf scene. Designer drugs, electromagnetic propulsion and artificial intelligence make up part of the book's intellectual landscape. Mike Gunderloy, of the late and greatly lamented *Factsheet Five,* called it "unexpectedly delightful."

Steamshovel must also apologize for last issue's typo concerning Blast Book's anthology of drug-inspired writing. It's called *The Drug User,* not *The Drug Abuser.* It's a good book, either way. Anticipating the desired location of the reviewer's head with precision, the publisher of that volume has now produced a text entitled *Guillotine: Its Legend and Lore* (Blast Books, POB 51, Cooper Station, New York, NY 10276-0051) by guillotine memorabilia and artifacts collector Daniel Gerould.

—reviewed by Kenn Thomas

4

Steamshovel Press #7, 1993

Conspiracy Writers Interviewed:
Jonathan Vankin, Robert Anton Wilson, John Judge

Jonathan Vankin: author of *Conspiracies, Cover-Ups and Crimes*

Q: Why are people interested in conspiracy theories and, secondly, if such conspiracy theories are valid, why bother to get up in the morning?

A: To take the second question first: I have heard that too, that the bad thing about conspiracy theories is that they'll create a feeling of helplessness and, as you say, if everything's a big conspiracy, why even bother? There's nothing we can do. We might as well just drop out. I disagree with that, but I understand why people say it.

I really thought that people I interviewed in my book are taking the exact opposite approach. They are activists in really sort of the deepest sense. They're constantly reading, thinking, some of them trying to do something about what they see as the problems that we face here, the Conspiracy, whatever you want to call it. And they feel that by educating themselves and others that's really the best weapon. So I think they are, in fact, trying to overcome the feeling of helplessness and trying to understand it. What I was trying to do in the book was understand it and I think, to go to the first question you asked, I think that feeling of helplessness that we all experience on a daily basis, I think a lot of Americans feel that really can't influence their government. I think that's one of the reasons that conspiracy theories are so attractive, it's really hard to understand what goes on, especially when so much of what goes on in this supposedly open, democratic society goes on in secret and it often seems are being manipulated by strange forces behind the scenes, or whatever. We're subjected on a constant basis to propaganda messages through not only the news media but advertising and entertainment. And we're sort of instilled with all sorts of conflicting wants and desires and emotions and it's hard to understand what's happening to us in this country and in the world right now. We're overloaded with information and events that move real fast. So I think conspiracy theories are an explanation of reality which I see in my book as, although not always an accurate one, often as accurate and as valid as the so-called official stories.

Q: How did you get interested in the topic and can you say a little about whether you started out as a believer and became more of one or vice versa?

A: I didn't start out as a believer. If anything, I didn't start out as a total skeptic of conspiracy theories, either. I started out as sort of an observer and an explorer of what I considered to be dangerous or heretical ideas. I've always been interested in why certain ideas are treated as heresy. Why is it that if you are a "conspiracy theorist" you are also by definition paranoid? You have some sort of a mental illness. That seemed to me like in Stalin's Soviet Union, if you disagreed with the revealed truth of the state you were committed to a mental hospital because, of course, you had to be crazy. I saw an analogy there, but then I also saw that with some of these theories there's at least a degree of validity. I wasn't all that familiar with things like the Kennedy assassination theories before I went into the book, but I didn't see how they were the nonsense that some of the Warren Commission defenders and some of the official sources make them out to be. It just seemed to me to be unfair.

So I went in trying to explore why that is, why these things are treated as stigmatized. Why they're not even considered valid. You're not even supposed to listen when someone comes up with a conspiracy theory, much less take it seriously.

Q: Kerry Thornley is one of the first interviews in your book. To get back to this idea of individuals feeling resigned to their destiny, Thornley seemed to take an almost light-hearted approach to being manipulated. Did you get that same kind of feeling from Thornley, that he kind of resigned himself to the fate of being manipulated?

A: I'm still a little puzzled about Kerry Thornley and I talk about that in the book, too. I also talked about that in an article that came out in July in a paper in New York City, the *New York Press*, where they did a story on Kerry Thornley and the writer there interviewed me. And I said that he seemed like he was serious to me but I also wasn't sure whether or not he might have been pulling my leg about all this stuff, since he has this history of sort of a Merry Prankster on a philosophical scale, going back to the *Principia Discordia* and all that sort of thing. He really enjoys intellectual jokes, satire on sort of a grand scale and I really wondered, and still wonder to some extent, whether his whole conspiracy theory is sort of a joke he's playing on himself as well as the rest of the world.

I said that in that article and I got a long letter from him and he was ruminating on that and seemed to be saying that, on the one hand he did take these things seriously, but on the other hand we can't really take anything seriously because of the nature of reality itself is so tenuous. How do we really know anything that we know? And you can sort of go on about that forever.

Q: Is that a principle that you can generalize about other people involved with conspiracy theory thinking, that maybe it's part of a lampoon or just a cock-eyed way of looking at the world?

A: I think that Kerry is probably the most self-aware. I started the book with him because he is on the surface the most crazy. He thinks that there's a bug implanted on his body and has been since birth. But at the same time, he's the most self-aware of all the people I talked to. There's other people in the book, one in particular I can think of, who take themselves extremely seriously.

Q: Who's that?

A: Dave Emory. I don't really want to say too much about it other than what I said in the book. He's a very dogmatic person and he really believes every word he says. To him, this stuff is just plain truth, even the stuff about the space shuttles possibly causing earthquakes and the whole bit. He takes it all with the utmost seriousness and, in fact, he's so serious about it that if you challenge anything that he says, especially anything about his self-image, which apparently I unwittingly did in the book, he really goes ballistic. He's done that on me since the book came out, the one person who responded that way.

Q: Did you find that attitude with the so-called "disciples" of Mae Brussell?

A: Actually, no. Which is why I was kind of shocked by Emory's reaction. Some of the other people who admire Mae Brussell admire her for the same reason that I admire her, which is that she was a real intellectual pioneer. Not in the sense of that she was necessarily coming up with some new truth but that she was exploring unexplored areas. In my introduction to the book I say consider the whole book to be a voyage, sort of like Darwin on the Beagle when he went out and stopped in lands that hadn't been widely explored before and took samples and came back with these samples with a new view of the whole world. That's what I was trying to do in the book and I think that was sort of what Mae Brussell was trying to do too. As wacky as she could be, she wasn't a proselytizer. She didn't tell people that if they didn't believe this stuff they must be agents themselves or they're part of the conspiracy. She really was a very deep thinker in her way.

Q: She opened so many different cans of worms. When you put together your book, how did you decide what to discuss and what to leave out?

A: A lot of it had to do with whether I could find, not necessarily verification, but at least corroboration. If I could track down some of the information that these people were presenting to me as fact. For instance, if they said Jonestown was a CIA mind control experiment, well I wanted to go back and see what facts they based this on. And they would cite them to me. They would say that the Guyanese coroner found that most of the victims were not suicides but murders. So I would go back and find a *New York Times* saying that very thing and I would cite that in my notes. That's just one out of hundreds of examples in the book. They would say it's known that there was a CIA agent present at Jonestown. Turns out that there's news reports saying that at the time as well. So I just wanted to go back to the public record and see what could be found.

Q: Were you in touch with the people that you discussed in your chapter on *Votescam* during the election? How did they take it all and how did the News Election Service work in this last election?

A: Well, it worked the same way it always works. Interestingly, on the night before the election I was on a show in New York on WBAI in which Jim Collier, the co-father of the Votescam theory, was also on and he's pretty much sticking to his theory. I haven't talked to him since the election but at that time he was definitely sticking to it, plus he added on the fact that, and this is a fact, that not only are election returns centralized now, exiting polling is also centralized. There's one company that handles all the exit polling. So when the networks announce the exit poll results early in the evening, which they were relatively conscientious about holding back on this year, those are all coming from the same source.

Q: Were either of the Collier brothers suggesting that this centralized process had been bought out this time?

A: I think they suggest that's it's been bought out from day one. That's why they are conspiracy theorists as opposed to simply political researchers or scholars.

Q: So if Clinton won then he didn't win by a general electoral landslide or a popular vote, he won because whoever controls these centralized processes of vote tallying wanted him to win. Or were they saying that Bush was going to win and they were wrong?

A: I didn't hear Jim Collier make a prediction, actually, but if they're going to stick by their theory it's kind of inevitable that they'd have to suggest that. And they're not the only ones that have that kind of theory. Mae Brussell always said that the President is picked twenty years in advance and presumably Bill Clinton would have been picked twenty years in advance. If you want to spin the whole scenario out, Bush certainly wasn't a very good president, I don't think, and so if you're the mastermind of this conspiracy you're going to want him out of there.

Talking about Clinton and conspiracy theories, to jump into another chapter in the book, about the Trilateral Commission, are your familiar with the book *Tragedy and Hope*?

Q: Yes.

A: To briefly explain it, the John Birch Society has this theory about the Trilateral Commission and these international...Council on Foreign Relations and all this stuff. And one of the books they often cite is by a Georgetown University professor named Carol Quigley, who I believe is now deceased, called *Tragedy and Hope*, which is about an eleven hundred page manifesto exposing in a favorable way this alleged conspiracy. And the Birchers cite this as evidence that this conspiracy is very real and that here's a guy who likes the conspiracy, thinks they're doing all these great things, the Rockefellers and the Morgans of the world are doing all these fantastic things, and just wanted to write about it. So anyway, the book *Tragedy and Hope* by Carol Quigley is a cornerstone of the Birch Society theory. Now in Bill Clinton's acceptance speech at the Democratic Convention, his acceptance of the nomination, he singled out Carol Quigley as one of the people who was one of the major influences in his life!

So here you have Bill Clinton who's sort of this "made" Trilateral man, a guy who is coming from outside the northeastern so-called liberal establishment, being brought into it, being trained by people like Quigley at places like Georgetown University and pub-

licly acknowledges Carol Quigley as one of the biggest influences on his life. As opposed to Bush, who is sort of a "born" Trilateral man, born into the family and pre-ordained that he would be part of the eastern establishment.

Q: Does Carol Quigley claim any affection for the Birch Society?

A: Not for the Birch Society, no. He claims affection for the insiders who are running the alleged conspiracy. The Birchers believe that there's this conspiracy of insiders, the Rockefellers, the Rothschilds, the Morgans, who pretty much have been running things through organizations like the Trilateral Commission, the CFR, for a very long time. Now in *Tragedy and Hope*, Quigley, who is a professor of politics, agrees with them, says there is such a conspiracy, but the thesis of his book is to say that these people have done wonderful, wonderful things. It's a benevolent conspiracy. "Yes, they operate in secret but I, Carol Quigley, think they are so wonderful, I want to tell the public about them." And that's what *Tragedy and Hope* is about. So Quigley is a Trilateralist, or was, he might have died even before the Commission was even founded, I don't know. Probably not, but he's been dead for a while. In any case, he was Trilateralist himself and Clinton cites him as this tremendous influence.

Q: Now that the paperback version of *Conspiracies, Cover Ups and Crimes* is out, what are your current projects?

A: I have a couple of other ideas for conspiracy-oriented books, but I haven't been able to sell them yet. I'm working on a novel.

Q: Is your novel conspiracy related?

A: Overtones, yeah, but it's not an out-and-out thriller. There's a lot of materials in here, though. I've certainly been tempted to spin some of them off but just haven't put my mind to it yet.

Robert Anton Wilson: author of *Reality Is What You Can Get Away With*

Q: Is the new book going to be published by New Falcon?

A: No, the new book is published by Dell Books, who've handled most of my fiction for the last ten years or so.

Q: So this new work is fiction.

A: Yes.

Q: And it's called?

A: *Reality is What You Can Get Away With.*

Q: Is this the latest volume in the current Historical Illuminatus series?

A: No, this is outside that series. The Historical

Illuminatus series is being published by Penguin Books.

Q: I see.

A: I've got four publishers. It's complicated, but that's the way it works out sometimes. *Reality Is What You Can Get Away With* is a novel in the form of a screenplay which has got as much structure as a Monty Python routine, at least.

Q: I'm always taken aback at how prolific you are. I think I just received a copy of *Cosmic Trigger II,* and for some reason I always think of you in terms of Thomas Pynchon, who writes similar kinds of things, but he does a novel every twenty years, and doesn't talk to anybody.

A: Yeah, somehow he makes a living from it. I don't know how. I've got to keep writing as fast as I can, or I'll go broke.

Q: And what are your audiences like these days? Are you getting any kind of feedback Post-Reagan that you weren't getting, say, in the late Seventies?

A: I still get largely young audiences. There's always a scattering of people of all ages, right up to my own age, which is sixty. But still, I attract mostly people around twenty, some under twenty.

Q: How do you see your early work, in terms of your present-day environment? Has a lot of what you predicted come true? Do you expect the same kind of things in the future?

A: The major thing I predicted was that there wouldn't be a nuclear war, and that humanity would survive. I feel vindicated by recent events on that issue, anyway. I write non-fiction, as well as fiction, and it's curious that in my fiction, some of the weird things in my fiction, have turned out to be true, and I wasn't even trying to be a prophet. In *Schroedinger's Cat,* a science fiction trilogy I did in 1979, I have America being overrun by armies of homeless people, and that was supposed to be crazy satire of the worst that could happen. And now it's really happened. Sometimes I feel a little bit guilty, like I caused it.

Q: Did you see *JFK,* the Oliver Stone movie and could you pluck your brain specifically about where you were on November 22?

A: I not only saw *JFK,* I saw the first show on the first day it opened here where I live, in Santa Cruz. I was very curious, I couldn't wait, and I had to get out and see it right away, before I could read any reviews, so I could make sure I was making up my own mind. And I think it's the greatest movie since *Citizen Kane,* fifty years ago. It's innovative in its film techniques like *Citizen Kane,* and politically it's hot as burning coals, just like *Citizen Kane,* and I liked it a great deal.

I can see, dramatically, why Stone picked Garrison. The more responsible conspiracy researchers don't make interesting stories, they sit and do research, and write books. That's not cinematic. Garrison took a man into court and had a trial. That's cinematic. So naturally, Garrison was the cinematic hero.

Q: So you don't have a very high regard for Garrison's research?

A: No, not at all. My feeling was that a lot of his evidence was very slapdash, and he didn't impress me very much. His evidence didn't impress me.

Q: Still, what do you think about Stone's basic premise - that JFK was killed because he was going to get us out of Vietnam?

A: Well, it's possible, but I don't believe it.

Q: Why do you think it did happen, then?

A: There are a dozen alternative theories that are just as plausible. I think the Mafia had a lot of reasons for wanting to get rid of Kennedy, especially their concept of honor. He took a lot of help from them to win Illinois, and then he double-crossed them and started throwing them in jail. That's the kind of thing they regard as dishonorable and worthy of punishment. And there's a lot of evidence pointing in that general direction, of the Mafia, but then again there's evidence pointing in the direction of the CIA, but I'm not at all sure you can distinguish the Mafia and the CIA any more. The two are so intertwined that it's like one entity rather than two.

Q: Some people have suggested that the CIA introduced LSD into the culture to de-politicize young people, the militants and the social activists became the image of the "hippy-dippy" stoned-out people just laying out in the grass.

A: Well, we survived. I'm not going to deny being a CIA agent. Hell, the more you deny it, the more people think that there must be some truth in it, like the story about LBJ spreading the rumor that, when he was running for congress, that his opponent was a *swinophiliac.* You can say that if you say it in Latin. That's somebody who has an inordinate sexual attraction to pigs, hogs, and other distinguished varieties of swine. And someone asked LBJ, "What do you expect to accomplish by all this?" And LBJ says, "At least I'll make him deny it!" I'm not going to deny every idiot charge that's laid against me, because that makes it sound like they were taken seriously, and there might be some truth in them.

Q: Let's talk a bit about the old motto: Space Migration, Life Extension, and the Intensification of Intelligence. Are these still three things that concern you, and how do you feel they've been developing?

A: I'm still very interested in all three of them,

and I'm glad more and more people have spent more and more time in space colonies, and more and more people are drinking smart drinks than booze, and that life extension research is moving along very rapidly. I think a lot of other things have to happen first before we're ready for space migration. I'm more interested in Bucky Fuller's plan to integrate all of the electrical grids in the world into one grid, which will make electricity cheaper for everybody, and show the governments and corporations of the world that they've got more to gain by cooperating than they have by conspiring against one another. I agree with Buckminster Fuller - when you show them something that works, and they see how they can make a profit out of it, you turn them around.

Q: Are you disappointed, say, in the breakup of the Soviet Union, and of the consequence that it had on their space program, and our own program sort of limping along the way it does?

A: No, I think the breakup of the Soviet Union was absolutely wonderful. It put the CIA and that whole segment of our government in a hell of a jam. How can you have an arms race when you're only racing against yourself? They've got to find some substitute for the arms race now, and they're desperately looking for something that won't involve improving the living conditions of most of us, because if we are allowed to develop the way technology could allow us to develop, then we'd all be billionaires, and they wouldn't feel superior to us anymore. It's the sentient primate drive to get higher on the tree than anybody else that governs all ruling classes. I also think the Soviet change began in 1989, with the collapse of the Berlin Wall, and it's just when Bucky Fuller predicted it would happen in his book *Critical Path,* published in 1981.

Q: So, you don't feel then that the space programs of the world are stunted, or not what they should be?

A: No, once the dunderheads in Washington begin to realize that there is no more Cold War, once they really understand it fully, I think that if we keep the economy going, they'll have to invest in space, which is the place where you can get the biggest return on new investment now, and there's more out there than there is on the surface of the planet, because there's more out there!

Q: Ireland recently went through a controversy involving a very young girl not being allowed to leave the country to have an abortion. Could I get your impressions of Ireland, and what kind of a culture allows this to happen?

A: In the first place, that was obviously a put-up job. I don't deny that the girl was pregnant, but women leave Ireland every day and have abortions in England. It's a well known fact. Every side in the abortion debate in Ireland admits it. The estimates of how many go to England every year vary from three thousand to six thousand. Four thousand seems to be the most popular figure. Nobody knows. There's no way they can control it. Ireland may be Catholic, but it's got a lot of common sense, and it's not totalitarian. So the idea of giving women pregnancy tests before they get on a ferry to Liverpool just won't float. Nobody knows how many women going to England are pregnant when they leave and not pregnant when they get back. Somebody for some reason decided that this girl should become a test case, and announced that was why they were going to England. So the government tried to stop it and the Supreme Court realized that this would make everyone look totally idiotic to the rest of Europe. There's also the economic factor there. If the case goes to the European Supreme Court, Ireland has to obey, or drop out of the EEC. And if they drop out of the EEC, that will cost them millions of dollars every year. So they'd rather not go to the European Supreme Court.

Q: Why did you leave Ireland?

A: Chiefly, my wife and I missed our children and our friends back here, and the climate. As much as I may like Ireland, the climate gets you down after a while if you're used to California weather.

Q: Did you favor any particular candidate in this race this year?

A: Wile E. Coyote.

Q: Wile E. Coyote! Beep-beep! Are there any last thoughts? Anything you want to communicate?

A: Yeah, a phrase from William Butler Yeats, a great Irish poet: "A statesman is an easy man, he tells his lies by rote. A journalist invents his lies, and rams them down your throat. So stay at home and drink your beer and let the neighbors vote."

Annual subscriptions to Robert Anton Wilson's newsletter, Trajectories, *are available for $20 from Permanent Press, POB 700305, San Jose, CA 95170.*

John Judge: Co-founder of the Committee For An Open Archives

Q: Can you tell us a little bit about the Committee for an Open Archives?

A: The Committee was formed by myself and researcher William Kelly, back in November of last year, before the JFK movie was out. We were kind of working behind the scenes, just trying to use what influence we could, in Congress, to kick open the House Select Committee on Assassinations records about John F. Kennedy and Martin Luther King. And after the movie, certainly, there was this tremendous groundswell of both media interest and response from across the country, wanting to get the files open. The movie makes mention of both the House Select Committee files, which were locked up for fifty years, until 2029, and the Warren Commission record, which was locked up for seventy-five years, by Lyndon Johnson, and so that stretches out until 2038.

Since then, a number of other researchers in the field have joined with us, and are on our advisory board, including Fletcher Prouty, Robert Groden, Peter Dale Scott, and Gaeton Fonzi, who was also on the House Select Committee staff; and we've sent invitations to a number of others who have come on. Bill Davis from the Christic Institute, out on the West Coast, is on our advisory board now. So it's an expanding number of people, those researchers that are doing the real work, and are willing to work together, have come along with us to try to make a national concerted effort to get the files loose.

They've also been, in the course of that, re-defining what we should ask for. Carl Oglesby, for instance, whom we spoke to, mentioned that there are remaining ballistic and acoustic and other medical tests that could be done, fruitfully, on the hard evidence in the case if it was to be released. It's under a slightly different situation than some of the other government documents, because it belongs to the National Archives only as a deed of gift from the Kennedy family, and Kennedy family attorney Burke Marshall has been in charge of who can see it, according to the terms of the gift, and I guess his opinions, since that time. So when Cyril Wecht got into the Archives in 1967 — one of the few honest doctors to see the record — he noted that the brain, and X-ray and slide photographs of the chest cavity existed in the record, but when he asked for them, he was told by the archivist that they weren't there — that they were missing. The archivist takes the official position that they never had any of this material, even though it's inventoried as being accepted in.

So there's that level, and then there are also additional investigative records, like in the Church Committee, which dealt with political assassinations; and the records of the FBI, especially Division Five, Domestic Operations Division; Office of Naval Intelligence records that would have concerned Oswald, and perhaps other key figures in the case; Defense Industrial Security Command records — another agency named in much of the good research that I've seen, as being involved, and a name that crops up later in other contexts; and of course, CIA and FBI in general. Those files, as well as all Senate and Congres-

sional investigative files, but the intelligence files as well, need to be released; and then, Peter Dale Scott has pointed out that there's not only what the House Select Committee had on hand, or the Warren Commission had on hand, but there were also files that they were allowed to see at the intelligence agencies that were then taken back from them. There's also a gag rule on all the House Select Committee on Assassinations employees. When they worked for the House Select Committee, they had to sign a lifelong secrecy agreement, due to the efforts of Mr. Robert Blakey, Chief Counsel to the HSCA and Louis Stokes, D-Ohio, the Chair of the Committee; and we would like to see that gag rule lifted as well, so that beyond seeing the documents, we could talk to some of these researchers about what they felt they found out from what they saw.

We do have lists of what was put in, at the time these rules for secrecy were applied, and we can compare that to what would come out. We have no doubt that other things may in fact be missing or destroyed, or partially revealed, but we are pushing for the strongest possible bill to make materials immediately public, fully public, without further review and without limitation as to which documents would be seen or who could see them. Over the years, for instance, they've tried to specify that only certain historical scholars, or qualified doctors that they would name, would be able to go in and look at these materials or photographs, and we think that it really should be a full, public opening. There's so much, since 1948, when the national security state came into existence, that's been buried.

Q: They've introduced the language again that only those files that don't endanger national security, or name specific agents, for instance, will be released.

A: Exactly, and the national security excuse was the door that they drove the truck through in the first place. So leaving that in — and that appears in another bill, also, "vital national security interests" — that was brought by Congressman James Trafficant, from Ohio [Dem.], that talks about releasing all the records, and making them public, unless vital national security is involved. Who is going to determine that, and how they are going to determine it, is laid out in the Stokes and Boren bill in probably the worst possible way. It will be a period of three years, possibly, and maybe even longer, but certainly up to three years, before a full review is done.

Now we've waited almost thirty years for some of these documents, and they want three years more. Their bill doesn't even touch the King assassination materials; it only talks about Kennedy. It talks about a broad range of agencies, but then they would appoint an executive director and a review committee. And these people would have to, currently, not be government employees, although there's nothing saying they couldn't have been government employees in the past, and they have to also not have been part of any investigation into the assassination of John F. Kennedy in the past. That's interesting, because it wouldn't leave out those that killed him, just exclude those that investigated it, although, in some cases, they were one and the same, I believe — the cover-up and the assassination people were the same.

But this group would then be chosen — and it's language that's reminiscent of the Warren Commission — people that the public would trust, and this is to restore public interest. I mean, the assumption is, there's nothing there, there was nothing to hide, they locked all this up for absolutely no reason, but if we, the public, insist on seeing it, well, let's do that, and then we'll show them that there was nothing there and that they've been suspicious for no reason, and we've got a great government, and the government can afford to be open to the public. But, in this document, they list about seven different reasons, including the ones you mentioned, for not releasing materials; another one that's quite interesting is if it would substantially invade the privacy of an individual. Now, privacy isn't a concern in a homicide investigation. And that's what this is, an unsolved murder, and the statute of limitations hasn't ended. But this goes so far as to say that the name of the person whose privacy is being invaded doesn't even have to be mentioned in the document that's being suppressed. Somehow, I guess, if you could figure out who they were talking about, they won't release the document on this ground.

All these decisions are made, first, by the executive director, and he's allowed to not only hire staff from outside, but to get detailed members of other executive branch agencies to come in: in other words, he could detail a whole group of CIA and defense intelligence agents to do this sorting. And that would fit under the bill's definition. Even though he is not currently working with the government, all the other hands-on people could be, and could be in fact in the intelligence network. Once those files are initially reviewed, this executive director would put some aside, and say these are to be postponed, or for review to see whether they should be postponed, and then the review committee can, for a definite but not determined period of time, postpone their release, even beyond the end of the three-year period. And there doesn't seem to be a limit on how long that would be; they would just have to name a year. They can also, under this bill, release parts of a document, or summarize a document, rather than release it, or substitute a document. This language is right in the bill. For the original document, that would not compromise these so-called security matters. So we have to, at public expense ...

Q: I'm sorry, John—substitute a document? You mean they can create a whole new document?

A: Yes, that's the language. It says that they can either issue part of a document, or substitute a document, or — here's some of the language; it says, "With respect to each assassination material, or particular information assassination material, the disclosure of which is postponed, or for which only substitutions or summaries have been released to the public pursuant to these subsections," — the bill would allow for that — "the review board will append the material with all records ..." And so it talks openly about the fact that they can give you another document and say, this is the one you can see for now. I mean, this is *1984* in print, this bill. And it's legalizing a whole process of needless review that, once again, obviously, is going to vacuum-clean this, scrub it one more time, just in case there's something in there that somebody might draw from.

Q: Wouldn't the most incriminating files have been destroyed a long time ago, and it's just blowing a lot of smoke trying to get these files?

A: I think that things have been destroyed. As I mentioned, I think we can track major sections of the files that, if they're no longer there, we can at least expose that fact. There are specific documents we know about, and that the research community knows about, especially concerning Oswald, the CIA and U2, and military intelligence connections, the Oswald-in-Mexico sequence, and background on Ruby and other key figures in the case, that have never been revealed, and really should be at this point. Some of the Warren Commission stuff has come out over the years, under the Freedom of Information Act, but of course that's been doctored under the provisions of that bill as well, in many cases. But it is the case that each thing that's been released has told us a little more, if not about the crime itself, at least about the cover-up, and about how the Warren Commission lied, and how duplicitous and conscious the cover-up was. So I would stand first just on the principle that these materials belong to us, even if there's no smoking gun. I would in fact be suspicious if we found a smoking gun. I would think that it was probably planted, and my guess at this point is, it would have Castro's fingerprints on it.

Q: John, who is served when Mark Lane writes a book like *Plausible Denial,* where he takes somebody like E. Howard Hunt to trial?

A: Well, if you want to focus the case on Mongoose...you have to understand that Lane, for many years, refused to say who killed Kennedy. He said he'd be as irresponsible as the Warren Commission. He gave the same lecture verbatim for over a decade, without any new information or facts. More recently, he's taken this position of fingering Hunt. And Hunt clearly can't explain where he was in Dallas. But it goes only so far as the CIA and Mongoose, and the anti-Castro Cubans, and quite possibly the idea of a "rogue element" in the CIA, that was working outside of known channels. But the solution to the case doesn't rest there. The anti-Castro Cubans and the CIA were used. The Mob was used. Dallas oil men were used. A number of people that had reasons to hate John F. Kennedy, or be afraid of him, were put in the position, I believe, of even being allowed to think that they alone had carried out the assassination.

But the strings that were being pulled were beyond the capabilities of any CIA schlepper, any anti-Castro Cuban, any Mob goon, in New Orleans or Miami or elsewhere. This was a military coup d'etat on November 22, 1963. The government was taken over. The defense of the United States was compromised. The Strategic Air Command bomber pilots in the air that hour had no codebooks in their lockers to respond to national emergency or nuclear alert. The plane bringing the Cabinet back from a meeting in Hawaii on Vietnam, similarly, was missing a codebook. The entire government phone grid in D.C., for all the Federal offices except the Pentagon and the White House, went dead. The Joint Chiefs of Staff were the only ones that could have coordinated those events. There was an entire division flying over the country, in Kansas, on its way back from Germany, that was on alert. The 112th Military Intelligence Group, out of Texas, which normally would have backed up the Secret Service in providing security on the Dallas parade route, was called down. These aren't things that a mobster or even E. Howard Hunt could pull off, much less to then create the Warren Commission and the top levels of people that were involved in that cover-up. Oswald was from military intelligence, from DIA [Defense Intelligence Agency]: these are initials that aren't usually heard. Army Intelligence, Navy Intelligence, all the branch intelligences, the DISC, the NRO, the National Reconnaissance Organization; the NSA, the National Security Agency.

Defense Industrial Security Command, DISC, is the largest police force in the United States, and has absolutely no civilian oversight, much less knowledge about it. It was DISC guards at Kerr-McGee that surrounded Karen Silkwood's house, and were responsible for poisoning her with radiation, and eventually for killing her, not because she was exposing plant safety violations, but because she had unearthed the fact that DISC guards were smuggling bomb-grade plutonium out of the plant. It was going through the Mossad and then on to South Africa. These people guard all the atomic energy installations, all the government's large military contracting sites, the Voice of America, the American information agency, and all the different key sites of the military-industrial complex, as well as Red Stone Arsenal, from the fifties. They were originally started as a police force to guard the secrets of the Manhattan Project, down in the Tennessee Valley, under David Lilienthal. And they've moved from that position forward. And there's nobody looking at these people, and these agencies don't come up.

You can get a charter of the CIA and see what you think about it. Its budget is ten times less than the DIA. CIA and FBI combined don't come to that budget. DIA employs thousands more agents than the CIA does. They're the largest and most effective domestic and international spy agency. They tap all phones, they monitor all electronic communications; they look at everything through satellites the world around. They can see a golf ball from the sky, you know. And they're the ones that really are in charge of Office of Naval Intelligence, it's the oldest intelligence agency in the United States. It dates back almost to the inception of the United States, and yet I can only find five books in print about the Office of Naval Intelligence. You can find hundreds of books in print about the CIA and what it did or didn't do. I'm not saying it's not dangerous. But I'm just saying it's not the only thing out there in the panoply of what runs American intelligence. And the military-industrial complex, that Eisenhower warned about, slapped Kennedy in the face and took over this country, November 22, '63, and they've had us in a death grip since that day.

The Committee for an Open Archives can be reached at POB 6008, Washington, DC 20005 or call 202-310-1858.

Science as Credo
by Roy Lisker

It seems to me that there are too many persons in today's intellectual agar-agar who discovered at some early stage in their career that they could feather their nest egg through merely the interminable cranking of a handful of dependable algorithms in obsessive-compulsive fashion, in much the same way as the Hindu peasant chews his betel-nuts, the cracker-barrel philosopher his wad of chaw, or the elderly Jewish housewife in Miami Beach her bag of sunflower seeds - and thereby concluded that any real effort towards a higher spiritual or cultural life was a waste of time.

For a great deal of science is nothing more than such forms of compulsive cud-chewing. truly original ideas are few; many famous scientists have built their entire careers on one or two ideas.

In mathematics (the science with which I have the greatest familiarity), those who developed two original and entirely unconnected trains of thought are given special mention in the biographies and histories of the science: Bernhard Riemann, for work in both complex variables and differential geometry; or Gauss for work in number theory, probability and physics.

Really independent ideas are difficult to come by in any field - and by "idea" I mean something like 'evolution' or 'the square root of minus one', or 'the atom.' Consider Thomas Hardy, capping a successful career as a novelist with a second career as a poet. Serving us as the exception which proves the rule, his poetry, though much of it be of a high quality, is monotone in its affect of dreary gloom. He is fond, for example, of grieving the miseries of children who aren't even born yet!

Most scientific work, to return to the point, is mechanical, methodical, repetitive and dull. A person may turn out several hundred papers in his lifetime of work without the grace of a single idea worthy of the name. It must be stressed that this in no way negates his competence, dedication or 'credibility.' He can indeed be quite a good scientist.

Yet one retains the impression, buttressed by numerous historic encounters with every sort of bully in scientist's clothing, that a lifetime of this sort will reinforce an impoverishment of the soul, stinginess of the heart and narrowness of mental vision that is really hardly any different from that of the medieval monk, scribe, soldier or peasant - whom to despise being one of the more thrilling blood sports of half a millennium.

A few months ago, I attended a poetry reading given by Czech poet/neurophysiologist Miroslaw Holub, at the Lamont Library of Harvard University. I liked his poetry quite a bit; I am sure he is also a good neuro (etc.), and know him also as a prominent activist in the years between Dubcek and Havel. Commenting on the differences between literary theory and scientific work, Holub related this conversation between Paul Valery and Albert Einstein:

Valery asked Einstein: "Albert, answer me this: when you get a new idea, do you run to your notebooks to write it down as fast as you can before it's forgotten?" To which Einstein replied: "In our profession, Paul, a new idea arises so very rarely, that one is not likely to forget it, even years later."

To support my thesis: that the scientists of the modern world are in no sense the torchbearers of true civilization, but are little different (in the majority), than the brain-dead scholastics of the Middle Ages, I have identified a Credo of thirteen articles resembling the dogmatic catechisms of various cults and creeds, such as the words of the Mass, the laws of Leviticus, the Nicene Creed, the Benedictine Rule, the Confessions of Faith, the Book of Common Prayer, and the like:

The Scientist's Credo

I. *That research be its own justification, whether its purpose be noble, silly or malevolent.*

We see this in particular in research on animal subjects, however there are many examples to be taken from all the sciences. The truism that many discoveries which were useless at the time they were made turned out to be of some use, even a century or two later, has, in our own day, been elevated into the above principles, which asserts that "All research MUST be valuable because it MAY be useful." Such an argument would, in the older religious credos, be equivalent to an exhortation to monks to commit murders because they might find something which, thirty years later, will give them some good reasons to instruct novices in the evils of murder.

II. *That there are hidden laws of Nature which* **guarantee** *that the fruits of All research must* **ultimately** *be of benefit to mankind.*

This is a stronger version of Article I: however, the emphasis here is on the "hidden laws," which posit a kind of ultimate "Moral Essence," or "Unconditioned Virtue," in research. There has been no attempt, as far as I know, made by anyone to discover these laws or to derive them from raw data. I may myself approach the NSF to underwrite a few decades of Research to validate or invalidate the belief that Ultimate Goodness lies at the bottom of All Research.

III. *That the unbelievable amounts of suffering inflicted on living creatures, including human beings, through research in biology, medicine, psychology, and related Sciences, have been as necessary to our Salvation as torturings were necessary to the Salvation of the victims of the Inquisition.*

The definition of salvation changes from one era to the next, but the facts of power and sadism undergo little alteration. As long as there exist so many highly qualified professionals in respected fields who enjoy causing suffering to the helpless, it matters little that they toil in this service of some given creed or another one. Ten minutes of rational judgement could cancel 50% of all the experiments in which living creatures are subjected to such horrible tortures. (It is my belief that this figure can be raised to 100%, but that constitutes another essay.)

Still, there is no arguing with Salvation.

IV. *That there exists a well-defined methodology known as the "Scientific Method," and that every intelligent person not only knows what it is, but has exactly the same idea of what it is.*

We are here confronted with yet another classical barge before the tugboat dilemma: the standard definition of intelligence as after all that mental factor which understands and uses the "Scientific Method." The vulgar definition of this method, that which is adhered to by most members of the scientific community, is some dreary mix of Positivism and Empiricism. Positivism claims that Universals can be proven by the accumulation of Particulars, while Empiricism claims that facts, and facts alone, are self-evident.

In point of fact, this author knows quite a large number of intelligent people who don't buy either of these viewpoints, but they are also not among the legions who recite the Credo every morning upon rising.

V. *That Science is not responsible for its creations.*

We all know that Szilard, Fermi, Ulam, Feynman, Oppenheimer, etc., didn't make the A-bomb: God made the A-bomb. One is reminded of the famous remark of Pope Clement II in the 15th century, when he was asked how he and his friends might, in good faith, throw all the gold plates used during their daily feast through the windows of the Vatican and into the Tiber River, while at the same time most of Europe was starving:

"God made the papacy; it's our business to enjoy it."

VI. *That Science has absolute control over its creations.*

Most of us go to sleep secure in the knowledge that genetic engineers are following all those guidelines (that they, in their superior wisdom also established), and that therefore Godzilla will not spring out of a test-tube, at least not while we're alive.

It might appear to the discerning that Principles V and VI cannot both be true: yet that is the nature of true Religion, which cannot be imagined without paradox and contradiction! Read, for example, Rudolph Otto's "The Idea of the Holy."

VII. *That the lifelong gratification of idle curiosity MUST produce all the raptures experienced by the mystics of the Middle Ages.*

What indeed is this much jubilated "Scientific Method," if not the promise of some delectation of infinite and perpetual bliss in the discovery, for example, that (Catalan's Conjecture), the Diophantine Equation, $xy - uv = 1$, has only one non-trivial solution in integers, namely $x = 3$, $y = 2$, $u = 3$; or that the uncovering of counter-examples, if there are any, would require more computer capacity than that presently available over the entire planet!

Alas, that Plotinus, Meister Eckhart, Heinrich Suso, Thomas a Kempis, St. John of the Cross, and so many others, were not born in our glorious age of scientific faith, so that they might achieve Union with the Ultimate Reality through computing 20 million roots of the Reinmann Zeta on the line $s = 1 + iy$, or through bashing in the brains of a thousand monkeys to learn about head injuries, or through counseling the world for more than half a century that it must find some way of copulating with its mothers to achieve psychological health, or through using the inhabitants of Bikini as guinea pigs for the study of radiation sickness, or through elaborating very complex and involuted theories with no experimental basis, no predictive power, and hardly any theoretical purpose, such as string theory in particle physics.

Twenty years of wasted effort in the elaborate gymnastics of string theory must be worth, in the free market, at least a dozen visions of the Virgin Mary in 10th century gold crowns.

VIII. *That Science is value-free.*

Most of these abominations are justified, sooner or later, by arguments to the effect that Science is unable to determine values. There is, in other words, a limit even to the great powers of the Scientific Method. A book of matches is also value-free; this hardly gives us the right to use it for the purposes of burning down someone's house.

The "ultimate benefit" argument, and the "value

free" argument are frequently employed by the same official personages, usually in the same paragraph.

IX. *That Science is the highest value.*

The metaprinciple: there is no contradiction in contradictory principles, is invoked with a high frequency in all organized religions; and, as a religion, Science is nothing if not organized, perhaps the most highly organized in the history of organized religion. One can well imagine, for example, that the author of this essay, sick unto dying from the gangrene of functional employment, would derive quite a lot of satisfaction and a good income by joining the ranks of Walter Sullivan, James Gleick, Gina Kolata, Isaac Asimov and so on, by writing a science column for some magazine or daily newspaper.

This is indeed true, the trouble being that he is unable to pay homage to the drivel demanded by the Religion of Science, a spiritually emaciated cult worship of such universal acceptance, that "science writing," "science proselytizing," and "science worship," are inseparable in the public consciousness.

The Article of Faith which requires us to believe that "Science," as a metaphysic and mass opiate, is the highest and most enduring value, has prevailed over two centuries that it has turned almost all of our schools and colleges, and certainly all of our big universities, into either technical schools or research institutes. Things have changed very little since the 12th century Sorbonne, when Theology was lord of all, and all other intellectual endeavors had to go begging. It is only the name of the game which is different.

In today's schools, Philosophy has been reduced to an inane, somewhat fecal, obsession with sententious doubt. Letters apologizes for its very existence. There's no money in an English degree, and the teaching of Languages for any profession outside the diplomatic corps has fallen to such a low level that even the pampered scientists of our day are in danger of losing their grasp on the scientific treasures of the past 500 years, almost all of which were written in Latin and Greek - indeed, scientists in today's America can't even speak a good French, German or Russian, something unimaginable 70 years ago.

Culture is ridiculed with a sorry yawn; mathematicians, physicists, biologists, or even chemists who imagine themselves on the slashing edge of knowledge will make comments about modern art, music or poetry that a poor lonesome cowboy, far from the centers of learning and art would be ashamed to utter.

Such is the power of FAITH.

X. *That non-scientific thought is ignorant, superstitious or crazy and merits ridicule and even persecution.*

Read Stephen Hawking's *Brief History of Time.*

His account of the history of Science is factually threadbare - yet quite valuable in presenting the "Standard Model" of European Science: *every advance was halted by obscurantist monks and Popes who burned Giordano Bruno, silenced Galileo, taught the unlettered that the Earth was flat, and so on.*

While not disputing the validity of these charges, it is very clear that the things which Hawking, or *Star Trek*, or *Nova*, or the *Shape of the World*, or Asimov, or Sagan (Carl, not Francoise), or Hofstader, or hosts of others really don't like about the Medieval Church, is the presence of a strong and well-organized competition.

This myopic view of history also fails to understand that the kind of world Science has created for us, and the kind of spiritual desert it wishes all of us to live in, is driving hundreds of thousands, millions of the "ignorant" into the arms of these simplistic, foolish, backward yet in many ways more spiritually enriching faiths; such as Creationism, which persons like Sagan and Stephen Jay Gould waste their time in hating and fearing.

As long as there is a well-entrenched, powerful intellectual Establishment trying to teach all of us that the pointless and sterile accumulations of silly facts has more spiritual merit than the compassion of a Mother Teresa or the courage of a Mahatma Ghandi, the legions of the "ignorant," and presumably, the "damned," are going to swell.

XI. *That anything but the latest theory ("the paradigm") is ignorant, superstitious or crazy and should be ridiculed or even persecuted.*

(I am indebted for this example to Dr. Andreas Ehrenfeucht, at the University of Colorado.) We know that the father of the theory of Drifting Continents, Hans Wegner, was ridiculed and ignored throughout most of his scientific career for his belief in this theory.

Imagine today, however, that there is a geologist who for lots of good reasons, believes that this theory is false.

He would probably be given much the same treatment that Galileo received, less brutal in its methods, perhaps, but with exactly the same results: a blacklisting and a silencing.

XII. *That social involvement interferes with pure thought.*

Why should the priesthood, the social elite who are carried on the backs of the society like Hindu Brahmans of old in the hoodhahs of elephants, worry themselves about the cow-dung that the elephants have to step in? Go to half a dozen science conferences and you will see that the academic scientific world lives in a kind of permanent merry-go-round from lectures to banquets to receptions to luxury hotels to jetliners to grants to awards to citations to publishing contracts to...

They are so much an integral part of the conservative power elite that the only thing which really distinguishes them is that they are too stupid to realize, as every politician and business executives does, how terrifyingly precarious their situation is, or that it can vanish with the flap of a butterfly's wing in the Amazon (what's left of it) jungle.

XIII. *That Science IS pure thought.*

Few words in our vocabulary are quite so impure as the word, "pure." The Burmese Buddhist tradition maintains that any person who is so advanced as to have no more than one sexually unclean thought each month is already a very high holy man and should be accorded deep veneration.

How much less can we expect of our modern day Western scientist? How often, even in a single day, does he (most of them being men, but this applies also to women), think of the path of the electron, or the structure of DNA, or the classification of all finite groups, or the hibernation of grizzly bears, without at least one reflection on how much money it can make him, or how many conferences he can travel to with it, or how much flattery his colleagues will give him, or how big his pension is going to be, or how handsome he will look in that photograph in the *Encyclopedia Brittanica* of the year 2024, or how much closer he is to the Nobel Prize, or how much better his theory is than that of the x,y,z group over in Illinois, or how his children will look up to him, or how bored his wife will be when he explains to it to her, or how, even though it has little about it that appears useful in any way, *somebody might just, in 200 years, discover a practical application that will earn him posthumous praise as a benefactor of Mankind...*

Of such does the purity of Science consist. It has about the same rating as the purity of the monks in the medieval monasteries, of which we have read many accounts. We see indeed that the "Credo of Science" is nothing but a long list of delusions on a par with the parting of the Red Sea, the immortal snakes of the Polynesian islands, the bodily ascension of Elijah, the material Ascension of the Virgin, the rebirth of Quetzacoatl, the immortality of the Pharoahs, and the like. It is therefore hardly surprising that the scientific community (apart from the many individual exceptions), have contributed nothing to the advance of civilization beyond their barbarian precursors.

Roy Lisker produces Ferment!, *a newsletter of commentary, poetry and fiction. Subscriptions can be ordered from his most current address: 1340 Ordway, Berkeley, CA 94702.*

Virtually Reality: Phenomicon in Atlanta
by Jim Keith

There are more things in the minds of men and conspiracy researchers than are dreamt of in your small philosophy, Bill Cooper.

After a depressing, rather macabre first night at the Phenomicon, a yearly conspiracy politics, cyberpunk, and marginals milieu gathering in Atlanta, where they had thoughtfully popped for my airline ticket and red-carpeted my every disoriented move, Saturday rose in mood and velocity with panel discussions and unscheduled gabfests, to climax in an impromptu party in the hotel bar around nine o'clock. Len Bracken, Situationist-influenced fiction writer, called from the lobby to tell me that he and Bob Black — well-known marginals writer/badboy — were hanging with a crowd of semi-clad and fawning professional strippers, camp followers eager to buy books, and publishers hot to sign contracts, and could I drop by and say a few inspirational words to the assemblage? Matt Love, freelance writer and pivotal figure in the Cabot Cabal research cult, and G.J. Krupey, author of any number of fiercely admired pieces in the underground press and regular contributor to *Steamshovel,* waded downstairs from our Fortress of Solitude on the third floor, and when we arrived in the lobby the place was boiling with a crowd that looked more like confidence men, call girls and probable spies. It was left for me to suggest that the bar was the only logical place to take our seemingly-bright-yet-undeniably-tarnished intellectual wares, and we did.

Until the wee hours of the morning the air, veritable aether of that unprepossessing booze parlor was lit with the fireworks of the intersection. The field of conspiracy research was represented by Stephanie Caruana (editor of the original *Skeleton Key to the Gemstone File,* lo these 18 or so years ago), Matt Love, Kenn Thomas (*Steamshovel* editor), myself, Monty Greene (who I didn't get a chance to talk with, but I've been impressed by his articles in the fine conspiracy rag *Zeitgeist*), and Joe Ionno (keyboardist for the Dr. Hook retro rock band, oddly enough, who blindsided me with his synthesis of psychology and politics: conspiracy research as scalpel for the scar in the collective unconscious). Having Stephanie at the shindig, both the convention and the party, was a treat; since the release (escape?) of the Gemstone File Skeleton Key years ago she had pretty well retired from the Public Eye, and I understand her reasoning. But it was good to belly up to the table with her and realize that she was a real person, amiable to a turn, and only given to grabbing the microphone away at panel discussions. Bob Black held forth at length (and breadth) while the Prime Minister of Livestock and Heavy Machinery (who I knew from his underground mag) and his compadre Mark (a blinkin' cryptographer from NASA! I collared him and told him I wanted an interview later...) banged in and began videotaping the proceedings, occasionally sallying forth to check out the cult religion Church of the Subgenius, who were holding a dance or pagan ritual of some sort in the basement. Len Bracken, an author portraying one of the most subtle aesthetics and wide-ranging knowledges of culture and politics around (read his superb anarchist science fiction novel *Free Play*) passed out copies of his new porn book *Stasi Slut* he'd done for a *Playgirl* publishing subsidiary, set among members of the East German secret police, and later attempted a demonstration of demonically possessed table surfing as the group launched into a rollicking retrospective of 60's surfing tunes (substituting improvised LaVey-derived lyrics), then abruptly diverted into a calm, cautiously-reasoned discussion of Wilhelm Reich when two hotel security guards ambled by. It was excellent meeting Adam Parfrey, owner of Feral House; if you're familiar with the astounding output of his publishing house, that will probably give you the best clue to what he's like. Adam and Kenn (a profoundly gentle and kind man, especially when it comes to proofreading) and I fell into competing for who could laugh in the most hysterical and non-stop fashion during most of the evening.

Oh, there were plenty of things about the Phenomicon political conspiracy-cyberpunk-marginals convention that I liked (meeting Kerry Thornley, Lee Harvey Oswald's buddy, was particularly enjoyable and enlightening), a few things I hated (too many gnawing black leather weasels haunting side corridors, for one thing), but the strictly exclusive (come back if you can find a chick to bring with you, sonny), catered (certainly Mr. Black, I'll buy you another round) conspiracy authors-publishers-and alleged perpetrators party on the second night of the con was the finest thing.

Jim Keith is the editor of The Gemstone File *from IllumiNet Press and* Secret and Suppressed: Banned Ideas and Hidden History, *from Feral House.*

Phenomicon
by Len Bracken

I'm sending this to everyone at the table...as if the conversation were going on and on...I was lucky to make it out of Atlanta alive. The lights seemed far off in the distance - only the most vague sensation of speed. Something snapped and I threw my Swedish clutch into second and locked up the brakes - swerved to stop with the nose of my car up to the shotgun door of another car, inches apart. Shadow boxing in the Viking - faulty auto-pilot. The occupants of a red Beamer piled out: "That girl's hair is so long she could piss on it anytime she wants." There were two guys and three girls.

"Looks like you've got an extra, well here I am."

I gave you guys classic Bracken in New Viking mode. Realize that I look over my shoulder and laugh at my macho parody. I make no claim to originality in my bad acting, which brings me to the most important lesson, for, me, at the con. Matt's comment about the enemy within, the painful self critique. I was begging to be taken to task for lifting lines and Adam was there, shrewd and engaging enough to do it. I'm grateful yet ambivalent. If I'm representing and recontextualizing Bakhtin, I leave hints and rationalize it the way he would: those who know, don't need footnotes; notes would be irrelevant for those who don't know. Think of Kosinsky's Hermit, bogged down in notes - high modern turned post-modern to a fault. I'd love to say to Adam, 'No more pastiche.' Bakhtinian dialogism makes it almost impossible not to lift value-laden terms that denote a given ideology. What I do is put various perspectives of interconnecting zones of speech...I like to bring marginal ideologies to life, have them sound off much the same way we did in Atlanta.

As for Bob's charge that I'm probably an agent, well, I answer with my art, and if that's not good enough I don't give a shit. *Ritual Intoxication* was originally called *Sons of Spies*. Total freedom and openness are the only real options for me - I became a writer, in large part, as a reaction to being spied upon by both the CIA and KGB since I was a teenager. They shouldn't care much about me now...I had several scrapes with them...It's stupid and boring, like the guy who wandered into the bar and offered me a job policy. Speaking of Holland...Ken Wish I ran into you sooner. Nobody saw my Dam VR photo play...As at least one photo attests, the beaches of the Netherlands are heaven on Earth.

As for *Stasi Slut,* you guys should know that I was edited line by line. They dutifully put verbs in my verbless phrases; turned dashes into "so"; turned carefully planned accumulation of past participles into the continuous present; took the quotes off the internal monologue in many places and used italics in others: edit by several raunchy hands. Key elements of the plot were altered. They censored my jokes about Germans and porn for marketing reasons. I wrote the rest of the book in two weeks while moving and dating a very edited delicate tautologies like: "Piss was the blood of life that she let place, once a month." Shit, I was just trying to give Erica Jong the guy she wanted, the one who would go down on her when she was having her period. Anyway...Bob, the Traven book I wanted to cite was Guthke's biography ('91 for the translation, '87 for the German edition). There are many takes on Bakhtin now. I say we marginals should appropriate him as the Bakunin for our times - he was one of us. Wanted to give you guys the two-minute Trocchi, but we never got around to it (at least not while I was lucid). *Flatland* has his new reader out of Scotland (Jim has one copy of his flawed, but interesting bio - a sample copy). All this garbage flying around the net, when what's of substance - books - takes half a year to order and at four times the local rate. The reader as Trocchi's sigma outline, which I think should be considered again.

The best part of Atlanta happened a week later - met Mary2 au contraire by chance in the subway in DC. Seems she was on stage during Stang while I was bending Adam's ear. One of my skin shots of this sexy witch with the Capitol as backdrop will make the cover of *INAUGURAL BALL* (forthcoming). Sexual outlaws of the world: unite!

The Promis Threat:
An Octopus Slouches Toward Mena, Arkansas, Area 51, and the International UFO Congress in Las Vegas
by Kenn Thomas

The first version of the Promis software—the software that figured prominently in events leading to the suspicious death of writer Danny Casolaro in a West Virginia hotel room in 1991—had a simple purpose: to track criminals in prosecutors' offices throughout the country. With the press of a button Promis provided district attorneys with up-to-the minute case histories. Inslaw, the company owned by St. Louisans Bill and Nancy Hamilton, originally began developing the software using taxpayer money as part of the Justice Department's Law Enforcement Assistance Administration in the late 1970s. When the Reagan White House nixed the LEAA in 1980, Inslaw became a for-profit corporation and continued modifying Promis as computer technology evolved. Inslaw signed a contract with the Justice Department in 1982 to supply the software exclusively to all U.S. attorney's offices. The contract was worth $10 million.

The Justice Department never paid and in 1985 Inslaw filed Chapter 11 bankruptcy and began a lawsuit. In 1988 Inslaw was awarded $7 million in damages. That settlement was upheld by the federal court but the U.S. Court of Appeals ordered it retried and Inslaw appealed to the Supreme Court. During these legal gyrations a software concern owned by Ed Brian, a friend of then attorney general Ed Meese, made a very hostile buy-out offer to Inslaw. The last legal action on this case came in the middle of October when Attorney General William Barr refused to authorize a special prosecutor to investigate the Inslaw allegations. Bill and Nancy Hamilton are no doubt studying further appeals.

The Promis modifications, of course, are what should concern the defenders of civil liberties. Even before it fell into the hands of the Justice Department, it had been shanghaied by the Navy to track and extrapolate Arctic Soviet submarine launches, which it reportedly did with extraordinary accuracy. Michael Riconosciuto, now in a Tacoma prison on drug charges and a key Casolaro informant, reports equipping Promis with a back door access, so the U.S. could spy on the police agencies to whom it illegally sold the software. The possible use of Promis in tracking political dissidents has been pointed out by Ben Price in the new IllumiNet book, *The Gemstone File*. It's not difficult to imagine other applications.

According to JFK assassination lecturer Bob Harris, Jack Ruby's closest contacts with the Dallas police were in the Criminal Intelligence Division, a division of the Dallas Law Enforcement Intelligence Unit, versions of which exist in every city and perforcely one must wonder what kind of software drives their work. (Harris' lecture notes are available for $8 from him at Box 4-18, 522 2nd Street, New York, NY 11215) The LEIU collects information on private citizens and gives it to Military Intelligence and the Domestic Contacts division of the CIA. Details of how the Los Angeles police's version, the OCIU, spied upon and harassed private citizens, can be found in the recent *LA Secret Police Files: Inside the LAPD Elite Spy Network* by Mike Rothmiller and Ivan G. Goldman ($5.99, Pocket Books). The celebrity status of these citizens, of course, is what made the book worthy in this instance.

Another connection between Casolaro and the JFK assassination concerns the Banca del Lavoro, a state-owned Italian bank that apparently the writer was investigating as part of the BCCI tentacle in his Octopus research. According to Sherman Skolnick, a researcher in Chicago, the Banca del Lavoro financed the training of an assassination team in Mexico, some of whom wound up in Dealey Plaza on November 22, 1963. At present, Attorney General Barr is considering the appointment of a special prosecutor in a case involving $5 billion dollars in loans to Saddam Hussein made by the Atlanta branch of Banca del Lavoro prior to the Gulf War, the so-called Iraqgate scandal. The Banca del Lavoro is indeed mentioned in the Torbitt Document, "Nomenclature of an Assassination Cabal" by William Torbitt, which has circulated among Kennedy researchers for twenty years, as is Ross Perot. That the Torbitt Document may have originated in the office of Lloyd Bentsen, now named by Bill Clinton as treasury secretary, as well as Bentsen's connection to Defense Industrial Security Command—culprits in the assassination according to the Torbitt Document—should leave the reader a long pause to ruminate over the connections spanning the years.

Back to Michael Riconosciuto: perhaps *UFO Magazine* editor Don Ecker summed up Riconosciuto's credibility best when he told *Steamshovel,* "If he told me the sun came up in the morning and set in the evening, I'd double check it." Last issue, *Steamshovel Press* reported on Riconosciuto's claim that a feud between intelligence factions, one headed by MJ-12 of Roswell saucer crash fame, had led to Casolaro's revelations. These claims were supported by Gunther Russbacher, the pilot who also claims to have video proof that he flew George Bush to a Paris October Surprise meeting.

Ecker notes in the latest issue of *UFO Magazine* (Vol. 8, No. 1, 1993) that Riconosciuto also claimed to have witnessed an ET autopsy with Robert Booth Nichols, another ominous figure in the Inslaw milieu. To be sure, everything Michael Riconosciuto says is meant to curry favor, to get money or to bring his story to someone in the entertainment industry who can turn it into a movie or a book deal. Nevertheless, Riconosciuto's claims about the modifications of the Promis software were supported by affidavits from Israel intelligence asset Ari Ben-Menasche (who offers more details of his own in a new book, *Profits of War*, published by Sheridan Square) and Iranian arms dealer Richard Babayan, both of whom came across pirated copies of Promis through Earl Brian and his friend, Reagan national security advisor Robert McFarland.

Riconosciuto is also one of the few and earliest sources for word on the airstrip in Mena, Arkansas used as a hub for the Iran/contra drugs and guns traffic, the investigation of which then-governor Bill Clinton soft-pedaled to the extent that he squelched it. According to the *Village Voice*, Riconosciuto claims association with Terry K. Reed, a self-proclaimed CIA asset who trained contra pilots at Mena ("Clinton and the Smuggler's Airport," by Frank Snepp, *Village Voice*, April 14, 1992). Reed's airplane, so goes the story, was stolen when he refused to give it to the Company's "Operation Donation", which was represented by John Cathey, aka Ollie North. Legal entanglements to recover the loss of the plane put Reed at odds with "Buddy" Young, Clinton's security chief. Reed's other associations include the downed contra pilot Eugene Hassenfus and JFK assassination veteran Felix Rodriguez.

Riconosciuto tells of a connection between the Arkansas Development Funding Authority (ADFA), from which Clinton fired contra player Larry Nichols— whose subsequent lawsuit led to the Gennifer Flowers revelations—and Park-on-Meter (POM), a company in Little Rock that made fuel tanks and helped develop chemical weapons at Mena. Riconosciuto's revelations supplement the small but growing amount of information about Mena, perhaps best summarized in the latest issue of Paul Krassner's newsletter, *The Realist* ("Clinton's Cocaine Connection" by Mark Giacomelli,

The Realist Number 122, Winter 1993). It appears that the strip was used as a major center for guns and drug smuggling since the early 1980s, most notably by a trafficker named Barry Seal, to the extent that Bill Clinton claims to have authorized the use of $25,000 in state funds to investigate and prosecute charges stemming from the activity there. The prosecuting attorney in the area claims the money never came. Other critics charge that even if it had, the amount is a drop in the bucket compared to what a full-blown investigation would have cost. Clinton's reactions to George Bush's Christmas pardons for Caspar Weinberger and other Iran-contra figures were limited to laments over Weinberger's lying to Congress. Clinton remained silent about the underlying policy issues, which many in the press identify only as the Reagan arms-for-hostages deal. As the Mena story emerges as an important one during the Clinton administration this identification perforcely will expand to include the role of drug trafficking in the nefarious Iran-contra affair.

Meanwhile, the Inslaw case lingers and spooks are doing untold things with the data collected through Promis. One such spook group, Wackenhut, was involved with both the Promis modifications and the contra resupply effort in tandem with the native American Cabazons in Indio, California, according to Riconosciuto. By 1966 Wackenhut had over four million files on dissident Americans collected at the direction of founder, George Wackenhut (see: "Inside The Shadow CIA" by John Connolly, *Spy Magazine*, Volume 6, September 1992). George Wackenhut was a former FBI agent who apparently patterned his world view after J. Edgar Hoover's collecting and storing information on as many people as possible. He founded and developed his private security firm through a legal loophole in the law preventing such groups from working for the government. As such, Wackenhut remains a private police force that in many ways stands outside the slim boundaries of responsibility ostensibly foisted upon the alphabet soup of government intelligence (CIA, FBI, DIA, ONI, etc., the agencies to which all top Wackenhut administrators belonged). It maintains private jails and contracts to take over police services, including surveillance. Don Ecker also notes that the oil consortium Aleyska hired Wackenhut to perform a variety of phone tapping and intercepts to disrupt a team of environmental whistleblowers.

Wackenhut has contracted to provide security services to Area 51, the site outside of the Nellis Air Force base in Nevada that has almost become a Mecca for UFO watchers. Sightings of unidentified flying objects are commonplace at Area 51, as are sightings of advanced conventional aircraft, stories of a nearby underground base manned by humans and aliens and rumors that a space shuttle launches from there on regular flights to bases on the moon. Reports have it that Wackenhut personnel have harassed skywatchers, chasing them by the van-load, physically threatening them at gunpoint and confiscating camera equipment. Indeed, Wackenhut played a role in covering up an illegal takeover of 89,000 acres from families near Area 51 in 1986-87 that eventually led to a secret congressional investigation.

At the invitation of Bob Brown, organizer of the annual International UFO Congress in Las Vegas, *Steamshovel* editor Kenn Thomas travelled to Las Vegas to speak on the UFO work of Wilhelm Reich. After the lecture he took the three hour trip into the desert with a group of UFO watchers that included researchers Rob Baldwin, Shawn Atlanti, Susan Low, German video documentary producer Michael Hesseman (whose documentary on crop circles, "The Mystery of the Crop Circles—Messages From Another World", won an EBE award at the Congress) and as many as a half dozen others, along with a video crew from television station KTNV Channel 13 consisting of reporter Steve Crupi and cameraman Clay Downey. As the sun went down, in a period from 6PM to 9:45PM, the group witnessed four unusual aerial displays. Some in the group speculated that one of these sightings might have been a truck-mounted, diversionary spotlight used by Wackenhut personnel to taunt ufologists. One of the other sightings was identified by Sean Morton, author of *The Millenium Factor,* who caught up with group at the Little A'le'Inn diner later in the evening, as an exotic SDI flare. (Morton witnessed it from a vantage point in Warm Springs, sixty miles away. Morton and his group, the Delphi Associates, have done a great deal of field work in Area 51. An interview with Morton will appear in the Saucer Section of the next *Steamshovel.* His book, *The Millenium Factor,* is available for $20 from the Delphi

Associates, 2207 Hermosa Avenue, Hermosa Beach, CA 90254.) The two remaining light-in-the-sky events that night remain unidentified.

In the discussion on the trip through the desert and at the Little A'le'Inn afterwards, many participants described incidents of harassment at the hands of Wackenhut personnel. One major common concern involved the youth of many rank-and-file Wackenhut recruits: teenagers dangerously armed and indoctrinated to believe they belong to an elite guard ("Wackenoffs," one observer quipped.) Signs now adorn the area announcing the authorized use of legal force by Wackenhut.

Wackenhut's presence as dirty-trick specialists was also felt when Robert Lazar defected from his work at Area 51 and began confessing to back-engineering captured alien spacecraft for the government to television reporter George Knapp. Similarly, *Steamshovel Press'* attempts to obtain a copy of KTNV's broadcast of the videotaped UFOs and interviews with members of the group met with an official stonewall. Reporter Crupi advised that a tape would routinely be made available through Channel 13's Shoshona video service. Shoshona said that the news division told it not to release that particular report. When contacted a second time, Crupi provided a weak explanation: station management did not want the footage falling into the hands of a competing station. Was this more Wackenhut spin control?

A tape of the broadcast, a camera transfer made from a TV set in the hotel room of a UFO Congress participant—did eventually circulate in the ufological underground. "Bootlegged" information artifacts such as this are perhaps the best defense against the threat of a surveillance tool like Promis. It is surprising, in fact, that hackers have not yet reproduced a copy of Promis for study somewhere in cyberspace.

A Party at Tim Leary's

Q: I understand we're in the middle of a party. We're crashing.

Leary: Welcome to the party! We certainly want intelligent people to join us. My son is living with a wonderfully brilliant dress underwear designer and we're having an off-the-rack show party for her. We have a lot of interesting people here. We've got Paul Krassner here walking around and Jerry Rubin somewhere in the house...we're loaded with talent here.

My daughter-in-law has designed silk underwear for men and women in robes and I'm modeling. I'm modeling a fantastic harlequin shirt right now.

I'm going to be the master of ceremonies of what's going on here. I'm going to give you the greatest minds of southern California, if that's not an oxymoron.

First let me introduce Paul Krassner, a culture hero from the 60s-70s-80s, started the *Realist* magazine and has been on the front lines fighting for pornography, freedom, good humor.

Krassner: Hello, this is me.

Q: Hi, Paul. We're crashing your party.

Krassner: Tim Leary is great for buck passing.

Q: How are things with the *Realist* and all?

Krassner: It used to be a magazine now it's a newsletter. I don't have the energy I used to put out a magazine every month. Besides, there's competition now. There never used to be competition.

Q: There's competition for the *Realist*?

Krassner: When I started it there was only *Mad Magazine* for teenagers. There was no *National Lampoon,* or *Spy,* there was no *Saturday Night Live,* there was no *Doonesbury.* So I had an open field of taboos to explode.

Q: You outlived Bill Gaines anyway.

Krassner: I know. In fact, the issue of the *Realist* that is on the press now is dedicated to Bill. It has on the cover a portrait of Alfred E. Newman being crucified. It says, "So Bill Gaines So Loved The World He Gave His Only Begotten Icon." You know *Mad* had these pages you could fold in a certain way. When you fold this up, there's an image of Bill Gaines.

One of my conspiracies was that the comedians conspired to make jokes about Dan Quayle as a diversion from the real reason he was chosen as vice president. During the Iran-contra hearings, a guy named Rob Owen testified and he was courier for Oliver North and he operated out of then-Senator Dan Quayle's office. So Quayle was not plucked out of obscurity as the *Washington Post* says. He had already proved himself to being a player in the game. In the series by Bob Woodward they said that he was actually campaigning for the vice presidency, which I just translate as implied blackmail.

Q: Can we collect your impressions of this party? Is Tim Leary actually modeling underwear?

Krassner: Yeah. This is a very pragmatic party. His daughter-in-law is a clothes designer. So somebody ask me which I would prefer her in and she showed me see-though pajamas and a see-through bath robe. And Tim himself is wearing a shirt with a price-tag on it. So it's getting hard for us satirists to make up things because reality keeps nipping at our heels. Somebody said Tim was modeling a t-shirt but it was really his own from the last political campaign. It said, "Think Green, Vote Brown."

Q: So he doesn't have the virtual reality gloves on and the goggles.

Krassner: No, no. I could use a little virtual reality myself. There's different circles of friends from different circles of Tim's and so they start off in different groups and sort of intermingle around the potato chips.

Q: Have you seen Gordon Liddy?

Krassner: No. Gordon Liddy must have rats to eat. Let me introduce Anita Hoffman, who was one of the founders of the Yippies and she wrote a book under the name of Ann Phetamine called *Trash. Trashing,* excuse me. "Trash" was the review.

Hoffman: Wonderful party here with many people who haven't seen each other in years and years. We all hope to have an impact in the 90s. And Abbie's certainly still here with us in spirit.

Q: Do you do any writing these days yourself?

Hoffman: With Tim, I'm sort of moving into the new electronic age. The computer-cyber revolution. I'm in the process of producing interactive multi-media software. I work for a very innovative company called the Voyager company. I think that part of the legacy is wanting to translate so much of our culture and our ideals into electronic form that it will be available in the future. I think everything is being transformed into that. The company I work for is a pioneer with electronic books, in fact. Translating many books. In fact, Ken Kesey's new book is going to come out in electronic form as well as print. CD-ROM. Even as we speak the interface becomes easier and easier. I'm not a technoid, unfortunately. But it's getting easier.

Q: Is it getting any cheaper, though? If these really are tools to empower people, how do you get them into the hands of people who can't typically afford them or typically afford even food to eat?

Hoffman: I totally agree. But they are coming down in price and I think we're moving in that direction. There is a vision behind this which Tim has been one the foremost articulators of, which is simply that a lot of us feel that we're helping build a new nervous system for the planet, which is electronic communication. So you hope that will have an effect like, for instance, in the Rodney King beating, which is on video. It had a huge effect as information. We were involved in this revolution in information with McLuhan way back. That was the beginning of it with television and it keeps moving forward. I think we hope that as the planet becomes smaller we solve some of the problems because people become more aware of the problems. You can't shut it out any more.

Q: We saw a lot references to the Persian Gulf War as the first Cyber War. A lot people watched that on their video screens and their cable TV at home. The technology always seems to fall so concretely into the hands of the people that make war.

Hoffman: I agree. It was like a video game. We have to change that. It's horrifying to have kids...I have a teenage son who grew up playing computer games and as we know those are sort of like bombing raids at your desk. That is a danger. But I know Tim and I and other people are trying to translate the good stuff into that electronic form so that learning becomes a fun experience. It's going to revolutionize learning. I think that basically it's a really good, positive thing and it's not all in the hands of the military. I think it's going to come out OK. The New Age that we're coming into is going to be interactive and you can create your own works by putting together different kinds of materials. I don't think that there's a way that it can be censored at a certain point. I don't think ultimately it can be controlled. I'm not saying that they aren't going to try.

I'm essentially an optimist, although I know there are terrible things happening in our world, as usual. I would like to introduce Jerry Rubin, another Yippie founder.

Rubin: I was just playing with a computer here and I got so scared. I lost everything but it just came back. I was playing with the Mac computer in his office and all of a sudden everything disappeared off the screen. The last thing I want to do is erase all Tim's genius, right? But it all came back, so I'm OK.

Q: Are you heavily into the computer thing too?

Rubin: Not quite as heavily as everybody else is. I use a Mac computer. I couldn't live without it. I can't imagine how I lived without it in the past. I can't imagine how I got through the sixties without a computer. I can't imagine how I wrote five books without a computer. I can't imagine how I would ever do business without a computer. I was one of the last people to get into the computer world. I don't put a lot of time into the advanced uses of the computer. I mainly use it for practical purposes. I send messages to people to get them to do what I want them to do.

I'm involved with teaching people how to be entrepreneurs and teaching people how to make money and how to improve their nutritional lives. I'm involved with a number of companies. I have seven or eight faxes on the desks of all my people before they wake up in the morning. I couldn't do that without the Mac computer.

Q: We were talking to Anita about how computer technology is used by the warfare culture.

Rubin: Computers are tools that can be used for good or evil. Like money, right? Money can be used to build the future or it can be used for destructive, wasteful things. The computer is no different in the advance of consciousness than...it can be a part of the war machine, it can be part of gambling and be a part of everything. Like any thing else, it's important that the right value system controls the computer world.

Q: One of the problems that computers have that, say, pencils don't is that they're money intensive. The poor, who really need to communicate with people better than anybody else, can barely get their hands on that kind of equipment.

Rubin: But that's not going to be the case in ten years. In ten years everyone's going to have a computer. There used to be a time when not everybody had a telephone. I remember a time when not everyone had a television. I'm old enough to remember the debate over whether or not to buy a color TV. That was an extravagant purchase. The computer now is becoming more and more democratic in the sense that pretty soon there's going to be hand-held computers and so forth and the cost will go way down. In the long run the computer will be a liberating instrument for people who don't have the financial means to own the expensive computers that now exist. Look how a television in every home has changed the world. So why wouldn't a computer in every home change the world? And why wouldn't a computer be cost effective for everybody? I think basically technology is democratic and liberating, except in the one example you used, when it's used in a war.

Q: Is the world you live in now one that you expected when you began your public life in the sixties?

Rubin: It's very different than I expected, but then all expectations never happen the way you expect them to happen. Instead what happens is a reality. So you have to accept reality. I never thought that the world going on today would be going on. I never thought that the black-white gulf would be as great as it is. Economics became such an overwhelming issue that people became survival conscious. And survival meant taking care of yourself first. And that was the wedge they drove between black and white. But here's what's happening: the baby boomers have not taken over yet. People in their thirties and forties who created the sixties, created the woman's movement, created the computer revolution, who Tim is a great example of a leader, although he's not a baby boomer, have not taken over yet. I believe that the changes you are going to see in America in the next four years will be the culmination of all the basic values of the sixties. The verdict on the sixties will be determined in the nineties. The key may not be Gore and Clinton but the forces behind them, people in their thirties and forties who still have the sixties dream in their heart. You can't imagine what's going to happen in the next four years. Awesome. I predicted every decade. I predicted the sixties. I predicted the inner development of the seventies. And five years ago you can go back to an Associated Press interview with me in which I said a yuppie would be elected in the White House in this election.

Q: Has anybody button-holed Dr. Leary yet?

Leary: Hello!

Q: Thank you for letting us crash the party.

Leary: These people all are doing state of the art stuff right now in computers and smart drugs and, of course, Krassner is always trouble making. We are happy to share the afternoon with you.

Q: Let's ask you: if computers are really empowering tools how do you get them into the hands of the poor?

Leary: You have a Nintendo on the market for about a hundred dollars. You add the CD-ROM attachment. You can give every school kid in the world, in the third world or the inner city, any poor kid, the equivalent to do this for ten percent of what they now spend on text books that kids don't read and that are causing the destruction of the Amazon rain forest. So wood pulp is out. They don't just read the book, they perform the book, they put it on screens. Imagine if a teacher was going to bring into the classroom a $69, any graphic video player, *Donkey Kong* player, with a CD-ROM and we're going to do a film about the Civil War. It's available right now. It's just that society and education and the bureaucracies have not caught up with it. But it's going to happen.

Once you have kids putting things on screen, they're not going to believe the screen anymore. It's truly revolutionary. We're also developing software that you can create your own trance state, you can re-imprint yourself, you can hypnotize yourself with your friends and not be hypnotized as the American public is who watch TV seven hours a day now. That's brainwashing and they know how to do it. They use the right brain trance state to tell you that the night belongs to Michelob and George Bush will save you from Willie Horton and blah, blah, blah. You can do it your self.

Anyway, it's been fun and stay in touch. We are here in Beverly Hills on Sunday afternoon putting the high back in high technology!

Saucer Section:
Winged Cats, Mothmen and Unidentified Flying Objects
by John Keel

Q: *Mothman Prophecies* **is regarded as a classic ufological work and it details your experiences in Point Pleasant, West Virginia in the mid 1960s but the book wasn't published until the mid-1970s.**

A: It took almost ten years for the book to be published. It came out around 1975. The New York editors had never heard about some of the things in the book and didn't care very much. They only know what they read in the *New York Times*. If they didn't see it in the Times then it doesn't exist for them. Although this material got nationwide publicity it didn't get much publicity in New York City itself. That was a handicap.

I happened to be in West Virginia when the story broke. I was there investigating a winged cat.

Q: A winged cat?

A: Yes, there was a famous winged cat down in West Virginia. A young boy had found this cat in a woods and he decided it was worthy of public attention and so he charged ten cents a look. All of his neighbors lined up to see this winged cat for ten cents. He came to New York and did the *Today* show. The cat's name, as I recall, was Thomas. And then one of his neighbors suddenly appeared and said, "That's my cat!" and demanded the cat back. There was a big controversy about this winged cat down in Beckley, West Virginia. And I was in Beckley, West Virginia when this story in Point Pleasant broke. So I went and talked with the witnesses there and got involved with this.

Q: The Point Pleasant experiences, of course, all involved a winged man.

A: This was two young married couples in an automobile, driving through an area outside of Point Pleasant called the TNT area. It was really a sort of lover's lane kind of thing, a sort of isolated area. It had been used in the Second World War to manufacture high explosives and had been closed ever since. They were driving through this area and they suddenly saw this large creature standing next to a building there. He was larger than a large man, they said, and he had fiercely glowing red eyes. And suddenly he spread his wings and he had a ten foot wing span and he started chasing the automobile. And these teenagers, they were all under twenty years old so I'll call them teenagers, they were so terrified that they drove as fast as their jalopy would take them to the local

police station. It takes quite a lot to get teenagers to go to the police in any town. They were terrified. And the police were very impressed by their story. So the police held a press conference the next day and the story carried on all the wire services. That's how it all began.

In the end, I had tracked down over a hundred witnesses, all of whom had seen this creature. Some of them very prominent people in the area. One was a local banker, the head of the Chamber of Commerce. Eventually the wife of one of the deputy sheriffs saw this thing. Quite a few people saw it. But nobody ever got a picture of it.

Unfortunately, the winged cat shed its wings. The wings fell off. That ended the controversy. When the wings fell off it was just another cat and so the neighbor said, "That's not my cat! I don't want that cat!" So the boy had the cat Thomas, I guess, until it died.

Q: The appearance of Mothman, of course, was just the beginning of the weirdness at Point Pleasant, right?

A: It got more and more complicated as time went on. The witnesses to this thing began to have other experiences, UFO type experiences. Interference with their television sets, strange phone calls, a multitude of things like poltergeist manifestations. It just seemed to grow and grow. And people began to see UFO type lights over the TNT area itself and finally great crowds of people would gather every night to watch the UFOs go over. You could almost set your watch by them. All up and down the Ohio Valley they were seeing things during that period anyway. Between 1964 and 1968 there were thousands of UFO sightings all over the country, in fact all over the world. It was a major UFO wave.

In the Army I studied psychological warfare. I was a propaganda writer in the Army. I know quite a bit about psychology and I certainly know a lot about these people in West Virginia and other areas. And they're usually not seeking attention and they're certainly not the kind of people who have that kind of imagination that would make something up. Most of them are often very sorry afterwards that they even said anything to anybody.

I've had a lifetime background in journalism and professional writing. I really don't have any major theories about any of this. I just find that none of theories that have been put forth work. The extraterrestrial theory does not work at all when you the study all of the aspects of the UFO phenomenon. It simply doesn't work. We're dealing with manifestations that have been reported throughout the centuries, not just in modern times.

Our version of reality is probably as wrong as an ant's version of its reality. The ant can only perceive things immediately around it and then it perceives it in a wrong way. People really have no sensory equipment at all. Our eyes are very limited in what they can see and our hearing is also very limited. Many animals have better hearing than we do. An eagle certainly has better eyesight. Our perceptions are very wrong in many ways.

UFOs and Fugos
by Terry Sofian

There has been some discussion in recent literature that a weapons system used by the Japanese during the closing stages of World War Two was responsible for the events now called the Roswell Incident. To judge this argument, the nature of the Japanese weapons, long range free balloons, and their operational use must be known.

The Japanese had begun experimenting with a series of secret weapons during the 1930s. Of these only the balloon bomb was to reach operational service. The idea was to design a weapon that could be produced cheaply and carry a useful military payload intercontinental distances. The payload could consist of small incendiary or high explosive bombs or biological weapons. The Japanese military had considerable interest in biological weapons during this period and may have used them operationally in China.

The project slowly faded in the period before Pearl Harbor, but was revived following the air-strike by Doolittle and his sixteen B-25 Mitchell bombers against targets on the Japanese Home Islands. This raid took place on April 18, 1942. The Japanese high command immediately instituted a number of reprisals against the areas in China where the planes, which had been launched from the aircraft carrier Hornet, landed. They also began an operation to destroy the remaining United States Pacific Fleet, which was to culminate with their stunning defeat at the Battle of Midway. The third program that the Japanese high command began was to attempt to develop a means to strike directly at targets on the American Mainland, without risking valuable resources.

The method that was finally chosen was to construct large numbers of cheap balloons and, when the winds were favorable, to release them. The high altitude winds would carry them to North America where they would release their payloads. The balloons, called Fin-Go by the Japanese, would then self destruct, leaving little evidence of their nature. The Japanese designers had to overcome a number of technical difficulties to produce a platform that could maintain a constant altitude for the fifty or seventy hour journey across the Pacific The aerostatic platform consisted of a gas bag or envelope with a volume of 19,070 cubic feet. Using Hydrogen as a lifting gas gave a ground level lifting power of almost 1000 pounds. The genius of the design was in a small mechanical device that allowed the aerostat to maintain its constant altitude. This device linked paired ballast bags with the gas release valve at the top of the envelope. When the balloon rose to high the automatic pressure release valve opened venting hydrogen lifting gas. When the balloon sank to low and altimeter sent a signal to small explosive bolts that held paired sand ballast bags releasing them and there by reducing the weight of the balloon. When all the ballast was released the military payload was dropped by the same mechanism. The payload on operational balloons consisted of incendiary bombs designed to cause forest fires in the great evergreen stands of the American West and high explosive bombs to cause direct civilian casualties.

Two types of envelopes were built by the Japanese, a cheaper silk paper one and one of more expensive rubbered silk. The rubbered silk balloons carried radio equipment to help determine the effectiveness of the weapons. They could be tracked to their targets by long range radio receivers. Unfortunately, the rubbered silk was more permeable to gas than was the cheaper paper and those balloons with that envelope type failed to reach the United States. Additionally, a news black-out imposed by the United States Army prevented the Japanese intelligence community from acquiring information on the balloons' effectiveness. After launching more then 9000 balloons the program was cancelled due to this inability to determine its effectiveness. The date of the program's deactivation was in March of 1945.

John Keel asserts that it was this news blackout that prevented the Army Air Corp from announcing the true nature of the device at Roswell. The news blackout had been lifted after the death of a woman and five children near Lakeview, Oregon, when one exploded while they were examining it. This was in May of 1945, two years before Roswell. Additionally a nationwide advisory bulletin was posted by the Defense Department on January 1, 1955 after the live payload of a balloon was discovered in Alaska.

There is little doubt that the mechanics of the balloon, with its automatic release valve and paper construction, would have made it impossible to remain aloft for two years. The majority of these devices could not survive even the seventy hours it required to cross the Pacific. It also seems highly unlikely that the balloon would have landed in New Mexico after having travelled for so long even had it been possible.

JFK Redux:
Oswald, Reinhard Gehlen and Clinton-Gore
An Interview with Carl Oglesby

Q: First, let me congratulate you for turning in a book on JFK that is shorter than an inch thick and still very comprehensive.

A: Thanks, I think. That was the thought. The publisher brought that idea to me and I would never have been smart enough to think it up. But he was of the view being a San Francisco publisher, that there was need for a book that you could read on that flight from San Francisco to Los Angeles. The book needed to be on some interesting subject upon which you felt some need of instruction so that you could feel good about yourself, you had used that hour and a half or whatever.

I hope the book finds the audience that was intended I think, well, the publisher's intent, was to get me to write a book for your basic, average, normal, sophisticated, urbanized spirit, intellect, who has always heard this argument about the JFK assassination going on over his/her shoulder and has never really wanted to pay any attention to it. For one thing because it's clear at a glance that there's an incredibly large information burden. If you take on the case you have to learn a lot. You have to develop views about lots of uncomfortable, exotic subjects. So I think a good many, can I say, general intellectuals or people of general intellectual spirit, have all these years tended to stay away from the Kennedy assassination case on the grounds that it's really too lurid, too gross, too complex for words and anyway Oswald probably did it after all. But now, I think, going on three decades later, it's finally clear to an overwhelming majority of well-educated Americans that we don't know the truth about what happened in Dealey Plaza in 1963. Period. We don't know it. And it's important. And we can't rest easy in ignorance. At least in that respect things have changed.

Q: What end does the opening of the government files on the Kennedy assassination serve?

A: First, I think, is the question of the documents from the Warren Commission, from various panels and other commissions that have investigated the case in whole or in part or reviewed it or reviewed the Warren Commission's work or listened to some new witness who showed up and then there was, of course, the work of the 1978 Select Committee. That generated an enormous amount of documentation which was classified and never released and never referred to and never developed in the committee hearings or in the

final report. I could give you one very important example of that: there was an investigator named Juan Edwin Lopez who worked for the Select Committee, the Assassination Committee staff. Lopez was given an assignment to investigate the stories that Oswald had been in Mexico City in September before the assassination and that he had made an appearance at the Soviet embassy on a few occasions and ditto the Cuban consulate. And, long story short, Lopez comes back from this investigation and writes a two hundred and ninety page report that says "that wasn't Oswald in Mexico City at all, that was somebody pretending to be Oswald. Oswald took a trip and maybe went to Mexico City, but it wasn't Oswald at the embassy or the consulate." Now that would have been a very explosive piece of news had it been allowed to come out in 1977 or early '78 when Lopez discovered it and wrote it up. The Select Committee, however, despite all its promises that it was going to let the sun shine in on who killed JFK chose to sit on that, it classified the Lopez report, didn't publish the Lopez report, never referred to the Lopez report, never gave even a half-sentence of a phrase to describe Lopez's amazing discovery and now these days, with all its pious talk of deciding to release these secret documents generated by all these public paid for investigations, they're not going to release the Lopez report. Suddenly. This was a news story just three or four weeks ago. Congress will not release the Lopez report.

Q: And did they say why not?

A: The CIA is going crazy about it because once it gets established that Oswald was in fact being impersonated not only in Mexico City but in Dallas, in El Paso, in Austin. Once that gets established for a fact then people are going to understand that Oswald, whatever else he was, was no loner. He was a...my goodness, one of the most totally controlled...he was a puppet on the strings of an elaborate intelligence operation whose roots, whose ultimate identity Oswald didn't know anymore than you and I do.

But the new consensus that's developing among at least the researchers that I pay most attention to was that Oswald was exactly what he said he was. He was a patsy. He was set up to take the blame for something that he never did. And part of the realization of this about Oswald is involved in understanding that he was impersonated by people obviously operating in an intelligence mode. He therefore has to be considered an intelligence operative on a set of strings and nothing that he does can be said to have been done out of his own private internal initiative. He's a totally controlled character. That has to be understood. We're going to have some trouble deciding whether he was controlled by the CIA, by some obscure military outfit called Field Operations Intelligence, or FOI, or by some branch of G2 or Naval Intelligence or the Russians or the Cubans. It's not going to be easy to figure out what Oswald's position actually was in full detail.

There's a long record beginning with intervention in certain union struggles in Greece and Italy and France and Britain and West Germany that the CIA, for a long time, has been building a record as being a rather nasty agent on the scene. Always under cover. In Latin America. It has a lousy record of backing every fascist in the house and doing everything it can do to bring down any government the least committed to reform and progress in the popular sense of the term. To the degree to which this true, the CIA has to be regarded as a political renegade. It has not been under the control of presidents. Rather, it has used its exclusive ability to manufacture the most secret information as a way to deceive, to hornswoggle presidents. I think Eisenhower got hornswoggled.

Q: So the President became the instrument of the CIA, not the other way around.

A: Sure, as long as you can control the information that is going to the President on the most privileged basis then you don't have to worry about what the President actually believes or desires or where his heart is. You can manipulate him easily into doing exactly what it is that you want him to do unless he is very strong willed. I think Kennedy was strong willed and that's what got him in trouble with the people who wanted to manipulate him and finally found out that they couldn't do it.

Let me just try to lay out the ABCs of this story. Reinhard Gehlen was Hitler's top spy master in the latter phases of World War Two and he especially soared to power in the period after the revolt of the generals and in a period when the SS took command of the entire government and all the military operations. It was during that period that this guy Reinhard Gehlen flourished and went from being the chief of an outfit called Foreign Armies East, which was a bunch of fascist underground groups in Eastern Europe and inside the Soviet Union, to being the head of western-oriented intelligence operations as well.

The war had already been lost on a chess board by early 1943 and it seems that early in 1943 the top Nazi command around Martin Bormann, who was number two under Hitler, made a secret decision, that is a decision kept secret from Hitler, to prepare for

defeat. The reason they were going to prepare for defeat was that they didn't beat the Russians in time to turn their forces around and get them back on the western front so that they would be there to meet the Americans when they came. Therefore, the Americans were going to be able to establish a foothold. They were going to invade France and therefore Germany was going to lose the chess game. So it was prudent at that point to begin planning for defeat, to make sure that you could undergo the experience of defeat with the maximum number of your resources in tact.

What was created was an organization called after the war, the Odessa, for Organization of Veterans of the SS. It had its war-time roots in several departments of the Nazi bureaucracy but let's just call it Odessa, it doesn't mean the city, it means this secret underground organization that the Nazis created in order to help them endure as a coherent organization the forthcoming defeat of Hitler's military forces. They basically were able to establish bases of retreat all around the world. Lots in South America. Lots in South Africa. Some important places in Indonesia and for a while Egypt. And these places were very well provisioned and victualed. The enormous wealth that the Nazis had plundered was moved out of the country. Important industries were moved out of the country, licensed to operate in neutral countries and therefore beyond the reach of war reparations and an enormous amount of gold. 350 tons you hear, sometimes 500 tons, an enormous amount of gold was moved out of Germany.

And there was one other component of the Odessa, which is where Reinhard Gehlen comes back into the story, the master spy. The Nazis knew that all these plans for escape would come to nothing if they weren't able to neutralize the opposition because the opposition would have an enormous military advantage and could basically do to them whatever it wanted. So they had to have some way to manipulate the American point of view in the post-War period. Their own intelligence gave them insights into a struggle going on inside U.S. intelligence between the military and the civilian. The military didn't like that there was this thing that Roosevelt had created called the OSS. The military did not like the OSS for being under civilian control. They thought that intelligence belonged under military control. So there was always a struggle during the war between the military and the civilian sides of intelligence. And Gehlen had good enough intelligence pipelines into the United States to know this. He was able to exploit this.

At the end of the war he comes to the United States with an offer, very secret. The offer was, "hey, you guys, everybody knows that now that you have beaten the Germans, you and Russia together, you and the Russians are going to turn out to be each other's worst enemies. Everybody can see this coming. Now in this struggle which is about to begin between you and the Soviet Union, a great advantage is going to accrue to the side that has the better intelligence capabilities. Now everybody knows that the Russians have spies everywhere in the American government and here we'll give a few that you never thought of before," and Gehlen passes a few names around and he says, "what we have here is an intelligence capability that's ready to go to work. That is to say, this organization that we set up here in Germany. We have spies everywhere in East Europe. We have spies inside the Kremlin very close to the top of the Soviet government. All you have to do is let us continue to carry on the fight against Bolshevism and we will go and work for you."

So the Army said, "Oh, wow, great, terrific. Let's do this." And after a period of several months having secret negotiations at Fort Hunt, very near Washington, with Gehlen and six of his aides, a deal was drawn up and implemented in the spring of 1946 which I think of as the Secret Treaty of Fort Hunt. As a result of it, Gehlen went back to Europe, set up headquarters with several thousand expert technicians to go to work again as in the old days, still spying on the Russians, still spying in Eastern European countries, still up to all kinds of dirty tricks but now ostensibly in the name of the United States. In fact, secret even from the United States, in the name of the Odessa. Everything that the Gehlen organization did when it went to work for the United States was done for the purpose of guaranteeing the survival of the Odessa and had nothing at all to do with the security of the western world from the Communist menace. The Communist menace was real, but it was always profoundly exaggerated by the Gehlen organization. I'm not saying that we can lay the blame for the Cold War at Gehlen's doorstep, but I am saying that it's a very important part of understanding the political transition from being in a state of alliance with the Soviet Union in to one of open hostility.

It should not be thought, however, that Gehlen's entrance into the American intelligence system represented the entrance of evil in the American foreign policy system or represented the first appearance of real malice in the government. That wouldn't be true. In fact, this is interesting. I know a guy who is writing a very important book, probably will come out this fall, Richard Russell. The book is currently titled *The Man Who Knew Too Much*. It's an unbelievably rich and highly documented and very novel contribution to this question of the Kennedy assassination. What he is showing us above all is that Oswald is part of an intelligence sphere where identities such as American, Russian, German, French, lose their meaning and everything blurs into a whirl of alliances and psuedo-alliances and loyalties and fake loyalties.

Q: You wrote a book called *Yankee-Cowboy War* where you identified these two political forces, the Cowboys and the Yankees. How did the Clinton-Gore ticket fit into that model of politics?

A: Actually the name of the book is *The Yankee and Cowboy War*. You are partly more correct than I in dropping the "and". Apparently if you have an "and" they're on the same side, like in the French and Indian War. If they are against each other, like the North-South, you just use a hyphen. In the re-issue of this book, which should be coming later this year or early next year, it'll be called *The Yankee-Cowboy War*. What it wants to say is that American politics is in an important respect a struggle between regions. And all our modernization and our jet airplanes and our telecommunications have not changed this fact. There still is an underlying regional component to our struggles and to our sense of who we are as people. And I think that happened, well in the Civil War obviously there was a fight between the north and the south and the one wins and the other loses, and the one that wins gets to run things for the most part if it wants to for a long time. Those are the yankees.

In our time it seems to me what's been happening is the center of dominance has been shifting further to the west and to the south. The rise of the Democratic Party under Clinton and Gore, I think what this shows is that the locus of political dominance is shifting away from the northeast and towards the southwest. This is in itself not good or bad. It's not even remarkable in a country that still is enduring growing pains such as ours is. The country hasn't filled up. The process of making America *America* all over is not finished. There's still an internal dynamic. And as that dynamic works its way out, power moves from the northeast to the southwest, I think. And I think that this is what the emergence of this kind of ticket in the Democratic Party represents. It means that New York is not going to be what New York used to be. It means that Los Angeles is going to be more and more important and the capitols of the states between are going to emerge. I think this could be very good. It could be very healthy. I suppose I'm a fool for wondering if it might not be possible that a ticket not based on the highly compromised political forces of the northeast, a ticket that is in some sense all scrubbed squeaky clean like the Clinton-Gore ticket, might not be able to harness some of the idealism that is latent in the American people and turn things around. I could hope a little bit for that.

Ustica Under-Reported
by Jim Cregan (with Kenn Thomas)

Critics viewing the media as an unquestioning transmittal of government disinformation, not reporting and under-reporting important events or otherwise distorting the news, should note with interest the role played by NASA spokesman James Oberg in the recent reporting of UFO events. Oberg debated Don Ecker on *Larry King Live* over the space shuttle video that apparently shows a UFO, making the doubtful claims that the maneuvering object was shuttle waste debris, with no apparent explanation for the beam that followed its right angle turn and high speed exit. Oberg appeared again on *Sightings* calling the famous crashed craft in Kecksberg, Pennsylvania a downed Soviet probe. Has Oberg been chosen by NASA as point man for the UFO cover-up?

The Houston space engineer is an expert on Soviet technology more than a public relations worker for NASA. Small wonder, then, that he was quoted by Reuters in support of the comments of Soviet air force captain and defector Alexander Zuyev, that blame for the 1983 crash of KAL 007 belonged to duplicitous bureaucrats of the Soviet Far East Command who failed to report radar outages in the Kamchatka peninsula. R.W. Johnson, in his 1986 book, *Shootdown* (Viking), and others have long argued that KAL 007 was a U. S. intelligence mission that sacrificed 269 lives, possibly for the sake of having the space shuttle Challenger monitor Soviet defenses. Johnson presents his best challenge to Oberg's previous analysis of KAL 007 on pages 157-160 of his books. L. Fletcher Prouty, in his new book, *JFK: The CIA, Vietnam and the Plot To Assassinate John F. Kennedy,* reminds those familiar with the tragedy that the CIA originally announced to the Korean Foreign Ministry—and the *New York Times* reported—that KAL 007 landed safely on Sakhalin Island, in part to ward off the investigative apparatus of the Japanese Air-Sea Rescue Fleet (Prouty, pages 342-343). This fact, along with the spy shuttle thesis, was notably absent from the Reuters report and Zuyev's subsequent *60 Minutes* interview of January 3, 1993.

Even more interesting was the *CBS Evening News* report on the Ustica air flight disaster reported upon in *Steamshovel Press #6.* How is it that after twelve years of silence, with *Steamshovel* apparently being the only magazine in America to report upon it at all, this air battle and massacre now warrants five minutes of *CBS News?*

As reported last issue, an Alitalia Itavia DC9 was shot down near Ustica Island off the coast of Sicily and 81 people died. The incident was not tracked on radar as all radar in the area mysteriously had been turned off. American military authorities stonewalled every investigation. Several new developments have happened since *SP6,* including the discovery of a recording of three radar technicians made one hour after the disaster suggesting the involvement of the American aircraft-carrier Saratoga, but the Pentagon denies the possibility, claiming that the Saratoga was not in the vicinity at the time. It also denies the presence of American war planes.

Rumors abound that the Air Italia flight got caught in a dogfight between American fighters and Libyan marauders. Wreckage from the incident was brought up last June thanks to advances in diving technology. In addition to parts of the civilian plane, parts of the wreckage were reassembled into the auxiliary fuel tank of a Corsair American fighter plane, the kind typically dispatched from aircraft carriers. This make of fuel tank only separates from the plane during combat action.

It was, perhaps, this last bit of hard evidence that occasioned the five minute blip at the beginning of *CBS News* in November. Nevertheless, the result of an intended inquiry from Italian minister of defense Salvo Ando to the U. S. Secretary of Defense Richard Cheney, went unreported in the U.S. The silence follows other curious clues of cover-up: despite the uncovering of the fuel tank, some researchers of the Ustica crash, notably Professors Pent and Vadacchino of the Polytechnic Institute of Turin (of all places), have changed their assertion that the plane was attacked by a missile and now claim that a bomb exploded within it.

The duty roster of the Saratoga on the night of the crash contains every signature in the same handwriting. The U.S. military explains that it is standard procedure to do a rough copy. Someone then copies the whole thing at the end of 24 hours for the official copy.

The latest development comes in the form of a wedding photograph taken on a hill overlooking the Ustica port near the time of the air disaster. The Saratoga can be seen in the photograph's background.

Book Reviews

" The trails are fresh. The clues are current. The case is open." So asserts Dick Russell in *The Man Who Knew Too Much* (Carroll & Graf, $27.95). Too bad the book existed only as a promotional post card at the Assassination Symposium on Kennedy in last October. Although the symposium did include an informative panel on Oswald, it would have only been enhanced if attendees had access to his remarkable addition to literature on the assassination. It builds on the working knowledge of Oswald previously distilled best in Philip H. Melanson's still available *Spy Saga* (Praeger, $21.95) through a minute examination of the author's correspondence and interviews with Richard Case Nagell, a spook with multilayered allegiances who shot up an El Paso bank in September 1963 to prevent himself from killing Oswald before Oswald killed JFK. Not that Nagell wanted Kennedy dead necessarily—Russell makes it clear that despite treachery by the intelligence world he served (admittedly only one level being U.S.) Nagell tried to do the right thing and warn the FBI of the assassination plot, warnings that went deliberately ignored. Despite the many revelations Russell pumped from Nagell, Nagell's name appears at the top of the list of potential "fresh trails" of people to be deposed. Indeed, Nagell is still out there balancing his government pension, along with the further manipulation it must represent for him (and the possibility—renewed by the publication of this book—that the government might want to end that pension early) against finally completing his life-long attempt to get the right thing done and tell all he knows.

Among the possessions Nagell has squirrelled away in a safety deposit box somewhere on foreign soil: a tape recording of Oswald's voice with Nagell and someone called only "Angel", discussing an assassination plot in August 1963. Russell also reports on a 45 RPM of Oswald on the phone line of the Soviet and Cuban diplomatic missions held by Winston Scott, CIA Mexico City chief. The tape apparently was retrieved after Scott's death by James Jesus Angleton, who no doubt lies in the grave clutching it with one hand while the other grips tightly onto Mary Pinchot Meyer's diary.

Another documentary artifact revealed in *The Man Who Knew Too Much*: an uncut copy of the Zapruder film possibly still extant, owned by the H.L. Hunt family. Robert Groden, renown for his enlargement and rotoscoping of the existing print, has long noted ten missing frames, and at the ASK conference David Lifton suggested in his Z-film workshop that many of the existing frames have been tampered with. At the ASK symposium also Groden promised good copies of the available film would be at videostores by the next conference, scheduled to begin on the thirtieth anniversary of the assassination this November, just as these suspicions and the existence of this pristine copy are beginning to become known.

Links between the government brainwashing program MKULTRA and Oswald and the assassination are brought out here in great detail and Russell also reports of another FBI memo from 11/22/63 showing George H.W. Bush—no mistaking it for the "second" Bush claimed by the White House as recipient of a previously discovered memo—trying to cast suspicion on a political rival. At the very least this puts the lie to the former president's supposed faulty memory about that date. For this and too many additional reasons in *The Man Who Knew Too Much* to list, and considering that in the current atmosphere of interest and anniversary, attendees will no doubt be quite anxious to hear an update on Dick Russell's research when he speaks at the Second Annual Midwest Symposium in Politics in Chicago, April 1-4.

Two new books, both entitled *The Gemstone File*, explore the Aristotle Onassis-kidnapped-Howard Hughes and took over the world conspiratorial view, in which the Kennedy assassination is one detail, explores the hidden machinations of the international Mafia that led to JFK's death, the takeover of the national security state via the kidnapping of Hughes and assumption of his defense contracts, the development of the Golden Triangle drug trade and its cover-up, the Vietnam War. Stephanie Caruana, a writer for *Playgirl* who came into contact with the file through Mae Brussell, distilled the enormous amount of data into a "skeleton key" chronology. She will be the subject of a *Steamshovel Press* interview next issue.

The first of the books to build on this data is edited by Jim Keith, *The Gemstone File* (IllumiNet, $14.95) and includes commentary by G.J. Krupey, Len Bracken, Robert Anton Wilson, Jonathan Vankin, X. Sharks Despot and Kerry Thornley, who has since modified his view that the Gemstone File is a hoax. The book not only presents the Gemstone material in a usable format, as opposed to the fragmented and xeroxed bootleg versions that have circulated among researchers for years, its commentary comes from writers familiar to *Steamshovel* readers. Each has taken the material in surprising and revelatory directions.

Richard Alan's *The Gemstone File* (Crown Publishing Company, POB 16261, Columbus, Ohio 43216, $29.95) is a contrast to the Keith edited volume. It seems to have developed in a vacuum a bit—it does not mention Stephanie Caruana, for instance. Apparently the author collected his archive based only on tracing the files through the public record, without collaboration or advice from the body of researchers also working on them. It also comes in a much larger format, much of which reproduces newspaper articles directly from the microfilm—advertising and all so cultural history can be examined as conspiratorial history is revealed. The primary material, Bruce Roberts' original correspondence, is still a cause for excitement among researchers as some of the original letters continue to surface, but these two volumes provide separate kinds of secondary support: the commentary of engaged researchers; and the extant public record from newspapers and magazines.

The Man On The Grassy Knoll by John R. Craig and Philip A. Rogers (Avon, $4.50) argues that the grassy knoll shooters included Chauncey Holt, Charles Harrelson and the psychopath Charles Rogers, who later killed and dismembered his parents when they discovered his involvement with JFK's death. The temptation is to put this in the same category as the Bonar Menninger/Howard Donahue *Mortal Error* book: possible, but not likely.

JFK: The CIA, Vietnam and the Plot to Assassinate John F. Kennedy by L. Fletcher Prouty (Birch Lane Press, $22), the former CIA-Pentagon liaison who has been taken to task over his association with Holocaust revisionists, presents Prouty's support for the thesis that Kennedy was killed because of changes he planned in the Vietnam policy. His relationship with the revisionists is no doubt the same as the one he had with the Scientologists, who also published his work when no one else would. Instead of Adolf Hitler, however, the philosopher that informs this book, remarkably, is R. Buckminster Fuller, who Prouty refers to constantly.

Finally, more tame spy fiction comes from the word-processor of E. Howard Hunt. His new *Chinese Red* (St. Martin's Press, $21.95) is curiously dull considering the wealth of skullduggery that characterizes his reality tunnel. One interesting note: the opening murder takes place in Charlottesville, Virginia—not too far from where Danny Casolaro, who was in communication with Hunt, met his demise. It's too much of a stretch to even qualify as a coincidence and otherwise the intrigue storied in *Chinese Red* is unusually distanced from that in the real world.

The most interesting offering from the Beat lexicon is *Pomes All Sizes* by Jack Kerouac (City Lights, $8.95), a previously unpublished manuscript, the first of four recently liberated from the legal entanglements of the Great Beat's estate, readied for publication prior to Kerouac's death in 1969. The new William Burroughs book, *The Cat Inside* (Viking, $12.50) is both slim and a bit domestic (Burroughs actually *likes* the animals) for readers anxious for another three volume epic of Burroughsian visionary madness, or at least the rumored Christ-virus novel. Nevertheless, it did inspire one reviewer to remark, "The fact that Burroughs lives with cats proves just how tolerant cats can be." And while the much anticipated Rhino anthology of Allen Ginsberg is still in the works, a new biography, *Dharma Lion* (St. Martin's, $32.50) by Michael Schumacher offers a wealth of detail missing even from Barry Miles' excellent 1989 Ginsberg bio. Schumacher sticks more closely to the biographical material surrounding the actual writing of the poems.

Another biography of a counter-culture figure, Marty Jezer's *Abbie Hoffman: American Rebel* (Rutgers University Press, $22.95) gives Hoffman a kind of *Rolling Stone* treatment with some obligatory criticism about his guerilla theater style, but no mention of the conspiracy theories surrounding his death.

Adam Parfrey's Feral House has published an anthology of material on Charles Manson, the two notorious editions of *Apocalypse Culture,* and a biography of Satanist Anton LaVey (containing incidentally, a curious photo of ufologist Jacques Vallee together with the master Satanist, unexplained as well in Vallee's recent autobiographical *Forbidden Science*), but it will no doubt receive more infamy for *Cad: A Handbook for Heels* (Feral House, $14.95). *Cad* produces cheesecake and nudie photos from "men's magazines" of the late fifties. As innocuous as *Mad Magazine,* it nevertheless includes enough female flesh to no doubt offend critics, moreso than prompt the obvious response of laughter.

Wilhelm Reich's name has re-appeared in two new weird science books. Preston Nichols' *The Montauk Project* (Sky Books, Box 769, Westbury, NY 11590, $15.95), written with Peter Moon, details the experiences of the author's involvement with a secret follow-up to the Philadelphia Experiment, which reportedly made the U.S.S. Eldridge move through time. The follow-up culminated at the Montauk Air Force Base on August 12, 1983 when according to authors, the Eldridge re-appeared. A reporter for *Newsday* documented an unpredicted electrical storm near the date. The book includes a slim appendix on Reich, more of a nod than an explanation of his work figuring into these experiments. Co-author Peter Moon explained to *Steamshovel* that "the scenario seems to be going deeper. We are planning a follow-up."

Steamshovel hopes the follow-up includes more on Reich.

Synchronistically, Leading Edge Research (POB 481-MU58, Yelm, Washington 98597) makes mention of "Reichian programming" in its examinations of "new electronic networks, use of the cellular telephone system, mind control projects and manipulations of the earth grid vortices," entitled *Matrix II* and *Matrix III* by Vladamar Valerian ($55 ea.). The one volume available to *Steamshovel*, *Matrix II*, contained brief mention of Reich's cloudbusting work and death in prison and much information on things conspiratorial and ufological, including primary documents on the Area 51 land grab and interviews with the likes of John Lear. In its discussion of "Reichian programming," a channel between the conscious and subconscious opened by a pre-orgastic state, *Matrix II* notes that this research was connected to Montauk but "it has not been determined whether the technology was a parallel development relative to Wilhelm Reich or whether the U.S. had acquired additional similar technology through alien contact after it became aware of Reich's work." The aliens seem the more likely culprit. Reich's life's work intended to heal mental suffering, not exacerbate it. It would be surprising to learn that Reich was involved in brainwashing. Before he further advances the notion that Reich was a mad scientist, it would be much appreciated if Valerian revealed the sources of this information. In any event, *Matrix II* is an admirable attempt at throwing a massive amount of data at the problems of alien abduction and manipulation. If the victims of such phenomena might be helped by orgone therapy, it would be too bad if this kind of information would cause them to avoid it.

Under the category of books-received-but-no-time-or-space-to review: *Marijuana and the Bible,* an educational look at the Ethiopian Zion Coptic Church view of the topic (available from POB 1161, Minneola, FL 34755-1161): and two more small entries from Odonian Press: *What Uncle Sam Really Wants* by Noam Chomsky and *The Decline and Fall of The American Empire* by Gore Vidal.

Holocaust Revisionism: "Myth" or Free Inquiry?
by Bradley Smith

Oliver Stone is up front about the falsehoods in his movie *JFK*. He admits he takes "artistic license" with the truth in order to tell his story. In his film, characters speak words that were not spoken by their real life models. Scenes are invented for the film that did not happen historically. A conspiracy theory is developed that he can not document.

As Stone would like to have it, as he has stated, he has created his own "myth" to stand against the orthodox myth formulated and institutionalized by the State. It sounds fair. What he has done in fact is to choose to address an historical issue with the most corrupt cinematic form exploited in Hollywood, the "docudrama."

The problems with the so-called docudrama have been discussed widely. The form does not require that anything whatever be documented. It does not require that truth be told or falsehoods denied. In short, the docudrama as a form is corrupt from beginning to end. Because of its easily accessed dramatic power, inherent in it being rooted in a real event that retains its own power to affect us deeply, it creates unnecessary intellectual and false spiritual burdens for those who take it seriously.

Oliver Stone appears to hope that myth can be shown to be politically committed to the Left of the 1960s. Not likely. Myth is a little grander than that. Better to call a Hollywood docudrama what it is, a chance for the least principled but most energetic people in that place to make unconscionable charges, which they can not demonstrate to be true against any person or any people they want. *JFK* then is a thirty-five million dollar movie structured on the sensibilities of the eighty cent super market tabloid. At the same time, while there are no documents that prove that the German state wanted to murder the Jews of Europe, and while it appears that it never occurred to the Germans to draw up plans or a budget for this little project, and while there appear to be no documents proving "gas chambers" and no documented proof of one man or woman having been "gassed" at any camp under German control, there is nevertheless a frenzy of holocaustamania whooshing like a storm through the front offices and back alleys of Hollywood calling for one Holocaust trash-epic docudrama after another.

All these Holocaust movies, whatever their form, are committed to promoting the myth of unique German monstrosity. That's how Hollywood "creates" myth. In other contexts it's been called the technique of the "Big Lie." This technique is made to order for an industry with unequaled access to mass audiences, based on expensive technology and mass distribution available only to a few, and with much of the industry in the hands of a minority that has convinced itself that a manufactured myth rooted in lies and falsehoods serves its own good.

Since the Holocaust story is so fantastic that no healthy man or woman would believe it if it were open to routine examination every other historical event in the history of the West is open to, it's necessary for the entertainment industry, acting as an agency of the Holocaust Lobby, to work like beavers to suppress every honest critique of the burgeoning Holocaust myth.

No two pursuits could be more opposite than the effort to create myth on the one hand, and the other to pursue the ideal of free inquiry. Inwardly, myth "makers" have an ill defined but unrelenting need for others to believe what they themselves want to believe, which may or may not benefit the others but which always appears to the myth maker to benefit himself as he wrestles with the pressures of his subjective life.

Free inquiry, however, doesn't make any promises to the myth makers or to anyone else either, and that's why Holocaust myth makers despise and fear it so. Free inquiry doesn't promise to reveal what truth is, but it does promise to reveal what it discovers is false and it is this promise that is such a terrible nuisance to the myth maker. The myth maker wants truth now and expects it to agree with what, inwardly, he pines for most desperately. He sees the projection of his own psychological set as a model that others would do well to guide their lives by.

Myth accumulates, it isn't manufactured by business men. Myth gathers unto itself what it wants century by century, paying little attention to the neurosis of individuals who don't like Arabs or Germans and use melodrama to punish people they imagine to be their enemies. Myth is always cooking, always cooking, no matter what any of us as an individual does or does not do. In that way too it's very different from free inquiry.

Free inquiry has to be cranked up by an individual who is willing to pursue it, with no guarantee where it might finally lead. Manufacture of myth promises comfort and success to the one who makes it up, particularly of others can be persuaded to believe it. What a comfort. Free inquiry promises that new understanding, which could wreak havoc in the life of the one who experiences it. The promise that new understanding makes is that in the moment you will become more vulnerable and less secure. Who needs it?

War crime trials where special laws were invented to try Germans for crimes that only Germans could be charged with were themselves filmed as docudramas, that is, without regard to truth. Here the State took over a vulgar cinematic form and used it to manufacture and institutionalize its own myth of World War II. The ideal of free inquiry, which is at the heart of any judicial process, was bitterly suppressed by the court representing the victories Allied military machines—the International *Military* Tribunal.

The products of the Nuremberg and other war crimes docudramas, film and text alike, were then made available to those who felt they could best profit from them. Truth was not an issue with the distributors of these materials, and has not become one since. The manufacture of a pseudo-myth was good enough for them, and that's what they got. Now, free inquiry, in the form of Holocaust revisionism, is revealing for all to see the fraud and falsehood that so much of the Hollywood and Hollywood-like Holocaust myth consists of.

A conspiracy theory can maintain its vitality even if free inquiry demonstrates that there isn't much to it, because such theory is rooted in the intellect of the few. Myth evolves from the experience of an entire culture. The irony in this instance is that the charge of conspiracy against Republicans and Democrats around the JFK murder holds a lot more water than the does the charge of "gas-chamber genocide" still being made against the National Socialist German Workers party.

In the 1960s it looks like a Democratic/Republican cabal used the Warren court to suppress evidence that contradicts much of the State's explanation for the murder of John Kennedy. In the 1940s it looks like the Democratic/Republican cabal cooperated with their friend Joseph Stalin in using the Nuremberg court to suppress evidence that would disprove the gas-chamber genocide charges. There's a kind of comfort to be gotten from such consistency of behavior, or don't you think so?

We don't need Hollywood docudrama myths-on-the-cheap to sort these affairs out for us. We need a celebration in action of the rights to free inquiry and open debate. That's what we promised ourselves at the very beginning.

Bradley R. Smith authored Confessions of A Holocaust Revisionist Part One, *published by Popular Reality, PO 2942, Ann Arbor, Michigan 48106.*

5

Steamshovel Press #8, Summer 1993

An Interview with Stephanie Caruana
author of *The Skeleton Key to the Gemstone File*

Q: Stephanie Caruana was responsible for surfacing the Gemstone File, a behind-the-scenes documentation of various power cabals involving Aristotle Onassis and Howard Hughes, among others, in connection with the Kennedy assassination. Thank you for being with us.

A: I'm delighted to talk to you.

Q: How did you first encounter the Gemstone File?

A: I was working with Mae Brussell. She was a conspiracy researcher in Carmel Valley, California for a number of years and I was a writer for *Playgirl* magazine. I got in touch with her because I wanted to find out more about the Symbionese Liberation Army's kidnapping of Patty Hearst and what was really behind it. So I went to see Mae and I began writing articles based on her research files. We began writing an article about Howard Hughes and Aristotle Onassis at the request of my editor at *Playgirl*.

Q: How did this grow out of your interest in the Patty Hearst kidnapping?

A: I was referred to Mae by a news editor of a radio station in San Francisco. I saw that she had so much information stashed away in her house in Carmel Valley, and I offered to move in with her as a sort of writing slave. My editor at *Playgirl* asked me to ask Mae if she knew anything about Howard Hughes. And Mae said, "Howard Hughes is dead. Onassis kidnapped him."

Q: This was well before it was officially announced that Hughes had died.

A: Yes. This was in 1974.

Q: What is the long and the short of what happened to Patty Hearst?

A: I was living in Berkeley about a mile from where Patty Hearst was living. When this happened, of course, everybody in Berkeley was quite shocked. It became clear that this was some sort of media event. I had never seen anything like it. There were these demands from the SLA leader, Cinque, battle

communiques; he wanted food giveaways in Oakland, which I watched. I felt that there was something going on that I really didn't understand. It seemed more media than anything else.

Q: Like an artificially constructed drama being played out on the TV news.

A: Yes. And that's when I went to see Mae. Mae had a great many interesting things to say, and we wrote an article about it which was terrific. Mae had done a lot of research on what was going on the California prison system, particularly at Vacaville prison, where there was a tremendous amount of mind control going on. I had a friend who had been there and they had given her shock treatments. It was something that was way beyond what was happening in other prisons. Mae's theory, and I believed her, was that Donald Defreeze, "Cinque", had been programmed at Vacaville through a series of classes in "Black Pride" and "Let's move along with the revolution," and possibly other forms of mind control such as drugs. He was also a three-time loser. They could have kept him in jail for the rest of his life. There was no chance that he could ever have gotten out. He was what Mae called a yo-yo, which is a prisoner that these people have on a string. They can let him out of prison for their own purposes and pull him back any time they want, completely under the control of the authorities.

Q: So you went to work for Mae doing research on Howard Hughes.

A: I was staying at Mae's house and she had these enormous files. She pulled out a file on Howard Hughes with all these clippings, and a file on Onassis and all these other clippings. And it was a tremendous rush job, a very fast deadline. It was supposed to be the major article for their Christmas issue. So I started reading and reading, but Mae's theory that Onassis had kidnapped Howard Hughes—I said, "Mae, I don't see it. I see articles about Hughes and Onassis, but I don't see any cross. So where are you getting this idea from?" And at that point, she said, "Well, I have these other letters from this guy. He gave me these letters back in 1972. I read them, and I thought maybe he's just a crazy-whacko kind of person, but I have since then received somewhat similar suggestions from a couple of other sources. So I tend to put more credence in it than I did originally." And she gave me a way of looking at things that I found was something I could accept. And I find myself using that. She said, "When I hear the same story from three different sources, I tend to think it may be true." So she had the story about Onassis and Hughes from one source, and then she had this Canadian tabloid and she had another source. If you have three vectors, you can locate a point in three dimensions.

Q: So the letters were the Bruce Roberts letters? What is the connection between Bruce Roberts and Mae Brussell? Who did Bruce work for?

A: He didn't work for anybody. He was his own man. And I would say without a doubt that he was the most incredibly amazing and fantastic person I have ever met in my entire life.

Q: How did you meet Bruce Roberts?

A: I read the letters at Mae's, and I was absolutely stunned by them. I was overwhelmed by them. There was so much information and it was written in such a brilliant style. I found it believable. Maybe I was different from Mae. I read it all over the space of one night or possibly two nights, but straight. Couldn't put it down. I was at the same time writing this article. I became very curious about Bruce Roberts. I asked Mae what he was like, and she gave me her impression. She told me that she had met him in 1972 and he had given her these letters. And she said that she didn't believe them at first, but she did now. By this time, it was 1974. After several months I decided that I didn't want to work with Mae any more; it was getting to be too dreary. I went to San Francisco, and the first thing I did was I went to Bruce Roberts' house and looked him up.

Q: *The Skeleton Key to the Gemstone File* is an outline that you created based on your review of all the Roberts letters.

A: He arranged for me to read some of his more recent letters, and I made notes. The *Skeleton Key* is a chronological outline based on my notes and my conversations with him, and whatever made sense to me. Believe me, I left out more than I put in.

It was a very dangerous situation for everybody. We were all living in a powderkeg and this man really was surrounded by murders. While I released the file, I didn't feel that I had any right to release a great many personal details about him or his sources, and that's why I didn't.

Bruce Roberts read the *Skeleton Key* and it seemed as though he approved of it in a way, which really amazed me. And he used to call me up sometimes and ask me to go to certain events, and bring copies along and give copies to people.

Q: When did he die?

A: He died in 1976. I would say that he was murdered. Supposedly, he died of a brain tumor, but that man was so healthy and so tough that I think he was killed. They almost killed him while I was there. That's why I released the *Key* in the first place. I was so upset. I was just enraged and I felt that I had to get the story out.

The Gemstone File is the best history we have of the Kennedy assassination and of that time. I'm not talking about my own work. I only wish I had the original letters. I have a couple of them but I don't have the whole thing. But this man was a historian in the real sense of the word. Of course, the people that are running our country at this point, one thing they want to kill is anybody who wants to tell the truth about what's going on.

Q: I realize the Kennedy assassination is only one detail in a long story about the hidden machinations of what's happening, the thrust of which is that the international Mafia with Aristotle Onassis at its head is the group that's calling the shots.

A: Of course, they have become so ingrained in the American society, can you call them Mafia? They all wear business suits. They've all got loads of money. They're all "respectable" businessmen—well, not all of them. The killers aren't, but the guys who tell the killers what to do and pay them, all of our big business people. I have a list somewhere of the hundred richest families or people in the country and it's probably the same people who are the Mafia. I'd like to compare notes.

Q: One of the criticisms laid at the feet of people who suggest Mafia involvement in Kennedy's death is that the Mafia couldn't do a cover-up over these thirty years. That may not necessarily be true when you consider that the Mafia and the high-ranking members of the intelligence community are basically the same people.

A: They are now. The factor that ties them together for me anyway is Onassis because according to Bruce Roberts, who I believe, he kidnapped Howard Hughes in 1957. And Howard Hughes was an extraordinarily rich and powerful man with a tremendous empire. And Howard Hughes had already bribed Richard Nixon. So Howard Hughes had vice-President Nixon in his pocket at that time. As I talk about this, in my mind I have this picture of the food chain in the ocean. A little fish gets swallowed by a bigger fish, who gets swallowed by a bigger fish, and a bigger fish...And Onassis was the biggest fish in the ocean. And along came Hughes, who was so huge that he became a tempting morsel for Onassis, who swallowed him up. And he got away with it. It was an imaginative stroke of genius by a man who was more powerful than Alexander the Great. He was the richest man in the world and the most powerful man in the world. And he ran the world until he died.

Stephanie Caruana lives on a mountain in New York. Three recent books have been devoted to the Gemstone File: The Gemstone File, *edited by Jim Keith and available from IllumiNet Press, POB 2088, Lilburn, GA 30226;* The Gemstone File *by Richard Alan, Crown Publishing Company, POB 16261-B, Columbus, Ohio 43216;* and The Gemstone File *by Stephanie Caruana, POB 192, Cragsmoor, NY 12420.*

Philip K. Dick and the Illuminati
by Jim Keith

The most fascinating account I have encountered of a possible contact with an alien intelligence is the book *VALIS* by Philip K. Dick. Aspects of the book which seem to be little understood are symbols which point to an encounter with what we can accurately term the Illuminati. The messages in *VALIS* are coded, and the meanings encoded are Freemasonic, comprising in fact a relatively exhaustive recapitulation of Freemasonic lore and agenda.

VALIS is a semi-fictionalized account of "Horselover Fat," Dick's alter ego (the name formulated from word derivations of his name), and Dick's meeting with what he takes to be God or at least a God, via the medium of a pink beam of light. Dick dubs this god VALIS (a Vast Active Living Intelligence System).

Dick's vision came about when, in March of 1974 and suffering from two impacted wisdom teeth, he waited in his apartment in Anaheim, California for a pain killer prescription from a local pharmacy. When the delivery person from the pharmacy arrived at the door it was a young woman wearing a golden fish-emblem necklace. Dick reflects that:

"For some reason I was hypnotized by the gleaming golden fish; I forgot my pain, forgot the medication, forgot why the girl was there. I just kept staring at the fish sign.

"'What does that mean?' I asked her.

"The girl touched the glimmering golden fish with her hand and said, 'This is a sign worn by the early Christians.' She then gave me the package of medication.

"In that instant, as I stared at the gleaming fish sign and heard her words, I suddenly experienced what I later learned is called *anamnesis* - a Greek word meaning, literally, 'loss of forgetfulness.' I remembered who I was and where I was. In an instant, in the twinkling of an eye, it all came back to me. And not only could I remember it but I could see it. The girl was a secret Christian and so was I. We lived in fear of detection by the Romans. We had to communicate in cryptic signs. She had just told me all this, and it was true."

The sudden influx of knowledge had been caused by a pink beam of light which shot out of the necklace, apparently penetrating directly into Dick's head and imparting a vast array of information, including knowledge of several languages which he hadn't previously understood. Aside from feeling a sort of hyper-rationality, Dick sensed that he had been taken over by a superior mind which had memories dating back in excess of two thousand years. Later Dick was to hear troubling, grotesque messages coming out of his radio telling him to die, and to have an all-night display of graphic inner visions similar to thousands of abstract paintings seen in succession projected upon his mind's eye. He also experienced a superimposition of the features of ancient Rome onto those of California in the 1970s, and formed the conviction that the present world was locked in a Black Iron Prison, a state of spiritual (and probably physical) entrapment.

From these experiences and others Dick evolved a complex body of speculation, from which he drew a trio of books including *VALIS* and a lengthy *Exegesis* of several thousand pages of handwritten notes about the nature of his contact with what he determined to be God.

Dick's experiences with VALIS were not altogether benign. After his encounter (and a breakup with his wife) Dick attempted to kill himself, ending up in a mental ward instead.

What Dick believed to be the source of his contact is particularly interesting:

"'Where did the plasmate [VALIS] originally come from?'

"After a pause Fat said, 'From another star system.'

"'You wish to identify that star system?'

"'Sirius,' Fat said.

In *VALIS* Dick relates the fairly well-known information on the Dogon tribe and their startling and unexplainably exact astronomical knowledge about the Sirius system (as described in *The Sirius Mystery* by Robert G.K. Temple —possibly a pseudonym?). The Dogon, Dick says, "got their cosmogony and cosmology directly from the three-eyed invaders who visited long ago. The three-eyed invaders are mute and deaf and telepathic, could not breathe our atmosphere, had the elongated misshapen skull of Ikhnaton and emanated from a planet in the star-system Sirius. Although they had no hands, but had instead, pincer claws such as a crab has, they were great builders."

Dick has Horselover Fat dreaming of these three-eyed creatures:

"They manifested themselves as cyborg entities: wrapped up in glass bubbles staggering under masses of technological gear...Soviet technicians could be seen, hurrying to repair malfunctions of the sophisticated technological communications apparatus enclosing the three-eyed people."

He also believed that:

"Our world is still secretly ruled by the hidden race descended from Ikhnaton, and his knowledge is the information of the Macro-Mind itself...From Ikhnaton this knowledge passed to Moses, and from Moses to Elijah, the Immortal Man, who became Christ. But underneath all the names there is only one Immortal Man, and we are that man.

"Real time ceased in 70 C.E. with the fall of the Temple at Jerusalem [i.e. the Temple of Solomon]. It began again in 1974. The intervening period was a perfect spurious interpolation aping the creation of the Mind. 'The Empire never ended,' but in 1974 a cypher was sent out as a signal that the Age of Iron was over; the cypher consisted of two words: KING FELIX, which refers to the Happy (or Rightful) King.

"The two-word cypher signal KING FELIX was not intended for human beings but for the descendants of Ikhnaton, the three-eyed race which, in secret, exists with us." Dick believed that "The person referred to by the two-word cypher KING FELIX is the fifth Savior who...VALIS had said, was either already born or would soon be."

Out of the VALIS communications, "...Fat deduced that he had a mission, that the plasmate's invasion of him represented its intention to employ him for its benign purposes."

Of Ikhnaton's three-eyed kin, Dick alter-ego Fat observes, "My God... These are the original builders...", to which statement another character replies, "We have never stopped... We still build. We built this world, this space-time matrix." These are approximately the same terms with which the Freemasons refer to themselves in such tomes as Albert Pike's *Morals and Dogma*. There is no mistaking the connection for anyone with the slightest familiarity with Masonic lore. And VALIS, we learn, employs the same mystical communication system as the Masons: "...all its verbal information is stored as Cabala..."

The Cabala (alternate spelling, Kabbalah) is an ancient form of Jewish mysticism which pervades Freemasonry, top of pyramid to base.

Dick describes the method by which VALIS initiates secretly communicate with each other: "During a handshake, a motion with one finger of two intersecting arcs: swift expression of the fish symbol, which no one beyond the two persons involved could discern." Unless, of course, you accidentally tried the handshake on a Freemason.

In his *Exegesis* Dick amplified on his beliefs:

"For the first time I have inferential evidence that a genuine secret fraternity of authentic Xtians exists, & has affected history... & possess supernatural powers & Immortality, due to direct links back to Christ - so they are the true hidden church. The two historic interventions which I am sure of collate: the secret fraternity fights the Empire (Rome in all its manifestations) & promotes the evolution of man to higher levels by inner & outer regeneration. The 16th, 17th century illuminati are connected with this secret brotherhood..."

Whether the godlike VALIS was involved at all, what was communicated to Dick seems to be approximately what the Freemasons and their brethren want us to believe about their mission: that theirs is an ancient tradition resting on an immortal bloodline from the star Sirius, and that the fulfillment of their plans (including the rebuilding of the Temple of Solomon, and the enthronement of a World King — their secret agenda hidden within their inner circle cant) is the only salvation for this soon-to-be One World.

Dick seems to have come to believe that VALIS took the form of a satellite, firing electronic beams of information down upon the Earth. Or perhaps crop circles? He has one of his characters say, "The satellite had control of them from the get-go. It could make them see what it wanted them to see...The satellite has occluded them, all of them. The whole fucking United States."

There are other indications that the actual VALIS which Dick contacted may have come from another source than Sirius.

"In Fat's [i.e. Dick's] opinion his apartment had been saturated with high levels of radiation of some kind." He theorized that "...the Rosicrucians [philosophic precursors of the Masons, with little if any connection to current groups of the same name] were telepathically beaming pictures at him, probably boosted by microrelay systems of an advanced order; but then, when Kandinsky paintings began to harass him, he recalled that the main art museum at Leningrad specialized in just such nonobjective moderns, and he decided that the Soviets were attempting telepathically to contact him."

Later Dick theoretically pinpoints the transmissions as originating from the schemes of a crippled rock musician named Mini:

"He [Mini] visited the Soviet Union one time; he said he wanted to see certain experiments they were conducting with microwave information transfer over long distances." Fat himself comes to believe within the pages of *VALIS* that "All that was involved from the start... was advanced laser technology. Mini found a way to transmit information by laser beam, using human brains as transducers without the need for an electronic interface. The Russians can do the same thing. Microwaves can be used as well. In March 1974 I must have intercepted one of Mini's transmissions by accident; it irradiated me."

Actually, I really doubt that Dick felt the source of his infernal "enlightenment" was a rock musician. It happens that information beam experiments of exactly the type that Dick speculated on were at about that time being conducted by both the CIA and the KGB.

CIA Director Richard Helms has described research taking place in the 1960s into "sophisticated approaches to the 'coding' of information for transmittal to population targets in the 'battle for the minds of men'..." as well as "an approach integrating biological, social and physical-mathematical research in attempts... to control behavior." He has described "use of modern information theory, automata theory, and feedback concepts... for a technology for controlling behavior... using information inputs as causative agents."

Anna Keel, in *Full Disclosure* magazine, writes that, "Due to [the CIA's] Project Pandora, it is now known that applied biological (and other) frequencies can also be used as direct 'information inputs' (e.g., of feeling or emotion) and to reinforce brain rhythms associated with conditioning and information processing. One way to get such a signal into a human may be through use of a high frequency carrier frequency. Results of research into information processing, unconscious processes, decision making, memory processes and evoked brain potentials would likely be exploited or integrated in an interdisciplinary system.

"For difficult subscribers...there are substances that have psychological or psychobiological effects ranging from subtle through devastating, and that cause increased susceptibility to conditioning. Some of these substances are similar to ones which are recognized by neurotoxicologists or behavioral toxicologists as occupational hazards; some are variations of substances used experimentally in laboratories to produce selective damage in certain neuronal tracts. Many substances needn't be injected or orally ingested, as they may be inhaled or applied with 'skin transferral agents,' i.e. chemicals like the popular industrial solvent, dimethylsulphoxide (DMSO), which can, in fact, enhance the applied substance's effect. For instance, some compounds cause damage that produces increased sensitivity to stimulus, distraction (or flooding of thought associations), and enhance susceptibility to influence, i.e., a state where automatic parallel information processing, which usually takes place outside of awareness, interferes with conscious or more intentional limited channel processing. While causing acute

mental symptoms wouldn't be the goal in groups, producing mild distraction, an ego weakened blurring between the sense of 'I' and 'you', would enhance some kinds of conditioning and promote suggestibility; then, perhaps transmitted 'thought associations, 'the voice of God', 'lucky advice' or whatever, can more easily get through and have an effect... [emphasis added] Convenient to the agencies involved in covert influence is that among primary syptoms of schizophrenia or mental illness are ideas that one is being influenced by 'transmissions' (e.g. radio frequencies), 'voices' or even telepathy; unless complaints about covert psychological weapons are well organized, they would tend to be discounted as indicative of mental imbalance."

Another approach which may have been used is the transmittal of "key concepts" to matters of which the subject is already conversant, creating a "realignment" of the subject's entire sense of reality by the injection of just a few bits of information, images, or sentences. In Dick's case this might have involved accessing his study into religious symbolism and history. A fast acting hallucinogen and a beamed transmission of religious concepts might have made him very susceptible to the idea that, due to an unexplainable event of "gnosis", he had tapped into the secrets of reality.

Dick describes a message broadcast "Out over the airwaves by one of the largest TV stations in the world, NBC's Los Angeles outlet, reaching many thousands of children with this split-second information which would be processed by the right hemispheres of their brains; received and stored and perhaps decoded, below the threshold of consciousness where many things lay slumbering and stored." He terms the message the 'KING FELIX cypher', and reports that, "The United States Army cryptographers studied it but couldn't discern who it was intended for or what it meant." Later he talks about a TV ad for a supermarket chain. "...on the screen the words FOOD KING appeared - and then they cut instantly, rushing their film along as fast as possible so as to squeeze in as many commercial messages as possible; what came next was a Felix the Cat cartoon...One moment FOOD KING appeared on the screen and then almost instantly the words - also in huge letters - FELIX THE CAT. There it had been, the juxtaposed cypher, and in the proper order: KING FELIX..."

I don't know whether the KING FELIX cypher or the Food King/Felix the Cat messages were actually broadcast (other than in *VALIS,* that is), but discounting the possibility out-of-hand would be unwise. Certainly similar messages have been sent over the airwaves, such as the Eye in the Triangle station break presented by CBS during 1992, or the subliminal image of the Statue of Liberty projected between the film frames of an ALF cartoon, as reported in *TV Guide.*

While the first example — the Eye in the Triangle — seems sinister enough, what of the second: the Statue of Liberty image? Surely that must have been slipped into the programming by some zealous right wing patriot skulking in the CBS editing room. So one would tend to believe, but check out what conspiracy researcher Norma Cox has to say in her *Secrets* newsletter on the subject of Lady Liberty:

"[This] is the statue of the Moon Goddess, Diana... This Queen of Heaven is also the Queen of Democracy... Diana's right arm holds a great torch (symbolizing the Sun) high in the air. The left arm (right and left symbolic of male and female), grasps a tablet which bears the date of the Declaration of Independence. A crown with huge spikes, like sun rays, rests on her head (the crown covertly represents our satellite, the Moon)... Note the similarity between Juno, holding aloft a sword and Diana, whose statue, symbolizing Freedom, Equality and Worldwide Brotherhood, stands in New York harbor. Worshipped as Juno Lucina, the Bringer of Light, Illuminism's [or Freemasonry's] adoration of this Moon goddess ranks only slightly below that of the god of the Sun who, in the case of Juno, is Jupiter (Zeus), her husband."

Ultimately the VALIS odyssey is difficult to interpret with any absolute sense of certainty about what took place that day in March of 1974. It shines with points of illumination whose meaning remains elusive against the explanations of prosaic reality.

What we do know is that, for whatever reason, in whatever fashion, Philip Dick had almost the entire Illuminist-Freemasonic mythos thrust into his forebrain, and that he struggled with it, trying to make sense of its symbolism, for the short period of time which remained of his life.

Either he was force-fed a massive injection of Freemasonic mythology via electronic beam, or in a moment of dreadful illumination — or perhaps hallucinogenic receptivity — Philip K. Dick saw the truth of the world.

This article is excerpted from the book Saucers of the Illuminati *by Jim Keith, forthcoming from IllumiNet Press, P.O. Box 2808, Lilburn, GA 30226.*

Mae Brussell: Secret Service Files on the Queen of Conspiracy Theorists
by X. Sharks DeSpot

" *We are identical to Germany in 1932...Nothing is natural today. Billions are going into creating divisions, terror, to make headlines, to spread confusion and fear.''(1)*

If ever there was a time Mae Magnin Brussell summed up her view of the world, that was it. The country, indeed the whole world, was being transformed into a police state, a gigantic conspiracy which was responsible for almost every disturbing event. As her obituary stated:

"Ms. Brussell contended that the Kennedy assassinations, Martin Luther King's assassination, the (Charles) Manson family murders, the Chappaquiddick affair and the Patricia Hearst kidnapping were all set into motion by the far right, the CIA, the FBI and the Mafia under a massive conspiracy to discredit the left and establish a fascist state.''(2)

This, along with her speaking style, condemned Mae Brussell to minority status. She may not have been, as an FBI agent said, a "crank", but she was on the political fringe throughout her twenty five year long career. Most people, regardless of political affiliation and ideology, simply do not see the country as being on the verge of fascism.

She did have several advantages. First and foremost is that she was a true believer. Most of the 120 pages which make up her Secret Service file were generated because she called the Secret Service. More than half the file's bulk would not exist if she had simply refrained from sending letters to presidents, calling up various police agencies, or visiting Maureen Reagan, daughter of the then-president Ronald Reagan. Someone who was only interested in the publicity would probably have lost interest in what she did as she became old news. If she had been trying to make money, she simply would not have invited trouble by annoying the Secret Service as often as she did.

This, I think, was because she was topical. She spent a large amount of time simply clipping magazine articles and cross-referencing them with her ever-growing collection of newspaper clippings and books. As a result, she was usually very up-to-date, focusing on Watergate and Howard Hughes during the 1970s, and then changing her emphasis to Contragate during the 1980s. She provided a fresh conspiratorial topic with each of her weekly radio shows: cattle mutilations; the House Select Committee on Assassinations;

Interpol; the Jonestown Guyana massacre; and on and on. There was hardly a conspiratorial topic which she did not cover. Her confidence in conspiracy theories never ended because conspiracy theories kept coming up.

Her United States Secret Service file begins some time after May 20, 1973. The first thing in the file is a letter from Mae Brussell to President Richard M. Nixon, asking that he stop by and discuss with her the problems of the nation. The letter gives one the feeling of having walked into the middle of a play but having missed the beginning. This is because of a fact in a memo on the same file, apparently typed on a piece of paper to which Brussell's mailing envelope was stapled:

"File on subject has been destroyed. Suggest we find out if subject's father known to administration. I believe this woman should be interviewed.''

Why was her file destroyed? And what was in it? The two most important facts are that Mae Brussell wrote the first real article about Watergate, in *The Realist* underground news magazine in 1972. The second is that her father was Rabbi Edgar Magnin, who had prayed for Nixon's presidency at his 1972 inauguration. It seems obvious that the Secret Service had spied on her because of *The Realist* article, or because the Secret Service agents in question felt it would be expedient to protect Nixon's friends.

In November of 1973, Brussell was scheduled to attend a rally at the Archives Building in Washington, DC, sponsored by the Committee to Open the Archives. "PURPOSE OF THE RALLY IS TO DEMAND ACCESS TO JFK ASSASSINATION MATERIAL" intones the teletype message. The San Francisco, California office of the Secret Service went out and bought a copy of *The Realist* and the *Mae Brussell Conspiracy Newsletter*. After that, there is no indication of any attempt to actually watch her. It was also one of the few times that the Secret Service seemed to be taking her seriously. She was the daughter of Nixon's good friend, and that was her importance to the Secret Service.

Aside from a few minor incidents, her file is uninteresting until she wrote a letter to Carter National Campaign Headquarters August 18, 1976. The subsequent interview by the Secret Service on December 4, 1976 said:

"Brussell stated that she was quite concerned with

President-elect Carter's leaving the country to vacation in the Virgin Islands, in that she felt that he, Carter, would be killed.

Brussell also stated that another assassination group that she is aware of is one that is located in the Los Angeles area. She further advised that this group has a member, a secret service agent, whom she did not name, and members of the California Highway Patrol, Los Angeles Police Department, have trained with the CIA in the Mohave Desert. The subject did not identify her source of information, however, it is known that she is a subscriber to at least eight daily newspapers representing various parts of this country.

The assassins seeking to kill President-elect Carter included "President Ford, Richard Helms, ambassador to Iran, John Connolly, (sic) Paul Laxalt, acting as Ronald Reagan's representatives from Summa Corporation (Howard Hughes Corporation)."

To people who had read her writings before, it was familiar. Evelle Younger had presided over the investigation in the murder of Senator Robert Kennedy in 1968, and she had asserted in the letter to the Carter Campaign that "Ronald Reagan was selected by American Intelligence and all the Pentagon and Intelligence powers to be their man. Nothing, not Jimmy Carter, can stand in their way." As she said in 1977, "I believe that the pecking order for front man Presidents always was Nixon, Agnew, then Reagan. Carter is an interim after Watergate."(3)

Since she was right, it should be pointed out that Ronald Reagan and the conservative wing of the Republican party attempted to take over the 1976 Republican Convention. They completed their task in 1980, and got Reagan elected.

But Presidential would-be assassin John Hinckley tried to undo Reagan with a .22 revolver. The "Duty Desk Incident Report" of "04-09-81" says:

"NARRATIVE: On 04-09-81 Mae Brussell called the San Francisco FO to report that she believes that John Hinckley may have been near her home in Carmel, California on 01-13-81."

Written in felt pen was the message:

"Note: this division is attempting to account for Hinckley's movements (all of them). Brussell thinks she sited (sic) Hinckley on 1-13-81, a day USSS (Author's note: United States Secret Service, probably) cannot account for re: Hinckley."

This was Brussell's finest hour in the Secret Service file. "San Francisco said that the subject, Brussell, appears legitimate." Of all the statements she made to agents of the Secret Service between 1975 to 1987, this was the only one treated with any seriousness at all. Brussell had provided them with a license plate number of a 1960 Alfa Romero BTM and the descrip-

tion of the couple driving it, including a man who seemed to be Hinckley. On "6-24-81," two months after being interviewed by the Service, a message was sent to "USSS Headquarters (ID-ACB REGION IV)": "Santa Barbara has determined the probability that the subject observed by Mae Brussell was not John Hinckley."

But Brussell didn't believe it, if she was told at all.

At 3:30 in the afternoon, January 30, 1982, she stepped up to the daughter of the President of the United States of America and stated "I have some information for you regarding the Hinckley family but the secret service won't let me talk to you. If you would just call me."

The next day she was interviewed by the Service: "Brussell made several remarks regarding her belief that vice president Bush was behind a plot to remove President Reagan from office..."

One of the obvious things about Brussell's Secret Service file is the lack of malice and ill will. In contrast to the FBI attitude towards, say Dr. Martin Luther King, Brussell and the Secret Service agents she met with seemed unable to create any hostility towards each other. On May 14, 1982 the Secret Service received a letter addressed to an agent with Brussell asking for a picture of an old girl friend of John Hinckley's she had read about in the May 9, 1982 issue of the San Francisco *Sunday Examiner and Chronicle*. Why should she trust the Service to do that? Apparently, she had trouble believing that the agent she wrote to could be evil.

In an interview with Brussell on 7/23/87, the report said:

"Subject stated that she no longer planned to publish handbills exposing the pope's criminal history because she realized it would therefore be a waste of money...stated that she planned to be out of town on the day of the Pope's visit."

Why did Brussell change her mind about publishing handbills? Most likely because the agent in question asked her not to.

The last entry in her file was her obituary from the San Jose *Mercury News,* October 5, 1988. The file itself has obviously been censored, but it is difficult to say what was left out of the pages released. Certainly, the Service would have talked to the local police department, and descriptions of two of her children were censored out of the December 29, 1976 interview. Brussell freely described over her radio show details of her own life that the Secret Service would have felt obligated to censor out, such as her children's names.

The bulk of the file consists of Brussell's talk of conspiracy theories, yet the agents in question obviously felt that personal information, not political world view, was most important. She frequently mentioned alleged "interlocking connections between Nazi activities and the takeover of the U.S. government" but not one word was said by the agents about this plot. The fact of the matter is, as Linda Hunt has shown in her book, *Secret Agenda,* the United States government had very little problem with recruiting Nazis after World War II for its crusade against Communism, and by the mid-1970s proof of this was available to anyone who walked into a public library.

The only thing certain is that it was the Queen, not her kingdom, which interested the United States Secret Service.

1. *Conspiracy Digest Interview,* Winter 1977-1978 issue.

2. *San Jose Mercury News,* B 1, "Conspiracy Theorist Mae Brussell Dies," by Ann W. O'Neill.

3. *Conspiracy Digest Interview,* Winter 1977-1978 issue.

4. *World Watchers International* Tape #360, 10/27/78.

Mae Brussell created a large amount of material, tapes and magazine articles, in life. Large amounts of it are now out of print. Audio tapes of her radio show are available from Al Kunzer, 348 English Avenue, Monterey, CA 93940. The *Conspiracy Digest* interview can be purchased from A-Albionic Research, POB 20273, Ferndale, Michigan 48220. A collection of Mae Brussell's essays, *The Mae Brussell Reader,* can be purchased from Prevailing Winds Research, POB 23511, Santa Barbara, CA 93121.

X. Sharks Despot has contributed to Steamshovel Press, Dharma Combat *and the IllumiNet edition of* The Gemstone File.

Saucer Section:
An Interview with Sean Morton
author of *The Millennium Factor*

Q: Sean Morton is a member of the group called the Delphi Associates, which has been involved in various forms of prediction and prophecy. We met in Las Vegas when I visited Area 51. Thank you for being here tonight.

A: Thank you for having me. I appreciate it.

Q: Your take on what I saw out at Area 51 was that it was some kind of SDI flare.

A: Yes. I had the advantage of driving down from Lake Tahoe at the same time you saw what it was you were seeing. I was looking at it from about sixty miles away up at a place called Warm Springs. I was ready for it because I knew something always happens at six o'clock. My friend John Lear had told me that Warm Springs was a good place for a sighting, so I had driven my car up at about 4:45 and parked it up on a hill and had my binoculars out and was ready for it when it happened. So right on schedule between 6:00 and 6:05, looking at it through the binoculars, what I saw was a triangle of helicopters and this triangle of helicopters flying in formation then had a red light that flew into it. Now this was a flashing strobe of some kind. I wasn't sure if a plane was attached to it but it didn't make the maneuvers that a "conventional" UFO would make. And all of this was very, very quiet. I'm not sure if I was too far away to actually hear the sound, but it is the open desert. What this did was that it flew into the triangle of helicopters, did an L-shaped curve, not a right-angle turn like the saucers do, but did a curve and then behind the curve, as it sped out, laid down behind it a row of five of these fireballs. Now they didn't look like the conventional military flares, which of course have smoke on them and float down. These things seemed to hang in mid-air as if they had some sort of propulsion of their own and then blinked out very rapidly one at a time, just bink, bink, bink. So I believe this was probably just a surface-to-air missile. It takes the heat-seeking missiles off the track. Of course, we saw this at six o'clock and I believe there was another demonstration of this at 6:45 and at 9:30 when we were up at the Little A"Le"Inn, the exact same thing happened to the west of the Little A"Le"Inn, very low. They weren't after-burners on jets, but looking at it through the binoculars, there was a lot of conventional activity around it.

I'm not saying that there aren't saucers there, but when you see the saucers they will appear and they will glow up very brilliantly and they will juke back and forth. They will zip very rapidly back and forth across the sky. They usually are not accompanied by those type of maneuvers.

Q: Let me explain that Sean is also an independent researcher who has worked with programs like *Unsolved Mysteries* and has done reports for *Sightings* and *Now It Can Be Told*. What exactly is your take on Area 51? It sounds to me like you seem to think that there's a combination of weird saucer activity and SDI research there.

A: Yes. Area 51 has been probably one of the most secret above-ground skunk works that the U.S. government maintains. 51 has been around for quite some time. Area 51 is a map classification that is part of what's called the Nellis Gunnery range, or also known as the Nevada Test Site. Quite specifically, it's also called Dreamland on all of the map classification charts, or Red Square because no one is actually allowed to fly over the area. For many, many years my dad was an experimental test pilot who actually flew the SR71 Blackbird out of Area 51. It was where the SR71 Blackbird was developed. It's where the U2 spy plane was developed. It's where they are currently testing everything from Russian Migs that we've captured to the Stealth bomber, both the B1 and the B2, and of course the F1-17A, which is the Stealth fighter, all fly out of Area 51.

Now this is, of course, the conventional warfare that we fly out of there. However, very interesting things began to occur in 1986-87 when the military decided that they wanted to expand their borders by 89,000 acres. After applying to the U.S. Congress and being denied, they simply took the land by force, throwing people out of their homes at gunpoint, in essence, confiscating this land. And right after was when they started moving what I believe is extraterrestrial technology, to be tested there. We found out about this from a scientist named Bob Lazar. We had actually known about the unusual activity before that, but the first time ever that we actually had somebody come forward, a scientist, this fellow Bob Lazar, came forward and literally defected from the project and said that we had nine captured alien flying saucers, that this was technology that was completely above and beyond the realm of anything that he'd ever seen, being at the top levels of our physics and our science, and that we were reverse-engineering these projects. We were taking them apart, trying to figure out how they worked, and that we actually had our test pilots inside these things, figuring out how they fly.

I did an interview with him for a documentary I was directing at the time, which was called *UFO Contactees,* which has now become the *UFO Magazine Library* and a whole set of home videos that this producer is now selling. Lazar basically stated to us, "Look, you don't have to believe a thing I say. All you have to do is go out on Highway 375, stand by this mailbox from about 6PM to about 1AM and you'll see flying saucers." And the first time, and really one of the only times I've ever seen anything that I couldn't explain, is out at Area 51. Since then, since February 1991 when I first went out there, I've literally seen hundreds of everything from discs to giant airplane-like craft, or should I say wedge-shaped craft, to triangles, all of which exhibit a propulsion system which completely defies any of the laws of gravity as we know them.

Q: Let's back up a bit: the military took over a large amount of land illegally? And there hasn't been any kind of protest?

A: There was originally by certain citizens groups who complained to Harry Reed and Floyd Lamb, who were the congressmen and the senators at the time. There were some hearings on it where they had the commandant of Nellis Air Force base and Harry Reed asked him, "Commandant, what gives you the right to simply confiscate public land?" And he says, "Congressman, we answer to a higher authority." And, of course, Reed said, "Well, what authority do you consider higher than the United States government?" And he sort of harumphed for a second and said, "We'd be happy to answer that question for you behind closed doors." What happened was that they then took anybody who was protesting, or anybody on this committee, and they took them on a tour of the base and after they showed them whatever it was they had up there, they came back quite happy and quite satisfied and said fine, the military can keep the land. It is out in the middle of nowhere and there were only probably about maybe fifty to a hundred people that were actually involved, who actually protested this. And Nevada is the military's playground anyway, so but whatever it is they showed them out there apparently impressed them enough that they said the military can do whatever they damn well please and all civilian protests were just ignored after that.

Q: So what you think they're doing out there is a combination of back-engineering these alien craft and also different forms of exotic SDI research.

A: They fly that stuff during the day. You can see the Stealth Bomber and the Stealth fighter flying up and down that valley during the day. Usually at night is when they test the saucers. One, they like a low cloud cover because satellites can't see whatever it is. Two, they don't want to have to explain it to their own people. Three, I think one of the reasons why so many of these saucers were not flying over the test site but were flying on the public side of the valley, where you and I were, is because of the fact that the Atomic Energy Commission has its base just up and sort of on the other side to the north of this. And there were some rumors that Nellis had actually requested the AEC to turn its back, to literally shut off its radar while they were testing some of the spooky stuff. And the AEC simply said no. So they had to start testing the stuff over public land where they couldn't actually be spied upon by any other government agencies.

Q: The sightings there take place on a regular basis. I understand that there's at least one that appears regularly at about a quarter after four in the morning.

A: Right, Old Faithful. It usually comes in, something comes in and it lands at exactly 4:50. Another project that you have going on there that's spectacular and has the most effect on people is the Aurora projects. Now we found out about Aurora because the military made a mistake and put Aurora in a white budget column when it was supposed to be in a black budget column. When Congress said, "What's this you're spending all these billions of dollars on?", the military panicked and said it's nothing, it's a clerical error, it's a mistake. But we found out since then that they have different surveillance and reconnaissance programs, which is why they're called "senior" programs. For example, the Blackbird was called Senior Crown. But they supposedly have a number of other projects called Senior Citizen and Senior Prom.

Senior Citizen is, and we've actually seen this thing land, is about eight hundred feet long and it looks like a huge wedge, like two door stops placed one on top of the other. The bottom half of it is black and the top half of it is white. It's cut off at the back and has a propulsion system that manifests itself as multi-colored lights. This thing creates a shock wave as it comes in from space. And it creates a .4 skyquake, which has been registered by Cal Tech. It actually creates an earthquake, between 3.4 and 3.7 as it flies in from space going approximately 18 to 20 thousand miles an hour, which is about Mach 10 or so, about Mach 8 or 9. It comes in from space, creates this massive shockwave, flies over southern California, just rattles the hell out of all the doors and windows, and then lands at Groom Lake. And, of course, the military won't admit to what it is and seismologists in the California area say it's not ground based, it comes from space.

My information on this is that this is actually a shuttle that is going back and forth from here to the moon. That this can actually make the trip from here to the moon in about six hours. It supplies the four bases that we have on the moon. We have two bases on the backside. If you don't believe what I'm saying, try to get some photographs of the backside of the moon—it's not the dark side of the moon, it's just the other side—but try to get these photos from NASA because they've recently been reclassified. I have two godfathers who walked on the moon, my dad was PR director for NASA. I can tell you as sure as I am talking to you now that this is not something that's nuts. We've got 'em there, and we've had 'em there since the mid-60s.

Q: There must be plenty of documentation, because it's happening on a regular basis. This is as well documented as the Kennedy assassination with all the 8 millimeter films, only this is the age of video.

A: Absolutely. You talk to dozens if not maybe over a hundred people or so who have actually gone out there themselves. I conduct tours to the area. Every month we get probably about fifteen or twenty people or so, some of them who believe, some of them who don't believe, and we just jump on a bus and go out and camp in the valley and they see UFOs. I forget, because I've seen so many of them myself now out there, what a religious experience it is for people to actually see these discs in the sky just start making all these wild maneuvers and zipping back and forth. So many of these people have said, "all I really want to do in my life is actually see one of these things" and there they are for all to see.

Sean Morton's book, The Millennium Factor, *is available from the Delphi Associates, which also publishes a newsletter, at 2207 Hermosa Avenue, Hermosa Beach, California, 90254.*

Puerto Rico, Nukes and UFOs
by Scott Corrales

Toward the end of October 1984, two commercial cargo vessels arrived at the small port of Arroyo on the southern shore of Puerto Rico, which faces the Caribbean Sea. The ships, Nautilus II and Caribbean Adventurer, unloaded a cargo allegedly "to be used by NASA", although its real purpose remains unknown. Word began to circulate among the ranks of UFO investigators that the equipment was space-connected, but hardly NASA related (1).

Nuclear weapons, the story went, were being tested in Puerto Rico against UFO bases allegedly nestled in the deep cavern systems that riddle the island. The story was decried as a groundless rumor: the Treaty of Tecamachalco, banning the deployment of nuclear weapons in Latin America, had been ratified in 1967 by the United States, and the Senate had, in 1981, approved of the inclusion of the Commonwealth of Puerto Rico into the Nuclear Free Zone guaranteed by the treaty. The fact that the rumor included the "nonexistent" but ever-present UFOs made it only worse.

But the very same naysayers were given something to think about when, on February 15, 1985, months after the arrival of the "NASA cargo" at Arroyo, the *New York Times* made it known that Reagan Administration planners had included Puerto Rico in a list of military emergency sites in case of a nuclear war (2). The nature of the emergency was left open, but it clearly involved the stationing of nuclear devices or the deployment of systems already in place. The Institute for Policy Studies issued a lengthy statement, saying that:

"There is real danger here [in Puerto Rico]. There is a military nuclear infrastructure so huge and complex that it has, in some ways, more power than policies. Those bases, facilities and plans obligate us to move in a certain direction in a conflict." (3)

If this part of the rumor was true, what kept the second half—the one involving unidentified flying objects—from being true as well?

A quiet battle against the UFO phenomenon has been conducted for the past few years in the blue skies over Puerto Rico, which has been notorious for the sheer volume of sightings that have occurred there since the 1950s, and particularly during the 1970s. UFOs have been plunging into the waters that surround the island (which happen to be some of the greatest depths on the planet) and emerging from them as well to the amazement of onlookers.

The sightings have been so numerous that they prompted the Civil Defense Agency of PR to issue Investigative Directive No. 1-91 on October 7th, 1991, which reads:

In the past and more recently there have been sightings of unidentified flying objects (UFOs) and unidentified submarine objects (USOs) in the territory of the Commonwealth of Puerto Rico. Pursuant to Article 6, clause F of Law No. 22 of 23 June 1976, we have deemed that it is fitting and proper for the Puerto Rico Civil Defense to investigate and study cases involving sightings of unidentified flying objects so as to determine that they pose no threat to the safety of the Puerto Rican people...(4)

One of the sightings which undoubtedly prompted the agency's unusual concern was the one witnessed in the town of Lajas in the southwestern corner of the island, where a sizable number of residents saw an aerial battle between a colossal UFO and two F-14 Tomcat interceptors. Even more amazing than the improbable dogfight was the fact that the Navy jets were "sucked into" the massive triangular intruder, which subsequently disappeared. The Tomcat Incident has been pursued vigorously by investigators Jorge Martin, Wilson Sosa and Amaury Rivera, the latter who happens to be the photographer of another battle involving an F14 and a circular, grayish UFO in May 1988. The photo, which stunned many due to its content and the fact that it was not another blurry UFO snapshot, was considered a hoax until analyzed by the NASA Industrial Applications Center in Arizona, which cast aside any doubts of trick photography or photo overlaying (5).

The Navy denied having lost any of its interceptors over Puerto Rico, although a carrier group was stationed off the island's west coast for a few months, ostensibly "on maneuvers", but more than likely maintaining surveillance on UFOs.

Into this highly charged atmosphere of UFO conflict and government installation of nuclear devices came Project Excalibur, a device to be employed in the destruction of subsurface UFO installations being perfected at the WX section of LANL (Los Alamos, New Mexico). The prototypes were to be used in Puerto Rico before being used "elsewhere." This experimentation, construed by many to be the actual offensive against the UFO bases, has resulted in a number of subterranean detonations and an increase in the number of tremors felt on the island in the past decade (6).

The alleged deployment of Project Excalibur coincided with the verifiable plan to deploy a type of tactical nuke or demolition mine known as the B-57, probably similar to those used in Western Europe as part of the NATO "tripwire" against any advance by the now defunct Warsaw Pact's forces. Tactical nuclear devices (kiloton-yield) go back to the days of the infamous "Davy Crockett"—an atomic bazooka a soldier was supposed to sling off his APC and fire at an approaching tank. These warheads are stored at the Roosevelt Roads Naval Base along with "in transit" weapons and specialized nuclear underwater demolition charges for the use of highly trained Navy SEAL personnel (7). The fact that the smallest of the Greater Antilles has been used as a testing weapon by the military cannot be overlooked either: chemical weapons have been tested in the Luquillo Experimental Rainforest (El Yunque), and the contraceptive pill was tested on Puerto Rican women in the 1950s.

Project Excalibur and all that surrounds it, then, no longer seems to be so improbable. The island is in fact riddled with caves, particularly the western end of the Cordillera Central, the range that splits the island in two. The caves found along the Camuy River extend along for some eight miles, and rank among the most important cavern systems in the world, and every year adds a newly discovered cave to the system. The discovery of the series of caves known as the Angeles system in 1972 coincided with the onset of the great UFO flap of '72-74 (8). With almost 2000 caves scattered over an area of 100 x 35 miles, one can say that Puerto Rico is virtually hollow inside! An excellent place to hide a squadron of UFOs.

Puerto Rico also boasts unexploited deposits of strategic minerals such as nickel, cobalt and copper, which are all vital to the nuclear weapons industry, even after the demise of the Soviet Union and the current lack of a clear-cut nuclear deterrent policy. As it so happens, UFOs have an interest in these metals: Since 1987, UFO sightings have been concentrated around the copper-rich municipality of Adjuntas, nestled amid the mountains of the Cordillera Central. There exists considerable photo and video evidence of landing marks and nocturnal activity in the area, including the destruction of enormous steel plates used to cover the test pits dug into the copper mines (9).

The scaling down of the arms race after the break-up of the USSR has also lessened fears of an East-West nuclear exchange, but what of the nuclear devices already in place, particularly those in Puerto Rico? Perhaps they will remain there, readily available for another no less ominous purpose.

Notes:
1. "OVNIS en Adjuntas". *El Programa de Carmen Jovet*. WAPA-TV, San Juan, 8/27/91.
2. *New York Times*, 2/15/85.
3. Cripps, L.L. *Calamity in the Caribbean: Puerto Rico and the Bomb*. Boston: Schenkman Books, 1987, p. 3.
4. Agencia Estatal de Defensa Civil, *Directriz Investigativa No. 1-91*. (San Juan, P.R., 10/7/91).
5. Dilettoso, Jim. Letter to UFO investigator Wendelle Stevens. 10 August 1991.
6. Freixedo, Salvador. *La Amenaza Extraterrestre*. (Mexico City: Editorial Posada, 1990). p. 130-131.
7. Cripps, p. 7.
8. Rimax, Orlando. *La Clave Esta En El Maya*. San Juan: Editorial Nucleo Alcion, 1986.
9. "OVNIS en Adjuntas". *El Programa de Carmen Jovet*. WAPA-TV, San Juan, 8/27/91.

Scott Corrales Writing Consultants do translations, briefings and creative writing and can be reached at 5423 Walnut Street, Apt. 1, Pittsburgh, Pennsylvania 15232.

An Interview with Lars Hansson

author of *UFOs, Aliens and Ex-Intelligence Agents: Who's Fooling Whom?*

Q: Lars Hansson is a professional investigator, an investigative reporter and a man who has co-authored books with Bo Gritz and has also written a book on George Bush. He is also a former deputy sheriff in north Idaho and a former customs agent. Lars has written an affidavit entitled *UFOs, Aliens and Ex-Intelligence Agents: Who's Fooling Whom?* which tells the story of John Lear and Bill Cooper, two gentlemen who have become popular in the ufological community. This affidavit explains some of the details of their more terrestrial activities. Lars, thank you for being with us.

A: Thank you. It's a real pleasure.

Q: Let's talk a little about Gordon Novel. Gordon Novel appeared on this television special a week ago, on J. Edgar Hoover, talking about these photographs that have been in the news. I think Novel described them as Hoover being in *flagrante delicto* with...

A:...his boyfriend.

Q: Right. You have some association with Novel. Tell us a little bit about him.

A: It's an unusual and pretty unexpected association. Maybe association isn't the right word. Interaction, I guess. Unfortunately, Lear is part of that equation. That's actually how this came about. As a longtime researcher on the Kennedy assassination, that's actually how I met John Lear initially in Las Vegas in 1988. At a certain point in late 1989, right after Bob Lazar had chosen to go public on a series of news programs on Las Vegas TV with George Knapp, I visited Bob and John at John's home and they both mentioned how Gordon Novel had showed up in Las Vegas and was intensely interested in meeting with Bob and discussing his knowledge and his experiences and so forth. It was an automatic, knee-jerk reaction on my part, I told them that my best advice was to steer completely clear of Novel because of what I had learned about him in the course of my fifteen years of research on the Kennedy assassination.

I must say right at the outset that in spite of everything I do have a begrudging respect for the man because despite the fact that he has been involved in a number of very questionable, if not criminal activities over the years, he is incredibly intelligent and resourceful and inventive. Like a cat with nine lives, he's managed to end up on his feet repeatedly throughout some of the most important scandals of the last twenty years. Just to recap briefly: he was involved with the group of people that were actively involved with planning for the Bay of Pigs operations around New Orleans and Miami. He was, according to many sources including his ex-wife at the time, a dead-ringer for Lee Harvey Oswald back then and according to other sources actually actively impersonated Lee Oswald during the period of time prior to the assassination.

Q: This was a period when a number of second Oswalds were noted in Dallas.

A: Two or three that we're quite sure of. Novel is one of them. More important, however, is the fact that he has openly acknowledged over the years that he was directly and actively involved in sabotaging district attorney Jim Garrison's investigation from the inside in New Orleans in 1967 to 1969, to such an extent that at one point Garrison actually tried to extradite him from where he had hidden in Columbus, Ohio. The governor of Ohio actually intervened to prevent his extradition. Since then, Novel has openly acknowledged actually being hired by Nixon's top aide, Charles Colson, to degauss the entire Watergate tapes and that he would have done it had not the White House capitulated to the forces arrayed against them. Since then he's been involved very actively on behalf of John DeLorean. He actually takes credit for essentially disproving the government's case against DeLorean, in securing his acquittal. He has been mentioned peripherally, very closely on the sidelines, in relation to the Vicki Morgan sex tapes, a big scandal in Los Angeles back in 1984. He claims that he got a hold of the tapes but that they were actually fakes, which may have well been the case, but Larry Flynt, in an issue of *The Rebel* magazine has a picture of him and Novel and he claimed that Novel actually came to him and tried to get him to sit on those tapes at the request of the White House. That's right in the cover of the magazine. There are a number of other activities that he's been involved in, but that gives you a sample of the flavor of this guy's activities.

Q: This is a guy who was identified only as an "electronics specialist" on this PBS special about Hoover.

A: It's absolutely known that he was working for the CIA during that period of time, at least from say '60 to '63, that he has worked as an FBI informant. If you pick up any good book on the Kennedy assassination and look in the index, you will usually find several if not many references to Gordon Novel. You will also find him in the Torbitt Document, one of the best descriptions of the actual command team and the way the operation went down. Novel's name is mentioned has having been very active in both the background and planning for the assassination and very active in the cover-up.

Q: According to this PBS special on Hoover, Novel was involved in a "complicated legal action" that is not described in any detail at all, when he was shown the photographs of Hoover and Clyde Tolson together. Do you know anything about that?

A: Yes, I know a great deal about that which I have gathered from other sources and directly from Novel himself. It was very revealing that he would even choose to go public on that program. Novel, unlike a lot of other people associated with the Kennedy assassination, has eschewed notoriety for many years. He's really tried to stay out of it, he doesn't like his picture in the press. He hasn't written books or come forth for the most part. And I think it is very illuminating that he chose to do that not only in this program but to actually serve as a source for the new book that inspired this program by Anthony Summers about Hoover.

In 1983-84, Dave Emory was doing a radio program in the San Jose area and was describing his various discoveries and so forth about the assassination and various aspects of the planning and the cover-up and so forth, and doing a good job of it. In the course of that, he brought up Gordon Novel, this shadowy character. Ironically, Gordon Novel calls up the program, this is about three in the morning, and at first I think Emory was trying to shine it on or pretend like it really wasn't him. Finally, he had to acknowledge that the caller was really quite conversant. At one point he offered his social security number if that would help Dave. It really wasn't funny because we know that a number of researchers have lost their lives or have been threatened and so forth. It was interesting, though, that from that point on Emory just stammered and was really very, very nervous. He kept protesting that he wasn't gunning for Mr. Novel on the radio. That was one of the first times I had ever heard Novel on tape and knew what his voice sounded like.

At any rate, Novel on that program said openly that he had been hired to degauss the Watergate tapes and that he would have done so had he been paid more and had a little more time. Emory was quite concerned about how he had just happened to call up and Novel explained that he happened to be driving down the road at that time and heard this thing on the radio and pulled off to a phone booth and just felt like

he really wanted to defend himself, that he was just so tired of being misrepresented in relation to this whole thing. And as hard as that may be to believe, he is the type of character that would do that at three in the morning.

Q: It is interesting that an intelligence spook would just pull over, pick up a phone in the nearest booth and offer his social security number to whoever was listening.

A: I have to say that even though the subject of that whole interview was very serious, it really was quite entertaining, talk-radio at its best.

But the point of this regarding Novel is that even then, now this was back in I believe '84, he was stating publicly that he was involved in these two very questionable activities.

To bring it up to the current time frame, in late 1989, when he surfaced in Las Vegas very anxious to meet with Bob Lazar and find out what he knew about this advanced UFO technology. Bob Lazar was a MIT trained physicist who was working up at the Los Alamos laboratories in New Mexico on a high-tech project. Apparently a lot of his background has been disputed but as far I know, from conversations with Bob and various other investigators, that much of his story does check out. He was listed in the employee's phone book at Los Alamos. He was at one point on the front page of the Los Alamos paper, a photograph of him working on his jet car and jet engine, which is one of his specialties or hobbies, describing his work at Los Alamos.

On the back page of that paper, ironically enough, was an article about Edward Teller who was coming to give a speech right at that same time in Los Alamos. According to Bob, and I believe this is true even though Teller has denied it, apparently Teller was impressed enough with him that he helped to facilitate his application and employment with EG&G, a very high-tech employer out at the Nevada test site, to get Bob a job working at Area 51 and what he claims is an even more secretive area called S-4, outside of Las Vegas, to do back-engineering on some very, very high technology aircraft. He claims that he worked on one of the seven or nine UFOs that had been captured or somehow or another they had possession of them. Apparently this whole project was run by Navy intelligence and he was paid by the Office of Naval Intelligence and apparently has a W2 form to prove it now.

Because of Lazar's claimed expertise in this area, once Lazar decided to go public with this information, Novel showed up in Las Vegas because he was and remains intensely interested in this type of technology. I have a copy, for example, of a letter he wrote from prison in 1978 to a Kennedy researcher describing his own ongoing research in anti-gravitational propulsion and so forth. At any rate, I advised both Lear and Lazar very strongly that I would avoid him. I didn't really trust his motives and I had a feeling that maybe he was there to try to get Lazar to reveal certain information that could have gotten him in trouble in terms of revealing national security secrets and so forth. That was my input and apparently that was one of the admonitions that Lazar took seriously because he never did meet or speak with Novel after that.

That was in November 1989. In January of 1990, Lear had called me up to his house because he had several things he wanted to talk about relative to the JFK assassination. He was very anxious to play this tape for me of his conversation with Novel. This figures in very directly with the current situation we were talking about with Hoover. As you pointed out, during the program about Hoover, it was really rather startling that Novel chose to appear at all. And as you have described, they said that he had a very serious problem and that he was directed to CIA counter-intelligence chief James Jesus Angleton and Jim Angleton showed him these photographs that were supposedly taken in 1946 by operatives of the OSS being buddy-buddy with Clyde Tolson. Now a lot of people around Washington and certainly those in the know, had been aware of his homosexuality and of the fact that Tolson, the number two man at the FBI for thirty or forty years, that they were live-in roommates for thirty or forty years. So it isn't that nobody knew that this was going on it but just that Hoover's power was so great that he could pressure people to not ever publicize it.

According to the PBS program, Novel had this problem and was shown the photographs by Angleton and so forth and they didn't really describe what he did after that. I wasn't aware that the program was going to be shown until just three or four days beforehand, but I spoke to Michael Sullivan, the producer, earlier that same day before it aired to ask him about the content and ask him about how heavily they had relied on Novel and if they had questioned him about this other aspect I'm about to go into. And he explained that he hadn't actually done the interviews with Novel and that they hadn't relied on him too extensively and that it was just a production decision for the program to not to go too heavily into the actual assassination of JFK because I guess they had so much ground to cover in one hour anyway and they felt that it was a little labyrinthine and if anything it would maybe the subject for a follow-up program.

Q: Are you saying that the JFK assassination was the "complicated legal action" that they referred to?

A: Essentially, yes. That's probably over-simpli-

fying, but what they chose not to go into in that program, that Novel actually discussed at length with John Lear during this taped conversation, which Lear gave me in January 1990 of a conversation that took place in December of 1989. Novel had called up John Lear to basically try to get him to persuade Lazar to sit down and meet with him and discuss all this stuff. And I honestly think that Novel's intent was genuine, that he just wanted to find out what Lazar knew and if they could utilize his knowledge and so forth, they were prepared to pay him and so forth. I think that was all pretty much on the level. What's so ironic about the conversation is that Lear meanwhile had not only been warned off on that but really didn't feel that he could persuade Lazar to do anything and said so. But Lear keeps asking Novel questions about the Kennedy assassination. And it's incredible.

He says that if you look at the overview matrix of this old boy network and who had the pieces in place to do it, and how they could affect control and how they could create this cover-up using one overt act covered up by a covert act and layer upon layer and to be able to force someone to do the cover-up of an enormous magnitude and the only outfit that could do that legally and jurisdictionally in the United States was the FBI. A little further on he comes back to that point again about how Watergate was essentially a frame-up of Nixon—he did have the plumbers, he did send them in, but James McCord essentially made sure that they got caught. Virtually all of the men who broke into the Watergate were members of the special assassination squad set up twelve years before in Miami through the agency of Richard Nixon, Robert Maheu and Sam Giancana and John Rosselli of the Mafia. So what Novel was saying was that Nixon and Helms were trying to blackmail each other with that information and Nixon lost.

All of that comes back to the fact that these elements of the CIA who were directly involved in directing and planning the assassination and engineering the cover-up were able to do that because they were able to blackmail Hoover. That was the key point to be made, whereas Summers is once again blaming the entire situation on the Mafia, that supposedly the Mafia had gotten hold of these pictures and was blackmailing Hoover into leaving them alone, the point that I'd like to bring into the argument that Novel was telling Lear three years ago and reiterated in a conversation with me was that, in fact, the CIA was able to use those photographs to pressure Hoover into going along with the cover-up of their members' role in the assassination. I think that's extremely important to bring out here.

When Novel found out that I had written just a

little bit about this in my affidavit, he became extremely upset about it a month before this PBS program and called me up repeatedly threatening me, threatening my life, threatening to bring legal action, et cetera, but then turned around and confirmed quite a few of those details and quite a few others.

After I watched it and thought about it for a while and I was wondering why he would do this. He told me himself that he currently has some problems with the IRS and the FBI and its very possible that this was his way of sending a message that, listen if I'm willing to come on TV and disclose these details, how much more might I be willing to say?

People who saw that program should be asking, if he had a "complicated legal matter" why would he be directed to the counter-intelligence chief? What was so serious that *that* would happen? And the problem that Novel described to me specifically, and I think that all of this needs to come out, he might think I'm betraying a trust or whatever, but all these people have betrayed our trust and I think it's time that all of this stuff come out because we can deal with it, and he explained to in advance of the program that the problem they were referring to was that he in turn had filed a lawsuit against Jim Garrison in *Playboy*, and he claimed it was done at the direction and the expense of the White House. I believe this would have been in 1969 in the Nixon White House, and it was one of many ploys that was used against Garrison to try to de-rail his investigation and his prosecution. Apparently Hoover had sent a memo telling him, I guess pretty flatly, to drop the lawsuit because Hoover did not want to have to be involved in taking depositions from the people that Novel was naming as witnesses because of what would have come out. So Hoover wanted him to drop the lawsuit and, as Novel said, he was twenty-seven years old, he was kind of arrogant

and he didn't realize how powerful Hoover was, so he confronted him at Harvey's Restaurant there in the Mayflower Hotel, right in front of Clyde Tolson, and said, you know, "Listen, you old fag, I'm definitely going to go ahead with this and I've got backing at the White House and if you don't like it, you can call these people at the White House." And I guess that Hoover responded with expletives deleted about what he could do with himself and what the White House could do with itself. And at that point Novel just said, "Well, you'll find out who really has the power here." And Novel found out because eight months later he was arrested on a trumped up charge of transporting specialized intelligence communications equipment and ended up spending two years in prison before he could prove that he was framed and railroaded by the FBI. So Novel has a very long-standing beef against the FBI.

But the most important point I'm trying to make here is that people should really look at what that problem was: why in the world would Novel have filed a lawsuit against Jim Garrison when Garrison just shortly before that had been trying to extradite him from Ohio and why would the Nixon White House be essentially bankrolling his lawsuit?

I cannot under-emphasize the importance of these revelations as far as research on the Kennedy assassination. I hope people take it for all it's worth and go back through their own files because I hope this may have opened a crack that'll bring the entire crumbling edifice down, the edifice of lies that has been built up. I think that Novel has always been a very serious wedge and think it's important at whatever risk to bring that out. I appreciate being able to elaborate sufficiently on it.

The Rose, The Cross, The Scimitar and the Unicorn

Folkloristic and Oriental Clues to the Medieval Origins of Rosicrucianism

by Timothy J. O'Neill

There is an aura of invincible mystery surrounding the origins of the Rosicrucian Idea in its historical framework, yet the persistent research of historians, following the lead of Frances Yates in her classic, yet now largely superseded *The Rosicrucian Enlightenment,* is beginning to push the time or rosicrucian "creation" ever backwards. Let us briefly examine some of the elements of this historical research which lead us to a Medieval setting for the origin of the Rose and Cross as an intellectual "constellation" of ideas.

There is a qualitatively distinct shape to the Rosicrucian idea...a unique and historically stable substructure which reveals significant vistas in our perennial quest for clues to its origins and ultimate purposes. Rosicrucianism is, after all, a form of Christianity. It is a Christianity fired by ideals of reform and universal renovation. To those who witnessed the embarrassments of the split papacy during the "Babylonian Captivity", the moral decline or the religious orders and the papal corruption and simonism that marked much of the period between the 10th and 15th centuries, there certainly seemed to be much that demanded renovation.

There was also a wide base of political and spiritual support for such change on many levels of European culture during that era. The Rosicrucianism of the early 17th Century, as made evident in the famous manifestoes, quickly aligned itself with the Lutheran Reformation as an expedient, however, there are two clear aspects to the Rosicrucian version of reform which place it decidedly outside the pale of mainstream Reformation Christianity. The Rosicrucian "Work" was to be a root renovation based upon the principle of *gnosis,* or direct and personal knowledge or the divine derived through principles and psychological practices founded in such contexts as Hermeticism, Neoplatonism and Neopythagoreanism. In a sense, this was derived from the Renaissance notion of the *Prisca Theologia,* or "pristine theology", which was supposed to have preceded the coming of Christ and to have been enunciated by the philosophs of Egypt and Greece.

The actual way in which such philosophies intersected with Rosicrucian Gnosis was focussed through the Royal Art of Alchemy, the particular interest of the Rosicrucian Manifestoes and the Chemical Wedding of Christian Rosenkreuz, the great Rosicrucian fable, along with *The Dream of Poliphilo* and the *Parabola,* another document associated with the "Work." Alchemy, as an art and science, *applied* the Hermetic, Platonic and Pythagorean philosophies to the practical business of cosmological transformation and transmutation. In a direct sense, the alchemist's fascination with animal, vegetable, mineral and spiritual transformation mirrored the Rosicrucian hope for a transformed Christianity. We can then begin to define Rosicrucianism as the idea of applying alchemical transformative techniques on the cultural and historical levels to the body politic of Christian culture. In poetic terms, the Rosicrucians hoped to follow Christ as the great alchemist in his form as "Elias the Artist" in his quest to evolve Lady Ecclesia toward Her true throne in the New Jerusalem.

This metaphor touches upon the other great peculiarity of Rosicrucian Christianity, beyond its use of gnostic alchemy, namely, its fascination with the Eternal Feminine. Lady Sophia, or "Wisdom", whether as the Black Virgin, Venus, Kundry, Astraea, Iustitia, Geometrica or Merlin's "Nimue", became the chief muse and point of balance to the overly masculine Mysteries of the Roman Church with their martial and political implications in the European power spectrum. Rosicrucianism became the subtle Moon, reflecting the harsh light of Rome's solar Christos from the mysterious Northern mountain of Abiegnus, a realm akin to the Blessed Isles of Arthurian myth, or the Greek Hyperborea. Interestingly, in this mythological context, the unicorn stands out as the Rosicrucian emblematic animal, appearing in such clearly Rosicrucian texts as the German *Book of Lambspring* which probably was produced around the middle of the 16th Century. The Unicorn becomes the symbol of Rosicrucianism, since it is the alchemical symbol for the purity of Spirit and it is only tameable by the Virgin, or Sophia. The unicorn's horn was also a chief ingredient in practical alchemical work, a hint which should help students of Rosicrucianism a great deal toward an understanding of how the mythological, spiritual and physical all interacted toward the ultimate end of the "Work"...a process occurring on many levels of reality all at once. In our terms, the solar "Lion" of Rome and the lunar "Unicorn" of the Rosy Cross became a subtle and powerful pair in the subconscious environment of European culture as early as the origins of heraldic usage, during the 12th century.

Moving further afield, the insistence, in the 17th century manifestoes, upon arabic and Islamic sources dating back to much earlier eras, as a key resource in the formation of the "Work", does seem to have much more than a merely legendary basis. The first Latin translations of Arabic alchemical texts began circulating through certain elite circles in Europe during the middle of the 12th century. The *Revelations of Morienus* is a clear example of a text with arabic versions dating back as early as the 9th Century. It is also clear that besides genuine arabic texts in alchemical field, Islamic sources were also important in the formation of such popular institutions as the troubadour songs, heraldry and the Arthurian legends. Wolfram von Eschenbach's description of the Grail Temple in *Parzival* may actually refer to a remarkable circular, zodiacal temple in Iran, whose remains still exist. (See *The Grail* by John Matthews.) His reference to Islamic sources derived through the agency of the mysterious teacher "Kyot" seem to have quite real bases, as discovered by the husband and wife team of the Kahanes in their volume *The Krater and the Grail* (see bibliography). The contributions of Islam toward the renovation of European culture, via the arabic influence in Spain, as well as the legacy of returning Crusaders, is now becoming more and more clear as a true and real source of ideas for Rosicrucian circles during the 12th Century. Indeed, another key aspect of the Rosicrucian Work is the idea of a *universal religion,* spanning Christianity, Judaism and Islam with the reality of Gnosis at the heart of outward structural elements.

We have already touched upon, in our discussion of the mythological elements of the Rosicrucian Unicorn, another key aspect which helps us to pinpoint Rosicrucian origins and purposes...their use of folklore, fantasy and popular culture in order to spread what might have been considered heretical ideas quickly and quietly with great efficiency. Every possible avenue, from board games and children's rhymes, to the more sophisticated literary devices of the Grail stories and troubadour songs were pressed into service to spread the "Work." Clearly, certain, though not all, of the troubadours addressed their songs of love to Lady Sophia, in quite the spirit of the Rosicrucian devotion to Her seat beside the Unicorn in the Garden of the Moon. Clear Rosicrucian motifs also abound in literary works ranging from the first part of the *Roman de la Rose, The Dream of Poliphilo,* the *Faery Queene* and a host of lesser epics and romances. Clearly though, it is in the Grail stories that a Rosicrucian-style Christianity is quite clearly enunciated to all those with eyes to see and ears to hear!

The medieval "Rosicrucians" were clearly well-educated, politically astute and far-seeing Christians, who looked ahead toward an astonishing vision of a universal polis and ecclesia in a truly *catholic* church of all mankind, united under both Christ-Elias the alchemist and his twin sister, Sophia, Lady of the Garden of Wisdom. The Rosicrucian empire of Lion and Unicorn gradually became something of a reality by the 17th Century and clearly mirrors the ever-present desire, still strong in our times for a new Golden Age of universality, which modern technology is making more and more possible each year, at least in terms of human communication over the globe, in quantitative terms. Undoubtedly, many of the medieval visionaries who looked forward to this day were well-hidden and highly placed forces within the very body of the highest churchly, political and social circles. There is every indication that we can firmly date the coagulation of Rosicrucian ideas into a working format during the middle of the 12th century, although these concepts clearly find their earliest origins probably during the 9th or 10th centuries. It is not impossible that they began to circulate in rudimentary form during the Carolingian era and that the remarkable culture of Aachen under Charlemagne may have been one of many focal points for these incredible ideas.

There is one final "Rosicrucian" element which is crucial to our understanding of history which is often overlooked. Rosicrucianism was in no way, shape or form, a secret society in the same sense that Freemasonry became. It neither initiated through degrees, nor taught through the Mystery catharsis. It had, further, no "official" outward structure at any point in its history. It was, always, a loose "collegium" of principles, ideals and hopes, shared at various times, perhaps by small elite groups loosely connected by the idea of master teaching pupil the essence of the art of alchemy. This is a far cry from groups today which call themselves "Rosicrucian" and which *all* uniformly date back to masonic fantasies of the 18th Century, which attempted to revive the truly unrevivable and uncapturable mystique of the true Rosicrucians; people who would never for a second have dreamt of organizing themselves into bands of initiatory political structures. The "Rosicrucians" of today are, without exception, bastardized masonic and theosophical fantasies, which, in the words of artist Hans Richter, capture "the fall, but not the drop" of the mysterious "rain" which was the misting cloud of true Rosicrucianism. Ironically, modern Rosicrucians simply stand as empty memorials to a project long since completed...the breaking of Rome's stranglehold and the planting of the seed of universal religion in the Rose Garden of the Philosophers; something much in evidence in the volume of scientific and cultural cooperation which flood the world each year. There will always be "Rosicrucians", however, they will always be anonymous individuals, quietly absorbed in their inner visions, seeking the universal Gnosis, penning their stories, drawing their fantasies, speaking out to each other across the Centuries, without regard for time or space...true students in the College of the Holy Spirit, tamers of the Unicorn all!

Bibliography:

The Rosicrucian Enlightenment by Frances Yates, Routledge & Kegan Paul, London, 1972.

The Rose Cross and the Goddess by Gareth Knight, Destiny Books, New York 1985.

The Symbolic Rose by Barbara Seward, Spring Publications, Inc., Dallas, 1989.

"The Path Toward the Grail: The Hermetic Sources and Structure of Wolfram von Eschenbach's Parzival" by David R. Fideler in *Alexandria,* issue No. One, published by Phanes Press, Grand Rapids, 1991, quoting from *The Krater and the Grail* by Henry and Renee Kahane, University of Illinois Press, Urbana, 1965.

Heraldic Symbols: Islamic Insignia and Western Heraldry by William Leaf and Sally Purcell, Victoria and Albert Museum, London, 1986.

The Grail by John Matthews (In the "Art and Cosmos" series) (Discussing the Taqt-I-Tardis, the Persian zodiacal temple which may have served as a model for the Grail temple in Eschenbach *Parzival*) Crossroad Publishing Co., New York, 1981.

Games of the Gods: The Origin of Board Games in Magic and Divination by Nigel Pennick, Samual Denis Weiser, Inc. York Beach, Maine, 1989.

Cinderella's Gold Slipper: Spiritual Symbolism in the Grimm's Tales by Samuel Denis Fohr, Quest Books, Wheaton, Illinois, 1991.

The Language of the Gods and *Hermes Unveiled,* both by Roy Norvill, Ashgrove Press, Bath, England, 1987 and 1986, respectively.

The Book of Lambspring, reprinted in *The Hermetic Museum* (originally re-edited by Arthur Edward White, 1893), this edition in two volumes, by Samuel Weiser, New York, 1974.

"The Transmission of Alchemical Knowledge: An Alternate View" by Timothy O'Neill, F.R.C., I.R.C. in *The Rosicrucian Digest,* Fall 1991, Rosicrucian Park, San Jose, California (discussing the *Revelations of Morienus to Khalid Ibn Yazid.)*

"A Very Medieval Renascence" by Timothy O'Neill in *Magical Blend,* Issue 25, January 1990, San Francisco, California.

"Century of Marvels, Century of Light: The Esoteric Treasures of the Twelfth Century" by Timothy O'Neill in *Gnosis,* Issue #18, Winter 1991.

"Hyperborea: Pathworking the Land of Summer Beyond the Northern Snows", in *Gnosis,* issue #9.

The Oak King, The Holly King and the Unicorn: The Myths and Symbolism of the Unicorn Tapestries by John Williamson, Harper & Row, New York, 1986.

In Pursuit of the Unicorn by Josephine Bradley, Pomegrante Artbooks, Corte Maders, California, 1980.

Unicorn: Myth and Reality by Rudinger Robert Bear, Mason/Charter Books, New York, 1977.

The Lore of the Unicorn by Odell Shepard, Avenel Books, New York, 1982.

Unicorns by Kristin Landon, Ariel Books, Andrews and McNeal, Kansas City, 1992.

The Bestiary of Christ by Louis Charbonneau-Lassay, Arkana Books, New York, 1992.

Timothy O'Neill is the director of the Athanor Institute, 236 West Portal Avenue, Suite 106, San Francisco, CA 94127-1101.

Ben Bradlee called this scene "one of history's frozen shots" (*Conversations With Kennedy*, 1975). Kennedy's September 24, 1963 stop in Milford, Pennsylvania complicated a tour primarily of western states that the *New York Times* called "one of the most complex he has made since his 1960 campaign." In Milford, JFK dedicated the ancestral country home of the late Gifford Pinchot as a conservation center. Twice governor of Pennsylvania and the first chief of the U.S. Forest Service, Gifford Pinchot was regarded by some as the father of conservation in America. JFK's tour was intended to promote conservation. Bradlee notes that Kennedy did not visit the governor's mansion but instead insisted upon going to "the poor relations quarters a few hundred yards down the road," home of Gifford's widow, Ruth, the mother of both Bradlee's wife, Tony, and Mary Pinchot Meyer. Mrs. Pinchot's daughers had arrived via Air Force helicopter with JFK. From left to right: Gifford Pinchot, Jr.; Tony Pinchot Bradlee; Ruth Pinchot; JFK; and Mary Pinchot Meyer. (Photo: Cecil Stoughton, John F. Kennedy Library (ST-C-310-87-63), a presidential library administered by the National Archives and Record Administration.)

Police examine the body of the murdered Mary Pinchot Meyer on a towpath along the Potomac River in Washington D.C., October 13, 1964. (Photo: Loren Coleman)

Mary Pinchot Meyer and Tony Bradlee de-planing for the visit to Milford, Pennsylvania.

John F. Kennedy and Mary Pinchot Meyer, September 1963. (Photo: Cecil Stoughton, John F. Kennedy Library)

John Meyer (left), attorney for Howard Hughes, assisting Elliott Roosevelt (right), son of FDR, against charges that Hughes paid the hotel bills for Roosevelt's wild parties. (Photo: Gerald Carroll)

Brian Redman, of the e-newsletter *Conspiracy Nation* (bigxc@prairienet.org), and Sherman Skolnick, at the River Flame restaurant near Chicago, April, 1995.

Mystery oil man Tom Slick (white hair) and friends. (Photo: Loren Coleman)

LBJ gets winked, November, 1963.

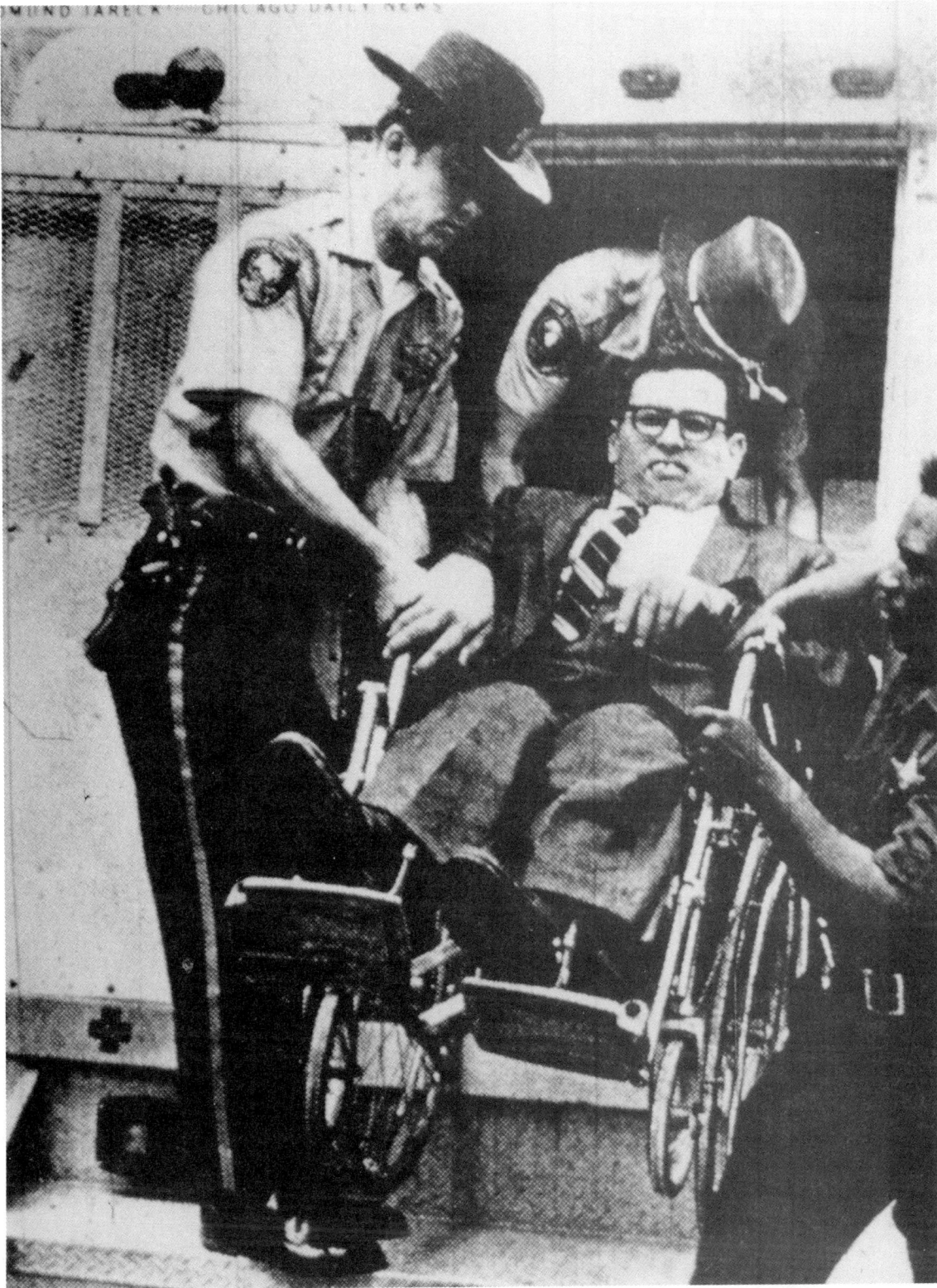

Police attempt to hoist Sherman Skolnick into a paddy wagon, Summer, 1969.

Steamshovel Press editor/publisher Kenn Thomas. (Photo: Linda Belford)

JFK Redux:
An Interview with A. J. Weberman
co-author of *Coup D'Etat in America*
by Kenn Thomas

Q: Your book was originally published in the late 70s and made the connection between the railroad tramps that were arrested behind the railroad yards at the Kennedy Assassination and the Watergate burglars E. Howard Hunt and Frank Sturgis. There's a new edition out by the Quick American Archives Press.

A: There were two sets of tramps that were picked up on November 22, 1963. The first set of tramps was John Gedney, a guy named Harold Doyle, and a guy named Gus W. Abrams. And they were picked up immediately after the assassination and brought into the Sheriff's office where Dallas homicide head Will Fritz set up temporary headquarters. He threw them right in jail, in the cooler, you know, didn't give them any hearing or anything like that and they stayed in jail for four days. And in 1992 arrest records on these guys were found, right? Then later on they searched the yards where these tramps had hidden and were about to get on the train. They searched the freights in the yard. They had a lot of law enforcement guys there by this time. All kinds of people from A.T.F., Dallas Police, Sheriff's office and F.B.I. They were all down there searching the yard.

They didn't find anything. They sounded the all clear, and one of the trains pulled out of the station. This was approximately an hour after the assassination. And Lee Bowers, who was in a railroad tower watching the whole thing, watched the train as it pulled out and when it was about a half mile away he saw a man crawling from one boxcar to the next. So he called back: "Bring that freight back in the station. There are some guys still on that train." And they brought the freight back in and they took three guys off and marched them through Dealey Plaza. And these are tramps whose pictures achieved wide circulation.

Now, what the FBI did at the Dallas FBI office was interview Doyle and Gedney. Abrams was dead, and they claim that these were the tramps who were picked up. It wasn't Howard Hunt, or Frank Sturgis, or Dan Carswell, as I've theorized. That was an attempt to put an end to the tramp theory thing. Now when I'm D.C. and I'm speaking with investigators who worked for the House Select Committee at one time and they asked me: "Well, what's the story? I

guess your tramp thing was wrong because they found it was Gedney, Doyle and Abrams."

These guys look nothing like the tramps! The only picture they ever published was of Doyle because he appeared on *A Current Affair*, a tabloid type TV show. And also on the show, they also purported that these guys were the actual set of tramps. If you study closely, you notice that this is just not the case. And what this reveals is even more suspicious because the arrest records of these guys show they were thrown in jail, never brought before a judge or anything like that but just, you know, thrown in the calaboose for three days and then released! Whereas the second set of tramps were picked up under even more suspicious circumstances and were released immediately.

We went down and asked Fritz what happened to the tramps and he said: "You'll have to ask the FBI about that. Ask the FBI. I don't know nothing," you know. So then the Rockefeller Commission questioned Fritz, and he says: "Gee, if I had questioned Hunt and Sturgis that day, I surely would have a record. They must have been absolved of all guilt and released." So this is very suspicious that one set of tramps was released when the other one was held for three days.

Q: I also saw Harold Doyle on another tabloid program called *Inside Edition*. And a couple of weeks later they did a follow up with this Doyle guy who works at a pool hall now in Klamath Falls, Oregon.

A: Right.

Q: For some reason he took an uncharacteristic Amtrak trip into Portland, where he was debriefed by some FBI people. That was their follow-up story.

A: Yeah, that was the story because the FBI did question him because they have the capability of doing this investigation realizing that there are two sets of tramps. They have access to the same materials that I do, in fact they have access to the undeleted form, and yet the Dallas FBI officer who used to work with the counter-terrorism unit of the FBI office in Washington, D.C., which corresponds exactly with the Central Intelligence Agency, disseminated this story which is just blatant disinformation.

Now I've just come back from Washington DC where I obtained documents that had been released by CIA in May of 1992. I want to report that one of these documents contains a stamp that says "see sanitized file A#4 for the sterile copy of this document". And this document concerns Oswald's trip to Mexico. And it's a cable message. Now what this indicates to me is that the CIA was producing sanitized documents on Lee Harvey Oswald. I've gone through twenty thousand pages of CIA documents, at least one hundred thousand pages of FBI documents in numerable states, this and that, I am an expert on government documents and markings. I've never seen a marking saying "see sanitized file, sterile copy". It's highly significant.

Q: Now this is the file that was just released that [former CIA chief] Robert Gates was talking about a couple of weeks ago in the press?

A: Yessir, that's it sir.

Q: And so they are admitting to sanitizing the files?

A: It's amazing. I couldn't believe my eyes. And the *New York Times* did an article on this and they overlooked the stamp on sanitization. Although they did indicate that it was very suspicious that up until two weeks before the assassination J. Edgar Hoover was sending all FBI reports on Lee Harvey Oswald to Richard Helms. And the CIA waited thirty years before releasing these cover letters that indicate that this was going on. Why was Richard Helms interested in Oswald? All Oswald did was print up a few leaflets and give them out. You know he did visit Mexico City, that's true. Which would indicate some interest there, but would that be planned necessarily?

Q: Mark Lane's book goes to great lengths to assuage this idea that Oswald went to Mexico City.

A: I disagree with that.

Q: In fact, he got David Atlee Phillips to say that in public.

A: Where did he get David Atlee Phillips to say Oswald was never in Mexico City?

Q: It was in *Plausible Denial*.

A: I'll look it up.

Q: Can you tell us the basic difference between the legal problems that you've had with E. Howard Hunt and what Mark Lane did with it?

A: What happened with me is that we never went to trial. Hunt just chickened out a day before the thing was going to come to trial.

He proceeded for five years. The *New York Post* ran a big article that it was very suspicious that he dropped it because he said that he was going to pursue this to the very end. He's made that statement numerous times. Yet when it came to trial, when it came time to face trial, he chickened out.

I have a letter from Lee Harvey Oswald to a Mr. Hunt dated November 10, 1963 asking for a position with the organization. I have copy of Lee Harvey Oswald's address book with the name Fiorini in it, which is Frank Fiorini, Frank Sturgis, one of the people who was picked up at Watergate.

Sturgis said to me, "Oh well, Oswald...I was on Oswald's hit list. You know he must have heard about me back then for my anti-Castro activities and Oswald must have heard about me and wants to assassinate me." Frank wasn't that famous. He was in *Parade* magazine, that was about it and he was a source for Jack Anderson. You know, like Oswald could have heard about him through the media.

So, when I was in Washington, DC I wanted to get a copy of this from the National Archives. I wanted to see the actual address book. But now I've found that you no longer are able to have access to the actual documents themselves. Everything is on microfilm. And when I asked them for recently de-classified documents I was told that no such list exists anymore. You know I used to go there once a year and say, "what's been de-classified? Give me a list." Now they tell me that you have to go through a hundred and thirty three rolls of microfilm, see what's been withheld and file a Freedom of Information Act request for each of these withheld documents. And then they'll tell me what's been declassified. So effectively, even though they're declassified, they have a period of five year declassifications. Now they've buried the documents back into the body of the Warren Commission stuff and it's impossible to find.

The letter itself was evaluated by a panel of experts for the House Select Committee on Assassinations and reluctantly they could not admit it was a forgery.

Q: It was Oswald's handwriting.

A: It was Oswald's handwriting. Absolutely. The House Committee did their best to discredit it. They couldn't find enough dishonest handwriting experts. Some people say that it was addressed to H.L. Hunt. I believe it was Howard Hunt.

Q: And the committee didn't discuss Howard Hunt at all.

A: No, not in relation to that letter. And the man that did it was aware of it because he questioned people about the Tramps shot. So he knew of the allegations about Hunt and the item and put two and two together.

Of Exiles and Exegeses
by Adam Sosostris

The mystery surrounding Ioan Couliano's murder threatens to overshadow the importance of his contribution to contemporary religious studies. Couliano, a professor at the University of Chicago until his death in May 1991 at age 41, was an intellectual prodigy, what the British call a polymath: he held three PhDs, spoke eight languages, authored over a hundred books and articles and held teaching positions at leading universities in the U.S. and Europe. He worked closely with Mircea Eliade, a towering presence in contemporary religious anthropology, and wrote thoughtful books about Renaissance magic and the history of out-of-body travel, among other topics of note.(1) He was one of the world's leading authorities on gnosticism, the name scholars give to a diverse body of early Christian heresies which radically reformulate Judaeo-Christian tradition, usually along dualistic lines.(2) Couliano was shot in the head by an unknown assailant on the University of Chicago campus. The murder took place in broad daylight without witnesses. It does not appear to have involved robbery and remains unsolved. Idle speculation has mentioned everything from disgruntled graduate students to—Goddess help us—witches as possible suspects.(3) However, police and FBI investigations are underway, and informed sources report that serious suspicion is focusing on the Romanian secret police.(4)

Couliano fled his native Romania and came to the West in 1972. When the 1989 Romanian revolution overthrew dictator Nicolae Ceaucescu, Couliano was enthusiastic. However, Couliano quickly came to see the new government as a betrayal of revolutionary hope, as something like a military coup disguised as a revolution. In numerous Romanian exile publications, Couliano published articles that were deeply critical of the new regime and of the secret police—the Securitate—in particular. The suspicion that Couliano was silenced was raised immediately after his death, by fellow emigre Andrei Codrescu, among others.(5) Police investigators, it now appears, take this theory quite seriously.(6)

Given this introduction, one might say that I am doing the very thing I complain about in my opening; i.e., letting the Couliano case overshadow the Couliano corpus. My reply is that it is difficult not to do so, given the packaging—and, in an eerie way, much of the content—of Couliano's new posthumous book, *The Tree of Gnosis: Gnostic Mythology from Early Christianity to Modern Nihilism.* (Harper Col-

lins, San Francisco, 1992; 296 pp., $24.95.) With *The Tree of Gnosis,* Harper Collins has brought out the first English translation of a work Couliano published in French in 1990. The edition is adorned with elegiac accolades from big literary names like Harold Bloom and Umberto Eco, as well as the aforementioned Messrs. Eliade and Codrescu. The blurb from Eco is given pride of place as an epigraph preceding even the title page: "If Ioan Couliano hadn't unexpectedly disappeared, he could have given us more seminal books like this. A masterpiece of scholarship." One can't help but think, when reading this, of *Foucault's Pendulum,* a novel by Eco which mixes occult studies, international conspiracies and yes, disappearing scholars. Strange to say, Couliano's death does look like something out of *Foucault's Pendulum,* at first glance anyway.

And this is not, I think, an inappropriate observation. Couliano had a hearty sense of the absurd, and was a fan of Jorge Luis Borges, whose scholarly fictions are Eco's prime inspiration.(7) Borges' work is full of references to kabbalism and gnosticism, and frequently plays with the conventions of those two deadly genres, the detective thriller and the scholarly article. Were he around to do so, Couliano would have noted the Borgesian dimension of his own death with pointed irony.

All this to say that context—the vicissitudes of personality, politics and history—positively surrounds the Couliano case, as well as the Harper edition of Couliano's last book. And yet it is precisely context—the vicissitudes of politics and history in particular—that is banished from Couliano's immensely learned discussion of gnosticism in *The Tree of Gnosis.*

Couliano makes clear at the outset that he is responding to earlier scholarship which has overemphasized the historical and social dimensions of gnosticism. Here he has in mind two powerful traditions. The first, the German School of Religion approach, goes off track, says Couliano, pursuing the genealogy of gnosticism, looking for an illusive origin in chronologically prior religions and civilizations.(8) The second is the approach of the philosopher Hans Jonas, who views gnosticism as a sociological phenomenon with affinities to modern existentialism: i.e., as a protest philosophy which emphasizes an absurd cosmos, man's sense of being "thrown" into it, and his resulting alienation; the sort of thing you can expect, suggests Jonas, in periods where empires are in decline, political institutions are moribund and people feel deeply disenfranchised.(9)

The German approach, argues Couliano, is doomed to fail because of its literalism. Religions are not people, and do not have family trees. Moreover, the intellectual search for origins is never disinterested and always serves some contemporary agenda. In this case, Couliano finds it suspicious that the German school has "found" a non-Jewish, Persian (read: Aryan) source for gnosticism. As for Jonas, Couliano gratefully acknowledges the elder man's work and his own indebtedness to it. However, he is concerned lest gnosticism be reduced to a kind of social pathology, a mere symptom.

For Couliano, gnosticism is a model of intellectual inquiry and a monument to free thought. Overly historico-sociological accounts threaten to obscure gnosticism's most interesting feature: the fact that when viewed "outside of time", as "a mental object", it appears as a complex, systematic intellectual activity whose closest analogues are games like chess and disciplines like theoretical physics.(10)

What this boils down to is that Couliano is proposing, in opposition to historicist interpretations, a structuralist account of gnostic myth. Now, even the best minds have come up short when asked for a succinct, pocket-portable definition of structuralism. For purposes of this discussion, let the following suffice: Structuralism is a twentieth century intellectual activity which downplays historical context, and views social phenomena in the abstract, as differential systems composed of layer upon layer of simple plus/minus binarisms. Claude Levi-Strauss has approached tribal myth in this fashion, and Ferdinand de Saussure and Noam Chomsky have put the structuralist stamp on modern linguistics. The approach has obvious affinities to information theory and computer systematics. Does this mean that *Pistis Sophia* or the *Apocryphon of John* (to pick two key second century gnostic texts) are just readouts? Primitive programs which spin out combinations and permutations of Biblical material the way your IBM crunches binomials?

Yes, sort of. And worth recalling in this regard is the remark of the early Church father Irenaeus, a bitter critic and contemporary of the gnostics: "Every day one of them makes up a new theory." (11) But what Irenaeus saw as a shortcoming, Couliano sees as the gnostics' great contribution. The various gnostic myths, traditions and teachers pursue ideas—ideas they view with the utmost gravity—without cessation and heedless of the stop signs thrown up by intellectual border guards (a species of which Irenaeus is a prime example).

The key gnostic move, says Couliano, is "inverse exegesis," a sort of reversal strategy which is brought to bear on founding texts of western cosmology like Plato's *Timaeus* and, above all, the first Book of *Genesis*.(12) This hermeneutic of suspicion, when confronted with ambiguities in *Genesis,* or the problem of squaring a fallen creation with an infallible godhead, leads the gnostics down some troubling religious roads. Almost all gnostic theorists divorce the true god from creation, attributing creation to a lower, subordinate sort of deity called a *demiurge* (craftsman). This much is straight Platonism. However, the gnostics typically identify Jaweh, the creator deity of the old Testament, with this second, inferior god, whom they place above a phalanx of baleful powers called archons (rulers). Most gnostic myths make the demiurge the author of evil, some attributing it to his ignorance, others to active malevolence. Some portray him as redeemable, others as the eternal enemy of good. In every case, the demiurge is the opponent—witting or unwitting—of mankind, which, in most scenarios, is not his creation so much as his hostage, humanity's home being the indescribable fullness beyond.

And so on. Given the rich ambiguities of *Genesis* (e.g., "Male and female created He them") or the existential problem of accounting for evil, the list of possible variant explanations is endless. And that, says Couliano, is exactly the point. Given certain premises (such as those mentioned above, or other experiential "facts" like the apparent separation of mind and body), thoughtful people, in any time or place, will derive certain propositions, questions and counterpropositions.(13) And this trend will continue even if the questioners are driven underground or burned at the stake and their questions erased or forgotten. It will continue not because there is some unbroken genealogical chain or some secret tradition or conspiracy. What guarantees its continuance is the dominant discourse, which implies all the gnostic variations as intellectual possibilities, at least to minds not completely cowed by dogma. Gnostic ideas "ultimately derive. . . not through: direct transmission"—i.e., genealogy—but "through a cognitive process of transformation." (14)

Two other key gnostic premises concern the idea of "ecosystemic intelligence" (the idea that the cosmos we inhabit is benevolent and purposeful) and the "anthropic principle" (the idea that humans are made for, and so can harmonize with, this cosmos).(15) In most (but not all) cases, gnostic scenarios say no to both. In doing so, they lay the groundwork for radical rejection of the world and a gamut of extreme responses that range from the ascetic to the libertine. However, Couliano cautions, gnosticism should not be considered pessimistic. By a strange turn, it is the most optimistic of religious mythologies, since it identifies human beings with the godhead itself; it simply says that the godhead is utterly out of and alien to this world. (It is this latter point which distinguishes gnosticism from modern existentialist nihilism. The two philosophies agree on man's complete alienation from the cosmos; however, existentialism stops there, whereas gnosticism invokes the most radical kind of transcendence.) "Gnostic myth originates in the transformation of other myth," writes Couliano.(16) Those other myths, typically, are the founding texts of Christianity. The act of rewriting such texts was, we know, a dangerous activity. It seems reasonable to suppose that it was also an impassioned one. On this point, Couliano acknowledges that gnostic revisionism is "a phenomenon of counterculture"(17) which guarantees gnostics "the tragic role of rebels caught and ground between the wheels of traditions." (18) Nonetheless, he says, their revolt had its beginning in genteel Platonic metaphysics: "What myth mirrors is only the play of the mind itself." (19) The gnostics were playing an elaborate intellectual game which required rolls of the die and the drawing of cognitive choice cards at every step. The fact that some of those cards turned up "Heresy: You die," is a historical horror. It should not, however, diminish our respect for the gnostic love of exploration for its own sake.

If you think this sounds more like John Stuart Mill than St. John of the Apocalypse, you're right. For Couliano, gnosticism is the prototype of modern, more or less "free" intellectual inquiry. The content of the inquiry—to say nothing of its price—is less important than the act itself.

This is not to say, however, that The Tree of Gnosis ignores the content of gnostic myth, or its history. Couliano sees theodicy, or the problem of evil, as the key gnostic theme, and he has sensitive chapters on the two mythic figures who dramatize gnostic theodicy: the aforementioned demiurge and the fallen Sophia (wisdom), a many-faceted female player in the cosmic drama. The book's cataloguing of gnostic inquiry proceeds chronologically, beginning with Nag Hammadi texts of the early Christian era and moving on through the teachings of Mani, Marcion and late medieval heretics like the Bogomils and the Cathars. A late chapter deals with modern transformations of gnostic myth as well as a persistent contemporary tendency to describe modernity itself as "gnostic." Among modern inheritors of the gnostic mantle, Hegel and Marx are foremost (consider their emphasis on alienation, fragmentation and transformation of consciousness). There is also a critique of philosopher Eric Voegelin, who appropriates the term to describe modern totalitarian movements like Nazism and Stalinism, a coinage that may seem strained (20); but

then, another day, another theory, eh, Irenaeus?

But despite such nods in the direction of history, Couliano's goal is to save gnosticism, not from heresy hunters or the Inquisition, but from historicism; from accounts which would see it as simply genealogical counter or sociological symptom. His encyclopedic—and eminently readable—book is an apt corrective to such tendencies. But, methinks the gentleman doth protest too much.

The Tree of Gnosis begins with a list of acknowledgements—like all such lists, placed first but composed last—which concludes thusly: "When I changed my area of study in 1973 from Indology to Gnosticism, and studied with Ugo Bianchi in Milan for almost four years. . . I felt myself attracted to Gnosticism in a way that Hans Jonas—whom I had the privilege to meet many times thereafter—would have defined as 'existentially rooted.' Now, after a dispassionate analysis of all Western dualistic trends, I think that my apprehension of the world during that period was certainly derived from the twenty-two years I had spent in one of the most totalitarian communist countries: Romania. I escaped in 1972, but the trauma persisted for roughly ten years and was not entirely cured until December 1989, when I saw on television the bodies of the executed Archon of that world and his equally evil consort. If I found healing, Romania has not yet, but that is an entirely different topic. Anyway, for my share of personal interest in Gnosticism I am bitterly indebted to the evil Archons who chased me into exile until I found a hospitable land."(21)

In other words, personality, politics and history had everything to do with Couliano's coming to the study of gnosticism. And when we place this passage in the context of Couliano's murder, our sense of the remark, and of Couliano's life and work, is transformed, at least a bit. It would seem that, try as he might, Couliano could not escape history or—to use the gnostic metaphor he employs—the evil demiurges of this world. They drove Couliano into exile and the study which shaped his life. No way around it, we have to wonder: Did they also, once he had penetrated the veil and questioned their false authority, reach out and strike him down?

Notes:

1. See Ioan P. Couliano, *Eros and Magic in the Renaissance* (Chicago: U. of Chicago Pr., 1987), and *Out of This World: Otherworldly Journeys from Gilgamesh to Albert Einstein* (Boston: Shambala, 1991).

2. For an introduction to the topic of gnosticism, see Elaine Pagels, *The Gnostic Gospels* (New York: Random House, 1979), or Hans Jonas, *The Gnostic Religion: The Message of the Alien God and the Be-*

ginnings of Christianity (Boston: Beacon, 1958).

3. The witch angle is mentioned, somewhat drolly, in Ted Anton, "Hyde Park Gothic," *Chicago,* Jan. 1992, p. 127.

4. For an initial report on the murder and various theories, including the Romanian politics angle, see Teresa Wiltz, "Romanians link politics, prof's death," *Chicago Tribune* 2 June 1991: Section 1, p. 1. For further background, see Anton, op. cit.

5. Wiltz, op. cit.

6. "The Couliano Murder Case," prod. Rich Samuels, hosted by John Calloway, WTTW, Chicago, 28 May, 1992. This discussion program provided a recent update on the case. Panelists included reporter Ted Anton (see 3) and Mircea Sebau, a Couliano colleague and fellow Romanian emigre. Both suggested that the Romanian politics angle has become the hottest lead. Anton further suggested that Chicago Police and FBI investigators are now pursuing this angle with the utmost seriousness.

7. Couliano discusses Borges in "A Historian's Kit for the Fourth Dimension," *Out of This World,* op. cit., pp. 13-16.

8. Ioan P. Couliano, *The Tree of Gnosis. Gnostic Mythology from Early Christianity to Modern Nihilism* (San Francisco: Harper Collins, 1992), p. 52.

9. See Hans Jonas, "Gnosticism, Nihilism and Existentialism" in *The Gnostic Religion,* op. cit., pp. 320-340.

10. Couliano, *The Tree of Gnosis,* op. cit., pp. 1-7.

11. Quoted in Benjamin Walker, *Gnosticism: Its History and Influence* (Wellingborough, Northamptonshire: Aquarian Press, 1983).

13. Ibid., p. 57.

14. Ibid., p. 59.

15. Ibid., p. xv.

16. Ibid., p. 63.

17. Ibid., p. 56.

18. Ibid., p. 126.

19. Ibid., p. 86.

20. Ibid., pp. 255-266.

21. Ibid., p. xviii.

Raiders of the Lost Shroud
by Preston S. Page

John Hayward's article "Has Carbon Dating Buried the Shroud of Turin?" in the Winter 1992 *Steamshovel Press* may be looking in the wrong place for a really fine shroud conspiracy. My view is to question why the Catholic Church allowed its use of the shroud relic. Ironically, the shroud's authenticity may not have been the point of any recent tests. Hayward also seems to ignore about twenty five years of compelling shroud scholarship, which is crucial to understanding the church's motivation.

A large part of Shroud scholarship over the past fifteen years has come not from Catholic circles, but from the Born Again and Evangelical camps. By the early 1980s Shroud "science" had become one of the major recruiting tools of the Catholic competition. By the time carbon dating of the Shroud was agreed to by its rightful owners, the religious TV channels were running marathons of Shroud shows between pleas for donations and ocular water shows by the likes of the now disgraced Tammy Fay and Jimmy Swaggart. Those curious about the Shroud could choose from more than 70 videos and literally hundreds of pamphlets and monographs. As nearly as I can determine, the church of the Pope had a very small cut of this business (three books, three videos) and was actually losing revenue to competing sects.

To understand the Vatican decision to perform carbon dating, it is helpful to examine claims of the miraculous applied to the Shroud in the light of work by critics. Mr. Hayward's article is a useful catalog of such claims — for instance his first paragraph points out that the image on the shroud is anatomically correct, "photographically" negative, contains three dimensional information (unlike any other picture in the world) and is superficial to the shroud cloth. This is fine. But he claims that no one can explain how, even if the shroud was manufactured somewhere between 1260 - 1390 AD, this seeming technological marvel of its time could have been produced. Mr. Hayward needed slightly more research on these points.

Mr. Hayward goes way over the top when he claims that no other picture in the world contains true three dimensional information. His life must be sheltered indeed if he has never seen a View Master (okay, that's really two pictures), the theatrical release of "Jaws 3-D," a contour map or at least the hologram on a major bank card. In fact, ever since the celebrated painting by Brunelleschi of the Baptistery across the square from the Florence Cathedral, 3-D perspective has been staggeringly popular in art and engineering. The Shroud image is a two dimensional Mercator projection of a three dimensional object (person), just like any ordinary map of an area large enough to be distorted by the curvature of the earth. No critic really questions whether the Shroud image is some sort of imprint of its onetime content; the debate is over the exact nature of that content.

Shroud researcher Joe Nickell in 1976 demonstrated that a technique of rubbing cloth wrapped around a three dimensional figure produces most of the characteristics of the shroud image, including a photographically negative anatomically correct three dimensional projection image that is superficial to the fabric of the cloth. By 1981, Mr. Nickell produced a forged Shroud image with iron oxide and vermilion pigments, used in North European cave paintings and available to 12th century artists, that passed the STURP (Shroud of Turin Research Project) 3-D mapping function used to "decode" the shroud image. It also closely matched the x-ray fluorescence and reflectance spectrum of the "real" shroud. It is worth mentioning the work of forensic microanalyst Walter McCrone who worked on the shroud image and found it to be composed of iron oxide and vermilion pigments. What does this prove? Not that the Shroud of Turin is a forgery, but that no superficial characteristics of the shroud preclude it from being a fraud. Since the shroud may have been languishing god-knows-where for 1300 years in less than ideal storage conditions before it burst upon the world stage in France, could 12th century conservators have touched it up a bit so the public could better see an image? Also, maybe we are looking at a faithful 12th century copy of the real shroud, which would have been too valuable to set before the public. The real shroud may be hidden or destroyed or non-existent.

In terms of looking for a conspiracy, it should be noted that the historical pedigree of the Shroud of Turin has always been suspect as far as the Vatican is concerned. The Shroud first appeared in the early 1350s when it was exhibited at a church in Lirey in North Central France, where a fee was charged to pilgrims who wished to view a holy relic. In 1357 Henri de Poitiers, a skeptical French bishop, launched an investigation into its provenance; as a result, the exhibitions were stopped. After Henri's death, however, the shroud was brought out again; and again it was generating substantial revenue for the Church; and again it was investigated by the Church, Henri's successor, Bishop Pierre d'Arcis.

The earliest known Papal communique with a reference to the shroud comes from Pierre d'Arcis to Clement VII, the Avignon Pope. In general, the letter voices concern that the Church is losing credibility and authority with the sideshow practice of charging pilgrims to see holy relics, many, if not all of which were obviously crude forgeries. Apparently the unwashed masses were becoming contemptuous of the Church and its cheap fund raising tricks. This was a period in Europe when life was becoming more cosmopolitan and trade was expanding at an incredible rate. Between 1350 and 1400 the number of bureaucrats needed to collect tolls and tariffs quintupled. Prosperity was breaking out and the "white collar" faithful were beginning to travel a great deal more than they had since before the Black Death. Pierre wrote of the investigations by Henri into the shroud and the "danger to souls" of those threatening to leave the Church because they felt the Shroud was a sorry excuse for a relic. The famous (to Papal and shroud scholars) letter begins:

The case, Holy Father, stands thus. Some time since in this diocese of Troyes the Dean of a certain collegiate church, to wit, that of Lirey, falsely and deceitfully, being consumed with the passion of avarice, and not from any motive of devotion but only of gain, procured for his church a certain cloth cunningly painted.

The letter describes in detail the painting on that cloth, which we today call the Shroud of Turin, along with the details of its exhibition and the wealthy patrons' complaints. The letter continues:

Eventually, after diligent inquiry and examination, he (Henri de Poitiers) discovered the fraud and how the said cloth had been cunningly painted, the truth being attested by the artist who had painted it, to wit, that it was a work of human skill and not miraculously wrought or bestowed.

Pope Clement, in response to this letter, issued a Bull, which, although it allowed the exhibition of the cloth (after all, it was generating revenue for the Church), ordered that it be presented only as a "copy or representation." The Bull was forgotten shortly after the watchdog Pierre left the area for a different appointment and the Lirey Church found it couldn't charge as much for admission to see a "copy". The painted cloth of Lirey gradually became thought of as a genuine relic. It should be noted that the Vatican, while it did not discourage popular veneration of the Shroud, never took an official stand on the question of its authenticity other than the aforementioned Bull.

Do Papal documents that refer to the Shroud as a man-made painting harm its provenance? It doesn't help. But let's be fair. The infallibility of Bishops is not a Church dictum. Pierre and Henri could have been persuaded to make their disclaims by a wealthy Church patron who just didn't like the Shroud. That seems rather thin, but who knows? So far we cannot rule out forgery and we cannot authenticate the shroud. What does the C-14 dating tell us?

What does C-14 dating ever tell us? I must agree with Mr. Hayward about the fallibility of C-14 dating. I have played with it myself, and I don't have absolute confidence in its reliability. I don't know of any scientist who does. Radiocarbon dating has occasionally yielded spurious results with samples of known age, so how on earth could anyone have confidence in the method for dating an unknown sample? While it has its flaws, C-14 dating methods are not as capricious as Mr. Hayward would have us believe. As the process becomes better understood, exceptions are noted and accuracy improves. So while deep sea snails are dated as coming from 100 years in the future, astounding as that sounds, the +/- 100 years accuracy range does cover this. Besides, I don't think Mr. Hayward is suggesting snails play a part in the manufacture of the Shroud. The radiocarbon chain is well understood for the component materials of the Shroud. So even if the test was not accurate even to +/- 500 years, it would be possible to place it well before the 12th century if it was 2000 years old. Still, questions about the Shroud history could affect the C-14 date. The storage conditions of the shroud for the past 500 years of its history would be important, but who can say what happened to it during its putative 1300 year unknown history. How was it stored and in what climate? Had it ever been soiled or washed or restored? Could an original image have been lifted from a deteriorating shroud by any of several known conservation techniques and deposited on a more contemporary cloth? How many times could this have been done? My question to Mr. Hayward is this: If radiocarbon dating is as inaccurate as he claims, why would the Vatican allow what could possibly be the most Holy of holy relics to be subjected to C-14 testing? Is this uncharacteristic carelessness, or part of a hidden agenda?

Mr. Hayward says that the raw data from the shroud dating is not available and that only a "final report" was issued, implying a cover up of some sort on the scale of the JFK assassination. All the data he could want is available from STURP proceedings and other journals where the data was indeed published. Carbon dating just doesn't generate very much data. The so-called final report was issued for the benefit of the non-technical press. Since carbon dating is relatively straightforward, falsifying the data would be easy (I have seen it done) and would easily pass any peer review process. That is why the test was performed at five different labs with slightly different equipment. No researchers could possibly double check the figures because they would need another shroud sample, which is safely not forthcoming. There might well have been a cover-up of some sort, but if C-14 dating doesn't generate serious data, who is going to waste time disputing it? You need only point out that it is, after all, only a C-14 date! Or come up with a lab that can guarantee more ancient results.

If the methodology for handling the shroud sample is unsatisfactory, or the motives of those involved in the testing is suspect, then there is only the Church to blame for being careless. A True Believer in the Shroud would see no reason for performing any kind of test. Only a critic would be interested in subjecting the shroud to mutilation for the idle curiosity of other critics. The notion that the Church was forced into allowing the test because it was being call "chicken" by a handful of what the Church would have considered crackpots seems unlikely. The Church and Science have been antagonists at least since that Galileo guy.

But remember, the Church never officially authenticated the shroud. Over the past thirty years or so "Shroud Science" has been an increasingly important recruiting mainstay of the more fundamentalist Protestant Christian cults, providing a physical link to the idea they are trying to sell to the more materialist holdouts. I think the Church spotted an opportunity to pull the rug from under the competition. If the shroud is genuine and failed any tests the Church allowed to be performed, then the Church must want it discredited. The C-14 date coincides nicely with the Church's own documentation that calls the Shroud a forgery. If there was C-14 chicanery, was it to assure these dates matched? Or has the Church known all along that the shroud was forged and just saw a chance to damage to the Protestant membership drive and perhaps absorb the disgruntled fallout? If the Shroud is a forgery, the longer the Church lent its guarded support to a worthless painted cloth, the harder the fallout when it finally is discredited. Why not look like the good guy, appear to embrace the age old enemy, Science, and remove a useful sales tool from the other guys? If the shroud is genuine, maybe the Church wants to put it away for a while until it can figure out how to keep Protestants from benefiting from its imprimatur.

Does the carbon dating effectively bury the Shroud of Turin? I think it depends on who you are. If you were a skeptic or an agnostic looking for any rebuff of a holy relic, the answer is "yes." If you are an atheist, none of this factored in your life anyway, but you would hardly be surprised that the Shroud was faked; and if the C-14 shroud date was 35 AD, who cares? It was just a C-14 date. If you were a True Believer in the Shroud, though, should you be despondent? Has your life just been turned upside down?

The answer is "no." And of all things, after a scientific inquiry to destroy the shroud, it is science that could rescue it! Yes, there is a theory (Stevenson and Habermas have a whole book on it) that an energy burst caused the formation of the shroud image. They formed the theory years before the carbon dating business, and while STURP is somewhat unhappy with their book, it could be the only way to rescue the shroud from the rag bin. The point is, what if that energy burst was heavy in neutrons and caused an extra thousand years or so of C-14 to form in the shroud cloth? C-14 is formed when a neutron collides with N-14 and displaces a proton. With the atmosphere being about 80% nitrogen, the shroud is virtually soaked in N-14 all the time. What would that do to carbon dating accuracy? Imagine surprised carbon dating technicians working on the shroud just before the fall of Rome, showing it would be created in about a thousand years!

So, even with modern experimental science running at full tilt, it still remains a matter of faith. There is no way to authenticate scientifically the shroud as there is, say, to verify quantum electron tunneling. We have built a jolly good scanning-tunneling microscope, but, sadly, the shroud doesn't seem to do much. The hypothesis can never be tested beyond doubt. Conversely, trying to prove a forgery seems like a waste of time as well. It is like trying to authenticate a painting with shaky provenance. Perhaps you are aware of the questions surrounding the Mona Lisa after it was stolen, then mysteriously returned. Is what we call the Mona Lisa genuine or a cunning forgery? Or is it authentic, just not the same, since Leonardo may have painted more than one. We think it is probably real, but no one will ever know for sure...

The shroud's biggest problem is that, as a miracle, it's a bit esoteric and not flashy enough. Ultimately, if the Shroud of Turin is truly a miraculous supernatural creation by the Judeo-Christian sky god, why should it hold up to any scrutiny, scientific or otherwise? Science can only test consistencies in the natural world. The supernatural, if it exists, is by definition inconsistent with the natural world. Could not a relic of faith be designed by a god to seem like a fake if questioned, just to test faith? Of course, most of us are less confident than the average god. I would have done a talking shroud that glowed, even in daylight, and it would sit up and accurately guess your weight. Radiocarbon dating on my shroud would always give the telephone number of the lab testing it. Too flashy? How does one design a restrained, tasteful, yet convincing miracle? Part the Red Sea, perhaps...

References:

1977-1988 *Proceedings of the United States Conference of Research on the Shroud of Turin,* Holy Shroud Guild, 294 E. 150 St., Bronx, NY 10451.

W.C. McCrone, *The Particle Atlas,* vols. 1-5, (Ann Arbor Science Publishers, 1973-79).

W.C. McCrone and C. Skirius, *Microscope* 28(3/4):105-14 (1980).

J.H. Heller and A.D. Adler, *Applied Optics,* 19:2742-44 (1980).

S.F. Pellicori, *Applied Optics,* 19:1913-20 (1980).

K.E. Stevenson and G.R. Habermas, *Verdict on the Shroud* (Ann Arbor, Michigan: Servant Books, 1981).

L.A. Schwalbe and R.N. Rogers, "Physics and Chemistry of the Shroud of Turin," *Analytical Chemistry ACTA,* February 1982).

Marvin M. Meuller, "The Shroud of Turin: A Critical Appraisal," *Skeptical Inquirer* (Spring 1982)

James Burke, *The Day The Universe Changed,* (Boston, Mass: Little, Brown and Company, 1985).

R.W. Rhein, *Medical World News,* December 22, 1980, pp. 40-50.

Ian Wilson, *The Shroud of Turin* (New York: Doubleday, 1978).

Kenneth Weaver, "The Mystery of the Shroud," *National Geographic,* June 1980.

Cullen Murphy, "Shreds of Evidence: Science Confronts the Miraculous — The Shroud of Turin," *Harper's,* November 1981.

Joe Nickell, *The Humanist,* November/December 1978; *Free Inquiry,* Summer 1981.

Pierre Barbet, *A Doctor at Calvary* (Image Books, 1963).

Quigley, Clinton, Straight & Reich
by Jim Martin

I have been reading a remarkable book called *Tragedy & Hope; A History of the World in Our Time* by Carroll Quigley. Quigley died in 1977, was a professor of history at Georgetown University. He has re-emerged among conspiracy researchers because President Clinton has, on several occasions, lauded Quigley as his "mentor", in particular during his acceptance speech at the Democratic National Convention. Clinton attended Georgetown and was a student of Quigley's.

The strange thing is, Quigley has long been a central figure among right-wing conspiracy theorists like the John Birch society, Christian rightists, and other cultists. This is because his main research has been into the existence of a semi-secret group founded by Cecil Rhodes in Britain. "The Rhodes-Milner Group" was a upper-crust cabal with financial and matrimonial connections to the world's most wealthy and powerful. In America their interests were fronted by the Morgans, and on the Continent things were handled by the Rothschilds. Rhodes was one of the wealthiest men on the planet, with an *annual income of over $1 billion* adjusted for inflation. Rhodesia was named after him, and we all know that he funded the Rhodes scholarships and that Clinton was a Rhodes scholar.

What is less well-known is that Rhodes scholarships were not set up to reward gifted students with a free ride at Oxford, but rather as one component of Rhodes' plan to create a one-world government based on British Commonwealth rules. He was actually, for those times anyway, a liberal, since he believed that the indigenous peoples within the British Empire should be given the same legal rights and political democracy as English Islanders. The function of the Rhodes scholarships was to identify future leaders, instill them with common values at Oxford, and send them back to their native colonies where they would spread these acquired traits.

Today, the "Rhodes-Milner Group" manifests itself as the Council on Foreign Relations (CFR), the Trilateral Commission and other "free-trade", "one-world" organizations.

RIGHT-WING CONSPIRACY THEORISTS want to believe that the Soviet Union is a creation of an International Jewish Money Cabal. They point to certain events where capitalists like the Rothschilds gave money to left-wingers and communists throughout history, but more important to them is the century-old master plan to end national sovereignty, consolidate all currency and institute the Global State. Quigley documents all this, which sounds crazy but Quigley is an insider himself, who had the opportunity to inspect the internal papers of Rhodes' group for several years and was well-connected with the various organizations in America which front for Morgan-Rothschild banking interests, such as the CFR. The whole "New World Order" idea originates with these think-tanks, which bring together leaders in the fields of finance, journalism, education and politics.

Obviously, while such groups do indeed exist, and have definite connections to the Rockefellers, Warburgs, Morgans and such, they aren't all Jewish. Yet this idea has a strong hold on people like those who publish the Spotlight newspaper. They are convinced that a Jewish cabal of usurers conspires toward world domination. Jewish, Protestant, Catholic, Scientologist, or all of the above, I doubt any such group could achieve the kind of harmony of purpose to really pull anything off. Then again, I just read where US troops are now under the command of German UN commanders. And when Clinton signs the NAFTA treaty, that abrogates whatever's left of our Constitution.

I don't go for the Birchite party line that the Soviet Revolution would never have happened without timely infusions of cash from finance capitalists. That doesn't mean such transactions never occurred, however. Taken as a whole, Quigley undermines the Birchers' thesis. What's important about the book is Quigley's suffocating sense of Commonwealth democracy being little more than a tool of control for global market planning.

SO IT IS VERY STRANGE that Clinton has gone out of his way on several occasions to say what a great guy Quigley was. Quigley's magnum opus, *Tragedy and Hope*, is truly fascinating. One section that caught my eye was a long discussion of *The New Republic*, which is of course familiar to any student of Wilhelm Reich. It was here, in the pages of *The New Republic*, that Mildred Brady wrote a smear article that served as a basis for the FDA's persecution of Reich. Theodore Wolfe outlined the steady spread of Brady's lies in various subsequent articles in his *Red Thread of Conspiracy*. In a nut, they all repeat Brady's whopper: that Reich claimed the orgone accumulator restored orgastic potency. To this day, you still hear this echo: that you're supposed to masturbate in the "orgasm box."

You may have noted that in my article on Reich's

prison files ("Wilhelm Reich in Hell", *SP #6*), I mentioned that Reich expressed a conviction to the warden that he was being railroaded by the Rockefellers. This sounded crazy to me at the time; but now I see his point.

The New Republic, Quigley explains, was founded by a full partner of the Morgan Bank. Quigley devotes a dozen pages or so explaining how Wall Street bankers funded foundations and lofty-purpose magazines in order to manipulate and monitor the left. *The New Republic* is cited as a sterling example.

Less than a year before Mildred Brady wrote her smear, Henry Wallace had been hired as editor of *The New Republic*. This was odd in itself because Vice President Wallace had just been dumped by Truman for breaking ranks over the Marshall Plan. Wallace wanted something more Stalinist for Europe. His political career was over, apparently.

Quigley says that Wall Street wanted to defeat Truman, and so they used Wallace to form a third party candidacy to draw enough support from Truman's left flank to elect a Republican. To do this they allowed many communists into the staff of *The New Republic* to promote his candidacy.

So what Reich told his jailers, specifically, that the Rockefeller Foundation "made me a tool of its socio-economic interpersonal relations" may not be so far from the truth. No one hates Reich as much as a communist; there were many, not a few, on the staff of *The New Republic*....

THE RELEVANT MATERIAL here starts on page 938 of *Tragedy & Hope*, and the following facts are presented:

The Straight Family, using Payne Whitney money, owned *The New Republic*. Since 1914, it had been managed by Walter Lippmann, a member of the Rhodes-Milner Group. *The New Republic's* "original purpose... was to provide an outlet for the progressive left and guide it quietly in an Anglophile direction", Quigley says.

Willard Straight died while attending the Paris Peace Conference in 1919. His wife moved to England six years later, remarried into nobility. "Lady Elmhirst of Darrington Hall" (the former Mrs. Straight) was sole owner of *The New Republic* until 1937 when she turned it over to her younger son, "Mike" Straight, setting up a dummy corporation in Canada with a grant of $1.5 million.

Quigley points out the close - incestuous - relationships between such families as the Straights, Paynes, Whitneys, Morgans and Rockefellers. For instance, Mike Straight started *United Nations World*, the original one-worlder bugaboo, which listed Nelson

Rockefeller, J.H. Whitney and *The New Republic* - among others - as owners of record.

In October of 1946, *The New Republic* hired Wallace, whose political fortunes were at low ebb, as managing editor of *The New Republic*. (In America, we always receive the first word about hitherto unknown "front-runners" just about two years before the election. Carter announced in the fall of 1974. Clinton likewise. So it would not be unreasonable to speculate that, for many years, Wall Street had begun playing its cards with a two-year lead time.)

Soon thereafter new funds expand *The New Republic* staff, which starts beating the Wallace drum.

The next fall, in 1947, Wallace, Mike Straight and Lew Frank Jr. (a member of the Communist caucus of the American Veterans Committee, Wallace's speechwriter, and a "fellow traveller," no pun intended) make a trip to the Mediterranean.

They are granted an audience with the Pope. (Huh?)

Wallace comes back "a changed man" and announces his candidacy in December.

Lew Frank, Jr., needing assistance in formulating a response to the Marshall Plan and the new Cold War, joins a "Communist research group" at the home of wealthy "Wall Street Red" Frederick Vanderbilt Field.

Wallace's candidacy severely splits the left.

Communists are driven out of former "Popular Front" organizations. CP marginalized long before McCarthy & Hoover.

Truman squeaks by anyway. After the election, the new "Wallace staff" of *NR* is fired en masse.

Quigley sums it all up thusly:

"The relationship between Straight and the Communists in pushing Wallace into his 1948 adventure may be misjudged very easily. The anti-Communist Right had a very simple explanation of it: Wallace and Straight were Communists and hoped to elect Wallace President. Nothing could be further from the truth. All three - Straight, Wallace and the Communists - joined in the attempt merely as a means of defeating Truman. Straight was the chief force in getting the campaign started in 1947 and was largely instrumental in bringing some of the Communists into it, but when he had them all on board the Wallace train, he jumped off himself, leaving both Wallace and the Communists gliding swiftly, without guidance or hope, on the downhill track to oblivion. It was a brilliantly done piece of work."

This is classic Quigley.

If you have a mind to, you could verify all of this evidence. (Frankly, trying to trip up Quigley's research may be a waste of time.) I think these facts would lead anyone to speculate, as Quigley did, that an ongoing pattern of manipulating left politics came into play here. What the hell was a *partner in the Morgan Bank* (Willard Straight) doing starting a "pinko" journal like *The New Republic* in the first place? Even Quigley doubts whether Straight (the manipulator behind the scenes) had anticipated all the wonderful results (the elimination of the CPUSA as a serious force in American politics thereafter) but the stark fact is that he cites not only Straight but a whole raft of big-money left-wing manipulators.

I'm not suggesting that the Rockefellers set out to get Reich, but rather that Reich was caught in a web of some seriously contorted parapolitics. There's no way, in 1947, Stalinist sympathizers like Henry Wallace, Mildred Brady and the gang at *The National Review* could have gained a national forum without big-time funding from people with a Game Plan. It would be like Al Gore jumping ship, joining the Greens and firing broadsides from the pages of the *Progressive*.

Reich could have gone on for years, working quietly, publishing privately and without fanfare. (In his best years, he only sold 500 copies of any one book.) From my own personal experience, most people consider Reich as a harmless curiosity, but Marxist materialists react with apoplectic stuttering - it's almost beyond their capacity to respond with words. Reich had them pegged in *The Mass Psychology of Fascism*: behind their facade of humanitarian caring writhed a seething tumult of sadism, unchecked lust for control, and contempt for the very people they claimed to champion. Did the staff of *The National Review* know about *Mass Psychology*? You betcha. Several months prior to Mildred Brady's hit piece, they published Frederic Wertham's review of it. In a textbook example of what the shrinks call "projection", Wertham accused Reich of "utter contempt for the masses". This is from a guy on the Morgan Bank payroll. So Reich indeed was a victim of an "emotional conspiracy" set to rolling by geopolitical interests of the Rockefellers.

Just keep in mind that Winthrop Rockefeller was a "father figure" to Clinton; and the next time you see Michael Kinsley "from the Left" on CNN's *Crossfire*, remember he worked at *The National Review*... Janet Reno loves the children... War is Peace... Taxes are Contributions...

ANOTHER INTERESTING SECTION of *Tragedy and Hope* is a long discussion of the situation in Latin America. Quigley argues that the poverty there is not a matter of lack of funds, or technological advances, but of a historical link via Spain to Saharasia.

He called it the "Pakistani-Peruvian Axis".

He said that Spain, although nominally Christian, never rid itself of its Moorish heritage; that patriarchy and militarism and machismo were the defining elements of Latin American society and until these patterns were broken, Latin America would remain as it is. He gives a long and lucid discussion of the sexual pathology of Islam, so astonishingly Reichian that I nearly fell off my chair. He explicitly mentions "the biological and character traits" of the region. Jim DeMeo is currently working on a book called *Saharasia*, which pinpoints the origins of patriarchy, militarism and mistreatment of women and children to climatic changes in the Sahara and Central Asia around 4000 BCE. This research is based on Reich's analysis of "the desert character" whose emotional desert projected itself onto the historical scene.

LET'S GET BACK TO BILL CLINTON and his "mentor" Quigley. Published in 1966, *Tragedy & Hope* would have been required reading in his class while Clinton was a sophomore. Clinton was, and is, the classic suck-butt. As a political aspirant, young Bill would have recognized the old professor's heavy-duty contacts. And if he was assigned to read *Tragedy & Hope*, you better believe he would have studied it thoroughly enough to ask the right questions in class, get noticed, invited to the old Prof's house for dinner. Or better yet, if he attended Georgetown *before* publication, he may have even helped with the research on the book (a la *The Paper Chase*). Clinton certainly used Quigley's good graces to secure his Rhodes scholarship. All it would have taken would have been a glowing recommendation.

What's less clear: whether Clinton was aware of the significance of *Tragedy & Hope* to the Birchite, Christian right, and other cult groups. As Daniel Brandt points out, Pat Robertson's *New World Order* cites Quigley as a central reference — Rev. Pat has a whole chapter on him. Robertson's book was published *before* Clinton's acceptance speech, so Clinton, or some of his sharp boys, should have known better than to choose this moment to enshrine Quigley as his main inspiration right up there with JFK. (Brandt is droll: "Reading Quigley may turn you into a student of high-level conspiracy, which is exactly what influential people around Clinton and elsewhere say you shouldn't be.") Another place I have just noticed Quigley referenced is in William Bramley's *The Gods of Eden*, a sweeping tour de force about ancient ET "Custodians", the Brotherhood of the Snake, Illuminati, Masons, JFK, Jonestown (it's all the aliens' fault, to divide us against each other and never rebel against being basically farm animals and big-game trophies), and this book has just been re-issued in mass trade paperbacks. And of course there's Eustace Mullins, Lyndon LaRouche, The John Birch Society, Skousens, etc. Carl Oglesby apparently based his *Yankee & Cowboy War* on Quigley's research. At any rate, I don't suppose Clinton was dropping a name to throw a red herring at the Birchers; nor was he tossing out a coded message Masonic handshake; rather, he was sincerely giving his due to Quigley for influencing his thinking and putting him in contact with the real power on this globe (and maybe others, if you follow William Bramley's *The Gods of Eden*).

A FEW DAYS AGO I was talking about Quigley to some former co-workers at the print shop I used to work at and a guy said, "That sounds familiar... I think my Dad was reading that book while recovering from prostate surgery." Subsequently, after phoning him, he told me that indeed his Dad had read *Tragedy & Hope*; a coworker had mentioned it as a fascinating book (not recommending it for its "conspiracy" value).

His Dad had trouble locating the book, and so he wrote to Quigley directly and received a letter (still has it) from the man himself, saying that MacMillan, the British publisher, had suppressed the publication because they didn't like its gist. (This was close to twenty years ago, of course, before Quigley's death in 1977.) Quigley wrote that MacMillan was preventing him from assuming copyright to his own book by keeping it "in print", but withholding it from the general public. Quigley *photographed each page of the book* and sent it to a printer; that's the only reason it was available at all in America. When I tracked down copies of the book through Bowker's *Books in Print*, I found that the rights are now held by Angriff Press (other titles: *Mein Kampf*, *The Eternal Jew*, *Protocols of the Elders of Zion*, Henry Ford's diatribes, etc.). The only way to buy Clinton's "mentor's" book today is from a severely fascist source. The irony at this point becomes a bit overwhelming.

Tragedy & Hope is over 1300 pages long and I must say it's one of the most lively and quirky history books I've ever read; Quigley was a genius. It's frustrating: all the "conspiracy" types I've talked to complain that it's "hard to find the Wall Street Commie stuff"; but there's so much more to the book than that. The last three chapters are stunning, covering the post-war period, the Cuban Missile crisis, Nuclear Rivalry and power-politics jockeying. There is a running subtext throughout that transcends Realpolitik, with his obsessive genealogy of wealth and power. It must be remembered that Quigley is no conspiracy nut, but rather an insider's insider, with personal knowledge of the groups he speaks of. Am I the only one who has noticed the strangest thing about the book: *there isn't a single footnote*? It's written in spooky Omniscient One style. But then, what's the point of footnotes when you're the official family historian of the global money cartel?

Tragedy & Hope (hardback, $44.00 postpaid), as well as Quigley's other book, *The Anglo American Establishment* (paperback, $17.00, postpaid) which is more specifically devoted to the Rhodes-Milner Group are both available from Flatland. Also: *The Gods of Eden* ($8.00 postpaid). Our complete mail-order book catalog is available for $2.00, free with any order. Flatland: POB 2420, Ft. Bragg, CA 95437.

Jim Martin publishes the Flatland Catalog.

Who Is Mike Straight?

When Quigley mentioned the name of Mike Straight, I knew I had heard it but couldn't remember where. After finishing this article I found my copy of *Mask of Treachery* by John Costello (Collins, 1988) where Straight is heavily referenced. *Mask of Treachery* is about the Anthony Blunt-Guy Burgess-Kim Philby spy ring dating all the way back to their days at Cambridge in the 1930s, when they all were associated with a secret fraternal society called "The Apostles". Entree into the group required an oath never to reveal the existence of the group or anyone in it, under penalty of death and "eternal damnation".

It turns out that Anthony Blunt, probably the Soviets' most important spook in Britain, was Mike Straight's recruiter and case manager. Straight, by his own admission to the FBI, was a Soviet agent. (Since the 20s, the Soviets had made a concerted effort to recruit members of the British elite while young students, realizing that the nature of aristocracy afforded a natural opportunity to create young "moles".)

"Sending the son of a J.P. Morgan banker to act as Wall Street agent of Moscow was the sort of bizarre plot that would have appealed to Burgess," Straight told Costello. "Anybody who knew anything about me would have realized that being a banker was the last thing I might want to do with my life. Unlike most undergraduates, I did not have to worry about making a living, the whole essence of my life at that time was Cambridge." Blunt pressured him to leave Cambridge just before finals, breaking officially with all his friends among ruling-caste socialists at Cambridge. Straight protested, but Blunt told him that these orders came from Stalin himself. Straight left for New York.

Lord Rothschild at Oxford: Vodka & Caviar

Get this: another recruit of the Apostles group, which at that time required a Marxist orientation, was Blunt and Straight's close friend, (Lord) Victor Rothschild. Guy Burgess, in fact, was being paid 100 pounds sterling a month as "investment advisor" to Mrs. Charles Rothschild while an active Soviet spy.

As an undergraduate, Straight was instrumental in bringing Haile Selassie, then under attack from Mussolini, to the Cambridge Union where he was inducted as an honorary member. "This anti-Fascist gesture demonstrated the Marxist ascendancy [in the Apostles group] and provoked heated controversy," Costello asserts. Straight gave the welcoming speech, while Anthony Blunt translated from French for the Lion of Judah. Afterwards, Straight and Blunt headed off to Victor Rothschild's where a going-away party for Straight was already in full swing. "When we arrived, a vodka and caviar supper was being served on the terrace," recalled Leonard Miall, ex-president of the Cambridge Union. Victor Rothschild was playing jazz duets with Cab Calloway.

Hi-de-hi-de-hi-de Ho!

Things Are Gonna Slide

While the disaster in Waco, Texas is being portrayed as a Jonestown-style mass suicide, many are still in a quandary about what actually happened. The curious aspects include Lloyd Bentsen's giving President Clinton a daily briefing on the affair. The Arms, Tobacco and Firearms authority reports to the Treasury Department and Bentsen is the Secretary of the Treasury. Researcher Penn Jones established early that Bentsen was a major recipient of funds from Defense Industrial Security Command, a police intelligence group connected to the Kennedy assassination by the Torbitt document. Other recipients of DISC money include Ronald Reagan. One analysis of the Jonestown massacre views it as a MKULTRA brainwashing experiment and mass murder. Incidents of mass suicide are rare in human history.

—Kenn Thomas

On the second Tuesday of February 1993 I had awakened to an NBC radio newscast which stated that witnesses across the entire Southeast United States had seen a meteor leave a blue streak across the sky from east to west. About a half hour later I turned on the television and saw a newscaster read a report that said the Russians had deployed a solar satellite, the purpose of which was to project sunlight back down to earth for nighttime illumination of ground operations. Later that morning I was watching CNN cover the story of both the meteor and a crashed Lockheed experimental "flying lab", which apparently had come to rest up against the Lockheed campus infirmary building in Dobbins AFB in Atlanta, Georgia.

Witnesses to the "meteor" phenomenon said that it caused an electrical brownout as it passed overhead—causing lights to dim. Then shortly thereafter two explosions were heard by witnesses close to Atlanta. One woman claimed to have found strange striated molten metal globules embedded in the sidewalk in front of her home that morning.

Not long after that the CNN camera men were in helicopters circling the Lockheed crash site and getting good telephoto video footage of what looked like a possible rear fuselage of an Aurora spy plane—*not* a modified transport C-130 as claimed. The firefighters were hosing down this plane with white detergent foam for retardant, and once the Department of Defense realized that the CNN crews were getting clear footage of an Aurora spy plane, the Tower at Dobbins Air base ordered the helicopters to back away from the site. This event was a major story for over three hours on CNN, but later that evening there was a news blackout on the entire event—including the meteor and Soviet satellite stories.

Newspaper accounts from the next day were from a Lockheed press release which stated that the crashed plane was a private, non-military modified C-130 type transport plane that was a "flying laboratory" of some sort, but what I witnessed on CNN was too small to have been a transport of that type—the plane had a rear-swept delta wing with odd winglets at the outer tips and a tall, narrow tail. The front of the plane was missing.

—Domingo Bugatti

You know how the KGB has been opening up records lately and telling the world about certain things they have done or known in the last years? Well, Russia now claims that its technicians were sitting in a top secret radar station in Libya on the night of the Ustica incident reported upon in the last two issues of *Steamshovel*. They claimed to have seen the whole thing on radar.

They claim that two U.S. jets took off from an Italian air base in Sardegna. There were NATO exercises planned for that period and the Russians were keeping all ships and planes in port, in order to not get in the way. The jets took off, intercepted the DC9 by mistake and shot it down with air-to-air missiles. The Russians claim that you can see such missiles on radar.

When asked why they didn't expose the whole thing to the world at the time, in the height of the cold war, an officer who was there responds that he doesn't know why. He imagines, however, that if they did not expose the Americans, the Politburo must have had even bigger geo-political reasons not to. Will the U.S. government give louder and clearer replies to Russian allegations or ignore it?

—Jim Cregan

Book Reviews

Anthony Summers' book on J. Edgar Hoover, *Personal and Confidential: The Secret Life of J. Edgar Hoover* (G. P. Putnam and Sons, 200 Madison Avenue, New York, NY 10016) was perhaps the only new contribution to assassination literature to be found at the Midwestern Symposium on Assassination Politics in Chicago, April 1-4, although many new projects, including Robert Groden's long-awaited JFK photographic and film evidence documentary, are slated for the fall. In fact, the discussion about the impending outcome of the John F. Kennedy Assassinations Material Act of 1993 included the observation that the research community did not need thirty more years of reading material. Although nomination of the review board for the assassination materials has been hindered by the changeover to a new administration, a cascade of documents was expected to be released in the weeks following the symposium.

The quip about reading material was made in the context of an important debate within the research community: should it push for the establishment of a special prosecutor, who would have power to hold back release of some documents, or should it be satisfied with the full release of assassination files? Should it move toward justice, or at least some kind of legal redress for the thirty-year old crime, or knowledge, as much knowledge as files buried and manhandled for thirty years can yield? Perhaps armed with new information from the released files, a special prosecutor might prove more effective than the government bodies (Warren Commission; HSCA) from which the files are taken. This seemed to be the sentiment by the end of the symposium, when those attending and panelists decided to form a new group to pursue avenues to getting a special prosecutor appointed. Carl Oglesby, author of *The Yankee and Cowboy War* and *Who Killed JFK,* and venerated veteran of the pursuit of the truth behind the Kennedy assassination, was selected by the participants to head the new group.

The medical evidence panel was the symposium highlight. Certainly this was the last stand of the discredited doctors from the *Journal of the American Medical Association.* Last year, *JAMA* attempted to authoritatively close discussion on the assassination by printing deliberately distorted memories of JFK's autopsy doctors. Despite the closure insisted upon by those *JAMA* articles, a new issue of the journal continuing the one-sided handling of the debate was available at the symposium. It contained a contribution by a formerly "pro-conspiracy" MD named Robert Artwohl, who was also a member of the symposium's

JAMA panel. He presented his view of how one of the autopsy x-rays might have fit into a view of the Kennedy motorcade. The *JAMA* panel also included John Lattimer, George Lundberg, and Michael West. The countervailing panel included David Lifton, author of *Best Evidence,* Cyril Wecht, Wallace Milam and Roger Feinman.

Artwohl was non-plussed by David Lifton over an abrasion collar to one of JFK's back wounds that autopsy doctor Pierre Fincke failed to note. Dr. Robert Lattimore gave a video presentation of his experiments demonstrating that a shot from the rear can cause a skull placed on (but not connected to) a ladder to fall to the rear, thus "establishing" that a shot to Kennedy's head from the rear could cause him to fall to the rear. The other side drew audience attention to the forward movement of the ladder and made a succinct and apt point. To its credit, the audience refrained from asking the most obvious questions, including those concerning the background of Johann Rush, who contributed to the video production of Dr. West from the University of Mississippi. The video ostensibly moves Governor John Connally's wounds backward in time to a point on the Zapruder film that might show his lapel flapping. Thirty years ago, Rush also was on hand to film Lee Harvey Oswald handing out Fair Play for Cuba pamphlets.

JAMA panel chair George Lundberg gracelessly (and suspiciously) attempted to cut short the discussion following the presentation by insisting on the strict timetable of the symposium's schedule. Other panelists caused him to relent, however, with Dr. West jokingly remarking that he was under time pressure: he had a Klan meeting to attend.

The debate between Lifton and Artwohl continued on the concourse outside the conference hall on April 4, the anniversary observance of the assassination of Martin Luther King. A large group crowded around the pair, primarily to hear Artwohl expand on his view that Oswald acted alone (an assertion that goes beyond the conclusions that can be drawn from the medical evidence), larger than the number of those in attendance in the conference hall to honor King.

Perhaps they were better off as the key speaker, the Reverend James Bevel, who was with King at the Lorraine Hotel at the time of the murder, extolled the virtues of Lyndon LaRouche and made a vitriolic and graphic attack on homosexuals. Former Chicago 8 activist Dave Dellinger, whose new memoir, *From Yale To Jail,* is available for $27.50 from Pantheon Books, a division of Random House) later told *Steamshovel*

Press that he and Bevel were instrumental in getting King to publicly oppose the Vietnam War. (The full interview with Dellinger, including his observations on Abbie Hoffman's death as a possible assassination, will appear in the next *Steamshovel*.)

In St. Louis a week after the symposium, Bevel's representatives distributed flyers protesting the Anti-Defamation League sponsorship of a King tribute performed by the St. Louis Symphony. The flyers including newsclips reporting upon a developing scandal over the ADL's alleged illegal collection of information on groups from the Aryan Nations to the NAACP, for sale to Mossad and South African intelligence. Carl Oglesby, who witnessed first-hand the deterioration and factionalizing of the SDS caused in large measure by COINTELPRO-style infiltration, complained openly not only about Bevel's remarks but also about the large LaRouche presence at a separate dinner sponsored by the symposium organizers. The LaRouche group did not co-sponsor either the symposium or the dinner. It simply purchased a large number of dinners.

Oglesby was nevertheless conscripted to chair a new group, as yet not named, organized to lobby for the appointment of a special prosecutor in the JFK case. The group's officers include: Committee for an Open Archives co-founder John Judge; the president of the Assassination Archives and Research Center in Washington, Jim Lesar; Mark Zaid, who was also attempting to organize The Association of Professional and Analytical Researchers (POB 6058) at the Symposium; and *The Man Who Knew Too Much* author Dick Russell, an ex-officio member appointed by the chair. This group is open to name, organizing and fund-raising ideas by contacting Carl Oglesby at 294 Harvard Street #3, Cambridge, Massachusetts 02139 or by calling 617-876-6558.

—**Kenn Thomas**

Secret Societies and Psychological Warfare by Michael A. Hoffman II ($8 from Wiswell Ruffin House, POB 236, Dresden, NY 14441) is the kind of book for which conspiracy buffs spend years scouring tiny little print in the backs of obscure magazines. Hoffman is certainly one of today's most unique and refreshing voices, his theories original and startling. The implications of this little tome are worldwide if even partially correct, and at the very least it will open one's mind to a new way of looking at the fast-paced technological society which we all share.

Secret Societies and Psychological Warfare is an expanded version of Hoffman's 1989 *Secrets of Masonic Mind Control,* itself a book-length rewrite of "Alchemical Conspiracy and Death in the West: An Introduction to James Shelby Downard's *King-Kill/33,*" which appeared in the first edition of Adam Parfrey's *Apocalypse Culture* (New York: Amok Press, 1987). Hoffman's article was unwisely cut from the second edition (Los Angeles: Feral House, 1990), but Downard's equally intriguing article was expanded and rewritten as "From Adam to Atom by Way of the Jornada del Muerto." It deserves looking up.

Hoffman's basic premise is by no means unfamiliar to conspiracy theorists and armchair researchers familiar with the field. That a global cabal of Masonic allies dating back to Europe's Middle Ages has become almost commonplace to the point of redundancy is soon plain to any who investigate the dark world that is conspiracy theory. It will surprise very few who encounter Hoffman's book. What is new is how Hoffman goes about outlining this cabal's methods and goals, and what highly visible events he interprets to document same. In this Hoffman has scored a first, for of all the accusers the Masons have had, none have ever understood their symbolism so completely.

I claim to make no judgement here on either Hoffman or the Masons; I only wish to present his impressive speculating in the most open light, and let the reader decide for his or her own self. I, for one, find it hard to comprehend humans being smart enough and harmonious enough to pull off such an international conspiracy for literally centuries without internal squabbling blowing their cover. More palatable to me is the idea of several competing factions, now joining forces, now double-crossing each other, but Hoffman's testimony speaks for itself.

The goal of the Conspiracy is this: the Perfection of Creation that is so much a part of Masonic doctrine. Hoffman implies in several places that this is tantamount to blasphemy, as God's creation must by definition be perfect, but ever since the Fall most Western religions have agreed on our imperfect state. Hoffman's first point comes here, where many have longed for the return of the Golden Age. He says the true Golden Age is not to be found in New Age paganism or some nostalgic return to Stonehenge days. Instead, that was the beginning of enslavement at the hands of those who would rule. Humanity's true Golden Age was spent as hunter-gatherers; the scythe of Old Man Time is the symbol of whom the Greeks called Chronos, the Roma Saturn. It is also the Soviet sickle (he should have pointed out the sickle-like "G" inside the Mason's logo of compass and square).

One thing Hoffman missed was the significance of the Pythagorean "Y", which represents a yoke between heaven and earth (hence "yoga"). The 33 degrees of the Scottish Rite are represented as going up the path on the right, while the 10 degrees of the

York Rite follow the *left hand path*. Such is Hoffman's work, that one is inspired endlessly to ever more intricate degrees of interconnectedness. His book could be expanded indefinitely.

The Catholic Church - and all organized religion - in actuality serves this false god, the evil gnostic *demiurge* who created the Earth and enslaves us all therein. Hoffman equates this deity with Saturn, but chooses to name him Lord of this World *(Rex Mundi)* rather than Creator, probably to justify the lack of need he sees for the Perfection of Creation. Recall that Saturn is the deity who rules over time, personified in the Mithraic Mysteries as a lion-headed man wrapped in the coils of a great serpent. Hoffman also sees a connection with the dogstar, Sirius, which plays such an important roles in occult - especially Masonic - doctrine. Once men stopped honoring their Mother (Earth) and turned with pride towards the heavens, his Fall occurred.

All this, of course, is mere background to the real problem. Hoffman states - without giving his source - that Elizabethan astrologer John Dee was the founder of Freemasonry. What is more important, however, is this: that during the Middle Ages occultism flourished in all royal courts, and by this the occult practitioners were able to influence history to their own inscrutable ends.

Ritual killings were one such method, performed in public to influence the public mind. Hoffman cites the Jack the Ripper killings; throats slit from left to right, entrails removed and placed on the left shoulder, etc. - all with Masonic significance. He then jumps to the modern Son of Sam killings, John Lennon's assassination, and more to show the same trend is still with us. By terrorizing the public with "lone-nut" setups, they have trained us to fear each other, Hoffman says, and thus set the stage for a future police state that has already begun. We are so far along this road that they have begun the Making Manifest Of All That is Hidden, an old Masonic doctrine that Hoffman gives a horrible new twist. In actually showing the public what is going on, they have gained our tacit acceptance. Our consent only makes them stronger, as they now have our implied permission to continue the tyrannical rule. Hoffman readily admits his part in this Making Manifest, but he has no choice but to reveal the *gnosis* in his possession.

Here's where it really gets interesting. Hoffman mentions three of the goals of the old Alchemists: 1. The Creation and Destruction of Primordial Matter; 2. The Sacrificial Killing of the Divine King, and 3. The Bringing of *Prima Materia* to *Prima Terra*. How he says these have been accomplished before our very eyes fascinates me to no end. Realize these are the three steps which must be accomplished prior to the total disintegration of base matter, and the subsequent Perfection of Creation which may then be completed. One must first destroy in order to build.

The Creation and Destruction of Primordial Matter took place at the Trinity Site in White Sands, New Mexico when the first atomic bomb was exploded in the 1940s. Hoffman engages in an intricate dissection of the symbolism, including the names of the important locations involved in the development and testing of the bomb, the location of Trinity Site on the 33rd degree of latitude, and more (a numerological feat worthy of a qabalist). Hoffman tellingly notes the 33 degrees of Masonry in the Scottish Rite, and compares then to the 33 bones in the human spinal cord, along which the kundalini force may be activated. He should also have related the 33 degrees to the 33 years of Jesus' life. (The 10 degrees in the York Rite correspond to the 10 *sephiroth* - whence our "sphere" - of the qabalists' Tree of Life.) Hoffman suggests the radiation from the first blast was used to animate homunculus; we'll return to this later. The Trinity, of course, is the form of God which most Christians are taught to believe.

The second alchemical act was the Sacrificial Killing of the Divine King in the form of John F. Kennedy. He was also killed at a "Trinity" site - Dealey Plaza in Dallas. this is where the Trinity River and the Triple Underpass run, also at 33 degrees north latitude. When Kennedy was sacrificed, Hoffman aptly tells us, something more died as well. The American public lost its idealism that day; its innocence was forever taken away.

The final step in the alchemical process was the bringing of *Prima Materia* to *Prima Terra* in the form of moon rocks brought back to Earth by (Masonic) astronauts. Hoffman says many have "disappeared" from NASA storage rooms since, and are being used in occult rituals. To what end he does not say, but this reviewer is aware of at least one occult leader whose authority in part rests on possession of a sacred tektite. Some interesting speculation follows here, as Hoffman describes Sharon Tate's murder as a Masonic ritual designed to appease the Moon Goddess after violating her body. He sees the jettison of the used lunar module into the sun as the alchemical Marriage of the Sun and Moon carried out on the grandest scale.

Now that the Masonic cabal has accomplished its three prime objectives, what does Hoffman see ahead? The ultimate pride of man, the highest aspiration of the alchemists, was the creation of life. He sees genetic engineering as working feverishly toward this end, citing artificially created "hupigs" (animals grown from pig embryos injected with human DNA, ostensibly for easily transplantable organs) as a shocking example. When man can indeed create life, he will no longer need God because he will have become a god, and Nature will be "Perfected". Some interesting comparisons to the Golem of Jewish lore are here made. It's a frightening scenario, to be sure. Once completed, the ashes of the last red heifer sacrificed before the destruction of the Temple in Jerusalem by Roman hands in AD 70 will be located by using the map engraved on the Copper Scroll (part of the Dead Sea Scrolls). Ashes will be used to anoint another line of priests, the Dome of the Rock will be reclaimed from the Muslims, and Solomon's Temple will be rebuilt.

I have, of course, only been able to give the briefest summary. *Secret Societies and Psychological Warfare* must be seen to be appreciated. Hoffman has certainly done his homework in this regard, citing many obscure sources of all kinds. Many of these I am quite familiar with, yet never have I thought to connect them in just this manner: Charles Manson, John F. Kennedy, Roman Polanski, Sharon Tate, Aleister Crowley, Kenneth Grant, Jack Parsons, Robert Anton Wilson, Philip K. Dick, Robert K.G. Temple, James G. Frazer, et al. That's where my appreciation of the man comes in, in his unique method of correlating previously known facts in a whole new light. I have long thought that most human endeavors draw from the same archetypal pool - or at least our perception of them does - and whether you accept any or all of Hoffman's theorizing or just appreciate his interpretation of modern history for the sheer mental stimulation, I feel certain the reader will have a thought-provoking experience in store.

—Paul Rydeen

Recommended Zine Reading
by Kenn Thomas

Conspiracy Update, 5715 S. Harper Avenue, Chicago, IL 60637. 314-324-2409. A four-page newsletter with a lot of good information on plots, counter-plots and political machinations. Editor Jon Arnold also does much to expose the deficiencies of the mainstream media, "be it left, right or middle of the road".

Crash Collusion, POB 492333, Austin, TX 78765. New ufological/psychedelic zine that urges, "Never take a drug you don't fully understand." A recent issue included articles on the Sonoran desert toad and 3 B-carboline containing plants, combined with new perspectives on the UFO and a long list of alternative publications and reviews. Wesley Nations, Crash Collusion editor/publisher, also encourages submissions.

Funny Pages, POB 317025, Dayton, OH 45437. Humor, sick, dopey, and funny, Funny Pages has become the source for the slimiest jokes that heretofore sprung spontaneously from demented minds. For instance: Why did Sinead O'Connor's parents smack her on the head so much? They thought they were spanking her. A recent issue included a section entitled, "Blonde Jokes, We Got Your Blonde Jokes Hangin'". Not terribly committed to non-sexist, non-ethnic expressions of the amusing.

Incite Information, POB 326, Arlington, VA 22210. Political discussions of great interest to Steamshovel readers. Updates can be found here on the debate between Chip Berlet, who has attacked "conspiracy" researchers for their associations, and David Brandt, who has come to their defense (The latest salvo, in fact, has the Berlet camp calling Brandt a LaRouchie.) Good material also on marijuana legalization, perceptions versus reality vis-a-vis AIDS, and an ongoing debate on the Holocaust.

Journal of Borderland Sciences, POB 429, Garberville, CA 95542. 707-986-7211. Founded in 1945 to examine "realms normally beyond the range of basic human perception", including Reich's orgone and other aetheric energies.

Lobster, 214 Westbourne Avenue, Hull HU5 3JB, UK. David Brandt's "An Incorrect Political Memoir" highlights the current issue, which also contains some interesting information about the UFO collections of renown Kennedy researchers.

Paranoia, POB 3570, Cranston, RI 02910. Newcomers with new energy to examine political assassinations, the Bilderberger connections of Bill Clinton and the information barrage of Kennedy assassination Research. The editor calls himself Al Hidell but he's not fooling anyone.

The Probe, Argus Research Foundation, POB 1082, St. Charles, MO 63302. Another periodical born out of frustration that the media, according to editor Alex Horvat, "has abdicated its responsibility to the public to inform with integrity". Includes new information on the October Surprise, MIAs & POWs and "JFK Cover-Up Continues To Flounder" by Keith Preston. The Probe is part of a network entitled the Argus Foundation, which attempts to "coordinate a catalog of esoteric knowledge."

6

Steamshovel Press #9, Fall 1993

J. Edgar Hoover, the Fall of the Soviet Union, the Drug War, and Teaching Poetry
An Interview with Allen Ginsberg

Q: What do think is the lesson to be learned by the relatively sudden disappearance of the Cold War?

A: First of all, everything changes fast in modern, accelerated, hyper-technological life. Capitalism certainly is not the answer to social reconstruction in either the east or west because it's wrecked the planet, actually. So that doesn't help. The capitalist solution is not a solution either. It hasn't done the eastern Europeans any good.

Although Tito and others were blamed for being tyrannical, maybe they may have killed less people than are being killed in the internecine and chauvinistic and nationalistic wars within their empires now. That doesn't excuse their dictatorships, but it makes the pressure more understandable. That the senseless, sick ideas that the *Readers' Digest* or anybody else had about Communists didn't make sense. That the CIA was incompetent. That the FBI was incompetent and corrupt and tied up with the Mafia and so was incapable of dealing with real subversion. That everybody was wrong, east and west, on both sides of the Iron Curtain and that the accelerated demise of the Russian empire bankrupted the United States too, so it didn't do us any good. And that the Russians are really weird, all the way around.

The other element of it is that the American left has been in left field all along and has not been very clear about what socialism is actually. They're still not very clear, the left, I think, is still probably confused about Cuba. What they should do is find some place for Castro to go, so that he'd be safe and they could make a change. I think the real problem is that we've been so bent that Castro can't leave because he has nowhere to go and will get killed. I haven't seen anybody discussing that aspect, that the way to resolve the problems, as we did with the Shah and as we did for the butcher in Haiti. Why not give him some place to refuge? That maybe would resolve the problem of

authoritarianism in Cuba. Obviously, he can't leave. It's not safe for him to leave. He's got to maintain his power. I don't know why nobody discusses that. It's like total amnesia on a subject that's totally obvious. Maybe because all those Cuban refugee politicians in Miami want to kill him. That's no way to resolve the problem. They don't deserve that much anyway because they ran Cuba down into the ground with narcotics before Castro came in.

Q: Do you think there are appropriate causes for political activism today?

A: Of course there are! The ecological situation. I think the left should learn to meditate, as I have been saying for about twenty years. Expansion of consciousness and the use of psychedelics as sort of little trips above and beyond meditation, just to look at the map. How to dig the planet out of the hole that we're in. Deforestation and desertification and the loss of relation to the ground and the loss of the family farm and all that. Those are major things to do. There's the problem of our having backed up the military death squads and police states in a number of countries. Finally we've got a president who wants to get rid of the dictatorship in Haiti, and in today's *Times* he says, "Well, we can always send in the military. We've always got that option". So we've allowed the wreckage of Haiti and the death squads of Salvador and similar death squads in Guatemala and Honduras. There's the War on Drugs that needs to be straightened out by legalizing grass and providing maintenance for junkies who deal with the Reagan drugs like cocaine. In America we put more people in prison than any other country and most of them are black and sixty percent are related to junk. I would classify those as political prisoners because they're in jail because of a wrong-headed political policy on drugs which the experts know is wrong-headed. It's not solving the problem. So the question of taking the twelve billion dollars a year that we give to the narcotics bureaus who are pedaling drugs, and put it toward rehabilitation. Many Betty Ford clinics all over the place. How to get off fossil fuel addiction, speaking of drugs. How to get to clean energy. Those are the things that the left should be involved with.

Q: Why do you think there seems to be around the country a new interest in poetry?

A: Because after so much public manipulation of propaganda and hype from the White House and Madison Avenue, the candid representation of private mind is more and more valuable as a touchstone of what's of value. Most public language has been manipulated if not predatory, which is the reason for that whole philosophy of deconstruction in language poetry. Burroughs stared it in a way but it was started before Burroughs even. Basic semantic examination of reference, of all these abstractions that the government uses. So you have the minute, particular details of real life coming from poets, it's a lot more valuable, a lot more information than what you can find in the *Times*. People are enthusiastic about having some real communication, when, particularly under the Reagan and Bush years, communication is totally blockaded deliberately, causing a kind of national schizophrenia. Language was used for manipulation rather than actual communication with people. It had this kind of predatory aspect to it.

Q: What is the main thing you hope to convey to your students?

A: Teaching poetry. Right now I'm in Brooklyn College teaching a course in beginner's Blake and the history of poetry. Historical Poetics. A lot of the MFA graduate students have never read Shelley's "Ode To The West Winds" or have never read Sappho or don't know anything about the quantitative verse that Pound spoke of or standard things that I took for granted like "Ode To Intellectual Beauty" by Shelley or Keats' *Odes* or William Carlos Williams.

At Naropa Institute, at the Jack Kerouac School of Disembodied Poetics, we emphasize that historical background plus the modernist background of post-Olson, Kerouac, spontaneous writing, relating that to meditative awareness of the mind, meditative scoping of the mind itself.

Poetry is considered in the Tibetan and Japanese tradition as a form of dharma communication. It's also a form of mental discipline or ordering your thoughts and being aware of the nature of your mind and the sequence of the thought forms as they pass through your head, the texture of your consciousness, the difference between language and the thing that language represents. So some teachers, especially my old teacher Chogyam Trungpa, a Tibetan Lama, thought that poetry was a form of practice, meditative practice, and related to it as he related to archery, flower arranging, tea ceremony, sitting practice, visualization and other techniques. I guess you can boil it down to you have to become familiar with your own mind and non-attached to your own thoughts. Looking at yourself and your thoughts objectively, from the outside and not contained within your own projections, which is a point in meditation, too. You don't get entangled in your own projections.

Q: What do you think of the supposed resurgence in LSD use among high school students?

A: You're talking about also a resurgence of interest also in the 60s and the Beat generation literature. They seem part of the same thing, feeding off each other. But I think there isn't so much of a resurgence as that people are acknowledging what's been going on all along. As far as I know, going around colleges and seeing a lot of high school kids over the last twenty years, there's never been a lack of granny wisdom in the use of drugs. People were just less overt about it. There's always been acid around. Many more people taking it than are publicly acknowledged.

Q: Whenever you hear a new report like that, I always get suspicious that there's going to be some kind of crackdown coming.

A: Yeah. But also there will probably be more open talk about it now that the neo-conservative government has fallen and that J. Edgar Hoover has been demystified. His secrets are out. So the authoritarian aspect of the American police state is a little bit more out in the open. The drug policy is obviously a great failure. The War of Drugs was hypocrisy and everybody knows that Bush and Noriega were dealing drugs together anyway. So I think it's just a disillusionment and deconstruction, disillusionment in the authority of the government on drugs, deconstruction of that authority and re-evaluation of what could be said in public and what couldn't be.

Q: So you think the new Clinton-Gore administration is going to take charge and liberalize drug laws?

A: I don't think so. No. Just like with the gay thing, there are more basic economic issues they have to deal with. One thing they might take charge of, however, is shifting the twelve billion dollar drug bureaucracy fund more in the direction of rehab and try to do something to decriminalize grass or at least get rid of the mandatory sentencing that we have in New York, I don't know if that's federal, but to decriminalize grass to the extent of bringing it back as a misdemeanor rather than a felony. And promoting more medical attention to drug problems, removing heroin from the police and giving it to doctors to figure it out. That would leave the field more clear to examine the Reagan-Bush drugs, how to deal with them, the cocaine and crack. Also, I think that everybody realizes that the government has been dealing in drugs now from the Vietnam War heroin trade to the CIA through the Contras dealing Bush and Noriega's manipulations of the drug trade to fund off-the-shelf military operations. Then there's the collapse of the whole myth of J. Edgar Hoover in terms of police authority. So I think kids might be more fresh, talk more fresh about it, with a fresh mind.

Then there's also the consideration that now people are slowly beginning to dig is that if twenty to forty thousand people a year die of illicit drugs in America, that's a small amount compared to the one hundred thousand people who die of alcohol and the four hundred thousand people—ten times as much, twenty times as much—that die of cigarettes. The real killer drug is the coffin nails, the licit drug, the agriculture of which is subsidized by the government. Jesse Helms, who sets himself up as the moral arbiter, is the one legislator who is the main lobbyist for that drug monopoly. He's now trying to redo the Opium Wars in retro by trying to force bad trade deals with Southeast Asia unless they accept our Marlboro ads and products. American cigarettes. I don't know if people realize that. He's trying to force Southeast Asian countries who are trying to prevent addiction to American tobacco, to open up. So that's a kind of interesting schizophrenic role for him, being like the purveyor of killer drugs...

Q:...the dealer.

A: The dealer and at the same time trying to set himself up as an ethical, moral operator.

Q: And specifically in Southeast Asia where a lot of the heroin traffic happens.

A: It's like the old Opium Wars where the United States and France and England starting bashing China physically with guns to let us sell them opium in exchange for silk or whatever they had.

Q: There's an effort now to get J. Edgar Hoover's name removed from the J. Edgar Hoover building.

A: I'm sure it will be soon.

Q: Do you think it's going to happen?

A: Of course, as people realize the consequences. It turns out that he was in cahoots with organized crime. After a while people will begin to realize the enormous consequences of that. It meant that organized crime got a foothold in America that it wouldn't have had otherwise. Maybe that has a lot to do with the drug plague, since organized crime dealt drugs. It has a lot to do with the destruction of the left in America since the labor unions were purged by J. Edgar Hoover from the 20s to the 40s. And who came into the vacuum but organized crime?

That's why that since everybody's been saying "how come England has a labor party, France has a socialist party, Italy has a communist party, every western nation has, Germany even, how come we don't?" That's one of the reasons. We have the mob instead, displacing it, and we have the CIA and the FBI dealing with the mob. The very police that were supposed to be controlling the mob, Hoover's FBI, were controlled by the mob by blackmail. It's enormous! They could not keep the J. Edgar Hoover building once people begin thinking this through. All you need really is the president to say this happened, or somebody important to say it, to talk about it.

Although I haven't seen anybody discussing the consequences of J. Edgar Hoover being a closeted queen aside from the hee-haw, the joke that he was a transvestite at times. He was the acme and icon of the right-wing, sour puss sector of the population and all of a sudden it turns out that he was a complete hypocrite. But I haven't seen anybody discuss the social consequences. And I think that's really important. I haven't seen anybody discuss it even. What was the effect on American politics of his displacement of an attack on organized crime to public enemy number one, the Communists and left-wing labor unions and blacks and the sabotage of minority leadership? It's an enormous trauma to the country.

People on hand to ask questions of Mr. Ginsberg included Susan Waugh, Andrea Murray, Michael Castro and Kenn Thomas.

King Co-Opted; Abbie Assassinated
An Interview with Dave Dellinger
by Kenn Thomas

Q: We were talking about James Bevel and you were saying that you and the Reverend Bevel were the ones who actually first convinced Martin Luther King to oppose the war?

A: We on the National Mobilization Committee, which at the time was organizing the largest anti-war demonstrations, decided that Martin, who a number of us knew and had worked with, that time was overdue for him to come out and really be against the war. But he was under tremendous pressure and he kept flirting with the idea during the time we were working with him. And I would have specific reports, sometimes from one of the other people on the staff because I was president, where somebody would come up to him and say, "Martin, if you march," except they called him Dr. King, that kind of person, "Dr. King, if you march in that demonstration next week or two weeks from now," whatever it would be at the time, "I have a check in my pocket here, or in my hand, for $20,000 that I was going to give you but I'll have to tear up or I can't give it to you." So he was under pressure that way.

Some of it came from very good intentions, namely that if he opposed his country when it was at war and added what seemed to some people, or would seem to some people, an unpatriotic element to the struggle for civil rights, that it would hurt the black people. It would hurt the cause of civil rights. But at the same time, in the mobilization that was putting on these demonstrations, we had people who were complaining that we had too many black speakers speaking about their problems and denial of justice. And we always used to have a Puerto Rican, not always the same one, but some Puerto Rican who would talk about the need for independence and cultural autonomy for his country instead of using its land as a bombing range and so forth.

And at the same time, King once wrote that unless we took off the name of Arnold Johnson, who was a known Communist, from our letterhead or from our list of signers and sponsors, that he would not take part. We had a terrible struggle over that before some of us could get the agreement of the rest of the board that we had to stand on principle. In that case it was non-exclusion.

Anyway, right around that time, Otto Nathan, who was a beloved friend of Albert Einstein, and was executor of his estate, was treasurer of our organiza-

tion and he resigned because we wouldn't agree to limit the number of speakers and speakers on issues other than just the war in Vietnam.

Q: Are you saying that King delayed his opposition to the war based on money considerations?

A: That was one of the pressures put on him. But also he was attacked. When he finally announced publicly, as he had told us earlier, when he finally announced that he was going to take part, he was attacked by the NAACP, by Ralph Bunche at the UN. Ralph Bunche was the most measured of them. He was the one who said that Dr. King must choose between anti-war and civil rights, he can't do both. And I'd have to say that it would be unfair to say that King wavered because of financial conditions, but that was one of the pressures that was put on him. I certainly would say—without hesitation—say that a number of his staff, whom I knew and who were not gradually becoming radicalized as King was, a number of them were severely influenced by the financial conditions and tried to get him based on them to refuse.

One of the things that I have done in this book, *From Yale To Jail,* I actually have three chapters on King in which I try to show King to be a person who was thrust into prominence before he was ready for it. During this period, when he was debating internally and also debating with his staff and a lot of his other backers about whether to take a strong stand against the war or not, he was changing his views, or developing his views, until he became so dangerous that he had to be killed. I've gathered together a few of the statements that he made during the last year and a half of his life, during that period, and here's one from the book (reads): "For years I labored with the idea of reforming the existing institutions, a little change here, a little change there. Now I feel quite differently. I think you've got to have a reconstruction of the entire society, a revolution of values."

We can't have a system where some people live in superfluous, inordinate wealth while others live in abject, deadening poverty. From now on our movement must take on basic class issues between the privileged and the under-privileged.

There are more, but I think that those two indicate the development that was happening. Actually, I believe that both of those were said shortly after he made the step of marching with us. A short while earlier, the same month, giving a talk at Riverside

Church in New York, in which he came out with a much stronger position not only on the war but on the American society.

When Martin Luther King did decide to take a militant stand against the war, and you asked whether he was deterred previously for financial reasons, we got word...the head of the New York police intelligence division came to me a few days before King was to appear on the platform and told me that the mob had a contract on King's life. And somebody went to his office, I think to Andy Young in Atlanta, from their department, and told him the same thing. And it did come out some bit later by the Assassination Committee in Congress that there was this actual contract, but it was by the mob. But that doesn't mean that the same people who used the mob to try to assassinate Castro, that some of them didn't also use it against King.

Q: When Abbie Hoffman died, in the press reports you were among the people who were suggesting it may have been something other than a suicide. Do you still believe that and why?

A: I never took a stand saying that he had definitely been assassinated. But I could spend a whole hour talking with you about that, how the coroner lied to Abbie's woman friend and to his oldest son Andrew. Andrew Hoffman came to every one of my events for three days in Boston on this book tour. He is absolutely convinced that his father was assassinated. He tells me that when he saw his father's body, lying there dead, that he had bruises on his face and that he had his fists clenched as if he had been resisting somebody. But meanwhile the coroner told him and the other family members present that Abbie had died of a heart attack, There was no sign of drugs or alcohol or violence. And Andrew wanted the body not cremated immediately, but it was cremated immediately. And after the body was disposed of, then the coroner switched his story and said that he'd been taking phenobarbital and alcohol.

And the other thing is that the newspaper stories and others who either were mislead or didn't want the thing dragged out, it was so painful for them anyway, let out that Abbie was discouraged because the youth weren't coming along and following his way of life and his thing and so forth. Abbie used to call me up every week or two, sometimes twice a week and sometimes it would be three or four weeks between them, but during that whole last year of his life, it was a pattern and it increased during that period. And he was very optimistic. And I have a letter from him, which came about five weeks before his assassination or death from other things, whichever it was, in which he says, "Everywhere I go I meet more people for

social change than at any other time in my life." Then, of course, in our phone conversations we would say that they're not exactly sure how to go about it or its all divided into so many issues now.

I could go on forever, but one final thing on that: I was in a program down in Champaign-Urbana, Illinois, where they bring in people off the beaten path, who haven't fallen into the...I don't know, "normal" thing, ruts of society or whatever...I never can remember the exact words...and they bring somebody in for two or three weeks to hold seminars, meet informally with the students, go to classes, work with them on various activities. When I was there I worked with the *Take Back the Night* march for women that I spoke at and participated in and so forth. And when they asked me on my second visit there who I would suggest to come in September, I suggested Abbie. I gave them the phone number, they called him up and he agreed to come. Now he would have come in September. He died, by whatever method, in April. And the second phone conversation with him, you know, going into details, he says, in his inimitable way, "Ya sure you want me? Because if I come there ain't gonna be no more CIA on campus!" Don't forget that he and Amy Carter had already launched a sit-in along with local students, en masse, and won a court battle on this. So there were plenty of reasons for somebody to get rid of him, and I've just touched on it. And there's a lot of evidence that *that* is what happened. But I know how easy it is to think that everything is a conspiracy and not to examine all the evidence.

Let me just say in conclusion that I found that Andrew, his oldest son, at his request, he and I worked together, from what he told me and other things, I got a coroner in Pittsburgh who had played an important role in some criminal cases by proving that the coroner's report was inaccurate, to agree that if he got the material which was used for, supposedly used for, the coroner's verdict, he could tell whether it was Abbie's or not, which was the kind of thing he could do, and secondly he could tell whether it was true or not. But the coroner refused to release the material without a court battle. And some of those dearest to Abbie, including his lawyer, who had worked a little more in the direction that Jerry Rubin worked in for a while, had become a little more on the inside and so forth...

Q: Yuppified.

A. Yeah. They basically would not allow that to go to court. And Andrew was overruled. But Andrew and Abbie's first wife, Sheila, are convinced that he was killed.

Dave Dellinger is the author of six books, among them Vietnam Revisited, More Power Than We Know; *and* Revolutionary Non-Violence. *His latest,* From Yale to Jail: The Life Story of A Moral Dissenter, *is published by Pantheon Books, a division of Random House. Dellinger lives with his wife in Vermont and lectures frequently around the country, especially before college audiences.*

Virtually Reality
by Jim Keith

Larouche strikes me as just one more scapegoat—like Koresh, Randy Weaver, Jim Garrison, the list is endless—yet the establishment media smearing of him is so pervasive that even the ragtag ranks of conspiracy research don't seem to have picked up on the fact. Sure, you can stand up on your chair at some convention wearing a hat made out of beer cans and shout that Milton William Cooper has got it all wired, but even suggest that Lyndon Larouche might have something on the ball, and watch out!

The fact is, I don't know if Larouche or his underlings were embezzling little old ladies out of their social security checks like the government says (if they were, certainly that crime pales next to something like the S & L debacle), but I do find it curious that the prosecution fell upon a guy who wrote one of the most interesting conspiracy books ever penned, and who maintains that Henry Kissinger is a homosexual KGB mole—not our Henry! Larouche's book is *Dope, Inc.*, which is credited on the cover to the editors of *Executive Intelligence Review,* Larouche's now-defunct (I believe) investigative mag.

Dope, Inc. links the huge world trade in drugs to a powerful and pervasive good old boys network centered in English aristocracy and banking, going back to the time of the Chinese Opium War in which Britain forced China to accept its opium trade. Larouche's thesis, which pinpoints a gnostic-Freemasonic cult underlying Britain's upper crust, engaged in a centuries-long conquest of the world and responsible for, among other things, the Kennedy assassination, may seem absolutely hare-brained...but then, that's what The Conspiracy would want you to think if he was right, isn't it?

If Larouche's belief that the high cabal is connected to British society and its imperial ambitions is crazy, then I suggest you check out a trio of 'scholarly' references which back up our boy to the hilt: these are Quigley's *Tragedy and Hope* and *The Anglo-American Establishment* (which primarily focus on the Cecil Rhodes Round Table penetration of world politics) and Francis Yates' *The Occult Philosophy in the Elizabethan Age.* While Quigley is better known to most conspiracy buffs, the Yates will launch you—in academic, heavily footnoted fashion—into the midst of the High Weirdness from which many of the conspiratorial plans of the current age were spawned. Yates, funded (significantly) by the Warburg Institute, gives a fairly detailed rendering of the Cabbalistic Isis cult which was founded by mage John Dee and centered around Queen Elizabeth I, and from which sprang Rosicrucianism, Freemasonry, and...British intelligence! This is pretty much exactly what Larouche has always maintained, only here we find the idea espoused by a leading scholar of the Elizabethan age.

Similarly, the idea that British interests may have been behind the Kennedy hit is not all that radical if you have checked out *Nomenclature of an Assassination Cabal,* by "Torbitt". *Nomenclature,* as far as I (and a number of other researchers, including Mae Brussell) am concerned, is the finest thing ever done on the Kennedy assassination, and places Canadian lawyer, Rhodes Round Table lawyer, and British Special Operations Executive agent Louis Bloomfield at the top of the heap in the assassination hierarchy. Now, what was it that Larouche was saying that was so nuts?

If Lyndon Larouche is crazy, it may have something to do with the fact that the world is crazy, a lot crazier than many conspiracy researchers seem to recognize.

Jim Keith is the editor of Secret and Suppressed: Banned Ideas and Hidden History, *available for $12.95 plus $2 postage from Feral House, POB 3466, Portland, Oregon 97208.*

"Europe Calling! Pound Speaking!"
by P.S. Waddell

Who remembers Ezra Pound? Once the *enfant terrible* of American poets and driving force behind the European expatriate intelligentsia movement back in the Teens, Twenties and Thirties when he helped discover himself, and Episcopal transcendentalist T.S. Eliot among others, restoring vigor and vitality to what was at that time the dying life/artform of poetry at a juncture when it drastically needed Muse to mouth resuscitation.

I first heard about our crazy Uncle Ezra in the book *Allen Verbatim* by another distinguished loon of American letters, Allen Ginsberg, that acid-gobbling/vision seeking hippie beatnik, hare Krishna chanting and oft times over-indulgent cosmic genius bard with commie and homosexual leanings. Back in the late great Sixties—when drugs were good and communicable diseases could be treated by a simple trip to your local pharmacy—Ginsberg paid a visit to our dear Uncle Ez somewhere in Italy methinks to sit at the feet of the Great Master and bless him for his good works and vitriolic rantings. There like a Tibetan holy guy Ezra sat in near total silence as Ginsberg fawned all over him, blathering beatitudes. Old Ez simply nodded his white-haired head from time to time while rubbing his knuckles raw with his aged and wrinkled hands. When pressed for specific answers concerning his poetry Ezra replied it was all pointless rubbish and a failed waste of time.

Ezra's—by all accounts—was a troubled life, though not without its interesting moments, to say the least. By the Thirties he was a well-renowned master of his art, but inevitably his preoccupations began to lead his poetic meanderings into uncharted waters in the brain. 'Social Credit' became his new passion around that time, an economic philosophy that turned into an obsession with him, becoming one of the driving forces in his life, eventually leading Ezra down the path of fascism. A path that ended tragically in an insane asylum for the psychologically treasonous at St. Elizabeth's Mental Hospital, in the District of Columbia, where he was finally released after twelve years of forced imprisonment.

Leading up to and throughout World War II, Dr. Pound felt passionately that the leaders of his native homeland, the ol' US of A, had betrayed their peoples with a monetary system that made the rich richer and the poor lesser, and in the process had masticated the Constitution into castrated confetti. The system, he felt, had been manipulated by rich Jewish bankers and greed mongering arms dealers whom Ezra referred to as the 'usurers'.

"I ask you WHY WAS CHRIST CRUCIFIED? He was crucified for trying to bust a racket," spoke Ezra to *The American Hour* microphone of which he babbled unto in his folksy and sardonic tongue in cheek manner, in the comic role of a cracker barrel philosopher with an exaggerated Yankee accent. It was the summer of '42 and Ezra was now under the delusion that a document called *The Protocols of the Elders of Zion* was the final truth and testament revealing the fact of a Jewish Conspiracy controlling mankind. (For a complete text of *The Protocols* see William 'Bill' Cooper's *Behold A Pale Horse,* Chapter 15.)

"For God's sake read the Protocols," he instructed his listeners, whomever they might've been. Military Intelligence for sure was one of the entities in on ol' Ezra, but for the most part it's very doubtful whether Ezra ever attracted much of an audience, and if he had anyway, very few would have been able to decipher his loony discourses that mixed a hodgepodge of literary criticism with economic theories and anti-Semitic conspiracies, praising Il Duce's "fascist experiment" as all the while he vehemently chastised FDR for selling America down the river. He liked to refer to Roosevelt's New Deal as "The New Steal".

Inevitably all these radio airwave rantings led Ezra near the War's end to be indicted by the U.S. for treason on propaganda charges, though Ezra denied up to the very end of his life that he was ever instructed on what to say by Axis Propagandists in these fireside rants of his. He insisted time and again that his programs were conceived and performed entirely of his own volition, which anybody with a modicum of common sense soon realized if they were fortunate enough to hear these bombastic broadcasts, so weird and wild his ravings. These "programs"— aimed at America via fascist Italian radio propaganda towers—were unlike anything else on the Italian Broadcasting System, or anything else for that matter in the annals of radio broadcasting history. He would begin these broadcasts by boldly shouting:

'Europe calling! Pound speaking!
Ezra Pound speaking!
'Old Ezra speaking! Pound speaking!
'Ezra Pound speakin' from Europe for the
American heritage!
'Dearly beeloved brevrrem, this is ole Ezra speaking.'

In the late Thirties, early Forties, Ezra had volunteered his services to the Italian Radio Broadcasting Service, and during those bleak years when he'd virtually alienated himself from the entire literary community, this was how he put bread on the table, by telling his airwave listeners the 'way it was'. But as the War drew to a close, and treason charges and a warrant for his arrest had been issued, Ezra turned himself in to the Allied forces, hoping to set the record straight on how he'd just been speaking his mind, trying to help his home country come to its senses so that it would throw the rascals out of power and restore the Constitution to its previous undiluted condition.

Ezra's major work throughout his life-span were *The Cantos,* a continuing body of work that traced his poetic growth and recorded his passions and beliefs for future posterity to ponder. In *The Cantos* he first brought to the attention of suffering humanity his outlooks on the world monetary system and the evils of 'usury', the detested practice of making money off of money, which Dr. Pound believed to be the root of all earthly evil. During the administration of Alexander Hamilton is when this detested practice first reared its ugly head in America. Hamilton turned the control of money from government to the manipulative hands of bankers. Banks at this time were able to lend out twenty times as much money as they actually held in gold reserves, thereby collecting credit on loans that were imaginary to begin with; a hallucinatory process manipulated by these economic hypnotists, the Usurers.

He first wrote of usura in the following section of *The Cantos:*

'With usura hath no man a house of good stone
each block cut smooth and well fitting
that design might cover their face,
with usura
hath no man a painted paradise on his church wall
harpes et luz
or where virgin receiveth message
and halo projects from incision,
with usura
seeth no man Gonzaga his heirs and concubines
no picture is made to endure nor to live with
but is made to sell and sell quickly
with usura, sin against nature,
is thy bread ever more of stale rags
is thy bread dry as paper,
with no mountain wheat, no strong flour
with usura the line grows thick
with usura is no clear demarcation
and no man can find the site for his dwelling.
Stonecutter is kept from his stone
weaver is kept from his loom

WITH USURA
wool comes not to market
sheep bringeth no gain with usura
Usura is a murrain, usura
blunteth the needle in the maid's hand
and stoppeth the spinner's cunning...
They have brought whores for Eleusis
Corpse are set to banquet
at the behest of usura.'

This poem speaks of the quality of life being cheapened by usura, as in the art of the painter where 'the line grows thick'. Where once the painted line was delicate, now it is painted quickly for the fast buck, without attention to aesthetic detail, thusly prostituting humanity for a fast fuck.

To quote once again Ginsberg from *Allen Verbatim* explaining Ezra's Usura theory: "This whole usura thing is a summary of his general economic theories and his attack on banks and the abuse of money, an attack which probably makes complete sense to you in other terms—like anybody building a university dormitory in order to make money out of it obviously is going to skimp," and "with usura the walls grow thin, with usura the ceilings grow lower'", as quoted his personal Prospero/Pound from another part of *The Cantos.* In another of *The Cantos,* around the time of his memorable Italian broadcasts, Ezra cuts to the chaff. This piece of inflammatory poesy was for years unpublished and only until recent years did his heirs see fit to release it to the general public:

'As soon as one begins to remember this shit war,/certain facts will rise to the surface again. In the beginning, God/the great aesthete, after creating heaven and earth,/after the fiery sunset, after having painted/the rocks with lichen like a Japanese print,/Shat the great usurer Satan-Geryon, prototype/of the masters of Churchill.'

A true master of language, yet at the same time a wee bit mentally deranged makes for one of the most interesting poetical talents in the annals of the planet. Pound was a man of deep convictions above all else, albeit he was crazy as a coot. In later years, when treason charges against him were dropped and he was released from St. Elisabeths, the wisdom of years made Pound regret certain things he had said and writ, and some of the extreme positions he had taken. Pound admitted to Ginsberg during their historic meeting in Rapallo that his "greatest stupidity was stupid suburban anti-Semitic prejudice".

But maybe Ol' Ezra wasn't as crazy as at first we surmised. Maybe just a wee bit confused but on the right track. In a short intro to *The Protocols* in Bill Cooper's aforementioned book, *Behold A Pale Horse,* Mr. Cooper shares his belief that in The Protocols where it mentions "The Jews" the document is, in reality, referring to the Illuminati. Was this another instance as in the annals of the Kennedy assassination when certain facts are served on a shining platter with an ounce of happy horseshit thrown in extra to obsfucate the big picture to throw the Searchers of Truth momentarily off track chasing tangent spectres and wasting precious time?

Maybe this is what happened to Ezra, who many agree was never really crazy at all but just another political prisoner, a dedicated artist who refused to toe the line and was punished for the folly of being too true to himself in his attempts to educate his fellow men.

Sources Cited:

Humphrey Carpenter, *A Serious Character: The Life of Ezra Pound*. Boston: Houghton Mifflin, 1988.

William Cooper. *Behold A Pale Horse*. Arizona: Light Technology Publishing, 1991.

Allen Ginsberg. *Allen Verbatim*. New York: McGraw Hill, 1974.

Eustace Mullins. *This Difficult Individual*. New York: Fleet Publishing Corp., 1961.

Saucer Section:
Secret Research on Antigravity and Space Flight Organized by the German Secret Societies During World War II
by Vladimir Terziski

In my research as a physicist I have gathered a vast collection of anthropological stories about antigravity flying devices from different cultures and times. Being fluent in Japanese, Russian, German and English on top of my native Bulgarian, and being able to read professional literature in several other languages has helped me tremendously in my research and my efforts to penetrate the veil of secrecy around this blacklisted advanced technology. As a rule, I do not discard any bizarre story when I hear it—I will simply post it in the big mental picture of such posted messages, until there is a second similar story, and so on.

In my public lectures on the West Coast I have traced with an extensive slide presentation of documentary evidence the general physical characteristics and theoretical arguments of antigravity and UFO propulsion through academic and tabloid sources; through modern UFO lore and ancient myths and legends, and again through some modern day revelations; through science fiction sources and contactee reports. The unexpected conclusion was that antigravity is extremely easy to produce with any advanced "alien" or Sci-Fi hardware: simple rotation decreases the weight of a spinning body, and if you spin 'the hell out of it', it will lift off and fly away. Antigravity as a physical variable is proportional to the rotational inertial momentum of the spinning body and to the angular velocity (in more colloquial terms, to the product of the mass and the rotational velocity of the spinning body).

Armed with this simple theory I was able to even answer the question of how to build a better flying saucer. From the slow spinning of "brute" heavy masses to the relativistic spinning of high frequency fine energy fields with very little mass around the stationary hull of the craft—this is the road towards the design of a solid state antigravity drive without moving parts.

The fact that antigravity is very easy to produce with the available hardware of our crude (by extraterrestrial standards) technological era is no surprise at all, keeping in mind the similarly easy to produce (hardware-wise) technologies from other blacklisted (for mass consumption) by the terrestrial secret societies fields of R&D, like free energy, alternative cures for AIDS and cancer, environmental cleaning technologies, etc., etc. Anyone who has studied extensively metaphysics and paranormology knows that the higher the mastery of the universal laws, the simpler the hardware to achieve the same technological goals becomes. The more advanced races in the universe achieve all our science fiction goals with the power of extremely small gadgets, and finally, with the power of their minds alone.

The blacklisting of an advanced space flight propulsion technology that is more than 100 years ahead of its time is not a very startling finding keeping in mind that this is the very mode of operation of the terrestrial secret power elite, the evilarchy that rules the planet from behind the scenes: how they usurp, hoard and lock behind triple vault doors the most advanced technologies that appear on the planet, until they make sure that all the patents are in their possession, and that the new technology will not undermine the already existing technologies, for which they also own the key patents and rights.

Close Encounters of the Foo Kind:
R&D In Antigravity and Flying Saucers in the Third Reich, Germany, 1925-1945

In my investigation on three continents, supported by numerous research associates from many countries, I have been able to retrace the genealogy of Nazi flying saucers with more than two hundred slides of original documentary photos, engineering drawing and sketches of more than 50 saucer models: from prototypes with gasoline piston and rotary engines and propellers, spinning the craft, through hybrid helicopter-rotor/antigravity lift and pure antigravity lift craft powered by outboard and inboard turbo-, pulse-, and ramjets, gyroscoping all, or the outermost part of the craft; to exoatmospheric saucers with rocket engines or with spinning magnetic fields, powered by U-boat oxygen-independent Walter gas turbines running on kerosene and hydrogen peroxide, that were designed for prolonged exoatmospheric interplanetary flights. My firm belief is that a rocket-spun 60-150 feet diameter craft was capable of going to the Moon on a truckload of kerosene and a truckload of liquid oxygen, due to the two magical keys to the saucer kingdom: the total negation of both gravitational and inertial masses, when the antigravity drive starts spinning.

Two months ago I was arrested and handcuffed by Pasadena and Caltech police for showing four panels with the first and very detailed and close-up photos in this country of low-flying German saucer-shaped craft over the testing grounds in Germany, and for demanding some *perestroika* and *glasnost* in the US space program. This happened after a lecture by Apollo-17 astronaut and ex-senator Harrison Schmidt in the central Beckman auditorium at the California Institute of Technology, the citadel of the party line in US science. The lecture was on the planned 21st century NASA flights to and colonization of Mars with the inefficient and gas-guzzling rocket technology of today.

First close-detailed photographs of Nazi Germany's free energy saucer dreadnoughts

After researching the German saucers for almost a year on faith alone without much of solid evidence (my faith only was strong because of my engineering intuition showing me the physical feasibility of these craft), suddenly several months ago my perseverance was rewarded when I received through private channels from Germany the underground video documentary by the secret German society, the "Thule Gesellschaft" about the most advanced free energy saucers, powered by Victor Schauberger's free energy water turbines (the so-called trout turbines) and Hans Kohler's tachyon magneto-gravitic drives, the "Thule tachyonators." Among them were shown in dozens of photographs of low level flights over the testing ground the ten meter diameter interceptor-fighters of the "Vril" series, 25 meter tank killers of the "Haunibu 1 & 2" types and the 74 meter "Haunibu-3" dreadnought for antishipping warfare. Drawings of 300 feet diameter "Haunibu-4" interplanetary craft and of a cigar-shaped mothership battleship 330 feet long dating from 1943 had also been uncovered by the authors of the German film.

German Space Flights to the Moon During WW2 without a Drop of Fuel

That Germans had in WW2 saucers with no moving parts, that could go to the Moon in one hour, is not even the biggest secret in this whole film. It is much more important that they managed to do that without using a single drop of traditional fuel for that purpose. The so-called free energy drives they were using were not perpetuum mobile drives, to use the dangerous word of the physics community, that were "producing" energy out of nothing, but converters of the practically inexhaustible for us gravitational energy of the Earth, Moon or other planetary bodies that these craft were flying by, into the electromagnetic energy necessary to propel the craft in space.

The well-known (in the field of alternative energy

research) Hans Kohler convertor was utilized to convert the inexhaustible gravitational energy of a planetary body into the electromagnetic energy of the flight. The convertor was coupled to a Van de Graaf band generator and to a Marconi ball vortex dynamo in an electro-magneto-gravitic, or tachyon drive—the so-called Thule and Andromeda tachyonators, that were mass produced on assembly lines at the AEG and Siemens plants in Germany in 1942-45. These converters were also used to propel their giant 5000 ton transport submarines or to produce energy in their underground bases around the world.

Recently I have uncovered some German and Japanese engineers that worked on the saucer projects in Germany and Japan and are still alive, but that will be a topic for a future article.

German South-Polar Colony, 1937-1992

The Germans started seriously exploring the South Pole with huge carrier ships in 1937. The Schwabenland ship was sent to the lands of Queen Mood, south of South Africa, and the Germans promptly dropped their swastika flags from the planes and claimed the land, as big as the whole continent of Europe, as belonging to the Third Reich. They gave it the name of Neu-Schwabenland. In 1942 a massive secret evacuation operation was undertaken by the Kriegs Marine to move people and materiel with submarines and ships to the secret underground base that was to become the last bastion of the Reich. Several hundred thousand concentration camp slave laborers, also scientists and young Hitler Ugend members, were evacuated with submarines and ships to the South Pole and to the extensive German colonies in South America, to continue the Nazi experiment at creating a pure racial society of Super Menschen. The rumors are that there is a vast underground city nowadays under the South Pole with a population of two million, that is called—you've guessed correctly—New Berlin. The major preoccupation of its inhabitants nowadays is human genetic engineering and space travel. Admiral Byrd is rumored to have secretly met with leaders of the German Antarctic colony in 1947, after his inglorious defeat, and to have concluded a condominium agreement with them about the peaceful coexistence of the German Nazi colony under the South Pole and the United States government, and for the exchange of advanced German technology for...American raw materials.

Half A Century of the German Moon Base 1942-1992

The Germans landed on the Moon as early as probably 1942, utilizing their larger exoatmospheric rocket saucers of the Miethe and Schriever type. The

Miethe rocket craft was built in diameters of 15 to 20 meters, and the Schriever Walter turbine powered craft was designed as an interplanetary exploration vehicle. It had a diameter of 60 meters, had ten stories of crew compartments, and stood 45 meters high. Welcome to Alice in Saucerland. In my extensive research of dissident American theories about the physical conditions of the Moon, I have proved beyond a shadow of a doubt that there is atmosphere, water and vegetation on the Moon, and that man does not need a space suit to walk on the Moon. A pair of jeans, a pullover and sneakers are just about enough. Everything NASA has told the world about the Moon is a lie and it was done to keep the exclusivity of the club from joinings by the third world countries. All these physical conditions make it a lot easier to build a Moon base. Ever since their first day of landing on the Moon, the Germans started boring and tunneling under the surface, and by the end of the war there was a small Nazi research base on the Moon. The free energy tachyon drive craft of the Haunibu-1 and 2 type were used after 1944 to haul people, materiel and the first robots to the construction site on the Moon. When Russians and Americans secretly landed jointly on the Moon in the early fifties with their own saucers, they spent their first night there as guests of the...Nazi underground base. In the sixties a massive Russian-American base had been built on the Moon, that now has a population of 40,000 people, as the rumor goes. After the end of the war in May 1945, the Germans continued their space effort from their south polar colony of Neu Schwabenland.

Vladimir Terziski was born in Sofia, the capital of Bulgaria, in Eastern Europe and arrived in the US as a political refugee in 1985. His degrees in physics and engineering were earned at Tokai University in Japan from 1974 to 1980. He currently teaches a course in Introductory Ufology, or "ET-101," at a community center in Santa Monica, California. He is the president of the American Academy of Dissident Sciences, 10970 Ashton Ave. #310, Los Angeles, CA 90024.

Bovmut: The FBI and Cattle Mutilation
by X. Sharks DeSpot

The actual story of cattle mutilations and the FBI's story of cattle mutilations are two different things. It seems almost like a story of competing subcults: the subcult of the FBI, the subcult of ranchers who own the dead cattle, and the subcult of various assorted conspiracy theories. And lost in here somewhere is the actual story of cattle and other animal mutilations.

Talking about the beginnings of the cattle mutilation affair is difficult. It's more like talking about certain points when ideas seem to have crystallized and then spread to other points.

On April 20, 1979, a conference was held at the Albuquerque Public Library at Albuquerque, New Mexico. The conference was held after an outbreak of cattle mutilations in the area. At it, according to the FBI file, "TOMMY BLAND, Lewisville, Texas" appeared along with other speakers and said, according to the FBI document, "...that animal mutilations date back to the early 1800s in England and Scotland."

That is the earliest factual account of a beginning to the animal mutilations. The problem is how do you trace an idea? In the late 1980s house cats started showing up dead in the city of Tustin, California. The local animal control people decided that the cats had been attacked and killed by coyotes who were being driven into the city by construction. At least some residents insisted that the cats were being killed by gangs of Satanists. The bad publicity forced one hundred necropsies to be performed on the cats, seeming to prove factually that the cats were, in fact, chomped on by coyotes. Apparently, the vocal minority that started all of this was unconvinced. Inevitably, someone, so it might as well be me, is going to compare this to medieval witch panics. Animal sacrifice to an alien God to bring about some sort of magic spell is a pretty old idea. Arguably, concerned meetings were held in ancient Rome to discuss the meaning of a cat found slaughtered one morning. Was it a religious sacrifice? An attempt to work magic?

So when books are published with accounts of helicopters using Satanic cultists killing and draining the blood from cattle for their rituals, it isn't exactly a new idea.

I've read accounts of the sacrifice of animals in the 1820s frontier New York in an attempt to make magic which would detect buried treasure. It was part of a folk-superstition at the time, pretty wide-spread, called "Money-digging", which was apparently dows-ing for buried treasure. The animal sacrifice was just a minor offshoot of the more general habit of digging for buried treasure. The point is that the idea that sacrifice would work in doing magic will apparently occur to some persons putting together freelance rituals. In 1984 seventeen year old Richard Kasso of Northport, New York, apparently practiced animal sacrifice with group of local youths called the Knights of the Black Circle before committing a murder which was first reported to have Satanic overtones. It was later attributed to an argument over a drug rip-off.

Having read about things like the panic over Satanism in Tustin, California and the Knights of the Black Circle's home-made Satanism, I expected the FBI file on cattle mutilations to be full of such accounts. In fact, that isn't the case. The FBI consistently bowed out of investigating cattle mutilations, being unwilling to enter into any investigation without a federal statute to back it up. It also wanted an increase in funds earmarked specifically for any such investigation. The FBI file stretches only from 1974 until 1980. Strange incidents took place both before and after that, but the FBI apparently never heard of them, or if it did, filed them away under a separate cover in its voluminous files.

One of the infuriating things about research into UFOs and cattle mutilations is the impossibility of distinguishing between a belief system and an account that resembles it. In 1896 people all over the United States began seeing an "airship" moving across the sky. When accounts were published of people meeting the airship's pilot, they usually reported descriptions of an ordinary American inventor. Almost all of these accounts seem to be stories made up as jokes. In 1897 a farmer named Alexander Hamilton made up an account of a strange, incredible looking "airship" crew stealing his cow, and then the next day leaving its hide on the ground on his property.

This made-up story by Alexander Hamilton in 1897, which got a lot of newspaper coverage from people who should have known better, appears to be the origin of the myth that "aliens" are stealing cows. Notice the complete arrogance of this statement. Because of the widespread belief in the UFO community that aliens are mutilating cows, it becomes a "modern myth". If someone sees a UFO then the next day finds his cow has apparently been mutilated, he has an entire UFO subcult to draw upon for ideas about underground base, etc., and an already established belief system exists to explain why cows are turning up mutilated: extraterrestrial pranksters wielding laser beams and surgical knives.

So what does the guy do if all he has actually seen are strange lights and dead cow? Does he make a connection? Does he assume the strange lights were space ships from another planet?

These two explanations, cattle mutilating aliens from space and Satanic cultists, represent ideas which both yours truly and the FBI reject as false. Judging from the FBI documents obtained under the Freedom of Information and Privacy Acts, the FBI concluded that the whole thing is misidentification of attacks by animal predators on cows already dead from natural causes.

The FBI file makes very dry reading. Basically it starts on September 4, 1974 when Nebraska Senator Carl T. Curtis sent a newspaper clipping to the FBI asking it to look into reports of cattle mutilations "stretching from Oklahoma to Nebraska". The FBI bowed out, stating "it appears that no federal law within the investigative jurisdiction of the FBI has been violated". On January 21, 1975 the Minneapolis, Minnesota FBI office reported that state veterinarians had attributed mutilations there to "other animals or varmints, believed to be foxes due to their sharp side teeth, which were described 'as shearing teeth like scissors'."

Colorado Senator Floyd K. Haskell was similarly told of FBI disinterest. The big change for the FBI came when New Mexico Senator Harrison H. Schmitt talked personally with the Attorney General of the Department of Justice, Griffin B. Bell on the telephone on January 10, 1979. Bell had the following typed onto a formal reply letter:

"Please have someone look into this matter at an early date. Sen. Schmitt is our friend and there have been about sixty mutilations in New Mexico in recent months. GBB."

It is very worthy of note that earlier FBI documents on this subject were listed as "cross-references", whereas this was the beginning of the main file. Schmitt's office sent along a copy of his file on the subject to the FBI. Along with clippings, most of it is reports prepared by Officer Gabe Valdez of the New Mexico state police.

Valdez's reports are weird and frightening. He himself was convinced at the time that the CIA or the Department of Energy was responsible, all of this in some way being related to "some type of research into biological warfare". "Information furnished to this office by Officer VALDEZ indicates that the animals are being shot with some type of paralyzing drug and the blood is being drawn from the animals after an injec-

tion of anti-coagulant. It appears that in some instances the cattle's legs have been broken and helicopters without any identifying numbers have reportedly been seen in the vicinity of these mutilations. Officer VALDEZ theorizes that clamps are being placed on the cows' legs and they are being lifted by helicopter to some remote area where the mutilations are taking place and the animal is returned to its original pasture."

Since Valdez did so much of the work, it may be that he was the catalyst for these ideas. I personally believe that he was not, that the ideas he proposed were widespread among the researchers at the time. Press reports in the file make clear that frightened cattlemen were taking up arms. On March 2, 1979, the Justice Department decided that since fifteen cattle mutilations had taken place on Indian land, it now had jurisdiction to investigate those fifteen. In this same memo, the FBI concluded that "It is obvious if mutilations are to be solved there is a need for a coordinated effort so that all material available can be gathered and analyzed and further efforts synchronized. Whether the FBI should assume this role is a matter to be decided". It was suggested that the investigation be code-named BOVMUT, obviously short for "Bovine Mutilations".

"A Conference directed by Senator Harrison Schmitt, New Mexico, and U.S. Attorney, R.E. THOMPSON, Albuquerque, was held on 4/20/79, at Albuquerque. This conference was opened to the public and was attended by law enforcement officials from New Mexico and other states, the news media and interested persons. Approximately 180 persons were in attendance" says an FBI report from "4/25/79."

The conference was attended by many speakers and the *National Enquirer*. Considering the fairly wide variety of things actually said at the meeting, the *Enquirer's* coverage was pathetically flat. All the emphasis was on UFOs, ignoring what was actually said by conference attendees. Some did talk of UFOs, but the point is that the *Enquirer* took the depth, detail and complexity of the event and reduced it to a UFO story. All the major theories were covered: predators, UFOs, "members of Satanic cults, or some unknown government agency." The Albuquerque FBI office "received a voluminous amount of correspondence from interested parties who have expounded their theories regarding this subject". The FBI got the fame but the actual result of the conference was that Kenneth M. Rommel, a twenty-eight year veteran of the FBI, retired and joined the First Judicial District, Office of the District Attorney, in the Animal Mutilation Project with a $50,000 grant from the federal government to investigate.

The result was anti-climactic. The fifteen cattle on the Indian reservation had not been preserved for examination, and no new mutilations came up for the FBI to investigate. Rommel came to the conclusion that nothing was happening. "He said to date, his investigative unit has determined that none of the reported cases has involved what appear to be mutilations by other than common predators. ROMMEL said he has traveled to other states and conferred with investigators in those areas regarding mutilations, and to date has received no information which would justify the belief that any animals have been intentionally mutilated by human beings. ROMMEL added that regarding all the dead animals he has examined, the damage to the carcasses has always been consistent with predator action".

The last page in the file is the FBI sending back Rommels' final report, finding nothing new or noteworthy about it.

If there is a real conclusion to be drawn, it is that the FBI produced a lot of paper work to please Senator Schmitt, and left the real work to the State of New Mexico. I personally believe that at least some human action was involved, that a small minority of cattle mutilations are the work of human beings. Most, as I've said, I believe are predators. Coyotes and foxes having lunch, dinner, breakfast, brunch, midnight snacks, et cetera, ad infinitum.

The big question is if the Kenneth Rommels investigation was accurate. The FBI itself never actually investigated anything, except some flakes of house paint found on the roof of a pick-up truck after a UFO sighting near Taos, New Mexico. The cattle mutilation investigation itself took place among the ideas of different groups and faded quietly away after a show of concern by officialdom in New Mexico. The actual answers to the cattle mutilation phenomenon are only in this file if you accept Kenneth Rommels, and the conventional.

viral def(l)ections
by Carl Steadman

> " *I think there is only one way you are going to cure the virus problem. Basically, we've got to have lots of them.* "
>
> **—Dr. Robert Lambert**
> **Computer Psychologist, Concordia University**

language is a virus

In the wake of the Michelangelo computer virus, we are presented with the opportunity to engage in a new analysis: the entire conception of the computer-virus-as-artificial-life appears little more than a stillbirth. Less than one thousand computers were struck by the virus March 6th; this, from the five million potential victims as reported in the March 5th *San Francisco Chronicle.*

What lies at stake is not the real effects, if any, of virulent computer code or the anti-viral software designed to combat it, but rather the veracity of the virus metaphor itself—that is, of the ability for language to foster a *living* analogy for the realm of the inorganic to the realm of the organic—this, against a more tenable but less interesting move to re-conceive the computer virus as a thing born unto itself. Perhaps, in the age of the binary computer, to fall on the side of the analog is only a nostalgia. But just as the binary computer can simulate the operation of analog mechanisms, so, too, can we simulate an argument for analogy which has all the outward signs of being true—so that we are no longer engaged in fabricating synthesis, but, more directly, what is synthetic. In the face of what is tenable, we will be tenacious.

a virus is structured like a breadbox

Computer viruses are usually defined around three criteria: that they be executable, that they be able to modify other computer code, and that they be capable of reproducing themselves. These criteria usually exclude that class of computer software known as worms, which are executable and proliferate themselves, but do not infect other programs, and Trojan horses, which perform, upon execution, a set of undesired operations (usually erasing or re-formatting a hard drive, or the planting of a virus), but do not necessarily modify other computer code, and do not proliferate themselves. The criteria would also exclude more well-received computer code such as the compression utilities *AutoDoubler* and *More Disk Space,* which, though executable and capable of modifying other computer code, do not proliferate.

But these triumviral requirements for the computer virus would, interestingly enough, exclude some of the first computer viruses (at least, what were then considered to be computer viruses) such as the 1987 Christmas virus, while doing nothing to promote the evolutionary process of the viral form. The viral metaphor would seem to dictate a different path than this focusing in and rarefaction of definition: it would instead seem to invite a scoping outward, itself following the logic of the epidemic, of that final overturning of the catastrophe. This is why some of the interior logic of the computer virus metaphor eludes us—though a virus, a cancerous threat, the computer virus has often been seen as an agent of good (hence the "universal message of peace" of the MacMug virus, and the experimental diagnostic viruses developed in the mid-1970s at Xerox's Palo Alto Research Center), and, beyond that, a precursor of artificial life (the probability shown to be *considerable,* though nigh to impossible, by Dr. Fred Cohen's 1987 computations on the spontaneous generation of computer viruses). The viral metaphor should be just that: a viral metaphor, adhering to its own extremes of logic, expounding exponentially, multiplying beyond the strictures of reason.

learning from los angeles

It was in early 1988, soon after the first outbreaks of viral code on personal computers, that Dr. Jan Brunvard of the University of Utah, under the headline "Computer Virus Called Fraud" in *Compuserve Magazine,* claimed the computer virus to be another in a long line of urban legends, in the same vein as the cat in the microwave oven. Peter Norton, "software guru", whose name belongs to the well-known data protection and recovery package, supported this view in a statement to *Insight* magazine later that year, saying "We're dealing with an urban myth. It's like the story of alligators in the sewers of New York. Everyone knows about them, but no one's ever seen them. Typically, these stories come up every three to five years."

Bernard's, and Norton's, description would lead us to an ideological analysis—one that would trace the meaning of such an urban myth in the face of its unreality. But the urban legend of the computer virus was specifically realized—and, while this does not, in itself, invalidate an ideological analysis—one that could point to a fear, or apprehension, of a new technologi-

211 / Fall 1993

cal form, and to the coping strategies, or investments of meaning, employed by such myths (here, one could read a simultaneous humanization and demonization of the computer, in that it is both susceptible to disease, and capable of being diseased [which leads to the corruption of data, usually expressed in a loss of man-hours])—it makes such an analysis one of the least interesting possibilities. As Jean Braudrillard, in his *Simulations,* rightly points out that "Disneyland is there to conceal the fact it is the 'real' country, all of 'real' America, which is Disneyland" (25), so, too, does the computer virus conceal the fact that it is computer software which is viral in nature, that the threat of the computer virus—as proliferate code, executable and modifiable—is there only to mask the true infestation, that of the computer software applications themselves (and computer systems they run on [which, it is important to remember, make no distinction between "authorized" software and viruses]), proliferating indefinitely, outside of any dialectic.

viruses cannot operate
when the computer is turned off

To the brute force of the computer virus, the computer application poses a sheer seduction, a seduction which is victorious in every sense. To the pale showing of the computer virus, the computer application poses a sheer proliferation and ascension to the limit (of hard drive space, of computing power). To the disguised presence and ultimate observability of the computer virus, the computer application poses a sheer presence, a ubiquity only recognizable in its lack of re-cognition, in its very immediacy. To the destruction of data of the computer virus, the computer application poses a sheering point, a true departure, based on the destruction of reality, in what is called the "virtually real". The realm of power is not the realm of seduction; to the blatant manipulation of the computer virus (which, in turn, invites a counter-power, that of the anti-viral efforts of the user) the computer application offers a subtle manipulation, one that relies on the user for the unauthorized reproduction of its code, in the form of software piracy.

The computer application then achieves an ascendancy over the computer virus, but only in being more virus than virus: as a true form of artificial life, based in a seeming indifference and ultimate vulnerability, which makes it all the more invulnerable. This is why we have the experience of the system crash: though the system crash can be claimed to be, as the virus, something foreign to the system—a result of "bugs"—this is certainly not the case: the system crash has the effect of making the computer more vulnerable, more indifferent, warranting all the more of the user's care and attention. In this, we have the true state of affairs; as in any seduction, we think ourselves the "users", but this is only an illusion.

"Only a Pawn..."
Bob Dylan, Lee Harvey Oswald and MK-ULTRA
by Bob Heyer and Kenn Thomas

❝ I'll stand up and to get uncompromisable about it—which I have to be honest...I just got to be, as I got to admit that the man who shot President Kennedy, Lee Oswald...I don't know exactly where...what he thought he was doing, but I got to admit that I, too—I saw some of myself in him." Bob Dylan stopped the Tom Paine Awards dinner of the Emergency Civil Liberties Union with this observation on December 13, 1963, according to Bob Spitz (*Dylan: A Biography,* McGraw-Hill, 1989).

Spitz does not make it clear whether he is quoting from a tape or has corralled quotes from various magazine reports about the incident, but it is a matter of rock music lore that Dylan embarrassed the ECLU in this manner just three weeks after JFK's murder. According to Spitz, Dylan's comments followed a drunken rant that defended student radicals in Cuba but attacked as too "respectable" the organizers of the 1963 March On Washington (in which Dylan had participated) and otherwise maligned the liberal left that sought to honor him with this award. In the end, he accepted the award in part for "the people on behalf of who went to Cuba". This was a reference to a group of 58 students led in part by ECLC employee Paul Luce who had violated the law in the summer of 1963 and travelled to Castro's Cuba. Some of the students were later called before the House Commmittee on UnAmerican Activities.

Just as the infamous John Lennon biographer Albert Goldman characterized Lenny Bruce's first crack after the assassination ("Poor Vaughn Meader") as the first sick joke about it, Dylan biographer Spitz put a similar spin on Dylan's ECLU speech, calling his lack of remorse for the incident symptomatic of Dylan's inability "to confront the people who he had disappointed". He reports the singer's explanation to the *New Yorker* that ECLU's members "had minks and jewels, and it was like they were giving their money out of guilt...they're trying to put morals and great deeds on their chains, but basically they don't want to jeopardize their position." Dylan had taken chances with his public life, not only writing popular and widely performed protest anthems, but as a performer at potentially explosive voter registration rallies of the Student Non-Violent Coordinating Committee. (Film footage of one such rally, in Greenwood, Mississippi in July 1963, appears in the 1965 documentary by D.A. Pennebaker, *Don't Look Back.)* His lashing out at the ECLU, albeit exacerbated by his inebriated stupor, was meant to convey more his distaste for its Old Left liberal membership, whose own involvements in social reform had long calcified into making charitable donations, but whose roots Dylan shared. Robert Shelton in his 1986 book, *No Direction Home* (Beech Tree Books, New York), gives a more thorough account of Dylan's ambiguous relationship with the ECLC and his regrets over the incident, including the entire Oswald speech taken from a transcript supplied by the committee.

Interestingly, Dylan's involvement with SNCC voter organizing in the South, done from deeply held convictions but also at the behest of his girlfriend Suze Rotolo, paralleled those of Lee Harvey Oswald. A month after Dylan's appearance at the Greenwood, Mississippi rally, singing "Only A Pawn In Their Game," Oswald visited a small town in Louisiana named Clinton, either to find work or to register as a voter. Witnesses had clear memories of Oswald's visit, being almost the sole Caucasian in a voter registration drive organized by the Congress For Racial Equality. Oswald did have two companions: the strange, albino pilot David Ferrie; and Oswald's New Orleans boss Guy Bannister (initially misidentified by the late Jim Garrison as Clay Shaw, the defendant in Garrison's ill-fated prosecution). One analyst has suggested that this duo's presence with Oswald was an attempt to connect CORE to the Fair Play for Cuba Committee, piling up leftist sympathies for Oswald to later tarnish them when he shot Kennedy.

Is this the real meaning of Bob Dylan's comments that "I saw some of myself in" Oswald? Did Dylan have an idea that Oswald was a patsy and that he, too, was being manipulated—into a public image as the spokesman for generation, into accepting an award from an entrenched leftist elite?

Support for this argument might be found in the life and career of John Robert Glenn, one of the 58 students upon whose behalf Dylan accepted the Tom Paine Award. In the current issue of the JFK assassination research journal *The Third Decade* ($20/year; State University College, Fredonia, NY 14063; the journal will be renamed *The Fourth Decade* in November), editor/publisher Jerry Rose notes similarities between the lives of Glenn and Oswald, including the possibility that Glenn had developed a faked pro-Castro background for himself via the Fair Play For Cuba

Committee. Glenn was also later connected to a rifle found in Indiana reported as being involved with the assassination. Glenn also had the honor of being one of three people on the "fink" list of the 58 students suspected of being an intelligence plant. "It is possible," concludes Rose, "that Glenn, like Oswald, was being groomed as a pro-communist patsy if Oswald did not for any reason work out in the role". It is also possible that Bob Dylan had more than one patsy on his mind when he gave his speech before the ECLC.

Little doubt remains that Dylan shared enemies on the right with the president who would be victimized by someone that official history names as Lee Harvey Oswald. In his book on intelligence spook Richard Case Nagell, *The Man Who Knew Too Much,* author Dick Russell describes the growth of the Anti-Communist Liaison, an extreme right old boy network that developed around Douglas MacArthur's aide Charles Willoughby. Russell characterizes one Willoughby associate, the evangelist Billy James Hargis from Tulsa, Oklahoma, as Willoughby's publisher and friend and a central organizer of the secret Anti-Communist liaison in September 1961, "to help save our country from internal communism" with financial backing from H.L. Hunt and other rich oil interests. Hargis also founded the Christian Crusade, which in 1966 published the paperback *Rhythm, Riots and Revolution* by David Noebel, a 352 page attack on the ills of folk and rock music with Bob Dylan featured prominently on the cover. "I want my woman dirty, looking as though I'd just found her in some alley", the cover quotes Dylan, "It triggers the animal emotion".

The book spends an entire chapter attacking Dylan and disses him throughout. Dylan accumulates guilt through association with such vicious radicals as John Hammond, Pete Seeger and Gil Turner but also as "a fellow traveler of the Broadside movement" and "a faithful disciple of identified Communist Woody Guthrie". These associations extend to Dylan's poetic influences, the evil Spanish Communist Garcia Lorca and the evil German Communist Bertolt Brecht (Noebel uses the more familiar "Bert"). The ambiguity of folk song lorist Irwin Silber's alternate admiration and jealousy for Dylan's *oeuvre* is used to cast aspersions in both directions, and even the inclusion of a Dylan song in a poetry anthology taints the songwriter because the publisher "has been identified as having been a member of the Communist Party". Praise from Allen Ginsberg and Gus Hall does not do much to improve Bob Dylan's reputation in Mr. Noebel's estimation. To the cover quote, taken from a 1966 interview in the *Des Moines Register,* Noebel adds "'I want dirty long hair hanging all over the place. I hate shaved legs or arms. I hate cleaning or astringent lo-tion because those antiseptic smells revolt me. I hate girls who like Rock Hudson.'" (p. 222)

Rhythm, Riots and Revolution says this about the Emergency Civil Liberties Union incident:

"For Dylan's usefulness to the Communist Party and his open and defiant attitude toward anti-Communists, the Communist front, Emergency Civil Liberties Committee, presented Dylan with its Tom Paine Award...Dylan was quite taken back with ECLC's display of finery, but took the award nevertheless...[according to a 1961 *Guide to Subversive Organizations and Publications]* the 'Emergency Civil Liberties Committee, established in 1951, although representing itself as a non-Communist group, actually operates as a front for the Communist Party. It has repeatedly assisted, by means of funds and legal aid, Communists involved in Smith Act violations and similar legal proceedings. One of its chief activities has been and still is the dissemination of voluminous Communist propaganda material'". (pp. 220-221)

Despite the temptation to dismiss *Rhythm, Riots and Revolution*'s cartoonish depiction of Dylan and the folk music movement of the mid 1960s as a quaintly funny reflection of bygone paranoids, and even allowing that its sentiments still linger in America's cultural atmosphere, it includes more disturbing elements and perhaps more clues to the JFK assassination. Published as part of a Christian Crusade book series (distributed primarily to the Crusade's own teen groups, like the Young Americans for Freedom) that included *Communism, Hypnotism and the Beatles,* David Noebel devotes half of *Rhythm, Riots and Revolution* to the topic of mind control. Chapter titles include "Communist Use of Mind Warfare", "Communist Use of Rhythmic-Hypnotic Music", and "Communist Use of Beat Music". These are the most heavily footnoted chapters and the research relies greatly on the work of Edward Hunter, specifically his 1961 book *Brainwashing.* Hunter served as chairman of the Anti-Communist Liaison and served also as a National Advisory Board member for the Young Americans for Freedom.

In *The Man Who Knew Too Much,* Dick Russell credits a September 1950 article in the *Miami News* by Hunter as the first printed use of the term "brainwashing" (Russell, p. 193) and otherwise notes that Hunter worked as a propaganda specialist for the OSS during WWII and afterwards for the CIA. In the article, Hunter decries that the Communist Chinese have established panels of experts in drugs and hypnotism to re-educate and reform its dissident citizens. "What Hunter did not say, then or later," notes Russell, "was that the OSS and Military Intelligence were investigating the same methods, starting in World War II. And that the CIA, starting in the late 1940s, initiated its own wide-ranging 'mind-control' program, to become known as MK-ULTRA" (Russell, p. 194).

Russell retraces Oswald's involvement in an attempt to shoot General Edwin Walker in Dallas prior to the JFK assassination—including such oddities as the eradication of a license plate number from an Oswald photo of Walker's driveway, and awareness of the event by the FBI and the CIA before the assassination—and suggests that, just as was possibly the case with Oswald's visit to Clinton, Louisiana, members of the radical right observed and perhaps manipulated the events surrounding the Walker shooting. Russell also notes that two weeks after the Walker shooting, the Anti-Communist Liaison held a 125 member meeting chaired by Edward Hunter, primarily to discuss mind-control, psychological warfare and "ideological conversion". (Russell, p. 327) Although originally skeptical of the mind-control scenario with regard to Oswald, Russell lists Hunter's brainwashing expertise and the Washington seminar as two chief reasons to re-examine it carefully.

As the Christian Crusade lambasted Bob Dylan and the folkies of the 1960s for brainwashing youth into Communism, bad personal hygiene and maybe even unsafe sex, new research suggests that it might have been more directly involved in events that did much more to change the country's political and cultural landscape. In presenting Dylan as a brainwashing tool of the Communists, the Christian Crusade instead revealed its own pre-occupation with the practice and, perhaps, its own affinity with the notorious MK-ULTRA.

Some of Dylan's friends suggest that the singer did become more cautious of the JFK assassination; it is a matter of record that his writing began moving away from overtly political protest songs. The simplified explanation is that the Beatles came along and signalled pop music's return to rock'n'roll. Dylan, however, gave up writing protest with the songs he wrote in early 1964 for the *Another Side of Bob Dylan* album, prior to the impact of the Beatles.

Sources Cited:
Goldman, Albert, *Ladies and Gentlemen, Lenny Bruce,* Ballantine Books, 1974.
Noebel, David, *Rhythm, Riots and Revolution,* Christian Crusade, 1966 (?).
Pennebaker, D.A., *Don't Look Back,* 1965.
Rose, Jerry, "Red Summer of '63," *The Third Decade,* Vol. 9, #6, September 1993.
Russell, Dick, *The Man Who Knew Too Much,* Carroll and Graf, 1992.
Shelton, Robert, *No Direction Home,* Beech Tree Books, 1986.
Spitz, Bob, *Dylan: A Biography,* McGraw-Hill, 1989.

On the Usefulness of Conspiracy Theories
by Len Bracken

66 *'The conspiracy theory of history' was in the nineteenth century a reactionary and ridiculous belief, at a time when so many powerful social movements were stirring up the masses. Today's pseudo-rebels are well aware of this, thanks to hearsay or a few books, and believe that it remains true for eternity. They refuse to recognize the real praxis of their time; it is too sad for their cold hopes. The state notes this fact, and plays on it."*

Guy Debord
Comments on the Society of the Spectacle

The evidence is so overwhelming that there is hardly any need to qualify the following statement: everything the cops on television tell you is 'terrorism,' is actually government provocation (only in rare exceptions is it genuine warfare). In other words, what you would be led to believe is 'terrorism' is simply politics. To cite a recent case, the World Trade Center bombing, those arrested for this deed would not have known how to make the bombs, or even considered the action, had it not been for the FBI infiltrator who was recently interviewed on National Public Radio. To what use can we put our knowledge of government/media conspiracies such as this?

When I say 'we,' I mean those of us who organize micro-revolutionary societies, and to answer the question I would insist on calling into question the intentions of anyone calling for armed struggle. Consider another example: a Black Liberation Army *agent provocateur* from the FBI facilitated the break-in and robbery of the Compton Armory in the early 1970s so that the BLA would have grenade launchers and other munitions. Beware of being given bombs by the powers that stage-manage the world. As Gianfranco Sanguinetti, author of the highly insightful *On Terrorism and the State,* knew first hand, the mere words "possession of arms" and "subversive conspiracy" can send you up.

A glance at few more cases of the government playing the terrorist card against the left. How much of a Stalinist was Oswald?

* Symbionese Liberation Army leader Donald DeFreeze was a specimen of U.S. intelligence brainwashing.

* A police infiltrator of the Weatherman was uncovered precisely during the "Days of Rage".

* It is well known that the Black Panthers were militarized by infiltrators.

* Bommi Baumann's *How It All Began* tells how the German underground was riddled with police agents; and in this book, this key figure in the June 2nd Movement renounces armed struggle.

* And - excuse me if I'm wrong - the Baader release from prison under a general amnesty, followed by his recapture and escape from a lightly guarded research institute; and the eventual death of both him and Mienhof in prison, reeks of provocation.

* The British government has admitted that it recruited the brothers Littlejohn to rob banks and run arms for the IRA.

* Right-wing militants (Posetta and Girotto and possibly others) infiltrated the Red Brigades and set the terrorist trap for naive leftists. Moro was killed by members of his party, who were simultaneously members of P2.

* And when United States began to lean left, the state killed Martin Luther King, playing the fascist card to justify its protection racket to African Americans and left-leaning people.

The list of artificial terror goes on and on (Mitterand hired gangsters to stage an attempted assassination in 1981 and some of you may recall Yeltsin's delirious jump from a bridge), but it's important to think of these points in light of Goethe: "In any case, I hate everything that merely instructs me without augmenting or directly invigorating my activity". No ultra-leftist worth his salt thinks in terms of murder, except in self-defense. Use the situationist outline for revolution - strikes, occupations, theorizing reality and realizing theory - in autonomous ways. Conspiracy theory is a theory of dialogue, a critique of society that begs for response in the world of historical deeds. To put it another way, anyone who works on Labor Day is a scab and is fucking up our struggle.

Len Bracken's work, Freeplay *and* East Is Black, *is available from him at 5723 N. 10th Road, Arlington, VA 22205.*

From the Other Side of the Pond: Ustica Tales
by Jim Cregan

It has been rumored that Luciano Benetton has been trying to buy the Milan Internazionale "INTER" soccer team and has offered around $120 million. The going value for a team of INTER's stature is around $65-70m and INTER has been on bad times lately.

This, to me, seemed to be peculiar. So I decided to sniff around a few days in a trench coat and see what would turn up. Pay Day! It seems that Lucky Luke is about to get an "Avviso di Garanzia", which is an official notice, informing one that he is under investigation by the state for high crimes and misdemeanors.

It seems that even he has been caught up in the "Tangentopoli" scandal in Italy. Systematic bribes to every party for public works projects. They have arrested hundreds now.

Reliable sources have it that Benneton was trying to get in on a mega clothing factory in one of those countless government-owned companies in every field, created by the Ministry for the Reconstruction of the South, a major source of income for the Mafia. In the new government policy of privatization, Our Hero was trying to get his super big, high tech factory that they never knew how to run right, and make money with it. He would also get huge tax breaks for investing in a high unemployment area. The deal was practically a give-away. But not only was it going to cost him a bundle up front, so the minister could grease the appropriate palms to get the deal through, but he also had to buy INTER at an inflated price because the Socialist party has got a lot of money tied up in it. Turns out also that he is gay and has always had a thing for Luciano, from when he did that "Do You Know Me?" commercial for American Express.

So there is a journalist who's locked up in jail in Treviso right now on charges of burglary. They claim he stole a bunch of documents from the office of L.B. Upon investigation, it turns out that: 1. He didn't break in to anybody's office; and 2. he had in his possessions pictures of ol' Lucky Luke in bed with the minister, playing Lone Ranger and Tonto, with spurs and everything. They stopped him and searched him because he ran a light. They found the pics and took him in. The local police are just Lucky Luke's lackeys anyway and now they're trying to switch the evidence and send this guy up, without having the photos come out. (Only one, which Benneton decided to use for his latest campaign.) Luke must have some big friends himself, because someone got to the minister and he suddenly can't find the negatives to the pics. Luciano can't find them either. Seems whoever went to get them, kept them.

Apparently, there are people of different political persuasions who would like to see the Socialists keep INTER and continue losing money. It is a real drain. If they can stop Luc from buying INTER, they hurt the Socialists, but Luke doesn't get the factory. He wants that factory.

So if the gay minister was in on the deal to sell INTER to Our Hero, why did he take those pictures on that blessed night? Extra insurance? And if the D.C. has got the pictures to persuade Luc from buying INTER, why don't they just hit him for another bribe and sell the factory to him anyway? They are the largest party in the coalition. Who cares about the minister? But the minister has lost his cool. He got an Avviso di Garanzia as well for other dirty things he's in. He's upset about those photos disappearing and the negatives by that gorilla. He's in the deal on INTER and needs to un-load. And Luciano probably hasn't called him again after that night and this has distressed him. So he freaked out when they questioned him on the other deals and told his whole story. Thus, Luciano's avviso.

There is an old story that at one time, about twenty years ago, when INTER was owned by the Communist party (and losing money), INTER's two "allowed foreign players" on the team were Russians on loan from the Russian sports ministry. Athletes at one time were a big money corner for the Reds. So apparently no one on the team knew about these kids' connections, but their fathers were both big honchos back home.

They say the CIA found out and was behind a lot of the financing when the Socialists bought the team. The money they used was a slush fund Nixon had left over after the Vietnam war. This was also tied in with Sinatra somehow, because it was right around that period when the Communists almost entered into the "Historic Compromise" with the D.C. when they had 33% of the electorate.

They got into a money bind with that electoral campaign and ended up selling INTER to balance accounts. Only that the Americans then passed the money through a bank in the middle east where it got frozen with all other western financial assets during one of the oil embargoes. So the Socialists got IN-

TER, the Americans got to the Russian players and the Communists only got their money a year later and were in formal bankruptcy proceedings. The government allegedly let them off the hook in exchange for an agreement not to try to get into the government for another ten years. Well Berlinguer died ten years ago and you know the rest of the story.

Now Luciano has come on the scene and it seems that the CIA doesn't want him to have the team either. They don't particularly care if the Socialists get their money back, but rumor has it that someone is buried out under the north goal zone. Luciano doesn't really want the team. He already has a Formula 1 racing team, a basketball team, Rugby and volleyball. But he has heard the story about the north goal as well and maybe there's a connection there.

Yuri Popanov, the striker and top goal scorer for INTER was the son of Boris Popanov, the one time Minister of Consumer Manufacturing in the Soviet Union. Every one knows that this Ministry is nothing more than the supply line for clothes, food and cars for the Russian Nomenklature. Anyone who is anyone has their vices supplied by the Ministry and no inconvenient lines to stand in. The delivery guys are full of KGB agents. Thus an interesting source of info for the CIA.

Years ago, Benneton tried to set up a little factory in the USSR. The factory would never have been able to produce any significant amount of goods. But it was a front for Benneton to import extra stock and end of series of defective goods from his clothing business in Italy. The Russians would pay a month's wages for one of his sweaters and the Ministry got its cut.

During one of his trips to Russia years ago, the KGB got some compromising pictures of Luke with the American ambassador. He seems to have quite a reputation about these things. The Ambassador left soon after with the closing of the Nixon administration

and the photos lost a good deal of their value. But there was still the Italian clothing magnate to squeeze. He let go of his part of the clothing deal to set up there and they sent the pics to Italy with a courier. The courier was Yuri Papanov. Was the KGB on to Yuri? Did they know that BENETTON would kill for those pics? Or was he a successful double agent?

One day Papanov simply didn't show up for practice and was never heard from again. But it's true when INTER fans say that the grass is always greener under the north goal. You should see it.

Yuri's "controller", the KGB agent assigned to keep an eye on him while abroad, was a female doctor on the training staff, Allesandra Pitchken. Yuri's teammates nicknamed one portion of his anatomy his "third foot". It is not known if he ever scored a goal with it. When Yuri disappeared, Allesandra took up with the other Russian player until the end of the season. The other player's contract was suddenly revoked and he went back to finish his career with RED STAR in Vladivostock.

Now she hadn't seen him in years and no one knows if she found out about the CIA putting the squeeze on Yuri. But it came out a few years ago that her name was on the passenger list of that famous flight from Bologna to Palermo. They say she had a reservation in a cheap hotel in Palermo for the night and a booking on the Palermo-Tunis flight the next morning. It's a very inconvenient way of going to Tunis. You change in Rome and be in Tunis for dinner time. The Palermo Tunis is by Tunis Air and is mainly to ferry immigrant farm workers back and forth to the citrus orchards in Sicily. They even let them take chickens on the plane! Is this a possible American motive for the Ustica disaster?

A Green Conspiracy
by Wayne Henderson

Few things, these days, seem more important to certain people than being "politically correct", adopting the stale vanilla language of the inoffensive, and most of all embracing "Green" politics. Far be it from me to denounce a good, ecologically oriented mindset—it's sorely needed—but can we really trust the "Green Movement"? Is it a coalition of disparate left-oriented proles bent on saving the planet, or the tip of a much more sinister iceberg?

I've done a minor amount of digging along those line and have unearthed some rather startling inconsistencies in the Green left.

Take, for example, the Fourth World Wilderness Congress, which took place from September 11 to 18, 1987. One participant, a Mr. George Hunt, was interviewed by *The Moneychanger* (formerly *Gold & Silver Update*) in its December 1987 issue:

"London banker Baron Edmund de Rothschild was at the meeting for six days...personally conducting the monetary matters and creation of this World Conservation Bank [WCB], in the company of I. Michael Sweatman of the Royal Bank of Canada...also, David Rockefeller [of Chase Manhattan Bank] was there, and gave a speech on Sunday...I think a lot of those Greenies were sponsored to be there. It was a contrived conference. So I called around and it turned out that the FINDHORN GROUP in Loveland, Colorado, were the official hosts..."

Now, I'll be the first to admit that the presence of a few people normally identified with the monied elite doesn't automatically mean *conspiracy*—it is entirely possible that there are in positions of power some few individuals with more than a passing concern for the state of the earth. Merely to point at the guest list of a Green gathering and shout "Aha!" doesn't cut the mustard. It's when we start delving into the actual business of the "Green gathering" that my interest is piqued:

"They're planning on re-financing, debt swapping [for assets] one trillion dollars of Third World debt into this new World Conservation Bank...The WCB will be enacted by the United Nations, and will need to be approved, I think, by every country participating. Let's assume that our senators and representatives allow this thing to happen: then the bank will be endowed with [roughly] 30% of the earth's surface...[the participating governments] will give title to the lands to the World Wilderness Land Inventory Trust. It will be entrusted...Then the WCB will have the power to act as a world central bank. It can create soft currencies [currencies good only within the country of issuance], not hard currencies [those which can be used internationally]...but...the soft currencies [according to the WCB scenario as set forward by the conference] can be spent outside for environmental and ecological equipment..."—G. Hunt, ibid.

Even an armchair economist can see what the WCB would mean: At last, an operational One World Bank that would hold, after only a brief amount of time, title deed to the majority of the earth's land surface. Now the debt would hardly affect First and Second World governments—the overwhelming majority of which are but fronts for the international banking clique, anyway; nor would Third World governments likely be overwhelmingly affected, either, as they exist solely at the pleasure of the banking cartel. The real victims of such a scheme as the WCB presents would be those outside the actual boardrooms and corridors of power, a description that, I think, covers 99% of the readers of this 'zine (intelligence agency employees excluded).

"...World Bank loans, as they stand now, are not collateralized; now they're entering into a new era of loan collateralization. They're stating, 'Okay, the next step is we want collateral, so that when we loan-swap this debt, we're going to own the Amazon if you default...as [Brazilian Finance Ministry official Dr. Jose Pedro] de Oliveira-Costa said, they're not going to be able to pay that off...'"—G. Hunt, ibid.

What we have here, in plain English, is a scheme to monetize land—the WCB would act, in concert with the World Bank and the International Monetary Fund [IMF], as the world's banker, and out of such a system would grow a one-world fiat currency system, placed in the hands of precisely those individuals who would benefit most from such a system, the international money-elite.

Not that this is an unprecedented move. Since the early part of this century, our monetary system here in the US has been in the hands of what is called the Federal Reserve System, a shady group that has, since its inception as the financial power here, increased prices on consumer goods 1200%. There's been a fair amount of speculation as to who actually owns this Federal Reserve System...the Federal Reserve Act of 1913 provides that the names of the owner-banks must be kept secret. However, I have been fortunate enough to find, via an unnamed but reliable source, a list of the eight banks that actually "own" our currency:

1. Rothschild Banks, London and Berlin
2. Lazard Freres Bank of Paris
3. Israel Moses Seif Banks of Italy
4. Lehman Brothers Bank of New York
5. Warburg Banks of Hamburg and Amsterdam
6. Kuhn, Loeb Bank of New York
7. Chase-Manhattan Bank of New York
8. Goldman, Sachs Bank of New York

Currently, at least one-third of Latin America's export earnings, taken as a whole, are devoted to paying the interest on a debt of roughly $400 billion to these very banks (though the 'fiction' is that these loans are from the US, in reality the US government merely guarantees the loan, meaning that if the debtor nations default—as they eventually must—the US people will be responsible for the debt—if you think this is impossible, console yourself with that thought when the S&L bailout is reflected in your 'tax debt')...Brazil, since the Wilderness Conference cited above, has made a deal to ameliorate the terms of its various loans, in return for allowing international interference with its development of the Amazon—perhaps on the very terms spelled out Rockefeller and Rothschild (Chase-Manhattan and Rothschild Banks) at the conference? One thing is certain: with the state of Third-World economy being what it is, *someone* will end up holding title deed to those lands, and a great many other lands besides-and *someone,* in this instance, would appear to be the same monied interests that were so much in evidence at the World Wilderness Conference.

"...they're going to be in back of the bank loaning currency and cash flow to the WCB to keep it alive, to give it the appearance of profitability...the bank will be running on an accrual basis. On paper it will be recognizing profits received on interest, but the interest will NOT be coming in because these countries can't pay...my hypothesis is that the...capitalists and moneychangers...will be in back of this bank in the position of *creditors*..."

The WCB is, essentially, the Federal Reserve scheme raised to the Nth power, on an international scale; not only will the world's cash-supply be controlled (as it is now, by the World Bank and IMF), but the land-area as well, by the WCB; while there is scant chance at financial security, let alone gain, in the current economic climate (making revolutionary change *very* hard), there is at least the opportunity, a thin thread of hope, in land-ownership, the ability to meet one's own needs through one's own labor, to be at least mildly independent of the whims of the market economy. Once the WCB is in full operation, land

itself—the only remaining means of 'opting out', of dis-attaching, will be gone, and rapidly. The "Green" complexion of such a WCB would appeal to the 'sheeple', the Politically Correct Greens and Semi-Greens, especially in today's climate—many, many otherwise well-intentioned people can be talked into switching their old mortgage into a subsidiary of WCB, under any number of pretexts—willingly surrendering control of their homes to the international banking cartel, perhaps in exchange for (apparently) lower rates and the 'feelgood' of doing business what appears to be a "Green" institution.

Such a scheme also dovetails beautifully with the elite's fear of real revolutionary movements. A guerilla band, hiding out in the rainforest a la Che Guevera, would find themselves trespassing on private property, hence subject to search and destruction by a private security force under no restraints (as if the current lot are anything to crow about); combined with the current dis-armament hysteria (the move to remove firearms from the citizenry under the banner of a 'war on drugs') and recent moves to more tightly control the flow of currency into and out of the US, we see a clear pattern of encirclement. Moves in the Senate and Congress are currently aimed at removing all 'large currency' ($100 bills) from the hands of citizens here—again, it's part of the 'war on drugs' package—such is the nature of what is a classic pincer movement, in three prongs:

1.: remove all private ownership of land, allowing the bank's security forces to 'sanitize' trespassers in any way they see fit;

2.: remove all offensive—and even defensive—firearms from the people, rendering them unable to resist; and

3.: remove all actual wealth from the people, rendering them unable to either 'opt-out' of the system (by moving themselves and their earnings from direct control into an 'underground' economy), or to purchase 'illegal' firearms in an attempt to wrest back control of their lives.

"Individuals who have decided that the operations of the government are not compatible with their own status as free and sovereign citizens may decide to 'drop out'—not all of them are criminals. Some have simply realized that an enemy need not speak a foreign language. They regard themselves as citizens of an occupied land, and as such wish to give no aid or assistance to their rulers..." *Full Disclosure* magazine #15, pg. 13.

Not only are the elite attempting to scarf up the land; there will always be those holdouts who will, under whatever circumstances, retain their property as long as possible; these few might even make a go of it! Such a scenario can hardly appeal to the monied interests. As such, those technologies that we normally see as "user-friendly", those intended to free us from, for instance, the energy (electricity) monopoly, are being bought up by those same interests at an alarming rate. Most wind-energy technology is now in the hands of the oil companies, and various solar-power suppliers are now following suit: Sunworks, Inc. of NJ and Revere Copper of NY are now owned by ASARCO (American Smelting and Refining); Solar-flex is now owned by Amoco (Standard Oil of Indiana), in conjunction with two related European firms; ARCO owns Northrup Solar and Energy Conversion Devices, Inc.; Exxon has acquired Solar Power Corp. and Daystar Corp.; Mobile-Tyco solar is now the property of Mobil Oil and Solar Energy Systems of Delaware is now owned by Shell Oil.

For years we've been content to moan and wail the 'slow erosion' of our rights—the left has become, in essence, a mutual whining society, nothing more. All the while, as we've cracked wise about Proudhon and Kropotkin, those whom we *claim* to oppose have been quietly, carefully, removing the last few barriers to total domination, rendering resistance futile.

No more "Green" politics. To hell with being "Politically Correct". From this point henceforward, I, for one, will trust no Greens—with the possible exception of the earth First!ers and related artists of eco-tage. Theory is fine and dandy, but our enemies are playing for keeps.

Book Reviews

Grace Beats Karma
by Neal Cassady

"You can work yourself into anything," Neal Cassady once told an acid test audience at the Berkeley Theatre, "How do you get out of it?" He ponders that question at some length during the early correspondence found in *Grace Beats Karma,* jail letters by Cassady just published for the first time by Blast Books ($12.95; POB 51, New York, NY 10276-0051). The earliest chapters reflect Cassady's frustration that he could not get wife Carolyn to use their house as property collateral to get him bailed out. After that resentment cooled, the letters practically turned into devotional sermons with Carolyn serving as the Muse to this great Muse of the Beats, if only in his alliterative salutations ("Dearest Devoted Deeply Disturbed Darling..., Carolyn").

Neal Cassady had indeed worked himself into a painful prison stretch for the crime of trading two joints to some undercover cops for a ride home. The way out was to get religion, or, rather, as Carolyn explains in her introduction to the volume, use the Catholicism of his youth to occupy his mind while serving the time. Carolyn Cassady's book, *Off The Road,* makes a good companion to *Grace Beats Karma,* as it details the events of Cassady's life during the time of the correspondence. Her introduction to this book also provides the needed buffer to reading cold the hard-hearted assessments by Cassady of those who admired him: "Pagan poet Allen, indecisive doodiller Jack [Kerouac], viciously degenerate Burroughs, utterly mad Celine...all the other pitifully distorted freaks I've known" (p. 30); and "ignoring all this Zen trash" while reading the early books of Alan Watts.

Instead, Cassady waxes heavy-handed with Catholicism, memorizing names of the popes, repeating endless novenas and prattling on, as Carolyn Cassady surmises, with a Catholic schoolboy's morality, even accepting his unfair imprisonment as a due penance. Throughout the volume, however, the *je ne sais quois* of Cassady's character—the ebullience, the hopelessly unfiltered openness remarkable in a convict serving time contemporaneous to the thoughts expressed—overcomes even those deep, early Papist imprints. Of sin, he explains to his godfather, Father Harley Schmitt, in one letter, "the sin delayed until conquered in time—is another inch upward, right? i. e., via this method, plus prayer naturally, I completely overcame masturbation some years ago..."; another

off-hand remark concludes that "a provocative study of the Holy Shroud of Turin by Rev. Wuenschel...ought to surely convince almost any skeptic of the resurrection".

Carolyn Cassady explains in the introduction that the two had in truth come to a more complex and personal interpretation of Christ through *Many Mansions* by Gina Cerminara, the Theosophists, Teilhard de Chardin, Meister Eckhart and others, including the clairvoyant Edgar Cayce. Struggling to combine this lofty mysticism with his in-prison need for religious expression and tangible spirituality, Cassady tells the priest that "*besides* proclaiming truth of Catholic Church *alone,* Cayce could dose, see auras, correctly analyze any piece of ground or metal alloy, &, in trance, performed 9 scientifically impossible acts..."

The Cassady spin on things conquers the facile Catholicism at which he groped throughout this correspondence. The book appears in advance of a full-blown biography of Cassady, the most comprehensive one perhaps ever written, researched and written by T.K. Christopher. Christopher and others involved in putting together *Grace Beats Karma* deserve great credit for a remarkable new look at Cassady, remarkable also in that it comprises virtually a third of all of Cassady's written output.

The Letters of William S. Burroughs, 1945-1959
edited by Oliver Harris

In another letters collection, *The Letters of William S. Burroughs* ($25; Viking, Penguin Books USA, 375 Hudson Street, New York, NY 10014), Burroughs looks at conspiracy more from the micro-management level, asserting that "it's like there's this vast, Kafkian conspiracy to prevent me from ever getting off junk". He calls Cassady "the very soul of this voyage into pure, abstract meaningless motion...ready to sacrifice family, friends, even his very car itself to the necessity of moving from one place to another", but this is as close as he comes to a compliment. His derogatory comments, however, include the insightful observation that Cassady "lacks any clear notion of how he appears to others". Later advice to Cassady from Burroughs, to stop his race-track betting, went unheeded, and after losing a fortune on the horses, one of Cassady's girlfriends committed suicide.

Many of these letters cover familiar territory, including Burroughs' life in Tangier and the development of the routines that later comprised *Naked Lunch,* although he seems surprisingly repelled by the products of his imagination in the early letters. The correspondence also reveals the removal as "irrelevant" of several *Naked Lunch* pages that include material on orgonomy-founder Wilhelm Reich, whose social and political theories Burroughs eschews (lauding instead a noxious red-bater named Westbrook Pegler) while calling Reich's work on cancer "of incalculable importance". While the work is still important and still obscure, Burroughs remains one of the great examples of the efficacy of the orgone accumulator.

Even though it covers well-known biographical episodes, such as the search for the yage hallucinogen and travels to Paris, London, Rome and Venice, and contains many familiar characters (Kerouac, Ginsberg, Cassady and Reich, but also Paul Bowles, Brion Gysin, Lawrence Ferlinghetti) Burroughs' great wit and sardonicism emerge here in more direct detail than anywhere else. Ted Morgan's *Literary Outlaw* would make a good companion book to read along with *Letters 1945-1959*, as would the *At The Front* anthology by Jennie Skerl and Robin Lydenberg, to which the editor of this volume, Oliver Harris, contributed. A second volume is planned and Burroughs is working on a new novel scheduled for a June 1994 release, as well as a memoir entitled *Evil River* (perhaps with the recent tumultuous Midwestern floods in mind?). Meanwhile, Grove Press has produced a color-coordinated trilogy of *Naked Lunch, The Ticket That Exploded* and *The Soft Machine* ($8.95 ea.; Grove Press, 841 Broadway, New York, NY 10003-4793).

Another Beat-oriented work good for a quick chuckle is *Growl & Other Poems* by David Shevin ($6.95; Carpenter Press, POB 14387, Columbus, Ohio 43214), which anthologizes the imagined poetry of the pets of great English writers, unfortunately mostly not the Beats. It includes the mystic insight of Ginsberg's dog, Solomon, "I saw the best mutts of my germination destroyed by badness...leashed along through the burbs at dawn looking for an empty lawn". On an utterly disconnected side note, the publishers also make available a book on the possibly hoaxed death of John Dillinger, *The Dillinger Dossier* by Jay Robert Nash ($12.50).

Extra-terrestial Friends and Foes
by George Andrews
Saucers of The Illuminati **by Jay Katz**
The Book of the Law **by Aleister Crowley**
Reich studies advanced a bit with two new books from IllumiNet, the Georgia-based publisher whose wares should engage deeply the interest of anyone wanting to explore the depths of alien-related conspiracy thinking. Although both books provide cogent overviews of this sort of mondo-theorizing, both also should appeal to audiences already up-to-speed and eager for details.

George C. Andrews, in *Extra-terrestrial Friends and Foes* ($14,95; IllumiNet Press, POB 2808, Lilburn, GA 30226) devotes an entire chapter to the "The Martyrdom of Wilhelm Reich", characterizing Reich's death in prison and the slandering of his work as "insane" because of its UFO component, as "specious and odious". The chapter provides a brief review of Reich's UFO work, and makes new connections between Reich's term for UFOs, "Ea", and a Babylonian god of the same name that may have been the basis for the Hebrew god Jehovah. This is a synchronistic analysis, of course, and Andrews does not suggest this was Reich's intent. By synchronicity also, Andrews relates anecdotes of recent saucer sightings involving *melanor,* an ash that Reich associated with UFO activity. The examples came to Andrews via newsclips as he was preparing the Reich chapter for *Extra-terrestrial Friends and Foes,* so he included them *in media res*.

Such a synchronistic organization scheme is both the flaw and the saving grace of Andrew's writing style. Andrews is a ufologist of some reputation, collecting enormous amounts of information to help him catalog and describe a variety of extra-terrestrial visitors, the ubiquitous greys as well as other benign and hostile off-earth presences that, he posits, interacts with mankind. The information—including information on Andrews himself—spins out like a spider web. The web's main arteries include a catalog of different types of aliens, speculation about their various agendas and examination of related phenomena like abductions and government cover-up. In between, however, are lesser threads that also tell a lot, like what happened to Gary Stollman, who put a BB gun to consumerist David Horowitz and forced him to read a statement on alien clones; and more support for the notion that Gordon Novel was the Umbrella Man in Dealey Plaza. While pursuing its main themes, *Extra-Terrestrial Friends and Foes* is packed with quantas of information, rumors, speculation, obscure facts, that really make it a page-turner to the end.

Whereas Andrews takes as a given the existence of the various extra-terrestrials, *Saucers of the Illuminati* ($10; IllumiNet; 8.5x11 spiral bound) presents author Jay Katz's critical view of the notion that flying saucers come from outer space. Katz offers a Freemasonic conspiracy as the source. "It is verifiable that Masons and their allied secret societies are hardwired into the corridors of control of government and intelligence agencies," argues Katz, "comprising a level of unseen motive and hidden intention". Katz' chapter of Reich, "Suppressed Tech" repeats speculation that

Reich's last work may have been smuggled out of prison and charges the American College of Orgonomy, founded to carry on Reich's work, with being a front for the Knights of Malta, attempting to "discourage or co-opt any independent interest in Reich's scientific legacy". *Saucers of the Illuminati* also directs criticism at the "gosh wow aliens are among us" people and at the panoply of widely known ufologists such as John Lear and Bill Cooper who apparently maintain ties with the intelligence communities. The book pursues its thesis through an examination of Philip K. Dick (previewed in the last issue of *Steamshovel Press)* and also relies heavily on the work of James Shelby Downard and Michael Hoffman. *Saucers of the Illuminati* is a thoughtful analysis and a fine addition to the anti-Masonic literature.

These two heavy-weight IllumiNet offerings should not obscure an Aliester Crowley cassette also available from the publisher. *The Book of the Law* ($9.95) was originally channelled to Crowley by an alien named Aiwass and here it is re-interpreted by Steven Ashe and Carolyn Hucker.

Bob Dylan, Performing Artist
by Paul Williams

The second volume of Paul Williams' *Bob Dylan, Performing Artist,* like the first, is a highly subjective work. In fact, Williams seems to regard the subjectivity of his text as its principle virtue. He tells in his preface:

"The idea of 'explaining a performance' is, in a real sense, absurd. What we can attempt to examine, however, is the experience of the observer, the listener, the person who is moved by the performance. If this can be described, however imperfectly, then we have the beginning of a common reference point for discussion of Dylan's work."

Happily Williams' survey offers a considerable amount of information about Dylan's work, in addition to telling us how Williams "feels" about Dylan's performances; for his thesis is in error on two counts. First, Williams' idea that he can describe what he feels as an observer is no less absurd than the idea that someone can explain what Dylan does in a performance. But the more blatant fallacy concerns the fact that Williams would have Dylan's admirers use his description of his personal response to Dylan as their "common reference point": it is Dylan's work, not Williams', that has potential to serve as a common reference point, for Americans and for people of other nations; and this is not brought out by Williams' text.

At one point, while comparing his views about a particular song to the views of another dylanologist named Clinton Heylin, Williams is so carried away by his notion of the importance of his enterprise as to remark that, "...history is made up of nothing more or less than the opinions of Heylin and me and the newspaper reviewers...etc..." Perhaps he meant to say "the historical record" rather than "history" is made up of opinion; but his book ignores, and almost obliterates, that fact that Bob Dylan, the man whose name appears as the title of his book, is an important historical figure. The closest Williams comes to speaking of Dylan's place in history is near the end of the book, where he speculates in passing that a particular song is the sort of song that would enable Dylan to "set the world on fire again". However, Williams does not offer a clue about what he means by this statement.

Williams' repeated insistence in both the first and second volumes of his text that the sounds Dylan has produced are all important, and that the words of his songs and their meaning are not so important, is perverse. So are his interpretations of the lyrics of some of Dylan's songs. He informs us several times that he does not share Dylan's faith in Jesus, and Jesus's power to save sinners from Hell; but Williams' skepticism should not inhibit him from seeing, for example, that in the song "Dark Eyes" Dylan is surely singing about the end of the world and the damned, as well as about his relationship with a woman. Williams' interpretation of this one song would hardly matter if it were not that he fails to discover the religious content of other songs as well, in this and the preceding volume. Williams speaks respectfully of Dylan's avowal of Christianity, but he does not seem to see that what enabled Dylan to "set the world on fire" in the 1960s may have been the way he brought the ideas preserved by the Judeo-Christian tradition to bear on a number of issues of burning interest at the time.

The volume concerns *The Middle Years: 1974-1986,* so Williams can be excused for not entering into an extended discussion of the 60s and the peace movement in this book; but he barely acknowledges Dylan's importance as a historical figure in the first volume either, which covers *The Early Years: 1962-1973.* Williams might defend himself by saying that he is not a historian, and that the history of the peace movement is not his subject; however, his disregard for the subject of Dylan's role as "the spokesman of his generation" and "the prophet of the peace movement," combined with his advice against the logic of Dylan's words, undermines his contribution to Dylan studies.

—Jenny Ledeen

Things Are Gonna Slide

Waco Revelations

The major media and mainstream pundits have all but forgotten the fiery destruction of the ninety-plus members of the Branch Davidian at the "Ranch Apocalypse" compound in Waco, Texas on April 19, 1993. Alternative sources, however, have only just begun to examine the event, attempt to resolve some of the contradictions news reports posed and present a truer picture of what actually happened.

Early among these was *Incite Information,* a small political newsletter published by libertarian Mark Hand out of Washington, DC (six issues/one year: $10; POB 326, Arlington, VA 22210). Its July-August issue includes "Licensed to Slaughter, An Examination of Governmental Crimes in Waco" by John Dingell III, which reviews the actions of the Bureau of Alcohol, Tobacco and Firearms personnel that led to the deadly blaze. In addition to noting a failed BATF raid in Tulsa, Oklahoma, two years ago, done under a sealed court order like Waco and failing to uncover any illegal arms as intended, Dingell lists information that has since become regarded as only the most obvious of BATF's *faux pas*. The BATF concocted the notion, for instance, that Ranch Apocalypse had a methamphetamine lab on its premises, as a legal excuse to engage National Guard helicopters, which can only be used in drug cases. Despite official pronouncements to the contrary, David Koresh could have been picked up nightclubbing or shopping at any point, making the raid unnecessary.

Dingell's report is not without its contradictions, however. He criticizes the Tulsa media of being in on the 1991 raid enough to have the cameras rolling as it happened, like Waco, and of not being there at all. He also reports that the Waco raid began when "an *unarmed* BATF agent shot himself accidentally" (italics added) and BATF agents in front "who could not see the accidental discharge" responded to the noise it made with gunfire, thinking they were under attack by the Branch Davidians. Dingell notes, however, that the BATF was armed with sound-suppressed H&K MP-5SD submachine guns.

"Licensed to Slaughter" is nevertheless supported in its broad strokes by a series of articles that have appeared on various computer BBs by Linda Thompson (America Justice Federation, 3850 S. Emerson Avenue, Suite E, Indianapolis, Indiana 46203; 317-780-5204). Thompson and her partner John Baird filed a petition to have Koresh represented by counsel while he was alive and trapped in the compound, one of eight such petitions (another perhaps filed by Mark Lane) denied by the court. Thompson's initial reports documented BATF and FBI abuse of the press, including her group's deliberate attempt to cross a road block inside the press area around the Waco compound to make First and Fourth amendment challenges to the expected arrests.

That attempt ended with the release of Thompson, Baird and a compatriot later discovered to be a paid government informant, being released without charges but slandered in the press as having been arrested for phony press ID. The one souvenir Thompson retained was a photograph of a BATF agent pointing a MP5 machine gun at them, safety off.

In the aftermath of the Waco conflagration, Linda Thompson's writings have expressed the extremes of anguish and frustration felt by many as official U.S. government authority openly murdered the Branch Davidians. "They are not glazed over moonie-type crazies", Thompson asserts of the survivors. "They are all well educated, articulate, very nice people. All of them had normal jobs outside the Mt. Carmel Center. None of them believed they were under David Koresh's 'control'". She ascribes the charges of child molestation at the compound as all originating from Mark Breault, a rival prophet ousted from the Branch Davidian who was hired by the ex-husband of a Branch member to make the allegations during a custody battle. Thompson also blames the false accusations on pressure from the Cult Awareness Network, headed by the wife of Leo Ryan, the congressman slain at Jonestown. As for the allegations of illegal firearms, Thompson writes, "No, it is not illegal to own a machine gun in this country. Even if the Branch Davidians had a machine gun, which it now appears they did not, if it was 'illegal' it merely meant that a $200 tax had not been paid on it. All it takes to legally own a machine gun in this country is to pay a $200 tax and fill out a form 4. The BATF is supposed to check that those taxes are paid."

Soldier of Fortune magazine repeats this observation, pointing out too that the warrant cites the legal definition of a "destructive device", not the legal prohibition of possessing one without payment of federal taxes, and has reported at length about other defects in the warrants used to begin the destruction at Waco. In the August 1993 issue of *SOF* writer James Pate explains of the arrest warrant that "Child abuse was only one of several innuendos...that were irrelevant to the two main crimes alleged against Koresh over which the ATF has jurisdiction, those being: the alleged conversion of assault rifles to permit full-automatic fire, and the alleged unlawful assembly of hand grenades and pipe bombs". Pate quotes a Washington, DC gun law attorney as being unequivocal that the affidavit did not show probably cause that Koresh and his followers had the necessary equipment and parts to make their weapons fully automatic. *SOF* also notes that in a sworn affidavit, one BATF agent claimed that Koresh made a statement that "the riots in Los Angeles would pale in comparison to what was going to happen in Waco", on April 6, 1992, three weeks prior to the LA riots.

Finally, the volume published by Feral House, *Secret and Suppressed* ($12.95, Feral House, POB 3466, Portland, OR 97208), contains an even more detailed view of the bungled BATF raid from Ken Fawcett, who, along with KGBS radio personality Ron Engleman, set up a satellite dish at Mt. Carmel. From the dish Fawcett videotaped an unedited newsfeed verifying the accidental weapons discharges described by Dingell, as well as a catalog of additional ATF offenses, including its "spray and pray" weapons discharges into the compound. Fawcett asserts that the video tape—as volatile as the Rodney King video if the mainstream media would take an interest—has been circulated for his protection. Linda Thompson may be one source to tap to get a copy. Feral House publisher Adam Parfrey reports that it's available for free according to *Williamette Week,* which ran an ad from a group initialed AFPL at POB 19691, Portland, OR 97280 offering it gratis under the title *Waco: The Big Lie.*

Parfrey also points out that Mark Richard, a top advisor to Janet Reno during the Waco ordeal, was instrumental in closing an investigation into the Edwin Walker/Libyan arms-sale scandal. Readers unfamiliar with Edwin Walker can look to the latest issue of *Back Channels* (POB 9, Franklin Park, NJ 00823) for a profile written by editor Peter Kross.

Parfrey also notes in the introduction to the *Secret and Suppressed* chapter on Waco that the affair gave police agencies ample opportunity to test new microwave weaponry. Linda Thompson has also pointed out sightings of trainloads of UN tanks going into Portland, Oregon. They were ostensibly returning from Somalia but a possible ominous intent seems obvious to anyone following the Waco story, certainly to one of the advertisers in *Williamette Week.*

On August 16, 1993 *USA Today* reported that the Treasury Department has conducted interviews with federal firearms officials about the BATF raid. Two officials plan to retire.

Thanks to Paul de Armond for information used in the above report.

Inslaw Revisited

A small portion of Danny Casolaro's Octopus work finally appeared in print, two years after the writer met an early death while embroiled in its research. The aforementioned *Secret and Suppressed* anthology, documenting the latest bad news in mind-control, power cabals, disinformation and the rest, includes a chapter entitled "Behold A Pale Horse: A Draft of Danny Casolaro's *Octopus* Manuscript Proposal", with an introduction by *Steamshovel Press* editor Kenn Thomas. The proposal is taken from a collection of Casolaro's notes for *The Octopus,* his fictionalized account of the Promis software double-dealing, the Cabazon murders, the Nugan Hand scandal, the October Surprise, etc. *Behold A Pale Horse,* Casolaro's first choice for the manuscript's title, echoes the title of William Milton Cooper's magnum UFOpus, interesting in that both writers had strong research interests in Area 51. Researcher Lars Hansson accused Cooper of plagiarizing the title from an earlier novel about gays, but all three actually follow the same inspiration: *Revelation* 6: 7-8.

The most significant new development on the Inslaw case, however, came in March when retired federal judge Nicholas J. Bua, appointed by then Attorney General William Barr to review the Inslaw allegations, filed a report with current AG Janet Reno clearing the Justice Department, the office for which he worked, of wrong-doing in the affair. News of the report did not surface until late May because, according to the *Washington Post,* it was being edited to take out information relevant to national security.

According to Bua, as reported by *St. Louis Post-Dispatch* reporters William Frievogel and Stephen Casmier in the *Post's* June 18, 1993 edition, the evidence was not sufficient to support the claim that the Justice Department, specifically Ed Meese crony Earl Brian, stole the Promis software from William and Nancy Hamilton and sold it illegally to police agencies around the world. Bua also apparently complimented Michael Riconosciuto's story-telling abilities ("a historical novel; a tale of total fiction woven against the background of historical facts") but poo-pooed his contention that he modified the software to give it a back-door access so its outlaw sellers could spy on its outlaw buyers. Bua also maintains that the removal from the bench of the judge who originally ruled in favor of Inslaw, George Bason, was only a coincidence; Bason was an inefficient administrator. Finally, according to Bua, Danny Casolaro committed suicide and there is no evidence that the Justice Department attempted to influence the investigation of his death.

Not mentioned in the report is the twenty-five million dollars Bua offered Elliot Richardson, attorney of Watergate fame now working for the Hamiltons, to settle the case—more than triple the amount awarded in the first federal ruling for Inslaw. Joel Bleifuss in the August 9 edition of *In These Times* offers these details, as well as highlights from the rebuttal to Bua's report. For instance, Bua failed to do a basic code comparison between Promis and the software currently being used by the FBI, instead relying on the expertise of a Georgetown University professor that such a comparison would be a waste of time. The Inslaw rebuttal also maintains that Bua's information on George Bason came in large part from Judge Roger Whelan, the judge from whom administrative problems were inherited by Bason, or so goes the House Judiciary Committee Testimony of U.S. District Chief Judge Aubrey Robinson. Whelan at the time also worked for AT&T, an Inslaw creditor.

Meanwhile, bodies continue pile up around the case. Jack Anderson was among the first to note that Casolaro wasn't the only person pulled into the murky depths by the tentacles of the Octopus when he reported on the mysterious death of British journalist Jonathan Moyle. Moyle was found hanged in his hotel room in Santiago, Chile after researching U.S. efforts to arm Saddam Hussein's Iraq before the Persian Gulf War, research that parallelled Casolaro's. Add to the mysterious death list the names of Ian Spiro and his family, who were found murdered in their San Diego home last November. Spiro reportedly worked for U.S. and British intelligence agencies and was talking to Casolaro informant Michael Riconosciuto up until a few days before his death, according to the March 1 edition of Liberty Lobby's *Spotlight*. Guenther Russbacher, another Riconosciuto contact, in prison now in part because of his claims that he flew George Bush to a Paris October Surprise meeting, reports now on the suspected murder of his *pro-bono* attorney, Paul Wilcher. According to Russbacher, he gave Wilcher videotape proof of his flight with Bush and shortly thereafter Wilsher was found dead on the toilet of his apartment. Details of the Russbacher/Wilsher story are available on a videotaped interview through Alex Horvat's Argus Research Foundation. The Argus Research Foundation also offers its newsletter, *The Probe,* for $20 annually at POB 1082, St. Charles, MO 63302.

Sherman Skolnick, long-time chairman of the Citizen's Committee to Clean Up the Courts, charges that nearly forty witnesses in the Inslaw case have been murdered and complained that Judge Bua failed to show concern over the safety of other witnesses. He also claimed that a Special Federal Grand Jury in Chicago planned to do an end-run around Bua and issue high-level indictments. Skolnick reported that three of the grand jury witnesses joined with Riconosciuto to

file suit against Bua for obstructing the indictments. Skolnick also charges that Bua had an FBI agent interrogating witnesses who was himself suspected of murdering Casolaro. The suit apparently included reference to Robert Booth Nichols, a Casolaro contact with alleged connections to U.S. intelligence as well as the Gambino crime family. On his popular Chicago phone-line (312-731-1100), Skolnick placed blame for the World Trade Towers explosion on Nichols, characterizing all the suspicion being cast on Arab terrorists as government race-bating in the search for enemies. *Newsday's* August 3, 1993 edition reports that one of the federal informants in that case, Emad Salem, surreptitiously recorded his conversations with federal agents that ostensibly show the FBI's role in instigating that plot.

Nichols' name appeared again as part of the legal blow-up between *Spy* magazine and actor Steven Seagal. Seagal filed a still-pending suit against *Spy* after it printed an article by John Connolly, who has done some of the most respected reporting on Inslaw, charging that the actor was involved in attempts to hire ex-intelligence agents to murder a former screenplay collaborator. One of Connolly's revelations is that Robert Booth Nichols had a cameo role in Stephen Seagal's movie, *Under Seige.* In the next issue of *Steamshovel Press,* researcher Lars Hansson discusses the Seagal controversy and its connection to his research project involving Bud Culligan, a man whose claims include having killed members of the JFK assassination team in Guatemala in 1965.

—Kenn Thomas

ADL Reviewed

In April 1993 police in San Francisco and Los Angeles seized evidence from the offices of the Anti-Defamation League suggesting that information in its files on nearly a thousand political activist groups, publications and unions had in part been illegally acquired from the police and had been sold to Mossad and South African intelligence. Authorities also released information concerning data collection methods of the ADL, including garbological analysis a la A.J. Weberman and the COINTELPRO-type infiltration of various Arab-American organizations, as well as activist groups from the left and the right. Because of his association with the ADL, the scandal eventually colored the reputation of researcher Chip Berlet, who has for years maintained files on extreme rightist, racist and anti-Semitic organizations, working diligently to expose them to the world at large. Berlet has been among the critics of assassination researchers, most notably L. Fletcher Prouty, for their connections to right wing groups. In May, Steamshovel Press *editor*

Kenn Thomas exchanged letters on the ADL scandal with Daniel Brandt, director of Public Information Research (POB 5199, Arlington, VA 22205). PIR maintains Namebase, *a database on international intelligence, foreign policy, assassinations and cliques of the full political spectrum. Following is a review of the ADL scandal, with citations, taken from that correspondence.—KT*

The ADL connection of Berlet is shown in the 5/13/93 issue of *Village Voice.* The same article includes a sidebar that shows how Dennis King, a colleague of Berlet, was a one-time paid agent for the ADL. King's book on LaRouche contains acknowledgements (Dennis King, *Lyndon LaRouche and the New American Fascism,* Doubleday) thanking the ADL, and acknowledging funding from the Smith-Richardson Foundation, which has CIA links (see: Friedman, John S., "Public TV's CIA Show", *The Nation,* 7/19-26/80) and the League of Industrial Democracy (ditto; Group Watch, published by the Resource Center, Box 4506, Albuquerque, NM 87196, offers a file on LID stating that its "pro-labor activities took on a different slant when the group became involved with the CIA in efforts to combat communism"). The ADL connection of Berlet himself is reiterated in *Israeli Foreign Affairs* (Vol. IX, No. 4, 5/11/93) and also in a deposition by Herb Quinde of the LaRouche organization (filed in the Commonwealth of Virginia, County of Loudon, 1/20/92).

In addition to the ADL connection, it can be shown that Berlet's tactics for collecting information are dubious. An article in *Forward* on 1/22/93 quotes Berlet bragging about infiltrating a meeting by posing as a racist. In Berlet's *Right Woos Left* (Political Research Associates, 7/28/92), he mentions posing as a paper recycler to get trash from an abandoned LaRouche office, which resulted in an investigation into LaRouche financial improprieties by the state attorney. His methods, in other words, are identical to the methods of ADL spy Roy Bullock. Webster defines "spy" as "one who acts in a clandestine manner or on false pretenses to obtain information usually for hostile purposes", so it's perfectly valid to consider Berlet a spy.

There are also some curious items about Berlet and Political Research Associate (PRA) that are not covered in Berlet's official PRA biography. One has to do with the fact that Berlet worked for the National Student Association from 1973 to at least 1975, and was apparently on good terms with Ed Schwartz, who appears to have been witting of the CIA connection to NSA before it was exposed by *Ramparts* in 1967 (see: Hinckle, Warren, *If You Have a Lemon, Make Lemonade,* W. W. Norton & Company).

Another is the fact that PRA lists the Beacon Fund as one of their donors in their Ten Year Report, and has stonewalled my efforts to determine if this is the same as the CIA conduit by the same name that was exposed in 1967 (and which was part of the NSA funding apparatus).

The money behind PRA is also curious. PRA executive director Jean Hardisty, Ph.D., gave over a quarter million of her own money over the past five years, but another substantial contributor is Chicago commodities trader Richard J. Dennis, through his Chicago Resource Center. Dennis is a major contributor to the Democratic Party (see: *Washington Post,* "The Federal Page," 3/8/93), and to a lesser extent so is Hardisty, leading the National Alliance Party to speculate that PRA's assigned task is to attack populist third party movements that threaten the Republocrat system (Salit, Jacquelin and Frank Solomon, "It's Beginning To Look A Lot Like Chip Berlet Works With The Cops," *The National Alliance,* 12/24/92). Meanwhile, PRA's literature sales are puny next to the Hardisty-Dennis contributions ($4148 on the 1991 Form 990), which certainly raises the question of just who they think they are representing.

The ADL situation leaves Berlet very vulnerable to criticism on the basis of his private cooperation with ADL (see also: Cockburn, Alexander, "The ADL Spy Probe," *The Nation,* 5/31/93), because at the same time he publicly criticizes groups like Public Information Research for allowing Fletcher Prouty on our advisory board (Brandt, Daniel, "An Incorrect Political Memoir," *Lobster,* 12/24/92; *Lobster,* 214 Westbourne Avenue, Hull HU5 3JB, UK). But beyond the question of hypocrisy, and the question of Berlet's methods of collecting information raised above, there is a deeper question of why Berlet has appointed himself a Thought Policeman of the New World Order. The hints of a possible intelligence connection to Berlet, as suggested above, and particularly as represented in: 1. the Quinde deposition; and 2. Berlet's long-standing relationship with Dennis King, invite some serious questions. His recent role as a critic of conspiracy theories (Berlet, Chip, "Big Stories, Spooky Sources", *Columbia Journalism Review,* 5-6/93) and of all associations between Right and Left, seems designed to defeat an emerging populism and anti-elitism that looks suspiciously at the two-party system. It's not a Left-Right problem we're dealing with, but a Top-Bottom problem. The populists know this, but the so-called "progressive" Left apparently hasn't received the message.

—Daniel Brandt

The ADL debate has continued in the pages of

Tikkun, the New York Times *and* The Nation. *A full defense written by Chip Berlet and Dennis King appeared in the July/August issue of* Tikkun. *Chip Berlet also admitted that a "subtle intolerance" affected the ADL in the 1970s and further criticizes the group in an Op-Ed piece, also written with Dennis King, in the* New York Times *on May 28. Berlet characterized the ADL leadership as having a "racist double standard for monitoring prejudice" in a letter response to Warren Commission defender Alexander Cockburn in the 8/23-30 issue of* The Nation, *explaining his attempts at bringing up "principled criticisms of the ADL that avoid...unfounded conspiracism found in the LaRouchians'* New Federalist, *the Liberty Lobby's* Spotlight *and the New Alliance Party's* National Alliance".—KT

JFK Files Released

Media hoopla over the JFK assassination began again in August with the release of the Lopez report and other documents as part of the Assassination Materials Review Act of 1992. As noted by Carl Oglesby in *Steamshovel Press Number 7,* the Lopez report was commissioned by the House Select Committee on Assassinations to determine the veracity of allegations that Oswald visited foreign embassies in Mexico City. Some researchers came to believe that Oswald spent as much time in Mexico City as he did on the sixth floor of the Texas Book Depository (that is, none at all). The 400-plus page report, written by investigator Edwin Lopez but not available even to him before this release, provides a detailed account of which claims about the Mexico City scenario have merit, which are bogus, and it makes some interesting new claims, all of which have been distorted to unrecognizable dimensions by the new wave of media interest.

The best place to get the real scoop on the Lopez report, and a worthy cause to support in general, is the Assassination Archives and Research Center. Center director Jim Lesar was in evidence in the newspapers and on television during this recent flap doing his best to ask questions that reveal the importance of the report. Was it Oswald at the Cuban embassy in Mexico City? Was it Oswald some of the time and someone else some of the other time? Was one of the ostensible contacts of Oswald, Sylvia Duran, an intelligence agent? AARC makes a full copy of the report available for $55 to its members and for a slightly higher fee for non-members. It costs a tax-deductible $25 a year to join AARC at 918 F Street NW, Room 510, Washington DC 20004, 202-393-1917.

Moreover, Lesar makes several good points that went virtually unreported: the overwhelming majority of documents covered by the Assassinations Material

Review Act have not yet been transferred to the National Archives. The FBI has not turned over a single page. The CIA is withholding 160,000 pages in violation of the law. Also, why has President Clinton's administration only now after long delay appointed just five of the six-member review board as required by the Act? The delay is unconscionable as the Assassination Materials Review Act gives the board only two years to complete its business.

According to Lesar, the review board has two fundamental decisions to make: 1. to determine what actually constitutes an assassination record (by late September the definition had included over 275 transcripts of Lyndon Johnson's phone conversations during the weeks following the assassination held by the Johnson library in Austin); and 2. to review the withholdings made by the various agencies to determine if more information should be released. AARC plans to produce a regular newsletter to report upon developments with the Assassinations Material Review Act and to help pursue and promote legal redress for the assassination, although Lesar is skeptical of calling for a special prosecutor for all the reasons noted in *Steamshovel Press Number Eight.* The effort for such a call, also as noted last issue, has not developed into anything formal, according to Carl Oglesby, the assassination scholar conscripted as its chair. Oglesby is still open to discuss it, though, at 617-876-6558 or through the mail 294 Harvard Street #3, Cambridge, Massachusetts 02139.

The thirtieth anniversary of the assassination is otherwise being met with the usual plethora of good and bad books. The most interesting of the former category include the memoir of Marita Lorenz and a book by HSCA investigator Gaeton Fonzi, both unavailable at press time for review. Unfortunately, the chief "bad" category book, *Case Closed* by Gerald Posner, is only too available, having been excerpted in *US News and World Report.* The book is a compendium of obfuscation, easily defeated "medical" evidence (especially with regard to the single-bullet theory), and other widely disseminated disinformation that even non-researchers and non-buffs should readily laugh off.

Posner even offers the Umbrella Man-as-Neville Chamberlain-protest theory in all seriousness, calling the umbrella a widely understood protest symbol. Readers of *National Review* during that time may have understood it, as the magazine often used the umbrella symbol when it perceived appeasement to the Soviets on some foreign policy issue. It is just as likely, however, that *National Review* used its intelligence community contacts to get an Umbrella Man on Elm as an advertisement as it is that he was finally taking his stand on Joseph Kennedy's support of Neville Chamberlain! Strangely, use of the Umbrella Man symbol at the *National Review* stopped after the assassination, an event described by the magazine at the time as an "awesome and splendid ritual of death." In a note to Gus Russo, JFK researcher Bob Harris summed up the career of *The National Review*'s William Buckley succinctly: "CIA official in Tokyo and Mexico City (sound familiar?); worked under Allen Dulles for years: first man brought to Mexico City by Howard Hunt...in 1950 as Nazi exiles are formed into U.S. assets...1952-3 assists in creation of H. L. Hunt's 'Facts Forum'; family money overlaps with Rockefeller's Socony Mobil; founded National Review; family owned Pantepac Oil, employers of George DeMohrenschildt. Coudert Brothers, Buckley family law firm, represented Schlumberger Corp., several members OAS, and the Nazi occupational Vichy government."

Harris, by the way, has been involved along with Jane Rusconi, Director of Research for the Oliver Stone movie, in creating a CD-ROM hypertext including the complete Warren Commission and HSCA reports and hordes of other data. Entitled *ZCI Encyclopedia of the JFK Assassination (Who Shot JFK?)*, ($29.95), the disc will be made available by ZCI Publishing, The Informat, 1950 Stemmons, Suite 6048, Dallas, TX 75207-3109. It was unavailable at press time but will be reviewed in the next issue of *Steamshovel*. (No comment on Gus Russo's current research efforts.)

In any event, Posner was recently caught up short in his arguments on *Crossfire* by Cyril Wecht, although the supposedly widely divergent views of Michael Kinsley and John Sununu once again coincided with the verdict of "no conspiracy".

Although it breaks little new ground, Shapolsky Books does currently offer a good current review of the assassination by James R. Duffy ($14.95; Shapolsky Publishers, Inc., 136 West 22nd Street, New York, NY 10011) entitled *Who Killed JFK?* It includes an introduction by Senator Alfonse D'Amato and high praise from Mafia-did-it theorists David Scheim and John H. Davis. Another Shapolsky offering, *The Mafia, CIA & George Bush* by Pete Brewton, follows the Mafia link through the Bush presidency with thorough analysis and documentation. Yet another Shapolsky offering, *The Crimes of President,* by Joel Bainerman ($5.50) not only further documents the criminal abuses of the Bush administration—including the almost utterly hushed-up Iran-contra related plane crash in Gander, Newfoundland in 1985—but also contains an entire chapter on the story of Bill Clinton's cover-up of the drugs-and-gun running operation at the airstrip in Mena, Arkansas. Shapolsky offers also a less convincing book entitled *Target America: Terrorism in the U.S. Today* ($5.99) by Yossef Bodansky, which seems designed to appeal to the same Arab-bashing mentality the American state seems to want to encourage.

—Kenn Thomas

Recommended Zine Reading

It remains one of the funnier, gossip-ridden rags of ufology, but Jim Mosely's *Saucer Smear* doesn't go out to the Preterite. "Dedicated To The Highest Principles of Ufological Journalism", *Saucer Smear* (POB 1709 Key West, FL 33041) pokes at some of the more glaring improbabilities among UFO claims, but it has sense enough to report at face-value the work of abductee claimant David Huggins, whose art depicts the hybrids resulting from his liaisons with alien women in the presence of insectoid voyeurs. Mosely will take love offerings but makes no guarantees that he will add to a subscription base that already costs him money.

Wes Nation's *Crash Collusion* ($3.50; POB 492333, Austin, TX 78765), a dynamite combination of reflections on UFOs and psychedelics, should have another issue available by the time this issue of *Steamshovel* hits the stands.

UFO Magazine ($3.95; POB 1053, Sunland, CA 91041-1053) has a new issue and its best article, "The Secret Life of Fred L. Crisman" by Anthony L. Kimery is squirreled away in the back. Kimery reports on a Puget Sound harbor patrol officer involved with the investigation of the 1947 Maury Island UFOs, which left a *melanor*-like substance over a large area. Crisman may have been involved with Operation Paper Clip, the government project to absorb Nazi scientists and engineers into U.S. intelligence. Jim Garrison subpoened Crisman in connection with the JFK assassination!

—Kenn Thomas

7

Steamshovel Press #10, 1994

Dave Emory Interviewed
by Kenn Thomas

Q: Dave Emory is a current event analyst and a person who is heard weekly on a radio program called *One Step Beyond* in the Santa Clara Valley. Dave also has another program called *Radio Free America* and his programs are available through a service called *Archives on Audio*. Dave, thanks for being with us tonight. I would like to talk a little bit more about what exactly you do on your program for those readers who haven't heard it.

A: I began the form of radio documentary that I do in 1984 in which I take research material and read it into the record and provide analytical discussion so that listeners could tape the programs and then use them as an audio study resource. People don't have a lot of time for reading. I do a great deal of it and I have access to a lot of comparatively rare source materials. So I do that as a public service. There's also a program called *Radio Free America* which began in 1987. It's run by the Sun radio Network and the Liberty Lobby, which I am not only not connected with but am fiercely opposed to. So please do not ever confuse the two names. I did not copyright the name. They used it three years later but mine is the original and, as far as I'm concerned, as the old rhythm and blues songs says, still the greatest.

Q: We won't confuse the two. Let's talk about fascism and its connection to political assassinations and maybe we can get back to talking about the Liberty Lobby. Dave has been an active worker in researching and exposing the connections between political assassinations in this country and the rise of fascism. He has traced the Kennedy assassination to forces that are connected to Nazis and other fascist groups. Is there more of an interest in this kind of thing now that this wave of Japan bashing has set in with Jack Anderson's new book and the *Rising Son* movie out?

A: I have not noticed any particular increase in interest in this kind of material because of that. I can't say that there isn't, but I have not noticed anything. I do think it's worth noting that the interests which dominate corporate Japan at this time, the so-called Zibatsu, the family trusts—Mitsui, Mitsubishi, Yasada and Sumitomo—are the main corporate interests which were behind, along with the imperial general staff, the rise of fascism in Japan in the pre-World War II and World War II period. I would note that many of those corporations, the Zibatsu, had links with American corporations and that many American corporations not only supported and did business with Japanese fascism but also supported and did business with Hitler and Mussolini. Names like Ford Motor Company, General Motors, ITT, Dupont, Standard Oil of New Jersey, Texaco, International Harvester. These are companies that actively did business with Nazi Germany and Mussolini's Italy and many of them not only supported or did business with the fascist powers of Europe but actually supported Hitler and Mussolini politically.

So as we analyze fascism we should note that the forces which generated it are major corporations which are very much dominant in all of the societies that exist today. The corporations which brought fascism to Germany and Japan are still very much in business in those countries. The corporations in this country which were supportive of fascism are the dominant elements in this country today.

Fascism is not something which is an aberration. It was not the result of some lone nut, Adolph Hitler or Mussolini, hypnotizing people. There is a very disturbing and very destructive tendency in our political culture to ascribe broad and very significant political forces to the actions of lone nuts. Perhaps Hitler could be referred to as the first lone nut.

In analyzing the pop view of fascism, which is that Hitler made 'em do it, one might almost use an Elmer Fudd accent: "Once upon a time, there was a vewy bad man named Adolf Hitler who hypnotized aaaall the Germans, made 'em aaaall go cwazy and den dey had a big war called World War II, and it was vewy, vewy bad but along came de Allies and dey beat dat ol' Adolf Hitler and de war came to an end and evewy body wived happiwy ever after! Or dey would have lived happiwy ever after but along came a vewy bad man named Joseph Stalin. Hypnotized aaall the Wussians. Made 'em all go cwazy." Again, it's attributing a very significant and broad-based political and social phenomenon to the action of a single individual.

Q: Could you give us a working definition of fascism?

A: Fascism as defined by Mussolini, who was the first fascist and who coined the term, is corporatism. Now Mussolini was operating on a couple of different levels. I am going to telescope things due to the limits of time here, so this might seem a little bit facile to some people. But on the one hand, Mussolini set up what he called the corporate state. The idea was to set up a country in which things were arranged in such a way as to benefit the corporations. Now when Mussolini spoke about corporations, as in his book *The Corporate State,* put out by Velecci publishers of Florence in 1938, when he talked about corporations he was referring to something that we might better term trusts or monopolies. Each major area of industrial manufacturing was grouped together in what might be termed a trust or a monopoly. In those trusts or monopolies there were the corporations involved in the manufacturing of the various goods in that field, but the idea was to organize a society in such a way as to benefit the corporations. The theory was that if the corporations prospered, the wealth and the prosperity would trickle down to everybody else, the middle class, the shopkeepers and the workers, would all benefit as the wealth was spread around.

In a very real sense, the corporate state of Mussolini operates on the same philosophical principle, or pretended to operate the same philosophical principle, as supply-side economics, or what George Bush, in a rare moment of lucidity termed "voodoo economics". The idea behind supply-side economics was that if the wealthy and the corporations had their taxes cut and were able to reap more capital then they would plow the capital back into the industrial process, expanding the industrial base with prosperity for all, and everybody, to go back to the Elmer Fudd accent, "Will wive happiwwy ever afta!"

Well, it didn't actually work that way. As we know, Ronald Reagan came into office with a national debt of nine hundred billion dollars. It was 2.6 trillion when he left. He almost tripled it. Then smilin' George put another 1.4 trillion on top of that. When he left office, the national was debt was 4 trillion dollars. It did not work at all. George Seldes, viewed by many as the dean of American investigative reporters and an individual whose work on the history and de-

velopment of fascism is absolutely vital, also an individual who is one of my personal role models, in describing Mussolini's corporate state described it as a "spoil system". The idea was that the wealth did not trickle down. The rich got richer and anybody who complained either got their head smashed or was killed by the *fascisti*. That, I think is analogous to what is going on today.

Q: I don't imagine that you recognize that much of a distinction between the major parties.

A: There are some significant differences but they are not nearly as significant as they should be. It's fairly well known that the same corporate interests finance both the Republican and Democratic parties so that they basically have a foot in each camp. No matter who wins they're in a position to dip their stubby little fingers knuckle deep into the pie.

Q: There has been a lot of debate over the Kennedy assassination since Oliver Stone's movie. Noam Chomsky and Alexander Cockburn have led the charge pointing to JFK as the person who created or escalated the war in Vietnam and who is representative of the same kind of powered interests. If that is the case, why was he assassinated?

A: I do not think much of either Alexander Cockburn or Noam Chomsky. Both have done some good work, however both are also not only individuals who blame the Vietnam war on Kennedy, which is simply ridiculous, and both individuals also endorse the Warren report. Alexander Cockburn endorsed Warren Commission counsel David Belin's view of that. There is a broadcast I did called "Observations on America's 116th Birthday" in which I read a letter from Noam Chomsky to a professional colleague of his, who gave me permission to read it on the air, in which he says, and I quote, "I can see no political forces which would have wanted to kill John Kennedy".

Chomsky, too, endorses the Warren report. Now the Warren report is simply fiction. It is not only wrong, but every one of its major contentions is physically impossible. It may be that Cockburn and Chomsky, who again have both done some good work, are simply too proud and too arrogant and also too entrenched as well-known and relatively successful progressive intellectuals, to admit that they have been wrong about anything. Pride has a great deal to do with intellectual reaction and intellectual culture is quite reactionary. At the same time, I think it is very important to realize how destructive those kinds of views are.

Now with regard to Vietnam, the notion that Kennedy "got us into Vietnam" is simply ignorant and both Cockburn and Noam Chomsky should know better. The fact of the matter is that Kennedy inherited an involvement in Southeast Asia, the genesis of which dates back to the second World War. During World War II the United States was a military ally of Ho Chi Minh and the Viet Minh. It's ironic that we ended up fighting Ho Chi Minh and that many American service men lost their lives there, because the Vietnamese guerilla forces in World War II, which fought the Japanese effectively and heroically, were trained by the U.S. Army Guerilla Warfare manual. It was given to them by operatives of the Office of Strategic Services, our World War II intelligence agency. The Vietnamese Declaration of Independence quotes at great length from our own.

We had advisors there in the 1950s. According to my own field work, our involvement there was much, much greater—and a number of observers have backed this up—was much, much greater than what the public was told. We had many more troops there than the seventeen thousand that were supposedly there as advisors when Kennedy was killed. And our involvement there dates well back before the Kennedy administration. So Kennedy actually inherited an on-going commitment in Vietnam. There's considerable controversy around some of the National Security Action memoranda that were issued during the Kennedy administration. Cockburn and Chomsky have both dissed the notion that NSA 263 and 273 represent respectively an order by Kennedy for a phased withdrawal from Vietnam and a reversal, a couple of days after Kennedy was killed, of his orders with scheduling of covert operations against North Vietnam and an escalation of the war.

Q: This is the thesis that John Newman has put forth in *JFK and Vietnam*.

A: Not only John Newman but before him many other people, including L. Fletcher Prouty, who was in charge of special operations for the joint chiefs of staff at the time that Kennedy was killed. He had drawn up the report upon which the recommendations made by Kennedy and then secretary of defense Robert McNamara, the actions in NSA 263, were based. Professor Peter Dale Scott of Berkeley, who I think merits serious consideration as the foremost political intellectual in America today, in a number of works has provided very detailed analysis of NSA memorandum 111 from November 22, 1961; NSA 249 from June 1963; NSA 263 from October '63; and NSA 273. I find his arguments and those of L. Fletcher Prouty and the aforementioned Major John Newman far more convincing. They are backed up by testimony from a number of Kennedy administration officials, including Arthur Schlesinger, former undersecretary of state for far eastern affairs Roger Hinsman, all of whom decry the Oliver Stone movie

among other things, but agree that Kennedy was in fact in the process of pulling us out of Vietnam.

Q: So you don't buy anything that Chomsky says that Schlesinger and Hinsman and these people have re-written history after the Tet offensive?

A: Well, the point is that I think that Chomsky himself is guilty of a fair amount of re-writing of history. In the personal letter that I alluded to, Chomsky admits that he has studied nothing, *none* of the record about Kennedy's assassination, but that he doesn't intend to do so because he finds the people interested in investigating Kennedy's assassination to be religious fanatics and does not consider them worth dealing with from an intellectual standpoint, which I think is rather hypocritical. His own analysis of the Kennedy assassination investigators would apply better to him than to them. He hasn't studied the record, he doesn't believe that there is anything to it. I think one should withhold one's opinion until one has examined the relevant information.

Going back to the "analysis" presented by Cockburn and Chomsky—and this is not to single them out as individuals but rather I think their viewpoint is representative of an intellectual viewpoint that needs to be very seriously considered and criticized from an intelligent and constructive standpoint. In order to put down just that one aspect of Oliver Stone's movie, which is backed up by analysis from such disparate parties as Arthur Schlesinger, Roger Hinsman, Colonel L. Fletcher Prouty, Major John Newman, Peter Dale Scott, all of whom are very, very different, with very different backgrounds and different motivations, what in effect that people like Cockburn and Chomsky and the others of that view are doing is that they are positing a conspiracy theory. They're saying that somehow all these people are conspiring to do—what? One of the things that they are supposedly doing is attempting to recapitulate some lost vision of Camelot. I have studied the Kennedy assassination among other things for the better part of twenty years and I've never heard anyone who considered Kennedy or his administration to be Camelot. Rather, the forces that destroyed John Kennedy considered him insufficiently vigorous in his pursuit of the Cold War. Those forces were explicitly fascist.

Q: There are those out there who accuse people like Fletcher Prouty of being connected to fascist elements. He's been connected to the Institute for Historical Review and Chip Berlet has written this thing "Right Woos Left" in which he tries to make a connection between all these people who don't fit so neatly in to the leftist perspective that's been carved out by mainstream people like Cockburn, Chomsky, etc., and tries to blacken their reputation

by their associations.

A: There has always been a tendency on the left to tar people with some sort of label: "You Stalinist, you!" or "You Trotskyite, you!" I don't think a whole lot of that viewpoint. I do think there is a need for intelligent, constructive criticism that should be made on the basis of the arguments presented.

Now with regard to Fletcher Prouty: he has had some dalliance with the Liberty Lobby, which I alluded to earlier. I think that's very tragic. I think that the progressive political sector itself bears some measure of responsibility for that.

The Liberty Lobby is making a considerable bid to co-opt a number of progressive issues, primarily by printing material on investigations relating to the national security establishment. There is a considerable degree of overlap between some of the things that the Liberty Lobby is looking into and some of the things that any serious investigator will look into, things like the Inslaw case, October Surprise, have been touched upon by the Liberty Lobby. Yet at the same time, when you examine the history of the Liberty Lobby, its founder Willis Carto and some of the other people involved with it, have documented involvement with the Institute for Historical Review, which denies the Holocaust happened. Willis Carto has gone on record as saying he felt we were on the wrong side in World War II, blaming World War II on the Jews. In the 1960s the Liberty Lobby used to open some of its meetings, according to some investigators, with the official song of the German Nazi party under Hitler. And they endorse people like David Duke, etc., and I think it would be quite fair to refer to the overall perspective of the Liberty Lobby as fascist.

Q: At the same time, it's extremely frustrating for researchers that the only information they can find, for instance, on Inslaw, is in the Liberty Lobby.

A: It is very important to take note of that phenomenon and also to understand what probably lies behind that. In the first place, I think that the investigation of many of these national security related scandals, such as the Kennedy assassination. leaves an observer in a relativistic political and philosophical universe. Once you understand that, in fact, Lee Harvey Oswald did not kill President Kennedy and Sirhan Sirhan did not kill Robert Kennedy, and that the official versions of so many of these cases are readily verifiable bald-faced lies, then it leaves people wondering, "Well, gee, maybe the Holocaust didn't happen". A recent poll found that as many as a third of Americans hold out the possibility that it did not. That leaves some in a state of relativism which plays right into the hand of those elements such as the Institute for Historical Review, which love to perpetuate the view that the Holocaust did not in fact happen.

Q: The utter failure of the major media to report accurately on any of these assassinations or stories leaves a vacuum that people try to fill any way they can.

A: Also the so-called "alternative" media for the most part stay away from these very same things. Many of the people who do work in investigating these national security related scandals want to get their information out and there are very few sources that will get it out. So they will both read and sometimes publish in something like the Liberty Lobby. Plus, in this line of work one does not make a lot of money generally speaking and if you can get paid for an article, hell, get paid for an article. In these days, when money is very tight, that will do it.

The progressive media itself bears a deep responsibility, though, for the relative success of the *Spotlight,* Liberty Lobby, etc., because they will not access this material to a considerable extent. Those progressive media forces occupy the same moral turf as the people in Nazi Germany who knew what was going on and did not speak up or act.

Q: Let's review a little of your research connecting the Kennedy assassination to the Reinhard Gehlen network.

A: One of the things that propelled me into committing my life to this type of research was the work I began doing in the early 1970s on the assassination of President Kennedy. It became very clear as the Watergate case unfolded that there was some very strong connecting links between the Watergate scandal and the investigation of the assassination of John Kennedy. As I moved from the Watergate scandal into an investigation of Kennedy's assassination, at the core of the Kennedy conspiracy, I came across both domestic and German Nazis and Eastern European fascists and fascist collaborators, which shocked me at first. I had no idea how such a thing came to be so I began studying history and what I came across at the core of John Kennedy's assassination were operatives who had served with the Reinhard Gehlen spy organization or had been involved in with the milieu during and after World War II.

Reinhard Gehlen had been Hitler's chief of intelligence for the eastern front in World War II. He headed an organization called *Frembe Heere Ost*, or Foreign Armies East. At the end of World War II, Gehlen and his entire organization jumped to the CIA and became in effect the CIA's department of Russian and eastern European affairs. They were sole purveyors of intelligence on the Soviet Union and eastern Europe to the CIA for the immediate post-World War

II period. They became the *de facto* NATO intelligence organization and ultimately in 1955 were incorporated into West Germany as the West German intelligence service, the *Bundesnachtrichtendiest*, or the BNB, which they are to this day.

The Gehlen organization paved the way for thousands of SS and Gestapo veterans to move up in to the US national security establishment, where a few of them remain to this day. Beyond that, it helped to provide the United States with a vastly distorted picture of Soviet aims and capabilities in the Cold War. The Gehlen organization did not operate in a vacuum in this regard. There were very powerful interests, very powerful corporate and financial interests as well as political and national security elements in this country, which were only too willing to hear the message that Gehlen had to provide.

In investigating the Kennedy assassination, I came across people associated with the Gehlen organization and the very closely related anti-Bolshevik block of nations or ABN. For example, when Lee Harvey Oswald returned from the Soviet Union to which he had supposedly defected with top secret information about the U2 spy plane and our radar nets, he was not only not charged with treason upon returning to the United States, which is simply ridiculous when you stop to think about it, he was met upon embarking by a fellow named Spas T. Raikin. Raikin had been the secretary general of the American Friends, the Anti-Bolshevik Block of Nations. He had been a prominent Bulgarian fascist prior to and during World War II. It should be remembered that Bulgaria, along with Hungary and Romania, were Eastern European allies of Nazi Germany. In addition to Germany, Japan and Italy, the Axis also incorporated Hungary, Romania and Bulgaria as well as Finland for a time.

In the Dallas/Fort Worth area also Oswald was handled by people associated with this Gehlen/ABN milieu. One of Oswald's intelligence handlers in the Dallas/Fort Worth area was a fellow named George De Morenschildt, nee George Von Morenschildt. His father had managed the Baku oil fields for the Nobel family in Czarist Russia. DeMorenschildt had been arrested on suspicion of spying for Nazi Germany during World War II. He had worked very closely for a time with Baron Constantine Maydell. Maydell had for a time been in charge of all *Abwehr* activities in North America, the *Abwehr* being German military intelligence in North America.

One of the other handlers of the Oswalds in the Dallas/Fort Worth area, an individual who was involved with the interrogation of Marina Oswald after the assassination, was a fellow named Igor Vashinin, who according to Peter Dale Scott was affiliated with

an organization with an organization called the NTS, that is the National Toilers Alliance or Solidarists. It was a group of White Russians or Czarist Russians, who saw the armies of the Third Reich as their ticket back into the Soviet Union. They sought a restoration of the old Russian empire and a political alliance with Nazi Germany. The NTS spied for Nazi Germany during World War II and worked with it and then jumped to the CIA, or US intelligence, along with the Gehlen organization, and they were an element for a time of the Anti-Bolshevik Block of Nations.

In examining the Kennedy assassination at the operational level, one come across links between graduates of the Gehlen spy organization and the Anti-Bolshevik Block of Nations working with sympathetic elements of our own political and national security establishment and domestic American fascists as well. George Lincoln Rockwell's name and address were in Lee Harvey Oswald's address book at the time of his arrest. No one has bothered to explain how the alleged Marxist Oswald, after having become a traitor to the United States and betraying American national security secrets to the Soviet Union, then came back to the United States and was never prosecuted for treason, promptly began trafficking around in a milieu involving the CIA's anti-Castro Cubans, aerospace and petroleum industry high rollers, ardently anti-Communist White Russians. Rather strange environment for an avowed Marxist to be trafficking in. Nobody has ever explained what George Lincoln Rockwell's Arlington, Virginia name and address were doing in Oswald's address book.

Q: These are sensible questions, just as they are when people bring up the notion, for instance, that the AIDS virus was caused by the Pentagon or that there may be something behind this disease that has been suffered by the Indians in New Mexico.

A: Yes. There has been an outbreak of an often fatal flu-like illness. It was initially noted in the Four Corners area in the American Southwest. It has now to a certain extent at least spread to Texas, Nevada and now apparently California. The illness is being blamed upon a virus called the Hanta virus, a virus which not incidentally has been a focus of U.S. Army biological warfare research for quite some time. There's a very important article in *Science Magazine* issue of June 11, 1993, discussing the Army's interest in the Hanta virus and its role in Army biological warfare research, terminated a few years ago because it supposedly was not bearing any fruit. But at least one researcher who is familiar with that program said it was a shame because the Hanta virus, which originally attracted the Army's attention because it produced Korean hemorrhagic fever, which killed some 400 GIs during the Korean war. That virus offered clear evidence of being a viable biological warfare agent. The article closes by noting that researchers may well decry the Army's termination of research because a vaccine to the Hanta virus may very well become necessary.

Biological warfare research was officially curtailed by Richard Nixon in 1969 except for "defensive" biological warfare research, a completely academic and fallacious distinction. There is no substantive difference between defensive and offensive biological warfare research. If you're developing a vaccine for "defensive" research, you still have to find out how the agent in question, whether a bacterium or a virus, infects its victims. So you wind up doing the same research anyway. There are substantive indications that biological warfare research has been carried on clandestinely and under civilian cover for quite some time. It is a matter of public record that biological warfare agents have been tested on unsuspected civilian population, including civilian populations in the United States. The U.S. and Britain, for example, have long conducted biological research on the populations of third world countries.

There is one account, which I am investigating, I have not confirmed this and this belongs in the category of what I like to refer to as "food for thought and grounds for further research", but there is at least one account that a military base near the Four Corners area, a place called Fort Wingate, had a biological warfare component associated with it. There were reports of suspicions on the part of some of the Navajos in the Four Corners area that perhaps some sort of agent had accidentally escaped from Fort Wingate. Now accounts on that differ. There was at least one broadcast account, at least one other news account that I have examined, maintains that Fort Wingate was closed in late 1992, that it was a munitions storage area. I do not know if there were any bacteriological agents stored there or whether the base was in fact closed or whether there is any relationship whatsoever between the allegations concerning Fort Wingate and the outbreak in the Four Corners area.

But given the fact, and this is a matter of record, at least according to *Science Magazine,* 6/11/93, the Hanta virus has been a focal point of U.S. biological

warfare research, given the fact that research was closed down a few years ago, there still is an element at Fort Detrick that's looking for a vaccine. Given the fact that many of the people involved in that research moved into the civilian sector, given the fact that the military did want to continue to conduct that research, and given the documented history of testing biological agents on civilian populations—people, for instance, can look at a book called *A Higher Form of Killing* by Robert Harris and Jeremy Taxman, there's a softcover edition put out by Hill and Wang in 1982. I do think that it is reasonable to ask the question about this outbreak of Hanta virus. Is it merely a natural occurrence or is there more to it? Is this perhaps some sort of research program or something of that kind, or was there an accidental release of some sort of biological agent?

Again, I am not making this statement in a definitive way. I want to make that very clear. From a methodological standpoint, in doing this type of research, one wants to gather information to form hypotheses and then test the hypotheses against the information that's coming in to determine if the hypotheses appear to be valid or whether an alternative hypothesis would appear to be warranted under the circumstances. For example, I cannot say that the Hanta virus outbreak had anything to do with the fact that the Hanta virus was a focal point of US biological warfare research. I cannot say whether the accounts at this point of Fort Wingate being in the area of where the Four Corners outbreak took place are accurate, whether Fort Wingate was closed, whether in fact there was a biological element to Fort Wingate. But if, and I say if with a capital "I", some of the information about Fort Wingate is true, if there was something released from Fort Wingate, whether accidentally or as a result of careless disposal of biological agents, or whether there was something deliberately released, we might be looking at Fort Wingate-gate.

Archives on Audio *address: POB 170023, San Francisco, 94117-0023. 415-346-1840. 15 page catalog lists all the sources with a synopsis of each program and the broadcasts are cross-referenced with other programs containing similar or related material.*

JFK Redux:
Shut Up, Roll Over and Go Back to Sleep: JFK's Assassination Has Been Solved for You, Gerald Posner Deconstructed
by John Kimsey

Don't be fooled by Gerald Posner or any of the media powers—*US News and World Report,* the Chicago *Tribune,* CNN, CBS—hyping Posner's new book, *Case Closed: Lee Harvey Oswald and the Assassination of JFK.* Since the book's September publication, Posner and Oswald have been in the news almost as much as Burt and Loni. In most of the publicity shots, the two are pictured together, Posner looking pensive before a photo of Oswald, whose face has been blown up to roughly the size of King Kong's. This is appropriate, since the book goes beyond the time-honored lone nut characterization to cast Oswald as a monster of mythic proportions, one with a penchant for mischief in tall buildings.

According to Posner, everything happened just the way the Warren Commission said it did, only uh, moreso. Oswald, acting alone, killed the President and changed history, all in the name of—what? Nothing really, except personal resentment at his sorry fate (the book, short on history and politics, is long on dimestore psychology): Oswald was a confused, chronically abusive mediocrity, a clever psychopath, a "man with a deadly smirk" in the *ad hominem* phrase of *US News;* one who unfortunately was ready, skilled and (considering the condition of the weapon) extremely lucky with a rifle.

Remember all that stuff the Warren Commission and its apologists said that made you wince, chuckle or seethe in disbelief? Remember all those insults to intelligence, credibility and Newton's second law of motion? The aerial ballet of the magic bullet? The Rube Goldberg intricacies of the jet effect (the scenario that "proved" that when JFK's head goes back and to the left, it's not because he's been shot from the front right—your eyes, common sense and the laws of nature be damned)? Or the claim that the first lone nut was eliminated by a second lone nut, one with no connections to organized crime?

Remember those golden oldies? Well, if you do then you don't have to fork over $25 for Posner's book, because you have its essence. This book, which establishment commentators find so incisive and devastating, contains nothing new other than a load of desperate attitude. It's a rehash of all the Oswald-did-it-alone arguments, dressed up in neoconservative rhetoric and high tech drag.

The publishers make much of the fact that Posner used computer models to plot bullet trajectories, etc. This is supposed to dazzle all us technopeasants and send us muttering, like so many Jethro Bodines, "Gollleee, Uncle Jed—they's got computers!". They neglect to tell us that no other layperson, engineer or scientist has duplicated any of Posner's vaunted results, a fact that puts his scientific credibility goshdarn close to zero.

Nor do Posner and his proponents mention the rule of GIGO—garbage in, garbage out—which every computer wonk knows. That is, before a computer can tell you anything, you have to feed it data; and the quality of the answers that come out corresponds precisely to the quality of the data that goes in. In setting up his model of the bullet's trajectory, the programmer (at the eerily named Failure Analysis Associates) has to give the computer information with which to work. So along with data about vehicles and buildings, heights and speeds, he tells it that there is an entrance wound in the back of JFK's neck, and an exit wound in the throat. Yet these are the precise points on which the controversy turns and about which there has for years been sober, educated debate. By telling the computer that "X is a wound of entrance," Posner and company prejudge what is perhaps the key question. What can such a computer possibly tell us? Only what Gerald Posner wants us to hear.

Random House, *US News,* Dan Rather and the others would have us believe that *Case Closed* is both the latest and last word on the crime of the century. This is because, thanks to one of those cute postmodern ironies, it really restates the *first* word on the case, the old Warren Report party line.

Actually, it's the Warren Report on steroids. Thus the Commission's portrait of Oswald as a crazed malcontent is inflated until we have a Psycho Killer the size of a Macy's Day Parade balloon. Schizoid tendencies; passive-aggressive behavior; sadomasochism; virtually every syndrome in the Psych 101 sink is flung at Oswald. It's as if the lone nut scenario is such a tough sell in the post-Stone 1990s that it must be staged on the scale of *Star Wars.*

The problem with the psychological profile angle

is that even if the profile is accurate, it doesn't make Oswald the killer of the President. Indeed, if the attitudes and outrages—truancy, tantrums, violent outbursts—ascribed to Oswald are any indication, the country must be brimming with assassins. Moody, arrogant loners like Frank Sinatra, Douglas MacArthur and Dan Rather would have to be prime suspects.

Besides, it's exactly like character testimony in a trial. The prosecution produces doctors who diagnose a devil; the defense parades experts who find the accused to be an angel; and both sides can do this until hell acquires a ski patrol. But Posner, the ex-Wall Street lawyer, presents only the prosecutor's brief.

The Warren Report did much the same thing; but then *Case Closed* is a medley of old standards. (Even the computer modelling angle has been tried before, in a 1988 *Nova* show.) Thus jiggles in the Zapruder film are trotted out as if they were the latest discovery and an infallible guide. But the jiggle theory—the notion that perceptible jerks in the film are traceable to cameraman Abraham Zapruder, who shook involuntarily in reaction to each shot, this occurrence making the jiggles an index of the number of shots fired—has been around a long while. Furthermore, the jiggle phenomenon has been read in differing but persuasive ways. Robert Groden, working for the House Select Committee On Assassinations, used it to sync up the sounds of *four* shots with the film. Posner is enamored of the jiggle factor because a jiggle around frame 180 allows him to claim a shot is fired earlier than the Commission has Oswald firing. (This idea was first proposed by Commission critic Sylvia Meagher in the mid '60s.) This in turn allows Posner to expand the lone gunman's killing window from the near-impossible span of 6 seconds to the vast, commodious luxury of 8 or so seconds. This 8 second span is supposed to make Oswald's alleged feat—2 hits in an incredibly short period under the most strenuous conditions-more, well, possible.

Leaving aside the question of whether a 2 second difference makes shooting from the sixth floor a cakewalk, we should note that many things in this world—outhouses in orbit, for example—are possible. This, however, does not mean they're at all probable; and it certainly doesn't prove they happened.

This emphasis on the possible is another old saw. When it comes to issues like the magic bullet's trajectory, the rifle's recycling time, or Oswald's presence on the second floor 90 seconds after the shooting—i.e., any scenario that might support the Oswald-did-it-alone view—the apologists apply a standard of evaluation that is very generous. The magic bullet scenario is *possible,* say the computers; the shot *could* line up; the evidence *does not disprove it;* it *can't be ruled out.*

On the other hand, when the apologists deal with evidence that would support, say, a shot from the grassy knoll—i.e., evidence they don't like—they apply a very strenuous standard. There is *no evidence that conclusively proves* a grassy knoll shot. Well, neither is there any absolute evidence proving the single bullet theory. But the double standard, with its equivocal language, implicitly favors the official view.

Regarding the grassy knoll, Posner's strategy is to cast certain witnesses—typically those like Beverly Oliver or Ed Hoffman who can be most easily discredited—as *de facto* representatives of the very possibility of a grassy knoll shot. Thus, when he has cast doubt on the claims of, say, Beverly Oliver, Posner pretends he has devastated the whole second gunman hypothesis.

But the second gunman theory doesn't need Beverly Oliver. (I could have begun the preceding sentence with "needless to say"; but Posner's omnipresence in the mass media makes the saying, sadly, a necessity.) Photo records of the scene like the Nix film show a horde of people running immediately to the knoll. Among this crowd are sharp-eyed reporter types like PBS's Robert MacNeil as well as numerous police officers—professionals trained to comprehend gunfire and its reverberational properties. And of course there's the Zapruder film, back and to the left; the splattered outriders to the limousine's rear; the testimony from Parkland medical personnel about entrance wounds in the front; to say nothing of the House Committee's acoustics evidence.

But as you might guess, the acoustics evidence is dismissed out of hand by Posner. He uses the same lame rationale the National Academy of Sciences used, in 1982, to refute the Committee's evidence: a rock drummer from Ohio said it was wrong.

This debate concerns the police dictabelt recording which was found by the Committee's experts to have recorded at least four rifle shots in Dealey Plaza around 12:30 pm. Furthermore, said the scientists, there was a 95% probability that one of these shots, the fourth one, came from the grassy knoll.

Scrutinizing a published copy of the recording, drummer Steve Barber was surprised to hear what sounded like a voice underneath the gunfire saying, "Secure the area." This was a police command that is documented as going out around 12:31 or 32, *after* the shots had ceased. Lone layman Barber presented his find to the NAS, who had been assigned by the Reagan Justice Department to review the acoustics evidence. Common sense, said the NAS, tells-us that if the voice command of 12:31 is simultaneous, on the tape, with the sound of the shots, those sounds must not be shots. (Interestingly, the same people who here tell us common sense is the key have for years been telling us that, when looking at the Zapruder film, common sense doesn't count.)

There are, however, other ways to account for this mix of sounds (needle skippage or tape print-through, for example) that don't rule out what the experts said was undoubtedly the sound of rifle fire on the tape. But the NAS and the Justice Department, obligated to review the HSCA evidence, did not do the scientific thing, i.e., conduct further tests; they simply embraced Barber's assertion and used it to dismiss the acoustics evidence as invalid. It was a convenient way for Ed Meese's Justice Department to get off the hook: no acoustics evidence; no conspiracy; no need to do a damn thing.

But the House Committee findings were based on elaborate scientific tests, just the sort of thing Posner is bowled over by. Furthermore, the Committee's tests were not confined to some plush-lined computer lab; they involved painstaking reenactments in Dealey Plaza. And, unlike Posner's computer results, the acoustics findings were verified by *two* independent studies and two sets of experts and criteria. If Posner or the NAS were serious about evaluating such evidence, they would conduct some serious tests. But these ministers of science march to a different drummer, one in step with their preconceived agenda.

And the doublethink doesn't stop there. Posner— like all Warren apologists today with the possible exception of Gerald Ford—admits what critics long have known, that the CIA and FBI lied to the Warren Commission, manipulating and derailing its investigation. One might think that simple arithmetic would apply here. Let's see: the Warren Report, minus the tainted evidence of the FBI and CIA, leaves—what? Answer: not much. But Posner, the apostle of science, is undeterred by such a calculus. No, despite a CIA/FBI coverup (which was, of course, innocuous and benign), the Commission somehow stumbled onto the truth—Oswald did it alone—in this matter. They were *that* honorable, these honorable men.

This touching faith in official bodies extends, in *Case Closed,* beyond the Warren Commission, the FBI and the CIA to include even the KGB. Posner relies heavily on the word of Yuri Nosenko, a KGB agent who turned himself over to the CIA in 1964, two months after the assassination. Nosenko claimed to be a defector, dissatisfied with life in the Soviet Union. He also claimed to have handled Oswald's file while Oswald was in Russia. The KGB, claimed Nosenko, had no contact with and indeed no interest in Lee Harvey Oswald.

In the CIA of the cold war 60s, Nosenko's claims

were dynamite. In ways too complex to explain here, they played into existing agendas and phobias within the Agency. Suffice it to say virtually no one believed Nosenko. A hardline faction, led by CIA Counterintelligence Chief James Angleton, held that Nosenko was a plant sent to disguise KGB involvement in the assassination. But even a moderate faction found most of Nosenko's claims—both about Oswald and other matters—dubious; the moderates simply ascribed nothing sinister to this fact. In the moderates' view Nosenko was mendacious and desperate but basically well-meaning, a boozy bureaucrat willing to say anything if it might get him out of the evil empire.

The war over Nosenko went on for ten years and tore the Agency apart. It involved isolation and interrogation techniques that seem right out of *The Prisoner* and yet it was only an interlude in the larger and weirder story of Angleton's Ahab-like hunt for a Soviet mole within the Agency. The Nosenko case was, to coin a phrase, closed in the mid 70s. This had little to do with any certainty about Nosenko's claims and much to do with exasperation about Angleton's. When it was all over, Angleton had been fired, the moderates had won and Nosenko was declared a genuine defector and made an officer in the CIA.

Nosenko's word on Oswald, which even his friends in the CIA doubted, is accepted by Posner as gospel. The same goes for retired KGB Colonel Maxim Nechiporenko, who was stationed at the embassy in Mexico City when Oswald allegedly visited there in September 1963. Like Nosenko, Nechiporenko says the KGB viewed Oswald as a possible provocateur and a definite nutcase and steered clear.

Fine, but what is the word of someone like Nechiporenko worth? He was renowned in Mexico as a master of intrigue and deception. Back in the not-too-distant days of the Cold War, establishment types like Posner would have regarded such a Soviet as the evil empire incarnate. Now, in the post-Cold War thaw, he has an American literary agent and admits close ties with *CBS News,* an outfit that has a history of patriotic cooperation with the CIA.

The bottom line? Simple: Agents Nosenko and Nechiporenko, like their counterparts in the FBI and CIA, should not be taken at face value. To do so is the height of naivete, or something worse. Of course if you do take them at face value, then you have further corroboration for Oswald's lonesome nuttiness. Anyone or anything that provides that is a friend of *Case Closed.*

Conclusion Foregone might be a better title for such a story than *Case Closed,* but no matter. Posner's real appeal with this bizarre argument is the neoconservative one: Aren't you tired of it all—the conspiracies, the weirdness, the wondering? Tired of the uncertainty and the horror, the horror? Well, guess what, shoppers? You don't have to worry anymore, because that's no longer the fashionable attitude. In interviews, Posner strikes a *Bob Roberts* pose, positioning himself as the lone outsider questioning an oppressive "establishment" of conspiracy theorists. Change "conspiracy theorists" to "liberals" and you have the same argument Rush Limbaugh is fond of using, and we all know what a Young Soul Rebel he is. It's been a stock right-wing strategy since the days of Reagan: it's hip to be square. It's even hip to believe the Warren Report.

As for conspiracy theories, they are dismissed with the usual psychological explanation of their appeal: They answer our need to find meaning in events. In fact, says Posner, there is no such meaning in events, and conspiracy thinking is analogous to the religious thought of primitives. In this view, conspiracy is the opium of the people: it's a balm for those not tough-minded enough to face a world where shit just happens and political leaders just up and die.

However, the appeal of a theory is not an index of its truth or falsity. And the no-conspiracy view has its own dubious appeal, to the American myth of the individual and his supreme importance. In this Great Man view, history is the function of personality and its mysteries. Such a view ignores the workings of institutions, classes and interest groups, and downplays context. At its best, it's an oversimplification; at its worst, it's history as *People* magazine.

Besides, the Oswald-alone view is itself opium for the people. It is very comforting, since it absolves us of any responsibility, including the need to question power and its workings.

But cutting off questions is Posner's real purpose in *Case Closed*. He pretends to be a disinterested party, calmly evaluating the facts, but start at the top and consider the title. It bespeaks the sort of shrill certainty about complex issues normally reserved for bad undergraduate papers. Other books in the assassination literature—*Inquest, Reasonable Doubt, Coincidence Or Conspiracy?, Who Killed JFK?,* to name a few—have titles that suggest openness and the spirit of inquiry. But *Case Closed* is about closure, of the most maligned sort. It wants to shut the door, shut off discussion and shut you up. Rest easy, America, it says. Our computers have figured it out. There is no problem, and certainly no politics here. You can all roll over and go back to sleep.

Case Closed is a work in an emerging genre, one focused on revisionist right-wing propaganda. Its nearest cousins are *The Real Anita Hill* and the works of D'Souza, Medved, Roiphe and company. We might call this genre "The Empire Strikes Back," most of its stars having been seduced by the dark side of the force. Many are the rewards awaiting the young writer willing to sell out truth to shore up conservative hegemony. And this is why Posner's picture is everywhere, even though his book is so slight.

Compare the Posner media blitz to the coverage, thirteen years ago, of the House Select Committee on Assassinations. At that time, the Committee released its finding of a "probable conspiracy" in the murder of the President. The Committee's report fingered Oswald, but said he was part of a larger plot. The report implied that this larger plot involved mobsters, probably anti-Castro Cubans and possibly individuals connected to U.S. intelligence. However, it said, the identification of these other conspirators would require more time and funding, as the Committee had run out of both.

This astonishing conclusion came at the end of the longest and most in-depth investigation to date. Yet the play it got in the mainstream media—in journals like *US News* and the *Trib*—was virtually nil. To this day, few Americans know what the House Committee found. I suppose a hype of Posner proportions might have been out of the question, but the conclusions of the House Committee were hardly covered at all. But then, the House Committee's verdict was: case open.

John Kimsey is a writer, musician and teacher living in Chicago.

Secret Service Masers Kill and Make Whores
by An Awakened Sleep Unit

Warning! Red Alert *Steamshovel* readers! All major news media have recently proclaimed that false memory syndrome is likely to be the next big problem in the mental health professions for the 90s. Do not buy into these particular news releases, which have been planted by clandestine spin doctors for the express purpose of covering-up a massive ongoing abuse of U.S. citizens at the hands of a variety of Federal level agencies who are deploying a variety of so-called "Novelty effects" which are classified as "Non-lethal" yet may still cause injury, health problems, and post traumatic stress symptoms. This non-lethal technology has been deployed for nearly forty years, and is used for many purposes—some of which are suggested below.

MASER, ma' zer (microwave amplification by stimulated emission of radiation), a device that produces highly stable electromagnetic waves by harnessing the natural oscillations of an atomic or molecular system. The Maser devices have been a staple of "our" National Security States of America since before 1955—the year that the maser was hailed as an important scientific achievement in the realm of psychological warfare. These devices have been deployed through the following Federal agencies: FBI, NSA, NRO, CIA, Army Intelligence, Naval Intelligence, Department of Energy, Defense Investigative Services, DIA, Justice Department, Department of Treasury, BATF, and probably others which I am not aware of in the Federal Reserve System and State Department. Deployment of this technology is a distinctly *federal* phenomenon! The so-called "Secret Government" will not allow mainstream media to speak or write the truth about the matter, and will deny this is the case at every turn. Masers are LPM (Low Power Microwave) directed energy weapons which are capable of causing the projection of auditory effects (either hearing "voices" or subliminal suggestion) into the occipital cortex. There is no way to shield oneself from this form of extremely high frequency directed energy—no shielding is adequate! One's only hope of protection is to be aware of the abuse as *external* to the self, i.e. not coming from one's own imagination or delusions, but invasive projections designed to effect *mind control.*

False Memory Syndrome is a scapegoat created by a consortium of Federal "spin doctors" bent on negating the believability and viability of the more than 12,000 unwitting citizens who have been on the receiving end of this technology. Since most persons on the receiving end have also been the types the government considers "enemies of the State" to begin with, the perpetrators have been allowed to use their victims *sexually* as well. That's right, rape, but a form of rape that is not available to the average rapist who hasn't access to the so-called "psychotronic" novelty effects weapons. Psychotronics allows the perpetrators to *sexually abuse and rape their victims and yet still have the victims enjoy and experience full sexual response. Yup, the victims have had their will power severed and give their abusers more pleasure than any unwilling non-consensual partner ever could!*

The mental health professions are currently swallowing this bogus media barrage on false Memory hook, line and sinker—and are preparing to ban all repressed memory therapies (hypnotherapies) as the main cause of these so-called "Lies of the Mind". The 12,000 victims of psychotronic abuse will then be dealt with as *mere schizophrenics,* just like they *always have been for over 40 years!* The media planted stories about False Memory syndrome will help "explain away" the memories of Alien Abduction/Ritual Satanic Abuse which are so prevalent in cases of government psychotronic abuse. The "Satanic" abuse being ritual *Masonic* abuse by the Illuminists who control the *Federalist World Government of the New World Order*/United Nations juggernaut! Are their eyes and ears *really* benevolent? *Not!* One of the main reasons that this form of atrocity is being so deftly covered up is due to the consistent abuse, sexual and otherwise, of the persons involved in the government's long standing "genetics vs. heredity" eugenics and genetics experiments which the imported Project Paperclip Nazi scientists have helped our government with since WWII!

These same covert arms of government are the ones who have coined the term "screen memories" to describe the obsfucational memories impressed by the abusers themselves! They must at all costs disguise their abuse in order to continue experimentation with psychotronics, and have given a fancy neutral name to their *enforced amnesia* which is designed to disguise abuse during *domestic* operations. Allowing the perpetrators their sexual reward is part and parcel of payment to the covert operatives in the field. Again screen memories are *enforced amnesia*. Since these Nazi inspired scientists must perform medical tests during the abuse event, such as implantation of bio-telemetric tracking devices into nasal cavities and ear canals, retrieval of gamete samples/tissue samples, they use alien abduction as a screen memory, inspiring terror in the populace they abuse, while the clueless "sheeple" will not believe in extra-terrestrials from space, those on the receiving end of the abuse are often convinced of space alien abuse or satanic abuse. This *con job* is fooling even the best of mental health professionals! The atrocities are so *outrageously unbelievable* that justice will *never ever be brought to bear on this most secret activity of "our" secret government*. The Biotelemetric implants are used to locate the victims via the Global Positioning System (GPS) satellites, they *cannot* escape *or* hide from their abusers.

Victims are typically selected for a variety of reasons: lifelong eugenics/genetic guinea pigs, children of secular humanist society members, enemies of the state, suspected spies, gypsy types (includes hippies, beats, deadheads), war protesters, civil rights activists, suspected terrorists, persons who use any drugs which the state cannot tax, feminists, homosexuals, socialists who differ from NWO objectives, firearms owners, or anyone doing anything which irritates the *powers that be*.

The Federalists have a special name for the select few abuse victims that they wish to control for clandestine objectives—*unit sleepers*—who can be made into "Manchurian Candidates" like the crazed gunmen with killing spree madness that are used in Post Office shootings, schoolyard shootings, Luby's Cafeteria shootings, New Jersey train shootings. They would have you believe in the old "lone crazed gunman" scenario in order to convince the populace that they must be disarmed for the national good. They will succeed.

Readers will note that this past Christmas season was one of the most violent seasons in history with regards to firearms mayhem. It is being engineered. The end justifies the means when it comes to disarming the populous as far as They are concerned. It matters not that they are really responsible for the atrocities attributed to crazed lone gunmen, since they believe the benefits will only come after they disarm the law abiding sheeple, leaving criminals armed in order to foster anarchy which must eventually result in bringing in the U.N. to perform peace-keeping duties within "our" own nation's borders. Martial law will be declared, and the Constitutional rights suspended under this national "drug and crime" emergency.

The Fox Network is currently using *The X Files* to reveal the government's position on these issues. However, the extraterrestrial hypothesis is the only officially accepted position. You will not see Special Agent Fox Mulder uncovering evidence of government abuse of citizens, except when the government is deploying crashed saucer retrieval teams!

Get a clue, sheeple, your time is short!

Of Steven Seagal and Bud Culligan
A Conversation with Lars Hansson
by Kenn Thomas

Q: The last time we had you in *Steamshovel* you were able to explain some of the background information concerning Gordon Novel and his connection to those photographs of J. Edgar Hoover in *flagrante delicto*.

A: I think your readers will find it quite fascinating how he re-enters the picture here.

I had been aware of Steven Seagal for about five years along with everybody else, since he entered the scene with his movie *Above The Law*. I happened to be living in Santa Barbara, actually commuting back and forth between there and Las Vegas, working with Colonel Bo Gritz. And I was very familiar with the Christic Institute lawsuit, so I was extremely impressed with that film when it came out. The director of that movie, and his most recent film, *Under Siege*, is a man by the name of Andrew Davis, who is a neighbor of mine in Santa Barbara. So I felt a fairly close tie. And I had a very good impression of Steven Seagal. I'm not that great a fan of martial arts *per se* but I felt that at least in his first film and perhaps in this last film he was trying to get a fairly decent message across.

A couple of years ago I was doing this radio program and we were talking about the JFK assassination. One of the listeners had sent some material which was released from a fellow by the name of Craig Hewlitt. I'm not saying this to endorse him or reject him, but one of the listeners had sent me this material concerning an individual by the name of Roland Bernard Culligan, or Bud Culligan for short. This was back in 1991.

I had first heard Culligan's name about a year or so before that indirectly from Fletcher Prouty. We were working on another case concerning Bob Lazar, interestingly enough, and in the course of it he had made a stray comment concerning the Culligan list. This was back in the middle of 1990. I had no idea what that was but I guessed correctly that this Culligan was potentially some sort of high-level hit man. The years go by and I get a tape of an interview that this fellow Culligan did from the East Ridge, Tennessee police department in, I believe, 1978, essentially going into some detail about his background as a US government hit man and some of these assassinations that he claimed to have performed.

I was extremely busy at the time working on a book about George Bush and covering the Noriega trial and a few other odds and ends and didn't really have much time pursue it. But after I got back from Iraq last year, we were supposed to start putting a documentary video together but the project fell through. So I had a little bit of time on my hands. This Culligan story had intrigued me so much during that year that I made all the various arrangements and I actually flew out from Florida to New Mexico to visit with him for the first time. It was a very interesting meeting. The man is 69 years old now. He stands about 6'4". Despite the fact that he's had open heart surgery and his hair is grey and he wears a beard, he's still an extremely formidable individual and extremely coherent and articulate. I thought that if this guy isn't what he claims to be, he certainly could play the role.

Q: Could you go into more detail about what exactly he claims and what is this Culligan list that Fletcher Prouty talked about?

A: What he claims, in fact, and what he has been claiming since roughly 1978, is that he was a very high-level, executive action specialist. That he was under orders directly from the CIA and he has in court documents named his case officer as having directed him in performing over a hundred international assassinations.

I have right in front me a copy of the most recent lawsuit he has filed in Asheville, North Carolina, against the Central Intelligence Agency. It's a very lengthy file. He's basically claiming that they are responsible for, I believe, 141 felony charges that have been leveled against him from Oregon to Rhode Island, Florida to New Mexico. He claims that he had loss of recognition, loss of retirement and several million dollars in damages. In goes into great detail after that. There are number affidavits attached.

On one six-page affidavit he claims that he had killed 117 persons from 1943 to 1990, claiming that it came from the official files of the US State Department as sent to the Federal court in Albuquerque in 1985. And some of the people he lists, which is what I heard on this tape two years ago, are people who most people would recognize: Patrice Lumumba, Rafael Trujillo, Dag Hammerskold, the Diem brothers in Vietnam, Jose Fuentes in Quatemala, King Farouk and Nasser in Egypt in 1970, with quite a few in between. He claims, and there is documentation to prove, that he's been trying for fifteen years to get the agency to come to terms, that he did not want to go public with any of it. He just wanted to be left alone and go into retirement.

There's an individual that I have come to know very well who lives down in Florida who has been following Culligan's case very closely for seventeen years. He has a phenomenal computerized database on this, catalogued audio tapes, including many, many tapes. One where Culligan is describing exactly how he killed King Farouk, or had Farouk killed in Italy, for example. A very, very extensive, exhaustive file.

The fact is that Culligan has filed, as I say, four Federal law suits against the Central Intelligence Agency. I personally have gone to two of those jurisdictions to verify those cases were on file and the contents. Interestingly enough, about a year ago when I went to Asheville, North Carolina to make sure that I had all the documents in the file, the court clerk claimed that there was no such case on file until I showed her the cover form that we had received earlier with her signature on it. She said, "Oh, that case!" Most of the people in these official capacities write Culligan off. Everybody seems to dismiss it, that he's a nut case and so forth. Yet right on the surface of it you have to ask yourself what kind of glutton for punishment would file cases like that if there weren't something to it? Not one, but four cases.

Q: And he hasn't written a book or tried to get publicity that way?

A: Yes and no. In fact, he actually had written a book, which I believe was published in Brussels in 1982 called *Highway Into Hell* but apparently the CIA prevented publication and distribution in this country. Interestingly enough, and this is something I have learned very recently and have not yet been able to verify it but I suspect it may well be the case, that he was supposedly the inspiration for the *Matt Helm* spy series of some years back. It was unfortunately played as a spoof by Dean Martin, but Culligan claims that he knew the people behind the writing of that and that many of those incidents were based on his own real life experiences.

Be that as it may, his overall thrust has been to try to just lay low and stay quiet and try to work out some sort of deal that would enable him and his wife, both in their sixties, to just fade into the sunset. He claims that because of what he knows and what he participated in there's no way that he would ever be permitted to do that. And so after trying to make contact with a number of people, I had gained his confidence and actually have made a total of six trips up to the prison. One of them, I might add, the second to last one, I made with Steven Seagal's attorney for five hours, during which we audio-taped three hours of

Culligan's jailhouse confessions, describing a number of these assassinations that he claims to have performed. Therein lies pretty much my dispute with Steven Seagal at this point. I should pronounce his name correctly, it rhymes with sea gull.

Q: One of Culligan's claims is that he rubbed out the JFK hit men in Guatemala in 1965?

A: Absolutely. He claims that there were three men, I don't have their actual names in front of me or I would give them to you, he claims that they were part of the hit team in Dallas and that all of these men were paid a great deal of money and given special treatment, but as he stated in one of his affidavits, "They were demanding more money and what they got was me." He describes how he had met with them in Miami and supposedly was assembling a team to perform an assassination. His cover story to them was that they were to perform an assassination in a South American country and he arranged for them to meet him down in Guatemala to set up the logistics for it. He has given me the names of the two men that he claims participated with him in these executions and that he then flew down to Guatemala and dispatched all three men. And what makes this especially interesting is that, as I say this a case that has an extensive track record for at least fifteen years that I'm aware of, the question is how much of it is absolutely true and real and ultimately provable. That's the difficulty. Frankly, that's why I got in touch with Steven Seagal, in about February or March of 1993.

Q: Before we get to that, Culligan also claims that the two surviving members of that hit team are E. Howard Hunt and Frank Sturgis?

A: That's correct. He has a habit of referring to, and I've noticed this with a number of these ex-agents, he refers to Sturgis as "Burgess". Apparently back during that time there was a battery called Burgess and I guess when he would make contacts or whatnot they'd make a sort of code. But, yes, Frank Sturgis. He claims that one of Hunt's many pay-offs was an incident where he was given something like $400,000 for a bunch of garbage art in his attic and so forth. But, yes, he claims that they are the only two surviving men.

Q: How does Steven Seagal fit in to this story?

A: As I say, he seemingly came out of nowhere. He has surrounded himself with this aura of mystery. Those people who have watched his films or follow him to any degree, are aware that he apparently ran an *aikido dojo* over in Japan. He has claimed in various interviews that he performed special works and favors for very powerful people over there with a heavy amount of implication that these were CIA people.

What has come out of these most recent articles

and in some of my own background investigation on Steve is that apparently one of the key people that he associated with over there, while he was actually running his mother-in-law's *dojo*, was a man by the name of Robert Strickland, who was an actual CIA agent and was involved in a number of very sensitive operations. Steven for a number of years had claimed him as a godfather type and Strickland apparently had unrestricted access to the film sets and so forth, until about 1989, when he claims, and the Connolly article quotes him as claiming, that Seagal tried to persuade Strickland to rub out was man by the name of Gary Goldman, who I know fairly well. Goldman had worked over in Vietnam, was a captain in the US Army and has been involved in a number of operations with Lieutenant Colonel Bo Gritz, the POW missions and so forth. In the period of time when I was helping Bo put his books together, I had gotten to know Gary fairly well.

Moving back a few months: I had contacted Seagal because I thought that he might be interested in this Culligan story. It seemed that it would not only make very good film fare but at that time I had the impression that Seagal was very sincere about wanting to try to bring the truth out about a lot of these covert operations. He's a very knowledgeable guy. He prides himself on having that sort of awareness and background. And we had a number of mutual acquaintances, such as Dan Sheehan and Andrew Davis. So I contacted him and was very pleased and surprised that he got back to me right away. And for the first two or three weeks he was extremely gracious and concerned and solicitous about my welfare and health. He seemed to be very genuinely concerned about the truth of Culligan's story or getting to the truth of it.

What I had originally proposed to him was that he underwrite a thorough investigation of Culligan's claims so that we could first and foremost find out how much of it really was provable before we did anything with it. Then, assuming that a lot of the claims that he had made were verifiable, then obviously this would have made tremendous background for a film, book, whatever, especially with the thirtieth anniversary of the assassination looming. If some of the stuff that Culligan is alleging in court could really be verified, obviously it could help to bring about a major breakthrough. So that was my primary goal and always has been, in terms of verifying these things through a very serious investigation.

What I noticed pretty quickly with Seagal was that he seemed to be much more interested and obsessed with the details and the intrigue and the sensational aspects than he did with really getting to the bottom of it. So much so that, and this is the first time I've said

this publicly, during two of the conversations that we had he seemed to be so enthralled with this idea of this incredible hit man that he actually started bragging about some of his own activities in that regard, which disturbed me tremendously, for obvious reasons. Number one: I don't support assassination for any reason. Number two: I'm very uncomfortable around somebody who is either bragging about something that either did not happen or, worse yet, that did.

So I started to become very uncomfortable. On two occasions, and I want this said for the record, Seagal actually made some fairly direct suggestions that I should consider performing some favors for him or, in the case of Culligan, that we should consider eliminating a particular general, who I mentioned earlier, who was working as his case officer and apparently Culligan claims is the one responsible for all the grief he has suffered over the last twenty years. I was extremely disturbed about that.

Q: Now Seagal is actually filing a slander suit against both John Connolly and *Spy Magazine* for these accusations, which you are basically supporting.

A: In fact, yes. That's why I wanted to put this on the record. He filed a slander suit against John Connolly personally and threatened to file suit if *Spy* printed it, which is a fairly apparent case of prior restraint. Part of the reason I want to put this on the record is that I turned this information over to the LAPD, which is investigating some of these claims by Goldman and myself, and they seem to be virtually non-concerned. As a matter of fact, I'm a fairly good investigator and I was really stunned that three weeks after Goldman made his report on this matter, even though they had contacted people around the country, they hadn't called me, and at that time the detective had to ask me what Seagal's phone number was, where he lived and who is attorney was. So anybody that sees anything here relating to what happened in LA in June 1968, the parallels seem slightly ominous here.

Q: That was the thing that made the reputation for the LAPD as investigators, the RFK assassination. John Connolly's credibility is very good. He's done a lot of good work on the Casolaro investigation.

A: In case anybody is ready to write him off or say that he is pursuing a vendetta, your readers should know that he has a law degree and was a former New York City homicide detective. So it isn't as if he doesn't have a certain amount of professional expertise in this field.

One of the names that has surfaced repeatedly in

the Casolaro investigation is a man by the name of Robert Booth Nichols. In the short period of time that I was attempting to negotiate with Seagal, I was stunned to learn that he had Robert Booth Nichols act as his technical advisor in his last film, *Under Siege,* and actually apparently plays a small cameo role as one of the terrorists. I thought that was appropriate.

I have actual documents from the First Intercontinental Development Corporation, when they were incorporating, in a letter to Robert Booth Nichols describing this corporation which includes Robert A. Maheu, which I'm sure many people will remember from the Hughes Intertel period, the guy who in many volumes now is described as having set up the hit against Fidel Castro, on behalf of Richard Nixon with Santos Trafficante, Sam Giancana and Johnny Roselli, under the JM WAVE program. Many researchers have alleged that it was members of that same team, which included Frank Sturgis and Howard Hunt, that later turned around and went after John Kennedy in Dallas.

Another person who is part of this corporation with Nichols was Clint Murchison, Jr. People who have done their homework will remember the name Murchison: his father was the very wealthy Dallas oil man who was involved with J. Edgar Hoover, at whose home both Hoover and Nixon were visiting the night before John Kennedy was killed. Of course, they later couldn't remember where they were that day.

For those who have been following recent developments in the Casolaro case, there was a letter written by Ted Gunderson, the former FBI man who has been investigating the Satanist and so forth, that was written to Robert Nichols back as far as 1983, to try to get him to get some information for him in Australia. It's my understanding from several sources that Ted Gunderson was actually involved in Meridian Arms Company with Robert Booth Nichols and Michael Riconosciuto. These are the kind of people that Steve has been associating with very heavily, employing in his films and so forth.

Getting back to the issue: what really concerned me tremendously was that in the middle of our discussion Seagal was actually bragging about his expertise in this field himself. His attorney was sitting right there when he was describing this in great detail. A close friend of mine was sitting there at a subsequent conversation where Steve was bragging to us, after we came back from interviewing Culligan in prison. Culligan claims that he actually fired the fatal shots at Raphael Trujillo in 1961 in the Dominican Republic using a 270 rifle, and he exclaimed "My favorite!" Apparently that inspired Mr. Seagal so much that he had to run out and buy two of them and then brag to us about it.

I was very concerned about all this and where he was coming from. As we were getting close to trying to complete the deal, which I was becoming more nervous about, I was told that apparently someone had contacted him and tried to warn him away from dealing with me. In hindsight, I was actually very pleased about that and I later found out that that person happened to be Gordon Novel.

Q: We discussed him in our previous interview. He was on the PBS special concerning J. Edgar Hoover and he's been on the scene for a long time, a guy who tried to de-rail the Garrison investigation.

A: Who actually brags about it publicly. One of the other people that both Novel and Robert Booth Nichols have been hanging out with over the last year or two is John Lear, who I have written about in a hundred and twenty page affidavit, *UFOs, Aliens and Ex-Intelligence Agents: Who's Fooling Whom?* John Lear, who lives in Las Vegas and goes around the country purporting to be a UFO expert, but who in fact was involved in flying six hundred tons of Soviet weapons to Somalia in 1977 to set up this problem we're now having to deal with. Lear bragged openly and showed me proof that he was involved in the shipment of weapons to Iran in violation of the embargoes in early 1981, which as you can see ties in closely to what Casolaro was looking into, what I believe was part of the actual payoff for the October Surprise election deal. I have also verified personally from first-hand experience, Lear was directly involved in the shipment of what ultimately amounted to 1.33 trillion dollars out of the Philippines in Guam, into Zurich, Switzerland. The latest reports that I have gotten from Las Vegas are that Seagal, apparently according to John Lear himself, hired Lear's wife as his casting agent.

Q: Lear, of course, throws stories out there about secret government manipulations with alien beings and so forth to entertain people while at the same time he is involved with moving Marcos gold and flying weapons to Somalia.

A: I just make the point again, not to get off on the UFO tangent, but certainly would hope that if any of your readers have an interest in that to look more closely into this and question very closely what the ulterior motives are of a lot of these so-called experts out there, to disinform and confuse. Pay attention to more of these mundane details. The reason why a character like Novel is so important to be looked at very closely, this is a guy who actively impersonated Lee Harvey Oswald thirty years ago and is still right in the middle of the situation here. Believe me, he is not the only one.

Thieves of Knowledge: The Vanishing of the Place of Muses
by John S. Craig

" *What is it, this unleashed fury of prince and priest, judge and soldier against these small monuments of clay or paper, against these sepulchres in which the dead say they have lived and loved, suffered and hoped?"*
— **Gilles Lapouge, 1988**

Of all the lost treasures of the world, the systematic and wanton devastation of the greatest sanctuary of knowledge in the ancient world, the Alexandrian Library, is the most stupendous of losses. The destruction of the world's great libraries has been commonplace through history; the great collections of Thebes, Nineveh, Baghdad, and Louvain were all destroyed, but none of these libraries can compare to the myth and legend surrounding the library and museum that was the jewel of the sophisticated culture of Alexandria, Egypt.

Legend tells us Alexandria contained a library and museum that eventually held every great work of literature in the world. The library and museum flourished from roughly 300 B.C. to 300 A.D. Every great literary work of the Greeks was there, as well as other collections of Roman, Jewish, and Arabian scholars. What became of all these treasures has been the collective wonderment of historical detectives for centuries.

The library, the greatest of man's inventions, has had a rocky history, built and accumulated by all great cultures only to be destroyed by conquerors who wished that fire and sword could change the past and obliterate the accomplishments of the vanquished civilization.

Aristotle, Plato's proud student and eventual tutor of Alexander, was one of the first scholars to collect and preserve the written word. Aristotle's collection included versions of Homer that were certainly different that what we know today. Aristotle bequeathed his collection to a favorite student who left the library to a relative (Nelius of Serpris). It is believed that Nelius eventually sold part of his collection to Ptolemy who was responsible for starting the Alexandrian Library.

When Alexander died there was tremendous infighting among his confederates as to who would rule his domain. Ptolemy, one of Alexander's generals and reputedly a half brother, seized control of a large part of Egypt, which included Alexandria. Ptolemy became the most successful of Alexander's successor's.

Alexander the Great, son of Phillip II and Olympias, inherited the crown of Macedonia at the age of twenty when his father was assassinated in 336 B.C. Until his death in India of malaria in 324 B.C., he conquered most of the known world in and around the Mediterranean and spread Greek culture into Asia, Persia, and Egypt. His astounding accomplishment in just twelve years, though at a tremendous cost of human life, left a mythical aura around his name. In 332 B.C. he established Alexandria which became Egypt's largest city for 2000 years.

Alexander was embalmed by eastern masters, swathed in malleable plates of gold to fit the contour of the body, and set in a golden casket that was paraded through his kingdom behind sixty-four gold-bedecked mules. For months the funeral procession journeyed from Babylon through Mesopotamia, over Syria, to Damascus and was eventually to end at Aegae Macedonia where Alexander would be placed with other royalty. But Ptolemy realized what a great political coup it would be to have the remains of the great king in Alexandria. He took an army to the procession and persuaded the leader to allow him to perform the last rites. While Alexander rested in Memphis, Ptolemy built a tremendous Mausoleum in Alexandria made of the rarest Greek and Egyptian marbles. This became Alexander's final resting place that lasted three centuries. In 89 B.C. Ptolemy IX, in a great need of money to continue his reign over Alexandria, had the gold sarcophagus melted into coin. The sarcophagus was housed in colored glass and eventually disappeared altogether in the centuries that followed.

Ptolemy went about creating the most comprehensive library known in the ancient world. The organization of the library was given to Demetrius Phalereus who was familiar with the library at Athens. Ptolemy went about purchasing scrolls and copying those he couldn't buy. Their goal was to accumulate 500,000 scrolls - all of the known literary works of the world. Ptolemy ordered that all books on ships that called on Alexandria were to be copied: copies were returned to the ships and the originals were confiscated and stored in the library.

A 120-volume catalog of the contents of the library was written by Callimachus, but nothing of the catalog has survived. Actually what was in the library will never be known for sure. It is estimated that the total accumulation swelled from 400,000 to 700,000 at the time of Julius Caesar's infamous arrival in 48 B.C. These works included every major work of the ancient Greeks. It was also the home of great sculpture and the workplace of distinguished scholars like Aristophanes of Byzantium and Apollinius of Rhodes.

The complex of rooms for the library and the museum containing art works was known as the Place of the Muses. In it contained the sacred writings of the Egyptians and Jews, music scores, medicine and science texts, and philosophy. It is believed that the entire works of Sophocles, Euripides, Aristotle, Plato, and Homer were present, though what was lost from these masters can only be guessed at. Claudius wrote a history of the Etruscans, a civilization occupying northeast Italy from 8th to 1st century of which we know very little at present. Pliny wrote the world's first encyclopedia from sources in the library during the first century A.D.; Euclid wrote the first textbook on geometry; Dionysius wrote *Art of Grammar* which became a model for much of the world's grammarian ordinances. Junius Venator, the last curator of the Library, wrote over a hundred books covering two thousand years of the world's known history to that time (350 A.D.).

What happened to the greatest collection of extant information, knowledge, and wisdom of the ancient world, the sculpture and the tomb of Alexandria is unknown, but the beginning of the end most certainly began with Caesar's arrival (48 B.C.).

For nearly two centuries the library had served as the greatest treasury of learning known to the world. It had escaped all of the threats of destruction until Rome's Caesar entered Alexandria. There were many reasons for Caesar to visit Alexandria: to collect debts; to gain political prestige with Egypt by settling a dispute over the will of Cleopatra's father, Ptolemy Auletes, which had created friction between Cleopatra and her brother Ptolemy; and to enjoy the culture and civilization of the world's most literate and aesthetic city.

Caesar, known as a scholar with a great interest in arts and letters, visited Alexander's tomb and the library. The love-struck Cleopatra offered the present day master of the world a great gift of hundreds of rare scrolls and art objects from the library and museum. How many Caesar packed onto some of his accompanying Roman ships is unknown. A banquet was scheduled to celebrate agreements to the will. As Cleopatra and her guests reveled, Ptolemy's general Achillas seized the opportunity to attack the palace with a force of Egyptian soldiers and slaves. Caesar sent for reinforcements but realized the Egyptian navy would cause the Roman ships difficulty in rescuing him, so he ordered some of his remaining soldiers to sneak into the harbor and throw burning torches onto the ships. His gift from Cleopatra was destroyed as were books stored in warehouses along the waterfront, but Caesar escaped with his life. It was estimated that 40,000 books were lost.

By the third century A.D., Alexandria had become a cosmopolitan population with conflicting philosophies and religions that eventually turned the city's cultural melting pot into a boiling cauldron of civil dissent. Under the rule of Aurelian (272) and Diocletius (296) the library suffered several destructive assaults. Areas that contained scientific, alchemy and other pseudo-science texts were burned, but much of the rest of the library remained intact.

In 391 A.D. Junius Venator, the last great director of the library, fell out of favor with the Christian Bishop of Alexandria, Theophilos. It is believed that Theophilos felt that the library was a hotbed of paganism and convinced the Emperor Theodosius, also a Christian, to burn the library. Junius Venator was rumored to be murdered by fanatical followers of Theophilos.

Since the library was stored in several buildings it is not known how much of the collection was destroyed. In fact there are reports that only one building was destroyed, and the main collection stored in the Library of the Serpeum survived. After all of these disasters the Alexandriana scholar Parsons wrote in his book *The Alexandrian Library*, " . . . if there is one outstanding characteristic of the library . . . it is its genius in surviving destruction."

The last assault on this paragon of written knowledge has been attributed to Islam. The Muslims conquered Alexandria in 642 under the leadership of Am ibn al-As. Like previous conquerors, the Muslims were fanatics in spreading their own philosophy. In this case they believed in spreading the word of the true god, Allah, and the one true prophet, Mohammed. Sometime between 642 and 646 the library suffered several fires by orders of Am ibn al-As's spiritual leader Omar, a Muslim fanatic who believed that there was only one book to read—the Koran.

In the end the destruction came from the pagan Caesar, the Christian Theophilos, the Muslim Omar, and the civil strife of Alexandria's own people.

Throughout the entire history of the library, scholars have found conflicting stories as to how much the library was destroyed during each assault. Only one thing is certain as of today—it has completely vanished.

Virtually Reality
by Jim Keith

The *Gods of Eden,* authored by William Bramley, is one of the more popular and talked-about recent books on UFOs and conspiracy. It's all over the place, and spoken of favorably by a lot of people who should know better. What has not been talked about is that there is a hidden purpose to the book, and that is to disseminate Church of Scientology concepts to the UFO field. It's not that Bramley glancingly touches upon material also covered in Scientology; he uses the bullhorn for basic, elementary Scientology principles without mentioning their source, and does it again and again in the pages of the book. I probably wouldn't even mention the matter except for the wide agreement which the book has engendered (even Milton William Cooper references the book like it was UFO gospel) — and people should know what they're agreeing with.

The Scientology message begins with the overall theme of the book: we are controlled, even "farmed" by extraterrestrials of evil intent. This concept has been put forward by a number of writers starting with Charles Fort, but Bramley's other theorizing makes plain where he got the idea: from L. Ron Hubbard, in such non-introductory Scientology texts as *History of Man, Creation of Human Ability,* and his taped Philadelphia Doctorate Course lectures. Hubbard specifically warned about passing this "advanced" (read science fiction-y) material on to the non-indoctrinated, and so Bramley carefully doesn't cite these or any of the other Scientology materials dealing with what Hubbard termed "space opera", i.e. tales of past life experiences with civilizations in advance of current Earth levels, except for a citation of the fairly homogenized *Have You Lived Before This Life?* By being tight-lipped about the wilder Scientology stuff, Bramley hews to the party line in this instance, as he does with his other covert treatments of Scientology doctrine throughout the book.

Chapter 2, "Orientation," pgs. 7-9, gets the ball rolling with a dissertation about the spiritual, as opposed to animal, nature of mankind. I won't argue the truth of this matter, but it is straight Scientology "orientation," one of the basic premises of the "religion." (Having spent 13 years in the organization, partly at an executive level, I can state that Scientology is less a religion than a very clever mind control operation, so clever in fact, that I think that Hubbard might have fallen for his own creation.)

In Chapter 6, pg. 74, Bramley discusses the existence of a mystical "Brotherhood" "engaged in a prag-matic program of spiritual education." Echoing Scientology PR terms he apparently identifies "the original uncorrupted Brotherhood" of ancient times with Scientology, or at least with the purposes of Scientology. It is "scientific, not mystical or ceremonial," which is precisely the claim that Hubbard made, hence the name of his group, and it was "...a considerable body of accurate spiritual data, but it had not succeeded in developing a complete route to spiritual freedom..." This is more Scientology jargon, as can be easily determined by reading any of the books pushing the subject or taking a look at the Scientology "grade chart" defining the various steps of counselling, claimed as the "road to spiritual freedom."

The same goes for Bramley's statement, again on page 74, that "Brotherhood teachings were arranged as a step-by-step process [a la the Scientology grade chart]. A student was required to satisfactorily complete one level of instruction before proceeding to the next one... This style of instruction was designed to ensure that a student did not prematurely atttempt difficult spiritual feats or become overwhelmed by advanced level information..." Again, this is straight Scientologese, but this time related to Hubbard's theories on study and the application of the "gradient" approach, i.e. easy before hard. This also provides a justification why everything but the introductory levels are secret: they would "overwhelm" someone who hadn't done all the preliminary Scientology counselling, and paid all the preliminary and considerable fees. How much does Scientology go for these days? Last I looked, which was about 10 years ago, it was something like three hundred dollars an hour for most of the counselling. This is why a goodly percentage of Scientologists choose the lockstep of virtually unpaid staff work: staff is promised free counselling, although in my experience they rarely get much of it.

Another point is taken from Hubbard's theories of study on page 76, where Bramley states, "With a word substituted here and a sentence omitted there, the semantic precision needed to communicate an exact scientific principle will be lost." Again, Bramley is virtually quoting Hubbard, particularly in the policy letter titled "Keeping Scientology Working", which rails on about people who change the materials of Scientology. Scientology makes a big deal about alteration of Hubbard's written materials by one jot or tittle.

Chapter 7, page 96 Bramley briefly touches upon "third parties" involved in wars and other conflicts. Hubbard insisted in his "third party law", covered in the book *Introduction to Scientology Ethics,* that third parties were always behind the scene in altercations.

In Chapter 9, page 108 Bramley chats about past lives, and shows that he again buys the Hubbard scenario in detail, with post-death disembodied spirits looking around for pregnant women to pick up new bodies.

Chapter 10, page 119 mentions the Buddhist legend of the coming avatar Mettaya, who would create "a religion that would bring about full spiritual liberation for all mankind... Mettaya would simply be an individual with the knowledge and ability to get the job done." More covert references to Scientology and Hubbard, provable by reading one of the three Hubbard books referenced in the endnotes of Bramley's book. This is Hubbard's *Hymn of Asia,* in which he claimed he was Mettaya come to deliver the planet. The text was originally supposed to be delivered at a Buddhist convention in the 1950s, no doubt in an effort to convert Asia wholesale to Scientology. Apparently the Buddhists got wind of Hubbard's plan, since the address was never given.

On page 220, Chapter 19, Bramley states, "A properly-done confessional can have a highly beneficial effect on an individual..." Bramley expands on the concept on pages 224-225 of the same chapter. Properly-done? Perhaps with an E-Meter? Bramley couldn't be talking about the elements of Scientology processing, which Hubbard started calling a "confessional" when Dianetics turned into Scientology and incorporated as a religion, could he? On page 225 he talks about improper confessions, terming them "quickie salvation," echoing the terminology employed in Scientology for abbreviated Scientology processing: "quickie grades."

Chapter 34, "Robo-Sapiens," is a rehash of Hubbard's take on the evils of psychiatry and psychiatric drugging. This was one of the things that Hubbard was right about, but don't get me wrong: Hubbard was right about a lot of things. This is the glue that sticks one so damnably well into the operation, that a lot of it works pretty well, and that a lot of Hubbard's insights were profound. And when you feel you have even a tentative handle on Truth with promises of a hell of a lot more to come (namely, the Advanced Levels), you're willing to ignore the absolute enslavement that you have to submit to in thought, word, and deed.

I could go on listing sneaky Scientology references in Bramley — there are no shortage — but frankly I'm bored with combing through the book. As an ex-Scientologist more than familiar with the in-group cant, I can tell you that Bramley is, without a doubt, a Scientologist who is trying to sell the Hubbard line throughout.

Gods of Eden is not that bad of a book, as UFO/conspiracy books go. A lot of his history is pretty shaky and dependent upon funky sources like AMORC, but I know the problems of sorting out truth and fiction amongst conflicting reports on what's been did and what's been hid.

On this account, Bramley did a decent job. Knowing the references that Bramley is utilizing, however, the originality of his cosmic conception pales. Bramley, like most other true believers, mouths the Scientology party line like a "Robo-sapiens," but then, if you've known any Scientologists, you'll find that they all do. Hell, I did for the 13 years I was a Scientologist, until I finally saw through the scam behind the space opera. Not to suggest that Bramley's intentions aren't honorable when he, like every other Scientologist in the world, attempts to get "raw meat" — i.e. the unprocessed in Scientology — to surrender their personal judgement and philosophy to the "pro-survival" doctrines of L. Ron Hubbard intended to recover the "spiritual being's" "total freedom." Everyone knows what the road to Hell is paved with. It may even be that Bramley won't deny what I have said, that his book is riddled with hidden Scientologese. The point is that he doesn't admit it in the book, and like the evil extraterrestrial custodians he blames in the book, he engages in some pretty sneaky mind control himself.

Jim Keith is the editor of Secret and Suppressed: Banned Ideas and Hidden History, *available from Feral House, and* Casebook on Alternative 3: UFOs, Secret Societies, and World Control, *available from IllumiNet Press.*

Quigley Live!
by Len Bracken

In casting a secret ballot, one casts a ballot for secrets. Like people involved in crime, those who use the ballot box are afraid that their acts will become known, or afraid to authorize a government to act in their name. The secret ballot is a way to avoid responsibility in much the same way that a well-kept secret protects a criminal. And if one is to believe the secret of Carroll Quigley's *The Anglo-American Establishment* - the strange tale of the semi-secret Rhodes-Milner Group by the late Georgetown University professor and Bill Clinton mentor - democracy is nothing more than a tool of control for global market planning.

Secret ballots, secret societies and secrets in general strike me as laughably childish in light of the fact that, eventually, everything becomes known. The world-wide money cartel described by Quigley was even referred to as "Milner's Kindergarten." Most of us are as curious as children when we see the smoke and hear the whispers - we want to discover the secret. Quigley says as much in reference to what provoked his study of the French Revolution of 1789: "I always had the eyes of a child."

According to the *Washington Post* Clinton has evoked Quigley lectures as "the rhetorical foundation for his political philosophy" as if they were an enchanted childhood memory revolving around the American dream like his trip to the White House to meet JFK. In speeches made a decade after Clinton was at Georgetown, Quigley sounds nothing like the convinced imbecile who would have him say "America is the greatest country in the history of the world."

Here's Quigley speaking for himself: "Secrecy in government exists for only one reason: to prevent the American people from knowing what's going on. It is nonsense to believe that anything our government does is not known to the Russians at about the moment it happens." The time was 1976, and retired professor Quigley returned to campus to deliver three lectures as part of The Oscar Iden Lecture Series.

It is testimony to the haughtiness of historians in general, and Quigley in particular, that he would attempt to present the sweep of human events from 976-1976 in three lectures: "The State of Communities," "The State of Estates," and "The State of Individuals." Quigley had the contemplative knowledge of the privileged academic, and the experience of being in the presence of his material, and by this I don't mean the archives in France he romanticizes in his lectures to inspire the young scholars.

It isn't very difficult to imagine young Bill Clinton once sitting at the feet of his favorite old professor, listening to the latter divide civilizations into Class A and Class B. The tone was that of an arrogant Princeton man, the voice of the establishment that belied the content and meaning of his words. Perhaps it was because he sensed the coming of the end of his life (he died the following year) that he let go with zingers such as this: "But, most significantly, out of the Dark Age that followed the collapse of the Carolingian Empire, came the most magnificent thing we have in our society: the recognition that people can have a society without having a state. In other words, this experience wiped away the assumption that is found throughout Classical Antiquity, except among unorthodox and heretical thinkers, that the state and the society are identical, and therefore you can desire nothing more than to be a citizen."

Quigley, the wannabe anarchist? At the end of the above quote, the tape and the pamphlet of the lecture differ. The transcript entirely omits the following: "And if you want to go down in a ghetto, or catacomb and be with your cozy co-believers and so forth and so forth, you are an enemy because you are violating a fundamental assumption." In giving us his list of aspects of sovereignty of states (cooperative defense, cooperative resolution of internal disputes, administrative power, taxation, legislative power, executive enforcement of laws, money control, incorporating power) Quigley underlines the sensitive points of states, and where to strike so as to repossess or destroy this aspect of sovereignty.

In what is perhaps a case of projecting his present on the past, as historians are wont to do, Quigley tells us there have been three periods in Western Civilization ruled by judges and lawyers: "The first period would be from 1313 to about 1480; the second was from about 1690 to the French Revolution; which was a violent response against a mass of confused, legalistic rigidity preventing necessary reforms. The third is our own day when judges and lawyers are running everything and we are obsessed by legalism and litigation."

At times Quigley sounds Marxist: "The fundamental, all-pervasive cause of world instability is the destruction of communities by the commercialization of all human relationships and the resulting neuroses and psychoses." Another cause of instability is that the world is dominated by elements of sovereignty outside of the structure of the state. Banks and corporations are, "free of political controls and social responsibility, and they have largely monopolized power in Western Civilization and in American society. They are ruthlessly going forward to eliminate land, labor, entrepreneurial-managerial skills, and everything else the economists once told us were the chief elements of production. The only element of production they are concerned with is the one they can control: capital."

Quigley attacks America on so many grounds that one is forced to ask if this isn't a latent radical showing all the bad cards held by the state on his death bed. The self-denial of living for the future that caused the protests of the 60s and 70s, the endless material desires, the mistaking of self-disciplined liberty for individualism, the fixation on quantitative change, the detriment of being "hung up on" vicarious experiences, the inability of missile weapons to control people that made the state vulnerable to terrorist attack, the reliance on a mercenary army recruited from elements of the population without internal controls, industrial production of medicine and food - in short, nothing works very well, least of all the Constitution with the Supreme Court ("we have to have someone supreme," he said facetiously) and Imperial Presidency.

Listen to this:

"Now I come to my last statement. I regret ending on what is, I suppose, such a pessimistic note - I'm not personally pessimistic. The final result will be that the American people will ultimately prefer communities. They will cop out or opt out of the system. Today everything is a bureaucratic structure, and brainwashed people who are not personalities are trained to fit into this bureaucratic structure and say it is a great life - although I would assume that many on their death beds must feel otherwise. The process of copping out will take a long time, but notice: we are already copping out of military service on a wholesale basis; we are already copping out of voting on a large scale basis. I heard an estimate tonight that the President will probably be chosen by forty percent of the people eligible to vote and that the percentage of voters who were registered and didn't vote will be higher for the fourth time in sixteen years. People are also copping out by refusing to pay any attention to newspapers or to what's going on in the world, and by increasing emphasis on the growth of localism, what is happening in their own neighborhoods."

And as a parting shot, he added: "And if a civilization crashes, it deserves to. When Rome fell, the Christian answer was, 'Create our own communities.'" Quigley studied the state and knew it was ugly, no longer the thing of beauty that Burckhardt described in Renaissance Italy. As Quigley expressed his long term view of the development of the state, it is precisely its hiatus in the Dark Age that stands out as "magnificent." Elsewhere Quigley relished the suicidal, for the state, campaigns of Ford and Reagan that promised to reduce government. If he seemed to pull this punch it was out of the need to keep the state in the ring with the corporations, even if he knew that the state had outlived its usefulness in every regard. In the end, he put faith in community. And by total omission of the word, Quigley did service to democracy.

What Aren't We Being Told, Exactly?
by Scott Corrales

To judge by the articles appearing in certain Central and South American magazines, we are certainly missing out on a lot of information. The "news that is fit to print" appears to be considerably different from what is heard and reported beyond the borders of the United States.

U.S. troops are on the move again—not against Somalia, nor Bosnia, nor yet another raid against Saddam Hussein. According to Puerto Rico's *Claridad* newspaper, the United States is planning the military occupation of the Amazon Basin, in a scenario straight out of Tom Clancy's *Clear and Present Danger*.

Articles which have appeared in the Peruvian and Brazilian press state that elements of the 37th Airborne, stationed at Fort Bragg, have set up a powerful transmitter near the town of El Beniá, in the dense Bolivan Amazon, in order to maintain vital radio links with the Southern Command in Panama and with the Pentagon itself.

The result of this information becoming public knowledge prompted the questioning of Bolivian president Jaime Paz Zamora by members of that country's parliament, concerning the issue of the illegal presence of well over a hundred American soldiers on Bolivian soil.

To judge from these reports, the 37th Airborne is currently erecting a permanent base in the heart of cocaine-producing territory. The official government explanation in the face of such an activity was that they understood that "a school was under construction."

Alfonso Alem and Gregorio Lanza, two politicians from La Paz, visited the area on a fact-finding mission. Their report to the parliament stated that U.S. military engineers were indeed in Santa Ana, studying high, medium and low-intensity warfare in drug-producing regions. This revelation caused parlamentarian Hugo Carvajal to state, "We must keep foreign military activity from turning our country into another Panama."

All of these revelations have come about at an odd moment, when the Bolivian government has embarked upon a massive campaign to legalize the use of cocaine and achieve industrial production of the leaf. This pro-cocaine sentiment is also very strong in neighboring Perú, where groups citing the historical and medicinal use of the narcotic have gone as far as to lobby the United Nations' Vienna-based commission.

Deputy Lanza, who formed part of the mission to Santa Ana, made public his belief that the U.S. forces have brought a large number of weapons into the country in order to train and to carry out swift tactical reaction operations, whose ultimate aim would be that of occupying either the Bolivian, Peruvian or Colombian Amazon under the pretext of counteracting drug-traffickers or fighting leftist guerrillas such as the *Sendero Luminoso*.

Carlos Saavedra, Bolivia's Minister of the Interior, released a statement on July 21 1992, confirming that U.S. forces were building permanent facilities in El Beniá as part of a pact between the two countries to intensify the "War on Drugs." This agreement, which excluded the use or training of Bolivian forces in the drug war, became a closely-guarded secret of President Paz's administration. A "consolation prize" for the non-involvement of the unreliable Bolivian military would come in the form of 15 million dollars worth of U.S. military matériel. Ninety per cent of the military activities to take place were to be of a repressive nature: enhanced police activity, military assistance, radar vigilance, indictment of aerial traffic and control over ports of entry. Implementation of the secret project allegedly involved the construction of a dozen new DEA bases as well as three military airstrips in the jungle.

The outcome of the fact-finding mission prompted the Bolivian parliament to demand of the Paz administration why it had acted in violation of the Constitution by bringing in foreign men-of-arms without prior approval. President Paz's goverment claimed that it had merely invoked the 1947 Inter-American Reciprocal Assistance Treaty, but a closer examination of the provisos contained within said treaty made it clear that it could only apply between neighboring countries repelling aggression from a third. The pretext that the U.S. troops were there for "humanitarian reasons" clashed with existing Bolivian legislation forbidding the use of military forces for humanitarian purposes. When asked why there had not been closer scrutiny of the weapon systems being brought into the country by the American forces, Chancellor Ronald MacLean declared that his ministry was not a customs' house, and that furthermore, "a gift horse should not be looked in the mouth."

In spite of the growing demands within the parliament, which is calling for the expulsion of the members of the 37th Airborne, Vice President Luis Ossio warned against precipitating a diplomatic incident that could provoke the wrath of the United States. This sentiment was also echoed by the ministries of Defense and State, and by the heads of the Bolivian armed forces, who feared the possible elimination of U.S. subsidies.

The upshot of the Bolivian situation has been the formal suspension of *entente diplomatique* for all DEA agents, a rearguard operation in the eyes of that country's political establishment, which has been largely opposed to U.S. military involvement in the drug war since Operation Blast Furnace (which took place in the summer of 1986 and was far from successful), which it now fears may have unwittingly led to the establishment of a U.S. garrison on its soil.

Was the CIA Involved in the Spadafora Assassination?
by Gabriela Selser
Taken from *El Día Latinoamericano*, Mexico, Translated by Scott Corrales

The trial against ten military men accused of having taken part in the assassination of Hugo Spadafora, physician and former guerrilla, has not gone beyond mere "window dressing": the core of the matter and the real culprits in the notorious affair, which took place almost eight years ago, remain hitherto untouched.

According to legislators and humanitarian agencies, the Endara government is trying to legitimize its judicial institutions thus, at a time in which nepotism, corruption and influence-peddling are on the rise in Panama's circles of power.

The trial on Spadafora's death is the fourth held this year in Panama against the former henchmen of deposed Panamanian strongman Manuel Antonio Noriega, who have involved former president Manuel Solís Palma (in asylum in Venezuela), three commanders of the so-called "Dignity Batallions" and four officers of the Defense Force, two of them members of Noriega's information services.

The hearing has been the most widely publicized of its kind in Panama in the past years: 17 attorneys, 45 witnesses, and 137 accredited journalists to cover it. According to opposition deputies, this and the previous legal processes are an effort to "wash the government's face before the people."

Set in motion on July 6th in the province of Chiriquí, the trial on the Spadafora case accused Noriega and nine other former military men (among them Luis "Papo" Córdoba, currently in prison) of murdering the distinguished physician, slain when he apparently was getting ready to expose Noriega's links with drug trafficking.

Spadafora, who fought alongside Amílcar Cabral in Guinea-Bissau and supported the Nicaraguans in their struggle against Somoza in the '70s, later joined the colorful dissident revolutionary Eden Pastora and his Miskito Indians in the "Misurasata" Contra group, which attempted to oust the Sandinista government. He was murdered on September 13, 1985 on the border between Costa Rica and Panama, his body decapitated and showing signs of torture and violation.

Colonel Luis Córdoba, who is identified as a close friend of Noriega's, would have been in command of at least 14 officers who participated in Spadafora's interrogation and torture. In his book *Noriega: Nothing But The Truth,* American journalist Frederick Kempe records an alleged conversation that took place between Córdoba and Noriega, in which the former advised: "We have the rabid dog." Noriega allegedly replied: "And what does one do with a rabid dog?"

In detail worthy of the yellow press, Kempe relates how Spadafora was beheaded by his captors "while still alive," after having pulled his fingernails, broken two ribs and severing "the groin muscles, with clean, symmetrical incisions worthy of the cleverest surgeon in order to facilitate anal rape. An autopsy showed Spadafora's rectum to be seriously deformed due to forced, repeated and violent penetration."

According to the author, "Noriega's friends didn't understand. They knew him and that didn't look like his handiwork [...] he had sanctioned political assassination as a tool, and under his leadership, Panama's repression had been relatively smooth and nonviolent."

Panamanian deputies also doubted that the assassination was the work of members of the Defense Force, although the possibility has not been discarded by the press. If Noriega's American critics classify him as "one of Bush's stooges," the assassination's brutality also reflects the use of methods germane to the military training provided by the U.S. to Panama, at the very edge of the national will and freedom of sovereignty expressed by the late Omar Torrijos and Noriega himself.

The CIA's best man?

In a video taken in his Miami prison cell and broadcast during the hearings, Noriega implicated Pastora in the crime (as "having differences" with Spadafora), as well as the Libyan government and the Palestine Liberation Organization (PLO), to whom the doctor allegedly owed 3 million US dollars destined to the Salvadoran and Guatemalan guerrillas.

In spite of the possible truth of his statements, the innocence of this version clashes with others—which are much more credible—in the sense that Spadafora had gathered abundant proof of the CIA-Noriega-Drug trade chain, which made him "a liability" in the eyes of the U.S. intelligence services.

Former guerilla Karl Raffo Coba, Spadafora's comrade-in-arms in Nicaragua, stated that the latter was assassinated "to keep him from revealing that Noriega was the CIA and DEA link in drug-trafficking operations." He also noted that Spadafora learned that the CIA supplied weapons to the Nicaraguan Contras with funds from the drug traffic between Central America and the U.S., as part of the operation known in 1987 as Iran-Contra.

"Hugo was with the Miskitos on the Atlantic coast and never received any of those donations. When backing was denied to him, he spearheaded a movement to point out that Noriega, the CIA, and the entire intelligence community in the area was involved in the drug trade. He faced the monster. That's why they killed him," Coba stated.

Attorney Arnulfo Escalona, a private prosecutor hired by the Spadafora family, also declared that the CIA plotted the assassination in order to protect Noriega. The CIA, said Escalona, did not want to lose Noriega, one of its best men in Latin America.

It doesn't appear to be mere chance that both men, Coba and Escalona, were pressured after having voiced their opinions on the crime. Three days after having made their statements, the former was arrested for the alleged theft of a vehicle two years ago; Escalona retracted on the following day, alleging that he had been "misunderstood" by the press.

The drug bridge

According to official reports, Panama is the main bridge for the traffic of narcotics stemming from South America to U.S. and European markets. Paradoxically, drug-related crime in Panama increased by 300% since the U.S. invasion in 1989 which deposed General Noriega, under the pretext of freeing Panama from the clutches of drug trafficking.

A week after the trial was set in motion, a group calling itself the *Movimiento 20 de Diciembre* (M-20) warned that "Spadafora's real assassin is on the loose" and that the next victims would be deputy Arnulfo Escalona and attorney Winston Spadafora, the slain guerrilla's brother, who has also expressed doubts about Noriega's exclusive responsibility for the crime.

The M-20's warning was contained in a note sent to the authorities accompanied by a skull, which they claimed was Hugo Spadafora's. The skull, which has undergone thorough dental exams, was presented in Chiriquí by former police agent Juan Sousa Betancourt, who is now under police custody and undergoing psychiatric examinations.

Beyond the grim twist that the judicial process has taken, there are many still-unanswered questions related with the true role played by General Noriega in the death of Hugo Spadafora and the implication of the U.S. intelligence services in the same.

According to Eden Pastora, who hastened to deny any personal ties with the events, the assassination of his then-comrade was due to "foreign interests", although "who ordered Noriega to carry out the crime still remains unknown."

On the sidelines of the guilt or innocence of the deposed Panamanian general and the nine accused ex-military men (who have already protested their innocence), there are persons and organizations linked to the market of the international drug trade, among them former participants in Iran-Contra, who are interested in keeping the truth from coming out.

As is always the case in these events, the identities of the true culprits will almost surely remain a mystery.

Who Shaped History: Vampires or Gods?
by William Meyers

Approximately 1400 B.C., according to classic Greek historians, a god, Zeus, had a son by the wife of a king. The son was named Hercules (or Heracles). After performing many feats of strength, including descending into the underworld and returning with the three headed dog Cerberus, Hercules was taken up into heaven by his father. The Greeks set up temples in Hercules's honor; there was even a temple of Hercules built in far off Rome, around the time of the founding of that city. But by Classic times (4th Century B.C.) many of Greece's leading thinkers considered Hercules, and indeed all of the gods, to be mythological characters with no base in history. Unfortunately the Greeks did not learn the art of writing until around 800 B.C., so there had been a gap of 600 years of oral history before the story of Hercules could be written down. Yet during that time, indeed until all pagan temples were destroyed by Christian zealots, people occasionally reported seeing and even talking to Hercules.

In contrast Dionysus appeared in Greece after writing had developed. In Dionysus, *Archetypal Image of Indestructible Life,* C. Kerenyi reassembles the fragmented and mostly lost historical record to show where Dionysus first came ashore near Athens c. 650 B.C., and to describe how he recruited adherents to his religion and established temples. But Dionysus was probably a Cretan god, husband of either a female ruler of the island or an Earth Mother god, at least a thousand years before he established his temples on the Attic Peninsula. Again, both classic Greek cynics and modern historians and pedants insist that first hand accounts were wrong, that there are no gods, that they do not take the shape of men, and they cannot live hundreds of thousands of years.

Add some facts (or legends, if you so insist): Dionysus slept underground for a year, and then was awoken to spend a year with his worshippers before returning to an underground vault. Equate wine, for which Dionysus was famous, with blood (which the Dionysians did in secret ceremonies) and you have the key ingredients of the vampire myth. But is it just a myth?

Romulus founded Rome, and after safeguarding the city ascended into the heavens to be with the gods. He continued to appear to Romans, beginning with a Senator who was an ancestor of Julius Caesar. His stated purpose was to make Rome the seat of a great State. About 700 years after his ascension into heaven Rome ruled the entire Mediterranean world. He was identified with the rather mysterious God of the Roman People, Quirinus. Go figure.

Mithras founded Persia and later came to be an important god of the Roman Empire. Osiris and Isis were an Egyptian king and queen who rose from the dead around 3000 B.C. and led the Egyptian religion for over 2000 years. Quetzalcoatl played an almost identical role in ancient Mexico. Krishna was an immortal warrior god in ancient India who still has a large cult following. Chang Ling and other Taoists claimed to be immortal and established a hierarchical church that was the true power in Western China for nearly 2000 years.

Should we leap to the conclusion that, because people seldom live to be 120 years old, that is an absolute limit on lifespans? No one is sure how long turtles live because they tend to outlive their human keepers. Respectable journals like *Scientific American* report a growing body of research on how to prevent aging. Could the ancient immortals simply have a different genetic program, one that allows them to survive ordinary death and to live for centuries or even millennia without aging?

Interestingly, most of the vampire-gods have similar ancestors: sky gods. The story of Zeus almost reads like an ancient version of the current story of UFOs with breeding agendas. Zeus would rape a woman, and have a son-of-god. That descendant would then have female children, who would in turn be raped by Zeus. One study of the ancestry of Hercules according to the old Greek stories indicates that most of his genetic material would have been derived from this sky god. Thus he was more god than man.

Even the Bible, that rude recorder of history and superstition both, distinguishes between the sons of gods and the sons of man. It is the sons of god like Methuselah who lived for centuries. And, as Von Daniken pointed out, there are spaceship like vehicles aplenty in the Old Testament.

Regardless of whether these gods came from UFOs or not, they are certainly the models for the vampire myth. The immortal god who eventually supplanted most of these other historical figures, Jesus Christ, is in fact a perfect match for the vampire myth. Like Dracula he is able to hypnotise people and has zombie followers. He can raise the dead with a kiss, and himself could not be killed. He can (and did) transfer his power to create vampires, though to a weakened degree, to his disciples. He came to rule a great empire: the Pope was the virtual dictator of Europe during the middle ages. And he was bloodthirsty. Most converts to the Christ cult converted at sword point. Many more pagans were tortured and killed by Christians during the decline of the Roman Empire than vice-versa. In fact the Christians, who loved to call each other heretics as much as they loved to see blood, killed more of each other in bloody sectarian wars than were killed by the handful of emperors who outlawed their religion.

The role of their religions in history is not ignored even by those scholars who would deny the vampire-gods a real existence. But some ancient historians attributed much more to these immortals than the establishment of religious cults. Most notably, the establishment of agriculture is attributed to Osiris and Quetzalcoatl; of wine making to Dionysus; and of laws and contracts to Mithras. Osiris, Jesus, and Mithras all had the power to anoint, or to cast down, kings.

Do the vampires still exist, and somehow rule us, today? I can't answer with total certainty, but there is much evidence that they do. The Catholic Church is still a remarkably strong institution despite its promotion of superstition, depression and alienation. But perhaps it is not exclusively in Churches and Temples that we should look for vampires. There are many stories about immortals posing in many other social roles, most notably as businessmen. For instance, it is remarkable how generation after generation of new Duponts appear to rule over their industrial empire.

I cannot even begin to cover the wealth of facts that need to be considered to properly study this idea in a short essay such as this. I must refer the reader to my book *Vampires Or Gods?*, which, despite its length, is also just bringing to light the most important facts and conjectures in an easily grasped manner.

William Meyers' book, Vampires Or Gods?, *is available at bookstores, from Flatland or for $15.00 postpaid from III Publishing, P.O. Box 170363, San Francisco, CA 94117-0363.*

Book Reviews

Defrauding Americas
by Rodney Stich

We have all heard the sorry tales of the corruption of our political system, our courts, corporations and military. While some justify an attitude of complacency by saying it's always been that way, others investigate and write of the details of this ever-expanding virus of criminality at high levels.

Rodney Stich has compiled in 538 pages what is perhaps the best documented effort of the extent of the pattern of this corruption. Stich's expertise stems from his career as a former FAA Flight Safety inspector and whistleblower of faulty airline practices in design and maintenance. This was detailed in his 1978 book, *Unfriendly Skies,* and gives the hard facts behind these practices, which have resulted in the deaths of thousands.

Stich breaches the wall surrounding the secret activities of the CIA and its many proprietaries. The disturbing news becomes abundantly clear as this well researched work gives you the connection between numerous scandals. Many of our nation's serious problems like the S&L stink, BCCI, Inslaw, drug trafficking, conversion of Chapter 11 courts into a criminal enterprise, the October Surprise and the prosecution and deaths of many whistleblowers have been linked by Stich's personal experience and research.

Part and parcel to *Defrauding America* is Stich's own journey into whistleblowing. In order to fund his activities, Stich relied heavily on the fortune from his real estate endeavors. He had built up a net worth of over six million dollars with properties that amounted to about ten million. Stich admits that he inadvertently gave his adversaries a clue as to how to stop his exposure activities, stating in a radio interview, "As long as they can't get to my money I'm OK." The scheme to silence Stich began in 1982 and got the illegal cooperation of the Federal government and authorities in California. Stich would lose millions and even briefly be imprisoned. Although he would be partially vindicated when a few of those who had committed crimes against him would be brought up on charges themselves, by then he had lost most of what he had accumulated. How this was done should be a lesson for us all to learn as this kind of insider racketeering is responsible for billions of dollars of looting nationwide. The irony of it all is that many of those affected rarely know the truth behind their dilemma until its over.

Due to Stich's investigative activities, he has acquired what appears to be one of the larger networks of insider information coming from US, Israeli and contract agents working for the intelligence agencies.

In *Defrauding America* you will see first-hand documented evidence from Michael Riconosciuto and his wife Bobby about the blatant piracy of the Inslaw software by the Department of Justice (DOJ). This theft could not have been completed without full cooperation from the highest official in the DOJ. Deputy Attorney General Lowell Jensend was amongst the first to refuse to pay for the successful program which resulted in putting Inslaw's creators Bill and Nancy Hamilton into Chapter 11. Stich documents the Inslaw cover-up, the buying off of pursuing attorneys, pressuring witnesses and alteration of testimony. Plus, the illegal sale of Inslaw software by Dr. Earl Brian and General (Iran/Contra) Secord to Korea, Chile, Canada, Iran and even George Bush's good buddy in Iraq, Saddam Hussein.

Stich follows this travesty of official criminality by corroborating testimony of those willing to talk about it, by the legal proceedings occasionally left in its wake and more.

The blatant abuse of power also manifests itself in the morality of sexual practices by those who apparently consider themselves above the law. One of the disgusting practices uncovered by Stich (with help from a former FBI agent and other intelligence sources) is the use of pedophilia to blackmail and control those who enjoy this deviate behavior. If you're wondering what is happening to a portion of those missing children, this could be one important area to check out. There may be hundreds, even thousands being abused or even killed every year for the amusement of this sick group.

If as a parent you can tolerate the aforementioned actions, or as a taxpayer you don't mind being robbed of billions of dollars through scandals and covert operations, then *Defrauding America* is not for you. However, if you really want to know the who, what, when, how and why behind these scandals, *Defrauding America* is what you've been waiting for.

Stich is certainly no Steinbeck and is periodically repetitive in his refrain of corruption, but he does seem openly honest about it. While many conspiracy researchers are quick to lump in these behaviors with the New World Order, the Rothschilds, Bildebergers, the Rockefellers or even the Illuminati, Stich does not point out any one point on the map of conspiracy. He states, "It is obvious that this is part of a greater scheme and higher power than I can comprehend at this time." Therein lies the problem for the average

American citizen in understanding the scope of this criminality.

There has been refusal by major US wholesalers to stock this book. Perhaps the reason for that could be how he exposes media and publishing complicity in these illegal activities.

—I. M. A. Dissident

Secret and Suppressed:
Banned Ideas and Hidden History
edited by Jim Keith

This book poisoned my dreams. Columns of HIV-infected crabs - each one bigger than the last - were released into my bed by the CIA...and when I woke up in a cold sweat, the eyes of the skinhead on the cover of the book were fixed on me in a menacing stare. Thinking back on what I'd read - from John Judge's dispassionate case that the U.S. intelligence services were involved in the Jonestown massacre, to Kenn Thomas' contextualization of "A Draft of Danny Casolaro's Octopus Manuscript Proposal" - I knew what had poisoned me: the truth. As the editor put it in his introduction: "It seems fair to warn you, however, that even a tentative scratching at the gargoyle-facade that passes for reality will likely unleash a clutch of demons from the far side of Truth."

The most disquieting essays are in the "Menticide" section of the book. Anna Keeler gives us the best exposition to date of "Remote Mind Control Technology" - if you doubt that it exists, *read this article!!!* To my mind, there is nothing so nefarious as targeting the brain with coded microwaves, which is what your friendly government did to the female peace activists of Greenham Common, England who were protesting the build-up of nuclear weapons, and to those under siege at the Branch Davidian compound at Waco. When you hear a madman yell "They made me do it" ask yourself what makes him so mad. And after reading Robert Naesland's "An Open Letter to the Swedish Prime Minister Regarding Electromagnetic Terror" (including X-Rays showing brain implants), Kerry Thornley's case for paranoia seemed very reassuring to this paranoid.

And then the book gets really weird. We have Downard's "Science of Symbolism" that Robert Anton Wilson described as "the most absurd, the most incredible, the most ridiculous Illuminati theory of them all." A nice compendium of the myths surrounding the death Jim Morrison. "The Last Testament of Rev. Jim Jones" with a picture of the Rev. kissing a chimp. "Secrets from the Vatican Library" from a Franciscan monk - a grandiose conspiracy theory that centers on the "Teutonic/Zionist clique" (a Vatican library chit is reproduced at the end of the essay). G.J. Krupey's article on the origin of AIDS is an extremely well-written, researched and reasoned report on the likelihood of Pentagon involvement in creating the disease. And to round off this tour-de-force of the unacceptable there's a long, riveting interview with an operative for the Nazi International chief, Otto Skorzeny.

Whereas the owners of the world use the mainstream media as the guardian angel of sleep, this dispatch from the margins is a wake-up call. *Secret and Suppressed* (Feral House, POB 3466, Portland, OR 97208, $12.95) gives you the poison of truth that will make your stomach turn, like a little dose of cyanide.

—**Len Bracken**

Things Are Gonna Slide

Aurora Erratum

The letter concerning the Aurora spy plane crash was in error. The crashed plane was *not* an Aurora, but was in fact precisely what Lockheed said it was in the following day's news releases—a four engine L-100, the civilian version of the C-130 military transport plane. The plane had a modification that made the wreckage of the tail section of the craft look like an odd delta-wing. This modification is supposed to reduce the stall speed of the L-100.

Much mystery still surrounds the crash, however. It seems that a "meteorite" with a long blue tail had been witnessed by many people *throughout* the South-East of the United States—*concurrent* with the crash. Also, there was without a doubt a news blackout in the major media regarding the crash. More recent cover stories have stated that scientists had been alarmed in early February by the close pass of a very large meteorite in the atmosphere. Of course, none of the "scientists" were referred to by name.

The blue tail of the supposed meteor may have been in fact the result of Lockheed's testing of new, unconventional armaments on board the L-100 aircraft. This aircraft is now being considered for use as a platform for mounting rail-guns, hypercannons, co-axial launchers, HPMs (High Powered Microwaves) and ram accelerators. This scenario differs from the Lockheed cover story in that the plane in fact would have been airborne when the accident occurred. Based on the fact that the witnessed "meteor" caused an electrical brownout in the region of the crash, suggesting that a powerful electro-magnetic pulse—such as that from a rail-gun or x-ray laser—was responsible for the brown-out and also probably malfunctioned resulting in the explosion of the aircraft in the air. This might also explain the several explosions noted by witnesses, one air explosion and one or two ground impacts from the fall to earth. The only portion of the aircraft visible on CNN had been the tail section—resembling a delta wing aircraft. The main fuselage was never photographed by civilians and must have fallen to earth in a remote location. Roff Sasser III of the National Transportation Safety Board said that a full investigation of the crash would take six months, but it is doubtful that the public will hear or read or see *any* further information on this particular crash, especially since it has been six months as of this writing and the only reports have been about those unnamed "concerned scientists" who were worried about the "large meteor" which made a close pass on the same morning as the crash.

Mr. Craig H. Smyser, principle investigator of advanced weapons systems integration at Lockheed Aircraft Service Company claims that today's gunship aircraft are too large and vulnerable to enemy fire to be completely effective. With current gun-powder based systems, a gunship may have to drop as low as 8000 feet to ensure an accurate strike on a target, but the new hypervelocity systems will allow the gunship to fly higher than 15,000 feet—well beyond the range of conventional ground based anti-aircraft weapons. Mr. Smyser claims that the leading candidate for development is the rail-gun. More sophisticated systems using directed energy, such as lasers and particle beams are "not mature enough for tactical applications". However, the use of high-powered microwave is already being investigated by Lockheed. Is the military now in the process of finding suitable platforms—air, land, sea and space—for placing HPM and particle beam systems that are likely responsible for the Crop Circle phenomena that has been growing more steadily complex?

(References: Smyser, Craig H., "The Future of Firepower," *Lockheed Horizons,* January 1993; "Hyperweapons: Goodbye Gunpowder," *The Futurist,* July and August 1993.)

Leary Smear

The Saturday, January 1 edition of the *Boston Globe* reported the "news" item that psychologist Timothy Leary had conducted experiments using psilocybin on prisoners at the Concord State Prison in Massachusetts in 1961 and 1962. The experiments are a fairly well-known episode in recent American history that Dr. Leary has discussed openly in biographies in 1967 and 1982. The *Globe* reported that former prison officials suggested that prisoners in these experiments may not have given fully informed consent.

Dr. Leary responded in the January 2 edition of the *Washington Post,* saying, "My God, whenever you do any kind of drug research...you have to give the patient every kind of [information]...This was not a researcher from Harvard who went in, dumped a lot of drugs on people and walked away." Leary's remarks did not appear in some syndicated versions of the news story.

The *Globe* article attempted to connect the prison experiments, widely acknowledged as having a positive effect on recidivism in the prison, to recent revelations about government radiation experiments conducted on citizens without their knowledge. A doctoral student at Harvard's Kennedy School of Government, Richard Doblin, who has studied prison records of the experiments, noted that all prisoners gave their consent. He characterized as "unethical" the attempt to link this work with the notorious radiation experiments.

Various syndicated versions of the news story called Dr. Leary a "drug guru" from the 1960s. Dr. Leary is a humanistic psychologist who currently lectures to large audiences and is actively involved with transforming computer technology into an educational resource. A book of his most recent writings, *Cyberculture,* edited by Michael Horowitz, is expected from Ronin Press in the spring. Leary described himself to the *Washington Post* as "a dissident philosopher from the school of Socrates."

Conspiracy in the Clinton Era
by Kenn Thomas

As a teenager I heard John Kennedy's summons to citizenship. And then, as a student at Georgetown, I heard that call clarified by a professor named Carroll Quigley, who said to us that America was the greatest nation in history because our people have always believed two things: that tomorrow can be better than today, and that every one of us has a personal, moral responsibility to make it so.
—from Bill Clinton's acceptance speech to the Democratic National Convention, 1992

As the tangled web of charges over marital infidelity and financial impropriety descended upon President Clinton at the end of last year, these remarks about moral responsibility echoed as irony only to those who took them at face value. Carroll Quigley, the Georgetown University professor whose memory was conjured by the presidential nominee, had already been flagged by conspiracy theorists as one of their own, a theoretician of the one-world secret cabal. Quigley's book, *Tragedy and Hope,* had long been regarded by right wingers (even cited in Pat Robertson's books) as a codex to the hidden ambitions of the Trilateral Commission and the Council on Foreign Relations. His pronouncements could only be regarded as cause for deconstruction. By invoking Quigley, Clinton had virtually telegraphed to the conspiratorial cognoscenti a signal to start massaging its database. A new age of conspiracy theory had arrived.

Response to that signal was impressive. By the time the former Arkansas state troopers made their claims about their former boss' alleged sexual liaisons, any scandal they might have caused paled in comparison. Bill Clinton already had been linked to the cover-up of a guns-and-drugs operation being run out of an airstrip in Mena, Arkansas. The body count around him had exceeded statistical norms even before the Vince Foster death. One researcher claimed that three of the four BATF agents killed in Waco were former Clinton bodyguards. Even mainstream sources, like columnist William Safire, had bought George Bush's silence with regard to criticism of the new administration by soft-pedaling the Iraqgate investigations. While the media focussed on Bobby Ray Inman's non-payment of his maid's taxes, the ill-fated nominee for Secretary of Defense was emerging as a personality among ufological conspiracists for comments he made to a retired NASA engineer regarding MJ12, the long rumored secret government task force on extraterre-

strialism. In fact, the Clinton administration bogged itself down in the Mother of All Conspiracy theories by dragging out the appointment of the JFK Assassination Materials Review Board. With three years left in his term, President Clinton had proffered enough raw material to keep conspiracy researchers busy well into his second term—if his secret masters deemed he would have another.

The conspiracy research community needed the feast set before it by the Clinton administration. On the JFK front alone it had waged veritable food fights in the media over the Oliver Stone movie, the Free The Files legislation and the passing of the thirtieth anniversary of Kennedy's demise. While the staid *Wall Street Journal* was characterizing JFK researchers as demented and primitively malicious, no less a hip source than Garry Trudeau began lambasting them in the funny pages, before moving on to such politically incorrect targets as the homeless and political correctness itself. The Fox Network co-opted one pet cover-up of the conspiracists, the secret Aurora aircraft project at Nevada's Area 51 and its concomitant UFO rumors, by making it the subject of its new spook show, *The X Files.* The 1992 elections ushered out the CIA president George Bush, and such Reagan offenses as the October Surprise seemed like history even as history finally was putting them into perspective. The conspiracy crumbs of the 1980s had virtually been nibbled away by the time the Clinton administration sauntered to the table.

The Quigley Connection

Before Carroll Quigley died in 1977 he had become almost a reverse barometer for the John Birch Society. Both agreed that the world was run by a secret cabal of Rockefellers, Rothschilds, Morgans and like-minded financiers. Quigley laid the conspiracy bare in an enormous book entitled *Tragedy and Hope.* Its thesis, however, was not critical of the super-cabal. Rather, Quigley viewed it as a "benevolent conspiracy", in the words of Jonathan Vankin, author of *Conspiracies, Cover Ups and Crimes.* The duty of a worthy academician was to describe, explain and praise to his students this secret arrangement of international affairs. The Birchers read *Tragedy and Hope,* became enraged at what they viewed as an insider's confessional and started listing it regularly in the footnotes of their books as proof of the monied interests behind their bugaboos, groups like the Trilateral Commission and the Council on Foreign Relations.

By quoting Quigley, though, Bill Clinton did more than renew the ire of the John Birch Society. That he referred to the late Georgetown University professor on a regular basis throughout the campaign and virtually enshrined him at the Democratic National Convention caused some to laud Quigley's work as the rhetorical foundation of the new administration's political philosophy. In the conspiracy realm, it caused others to review Quigley's research.

Writer Jim Martin, whose *Flatland* book service remains one of the few places where copies of *Tragedy and Hope* still can be purchased (POB 2420, Fort Bragg, CA 95437), notes that Quigley's main research involved the Rhodes-Milner Group, a real elite with real connections to both the Morgans and the Rothschilds, founded by Cecil Rhodes. In the latest *Flatland* catalog, Martin also points out that Cecil Rhodes was one of the world's wealthiest men, that he had a country named after him (Rhodesia), that he founded and funded the Rhodes scholarships and that Bill Clinton is a Rhodes scholar. "The function of the Rhodes scholarships," explains Martin, "was to identify future leaders, instill them with common values at Oxford, and send them back to their native colonies where they could spread these acquired traits."

More alarming to Martin, however, is Quigley's documentation of the money given by Rothschild-styled capitalists to left-wing causes and communists, part of the realization of a "century old plan to end national sovereignty, consolidate all currency and institute the Global State" according to the Birchers, but the cause of "some seriously contorted parapolitics" to the less paranoid. According to Quigley, progressive journals, specifically *The New Republic,* were funded by financiers, specifically the Morgan Bank, to manipulate the left. For instance, "Quigley says that Wall Street wanted to defeat Truman," according to Martin, "and so they used Henry Wallace [recently hired as editor of *The New Republic*] to form a third party candidacy to draw enough support from Truman's left flank to elect a Republican. To do this they allowed many communists into the staff of *The New Republic* to promote his candidacy." Whether Quigley's analysis is right or wrong, the admiration he expresses in *Tragedy and Hope* for the "piece of work" that he thinks led Wallace to his defeat hardly squares with the mantle of moral responsibility President Clinton bestowed upon him.

Researcher Len Bracken explores this disparity further in an upcoming issue of *Steamshovel Press,* a nationally distributed print forum of "conspiracy"-oriented writing. In a study of speeches by Quigley made ten years after Clinton left Georgetown, Bracken comments that "Quigley sounds nothing like the convinced imbecile who would say America is the greatest country in the history of the world." Bracken echoes Jim Martin's observation in *Flatland* that Quigley viewed democracy as little more than a control mechanism for global market planning but holds out the possibility that Quigley became radicalized in his last years. Of these later speeches, Bracken writes: "Quigley attacks America on so many grounds that one is forced to ask if this isn't a latent radical showing all the bad cards held by the state on his death bed." In one of his last speeches, Bracken quotes Quigley as having this assessment of the American state: "Today everything is a bureaucratic structure, and brainwashed people who are not personalities are trained to fit into this bureaucratic structure and say it is a great life—although I would assume that many on their death beds must feel otherwise. The process of copping out will take a long time..." Again, this is a far cry from the Carroll Quigley that exhorted Bill Clinton to make each tomorrow better than today.

The Mena Mess

Less intellectual entanglements with the conspiracy nether world have occupied the attention of researchers since April 1992 when a decidedly non-intellectual source, Geraldo Rivera's old *Now It Can Be Told* infotainment tabloid, ran two stories on drug smuggling, money laundering and possible Contra war troop movements in and out of an airstrip in the small Arkansas town of Mena. The case had been written about early on by Alexander Cockburn and has since been reported on and expanded upon in *Village Voice,* Paul Krassner has brought it to the attention of the readers of his satirical newsletter *The Realist,* and it took up an entire chapter of John Bainerman's book, *The Crimes Of A President* (SPI Books), which ostensibly intended to expose abuses of the Bush administration. Before recent developments regarding the Vince Foster suicide, the cover-up in Mena promised to be the weak link in a chain that entangled Bill Clinton not only with George Bush but also with Oliver North's secret network of operatives running off-the-shelf projects to finance the Contra war.

The Mena story begins with a drug dealer named Barry Seal who apparently began smuggling drugs through the airstrip in 1982. The operation continued past Seal's 1984 drug conviction in Miami. As Seal was working deals with the DEA and Ollie North's network trading undercover work against the Sandinistas for immunity, as the story goes, a second wave of mysterious businesses descended upon the Intermountain Regional Airport at Mena. These businesses described themselves variously as aircraft and parts delivery services, but rumors of drug traffic continued and new rumors, that the airfield was also being used for commando training, began. The Arkansas state police investigated and reported to the U.S. attorney but expected indictments were never returned, leading to the suspicion that the Reagan administration could add one more small cover-up to its tally.

Bill Clinton did not become involved until a pair of students at the University of Arkansas, Mark Swaney and Tom Brown, appealed directly to their then-governor to investigate. The appeal, and another call for financial assistance to help the state conduct a grand jury investigation from the Deputy State Prosecuting Attorney, met a stonewall. When Arkansas Congressman Bill Alexander met with Governor Clinton, he was told that $25,000 in state money had been set aside to investigate Mena. The amount was slight enough for an effective investigation but even that was never delivered. The prosecuting attorney in Mena's Polk County at the time said he never received the offer from the then-governor's office.

The IRS began an investigation of Barry Seals' operation in Mena after Seal was murdered in Baton Rouge by Colombian drug traffickers, but investigators were warned off, causing one to quit and testify before a House committee about all he had learned of money laundering, covert operations and drug smuggling in Mena.

The man who introduced Gennifer Flowers to the world, Larry Nichols, was first responsible for revealing the Clinton-Mena connection. Clinton had hired Nichols as marketing director for the Arkansas Development Finance Authority (ADFA) but fired him when his contacts with the Contras became too apparent. The governor's office used the charge that Nichols had made unauthorized phone calls to Central America as a pretext for the firing. The Mena allegations, and the claims of Gennifer Flowers, ensued from Nichols consequent defamation lawsuit against Clinton. Another court case, that of CIA contract operative Terry Reed, also added much to the Mena story. In 1988 Reed was charged with postal fraud for receiving insurance money on a false claim. Reed claimed that his airplane had been stolen as part of an Ollie North-styled project called "Private Donation", wherein "donations" to the Contra cause were filed as lost or stolen with insurance companies and then reimbursed. According to Reed, he had no awareness of "Project Donation" at the time of his plane's disappearance, and so reported it as a legitimate loss. The plane reappeared after Reed learned of the Donation project and warned his contacts in the Ollie North network that he would have no part of it. The person who found the reappeared plane was Buddy Young,

then working for Bill Clinton as security chief. Young later admitted to tampering with the plane, and charges against Reed were dropped. Reed has since put forth his entire story in a new book, *Compromised* (Shapolsky).

Terry Reed made one other interesting claim about his work with the North operative network: that he was approached to begin a front company that was to be headed by Felix Rodriguez, the Iran-Contra player who figured prominently in establishing that George Bush had indeed been inside the Contra supply loop. Rodriguez had been a leading police authority in Batista's Cuba in the late 1950s and his name comes up often in JFK assassination research as a suspicious anti-Castro Cuban with ties to the events of that day in Dallas. The Clinton and Kennedy conspiracies had met a crossroad.

The Kennedy Conundrum

Candles were passed around at the night vigil in Dealey Plaza during the thirtieth anniversary observance of the JFK assassination in Dallas last November. The event had been organized by Citizens for the Truth about the Kennedy Assassination (CTKA) as part of the Assassination Symposium on Kennedy (ASK), the annual convention of researchers who feel they have left the Warren Commission at the starting gate in the rush toward the truth about this topic. Jim DiEugenio, the author of a critical study of the Jim Garrison investigation of JFK's death and head of CTKA, suggested to participants that they hold on to the remains of their candles until Bill Clinton comes to Dealey Plaza to acknowledge the tragedy and leads an effort to expose the conspiracy. During the campaign, Clinton had deferred to Al Gore on the question of conspiracy and Gore's statements made him seem sympathetic to the cause. Gore's college roommate, actor Tommy Lee Jones, played Clay Shaw in the Oliver Stone movie and, like most in Stone's retinue, was outspoken in his contempt for the findings of the Warren Commission. A suggestion was made at the candlelight vigil that Clinton might even appear in Dallas the next day to lead the charge for a renewed investigation.

The suggestion was not met with the response one might expect from impassioned enthusiasts for a reformed and restored America. It consisted of a lukewarm spattering of applause. Had not the Clinton administration emasculated the Assassination Materials Review Act of 1992 by dragging its feet in making nominations to the review board? The last of those nominations had just been made and all the nominations were pending the long congressional approval process. The nominating process had taken one year of the board's proscribed two year life. Neither the FBI nor the CIA had been cooperating with the spirit of the Free The Files legislation, and Bill Clinton had not even deferred to Al Gore for a criticism. The last review board nominee suggested to the *St. Louis Post-Dispatch* that he had gleaned an opinion about Oswald acting alone from a *Frontline* television documentary he had seen two weeks earlier.

The audience that had such slight excitement over the prospect of Bill Clinton as its avenging hero was not disappointed. President Clinton finally asserted himself during his press conference on the anniversary day: Lee Harvey Oswald had acted alone in his estimation. The delay in appointing the Board was first ascribed to the changeover in administrations; the continuing delay had caused some suspicions; this final pronouncement had put Bill Clinton solidly back into the fog of shadow government with only Carroll Quigley as a moral compass.

Waco Weirdness

Many of the participants at the candlelight vigil at ASK made these connections, though many did not. Of all the gatherings that discuss current issues, the conspiracy scuttle-butt foments best at events like the ASK symposium (its narrow focus on an historic event thirty years gone only tangentially disqualifying it as a current events forum), if not as part of the program then certainly as part of the break-time conversation. Jack White, who has done an enormous amount of work analyzing a large inventory of Oswald photographs, flashed a slide before his presentation showing a tank backing away from the destruction at the Branch Davidian compound with flame ostensibly spewing from its cannon. "The cover ups continue!" exclaimed White.

The scene came from a videotape entitled *Waco: The Big Lie,* circulated by the America Justice Federation (3850 S. Emerson, Indianapolis 46203), headed by Linda Thompson, who filed a petition during the Waco siege to represent David Koresh and his followers. The tape contains a detailed view of the bungled BATF raid taken by Ken Fawcett and local radio personality Ron Engleman from an unedited satellite feed. The flame-throwing tank has been challenged by others as misidentified debris from the conflagration falling in front of the tank as it backs out from destroying a wall of the compound. What has not been challenged, however, is Thompson's assertion that three of the murdered agents had been bodyguards for Clinton during the presidential campaign.

The tape also claims to show that the alleged former bodyguards were actually killed by a fourth BATF agent, either deliberately or with reckless application of the "spray and pray" method of gunfire used after the three had entered a rooftop window. According to the tape, the raid itself began after this fourth agent accidentally shot himself in the leg while climbing the ladder to the rooftop. The rest of the gunfire from the BATF was simply responding to that accidental discharge. CNN interviewed a survivor of the initial raid who was indeed undergoing therapy for a leg injury, but a broken one, not a wounded one.

The Body Count

Dave Emory does a radio program in California's Santa Clara Valley called *One Step Beyond* in which he reads into the public record various kinds of research material he has collected from newspapers, magazines and books, puts it into a context by linking similar and connected stories and offers it to listeners on tape for review (POB 170023, San Francisco, 94117). Through this method, Emory has reached an interesting conclusion about the mortality rate in the Clinton campaign and administration: it exceeds what would ordinarily be expected from a study of the laws of statistical probability. In addition to the Foster suicide, Emory notes that two important Clinton campaign aides died during the campaign. Also, the woman who had been doing sign language interpretation of Clinton's speeches for the hearing impaired and was scheduled to do the same at the inauguration died unexpectedly before Clinton took the oath, at age 36. Presumably, the statistical wave now includes the bodyguard deaths at Waco. Emory offers a reminder that natural deaths and accidents can be easily faked with the resources available to the intelligence community. Although he makes no direct charges in this regard, he does place the statistical anomaly in a category familiar to his listeners: food for thought and grounds for further research.

Inman The Spaceman

Extraterrestrial theories are frequently thrown in to the conspiracy milieu as comic relief, although in many instances conspiracists note that flying saucer rumors are often injected into situations where real leaks of government secrets occur in order to deprive those situations of any credibility. This theory has been used to explain the UFO stories emanating from the military testing site outside of Rachel, Nevada known as Area 51, from where the sub-orbital Aurora craft is said to launch despite denials from the Air Force that it even exists. (Enough information on the Aurora has leaked to allow a toy manufacturer to produce miniature models of it, and, of course, it was a plot element in X Files.) Flying saucers of every geometric description have been witnessed by hundreds ever since bus tours of Area 51 have been organized by amateur skywatchers in the past few years. But the disinformation theory has yet to be applied to President Clinton's failed nominee for Secretary of Defense, Bobby Ray Inman, since the only known improprieties of his past at the time of his nomination involved tax discrepancies apparently shared by many Clinton nominees (save for the suggestion in Jim Hougan's 1984 book *Secret Agenda* that Inman might have been Deep Throat of Watergate fame). Inman figures prominently in at least one UFO researcher's tale, however.

Alien Contact (Morrow) is a follow-up to author Timothy Good's *Above Top Secret,* a book well-received among ufologists for its documentation of international government interest in UFOs. In it, he describes the efforts of a retired NASA engineer named Robert Oeschler to contact Admiral Inman and discuss military knowledge of extraterrestrial craft because of Inman's extensive background with technology-related government projects. Oeschler approached Admiral Inman after a speech and handed him a note requesting that the admiral help get him in closer contact with MJ12, a secret government liaison group with space aliens of longstanding repute in the UFO lore. The Admiral said OK.

The two men did not talk again for over a year, when Oeschler, who occupies some of his retirement with the responsibilities of being assistant state director for the Mutual UFO Network (MUFON) in Maryland, called to discuss MJ12 and perhaps gain some access to government data on extraterrestrial craft. Admiral Inman demurred that he had retired from intelligence work and was seven years out of date on any such information.

Oeschler continued, "Do you anticipate that any of the recovered [extraterrestrial] vehicles would ever become available for technological research—outside military circles?", according to Good, who was present during the phone conversation. "Ten years ago the answer would have been no," replied Admiral Inman, "Whether as time has evolved they are beginning to become more open about it, there's a possibility." Good also notes that while Admiral Inman now denies any knowledge of UFOs, he has admitted in a signed letter that this was in fact the topic of his phone conversation.

The Foster Death

The suicide of assistant White House counsel Vincent W. Foster last July left the sad legacy of a lost friend for President Clinton but also a conspiratorial quagmire that lingers like a ghost spooking his administration. The circumstances of the death, a wound inflicted by an untraceable antique gun, were quickly overshadowed by questions of motive: what aspect of Foster's involvement with Hillary Clinton's Rose law firm in Little Rock drove him to such an extreme? Just before Christmas, law enforcement officials were pre-occupied with files removed from Foster's office just two days after his death which reportedly documented the Clintons' involvement with an Arkansas real estate partnership called the Whitewater Development Corporation. The files also contained information on James B. McDougal, a Whitewater partner and owner of a failed S&L in Arkansas, the Madison Guaranty Savings and Loan. The extent of any financial improprieties, the legal dimensions of this developing drama and the impact it will have on the Clinton presidency remain to be seen, but the conspiracy mill already has attached the scandal to international murder plots and long-standing connections between Clinton, George Bush and the Atlanta branch of the Italian state bank, Banca Nazionale Del Lavaro (BNL). Researcher Sherman Skolnick states flatly that Foster died trying to prevent the assassination of Saddam Hussein.

Skolnick offers press releases and a telephone recording (312-731-1100) through his Citizen's Committee To Clean Up the Courts in Chicago and is a respected veteran of the research community. He claims that the White House registry records a July appointment by Vince Foster that he did not live to make and speculates that Foster planned to urge the president to forestall a plan by the CIA to kill Saddam Hussein. This plot was later reported upon by the *Chicago Tribune.*

Foster did not attempt to do this out of love for Saddam Hussein or even to make tomorrow better than today according to Skolnick's scenario. He did it to prevent Saddam's half-brother from releasing bank records revealing the extent of Clinton and Bush involvement with BNL. The Atlanta branch of BNL recently had an official, Christopher Drogoul, sentenced for laundering money used in Saddam's military build-up before the Persian Gulf War, but it had been fingered also as a presence in the JFK assassination in a 23 year old document of some repute among JFK researchers. Known as the Torbitt Document, it claimed in 1970 that BNL had financed the training of the hit team used against Kennedy. Once more, a crossroad had been reached connecting the labyrinth of the Kennedy assassination with the burgeoning labyrinth of the Clinton conspiracies.

In the end, Skolnick is not clear on what exactly kept Foster from making that fateful appointment, or how the CIA plot against Saddam failed anyway. He also asserts, however, that former FBI director William Sessions was removed for something related to the Clinton-Bush-BNL connection, and that Foster was actually a victim of an assassination team from Germany.

If indeed President Clinton is as immersed in these plots, counterplots and various intrigues as some of the research in this New Age of Clinton conspiracies suggests, the need for the kind of moral certitude he ascribed to Carroll Quigley seems obvious. Like the research, however, its litmus test will be the degree to which that certitude is real or the imaginative projection of those who put it forward.

Kenn Thomas is a free-lance writer in St. Louis.

8

Steamshovel Press #11, Summer 1994

Zero Waste: From Phalanstere to Biosphere
by Jim Martin

What's going on in Oracle Junction, Arizona? By now, you may have heard about the hermetically sealed, glass-and-steel enclosure called Biosphere2, built in the Arizona desert near Tucson as a radical environmental experiment in total recycling. Since 1991, the 7.2 million square foot terrarium, which leaks air at a rate of 1% per year (the space shuttle leaks 300% per year) was built at a cost of $150 million of the Bass banking family's money. It has been inhabited by two different crews of researchers who raise all their food within the Bio2 complex, recycling air, water and waste in an effort to study the feasibility of launching a similar project in the not-so-distant future on the surface of Mars. Billed as a research station, tourist attraction, and ongoing R&D center in environmentally sound science, the project has lost millions of dollars while producing little in the way of marketable new technology.

I happened to visit Biosphere2 just before the recent managerial shake-up. This spring I took a "working vacation" in the Tucson area to revisit some of the sites of Wilhelm Reich's final experiment, "Desert OROP Ea", conducted around Tucson between October 1954 and March 1955. Reich was under an injunction by a court order to refrain from distributing orgone accumulators and during this time he had every intention of abiding by the court's decree. The emotional plague was closing in, however, and Reich was beginning to behave like a caged animal. He had long since abandoned individual psychotherapy in favor of new pursuits in natural science, and his trip to the desert was a last-ditch effort to force the world to recognize his discoveries.

Reich's last published work, a scarifying document called *Contact With Space*, is a full report on this desert expedition, undertaken with his son, Peter, his daughter, Eva (then a twenty-five year old medical doctor), and the few remaining coworkers whom Reich could press into service. His daughter didn't want to go, but Reich insisted: "The harvests are plenty, but the workers are few."

Reich had successfully used his cloudbuster, a set of hollow metal tubes that he grounded in water, to restore atmospheric pulsation and bring rains to droughty regions around his research center in Rangeley, Maine. He sought to extend this research by testing the device in some of the most arid lands in the U.S., found near Tucson, Arizona along the border with Mexico.

Contact With Space describes the long journey west, where he set up a temporary base about 8 miles north of Tucson. Reich explored the region while taking ambient radiation readings with his Geiger counter, working with the atmosphere using his cloudbuster while parrying with UFOs, which he sensed were responsible for at least some of the atmospheric stagnation in that region. The experiences he describes in his last book are too heavy with implication to do justice in a brief article, but I hope to pursue a book on Reich's final years, tentatively titled *Am I A Spaceman?*

There are many parallels between the Biosphere2 project and the "Desert OROP Ea" expedition Reich undertook 30 years ago in the very same region. Both experiments approached atmospheric research with an understanding that the Earth functions as an organic whole. Each research team assumed that the Earth's atmosphere is undergoing severe strain, and sought answers to prevent an apocalyptic ecological collapse. Interstellar travel was a key component to both experiments, with Bio2 exploring the possibility of a self-contained "biome" which could sustain a small population of humans and other life-forms in outer space. Reich has always been ridiculed for his interest in UFOs, and he and his co-workers reported seeing many in the desert around Tucson. Rather than argue for the reality of flying saucers, Reich sought to understand their propulsion system.

In many ways the Biosphere2 experiment is an embodiment of a wrong turn taken 30 years ago.

I had first heard about Bio2 in a series of glowing reports written by Kevin Kelly in *The Whole Earth*

Review. Based in part on the work of J.E. Lovelock's "Gaia Hypothesis" as well as earlier work by Russian geologist Vladimir Vernadsky, who was the first to use the term "biosphere", the project intended to investigate whether a closed system, properly stocked with a variety of plant, animal and insect life, could sustain a human community in isolation from the surrounding atmosphere. Completely funded by private money, the Bio2 complex would receive funds from visitors and technological spin-offs in the areas of recycling, air and water purification, and space technology.

Bio2 was the brainchild of John Allen, one of the members of the first "biospherian" crew that entered the sphinx-like pyramid on Sept. 26th, 1991. Dr. Roy Walford, author of *The 120 Year Diet* (a reduced-calorie, high-nutrient diet which Walford found to increase the life-span of rats to the equivalent of 1.2 centuries) was another important member of that first crew.

The Psychozoic Era

Much of the material published by Synergetic Press, the publishing arm of Bio2, refers back to the work of "Academician" Vernadsky, the Russian scientist who taught with Teilhard de Chardin in Paris during the 20s. Vernadsky's intriguing theory, that the Earth's "crust" has been formed not by mineral processes, but by succeeding layers of biological detritus, seems to be the main inspiration for the Bio2 group. Vernadsky held that the earth's geology and atmosphere cannot be separated from the process of life, and that the earth must be taken as an organic whole along with the atmosphere and ozone envelope. The earth functions as a kind of receptor of cosmic energy, said Vernadsky, and he even seems to make a distinction between solar rays and some kind of "luminous energy" on earth, much like orgone. He describes his theory as different from previous vitalist and materialist ideas about life. "Considering living matter as a unity, a planetary phenomenon, this feature called civilized man cannot be regarded as an accidental one. Hence we must treat with caution any idea which suggests that the present limits to life are immutable," Vernadsky wrote in *The Biosphere* (1929).

Late in his life, in 1944, Vernadsky suggested that the planet is entering a new geological era, which he called the *psychozoic era.* "The historical process is being radically changed under our very eyes. For the first time in the history of mankind the interest of the masses on the one hand, and the free thought of individuals on the other, determine the course of life of mankind and provide standards for men's ideas of justice. Mankind taken as a whole is becoming a mighty geological force. There arises the problem of the re-

construction of the biosphere in the interests of freely thinking humanity as a single totality. The new state of the biosphere, which we approach without our noticing it, is the noosphere."

This concept of the noosphere fascinates me. Like a mystical envelope of mass mind, it envelopes the Earth and molds it. "The problem of planned, consistent activities which will aid us in mastering nature and accomplishing the correct distribution of wealth, connected with the comprehension of the unity and equality of all people, of the unity of the noosphere, is now on the agenda." Utopian, to be sure, but reminiscent of a termite nest. That Vernadsky delivered this paper, which turned out to be his last, in 1944 is an indication that Stalin had no serious disagreement with Vernadsky's ideas.

Synergetic Press literature also reinforces the idea of a yawning gulf between man and nature. Like the most misanthropic of environmental activists (like Edward Abbey and some members of groups like Earth First!), humankind is viewed as a kind of "plague species".

As I undertook my plans to visit Arizona, I noticed the news reports of a new crew entering the Bio2 and thought I'd take a look. While the project's environmental goals appeared laudable to me, I was interested more in the Utopian aspects of such a community. How did they make decisions? Kelly didn't say. The whole thing reminded me of the great French post-revolutionary thinker, Charles Fourier. Beginning in 1800, Fourier had begun a life-long blueprint and constitution of an ideal, Utopian community, which he called the "Phalanstere", based on the novel theory of "passionate attraction" on which all life turned. He envisioned a society ruled by the metaphor of harmonious musical chords. Different strokes for different folks is another way of putting it. His "unitary architecture" anticipated the Situationists' "unitary urbanism" by nearly two-hundred years, and his work was revisited frequently by sixties radicals in search of historical antecedents. The young Marx claimed Fourier as one of the first true socialists. He was a champion of sexual freedom and enemy of boring work long before these icons became common commodities in the intellectual marketplace. Fourier spent his whole life seeking a rich patron (such as the Bass family) to fund a trial "Phalanstere", which would return the investment through technological spin-offs (generated by the total engrossment Phalansterians experienced when an entire society was set up to anticipate their desire for meaningful work, delicious food, and gratifying sexual encounter) as well as selling trinkets and mementoes to the curious visitors who would undoubtedly be drawn to the interntional community.

From Phalanstere to Biosphere

My friend Alex Hamann accompanied me on the back-road journey toward Oracle Junction from Phoenix. Along the way, we spotted a black, unmarked helicopter hovering 30 feet above the desert in a desolate stretch, just hovering over nothing. The Bio2 complex presented itself as a sprawling neo-Bauhaus shopping mall nestled in the rolling foothills of the Catalina Mountain range. Parking our rented white Sunbird among dozens of Winnebagos, we awaited the tram to haul us uphill to the attraction. Signs warned against walking in.

After forking over the $13.50 admission fee, we oriented ourselves in a room with a scale model of the complex. "We ask that you take no photographs of the model, since Space Biosphere Ventures retains the copyrights. You may take pictures of the complex itself, however". Further on, in a movie theatre not unlike that at Disneyland, we "Meet The Biospherians" in a multimedia experience revealing the plucky pioneers and their project. "No public funds have been used to build Biosphere2."

At the bookstore, I found many of the original Synergetic Press books, including one by Vladimir Vernadsky (published by MIR Press in Moscow), which I bought in lieu of any real information about the origins and intentions of Bio2 presented thus far. Outside, we strolled around the massive complex, taking pictures as we walked. No Biospherians were visible through the glass pane enclosure, which was dripping with condensation on the interior like a cold sweat. I suppose I wanted to find some Biospherians, draw their attention by tapping on the glass.

I left feeling like they were hiding something. It was too damn quiet there. They were silent, in words, writings, and multimedia on the issue of decision-making within the group.

Hostile Takeover in Utopia

No sooner had I returned from the trip when all hell broke loose at Bio2. Ed Bass, financial angel for the project, got a court order to ban John Allen, Margret Augustine, Mark Nelson and others in Decisions Team Inc. (DTI) who headed the management at Bio2 from the premises. On April Fools Day (and also Good Friday) federal marshals appeared, the locks were changed, the attraction closed for the day, and the whole deal was placed under the receivership of Martin Bowen, a Bass associate. In a written statement, Bass indicated he was fed up with the recalcitrance of the management team and ready to recoup his investment, although he was committed to the basic research being done at Bio2.

[While Bio2 publicity assures us "no public funds" were used in the Bio2 complex, the same cannot be said of Bass' bank holdings. Bass made most of his estimated $2.2 billion net worth in a single deal, in which he acquired the failed American Savings & Loan in 1988 for $350 million while the government put in $1.7 billion to sweeten the pot. If I am reading the news reports correctly, Bass was actually paid $1.3 billion to "buy" American. Before Bass bought American Savings, it was stripped of all bad loans in its portfolio and these liabilities were assumed by the taxpayers. These liabilities are now estimated to be $4 billion by federal regulators, making the S & L's failure the costliest in American history at $5.4 billion (sic). AP reports (5/21/94) that Bass is putting American up for sale. I'll buy it Ed, if I get the same deal you got!]

Next, on Easter Sunday, two members of the original crew which entered Bio2 in 1991, Abigail ("Gaie") Alling and Mark Van Thillo, opened four of the five doors into Bio2's air-tight enclosure and broke five panes of glass in the "lungs" (a huge dome housing a pump which regulated the expanding and contracting air inside the enclosure). Reports indicated that the seal was broken for about 15 minutes, but my guess it was far longer than that. On Monday, Gaie Alling placed calls to Bio2's new management and the press, including the AP news service, explaining her actions. She cited a deep concern for the welfare of the remaining crewmembers and said "I did not sabotage the Biosphere". Alling and Van Thillo had been suspended in the management shake-up, and had been seeking $10,000 in back pay. "At any moment in time something could go wrong," Alling told the press. "It's like sending the shuttle up and in midstream you replace the captain and the mates."

"I've no remorse for what I've done. I've acted for the safety of the Biosphere." Alling denied the act was sabotage or revenge. Acting as "assistant vice president of Space Biosphere Ventures" she wanted to protect the seven people remaining inside.

While Alling was making these statements on Tuesday, April 5th, John Allen, the head of the team ousted by Bass, was issuing similar eery statements clear across the world in Tokyo on Wednesday. "There is not now a single person left in power by Mr. Bass... who knows why anything is being done. They have done all this without concern for the safety and well-being of the seven human beings inside Biosphere2." Reuters also reported that Allen was "worried the project would be trivialized and turned into a Disneyland-type attraction to make money."

Vernadskyland

Indeed. To me, one of the most heartening aspects

of the project was always that a Utopian community had adopted the methodology of Disney, and might serve as a model for more experimental projects that could be self-sustaining without government support. Just think of it: Cooperburg, L-Ronville, Situland...the possibilities are endless. You may think I'm being sarcastic, but I'm not. This nation was founded on cults too strange for Europe. I can honestly say that I love America, warts and all, for precisely this reason. After Fourier's death, several communities based on his ideas appeared only here.

But who is John Allen, the main force in charge of the group of managers forced out by Ed Bass? According to sources who would rather not be identified because of safety concerns, Allen was a fixture in new-age, occultist circles in Santa Fe since the early seventies, where his wife still owns the "Synergia Ranch". Allen served as the guru for this New Mexico commune under the rubric "Institute for Ecotechnics". A British subject, Allen was a student of J.G. Bennett (author of *Meetings with Jung*) who was the major promoter for Gurdjieff until he discovered the Polynesian Muslim Pak Subid. "Ecotechnics" is a non-profit foundation operating privately owned enterprises (apparently for tax advantages), including two farms in Australia, a conference center in France, a gallery in London, hotels in Katmandu & Houston, along with ranches in Texas and Arizona. Started in the early 60s in New York, this secretive guru-system views itself as an evolutionary vanguard, based on the works of Gurdjieff, the Russian geologist-marxist-mystic Vernadsky, and J.G. Bennett.

Essentially, Allen's group believe the Earth is doomed, and the evolutionary forefront (Allen and his followers) have prepared to create Bio2 as a mode of transit by which they will shove off from the rest of us sleepwalkers. There is a suspicion that "Ecotechnics" group-dynamics involves the typical sex-drugs-hypnosis forms of guru manipulation. Allen attracts a "high-level" type of person: rich & bright; Gaie Alling fits the bill perfectly. In fact, her mother (Gail Alling of Kennebunk, Maine) was quoted by the AP wire as saying "She's a victim of mind control... The people who have been kicked out are members of a cult." Reportedly, one of the Bass brothers fell under Allen's sway; thus the $150 million start-up money.

So we need to take a closer look at the striking similarities between Alling's statements of concern for the remaining Biospherians after the sabotage of Bio2's seal and John Allen's similar statements issued from Tokyo within a 48-hour period. Certainly this indicates a close communication, perhaps even some discussions before the event? But it gets even stranger. The next day, Allen faxed a "rambling four-page letter to drug-culture guru Timothy Leary, asking him to distribute it on a computer network" according to the Associated Press. Although they didn't name it, this computer network is sponsored by the *Whole Earth Review*. "The WELL" is one I check in with regularly and it has a forum wherein e-mail and bulletin board postings can be sent to the Biospherians. Leary posted a message saying he had received the fax, and uploaded it in his "home directory" but gave no indication how to access it. After many requests to post it openly (and not just from me), Leary has not responded. It's clear from the excerpts from this fax, related in the AP article 4/15/94, that Allen may have implicated himself along with Alling's sabotage. As of this writing, Leary hasn't posted the original fax. Leary was an early convert to the Bio2 project. I suspect he knows how it would sound now.

Especially since the matter has since been settled quietly in court, with Allen and the others, save Margret Augustine, having all backed out and issued statements of support for Bio2's new management. Terms of the settlement were not disclosed. What has happened to the overwhelming concern for the Biospherians that caused Gaie Alling and Mark Van Thillo to break the seal? What's changed in the situation, now that John Allen has settled? Why would Allen choose Tim Leary as his press agent? Would you choose Leary when criminal charges were in the air? Why would Allen think well users would support his side in the dispute?

Returning to the original reason why I visited Tucson, it's ironic that here, in Oracle Junction, where the Biosphere2 experiment involves a controlled, manipulated environment and atmosphere, is the same place where Wilhelm Reich was doing his atmospheric experiments with the cloudbuster exactly thirty years ago. The two approaches could not be more completely opposed. Reich sought to heal the environment and prevent a catastrophe, while the Biospherians sought to privately seal off from the catastrophe while openly and cynically preparing for final lift-off, leaving us suckers behind. While Reich committed no crime, he died alone in jail; John Allen apparently is implicated in an adolescent vandalism while walking away with a pay-off and/or blackmail. Tim Leary once again has the onus of mind-control hanging over his head. Biosphere2, a sick and perverted monument to isolation, separation and evasion of the life energy continues to herd the suckers in at $13.50 a head. Yet if I were to advertise the health benefits of the orgone accumulator and offer to sell one to you, feds would roll. The Dome of Doom prevails.

Sherman Skolnick Sounds Off!
An Interview by Kenn Thomas

Steamshovel Press editor Kenn Thomas recently had the distinct pleasure of having dinner with legal researcher Sherman Skolnick at his usual haunt, the River Flame restaurant off Highway 94 outside of Chicago. Sherman Skolnick has been on the scene since his early courtroom victories regarding the corruption of Illinois state courts and congressional re-apportionment in that state. His research has made him a perennial figure in national politics. He helped expose the existence of a Chicago-area assassination plot against JFK involving Lee Harvey Oswald. He demonstrated that sabotage was the probable reason for a United Airlines crash that killed the wife of E. Howard Hunt and eleven other Watergate figures. He surfaced a great deal of information regarding witnesses to events surrounding the Inslaw investigation. In fact, he continually exposes interesting and under-reported details about current political scandals on the hotline of his group, the Citizens Committee to Clean Up the Courts (312-731-1100), which also has helped many people with their struggles in bankruptcy court. Sherman also produces a Chicago public access cable television program that further documents the issues and cases he has brought to public scrutiny. Virtually dismissed entirely by the mainstream and often labeled a kook even by some in the conspiracy research community, Skolnick's work has nevertheless had a remarkable staying power and his successes in court and in the media have earned him much respect as a champion dirt-digger and exposer of hidden truth. This interview provided a rare opportunity to discuss history with him, his own as well as that of the people and events he has investigated over the years.

Q: How did you get in to this line of work, Sherman?

A: It's not a line of work. It's unpaid work if I ever saw it. I lived all my life with my parents. Since the age of six I have been a paraplegic from polio, similar to the late President Roosevelt, who was a hero when I was a child. In later years, I didn't consider him so much of a hero, I considered him one of the greatest counter-revolutionaries of American history in that he prevented a genuine upheaval against the ruling elite in this country which was overdue.

Q: They also went to great pains to hide his disability.

A: Right, although the *Chicago Tribune* used to call him the cripple in the White House. In some ways the *Tribune* wasn't nicer to me either. What I should have learned from Roosevelt about the media because I was often videotaped sitting in my wheel chair and I didn't realize they were looking at me as a crippled bug in a wheelchair, a nut, a crackpot.

Q: That's precisely why they tried to cover up Roosevelt's disability, so he wouldn't look weak or infirm.

A: It took me up to about 1979 to figure this out, after my friend says, "Hey, no more videotaping by the media, only sitting at a table in a restaurant like everybody else. None of this standing on your crutches, none of that sitting in the wheel chair, and stuff like that."

My father was a Ladies Garment Worker and I was born in the bad years, 1930, and my folks had a very great problem in taking care of me. In fact, the only way I could get hospital treatment—no hospital would let me in and my folks didn't have any money—so my mother took a long shot and she wrote directly to Roosevelt. She said, "I got a son that seems to be like you. What do you want to do about this?" And we got a letter back from the labor secretary, Francis Perkins, and that letter opened a lot of doors for me. It got me into the HDCC, which is the Home for Destitute Crippled Children, which was a hospital on the University of Chicago campus.

Q: So you do owe Roosevelt a debt.

A: Yeah. He was a hero because he looked very much like me, he had braces, he was paralyzed from the legs down just like me and he needed a wheel-chair. But he could walk a hundred feet, like I can. I can walk a hundred, two hundred feet max. The only difference was that I was poor and he came from a rich, aristocratic, up-state scene.

So my parents were always concerned over the years with what will be with me. I had sixteen experimental operations and I thank heaven that I didn't get into the anti-doctor field, as some people are, you know, rapping doctors, because there is no way I could be objective.

One of my doctors was Mary Sherman, who was murdered as a result of the Jim Garrison investigation in New Orleans. She was my doctor until about 1954. She was an orthopedic specialist. (*Steamshovel* Debris: a new book, *Mary, Ferrie and the Monkey Virus* by Edward Haslam, not available at press time, connects Mary Sherman and Oswald associate David Ferrie with an underground medical laboratory experimenting with monkey viruses to develop a biological weapon.)

As I got older, I was very good at the special school I went to. Early on my folks bought a car and had it equipped with hydraulic controls. So as a teenager, I drove all over.

Q: In the late 40s you had that?

A: Oh, yeah. At the end of the second war they came out with the special cars for legless veterans. They put in an electric clutch, because they didn't have automatic transmissions. And they had hand controls for the gas and so on. So I learned how drive and I drove until 1959, when the car got too old to go anymore.

I learned from an early age that there are what's now called "politically incorrect" people. I don't know what they called them years ago. My teachers at the Spalding High School for Crippled Children here in Chicago were political outcasts. For example, my teacher in mathematics, Dr. Bernard Anderson, was politically incorrect. Previous to this, he was a protege of Albert Einstein but there was something wrong with his politics. So they had him previously teaching at the jail. I had Einstein's protege teaching me mathematics in small school and I was at the top of the class!

Q: You graduated from Spalding in 1948?

A: I graduated salutatorian in my class. I would have been first in my class except for my politics. I was forever railing against the government. In high school I had a small mimeograph machine and I used to print an underground thing investigating all the teachers except my math teacher.

I learned at an early age that if you find out the secrets, you have got a weapon bigger than a sixteen inch cannon on a battleship. I suppose that's what I have been doing the rest of my life. If you can't persuade them on the law, the facts and the merit of a thing, then you better do closet work. You go into their closet, "what about your bank?", etc.

I took a city-wide scholarship test from Roosevelt College, a so-called left-wing school, a hotbed of liberal politics, and I scored first place. So they said I could go for five years but after three semesters I gave it back to them because getting there was such a problem. It was hard to park my special car. I had to bribe the policemen to do that.

So for a few years thereafter I ran a small printing business in a basement.

Q: You weren't producing radical literature then?

A: No, just printing jobs for people in my neighborhood. So as my parents got older, they became worried about what was going to happen to their life savings. They didn't save much. How could they have saved much with the limited income my father, as a Ladies Garment Worker, you know?

Q: They were surviving mostly.

A: Yeah! I don't think he made more than $5000 in the best year of his life. So they had saved up $7500, which was a fantastic sum, by not taking vacation, not buying a new car, all that, and by living in a very reduced house. So they ran into a broker that was Jewish who talked their lingo from the old country. And he sweet-talked them into turning their life savings over to him and he's going to make it into something with me as a beneficiary. Well, he lost all the money on margin, without us ever signing any papers authorizing him to gamble with the money on margin. When he got through with it, not only was the $7500 not there anymore, he claimed my folks owed him $20,000.

So we hired a lawyer and we spent I don't know how many years fighting. I used to go myself all the time with the lawyer.

Q: This was your first experience with the court?

A: Yeah, and my lawyer used to say, "Look sad. Tell your parents to cry a little bit." And I thought this was humiliating. In other words, a cripple and his parents are coming there to get their money. So he says, "Go to your ward committeeman." And I say, "What do you gotta do?" And he says, "You got to give him something. He's got to intercede with the judge." And I says, "What does that mean?" "He's got to go and do something. There's so many voters for the Democratic Party at your address. You're willing to contribute to the judge or the Democratic Party or his campaign. You gotta send him about $300 minimum." And I says, "To do what?" "For a proper hearing!" And this first lawyer urged me to study law, which I did.

Q: After he introduced you to corruption.

A: Yeah. Well, the first trial we had by jury was fixed.

Q: So you hadn't come up with money for the judge?

A: No. First of all, we didn't have it and number two, we wouldn't do it!

The bailiff in charge of the jury was the neighbor of the forelady that ran the jury. The judge goes home and puts the bailiff in charge and the bailiff tries to kick me and my dad out of the courtroom. We stood there and the bailiff lets Hornblower and Weeks, that's the stock broker's lawyer, big-shot, stand by the jury door to talk and tell them that Skolnick is a rat, he's no good, he's a liar all his life—at the jury door! Right there at the keyhole! This is all documented. It became a federal lawsuit.

I says, "Hey, bailiff! Me and my father, we'll

come there and talk how nasty *they* are!'' ''No, no, no, get the hell away.'' When the trial ends, I call up my lawyer at 11:30 because the jury comes out of there with no verdict, and I tell the bailiff, ''Hey, before we go home, where are the papers?'' ''I didn't find any.'' ''Wait a minute, they went in there with evidence.'' ''It's all gone, we don't know where it is.''

So I call up my lawyer at home and I wake him up. He went home. He left me and my father to be in the courtroom near the jury door. He says, ''Listen. What are you, tired of living Skolnick? The sheriff is in with the mob here. What's with you? Are you and your parents tired of living? You got paid up insurance? If you go and complain about these methods, which have been going on for decades, you're dead.'' I say, ''what are you going to do tomorrow morning?'' ''I'm going to go there and ask the judge if he knows if there's a verdict.'' So the next morning he goes there and the bailiff says, ''I didn't find any verdict. I didn't find any papers. The jury went home.'' And that was the end of it.

Q: No verdict?

A: Somewhere down the road some judge got the case and they called for a status hearing again and he suggested a settlement. We were out $7500, which was a lot of money in the 1950s, into the early 1960s. And so the judge suggested $500. Hornblower's lawyers are very big, Bell Boyd and Lloyd, and they say ''we ain't giving Skolnick $500 now or ever. We've never lost a security case in Illinois and we're not starting with Skolnick.'' When I heard that, I figured that's the end. War! So I told my parents I'm going to wreck them. They say, ''how can a small man like you in a wheelchair wreck them? You don't know what you're doing.'' I says, ''I don't know, I'm good in math and I'm good in all these things. I'm pretty clever. I got a high IQ. There must be something I can do.'' So I started in about 1963, I began to run into other victims of injustice. I found out that the woods are filled with them, and I became the beacon, where they can come to me, cry on my shoulder, ''look what happened, I lost my wife, I lost my house, I lost my this, my car, and on...''

So we formed this little group. Now the original name of the group was the Committee To Smash the Courts. And my friend says, ''No, no, no, no. That sounds bad. It's got to be a name that's acceptable.'' So the next name was the Committee To Protect Patent Owners. The first group that I helped were all patent owners that had been swindled out of their patent through the corruption in the courts. At one time I had the attic in my house filled with prototypes—the butterfly bandage, the high speed ice machine. We finally changed the name to the Citizens Committee, not

to Smash The Courts, that was too strong, Citizens' Committee To Clean Up The Courts. It sounded rather...

Q: You're cleaning now, not smashing. This was 1963, the year Kennedy was shot?

A: Yeah, but I wasn't interested in that. I was looking for a way to get in the public eye. A family friend was telling me, ''you're not objective anymore about the Hornblower thing. Nobody wants to listen anymore. Certainly not your friends, not your relatives.''

Q: So your case was not resolved and you were taking on all these other cases.

A: It went on for years and years. A couple of my cases ended up before the state supreme court in 1960s. I argued my own case. They had to carry me up twenty stairs because the crooked judges wouldn't allow me and the wheelchair through their entrance that had an elevator in Springfield. The high court in Springfield is on a hill.

Q: Literally a high court.

A: Through a series of circumstances, in 1969, we continued our closet work. We found out that there are little-known bank ownership records that only Illinois has. Illinois requires public disclosure of bank ownership, which was so secret that it was in the basement of one of the government buildings on microfilm so dusty that nobody knew it until a lady friend of mine discovered it. She said, ''Look at this. Across from the local courthouse there's a bank and thirty judges and nine gangsters own the bank.'' So we start checking and found out that most of the state supreme court are owners of this bank with mafioso.

Anyway, I got to know some Springfield reporters and I made a mimeograph list of this and I offered to show them the microfilm pages.

Q: Falling back on your high school experience here.

A: Yeah. Closet work! We can't deal with them on the law and the facts, we've to deal with them on the dirt. So I found two young reporters from the *Alton Telegraph,* real old newspaper, and they ran a big story about the bank across from the courthouse. At that time the local courthouse had the local office of the Supreme Court on the top floor. The main state supreme court courthouse was in Springfield on a hill. But they had an office in Chicago called the Civic Center. Diagonally across the street was a bank called the Civic Center Bank. It was owned by thirty judges and nine gangsters. And we had the proof. I told this to the *Alton Telegraph* and they started a series of stories that implicated the local newspaper guy. The editor in chief of the *Sun Times* and the *Daily News* was one of the largest stockholders with the gangsters and the thirty judges.

Q: He also happened to be a competitor of the Alton newspaper.

A: I don't know about that, but they wouldn't run the story. So they found a way to get around it by running the story on the Associated Press hub in St. Louis. The governor was a stockholder, who later became a federal appeals judge. By the time I started the scandal, he was no longer the governor, Otto Koerner, Jr. So the story started running with big headlines.

I filed a motion to be appointed *amicus curiae*, friend of the court, and as a friend, I would point out that I was not a party to this case but the judges in this case took a bribe. I found the leading case that this bunch of judges who were stockholders in the bank, the largest stockholder was the former revenue director, Theodore Isaacs. So I found that he had a case in their court on criminal conflict of interest. Two weeks before they heard the oral argument in the state supreme court he does a thing natural for Illinois, he brings all the judges of the court into the bank as stockholders.

So I filed a friend of the court petition in the Isaacs case. They got upset and wanted to know how I knew. They claimed that the *Daily News* had instigated me and had paid me, which was false. Then they said that if I don't tell them exactly how I found this. . . . They didn't know that this was in the public record. I didn't want to tell them. I accuse you of bribery and you want to know how I found out?

So they put me in jail and the picture made *Time* magazine because they couldn't get me into the paddy wagon. So there were four sheriffs trying to put me into the paddy wagon through a narrow door. They took me from the courthouse where the judges put me in contempt for not telling them how I knew they took a bribe, they wanted to put me in this paddy wagon to take me to the jail.

Q: To make a public display.

A: Two got on one side, two on that side. I didn't fit through the door. The sheriff was the brother of Rosemary Woods, Nixon's secretary. He liked me.

For every hour I was in jail, I was in four hours, one judge bit the dust. They put up a special commission that investigated judges and found that most of them were guilty as charged and recommended that they all leave. They resigned August 4, 1969. The third judge I accused died. So they got three of them, the chief judge, the associate judge and a third one. But the fraud is still going on all these years later.

They committed a fraud on the court for the benefit of the governor. There was a lawsuit challenging the validity of the state income tax being pushed by the governor. It was pending in their court at the time of my scandal. In the name of the judges, they issued a decision August 14, 1969, ten days after they weren't there anymore. You can't do that. I recently asked state attorney general Rollin Burris, about this and he got all puffed up and said, "If any of you don't pay your state income tax, I don't want to know about this. I'm going to put you in jail." I said, "This is a fraud upon the court!" I have been talking about this for twenty years and nobody's listening. A fraud upon the court doesn't go away.

Anyway, that's what made me world famous. It was the biggest judicial scandal in the history of the United States. I had collapsed the state supreme court and as result I got to know victims all over. What I did over the years, I didn't want publicity to make money, I wanted publicity so that the press would listen to me. I got in to the biggest controversies because it enabled me to get publicity for my point. For a while there I was able to say whatever I wanted about the courts, about voting and reapportionment, corruption, and so on, up to a point. And I got to know all these victims that came to me.

Q: How do you make that leap from working on local court cases to these national things?

A: Well, for instance, I taught civic investigation for would-be journalists and in the same building where the college was, on the third floor was a strange outfit with no name on the door. And they filmed or taped every talk show in the Chicago area and then sold the tape, the film or the transcripts to certain offices in Washington and the Pentagon. And the courier for that got to know me and he says, "I got something for you, some documents about the Kennedy thing." I says, "I don't have any money to go to Dallas, don't tell me about no Kennedy thing." This was 1970. So I met him and he gives me this pile of documents about the Chicago plot against Kennedy, that there was a plot two and half weeks before. So I was worried and I wrote him a $5 check for xerox expense and on the back I put down "For the Kennedy documents, full payment." The $5 check saved me from the rope, I tell you! Because what they wanted me to do was to blow the cover of certain police that worked for CIA in Chicago. And if I could they would terminate these police. They never intended that I as a loud-mouth would get into the courts.

When I started the plan to go to courts is when I got in trouble. Harold Weisberg says, "Skolnick, come to my goose farm." I say, "I don't know you." He says, "Oh yeah, I'm a leading writer of books about the Kennedy assassination." I say, "I'm not into the Kennedy thing. I'm on the Chicago thing. I don't know nothin' about Dealey Plaza." I never went to his goose farm.

These were all the secret documents that a black secret service agent put together, Abraham Bolden.

Q: You got documents directly from Abraham Bolden?

A: No, not from him. I got them from this guy, this mysterious courier that delivered the film and tapes to a secret office in the Pentagon which he thought to be the CIA.

Q: But they originated with Bolden.

A: What I later found out was that this was the first time in the 200 year history of the National Archives that someone stole this out of the archives. So I was planning to go to court, and luckily I didn't go to Weisberg's thing because Weisberg, after I went to court, threatened to sue me that I stole the documents from him. Luckily, I had this $5 check endorsed by the one that I bought them from, full payment for the documents. David Lifton, who was just getting started on the west coast, I never heard of the guy, I got a letter in the file from 1970 saying "You stole the documents from me!" Lifton writes me from the west coast, Weisberg writes from his goose farm, both say that I stole the documents from them and I bought them from this strange character.

Through my late friend, James Albright, who owned the patent for the high speed ice machine, he knew where to find Bolden at an unlisted address on the south side. So he arranged for me to meet with Bolden. So I went with a lady friend of mine in her car to meet Bolden.

Q: I should say for the readers that Abraham Bolden was the first black Secret Service agent, appointed by Kennedy, and after the assassination...

A: First black in the White House guard.

Q: ...he was apparently thrown in jail on trumped up charges.

A: So I came with my lady friend in her little red car and we sat in front of Bolden's house and I had these documents, eleven of them, mounted in one of those salesmen's books with the plastic pages, under celluloid. And Bolden sits in the back and looks at them and looks at each one and says, "I knew it. You are here to put me back in prison. I'm on parole!" I says, "Bolden, I want to clear you." "Like hell you do! You're part of a government effort to put me back." And I say, "I think Mark Lane didn't do right for you when you were down there in Springfield, Missouri. I think all your lawyers put together have not done right for you. I am here to clear you." "Like hell you are. You got my secret report. It's not supposed to be out until 2039. You got it. You stole it. And I'm going to be blamed that I gave it to you and I'm going to be sent back to jail and you are going to

get publicity and I am going to get jail." I says, "For godssakes Abraham Bolden, I am here to do good for you. I'm going to court and attach all these documents and I'm going to confront the goddam government and I'm going to put in there how they framed you." I didn't know anything about Garrison or Dealey Plaza, I kept no clippings, I was not interested in that.

Q: Garrison tried to do something and failed and here you're coming to this guy saying you're going to do the same thing, take it to the courts. If he was following the Garrison case, I could imagine that he would not have the same faith that you had that you could do something in the courts.

A: And so I went to court and I sued, *Skolnick vs. National Archives and Records Service* and I set forth the whole thing about Cuba, about Kennedy, about Bolden and the fact that Bolden was framed. On the day we brought the lawsuit, one of the major 50,000 watt stations here had a good young reporter, Stuart Pahn, that I knew and he put a major story out on it. He eventually was run out of Chicago. There aren't any happy endings to any of this. Stuart Pahn went into the brokerage business.

Q: What was in Bolden's report?

A: It was on the plot to kill Kennedy in Chicago by a person named Lee Harvey Oswald and an Oswald double, Thomas Arthur Vallee, both of whom were apprehended. Vallee was arrested on a $5 traffic rap and the traffic ticket was suppressed and put in the National Archives. Two blocks off the Northwest Expressway, which is now called the Kennedy Expressway. And they were going to go through a hairpin turn just like they ended up going in front of the Book Depository. They found a hairpin turn in the route from the airport to the college football game where on November 2nd Kennedy was to go to a football game in Chicago. He didn't come, but his route was to go through a hairpin turn where they had another guy who was working at a CIA printing office with the window looking right down at Kennedy. The complaining witness against Vallee was Daniel Groth, not listed as policeman, listed as a witness. Later Groth came with a machine gun, kicked in Fred Hampton's door and assassinated people there.

Q: The Black Panthers.

A: 1969. The same guy. But no author has ever called me to ask for copies of Bolden's documents. A day after I filed the lawsuit in April of 1970, they tried to revoke Bolden's parole. And my friend on a major radio station here went on the air and saved him.

Q: So Bolden was right. They came after him.

A: If it wasn't for the radio station, Bolden would have gone back to jail. I got world-wide publicity, except in Chicago. The Chicago press ignored it. But I also got on the crap list with almost every assassination researcher. Sylvia Meaghre, who wrote *Accessories After The Fact,* called me up and says, "Who the hell are you? Do you know about the Dallas thing?" I says, "Not a word." "Did you read the Warren Commission documents?" "Does not pertain to my thing." "You're a fraud, Skolnick." I says, "I am not investigating which way the bullets went in Dealey Plaza. I'm only on the Chicago plot."

Q: So she took it as intruding on her turf.

A: Yeah. David Lifton writes me a letter, and I can give you a xerox copy, "You are a fraud and you stole the documents from me." "I don't know who the fuck you are, David Lifton!" Weisberg sends me a thing in the form of a legal paper which he never filed, *Weisberg vs. Skolnick,* he wanted damages for me stealing the eleven documents from him. Nobody to this day has made an accurate chapter or sub-chapter on the Bolden thing.

Q: So the researchers all converged on you even though you're making a contribution to a case that they're supposedly trying to help solve themselves.

A: They've all got a vested interest. Peter Dale Scott, for reasons I do not know, has taken to the lecture platform and accused me of being a fraud. As you know, when I come to the assassination conferences, I'm the one they always want to throw out of the place. Now why is that?

Q: Carl Oglesby still likes you, doesn't he?

A: In 1974 or '75 I was giving a speech in Boston and I met him for a couple of hours while I was there. He lives in Cambridge. I raised the issue about Rennie Davis, the Chicago 7 and the CIA and I tell you, Carl almost took my crutch and wrapped it around my throat. He says, "That's a forbidden subject. You are not asking this!"

Q: Could you restate what you said about Rennie Davis?

A: I came out with a documented thing about all the CIA front foundations, which I'm an expert on. I found a way to identify CIA front foundations through 990AR, which is the foundation tax return that's a public record. I proved that the CIA financed Rennie Davis and the Chicago 7 to down the Democrats and put in Nixon. And when I raised this with Oglesby, he had been a big shot with the Students for Democratic Society, and when I was in Cambridge in '75, he got livid. So he's got this mixed feeling about me. He's always worried that at some public place I'm going to say something about that and I'm going to get around to him.

Q: So Rennie Davis, Jerry Rubin, Abbie Hoff-man, Bobby Seale, all on the payroll?

A: Not Bobby Seale, but the others were part of the game. They were getting money from CIA foundations. I got arrested confronting Rennie Davis on a local TV station on a live program. Rennie had me arrested.

Q: The Chicago police came to the defense of Rennie Davis?

A: Eighteen police, yeah. Channel 44.

Q: I didn't realize until recently that it was your work that helped expose the story about E. Howard Hunt's role in the downing of the airplane that killed his wife Dorothy.

A: I sued the National Transportation Safety Board and I didn't tell them that I had their file, all the pictures, all the documents, showing they knew it was sabotage where Dorothy Hunt and the eleven other Watergaters died. So in front of 250 reporters that gathered from all over the world for the re-opened air crash hearings, I laid all the documents on the table and I says, "Alright NTSB, now is the time to arrest me. This is your stuff. My friend swiped it from you. What are you going to do about? Arrest me in front all these reporters?" The Associated Press ran a story on the A wire: "Chicago legal researcher Sherman Skolnick presented today a heavily documented case of what he claims is sabotage based on government documents." Only one paper in the country ran the story, even though it was on the international wire. The *Seattle Intelligencer* is the only one that ran the stories. The *Tribune* ran a cropped picture of me sitting at the table and says "Skolnick has no documents to support his contention of sabotage." CBS had a live thing closed circuit, that they didn't use on the air, for their executives. It was UAL Incorporated, the parent company of United Airlines, whose flight 553 crashed, exactly one month after Nixon's re-election. A month before they killed Hale Boggs, from the Warren Commission. Dorothy Hunt and the eleven Watergaters, who had blackmailed two million dollars out of the Nixon White House.

During the hearings, on the second day I was tired and told this joke. I says, "I'm here to absolutely and categorically admit that I have no proof whatsoever that Edward Carlson, the head of United Airlines and Richard Nixon were on the plane with a .38 and shot Dorothy Hunt. I admit it!" I figured it was going to be a joke and everybody was going to laugh. The next day it comes out: "Skolnick has no proof whatsoever." And they show this cropped picture, I'm sitting in front of the table and I figured the photograph was bound to show the documents. No way: they cropped to where the documents are not shown.

Q: That's what you get for being funny. At

that time, Hunt was known only as a Watergate figure. This whole business about him being one of the tramps and all that had not happened. You weren't making connections between Watergate and the Kennedy assassination, were you?

A: The one who was working on that was my friend A.J. Weberman. When he went on the road with Mike Canfield after the publication of their book, *Coup D'Etat in America,* his editor was from Nigeria, Opaku, and for reasons that I do not know, insisted that he put in a thing there condemning Skolnick. Weberman says that they insisted that the book wouldn't be published if he didn't allow them to condemn me. I am not pertinent to the Dallas thing. Why was it necessary to say that Skolnick is a complete liar? A year ago I talked to Weberman and he didn't even remember it.

Q: Weberman is virtually called an agent for Mossad in a new book published by the Liberty Lobby. Could you describe your relationship with the Liberty Lobby?

A: Many in the left wing and the liberal press are tied in, like Chip Berlet, with that Cambridge group, that are in with foundations connected with the CIA, *Z Magazine* and that, and they accuse me and my late friend Mae Brussell of being Nazis. If time permitted, I could tell you how in 1976 I ran the first large seminar in America about Nazi war criminals in the United States—before Howard Blum's book came out, before all this stuff came out—and at my own expense came up with every rare book on the Nazi question and the companies that were in with Hitler and the American connection. I was condemned all the way around. I mean, I've been condemned by Chip Berlet that I am a Nazi and yet I ran the first seminar and nobody in the liberal press gave a single word to it. I was the only knowledgeable journalist that came to a press conference of Simon Weisenthal and they took me away under arrest because it was a private club.

I deeply resent Chip Berlet, *Z Magazine,* various books, that run stories that I am a Nazi. The problem is that the liberal press will not run stories about what I do. The CIA and Rennie Davis. The CIA and the foundations, the 990AR, the public tax returns. Most of the so-called left press is financed by the intelligence agencies. I can prove that. So they're not independent. I know it's a terrible thing...and I could go into a long rap about how the ACLU has been taken over by the Baldwin Foundation, which runs *The Nation* magazine, which is very liberal and runs a lot of good stories but heaven help you if you raise a thing about the CIA and the Baldwin foundation. It's because of my work in that area that I get rapped by the left. So they won't publish me in any of their magazines.

The only one that would publish my stories, about the Banca Del Lavaro, this different stuff, is the right-wing press. I'm an orthodox Jew. My mother and her whole family died in the Warsaw ghetto, the Lubesky family. To say that I'm a Nazi and promote the Nazi cause is the most horrendous thing that you could say about me. Also, Mae Brussell. She's dead and can't speak. She showed how the Nazis were involved with the JFK thing. To say that Mae Brussell and Sherman Skolnick are Nazis, this is the worst defamation!

Q: The left won't listen to you so you're kind of pushed into the arms of the Liberty Lobby.

A: Since 1987 we have passed out these leaflets about the judges and the CIA but the public doesn't dig leaflets. It's seventeenth century stuff. They want TV, they want radio. And none of the liberal press would have me. *In These Times,* Joel Bleifuss, you know what that guy did to me? Sent a letter to all my friends that Skolnick is a Nazi, stay away from him. Leaflets don't do the trick. I've got to be in the media eye. I have been blotted out since '71. So I started with my five minute recorded message. And then in the 70s I got to know Tom Valentine and he wrote about me in his magazine, *The National Tattler,* and then he became the associate editor of *The Spotlight* and through him they would run my stuff verbatim. He'd get me on his radio program and they did an accurate transcript of what I said. They didn't butcher up the words.

There's no free press in America. We must face that. A magazine like yours is rare. So the press is the bus company. What my left wing critics are saying is that before you get up on the bus, you must investigate the politics of the bus company. Otherwise, walk. Pass out leaflets! Holler on the street! With no free press in America, if they print my stories verbatim, the fact that they got naked women on the other side, like the *LA Star* which used to run my stuff verbatim with the naked pictures on the other side. So Chip Berlet and others say Skolnick is a Nazi, he's in with a paper that repudiates the Holocaust. And Tom Valentine has mentioned on his program that Skolnick does not repudiate the Holocaust. It happened. I prefer to talk about the major companies in America that financed Hitler. To call me a Nazi...I can't think a worse thing you can call me, honestly. Even A.J. Weberman calls me up and says, "Skolnick why aren't you at the Holocaust Museum? Why are you with *Spotlight,* which repudiates the Holocaust Museum?" So I says, "Listen, they're the bus company. They print my stuff verbatim!" "But you're in with Nazis!" I can't help it. Find me a better place. I'd like to be printed on the front page of the *New York Times* and a cover story of all my friends on *Time* magazine. What can I do?

Following this interview, Skolnick discussed his recent work with the involuntary bankruptcy case of caulking contractor Joseph Andreuccetti, which has led to his involvement with scandals of the Clinton era. Mr. Andreucetti was present at this dinner table discussion, as was Skolnick associate Mark Sato and Michael Scott Dugan, another person helped by the Citizen's Committee To Clean Up The Courts. They explained the connection between Mr. Andreuccetti, a descendant of Italy's House of Savoy, and over $10 billion in gold stolen from the Italian treasury by the OSS in 1943 and now located in Building 4 of King's Point Condominium in Addison, Illinois, a western suburb of Chicago. The story is rich with detail and suitable for expanded treatment in a future issue of Steamshovel. It includes charges by Inslaw informant Michael Riconoscuito that gold mesh filters made by a company named Wirecloth Products was used as a

currency within intelligence circles. The story also suggests that the gold was used as collateral in the early 1980s to support the opening of the Chicago branch of the Banca Del Lavoro, long connected to the JFK assassination, BCCI and Household International, a successor to Nugan Hand Bank of Inslaw infamy. From the gold as well, a $50 million contingency fund was established by the Resolution Trust Corporation to cover liabilities from the liquidation into Household Bank of American Heritage Savings and Loan, the S&L that purported to lend Mr. Andreuccetti money to finish the King's Point condos. According to Skolnick and associates, the fund disappeared and ended up in Little Rock to make the Madison Guaranty S&L just look incompetent (instead of criminal) when its financial improprieties are finally examined closely. The Committee To Clean Up The Courts can be reached at 9800 South Oglesby Avenue, Chicago, IL 60617.

JFK Redux:
Can Anyone Verify Fletcher Prouty's ID of Lansdale and Conein in Dealey Plaza?
by Jack White

I have always had the utmost admiration and respect for Col. L. Fletcher Prouty when it comes to integrity, patriotism, and his insider's personal knowledge of the personnel and workings of the "Secret Team" based on years of first-hand participation.

Therefore I take very seriously his identification of two persons photographed in Dealey Plaza on November 22, 1963, as being Ed Lansdale and Lou Conein. He knew Lansdale personally and worked closely with him over a period of years and through Lansdale he knew Conein.

As a researcher of JFK photos extremely interested in identifying persons in the pictures, I have corresponded with Col. Prouty in an attempt to develop definite proof of his allegations, and herein I will quote directly from some of his letters with his kind permission.

I sent Fletch xeroxes of the photos in question for his comments. He identified them as Lansdale and Conein, but volunteered no further proof than his own personal acquaintance with the two.

The photos include (1) the George Smith photo of the three tramps, which shows a man Fletch identifies as Lansdale, in a suit and wearing eyeglasses, strolling westward by the Texas School Book Depository as the tramps are loosely escorted eastward by Officers Wise and Bass; (2) the James Altgens photo, which shows a stocky man wearing a construction helmet who Fletch says is Conein, standing on Elm Street with his arms folded across his chest, looking not at the motorcade, but more toward the Dal-Tex Building; (3) the same individual as seen in Phil Willis slide number 5; and (4&5) the same man strolling westward on Elm past the Umbrella Man, as seen in two slides by Wilma Bond.

Here are direct quotations from some of Prouty's letters about his identification of these persons. (All are direct quotes, but in some cases paragraphs have been rearranged or combined with other paragraphs from a different letter for clarity or continuity, as indicated by ellipsis.)

"...the first time I saw the 'tramps' photo series, I recognized Ed Lansdale in #1, for sure. So, because I knew Ed so well and what his type of work was, and what he was best at, I knew right then, for sure, what he was there to do and how he would have done

it. He was a true professional. Do you recall that he had 'retired' as an Air Force Major General on Oct. 23, 1963? Of course that was an entirely 'notional' retirement. He was never in the Air Force. He was always an agent of the CIA.

"Furthermore, this leads to the source of the decision. Ed's role would have been the script-writer and leader of the band; but he would only have been working on the orders of someone above him. Ed had many deep and important links to big business. It is easy to visualize that within his circle, which would have included Allen Dulles, among others, word was received that a decision to get rid of JFK had been made. That fact, the decision, would trigger a chain of events that would assure the death of JFK, or anyone else, anywhere in the world. These are not "terrorists" on the streets. They are superior professionals who are on salary, highly skilled and trained, and thoroughly covered. They are never arrested. They certainly are not 'lone gunmen.' The lone gunman is always a selected 'patsy.'

"I had known Ed since 1952 in the Philippines...and throughout my service in the Far East, 1952-1954, I kept meeting him frequently in Manila and Saigon. My Air Transport Squadron flew there on regular schedules out of Tokyo and we supported his Saigon Military Mission (a 100% CIA unit).

"When he returned from Vietnam he was assigned to the Air Force Directorate of Plans where he worked for a very good friend of mine in that shop...in the Pentagon in 1957...His office was in a parallel hall just opposite mine. He was a fish out of water there, and I was a very handy old friend for him...In other words I saw him frequently...and I was one of the few persons in Plans that he could speak to easily.

"Then in about 1959 he got reassigned to the Office of the Secretary of Defense in the Office of Special Operations. That is the office that takes care of CIA matters and manages the NSA. The Air Force transferred me to that office in 1960, so Ed and I were together again in the same office...I worked with him daily...in 1960-1961...I knew him well...In 1961, I was transferred, this time to the Joint Staff. I did the same work there that I had done in the Secretary's Office. In fact, because they had eliminated the Office of Special Operations, I was now head of that work for all services all over the world. Ed stayed with the Secretary doing CIA work. We still saw a lot of each other.

"I say all this to tell you I knew the guy very well. I worked with him, have visited with our wives in each others' homes, have traveled with him when I was the pilot of Air Force planes, etc.

"Then one day someone showed me the 'Tramp' pictures. I think it was (Richard E.) Sprague. I recognized Lansdale immediately in the first photo. Being trained never to 'uncover' a CIA man, I didn't say a word; but as soon as I could, I got a set of the pictures. I had no doubt whatsoever about his identity...the 'tramps' photo is unquestionably Lansdale...Then I got a letter from a man who was quite senior in the Pentagon and who knew Ed and me very well. (*Steamshovel* Debris: Fletcher Prouty declined again to name this official when contacted by *Steamshovel Press*.) In responding to the letter, which had nothing to do with the assassination, I slipped that single 'Tramps' photo in the envelope and asked if he had seen it. I told him about the 'Tramps' and then said do you see anything you can tell me about in the picture. I gave him no names at all.

"Immediately he replied and much to my surprise began by saying, 'That is Ed. I could tell him anywhere. What the hell was he doing there?' He went on with more and described the strange costumes of the 'police', the weapons and the rest...his details were more complete than mine...That was all I needed. That senior person is unimpeachable. I had not suggested the name. He and I knew!

"I have carefully put that letter away and never revealed its source...I made Mae B. (Brussell) and Charles S. (Spears) aware of all this years ago, and asked them to keep it confidential...

"Because I knew that was Lansdale I then knew why I had been sent to the South Pole at the time of JFK's death and what his role in the whole thing was. He was an absolute genius. He could plan the Cover Story, such as Oswald, such as Ruby, such as the Tramps, etc. That was his specialty.

"...In keeping with our work, Lansdale's and mine, I have a good idea of what he was doing in Dallas. It is a most professional and demanding type of work. He was using certain of his highly trained MONGOOSE people to perform roles in Dallas and he was orchestrating the whole thing. In such a capacity he may or may not have had a thing to do with the shooting team. They are always 'faceless', highly professional and from out of the country. He simply created the 'smoke screen' under which the professionals worked. In fact the actual smoke screen on the Grassy Knoll, the Umbrella Man, the Tramps and other such

events are among the things he would have been directing. The phony police and Secret Service men would have been his actors. Ed was very good at such things and had a world-wide reputation for it. Note: people have noted that Ed had eyeglasses on in the photo. They are more likely his ear-pieces for radio transmission. The cops are wearing normal (hearing) devices.

"After the job in Dallas, Ed would have had to work with the perpetual 'Cover Story' people so that they could keep it alive and vibrant as it is today, nearly thirty years later. That is the most difficult part of any 'assassination.'

"...Oswald had been in the Philippines when the CIA was supporting the Indonesian rebellion against Sukarno. Ed and I were deeply involved in that. I would not be surprised to learn that he had met Oswald there. It was all CIA, not military, and Oswald was one of the selected Marines from the Atsugi unit. Perfectly normal. He might have been the only Marine Ed ever knew that well. So he 'created' a role for him. Oswald would trust Ed because he had known him before, knew that he worked for the Secretary of Defense and all that. So when asked to go to Russia for a good cause, to go to Dallas for a good cause, and to sit in that theater after Tippit and the President had been killed, for a good cause, he did so. He had no idea the President's death had been pinned on him, or Tippit's. He just fell into that as a 'patsy', just as he said. He did it all for his good friend 'Major General Lansdale.'

"...It is my belief (unverified to date with other associates) that the fellow in the white hard-hat who is shown in the Altgens photo, the man almost in line with a pole and to the left of the Depository door area, with his arms folded over his chest and staring, not at the President, but at the shooter in the Dal-Tex building, is Lou Conein. He, (E. Howard) Hunt and Lansdale frequently worked together on major projects and we know they were in Dallas.

"...Quite obviously there are few good pictures of Lou Conein...look in a copy of the Cecil B. Currey biography, *Edward Lansdale, The Unquiet American*, published by Houghton Mifflin 1988.

"Now I'll reveal something strange for you. Turn to the set of pictures that follows page 206. On the top of the tenth photo page you'll see a picture of a house in Saigon. On the bottom half you'll see two guys and the inscription, 'Lucien Conein and Joseph Baker, Lansdale teammates on Vietnam, relaxing.'

"So now you know who Conein is and what he looks like. Not at all! The CIA put out this book and it is full of untruths. They very cleverly found the worst picture of both these men they could find and then REVERSED the names. Conein, not a good picture, is the guy on the right holding the drink in his left hand. He's not the guy on the left of the photo.

"That's the way the CIA works. They take advantage of every detail, to their own interest. That is a poor picture of Lou. I'm going to see if I have a better one. (I should have put one in my own book). Here, I found one. In the Karnow book, *Vietnam* go to the set of photos after page 269. Then go to the fourth photopage. You'll see Conein, again not specifically located, but he is the guy right in the middle and up one step. All the others are Vietnamese. That is a much more typical shot of Conein. Now see if you agree with me that this man is the same one as in the one in the Altgens photo.

"You'll see in this bit of work how the CIA plays the game. Both books are contrived trash...so that no one will know the truth about Lansdale and Vietnam...This is the CIA and its allies in their efforts to teach all of us history."

There you have Col. Prouty's amazing allegations. He says that two high-ranking CIA officials were photographed in Dealey Plaza on November 22, 1963. He speculates that Lansdale and Conein were there as planners and supervisors of the "cover story" aspects of the assassination. Does he have proof beyond his own personal observations? No. Should these allegations be investigated? Yes.

If it can be shown that either or both of these men was in Dealey Plaza on that Friday noon 30 years ago, who in the entire world would believe it to be just another harmless coincidence?

Can we prove or disprove Prouty's claim that two of the planners of the assassination were on hand in Dallas on 11-23-63?

Jack White lives at 704 Candlewood Road, Fort Worth, Texas 76103.

Readers will remember Edward Lansdale as a Vietnam-era guerilla insurgency expert, an adviser to the Diem regime in South Vietnam and the central figure (as "Colonel Edwin Barnum Hillandale") in William Lederer and Eugene Burdick's 1958 book, The Ugly American *(New York: Norton). Marlon Brando played Lansdale in the 1963 movie version of the book.*

Not surprisingly, Lansdale's high opinion of Fletcher Prouty did not go beyond his assessment of Prouty's skills as an airman. "He was a good pilot of prop-driven aircraft," Lansdale wrote to Lt. Charles T.R. ("Bo") Bohannan, "but had such a heavy dose of paranoia about CIA when he was on my staff that I kicked him back to the Air Force." This opinion is reported in a 1988 biography of Lansdale, Edward

Lansdale The Unquiet American, by Cecil B. Currey (Boston: Houghton Mifflin Company), an official biography no doubt rightly regarded as unreliable. (Currey was not unfamiliar with the clandestine life of folk heroes. He wrote a book in 1972 eititled Code Number 72/Ben Franklin; Patriot or Spy.) *For instance, Prouty denies ever being on Lansdale's staff. Factual errors aside, the book also notes Lansdale's opinion that Prouty had a "whacky imagination", and in comparing him with Daniel Ellsberg of* Pentagon Papers *fame who* did *work on Lansdale's staff at one time, ostensibly noted, "I sure pick 'em, huh?"*

The biography contains no reference to Prouty's assertions about the Kennedy assassination, of course. It contains no reference at all to the Kennedy assassination, another glaring factual problem. It does, however, acknowledge Prouty's charge that Lansdale worked for the CIA throughout his life. According to Currey, "While he was never anyone's lap dog...it is evident that [Lansdale] certainly shared information with the Agency when he believed it would be useful to them." In a phone conversation with Steamshovel Press, *Prouty again maintained that Lansdale worked throughout his life for the CIA using the Air Force as cover.*

In his book The Secret Team *(Englewood Cliffs, NJ: Prentice Hall, 1973), Prouty suggests that Lansdale's clandestine ops played a role in the Huk rebellion. The Huks were socialistic, anti-Japanese Philippines natives that sustained guerilla warfare in the Philippines from the end of World War II until 1954. In correspondence with Bohannon, Lansdale remarked that Prouty "has claimed that I invented the Huk rebellion, hiring actors to pose as guerrillas just to get RM [Philippines Congressman Ramon Magsaysay] elected."*

Debate surrounding the relationship between JFK's murder and his plans for Vietnam, while not new, took center stage again with the release of Oliver Stone's movie, JFK. *One often cited suggestion that Kennedy planned to withdraw the US from Vietnam after the 1964 election comes from Democratic senator Mike Mansfield, described in* The Unquiet American *as an old friend of Lansdale's. According to* The Unquiet American, *Lansdale was forced to retire from the Air Force on October 31, 1963, in real life retiring only his cover story, according to Prouty. Lansdale immediately began work as an "agricultural specialist" for a Kennedy program called Food For Peace—a CARE program, and a job that Currey admits was noted by friends as "ill-fitting" Lansdale.*

Twenty eight days after his "retirement," however, just under a week after the assassination, Lansdale launched plans to create Liberty Hall, a non-

profit speakers bureau and educational service intended to promote traditional military values. Lansdale gave up on Liberty Hall, according to The Unquiet American, *when he found that most of its supporters came from extreme, Bircher-type rightists, if the reader believes Currey. Fletcher Prouty suggests that* *readers turn to notes in* JFK The Book of The Film *for better documentation concerning Lansdale's whereabouts during the assassination.*

The Fate of Lew Welch
by Chris Roth

Lew Welch, who was born in 1926 and disappeared in 1971, is one of the lesser known names of the Beat movement of the 1940s, '50s and '60s but he was also possibly its finest poet. His is also one of the mystery stories of the milieu that gave rise to more recognizable names like Allen Ginsberg, Gary Snyder, Jack Kerouac, and William Burroughs. Welch seemed torn between the two sides of the Beat personality—the urbane *vs.* the bucolic; the reckless *vs.* the sagacious. Scholars argue whether the very term *Beat* comes from the word *beatific* or from *beat* meaning "fatigued," "defeated." Both etyma make sense for Welch. He combined Ginsberg and Kerouac's jazz-inflected ribaldry with Snyder's quiet mysticism. His verse has the hip slangy rhythms of William S. Burroughs but also the Zen ineffability of Snyder and Philip Whalen. Like his life, his death is full of contradictions. Some wonder whether he died at all.

As Snyder writes, Welch "drank far too much, had a way with guns, and took one with him into the woods, never to be seen again, in May of 1971." But these woods were Snyder's neck of them, in the mountains of northern California. Snyder doesn't quite say he died there. There are clues that he may still be alive, perhaps in hiding, perhaps abroad.

Before Welch became renowned as a poet on the San Francisco scene, he knew Snyder and Whalen at Reed College in Portland, Oregon. His B.A. thesis—praised by William Carlos Williams, on whom Welch foisted a copy during a lecture appearance—was on Gertrude Stein, matriarch of a generation that was Lost if not quite Beat. Welch went on to write ad copy for Montgomery Ward in the 1950s, where he actually penned the pithy slogan worth of Stein, "Raid Kills Bugs Dead" (still in use today of course). For Welch, this phrase was a sort of Zen *koan* about the food-chain at its most unnatural. He was to develop the theme in his later work, as he studied mysticism with Snyder and, in his poems, tried to reconcile his hard living with the path of enlightenment. He became a rising star of the Beat scene.

By 1971, he was drinking too much to function at all well. He was often in the throes of yo-yo-ing between Jim Beam and Antabuse, but he had moved next door to Snyder in the Sierras and was trying to live in the ways taught by Eastern meditative traditions. What is generally taken as Welch's "suicide note" was his final published poem, "Song of the Turkey Buzzard," which sang of the food-chain in more beatific terms than killing bugs dead:

> The very opposite of
>   death
> bird of re-birth
>   Buzzard
> …
> Hear my last Will & Testament:
> …
>   On a marked rock, following his orders,
>   place my meat.
> …
> With proper ceremony disembowel what I
> no longer need, that it might more quickly
> rot and tempt
>
> my new form

The reference is to the ancient Tibetan custom of disposing of the dead by leaving them in aeries for scavenging birds. His poems had become morbid, but not dark.

Whether "Turkey Buzzard" was intended as Welch's last will and testament became moot, for his body was never found. In May of 1971, suffering from morbid depression but at the peak of his career, Welch disappeared with his rifle into the woods. Before long, Snyder found an entry in Welch's journal, appointing a literary executor, Donald Allen, and lamenting a wasted life but adding, "I went Southwest. Goodbye." Search parties were unsuccessful, even with their field narrowed to a quarter of the compass. It is still a matter of debate whether Lew Welch managed to kill himself where no one would ever find him or whether he simply "dropped out" of society.

This has given rise to a number of rumors as to Welch's whereabouts. Four or five years later, Snyder, zoning out in his sauna, had a "vision" of a visit from Welch, described in his poem "For/From Lew":

> Lew Welch just turned up one day,
> live as you and me. 'Damn, Lew' I said,
> 'you didn't shoot yourself after all.'
> 'Yes I did' he said,
> and even then I felt the tingling down my back.
> 'Yes you did, too' I said—'I can feel it now.'

The whole mystery is reinforced by the posthumous publication of a talk Welch gave at Reed College on March 30, 1971, short months before his disappearance. In it, he waxes enthusiastically about poetry but then cuts short at the height of an angry tirade against society and organized religion. Don Allen, who edited the volume, referred in his preface to the "faithful transcription" but it was later discovered that the second half of the talk had been omitted without comment. Allen says he knew about it but didn't think the deleted parts added much. However, it's all there on the cassette tape from which the transcript was made, on Side B. Some think the clues to Welch's plans for himself are in this suppressed material.

And Gary Snyder's odd remark in his preface to Welch's *Selected Poems* that "of *his forty-five years of life in the west* [Welch] gave twenty-one to poetry" (emphasis mine) confuses the issue. Now, Welch was *forty-four* when he disappeared into the woods. That discrepancy aside, it's unclear what Snyder means by "the west": Welch never went to the Orient as Snyder did, and yet he lived all over the U.S. in his forty-four years, including the Midwest and the Northeast. Snyder's phrasing would make sense, though, if Welch had continued to pursue his interest in Eastern mysticism by escaping somehow to Asia (roughly *southwest*), sometime, say, after his forty-fifth birthday, which was three months after he disappeared. His plans in 1950 to escape to Chile to avoid the draft, revealed in letters written to his mother at the time, would support this tendency in Welch. There's no proof that he went to Asia, but it's the only scenario that makes sense in light of Snyder's odd statement.

The strangest part of the whole story was sworn to me by an acquaintance of mine, the one who tracked down Don Allen in a rather aggressive way in the early 1980s to try to get to the bottom of the issue of the missing parts of his Reed talk. This acquaintance was working at a diner in Madison, Wisconsin, shortly after his communication with Allen and was startled by a grizzled-looking customer who came in, walked right up to him, and said, peering into his eyes, "If you have something you'd like to ask me, ask it now." My acquaintance thought the stranger looked familiar but was too taken aback to say anything except that he had nothing to ask him and didn't know what he meant. The customer hung around for a few minutes and then left and never returned. My acquaintance claims the man looked like an older, more bedraggled version of Lew Welch.

Whether he's in Japan, Tibet, or Wisconsin, or in a ravine in the Sierras swept unrecognizably back into the food-chain he revered, Welch's poetry still speaks to us. He was a tireless critic of mechanized American society, and maybe after all he did fulfill the promise of one of his earlier ruminations:

> *You can't fix it. You can't make it go away,*
> *I don't know what you're going to do about it,*
> *But I know what I'm going to do about it. I'm just*
> *going to walk away from it. Maybe*
> *A small part of it will die if I'm not around*
>
> *feeding it anymore.*

Chris Roth's radio program, In Advance of the Landing *can be heard on WHKP in Chicago and surrounding environs of Monday afternoons.*

The Encryption/Decryption Dickwads of Cipherspace
by Raleigh Muns

" At White House Policy meetings, it appears, the economic side of the table is out getting coffee whenever the national security squad turns on the overhead projector." Thus spake James Aley in *Fortune* (May 16, 1994, "How Not to Help High Tech", p. 100) in reference to the worldwide battle involving one man's efforts to bring uncrackable cryptography to the unwashed computer masses.

Philip Zimmerman, owner of Boulder Software Engineering of Boulder, Colorado, utilized a public domain mathematical formula called the RSA algorithm (for its inventors, Messrs. Rivest, Shamir, and Adelman) to independently develop state of the art "guerilla freeware" for the masses called PGP (for "Pretty Good Privacy"). Zimmerman has rationalized that since the military, the government, and organized crime all have access to cryptographically secure communications, that the common person should have the same capabilities. "When cryptography is outlawed, only outlaws will have cryptography." Note that Zimmerman did not produce a piece of software that would be sold. He publicized the RSA algorithm and the PGP source code, and waited (successfully) for the information age axiom "information wants to be free" to take over. It did.

In a world where companies routinely claim the right to monitor employee electronic mail and telephone calls, and where post-Nixonian governments typically use illegally obtained information as leverage for attacking opponents (the media calls these "high placed anonymous sources"), the citizenry is the last to be able to communicate privately.

In a recent *Wall Street Journal* article (April 28, 1994, p. 1), author William Bulkeley cites electronic mail from Latvia thanking Zimmerman for creating PGP which is used to keep politically unpopular information from the local Polizei. "If dictatorship takes over Russia, your PGP is widespread from Baltic to Far East now and will help democratic people if necessary."

A common rallying cry by the "cipherpunk" community on the Internet discussion group *alt.security.pgp* is "They'll have to pry my PGP from my cold, dead fingers." This is the first Usenet discussion group in which I have seen the term "dickwad" applied to correspondents. Zimmerman himself has chimed in on occasion, though his lawyers have advised he keep mum while a Federal Grand Jury probes his role in exporting prohibited munitions. You see,

PGP as "public key cryptography" has been classified by the State Department as a prohibited munitions. In the borderless world of the Internet terms such as "international export" are absurd.

While Zimmerman may be under the Federal gun for exporting weaponry, the Feds themselves have apparently exported the RSA algorithm and public key cryptographic software in various engineering proceedings with no qualms. The war being fought is fraught with yet stranger and stranger twists and turns. Those unaffiliated with sanctioned business or government agencies seem to be most likely to come under attack. If you purchase the cryptographic software from any of the companies holding the patents and copyrights, you are safe from harassment - but are your communications safe? The same people bringing you the trust-us-we-won't- look-at-your-messages-without-a-warrant Clipper Chip only seem to have a problem with software, like PGP, which is independently developed and verified by an amorphous cadre of international cipherpunks as being free of trap doors. A "trap door" is a hook in the software which would allow "someone" to decode a message. The whole point of the Clipper Chip is to allow the government easy access to Clipper encrypted information. Examples of harassment against PGP users abound on the Internet. In the Usenet discussion group *alt.security.pgp* a user utilizing the name of David Sternlight has even examined a pro-PGP user's computer files in order to report that said user has illegal PGP software on his computer account and thus should have his Internet contract revoked. "Sternlight" has become notorious as a well-spoken, literate, clean-cut opponent (who claims *not* to be an opponent) to the use of what he considers illegal software in violation of copyright and patent law (sounds innocuous).

Until recently, copyright and patent issues were the primary weapons used by the anti-cryptography cabal (all upstanding citizens). Stranger twist is that the copyright on the RSA algorithm isn't valid outside the United States. The Europeans have independently developed compatible versions of PGP which are legal abroad. So Zimmerman may be accused of exporting "munitions" (cryptographic software) to countries that already have legal versions of those same "munitions"!

The current whirlpools in the rapids have found the original developers of the RSA algorithm, The Massachusetts Institute of Technology (MIT was originally funded by the U.S. Government), releasing an apparently copyright and patent safe version of PGP for the public to use. This PGP version 2.5 lasted only three days on the Internet before it was pulled by MIT or their handlers. Version 2.6 is due any day. What happened? Was there an obvious trap door that would indicate collusion by parties interested in a weakened version of PGP for the masses? *Alt.security.pgp* cipherpunks will be adding grist to the mill, and I will be reading it, as the next weeks pass.

Final note: Rep. Maria Cantwell (D-Washington) via the House Foreign Affairs committee, has introduced legislation which would allow the legal export of encryption software. The Clinton administration, to no one's surprise, has gone on record opposing this relaxation of the export laws. It will also be interesting to see what happens to Cantwell as time passes. Skeletons, real or otherwise, have a habit of coming out of closets around Halloween.

Raleigh Muns publishes Fugitive Pope, *which* Playboy *recently characterized as "Ranting attempts at reincarnating a wacky librarian as a foulmouthed folk hero" that "recalls questions you had in grade school but forgot when you matured."*

Book Reviews

So Cool, So Reichian
Jack's Life: A Biography of Jack Nicholson
by Patrick McGilligan, Norton, 1994.

Writer Saul Bellow, another Reich-influenced personality (see his short story, *Henderson the Rain King*) described, in his recent collection of essays, a visit from Jack Nicholson:

"His white stretch limousine could not make the narrow turn between my gateposts. Silent neighbors watched from a distance as the long car with its Muslim crescent antenna on the trunk. Then Nicholson came out, observed by many. He said, 'Gee, behind the tinted glass I couldn't tell it was so green out here.' He lit a mysterious-looking cigarette and brought out a small pocket ashtray, a golden object resembling a pillbox. Perhaps his butt ends had become relics or collectibles. I should have asked him to explain this, for everything he did was noted and I had to answer the questions of my neighborhood friends, for whom Nicholson's appearance here was something like the consecration of a whole stretch of road."

I was first alerted to the new biography of Jack Nicholson when Christopher Lehmann-Haupt's review appeared in *The New York Times*. One of the reviewer's comments stood out: "But less engaging sides of the star emerge: his taste for drugs and one-night stands; his indulgence of crackpot thinkers like the orgone-box psychoanalyst, Wilhelm Reich; his habit of mooning in public places like the Boston Garden..." (Funny he should call Reich a "crackpot" since, in a 1971 review of *Mass Psychology of Fascism*, he claimed, "Perhaps it is time to reconsider all of Wilhelm Reich...and to reopen the question of cosmic orgone energy, its effect on cancer, and other theories Reich died in Lewisberg Federal Penitentiary defending.")

Jack Nicholson is a Reichian? But I guess I knew that.

Normally, I am no fan of celebrity biography, but I ran out and bought this one. And I can't say I was disappointed. Well-researched, lively and impeccably documented, McGilligan's book is a breezy read which captures the reader's attention from the start and rarely lets go. Nicholson, the most highly paid actor in film history ($60 million including "points" on merchandising from *Batman*), has fashioned himself into a cultural icon of "cool" despite humble origins as a nerd from Neptune, New Jersey.

McGilligan makes much of Nicholson's Oedipal conflict: Jack remained unaware until his mid-thirties that the sister he always called "June" was actually his mother, and that the couple he thought of as his parents were actually his grandparents. But fortunately McGilligan spares us the expected heavy pseudo-analysis, and places more emphasis on Nicholson's real achievements. I mean, did Jack ever play a *bad* role that you can remember? He's rescued many a film.

To be honest, my main reason for buying the book was to find out about the extent to which Nicholson is indebted to Reich's ideas. And I wasn't disappointed. Nicholson first started talking about Reich in his boho days as a semi-employed actor in Roger Corman's low-budget biker epics; a friend from those days cites Camus, Nietzsche, and Reich as Nicholson's main intellectual reference points. Nicholson comes through clearly as a sophisticated guy. While McGilligan portrays Nicholson's interest in Reich as a rationalization for womanizing common among 60s hipsters, it's also clear that Nicholson's appreciation went far deeper than that. By the 1970s, Nicholson repeatedly stressed the importance of Reich's sexual-political ideas, and the star's biographer told me over the phone that Nicholson had "replaced Catholicism with Reichianism".

In 1987 Jack told *Rolling Stone* magazine that he had been a supporter of Gary Hart, the U.S. senator from Colorado who dropped out of the presidential race after it was revealed that he was carrying on an extra-marital affair. "I'm a Hart supporter because he fucks," Nicholson told *Rolling Stone*. "Do you know what I mean?"

Fucking took precedence over politics for Jack. Indeed, from his point of view, fucking was politics.

One of the people Nicholson began to quote often—either he was making a study of him or doing a good job of faking it—was Wilhelm Reich, the former colleague of Freud's who developed the theory of "orgone power" or orgasmic energy and later went to jail for merchandising sexual vibrations in dubious "orgone boxes." Everybody in the later Sixties seemed to be imbibing Reich, who in his writings prescribed sexual freedom as a cure for most of society's ills.

To Jack, Reich was "the most important *political* writer and thinker of the last century." Reich became like a new religion for Jack, a counterpoint to Catholicism, and one that, like the Mother Church, contained articles of faith that might be utilized in every area of life.

When he was promoting *Drive, He Said,* his definitive movie on the Sixties, Jack continually brought up Reich's name. "I do feel that the country is hung up in a sexually repressive society," Nicholson said in a 1971 radio interview, expounding on his belief in Reichian theories, which in his mind were linked, intriguingly, with infant psychology and familial relationships.

"The way Reich describes it—the very description of the convulsion of an orgasm, of a change, of an expansion and contraction...He believes that from infancy it is incorporated into the psychology of every person; that they deal with the flow of 'sexual energy' by either holding it down—as you do with breathing...You control its expression by how much 'fuel' you give it to express itself...You then develop 'familial relationships' around these attitudes of tension— and the 'family' then develops it into towns, cities, and societies."

Jack may have been standoffish about some aspects of the Sixties, but he understood what would work for him. Drugs and sexual liberation yielded positive results, in his case; and the personal and professional growth, which he boasted about, was obvious to close friends.

Nicholson's little known *Drive, He Said* was an explicitly Reichian movie, according to the actor's interviews promoting the film. Throughout his career, Nicholson has eschewed traditional politicking so ridiculous and rife among Hollywood stars. His consistent ability to capture free—even explosive—emotional expression on the screen casts a whole new light upon his experiences in Reichian therapy, in which patients are encouraged to break down their resistance against feeling deep emotion.

In most ways the character of Gabriel, who "goes crazy under the stress of his vision," in Nicholson's words, was closer to Jack: like Jack, a loser with women, with a history of premature ejaculation. (Nicholson wrote a scene, not in the book, that implied as much.)

"Gabriel is a Reich-influenced, young, politically revolutionary character, who believes what Reich said about politics," Nicholson said in interviews following the film's release. "His action through the film is the life of Reich; he was right, what he was saying was right, no one believed him, it drove him crazy and he was institutionalized." (p. 216)

Of course, Jack Nicholson wasn't the only celebrity Reichian; those were different times.

"I kind of admired the way Jack was able to bring everything down to the bottom line," [Susan] Strasberg continued. "He didn't complicate things in the way that some actors do. When we were filming

[the sex scene]. for example, I discussed Reichian therapy with him. I had been in Reichian therapy, and so had Jack, I believe. Reich was a brilliant man with complex theories, far ahead of their time, about the bio-energy of the body. And I remember Jack distilling it all down to 'You fuck better.'" (p. 186)

—Jim Martin

Votescam: The Stealing of America
by James M. Collier and Kenneth F. Collier
Victoria House Press, 67 Wall Street, New York, NY 10005. ($6.99)

Shocking, outrageous and definitely too controversial for prime-time nooz, *Votescam: The Stealing of America* is one of the most important stories of the year.

The premise? "Computerized voting gives the power of selection, without fear of discovery, to whomever controls the computer."

Former rock impresarios, New Wave entrepreneurs, and investigative journalists, Jim and Ken Collier stepped into a virtual netherworld of political and bureaucratic corruption ranging from Dade County, Florida to Washington DC.

The Collier brothers' long strange trip began in the heady 1970s. Before they got involved in politics, the brothers put on the Doors concert in Dade County where Jim Morrison got arrested for obscenity doing his infamous jerk-off routine.

Then, almost on a lark, Ken decided to test the American political process by running for Congress against Claude Pepper. They simply wanted to "use the system to see if things that needed to be done actually could get done." They even got a book deal from Dell Publishing to write about their adventures, *Running Through the System: Ballots not Bullets.*

Spending almost no money on their campaign, they were surprised to hear on election night coverage that Ken's vote had jumped to 31%. Then mysteriously by the next "projection", the vote had dropped to 16%. And not too surprisingly Ken lost.

Investigating further, the brothers began looking for anomalies, a pattern in the official hand-written records of the voting machine tallies. They soon recognized a bland gray sameness to *all* of the signatures of the vote canvassers. Yup, they were forgeries. They even found the guy who wrote an article about it, "How To Forge Documents with a Bank Rapidograph" for *Police Magazine.*

Votescam is a true-crime real-life detective story as the brothers uncover more low-tech vote-stealing techniques like: 1. shaving the plastic wheels inside voting machines; 2. printing blank canvass sheets which could be filled in later; and 3. the ubiquitous

Printomatic voting machines which can be pre-arranged for a win by the candidate of choice.

And then there's the News Election Service (NES) of New York. Never heard of it? According to a CIA-sponsored think tank study unearthed by the Collier brothers, "NES is a wholly owned subsidiary joint-venture of national television networks ABC, CBS, and NBC and the press-wire services AP and UPI. This private organization performs without a contract, without supervision by public officials. It makes decisions concerning its duties according to its own criteria. The question of accountability of News Election Service has not arisen in the nation's press because the responsibility NES now has in counting the nation's votes was assumed gradually over a lengthy period without ever being evaluated as an item on the public agenda."

According to the Colliers, "the NES mainframe computer has the capability, via telephone lines, of 'talking' back and forth with county and state government mainframes. During the important 60-day certification period after an election, the counts in the county and state mainframes can still be manipulated by outsiders to conform to earlier TV projections."

When asked by our reporters how NES counts and disseminates the vote nationwide, the president of NES replied, "This is not a proper area of inquiry." Oh, zat right?

With an answer like that, try to figure out the odd coincidence of *all* the networks coming up with the *same* "projections" at the *same* time. They do.

And what if "deniability" and "untrackability" were built into the secret source codes that run the machines?

Votescam is a real page-turner as the brother practice their take-no-prisoners brand of reporting, even getting the League of Women Voters on video doing the dirty deed.

Describing the Collier brothers' video, attorney Ellis S. Rubin in the Voters' Ombudsman report, writes "you will be shocked and sickened to see seventy workers from the League of Women Voters sitting at long tables at the Dade County tabulation center using pencils to punch holes in thousands of paper punchcard computer ballots prior to their being counted." The LWV were quietly dropped after this revelation.

This book is an absolute must-read because it names names—a Supreme Court justice, the most powerful female publisher in America, and the current US Attorney General—all culpable in withholding evidence of massive vote fraud in America.

Votescam: The Stealing of America is a troubling look at the corruption of the American vote that most

people don't want to believe is even partially true. It asserts the unthinkable—the ultimate computer crime.

And you keep wondering why you vote and the rascals never seem to get thrown out? This book will set your mind a'spinning. Guaranteed.

—Uri Dowbenko

Project Seek:
Onassis, Kennedy, and the Gemstone Thesis
Bridger House Publishers, Inc, 1994.

In *Project Seek* one seeks in vain through its 388 pages to find much that is new on the subject of the Gemstone File. Gerald A. Carroll, "program assistant and adjunct assistant professor...at the University of Iowa," has written what the publisher touts as the first treatment of Gemstone to be "seriously researched and confirmed through independent, objective means." But Carroll is playing hide-and-seek when he hides the fact that one third or more of his book was previously published in my own *The Gemstone File* (Illuminet, 1992). Carroll says, "The Skeleton Key appears here, for the first time, in annotated form." Not.

Beyond *the Key* and the *Kiwi* and a lot of paraphrasing from my book, the book is mostly padding.

Carroll also implies that my interview with Stephanie Caruana, the person who most likely penned the *Skeleton Key to the Gemstone File,* is a fabrication by me. "It was only through Keith's narrative in *The Gemstone File* that the breakthrough was achieved—that the Skeleton Key editor at long last had been 'found' and that some original Roberts scripture was suddenly extant," according to Carroll.

If Carroll doubted the authenticity of my interview with Caruana, might he not have exercised some of his "objectivity" and dropped me a line, asking to review my file of Caruana correspondence? Perhaps he might have inquired about Caruana's phone number? Or might he not have collared her after her rant as a participant on my Gemstone panel discussion at the Phenomicon in 1992?

Along with a few new observations on Gemstone, we are mostly given material without much bearing on the subject: page after page of Carroll's partially-informed views on the JFK hit, BCCI, Paul Wilcher, Casolaro's Octopus, the Illuminati...There are even several pages comparing the Gemstone material to the Indiana Jones films.

A "Conspiracy Network" chart at the back of the book provides a handy index to the muddle that is Carroll's view of conspiracy politics—you're going to want to laminate this one for your billfold. The Illuminati and Freemasonry (which Carroll swings into action against with two sentences in his book) are depicted at the top of the conspiracy heap, branching downwards to the Gemstone Files, which branches into the Committee of 300, the Olympians, and the Trilateralists on one hand, and Torbitt, Brussell, and Onassis/Nazis on the other.

Is all this willful disinformation and obsfucation? Or is this just a book which is miles from the original spirit of Gemstone, muffling whatever original message which might have been contained in the 'Stone with layer after layer of conspiratorial cotton wool?

—**Jim Keith**

(*Steamshovel* Debris: Jim Keith is the editor of *The Gemstone File* and *Secret and Suppressed: Banned Ideas and Hidden History*. His new book is *Casebook on Alternative 3: UFOs, Secret Societies, and World Control*. All of these books are available from Illuminet Press, PO Box 2808, Lilburn, GA 30226. Phone: 1-800-680-INET.)

Kennedy Round Up

Of the new JFK assassination books, the one that adds the most to the libraries of novices *and* veterans of the topic is Robert Groden's *The Killing of the President* ($30; Viking Studio Books, Penguin Books USA Inc., 375 Hudson Street, New York, NY 10014). Groden, of course, has done more than any other researcher to expose the intricacies of the Zapruder film to researchers, through rotoscoping and enlargements that appear now on virtually every amateur video documentary of the assassination—sometimes dubbed to smudges by many generations. His enlargements of the Zapruder frames as well as other films he has collected and has been working on, most notably the Charles Groden film containing a previously unknown view of the Elm Street sequence, can be found in this coffee-table edition. The commentary will not only enlighten uninformed coffee-table guests, but it presents new and under-reported information that will inform some buffs and remind others of significant, fascinating and unresolved aspects of the crime. For instance, Groden reproduces the "tramps" photos and seems to have no problem stating flatly that they picture E. Howard Hunt; his enlargements even reflect what he labels as a radio control device behind Hunt's ear. *The Killing of the President* is a plush, bountiful presentation of the visual elements of the JFK assassination that really sets a new standard for research in the photographic materials. (An accompanying video release was unavailable to *Steamshovel* at press time.)

Michael Collins Piper brings a perspective that is relatively new to JFK studies but an old saw to his publishers, a subset of the Liberty Lobby. *Final Judgement: The Missing Link In The JFK Assassina-tion Conspiracy* ($20; The Wolfe Press, Washington, DC) looks at the involvement of the Mossad, the Israeli secret police, in the JFK hit and makes the case that it was a pre-dominant element. The thesis certainly has been under-examined in the past and raises some interesting historical questions about the relationship between the Kennedys and Israel that date back to Joseph Kennedy's Neville Chamberlain-like nods to the Nazis. The book cannot be read, however, without trying to identify the fine line of an anti-Israel/anti-Zionist critique with old-fashioned anti-Semitism.

The main thesis of the book is not what recommends it, however. Included in its pages is a discussion of Mark Lane's defense of the Liberty Lobby against E. Howard Hunt's defamation suit. It condenses and in some ways makes the trial more clear than Lane's own *Plausible Denial*. Readers will recall that Hunt brought suit after Victor Marchetti published an article in the Liberty Lobby's *Spotlight* suggesting that the CIA was about to issue a memo charging Hunt with complicity in the assassination. Marchetti's article stated explicitly that this memo was created for purposes of limited hangout, to sacrifice Hunt as a rogue element and deflect criticism of the CIA as an institution. The Liberty Lobby claimed no malice in publishing the story but Hunt won the original case. Lane took it up on appeal and won by changing the defense to proving that Hunt was in Dallas and was complicit in the conspiracy, a charge never made in the original Marchetti article. If for no other reason, *Final Judgement* is worth the readers' attention to discover what a piece of lawyer work that trial became.

Ron Lewis' book, *Flashback: The Untold Story of Lee Harvey Oswald* ($14.95; Lewcom Productions, POB 2429, Roseberg, Oregon 97470), has the most to offer in terms of local color and period detail about the assassination. Lewis met Oswald in October 1962 and had an intermittent relationship with him through October of the next year. In August 1963, Oswald confided in Lewis the plan to kill Kennedy and Lewis failed to bring the information to authorities. Like Robert Morrow (*Steamshovel* Debris: whose claim that Robert Kennedy was killed by a Mossad agent with gun disguised as a camera recently cost the *Globe* tabloid $3 million in a defamation suit), Lewis has confessed publicly to this complicity and has been investigated by the FBI, which does not prosecute for fear of exposing the conspiracy.

Lewis was first incarcerated at age 18 and was living under an assumed name in fear of being prosecuted for check-bouncing when he met Oswald. After the assassination he hid for years in Del Rio, Texas, with his family thinking him dead. In addition to reflecting his life in the Oswaldesque under-class, Lewis' account contains a vivid reflection of its banal detail. In complaining about his meager pay as a messenger boy for Guy Bannister, for instance, Lewis quotes Oswald: "'If I had to depend on thirty-three dollars a week, I couldn't even buy Marina a thirty-nine cent pair of panties,' Lee told me. He discussed Marina's panties in his half-kidding, half-serious manner, saying, 'I'm serious...you should see her panties! The elastic is giving out and she wants some new ones'...the panties she wore obviously weren't designed for the latter stages of pregnancy."

All The Rest

On the UFO publishing front, two offerings should grab reader attention: Linda Moulton Howe has produced a glossy, slick, large, comprehensive and copiously illustrated volume on crop circles, animal mutilations and human abductions entitled *Glimpses of Other Realities, Volume 1: Facts and Eyewitnesses* ($39.95; Linda Moulton Howe Productions, POB 538, Huntingdon Valley, PA 19006); and Bill Barker has released a two-package kit of his eerie, all-too-real alien cartoons, *Schwa and Counter Schwa* (send SASE to Schwa, Box 6064, Reno, NV 89513 for more information). Howe's book gives alternately beautiful and repugnant color photographic images of crop circles, dismembered cattle and abductee impressions of alien presence.

Glimpses presents the view that these phenomena may reflect "another intelligence that is facing environmental survival issues as we are on our own planet", but does it more with a presentation of evidence than persuasive argument. *Glimpses* attempts to report on overlooked local stories from a large variety of locales to reveal common patterns that may, in turn, reveal something of this other intelligence. Nothing here, however, really contradicts the notion that the aliens are just dicking around with us.

The only real defense, of course, is *Schwa,* the unwieldy packages of key-rings, tokens, pins, bumper stickers, booklets and cartoons put out by Barker. These new materials note that "Alien Is Beautiful" and that "This Planet Contains Life Of An Unusual and Graphic Nature", and present a variety of keyhole gizmos and charms to detect and expose such alienism. Amidst the ubiquitous Grey visage in Barker's drawings, which comprise two large booklets in this latest outing, is the stick man—a one dimensional ordinary guy overwhelmed by the alien madness. Steve Ditko comes to mind as an antecedent in the graphic arts. Jacques Vallee promises to use the Alien Detector at the next MUFON convention.

More serious students of alien land/timescaping would do well to boot up the *Timewave Zero* software ($49; Dolphin Software, 48 Shattuck Square #147, Berkeley CA 94704). Based on Terence McKenna's millenial/apocalyptic theories, which were laid upon him by aliens after a heavy mushroom encounter in the Columbian Amazon in 1971, it currently projects the singularity event at the end of history coming in on December 21, 2012, after which hopefully we can all relax. This software displays any part of McKenna's timewave as a western calendar graph. The user can see the 4.5 billion year history of earth or zero in on portions as brief as 92 minutes. It was developed by Peter Meyer in consultation with Terence McKenna. It's IBM PC compatible (graphics adapter or not) and requires MS-DOS 2.10 or later.

Robert Anton Wilson writes, "I don't care what you say about the video—as long as you get the ordering information correct!" as if to suggest *Steamshovel* would have anything but high praise for *Fear in the Night: Demons, Incest and UFOs* ($14.95; Permanent Press, Department S, PO Box 700305, San Jose CA 95170). Any chance to be regaled and enlightened by this great professor of the higher circuits is a bargain at almost any price—it's surprising really that recent Wilson-is-Dead rumors haven't put the price for this tape through the roof. (In fact, *Steamshovel* is still waiting for the effect of the Wilson-Is-Orson Welles rumor to impact on the back issue market.) On the tape, RAW tackles issues surrounding false memory syndrome, where sham psychotherapy meets the tribulations of abductee victims, but the lecture is also almost a picaresque of many wide-ranging amusements—including Wilson's report on how Berkeley (as in "Berkeley, dooood") got its name and his take the Budd Hopkins crowd. The tape runs just under an hour, which is palatable for a lecture, and it will hold over viewers/readers/thinkers-of-things until an expected new anthology from R. A. Wilson this year.

Growing out the Potlatch Lecture series, *Extraphile* expresses in zine form the "no nation, no work" ethic Len Bracken and Bob Black have attempted to articulate in their First Extranational manifesto "Provisional Resolutions Towards a Union of Egos". The Spring 1994 issue includes that manifesto as well as Peter Lamborn Wilson's "An Immediatist Potlatch", Black's postscript to "The Original Affluent Society" by Marshall Sahlins and much else, some of it taking a bit of, well, work to deconstruct. Available for $12 annually, $3 per issue from POB 5585, Arlington, VA 22205.

—**Kenn Thomas**

Things Are Gonna Slide

Tramp the Dirt Down

Richard Nixon, of course, is now dead. Media pundits were obligated to come up with some rationalization for his life, of course, so little enough was said about even the disgraces accepted by the mainstream, the misbegotten escalation of the Vietnam War, Watergate, the resignation. "Well, he opened up China, dammit!" seemed to be the refrain as television commentators coughed their way through their eulogies. Even less was mentioned about, for instance, Nixon's role in approving Gary Powers' ill-fated U2 flight as means to interrupt a US/Soviet summit that might have ended the Cold War thirty years earlier, or Nixon's involvement with various assassinations. Nothing was said about the synchronistic wave of deaths connected to the JFK assassination now happening—in the wake (still) of the Stone movie, the passage of the Assassinations Material Review Act and the observance of the thirtieth anniversary of the assassination. Nixon, John Connally, H.R. Haldeman, Frank Sturgis, Bill Hicks (the JFK assassination comedian recently kicked off the Letterman show, another fast-acting cancer) and now Jackie Kennedy Onassis, all dead within less than a year. Few even noted this as coincidence.

(*Steamshovel* Debris: The best commentary on Nixon to pass this editorial desk came from Mark Zepezauer of the *Tucson Comic News*. Zepezauer wrote a comprehensive overview of Nixon's public life, noting the doubling of US deaths in Vietnam by Nixon for no discernible change in the war's final settlement terms; the transformation of Chile into a fascist state; the mindless support of the Shah of Iran, consequent oil crisis and all the attendant economic woes of the 1970s; Nixon's ties to the mob. He concludes that "Richard Nixon, a dismal, loathsome toad of a man, left this world a much nastier place than he found it, in large part due to his career." The *Tucson Comic News* is available for $10.70 for twelve issues from POB 2111, Tucson, AZ 85702.)

Nixon's lawyers and family vowed to continue their effort to deprive the country of its own history through lawsuits to stop the release of his presidential papers and tapes. One lawyer, R. Stan Mortenson, told a *New York Times* reporter that Nixon had posthumous privacy rights. "He could not cite a legal basis for that concept," commented the reporter.

Assassination Coalition

Meanwhile, the effort to locate and examine documents that reflect a truer picture of recent history continues in the wake of the Assassination Materials Review Act of 1992. At press time, legislation was pending that would extend to two years the life of the Assassination Materials Review Board, currently slated to close-up shop in October despite the fact that its members had only finally been confirmed in April. According to Steve Tilley, JFK Assassination Records Collection liaison for the National Archives and Records Administration, the board has authority to extend its own life by a year if the pending extension legislation is delayed past October. A description of the Assassinations Records Collection and its work to create an electronic database of the newly emerging records can be found in General Information Leaflet 42 from the National Archives and Records Administration, Washington DC 20408.

The question of what is an assassination record has helped researchers in sifting through new releases, but an equally important question may define the legal parameters of what will be made available through the Materials Review Act: who decides what is an assassination record? The claim of H. R. Haldeman (whose newly released book/CD-ROM was unavailable at press time) in *Ends of Power* that Nixon makes coded reference to the assassination in a Watergate tape should qualify all Watergate tapes as assassination records. The logic would be lost on Nixon's lawyers. Who decides?

Fortunately, a new organization, the Coalition on Political Assassinations, has formed including representatives of many important research organizations (the Assassination Archives and Research Committee, the Citizens for Truth in the Kennedy Assassination, the Committee for an Open Archives, the Fourth Decade and the Fund for Accountability) to analyze released documents, assist in public education and influence the Review Board. John Judge is one of its principal organizers and its governing body includes Cyril Wecht, Jim Di Eugenio, Jim Lesar and John Newman. The group conducted an organizing conference in April and plans a national conference on the thirtieth anniversary of the Warren Commission Report, Oct. 7-10, at the Sheraton Washington Hotel in Washington, DC. The Coalition On Political Assassinations can be reached at POB 772, Washington, DC 20044.

Mack Facts

John Mack's new book, *Abduction: Human Encounters with Aliens,* published by Scribner's, is being hailed as the best thing to happen to ufology since Jacques Vallee. Mack is a Harvard psychiatrist and a winner of a 1977 Pulitzer Prize for a biography of Lawrence of Arabia. His four hundred page book takes the UFO abduction phenomenon into realms undreamt of by its original guru Budd Hopkins. Finally, say UFO buffs—legitimacy.

But the backlash has already begun. Long-time UFO-scene observer Jerome Clark calls Mack's book a throwback to the 1950s "space brother" craze, when suspect characters like George Adamski told stories of Aryan-looking Venusians bringing messages of peace. That was a far cry from the supposedly more believable tales of emotionless, robot-like Greys performing experiments on hapless abductees. Mack's aliens bring messages of peace, messages surprisingly similar to Mack's own radical-left, anti-"Western" political views.

That's no coincidence, according to Donna Bassett, a journalist recruited to infiltrate Mack's support-group pretending to be an abductee. Philip Klass and Bassett both claim Klass did not put her up to it, although Bassett's husband is a fellow editor of Klass' at *Aviation Week and Space Technology*. *Time* (April 25) reported on the shoddy research methods and indifferences to clients' welfare that Bassett found in Mack's "UFO cult." But she also says Mack is creating alien "split personalities" in his abductees and using what she likens to "Chinese brainwashing techniques"—including the Grof breathing technique, which Mack calls "LSD without the LSD." That sounds less like a dispassionate way to get at the truth of what's causing abduction trauma and more like classic MKULTRA "spy-chiatry." Mack's colleagues at the Center for Psychology and Social Change include not only Yale professor Robert Jay Lifton but also parapsychologist and former Naval Intelligence official C.B. Scott Jones, reportedly the "Falcon" of William Moore's "aviary" of UFO-U.S. intelligence turncoats. Mack has ties to EST and reportedly to the CIA and the Rockefellers as well.

In the next few months we may be learning a lot more about John Mack.

—**Chris Roth**

(*Steamshovel* Debris: The *New York Times Book Review* of March 20 compared John Mack to Timothy Leary and quoted an anonymous friend of Mack's as raising "the specter of Wilhelm Reich, the psychiatrist whose notions about orgone energy destroyed his career." In the same article Philip Klass sniffed that abductees are "little nobodies."

In December 1992 John Mack's name appeared in an article entitled "Microwave Harassment and Mind-Control Experimentation" by Juliane McKinney in *Electronic Surveillance Project,* published by the As-

sociation of National Security Alumni. The author reports upon the experiences of a woman referred to a hospital near McGill University in 1973 during the period when the university housed MKULTRA experiments. The woman was later physically subdued by personnel of a medical center in New York but resisted their attempts to force neuroleptic drugs upon her. She later found herself in one of John Mack's support groups for alien abductees. The article suggests that the woman was "an MKULTRA experimentee being kept on the books" and concludes that "drugs, externally induced auditory input, holographic projections...appropriately focused directed-energy targeting, device implantations, special effects and abductions are all within this government's capabilities and can be used for purposes of creating illusions of UFO experiences." The Association of National Security Alumni is a private group focusing on directed energy and mind control issues. It can be reached at POB 13625, Silver Spring, MD 20911-3645.)

Skip Clemens and the Finders

Skip Clemens says the more he looks into the possible involvement of the U.S. Customs Service, the FBI, and the CIA in an international child-abuse ring, the more it resembles the Washington, DC based "Finders" ring uncovered in 1991. In fact, he has come to suspect that it might all be connected.

Clemens used to be with the CIA but now he says he's with a private company in Stuart, Florida called Technology Strategic Planning (TSP), that is staffed by former intelligence employees (although, unusually for a private company, its telephone number is unlisted, and Directory Assistance told me that its prefix did not exist in that area code). Clemens says the capacity he works in now is not as an agent but as a "parent." Clemens' own child was one of the victims of the Glendale Montessori School in Florida, which was busted in the mid-1980s in what has been the only successful prosecution ever in the U.S. for ritual abuse (*contra* Ken Lanning, the FBI's False Memory Syndrome advocate, who denies ritual abuse exists).

Numerous other ex-CIA officials' kids were victimized in that case, too, but once the true scope of the operation became known prosecutors hands were already tied. James Toward, the school's founder, and his secretary were sentenced to 25 and 10 years respectively in 1986, but only on condition that anyone else discovered in the operation be immune from prosecution. That odd plea-bargain should have been the tip-off, Clemens says. Beyond the five victims known at the time, TSP is now discovering that Glendale was connected to a ring of Montessori schools in Kentucky, Mississippi, and elsewhere which routinely chloroformed and hypnotized children—some as young as 18 months—and shipped them as far afield as Mexico on "field trips" featuring sexual abuse and full documentation on film and video. According to Clemens, multiple-personality-disorder programming also features in their repertoire of mind-control techniques.

Clemens claims TSP has been finding similar connections and patterns as in the Finders case. In that case, Tallahassee police in 1987 busted what seemed at first to be a small kiddie-porn operation that they managed to trace to a warehouse in Washington, DC. There a full-on studio was in operation, involving not only child victims but also mutilated animals and other paraphernalia indicating ritual abuse. It was shaping up to be the kind of multi-jurisdictional bust that would make the Tallahassee cops famous; the FBI and Customs were cooperating on cracking the whole ring. That is, until the CIA stepped in and squashed the bust—and the story. That's why you haven't heard about the Finders in the mainstream press: it's tentacles went too high into federal agencies.

The cover-up of the Montessori ring, Clemens maintains, involves not only the Custom Service's child-protection team but also that agency's executive level and the highest levels of the FBI and CIA as well. But TSP's people have high connections in the CIA too, and that's the only reason they haven't shut down as quickly as the Finders investigation. The IRS tried to crack down on TSP in April, and they've been harassed by Finders agents as well. But Clemens insists the scandal reaches too far and the documentation is too extensive to deny: even paperwork from Customs' own investigations implicates their involvement.

That much is confirmed by a 1993 Associated Press report that the Justice Department was investigating Customs Service allegations that the Finders was not only a Satanic "commune" but a CIA "front company." The CIA, according to the report, has tried to obstruct the investigation, but the CIA denies everything. The Finders are in this connection identified with a computer company called Future Enterprises, which trained CIA employees in the 1980s.

Clemens says TSP has been in touch with Attorney General Janet Reno, NBC, ABC, CNN, *Newsweek,* and others. At *Steamshovel's* press time he was promising that America would be reading all about it within a few weeks. Then again that's what Clemens told me in December 1993. But he isn't making it all up. A spokesman for one of the two Congressmen cooperating in Clemens' investigation, Charlie Rose of North Carolina (the other is Tom Lewis of Florida), confirmed the main outline of what Clemens said. The spokesman added though that it was too early to talk about "ritual abuse" or to start setting dates for any big revelations. The investigation is still in the early stages, Rose's office said.

But if half of what Clemens says is true, there's a government-run ritual abuse ring whose discovery could shake up the corridors of power like no other scandal since Watergate. Let's hope that if he's right the CIA doesn't get to him first.

—**Chris Roth**

Post Partum Suppression

In an announcement for its address change, *Steamshovel Press* reprinted the words of subscriber Mike Sylwester, a JFK assassination researcher, as they appeared in the letters page of the *Washington Post*: "[the *Post*] printed a piece by humorist Charles Paul Freund on the theme that all books about the assassination are equally stupid and laughable. Which comic gets the assignment this year?" Through the good offices of Mr. Freund, who was otherwise occupied when the *Post* decided to again look at conspiracies and so passed on the chore, the comic ironically turned out to be *Steamshovel Press* editor Kenn Thomas.

Steamshovel's best attempt at documenting the *Washington Post's* notorious relationship with the intelligence community appears in its sixth issue. *Steamshovel Press #6* contained an interview with Deborah Davis, author of *Katharine The Great: Katharine Graham and Her Washington Post Empire*. Ms. Davis reviewed much of the known record about the relationship between *Post* publisher Phillip Graham and CIA head Allen Dulles; the CIA's project to staff the *Post* and other newspapers with its assets (Operation Mongoose); Phil Graham's mysterious death after making a public announcement about the JFK/Mary Meyer liaison; and the military intelligence backgrounds of such *Post* luminaries as Bob Woodward and Ben Bradlee. "The most important thing to [the publishers of the *Post*]," Ms. Davis noted, "is putting forth this myth about themselves, that they are supremely moral, supremely powerful, all-knowing, all-caring, that they'll take care of the rest of us and anything that they do that is questionable they try to cover up". So the *Washington Post* did not patronize an unknowing or tacitly collaborating ally in the alternative press when it offered this opportunity for *Steamshovel Press* to provide a wrap-up of "conspiracy" research.

The newspaper's intention was to present a tongue-in-cheek feature heralding in the "new age" of conspiracy theories wrought by Bill Clinton's first year in office. The *Post* editor did offer caveats that the writing "had to be more careful" than what ordinarily appears in *Steamshovel* (in the *Post's* view)—but otherwise it made a rare verbal commitment to present the material with as little varnish as possible—within the limits of its editorial mission. Anxious as ever for publicity and never adverse to exploring dimensions of humor in conspiracy research, *Steamshovel* editor Thomas took the challenge to present the often suppressed conspiracy material to the *Post* readership with minimal distortion. The result, "Clinton Era Conspiracies!" appeared in the January 16 edition of the *Post*.

Thomas views the final article as 80% successful in identifying currents within "conspiracy" research and keeping at a minimum the *Post*'s propensity to ridicule researchers. This success came as a result of three weeks of haggling with the editors, however—abandoning some good ideas, changing others, and resisting attempts at putting in parenthetical jibes against the research community. A flippant query not written by Thomas, "Was Gennifer Flowers On the Grassy Knoll?", headed the article, and it included the opinion, not shared by Thomas, that the Trilateral Commission and the Council on Foreign Relations are "generally well-regarded pillars of the foreign policy establishment". To give interested readers the best view of the differences, *Steamshovel Press* offered two versions of the article to anyone purchasing its *1994 Assassinations Calendar,* the one that appeared in the *Post* and the original draft.

In the published version, *Post* editors removed every reference to Area 51, ostensibly because it had already examined that topic at length in recent editions. Cut also was Len Bracken's comment that Carroll Quigley's speeches made him seem less the convinced imbecile that Bill Clinton made him out to be in his acceptance speech at the Democratic National Convention. The *Post* also trimmed a long section reviewing the 1993 ASK symposium and the Clinton administration's incompetence in establishing the review board required by the Assassinations Material Review Act of 1992. In addition to space considerations (the chief culprit for most of the cuts), the *Post* maintained that too much JFK material would rob the article of its focus on Clinton conspiracies.

Indeed, the *Post* was most rigorous in asking for rewrites of the section on the airstrip in Mena, Arkansas apparently used in an Ollie North-styled drugs-and-guns scheme that then-governor Clinton failed to investigate properly. The *Post* insisted that this section be flushed out with details and sources, even inserting reference to Alexander Cockburn's early work in breaking the Mena story. "Clinton Era Conspiracies!" appeared before the Whitewater scandal began to flood the daily news and, although the death of White House aide Vincent Foster did comprise one section of the essay, the Mena story seemed the most substantial.

(By March even *CBS News* could no longer resist and did a two-part broadcast on Mena, albeit depriving the story of important details.)

If a similar rigor had been applied to the earlier article by Charles Freund mentioned by Sylwester, the Clinton conspiracy essay may have never reached print. Freund had exaggerated comments Thomas made in the book reviews for the *Flatland* catalog about charges of "agent baiting" made by John Judge against Mark Lane. The resulting phone conversations and correspondence between the two resulted in Freund's recommendation of Thomas for this assignment.

Two days after the publication of the essay, Bobby Ray Inman withdrew his name from consideration as Secretary of Defense in a news conference that made him look like a conspiracy wonk. His complaints were made primarily against columnist William Safire, but some *Steamshovel* readers suggested that the Clinton conspiracy essay also may have contributed to Inman's decision to withdraw. The essay had repeated Jim Hougan's suggestion that Inman may have been Watergate's Deep Throat, reflecting a general criticism of Inman as a source for leaks. However, the essay also reported upon Inman's exchanges with ufologist Robert Oeschler in which the Admiral seemed to be acknowledging the existence of alien spacecraft and the MJ12 group of UFO lore. This report appeared and was read widely in Timothy Good's book *Alien Contact*, but readers suggested that its appearance in a Washington daily may have caused MJ12 to force Inman out! Holding out the possibility that such attention may indeed have been one more aggravation underscoring Inman's dislike for the Washington spotlight, *Steamshovel* nevertheless could find no evidence that he had mentioned the essay in his press conference or on *Larry King Live,* as some readers suggested.

The parenthetical swipes at researchers that did creep into the text included mention of the relationship of Jonathan Vankin's publisher to the Unification church and Sherman Skolnick's view of Watergate. That Vankin's book, *Conspiracies, Cover Ups and Crimes* was published by Paragon House, which is owned by Sun Myung Moon's church, has been widely discussed. This brief parenthetical nod, however, allowed no opportunity to discuss the issues of publishing compromises that surround the provenance of that book—issues that also obviously involve the publication of the Clinton conspiracy article by the *Washington Post* as well.

The *Post* asked several times about Skolnick's take on Watergate, unknown by the author but presumably having something to do with the JFK assassination/Watergate link often scoffed at by the mainstream but accepted as canon by certain segments of the research community. Hence, a non-parenthetical and marginally relevant statement that Skolnick "who has been prominent in conspiratorial circles since Watergate" (Skolnick's work actually pre-dates Watergate) appeared in the article. The article reported Skolnick's view that Vince Foster had been killed by a team of German hit men to prevent him from having Bill Clinton stop an assassination attempt against Saddam Hussein. Details about the plot against Saddam Hussein were supported by news reports in the *Chicago Tribune* faxed by *Steamshovel* to the *Washington Post*.

The last significant change made by the *Washington Post* underscored the differences between the pre- and post-published versions of the article. After the article concluded that "If indeed Clinton is as immersed in these plots, counterplots and various intrigues as some of the researchers suggest, the need for the kind of moral certitude he ascribed to Carroll Quigley seems obvious", the *Post* chose to end the article with its own invention, "The president will also be hard pressed to find time for reforming health care, never mind NATO", a glib observation for what the newspaper viewed as a frivolous piece. An important point was lost from the original article, which nevertheless emphasized an ironic relationship between the material it examined and the view held by Clinton that Quigley was a paragon of morality: "Like the research, however, its litmus test will be the degree to which that certitude is real or the imaginative projection of those who put it forward."

One last exchange with the *Post* provided some measure of how the publication of "Clinton Era Conspiracies" might affect the *Post*'s future reporting of similar types of research. After the Whitewater scandal erupted, several interesting connections between it and the Inslaw case became apparent. These were communicated to the *Washington Post* when Mike Issikoff, a reporter pursuing the "conspiracy" angle on the Foster suicide, called. *Steamshovel* faxed articles to Isikoff showing that Webster L. Hubbell, the White House counsel and associate attorney general who resigned under one of the Whitewater waves, had been recently assigned to re-open the Inslaw investigation. The articles also reflected that Park-On-Meter, the parking meter company central to the allegations leading to Hubbell's resignation, had curious contracts with the Pentagon to develop more than just parking meters (it built MX missile cones for one) and that information about the company had surfaced with allegations made in part by the notorious informant of Danny Casolaro's Inslaw investigation, Michael Riconosciuto, regarding the Mena airstrip. Isikoff responded that he had been satisfied with the report on Inslaw issued by Judge Nicholas Bua last March stating that Danny Casolaro had committed suicide and that no wrong doing was evident in the Inslaw affair. *Steamshovel* had faxed its report from *SP9* that Judge Bua made a twenty-five million dollar out-of-court settlement offer to Inslaw attorney Elliot Richardson (who rejected it) before issuing the report and that Bua's report failed to do even simple things like a code check of the Promis program. Nevertheless, Isikoff remained convinced by Judge Bua and found no merit in pursuing the Inslaw/Whitewater connection and instead wrote a piece emphasizing Sherman Skolnick's theory on Vince Foster. (Isikoff did brush against the Inslaw/Whitewater link by reporting that one of the last phone calls received by Foster was from Brantley Buck, the Rose law firm partner responsible for looking into its troubles with Webster Hubbell.)

"One excellent historical lesson [learned from the JFK assassination researchers]," Mike Sylwester wrote to the *Washington Times* last November, "has been the ability of independent but informed citizens to defeat government and media elites who try to impose an Official Truth by pretending infallibility and by ignoring, mischaracterizing and hooting down dissenters." Certainly this process was evident in *Steamshovel*'s relations with the Washington *Post*, but *Steamshovel* takes some credit—and gives credit as well to the editorial department on the *Post*'s *Outlook* section—for minimizing it in this instance.

In All Directions

We's all cuzzins! Federal approval of the bovine growth hormone in milk was passed with the participation of FDA officials who also held interests in Monsanto Company, the hormone's producer; and a campaign promise to shut down Waste Technology Inc.'s toxic waste incinerator in East Liverpool, Ohio (the world's largest) was ignored because of campaign contributions by Arkansas investment firm Stephens, Inc., one of four original investors in the incinerator...*Isn't that what happened to RFK?* The murder of Mexican presidential candidate Luis Donaldo Colosio must have set a speed record. He was assassinated before he was actually president. The Mexican government first characterized the assassin, Mario Aburto Martinez, as a lone gunman, then conceded that at least six other people blocked and distracted Colosio's bodyguards, and then backed away from any notion of conspiracy...*Of course, he couldn't see anything from the floorboard.* Tapes released by the LBJ Library in Austin demonstrated that Johnson didn't believe the magic bullet theory either. John Maher failed to bring it up during Arlen Specter's recent appearance on *Politically Incorrect...It would happen if Spike Lee teamed up with Oliver Stone.* At the end of last year a lawyer named Wayne Chastain sought to present new evidence on the Martin Luther King case but was refused a hearing by a grand jury in Memphis. This followed a confession published by the *London Observer* of a US businessman claiming to have hired the murderer. James Earl Ray lost his bid for parole on May 26, despite pleas from two former MLK associates...*A Moose of a man.* Still no trace in Alaska, or anywhere, of Joe Vogler, the malcontent, anti-environmentalist and founder (in 1973) of the secessionist Alaskan Independence Party. It looks like murder and conspiracy...*Garbologists on the run.* One of the deals considered by the San Francisco district attorney's office over the ADL spy scandal prevented it from receiving confidential information from police sources but didn't stop any of its other "fact-finding" activities...*Garbologist on the run II.* A Long Island judge subpoenaed Yoko Ono to testify against Frederic Seaman, a former assistant to John Lennon, in a suit brought by one of the bodyguards that Seaman alleges beat him up after the Ono camp discovered his theft of a Lennon diary used as the basis of his book, *The Last Days of John Lennon* (reviewed in *Steamshovel Press #4*)...*Better safe than sorry.* The Justice Department requested that files relating to the botched raid and unnecessary deaths at the Branch Davidian compound be exempted from the Freedom of Information Act for the sake of national security...*What'd I say?* The National Reconnaissance Office launched a $1.5 billion-plus satellite in April but did not give its name, mission or exact cost to the taxpayers footing the bill. "Spy satellites are enormously expensive," says the *New York Times*, "in part because they are technologically exquisite devices capable of plucking a single conversation from the babble of telecommunications, and in part because the secrecy that surrounds their existence adds significantly to the cost of building them"...*Anything you want, we just don't want to see him naked.* Siddig Ibrahim Siddig Ali, the alleged World Trade Center bombing villain who just happened to be under FBI surveillance prior to the bombing, planned to kidnap Henry Kissinger, strip him because he might have been wearing electronic eavesdropping devices, and offer him in trade for the freedom with those charged in the blast...*You won't see it on X-Files.* The White Sides Defense Committee is fighting to prevent further government takeover of land at the infamous UFO sight Area 51. The government can only take 4000 acres at a time without running into Congressional oversight. It has now set its sight on one critical hill, White Sides, one of the last

places where visitors can still look on the Groom Lake facility, supposed home of the alien spacecraft and genetic labs. Contact the White Sides Defense Committee, POB 448, Alamo, NV 89001. ...*For real, now, what's going on with this?* The fumes that overcame emergency workers at Riverside General Hospital after the death of cancer patient Gloria Ramirez still have no official explanation, only rumors that the 31 year old woman belonged to an abductee or ritual-abuse survivors support group...*Liddy lifts the lid on Foster.* G. Gordon Liddy led the FBI to the "man in the white van" who originally found Vincent Foster's body (the National Parks maintenance worker who claimed to have seen the man in the van later recanted). The witness says Foster had no gun and Liddy is convinced of his veracity. In St. Louis recently to promote his radio show, Liddy also claimed that his program provided a needed counter-balance to the liberal media. The radio station boasted that it brought in Liddy's program in as competition for Rush Limbaugh, who appears on a rival station. Liddy once busted Timothy Leary for possession of peat moss... *It's Rodney King all over again.* An airport cop in Austin now shares a distinction with Liddy by arresting Dr. Leary for an association with non-criminal plant life. On May 10 Leary was arrested for lighting and not quite smoking a tobacco cigarette in protest against the lack of a smoking area at the airport. He later explained to Greg Kinnear on NBC's *Later* that as a smoker he pays heavy taxes and airports *are* tax supported facilities. Leary also brought video of the bust showing the cop snatching the cigarette before he could inhale. Leary will pay as much as $500 in fines for this act of social protest (in typically 1960ish-styled show of solidarity, Allen Ginsberg went on the Conan O'Brien show and did "Don't Smoke.")...*It means "Editor's Note".* The *American Heritage Dictionary of the English Language* includes this quote from Jack Kerouac in its definition of debris: "The whole library groaned with the accumulated debris of centuries of recorded folly."

THE HITS JUST KEEP ON COMIN' (News that happened while the current issue waited out its production delays.) *Shut down with an endorsement by the FDA.* The psychedelic-mimicking relaxation devices that look like a cross between a Sony Walkman and a pair of Foster Grants have been busted by the Food and Drug Administration. Production of the light and sound devices by Synetic Systems of Seattle has been shut down and its inventory confiscated, although other manufacturers still exist and the device is still being sold. Synetic had altered its descriptive literature for the machines several months prior to the FDA seizure to avoid the appearance that it made medical claims for the device. (Readers should recall that the characterizing of Wilhelm Reich's books as labeling for orgone devices by the FDA is what led to them being burned.) The FDA proceeded with its raid against Synetic despite its approval of the wording changes. FDA compliance officer Daryl Thompson stated that it is against the law to market devices "that affect the structure or function of man", certainly a larger claim than has ever been made by the device's manufacturers. The best version of the spinning-lights and synchronized sound machines tested by *Steamshovel* is the Voyager XL, available from Theta Technologies, POB 130, Fall City WA 98024. It includes a program written by Thomas A. Budzynski, an aerospace engineer and psychology PhD who at one time served as crew chief of the inertial navigation team of the SR-71 Blackbird, which was developed at Area 51. (Last June the Senate Armed Services Committee approved $263 billion worth of defense authorization, including money that takes the SR-71 out of mothballs for service in spying on North Korea's nuclear program.). *Simpson Twists of Fate:* One week after the *Buffalo News* printed a recap of O.J. Simpson's connections to former Buffalo bar owner Casimer J. "Casey" Sucharski, he and two women were found murdered at Sucharski's home in Miramar, Florida. In April 1975 Sucharski was arrested on drugs and guns charges at the home of Michael Militello, another Buffalo bar owner. Militello and Simpson were subjects of police investigation for cocaine but charges were never brought against either of the prominent, well-connected citizens of Buffalo. Militello paid a visit to Simpson in jail on July 17, shortly after Sucharski's death. *Adventures of Robert Morrow:* NBC interrupted its Simpson coverage to report an assassination attempt against the PLO chairman. Israeli radio had reported that shots were fired from a gun disguised as a camera—a scenario identical to author Robert Morrow's take on the RFK assassination. The *Globe* tabloid lost a considerable sum when it repeated the tale from Morrow's book, *The Senator Must Die*, that Robert Kennedy was shot by a gun disguised as a camera wielded by a Mossad agent named Khawar. Khawar sued and won $3 million. Meanwhile, last November Morrow announced that he had the financial backing to build a $90 million sports arena in Cincinnati for a National Hockey League team. The money, the arena and the team never materialized. *Soccer Star Killed by Group of Lone Nuts:* After "accidentally" kicking an own-goal that lost the pivotal game for the highly-rated Colombian team during World Cup soccer, Andres Escobar was shot to death by a group characterized in the media as disgruntled fans of the sport. The Colombian loss allowed the U.S. team to play against Brazil on July 4. Henry Kissinger was one of the prominent sponsors of World Cup Soccer in the US. *Add to the Clinton Body Count:* The police informer who testified against the son of Surgeon General Joycelyn Elders during his trial for selling cocaine was found dead of an apparent suicide in July. Police do not suspect foul play (as ever) in the death of Calvin R. Walraven, who admitted helping police entrap Elders' son in a cocaine deal.

9

Steamshovel Press #13, Summer 1995

Sagan Sees a Moonbase

" Prof Says Beings From Outer Space Visited Earth," from *Stars and Stripes*, Monday, November 26, 1962:

Some of the best scientific minds in the country were stumped when a slender, dark-haired young man chalked on the blackboard this equation:

$$N \text{ equals } R \text{ } FP \text{ } NE \text{ } FL \text{ } FI, \text{ } FC \text{ } L$$

The speaker was Dr. Carl Sagan, a 28 year old assistant professor of astronomy at Harvard University.

His audience consisted of several hundred members of the American Rocket Society, gathered for his luncheon address.

The equation was his way of expressing the mathematical probability that intelligent beings from outer space have visited earth.

Sagan soberly explained that in his equation N stands for the number of advanced civilizations in the universe possessing the capability of interstellar communication.

R is the mean rate of star formation averaged over the lifetime of the galaxy.

FP is the fraction of stars with planetary systems.

NE is the mean number of planets in each system with environments favorable for the origin of life.

FL is the fraction of such inhabited planets on which intelligent life with manipulative abilities rises during the lifetime of the local sun.

FC is the fraction of planets populated by intelligent beings on which an advanced technical civilization rises.

And L is the lifetime of this technical civilization.

Sagan said information in his formula is based on current estimates by astronomers. In making calculations, he assigned each symbol an arbitrary numerical value.

As expressed in numbers, Sagan said, the formula means that at least 1 million of the 100 billion stars in our Milky Way galaxy have planets which have developed civilizations capable of travel between the stars.

"Let's say that each of these civilizations sends out one interstellar expedition per year," he said.

"That means that every star, such as our sun, would be visited at least once every million years. In some systems where these beings found life, they would make more frequent visits. There's a strong probability, then, that they visited earth every few thousand years.

"It is not out of the question that artifacts of these visits still exist or even that some kind of base is maintained, possibly automatically, within the solar system, to provide continuity for successive expeditions.

"Because of weathering and the possibility of detection and interference by the inhabitants of earth, it would be preferable not to erect such a base on the earth's surface. The moon seems one reasonable alternative.

"Forthcoming photographic reconnaissance of the moon from space vehicles—particularly of the back—might bear these possibilities in mind."

At a news conference Sagan predicted man himself would be capable of interstellar flight at close to the speed of light "within a century or two."

Asked if he believed in flying saucers, he said: "I do believe there are objects which have not been identified."

Steamshovel *Debris: "It's never been, 'Oh, gee, this is nothing like what I had imagined,'" comments Carl Sagan about the growth of his scientific understanding in the January/February 1995 issue of* Skeptical Inquirer, *"Just the opposite: It's exactly like what I imagined." Whether Professor Sagan is embarrassed by his early equations about life in space or MJ12 got to him, as some* Steamshovel *readers have suggested, his SI article underscored his real fear that others still add it up the same way he did in 1962: information overload, bane of the acid head. "If you are awash in lost continents and channelling and UFOs and all the long litany of claims so well exposed in the* Skeptical Inquirer, *you may not have the intellectual room for the findings of science." While this does not really* seem to be a problem with those interested in such "fringe" topics, the skeptics do seem to have their problems managing information. In the following issue of SI, a review of a panel on conspiracy theories identified the author of Crossfire, a much respected work on the JFK assassination by Jim Marrs used in part as the basis of Oliver Stone's JFK movie, as Jim Morrison. Jim Morrison, of course, sang with a rock band called the Doors and served as the subject of another Oliver Stone movie.

Johnny Meyer: Gemstone's Link
Between Howard Hughes and Aristotle Onassis
by Gerald A. Carroll

Aristotle Onassis carries out a carefully planned event: He has [Howard] Hughes kidnapped from his bungalow at the Beverly Hills Hotel, using Hughes' own men (Chester Davis, born Cesare in Sicily, et al). Hughes' men either quit, get fired or stay on in the new Onassis organization.

Gemstone 1:9

One of the more amazing, and seemingly implausible, aspects of the long-maligned Gemstone thesis is this wild tale about Greek shipping tycoon Aristotle Onassis masterminding a kidnapping of billionaire defense contractor Howard Hughes in 1957. Researchers who have bothered to dig around in the Gemstone legend have often kissed it off as a fabrication because of a lack of "proof" that any of the events described actually took place—the most flagrant falsification being this "kidnapping and switch" of Hughes, by Onassis or anyone else.

But a closer examination of the Gemstone language and some cross-referencing with news accounts of that time paint a dramatically different picture, one of deception of the highest degree.

For example, the Gemstone thesis states Hughes men either quit, get fired or stay on in the new Onassis organization—following the alleged kidnapping of Hughes in the Bahamas in the spring-summer of 1957. Indeed, key people did peel off quickly and suddenly in 1957. Noah Dietrich, one of the Hughes Corp.'s mightiest chief executives, was suddenly "fired" by Hughes in 1957. (1) Long-time aide William "Bill" Gay abruptly resigned, citing "mononucleosis" as the cause (2) under mysterious circumstances. Even publicist Carl Byoir mysteriously died right before that ill-fated trip to Nassau (3). It was Byoir's public relations firm—which served the Hughes Corp. for years, even after Byoir himself passed away—that provided "doubles" including L. Wayne Rector. These doubles were well-known to Hughes's aides.

Also well-known was a special man named Johnny W. Meyer, who started out with Hughes in the early years as a personal driver and became one of the billionaire's closest confidantes. He set up elaborate Hughes parties, including attractive female escorts, with such high-rollers as Elliott Roosevelt, President Franklin D. Roosevelt's son and a maverick arms dealer on the side.

Meyer is clearly one of the men who "stay on in

the new Onassis organization" after the events of 1957. In fact, it was Meyer who broke the news to Jacqueline Kennedy Onassis that her husband, Aristotle, had died of respiratory failure on March 5, 1975. (4) Strangely, Jackie had left her sick husband's bedside and was skiing in New Hampshire when Ari passed on. Meyer, like he did for Hughes, had to do the dirty work. He notified Jackie of yet another dead husband.

Mcyer himself died under even more strange conditions. He allegedly got out of his car one night in Florida in 1983 to relieve himself following his attendance at a party—and the car rolled over him, killing him. (5)

Clearly, it was Meyer who was the common thread between Howard Hughes and Aristotle Onassis. He was a skilled public relations expert, and manipulated the media at every turn for both men over the years. If Onassis ever wanted to conquer Hughes—even kidnap him and replace him with a double—he would need the help of Meyer to cover it up and keep a lid on it for years. The existence of a man of Meyer's abilities is enough to give the Gemstone passages a sense of truthfulness regarding this bizarre kidnap story. The skills that propelled the rotund Meyer to prominence in the Hughes organization peaked when he covered for the billionaire in embarrassing situations, particularly the so-called Brewster Hearings of 1947, engineered by muckraking Sen. Owen Brewster (R-Maine) when it had become known that Hughes' airplane contracts with the government were questioned.

It was intrepid Hearst Corp. Newsman Bob Considine who blew the lid off this story, exposing Hughes, Elliott Roosevelt and the velvet cover Meyer had placed over the whole sordid mess. Hughes and Elliott loved to party together and Meyer set up these affairs. Brewster and others were convinced that Elliott used his influence as the president's son to seek "the intercession of his father in order to override Army Air Force objections" to aircraft supplied the U.S. armed forces during World War II. (6)

Hughes was angry that an earlier warplane design of his was rejected by the Army Air Force—a record-breaking design that later became the model for the Japanese Zero, one of the most deadly warplanes of the war. (7) Meyer got tangled up in the mess when he allegedly "entertained" high government officials lavishly in order to sway their opinions of Hughes' airplane deals. Many of those parties also included Elliott and his new wife, Faye Emerson.

Considine, with some help from The Associated Press, originally broke the story on Aug. 3 by releasing a lengthy expense-account list of Meyer's excesses "duly recorded by Hughes' bookkeepers. (8) Meyer's P.R. skills were evident when he was accused of ordering Elliott to stay in Europe—and out of the U.S.—until the 1944 elections were over and his dad was safely re-elected.

Then, astonishingly, at the height of the Brewster Hearings and the public outcry they were precipitating, Johnny Meyer disappeared. With the key witness gone, the hearings collapsed. (9) An international manhunt was launched to find the portly Meyer. The next day, Hughes triumphantly left Washington for California to the cheers of a supportive public (10). Meyer resurfaced in Hollywood on Aug. 17, 1947, but by that time, the hysteria over the Brewster Hearings had subsided and his client, Howard Hughes, was temporarily off the hook.

Three years later, Meyer dabbled in oil-rig investments in Wyoming, a deal that would inevitably lead him to Onassis, who at that time in 1950 had tried to monopolize the oil-shipping routes from Saudi Arabia. (11)

Fast-forward to 1957, and it was duly noted that Meyer received a $104,666 "loan" from Equitable Plan Company that he was under no obligation to repay (12). The timing, September 1957, is absolutely vital, for that was just after the kidnap and switch of Howard Hughes was rendered complete in August, according to the Gemstone thesis, and Hughes' personal aide Donald Neuhaus (13). Was that "loan" part of a payoff to Meyer for his cooperation?

And that was not the end of the story. Another disclosure of an additional $125,000 "loan" to Meyer from Equitable was made on Sept. 6, 1957. Congressional investigators, weary of Hughes-related probes, gathered sketchy, hurried testimony from Meyer and others and ended up clearing Meyer of any wrongdoing. The coincidences, however, are disconcerting and lend more credence to the Gemstone account (14).

Another damning piece of information that would link Meyer to any kidnap plot is the fact that he, along with Bill Gay, accompanied Hughes on that ill-fated trip to Nassau by way of Montreal—from Hughes headquarters in Beverly Hills (15). Meyer stayed with the Hughes party the entire time the billionaire stayed in Nassau.

Later, when he openly switched to Onassis, one of Meyer's chief jobs was to keep a full-time watch over Jackie (16). As always, Johnny Meyer did his boss right.

Notes:

1. Carroll, Gerald A., *Project Seek: Onassis, Kennedy and the Gemstone Thesis* (1994, Bridger House), p. 78.

2. Carroll, p. 334.

3. *San Francisco Examiner,* Feb. 4, 1957.

4. Heyman, C. David, Cosmopolitan, August 1989, p. 164, *Jackie: The Onassis Years.*

5. Davis, L.J., *Onassis: Aristotle and Christina,* 1986, St. Martin's Press, p. 273.

6. Considine, Bob, *San Francisco Examiner* (International News Service), Aug. 5, 1947.

7. Considine, *Examiner* (INS), Aug. 10, 1947.

8. Associated Press, *Examiner,* Aug. 3, 1947.

9. Considine, *Examiner* (INS), Aug. 12, 1947.

10. *Examiner,* INS, Aug. 13, 1947.

11. Lloyd, Ed C., *Examiner,* "Reports from the Oil Fields," July 15, 1950.

12. *Examiner* (INS), "$104,666 Loan Sans Obligation Told at Hearing," Sept. 4, 1957.

13. Carroll, p. 89.

14. *Examiner* (INS), "Johnny Meyer's Equitable Co. Loans Revealed," Sept. 6, 1957.

15. Serling, Robert, *Howard Hughes' Airline, an Informal History of TWA,* 1983, St. Martin's Press, p. 121.

16. Caruana, Stephanie and Brussell, Mae, *Playgirl,* November 1974, "Is Howard Hughes Dead and Buried Off a Greek Island?"

Tom Slick - Mystery Man
by Loren Coleman

The study of hidden animals, zoological species as yet not scientifically accepted but for which testimonial and circumstantial evidence exists, was, during the 1950s, formally given the name "cryptozoology" by the French zoologist Dr. Bernard Heuvelmans (1993). Early in the history of cryptozoology, an unusual man was attracted to the young science. His name is Thomas Baker Slick - Tom Slick to his friends, and as it would turn out, to most of the rest of the world for a brief time. What little is remembered today about Tom Slick is associated with his expeditions in 1957, 1958 and 1959, in pursuit of the abominable snowmen of the Himalayas, the elusive yeti of the Sherapa. But there seems to have been other sides of Tom Slick. As the Texas writer Dennis Stacy once noted, Tom Slick is today Texas' "forgotten millionaire." Indeed, Tom Slick was a shadowy figure who died very mysteriously in 1962, but looking at his life and his death, as I have done in the last twenty years, has turned me down many intriguing paths. As one treks down the trail of Tom Slick, a lurking question keeps popping up: was cryptozoology used as a front to hide a covert cryptopolitical agenda?

Beginnings

We really do not know much about young Tom's early life. Born into a wealthy Texas oil family, his choices were clearly already set up for him - to go into his father's business, but young Tom had other ideas. He was an adventurer at heart. However, the beginning was a classic privileged one. His first two years of high school were spent at Oklahoma City's Classen High School. Tom's father died in 1930, and the next year Tom went to Phillips Exeter Academy in Exeter, New Hampshire. Dating from 1781 and nestled among stately elms in the 1930s, Phillips Exeter was and is an old college-preparatory school of the highest academic and social standing. The sons of Presidents Lincoln, Grant, and Cleveland attended the school. Politically forward thinkers from Daniel Webster to the Democratic Senator from West Virginia, Jay Rockefeller, attended Exeter. Cofounder of the Americans for Democratic Action Arthur M. Schlesinger, Jr., for example, was an upperclassman at the same time Tom Slick was there.

While at Exeter, Tom was mainly involved in his studies and chasing young women, according to a friend he made there who would remain close to Tom until his death. Stewart Strong ("S.S.") Wilson, who I interviewed in 1989, was Tom's closest friend at Exeter, then also at Yale. Coming from Oracle, Arizona, Wilson found that Slick and he were immediately drawn to each other because of their common interests in the Spanish language, Mexican food, ranching, and dating. Wilson recalled that Slick was very handsome, and rather popular with "the ladies." Tom did have time to be a coxswain on the Academy's rowing crew team, as well (Slick, 1989). Tom also was the President of the Southern Club (Exeter, 1934). On campus, Tom Slick wore a long black overcoat and black Stetson hat, and is said to have relished the label of Southwestern nonconformist he was given at Exeter (Lubar, 1960). In 1934, Slick graduated from Phillips Exeter Academy.

The Young Man and The Loch Ness Monster

After his graduation from Phillips Exeter, Tom Slick would go to Yale University in New Haven, Connecticut. Here, Slick was a member of the residential college of Pierson, and became a member of the Political Union. Tom's academic record was good; he ranked a second or third during his first three years, and eventually graduated Phi Beta Kappa in 1938, as a pre-medicine biology major (Yale, 1989). I have been unable to determine what secret society Slick joined, if any, although he is not listed on any of the published Skull and Bones lists.

S.S. Wilson, Slick's friend from Exeter, as noted, was at Yale, and roomed with Slick. The two buddies were constantly together, and most of their activities overlapped. For example, Wilson managed the Pierson football team on which Slick played. But mainly, according to what Wilson remembered, Slick, Wilson, George Nichols, John Francis, John Nelson, and Rawson Goodwin all were members of an informal group who would get in Slick's car and take trips to Vassar, Smith, and Wellesley to spend weekends socializing with "college girls" (Wilson, 1989).

In addition, I discovered from casually talking to Wilson that during their Yale years, Slick actually went to Loch Ness and looked for the Loch Ness monsters, the large humped beasts said to resemble gigantic long-necked seals or waterbound dinosaurs. Since a new road was dynamited around the hills of Loch Ness in 1933, scores of sightings have occurred. During the summer of 1937, Slick, Wilson, Nelson, and Goodwin took Slick's 1934 maroon Buick sedan aboard the *Bremen,* debarked in Germany, and then drove 10,000 miles all around Europe. During August, 1937, the group, at Slick's urging, traveled to Scotland's fabled Loch Ness. They spent a few days talking to residents about the reported monsters, and searching the water's surface for any signs of the creatures. They definitely stayed for a time in Inverness and Drumnadrochit. The latter village is located on Urquhart Bay, site of the ancient Urquhart Castle and location of numerous monster encounters. Around the time Slick and his party were at Loch Ness, one of the more memorable monster sightings occurred from a tea-room at the Halfway House near Foyers. In August, 1937, the Reverend William Graham saw two separate four feet high humps, the color of an elephant, creating a heavy wake as the creature moved along at thirty-five miles an hour (Whyte, 1957). But the Slick group was to see nothing. For Slick, however, his search for unknown animals had begun. The Loch Ness monsters really got Slick excited, his friend told me (Wilson, 1989). From Europe, Slick's friends would return with his car to America while Tom went on to Russia to allegedly see what it was like there before going home. We do not know what Slick did in Germany or Russia during his pre-War World II visits to these politically important nations.

Playboy Slick and Howard Hughes

For a year or so after graduating, Slick lived in Oklahoma City, but in 1939, he established his home in San Antonio, Texas, and remained there for the rest of his life. By his late thirties, Tom Slick, like his father, had turned prematurely white-haired. This did not diminish his good looks, and in his bachelor days (and apparently during his marriages) he kept the company of many attractive socialites and budding Hollywood starlets. Thomas Baker Slick, Jr. was an attractive man, and he seemed to have known it. Some five feet, eleven inches tall, he was always fit and trim, never weighing much over one hundred and seventy pounds, even into his forties. An early contact in California was Howard Hughes. They both were from Texas and shared much in common including traveling, women, Hollywood, inventions, the oil and airline industries, and the intelligence business. Tom Slick and Howard Hughes became such close friends that they had adjoining cottages at the Beverly Hills Hotel. Like Hughes, Tom was not your typical jet-setting playboy, for he was excited by stimulating conversations with his female associates as well as by his allegedly frequent sexual encounters.

One of the many stories about Tom Slick is that he, like Hughes, had more than a passing interest in Las Vegas. Slick, it was rumored, had a large financial interest with Mickey Cohen in the town's first casino, La Rancho Vegas, until it burned down. Slick is even reported to have known Jack Ruby and assisted with the early running of guns to Cuba for the Mafia, using a Florida branch office, Transworld Resources as his avenue of delivery for the mob and, possibly, some hidden federal agency. Transworld Resources, a Slick-owned company, publicly was said to hold mineral rights to locations in Mexico, Alaska, and California. What is known for certain is that Tom Slick had been involved with the CIA for a long time, via Slick Airways.

Saipan and the CIA

During World War II, Slick volunteered for Navy Service immediately after Pearl Harbor was attacked on December 7, 1941. Turned down for poor eyesight, he served as a "dollar-a-year man," in the role of a shipping officer of the War Production Board in Washington, D.C. for six months. After that he transferred and served for one year as a cargo officer of the Board of Economic Welfare in Chile. The official record tells us that when the Navy relaxed its eyesight requirements, he served in Hawaii, in Saipan, and with the occupation in Japan (Coleman, 1989).

In reality, Tom Slick's military record is not too detailed in the archives I was able to examine. In Saipan, Slick wrote in his short resume, he was a commanding officer of an oil tank farm. The Japanese built a naval base at Saipan when it became their territory in 1919 and maintained it until the United States captured the site in July, 1944. What has only become known years later is that the Central Intelligence Agency's "Special Operations Division had 'a home away from home' under Navy cover on the Pacific island of Saipan" (Marchetti and Marks, 1974). In the early 1950s, Koreans and Taiwanese were the recipients of the CIA's advanced training on Saipan, and apparently starting in 1959, Tibetans came too. "The CIA facility used a military designation, Naval Technical Training Unit, for its cover. Recruits were flown in at night by C-47 aircraft like those of Civil Air Transport. New arrivals were blindfolded on the ground enroute to the base. But the CIA facility had been built on the highest mountain on the island, with surroundings plainly visible to the trainees" (Prados 1986). What was the extent of Tom Slick's involvement with the intelligence community's early development of the Saipan training center? One wonders-was the oil tank farm merely part of the cover story? And how involved was Slick?

Flying Tigers, CIA and Slick Airways

Tom Slick joined his brother Earl in founding Slick Airways in January 1946 to allegedly fill the void in air cargo freight delivery. Slick Airways and Flying Tiger Lines, during the late 1940s and 1950s, had the corner on the market, and flew many fast-paced and exciting jobs, recalling images we all have from the early scenes in the *Indiana Jones* movies, and John Wayne's 1942 film, *Flying Tigers*. Coming out of the adventurous days of pre-World War II "flying tiger" pilots who "flew the Hump," that is, took cargo over the Himalayas to China, Slick Airways carried on a thrilling tradition. OSS-connected men have had many strange links to these times. The OSS's Colonel Merian Cooper would, in 1942, become Chief of Staff of General Claire Chennault's Flying Tigers in China (Smith, 1972). It was Cooper who was the adventurer and the writer/producer/director of the first *King Kong* movie (1933) starring Fay Wray.

Incredibly, little discussion has ever been made of the similar evolutionary beginnings of Chennault's and the CIA's Civil Air Transport and Air America, and the origins of Earl and Tom Slick's Slick Airways, Inc. Claire L. Chennault, who was born in Texas in 1890 and trained as a military aviator at San Antonio's world-famous Kelly Field, was destined to embody adventure and derring-do. After years of rebuilding the Chinese Air Force, Chennault took command of the Chinese-based American Volunteer Group (AVG) during the summer of 1941. The AVG (or Flying Tigers as they soon came to be known) was initially created to insure the safety of the land supply route from Burma to China. These were the famed pilots who overflew the Himalayas, protecting the transportation of valuable supplies (Leary, 1984).

At the end of World War II, Chennault set about to create a Chinese-based American-owned airline, the Civil Air Transport (CAT). Meanwhile, former members of the AVG in the United States decided to establish two pioneer air freight companies. Robert Prescott, one of Chennault's men, was to head one, Flying Tigers, Inc. The other company was Slick Airways, Inc., which originally started as an idea of Earl Frates Slick, but was something in which Tom Slick quickly became interested. Hiring pilots Earl had once worked with, and buying planes from the military, Slick Airways was the number one air cargo transporter in the 1950s (Davies, 1972; *Business Week*, 1951; Coleman, 1989; Leary, 1984).

In 1950, the CIA secretly purchased Chennault's CAT, and then in 1959, CAT became Air America (Leary, 1984). Other airlines that are connected to the CIA have been mentioned in the public record, such as Air Asia, Southern Air Transport and Intermountain Aviation, but the CIA had retained the right to delete at least one airline from an expose of their proprietary

organizations (Marchetti and Marks, 1974). How deeply involved was Slick Airways in this interwoven network of CIA companies and contracts? Intriguing hints always existed. One individual who evidences a direct connection between Slick Airways and CAT is Robert Rousselot, who worked for both (Leary, 1989). Rousselot was highly regarded by the Central Intelligence Agency:

"Chief Pilot Rousselot was the key link between CAT and the CIA for covert missions.... Rousselot took charge of operational planning and selection of crew. The chief pilot looked for capable, responsible individuals, who would complete a mission if at all possible but would abort when necessary.... As one former case officer recalled, Rousselot always delivered'" (Leary, 1984).

Slick Airways was a good idea. It was the cargo freight leader of the U. S., and on April 16, 1951, the company became the world's first operator of the highly revolutionary and specialized cargo plane, the Douglas DC-6A. Shortly American Airlines, then most of the rest of the passenger carriers were jumping into the freight business. Opposition from the commercial airlines seemed to have been behind Slick Airways losing an important decision regarding their merger with Flying Tiger Lines in the late 1940s. Slick Airways never regained its central position, supposedly. The company spurted along through trials and tests in 1959 and 1965, and was finally bought out by Airlift in 1966. The holding company, Slick Corporation, still has some Airlift stock, but in the 1970s also had interests in Drew Chemical Company and Pulverising Machinery plant (Davies, 1972). Flying Tigers was purchased by Federal Express (now FedEx) in the 1980s.

The CIA expert Professor William M. Leary notes in his book *Perilous Missions* (University of Alabama, 1984) that the Air America precursor, Civil Air Transport (CAT) was very involved with Standard Vacuum Oil Company, as their main supplier of air fuel. Standard Vacuum Oil Company was the employer of Harry Gillmore, Peter Ryhiner's and Tom Slick's man in Sumatra trying to track down more on the orang pendek, the little hairy bipedal unknowns of the woods. From at least the summer of 1958 through the spring of 1959 the Slick-sponsored Ryhiner-Gillmore team operated in Sumatra looking for the orang pendek and the special little hairy rhinos of that island nation. Interestingly, in the secret history of the CIA, 1958 was the year that the intelligence organization supported an anti-Sukarno coup in Indonesia with a fleet of B-26 bombers. On May 18, 1958, one American pilot, Allen Pope, was shot down and captured. According to Victor Marchetti and John D. Marks

(*The CIA and the Cult of Intelligence* 1974, p. 29): "Although U.S. government officials claimed that Pope was a 'soldier of fortune,' he was in fact an employee of a CIA-owned proprietary company, Civil Air Transport. Within a few months after being released from prison four years later, Pope was again flying for the CIA-this time with Southern Air Transport, an agency proprietary airline based in Miami...The CIA later produced a pornographic movie using a stand-in for Sukarno in an attempt to discredit the leader."

What we now know from the release of information in a 1993 Supreme Court case involving the Central Intelligence Agency and E-Systems is that Tom Slick was involved with the CIA via Slick Airways soon after its creation. The case concerns Erwin Rautenberg and his Los Angeles air freight company named Air-Sea Forwarders. Rautenberg agreed in 1956 to let the CIA use his company's name. It became a subsidiary of the CIA proprietary, Air Asia, which was in turn part of Air America and was finally purchased by the covert military intelligence company E-Systems in 1975. Rautenberg sued the CIA because they had walked away from millions of dollars in debts left when they were really using Air-Sea as a front. Almost in passing some interesting notes for our story appeared in the midst of the *New York Times'* May 17, 1993 article on the matter. Edwin Rautenberg is quoted as explaining: "Until 1956, the C.I.A. proprietary worked through a company called Slick Airways. Then they started their own operation and ran immediately into tax problems with the state of California. As a Federal agency, they were tax-exempt, but they couldn't say so. They wanted to maintain their secrecy and still not pay taxes." Rautenberg noted the government did a little research and found that an international freight-loader is tax-exempt in California, looked around and discovered Air-Sea. "They made a deal with me in the late fall of 1956, " he said. "An operation would be conducted under the name of Air-Sea Forwarders, it would be an entirely different business." During the Vietnam War, business boomed, but with the fall of Saigon in 1975, the CIA sold Air Asia for a huge loss to E-Systems. Rautenberg, by the way, lost his case because the Supreme Court refused to unseal a secrecy order governing the case. (As a sideline here, President Clinton's very own US Trade Representative Mickey Cantor was Rautenberg's lawyer and it was in his offices where, on behalf of the CIA and the Justice Department, the secrecy order was presented for Rautenberg. A government attorney and Cantor told Rautenberg to sign. Under protest he complied, then sought a new lawyer.)

E-Systems remains in the news. Raytheon (makers of the apparently less-than-successful Patriot anti-missile rockets) recently took over E-Systems of Dallas, Texas. It will cost Raytheon 2.3 billion dollars in cash. In the story in *The Boston Globe* (April 4, 1995), E-systems is described as "a successful maker of electronic surveillance and communications systems." While Raytheon is noted as wanting this company as a defense industry purchase, Raytheon is painted as a commercial company that has recently been buying "construction, computer networking and washing machines" businesses. It is not until page 22, that we learn "E-S is an oddity in the defense industry: It is a growing company in a niche largely protected from US budget cuts. The company specializes in electronics for reconnaissance and military intelligence." This is "a part of the defense budget that is probably more stable than others," Lowell Lawson, E-Systems chairman and chief executive officer is quoted as saying (p. 22).

E-Systems will retain its name and corporate headquarters in Dallas where it employs 16,000 people. "Besides spy planes, the company provides electronic systems for Air Force One, the president's plane," noted *The Boston Globe*.

Connections and the FBI

Slick Airways was not Tom Slick's only venture, however. Following the lead of at least three generations of Slicks, Tom was Chairman of the Board of the Slick-Urschel Oil Company, later renamed the Slick Oil Company. Shortly before Slick's death, this company was worth about nine million dollars and Slick owned twenty-five percent of it.

Slick was deeply involved in many other business enterprises as well. He was a partner in Slick-Moorman Land and Cattle Company; Chairman of the Board of Transworld Resources Corporation; Director at Dresser Industries, Bailey-Selburn Oil and Gas Ltd., Dynamics Research, Inc., Dynamics Iron & Steel, Inc., Quanta Electronics Co., Summit Valley Land Corp., Guinea American International Corp., Slick Airways, Inc., Slick Corporation, and Beatrice Perry, Inc. Tom Slick was making major achievements that would be recognized by his being chosen "Young Man of the Year 1948" by the San Antonio Chamber of Commerce, and receiving an honorary Doctor of Science degree from Trinity University in 1953.

Slick had many opportunities to travel to such locales as the Soviet Union, South America, and India, and was in many international networks. In the area of world affairs, the public Tom Slick was supportive of an innovative idea leading to the possibility of international disarmament. Slick wrote two books on the topic. *The Last Great Hope* was privately published and disseminated in 1951; *Permanent Peace* was printed and distributed fairly widely by Prentice-Hall in 1958. He proposed in these books a plan that promoted world disarmament by way of small national armies slowly decreasing in strength as an international police force backing a global rule of law grew bigger. It was an early version of "The New World Order."

Slick founded the Strategy for Peace Conference. The first and second meetings were held at the Arden House in New York in June 1960 and January 1961. The third took place at the Airlie House in Virginia in October 1961. The fourth was scheduled for November 1962, but with Slick's death in October, it is not certain if the last conference ever took place. It seems rather obvious that he was under watchful eye of the FBI during this time, as my FOIA search reveals documents showing an active investigation of Tom Slick was taking place from January 1961 through February 1962. A memo, with much blacked out, dated January 5, 1961, has the FBI looking into any subversive activities in his background regarding a request from the Army War College National Strategy Seminar, scheduled for June 1961. On February 21, 1962, the US Office of the Attorney General in Washington D.C. has the FBI checking on Slick and fourteen other blacked out individuals for reasons that are so heavily masked as to be unknown. A CIA FOIA came back denying anything was in their files on Tom Slick or Slick Airways!

Slick was a member of an elite circle of internationalists in such organizations as the U.S. Committee for the United Nations - Member Advisory Committee on Education and Public Affairs, as well as the National Advisory Board of the United World Federalists. He joined together such individuals as Cyrus Eaton, Norman Cousins, Jimmy Stewart, Albert Schweitzer, Jawaharlal Nehru, Dwight Eisenhower, Henry Cabot Lodge Jr., Winston Churchill, and John Foster Dulles (whose brother was Allen Dulles, Director of the Central Intelligence Agency) in his informal group discussions on world peace.

Cryptopolitical and Cryptozoology

Intriguingly, as Tom Slick's role in internationalism began to increase and his CIA covert role with Slick Airways supposedly was on the decrease, the secret war in Tibet appears to have figured in some new interests of his - the search for the abominable snowmen in the Himalayas of the Nepalese-Tibetan border. But what if some of these yeti searches were espionage operations aimed at spying on Chinese military and political activities in Tibet? Before we move into

looking at the Slick expeditions, let us pause and see if there are percursors in the past for such activities. Have cryptozoological pursuits been used and wrapped within elaborate cover stories for politically motivated covert operations?

Historical Background

Individuals important to cryptozoological chronicles have been involved with secret intelligence networks for over two hundred years. For example, in 1769, South American reports of the five-foot-tall ape-like creature called the *didi* were collected by the botanist, naturalist and doctor, Edward Bancroft (Heuvelmans, 1959). Bancroft also called himself Jacobus Van Zandt (Sanderson, 1961), and was an espionage agent.

Dr. Edward Bancroft, internationally known as an expert on tropical plants, is an interesting figure in cryptopolitical history. Benjamin Franklin had sponsored Bancroft for membership in the Royal Society of London. When Franklin was at the American Embassy in Paris, Edward Bancroft, Franklin's friend and chief assistant, organized a cell of British spies, beginning in 1772. During his sojourn in Paris, Bancroft left weekly dispatches for the British written in invisible ink between the lines of love letters of a "Mr. Richardson" and placed in a bottle in a hollow tree at the Tuileries. Franklin, who was involved in occult circles, such as the Lodge of the Nine Sisters in Paris and Sir Francis Dashwood's Hell-fire Club outside of London, is viewed by Richard Deacon in his *A History of British Secret Service* as merely part of the British intelligence network set up by Bancroft and others (Coleman, 1985). Furthermore, Dr. Bancroft's associate, Sir Francis Dashwood, was thought to have traveled to Calcutta and Bengal (Silver and Lasky, 1977), thus even placing him in the sphere of Tibet, the location of our story.

Tibet, Pandas and Spies

Tibet certainly was worthy of a Tom Slick adventure. The recent history of this snowy Asian plateau-fenced in by the Himalayas to its south and surrounded by the body of China to its north and east-is central to gaining insights into the interplay between the cryptozoological and cryptopolitical. Before we delve too deeply into the late 1950s and early 1960s web of yeti searches and secret intelligence, let us step back over sixty years ago to the days when the giant panda was still a cryptozoological wonder, quickly becoming a zoological prize. Tibet's lands guarded the secret of the giant panda from the West until the numerous American expeditions of the 1930s began to return with specimens for natural history museums.

The first expedition to obtain a dead giant panda for mounting was led by Kermit Roosevelt, Teddy's son. The second expedition to kill pandas was headed by Brooke Dolan of the Philadelphia Academy of Natural Sciences during 1930-1932 (Morris, 1966; Perry, 1969).

Early giant panda collector Kermit Roosevelt's son, Kermit or "Kim," was later involved in Wild Bill Donovan's Office of Strategic Services (OSS), and the postwar Central Intelligence Agency (CIA). Kim Roosevelt is credited with living an almost James Bond-like existence and being the one man responsible for the 1953 CIA coup against and overthrow of President Mossadegh and his Iranian government. In 1942, when the United States decided they needed a post in Tibet to assure the Dalai Lama of American friendship, they picked the OSS for the task. Chosen for this specific assignment were the agents Lieutenant Colonel Tolstoy (emigre grandson of the famous Russian novelist) and guess who-Captain Brooke Dolan, the accomplished adventurer, Far Eastern explorer, and giant panda hunter. In later years, Tolstoy would become a general manager of Florida's Marineland, a movie producer, and cultivator of Bahamian sponge beds (Smith, 1972).

During the secret mission, Tolstoy and Dolan had first flown into India before traveling through Nepal to the Forbidden City of Lhasa, Tibet. There they exchanged gifts with the Dalai Lama, and thus cemented the American intelligence community's toehold in the region. From Lhasa, their caravan set out across unexplored Eastern Tibet toward Chungking, studying the potential route for a military road and noting on their map the sites of possible airfields (Ford, 1970). At Chungking, Tolstoy and Dolan would have no doubt run into an OSS staff member and jolly amateur chef named Julia McWilliams Child. Today, Julia Child is best known as the public television's "French Chef" (Smith, 1972). Upon their return to the States, Tolstoy and Dolan secretly received the Legion of Merit.

OSS veteran Leonard Francis Clark mentioned being in Tibet as the first foreigner since Tolstoy. Clark went on an expedition to Tibet in the late 1940s in an attempt to rally the Chinese Moslems against the Chinese Communists. In his book *The Marching Wind*, he made mention of abominable snowmen and apparently believed in them.

Yeti Searching and Covert Operations?

The vortex of intelligence operatives connected with cryptozoology seems to be especially concentrated around the mysterious figure of Tom Slick, forgotten Texas oil millionaire and yeti searcher.

How involved, therefore, was Tom Slick in covert operations? Did the search for the abominable snowmen serve merely as a cover? We know, for example, Slick was in the foothills of the Himalayas many times throughout the mid-1950s. Was he there only for mind science research and yeti investigations? In the literature about the unknown war between the Chinese and the Tibetans, there is a mysterious episode concerning an apparent CIA agent who comes to a famous Indian bordertown to discuss setting up an arms supply line with the Tibetans. "It was in the guise of a tourist that an American came to Kalimpong in the spring of 1955.... The American who came in 1955 may have been a diplomat but he was most probably a spy. He is not further identified by the man who tells the story, George N. Patterson, a Scottish missionary who had worked in eastern Tibet, spoke the language, wrote several books about the country, and resided in Kalimpong" (Prados, 1986).

By 1958-1959, Tom Slick was running the expeditions in pursuit of the abominable snowmen from his home in San Antonio. Peter and Bryan Byrne were Slick's agents in the field. Most of the time, the Byrnes were not in the field. Instead, they would stay in West Bengal, Calcutta, Darjeeling, or other eastern Indian cities. One West Bengal city, Kalimpong, the site of the meeting between the mystery man and George Patterson, was actually viewed as a "spy center." *The New York Times* of April 4, 1959 detailed Prime Minister Nehru's one-hour news conference held to answer Chinese Communist charges that Kalimpong was being used as the base for Tibetan subversive activities. Nehru said that the city was often described as a nest of spies of innumerable nationalities, and he had been told by an informed source that there were more spies in Kalimpong than the rest of the inhabitants. The Prime Minister continued, stating that after the Communists took over in China all kinds of people went to Kalimpong under assumed identities-some as technical people, some as bird watchers, some as journalists and some as just scenery admirers.

Ornithology and Espionage: The Old Boy Network

It appears that birdwatching and spying were never far apart in the secret world of intelligence operatives. Former CIA director James Schlesinger and covert actions expert Desmond FitzGerald enjoyed both pastimes. Birdwatching could be a useful cover. Take, for example, a person like S. Dillon Ripley. Ripley, a noted ornithologist and postwar Secretary of the Smithsonian Institution in Washington, was the chief of the OSS counterintelligence branch for southeast Asia.

Film fiction has picked up this thread. In the film, *The Dogs of War,* based on Frederick Forsythe's novel about covert operations in an African nation, the hero, played by Christopher Walken, goes to this country, disguised as a birdwatcher, to do reconnaissance for a mission. The Walken character is shown reading an African bird field guide on the flight over, to familiarize himself with the names of the local birds.

The most famous (though fictional) agent in modern popular literature is based on this ornithology-espionage connection, and the creator of this character has links to our yeti story. Peter Byrne, thanks to Tom Slick, met with many "former" intelligence individuals in West Bengal, including World War II British Intelligence officer Ian Fleming. Fleming was to become famous for his series of fictional spy books featuring the British secret agent 007, James Bond. And, of course, as most people know, the name "James Bond" was actually the real name of the author of the book *The Birds of the West Indies,* lifted by Fleming for use in his novels. The "original 007," by the way, was the English mathematician, astrologer and occultist Dr. John Dee (1527-1608). Dee served as Queen Elizabeth's personal spy. "007" was, in fact, Dee's code number, and was adopted by Ian Fleming for "James Bond" (Rosenblatt, 1989).

The networks and connections between the 1950s explorers, ornithologists, cryptozoologists and spies are under-studied, yet revealing. Ian Fleming was the brother of Peter Fleming, explorer and writer. One of the latter Fleming's most remarkable books is *Brazilian Adventure,* a work in the tradition of Percy Fawcett. Another classic is Fleming's *Bayonets to Lhasa,* an account of the British invasion of Tibet in 1904. Peter Fleming was a school-years buddy of Ralph Izzard, Gerald Russell, and Ivan Sanderson-all individuals deeply involved in the search for the yeti and, to varying degrees, friends with Tom Slick. Izzard led the 1954 *Daily Mail* expedition to the Himalayas in search of yeti, Russell was a member of Izzard's 1954 trek and headed the 1958 Slick-Johnson Snowman expedition to eastern Nepal, and Sanderson was involved in all manner of cryptozoological investigations (including an African expedition with Russell in the 1930s) and writings, authoring the classic *Abominable Snowmen* in 1961. Sanderson was a consultant member of Slick's 1960-1962 search for Bigfoot, the so-called Pacific Northwest Expedition headed by Bob Titmus, then Peter Byrne.

Ivan T. Sanderson was a commander in the British Naval Intelligence Service from 1940-1945, assigned to the Caribbean because of his zoological experiences there. The famed cryptozoologist's wartime connections to spying apparently did not end in 1945. Sanderson gives a hint that some of his information sources remained in the realm of the intelligence network in one passage in his book Abominable Snowmen. Therein Sanderson (1961) details two curious encounters with the giant hairy Tok, given to him by "a young American, then in the service of his country, who had been born in the Shan States and brought up there, his parents having been missionaries." Sanderson "was asked not to publish" the man's name.

This individual, it appears, was probably a member of the extraordinary Young family who were responsible for setting up the Burma Baptist Mission. The Sanderson contact was, no doubt, William Young, who was:

"...perhaps one of the most effective agents ever, [who] was born in the Burmese Shan States, where his grandfather had been missionary to the hill tribes. Arriving in Burma at the turn of the century, Grandfather Young opened a Baptist mission in Kengtung City and began preaching to the nearby Lahu hill tribes. Although they understood little of his Christian message, a local oracle had once prophesied the coming of a white deity, and the Lahu decided that Reverend Young was God. His son, Harold, later inherited his divinity and used it to organize Lahu intelligence gathering forays into southern China for the CIA during the 1950s. When William was looking for a job in 1958 his father recommended him to the CIA, and he was hired" (McCoy, 1972).

In the book *Uninvited Visitors,* Sanderson (1967) discusses how he was called to the Pentagon for a briefing; this is an odd event for someone who supposedly has no official ties to the government. Sanderson appears to have maintained an open line to some members of the espionage community.

Carleton Coon:
Spying, Anthropology and Cryptozoology

Peter Byrne and Tom Slick also had contact with elements of American intelligence. One of Tom Slick's earliest yeti consultants was Carleton Coon, professor of anthropology and former Office of Strategic Services agent. Coon was consulting for the Slick yeti expeditions from the very beginning, having been at one of the first meetings attended by Tom Slick's assistant Cathy Maclean, Peter Byrne, and *Life's* Jim Greenfield in Darjeeling, India, on January 16, 1957.

Within espionage circles Coon's work for the OSS was legendary. One of the first missions of Donovan's spy organization was operation TORCH, the invasion of North Africa, involving agents such as Peter Tompkins who has gone on to write about pyramids. Carleton Coon was in charge of TORCH and the affair was such a success that it insured the future of the OSS. OSS's leadership, who were later connected to the

Central Intelligence Group, then the Central Intelligence Agency, would never forget Coon for his contributions to the budding American intelligence community.

Gambit, Inc. of Ipswich, Massachusetts (Coon's residence in his late years) published the small book, *A North Africa Story: The Anthropologist as OSS Agent 1941-1943* by Carleton S. Coon, in 1980. It is filled with Coon's 1940s writings of his exploits, with historical background supplied by the editors at Gambit. The book is an interesting insight into the dual life that Coon led. And the mostly code-named characters along the way hint at the overlaps that intrigue us, as well. There's "Levy," for example, a young Frenchman who Coon did not like because of the way he treated the Arabs. Coon noted, nevertheless, that this individual "claims to have been a member of a Himalayan mountain climbing expedition."

A North Africa Story details Coon's thoughts on the kind of legitimate front that worked best for OSS agents during wartime. "The question of cover is one that can only be settled by experience. We have had, however, enough experience to determine a few principles. There are two things good cover should avoid; tying the agent down with cover activities, and making him conspicuous," Coon wrote. He went on to make some further points:

"State Department cover is good in that it allows the agent to go places where he could not otherwise get; it does not take up too much of his time. It is bad in that he is conspicuous and constantly under enemy surveillance. They undoubtedly know he is an agent, but don't dare harm him in neutral territory.... Special civilian covers are useful only for special jobs of brief duration.... To be an archaeologist is silly, even if the agent is really a well-known professional archaeologist in peace time. All archaeologists are inevitably suspected of being agents anyhow even in peace time; and who cares about archaeology in wartime? An archaeologist may be very useful for his knowledge of the country, its people, languages, etc., but he must not pretend that he is still an archaeologist in war (Coon, 1980).

Coon used the cover of the diplomatic corps during World War II. Carleton Coon tied his public exit from the OSS to the time that the organization was disbanded at the end of the war. Many former OSS agents, of course, were later employed by the operations division of the CIA. Was Coon one of them? Did he change his mind and allow his anthropological career to dovetail with some clandestine activities after 1945? Coon always seemed to be working right on the fringes of the Communist bloc countries, in Iran, in Afghanistan, and so forth. Or in India and Nepal, near Tibet.

Carleton Coon's autobiography, *Adventures and Discoveries,* extensively deals with his Office of Strategic Services (OSS) tenure and briefly with his Slick involvement.

From October 17, 1956, until March 26, 1957, Carleton Coon conducted his "Faces of Asia" trip of eleven countries. Coon wrote that a "*Life* side mission" investigating Tom Slick "was a minor effort during his multinational Faces of Asia" research tour. Coon called the Slick matter "sticky" because *Life* had hired him to see what Slick was up to. The names cropping up in this one-page-long section of the autobiography sound all too familiar. There's Jim Greenfield, "the New Delhi representative of the Luce empire," who seems to always be there in the background for *Life*. Was he gathering information for anyone else? Coon shows up to investigate Slick in Kalimpong, the so-called spy center of the area. When Coon moves on to Gangtok in Sikkim, he cannot be housed at the Raj Kumar's, because his guest quarters were already full to overflowing with the Dalai Lama and his entourage. Returning to Kalimpong in the dark, Coon then was hosted by Prince Peter of Greece, a shadowy figure in the yeti and intelligence story if ever there was one. Nevertheless, Coon had the unenviable position of telling Slick that Slick's search was inadequately staffed and "his plans to use helicopters, bloodhounds, and the like, were impractical."

Coon's retelling of the Slick-yeti events is confusing. From what Coon wrote, he arrived in India on December 8, 1956, and stayed in that country for 88 days before going on to Ceylon. His tour ended there in March 1957. From my Slick records, we know that Coon met with Greenfield, Peter Byrne and Slick associate Cathy Maclean on January 16, 1957, in Darjeeling, India. Coon stated that he met with Slick. Did he? Where and when? *Newsweek* noted in its February 18, 1957, issue that Slick was enroute to Nepal. On March 14, 1957, Slick arrived at Biratnagar, Nepal, to start his yeti trek. By March 26, 1957, Coon was back home. When and where did their paths cross?

What Coon was really doing in India and Sikkim with Slick, Greenfield and Prince Peter may never be revealed, but an interesting bit of data has come my way regarding his son, Carl Jr., as Carleton Coon referred to him, who was the station chief of the CIA in India during this time. When the elder Coon flew into New Delhi late in 1956, he was met at the airport by Carl Jr., Carl Jr.'s wife Janet, Major Brooks (the air attache), and John and Barbara Waller.

Here is one more noteworthy Coon tidbit. Coon wrote: "As soon as we had arrived at Clark Field [the military airbase in the Philippines] I cabled both the air attache and Jim Thompson in Bangkok warning them of our arrival date [of December 7, 1956], but neither received the message. All hotels were full because of an international fair, but Jim wangled us a room at the Arelan Hotel, where we had as fellow guests Senator Jacob Javits and Benny Goodman's entire orchestra.

"Jim Thompson was an old OSS man who stayed on to found the extremely profitable Thai Silk Company. One day, not long after we passed through, he suddenly vanished into thin air; as far as I am aware no one knows yet what happened to him. His disappearance remains one of the most fascinating mysteries of the East" (Coon, 1981).

The Dalai Lama, Slick Denials and the CIA

While a great deal of information has surfaced over the years about the Central Intelligence Agency's worldwide covert operations activities, little is known about how deeply the CIA was involved in Tibet in the 1950s and 1960s. "It is impossible at this writing," John Prados noted in his 1986 book, *Presidents' Secret Wars,* "to give a detailed analysis of the Washington decision making for Tibet. The appropriate records remain security classified. If not for the courts, in fact, the entire discussion of Tibet in the Marchetti and Marks book, *The CIA and the Cult of Intelligence,* would have been deleted by Agency censors."

We are forced to read accounts of the conflict in Tibet closely to get some insights into how involved some of the yeti searchers may have been. Let's start with one critical incident, the escape of the Dalai Lama from Tibet. There are denials, for example, of the rumors circulating that Tom Slick and Peter Byrne were responsible, in some fashion, for the safe passage of the Dalai Lama from Lhasa. Since the time of Tom Slick's first official yeti reconnaissance of eastern Nepal in 1957, in which he was actually a member of the trek, the rumors of his expeditions' involvement in spying have been rampant. The *New York Times* even saw fit to publish an article reporting on the Russians' promotion of this story in an item entitled: "Soviet Sees Espionage in U.S. Snowman Hunt." The April 27, 1957 piece claimed Slick was behind an effort to subvert the Chinese, and free Tibet.

What can we find in the record about the Dalai Lama's rescue? Who was behind the exit or with the Dalai Lama? Fletcher Prouty, an Air Force colonel who supervised secret air missions for the Office of Special Operations, has written: "This fantastic escape and its major significance have been buried in the lore of the CIA as one of those successes that are not talked about. The Dalai Lama would have never been

saved without the CIA" (Prouty, 1973). On March 17, 1959, all three groups, the Dalai Lama, his immediate family and senior advisors escaped from Lhasa. Tenzin Gyatso [the Dalai Lama] was disguised as a common soldier of the guard.... The best information [about the fleeing Dalai Lama] came from the CIA.... The CIA was so well informed because it had furnished an American radio operator, who traveled with the Dalai Lama's party...There may have been other CIA agents with the party as well (Prados, 1986). Who were these individuals?

George Patterson might know. Remember, he is the guy who had the mysterious meeting with an American tourist during 1955 in which parts of the CIA's war in Tibet were mapped out. Patterson, who used the cover of being a missionary (but drank, smoked and chased women with the best of the guys) was part of a unique foray into Tibet in 1964. Setting out secretly with Adrian Cowell, a British filmmaker, Patterson took off from Nepal to coordinate and film an attack on a Chinese convoy by Tibetan Khamba commandos. Patterson and Cowell were successful, but upon their return they were briefly jailed in India, and their film was suppressed and not shown for two years.

Now here's the interesting part: Who helped them get into Tibet? None other than Peter Byrne, Tom Slick's man in Nepal.

And who has written the most concerning the Patterson incident without saying too much in depth about it? None other than Michel Peissel. In his book, *The Secret War in Tibet* (1973), Peissel mysteriously kept his references to the CIA to only four small mentions in this 258-page book. Peissel discussed a good deal about the secret war in Tibet but strangely never mentioned some amazing points now well-known (due to recent CIA limited releases of information), such as the fact that the small kingdom of Mustang was the CIA-run base of Tibetan guerrilla operations. Peissel revealed that he first went to the area in the spring of 1959 with a letter of recommendation from Thubtan Norbu, the brother of the Dalai Lama, to the Prime Minister of Bhutan.... "I was off to meet Jigme Dorji, the Prime Minister of Bhutan, in the small border town of Kalimpong" (Peissel, 1966). We, of course, understand a little bit more about the importance of Kalimpong in the espionage game, as was mentioned above.

Also, we now have some facts about Thubtan Norbu. The eldest brother of the Dalai Lama was connected to the "American Society for a Free Asia," a CIA-funded organization that sponsored a series of visits to and lectures in the United States by Norbu, beginning in 1956 (Prados, 1986). Secretly, the Dalai

Lama's family was very involved with the CIA in fighting the Chinese. Gyalo Thondup, the Dalai Lama's second-eldest brother, based in Darjeeling, established an intelligence gathering operation with the CIA in 1951. Six years later, he upgraded it to an advanced CIA-trained guerrilla unit whose members were introduced to commando techniques on Guam for example, and then parachuted back into Tibet (Avedon 1984). What was Peissel's connection to the CIA? It's difficult to say.

Peissel was apparently able to obtain much "Tibet file" (as he called it) information from American and British intelligence contacts. He even reveals names that sound familiar - such as "Nyma Tsering," said to be one of the most trusted officers among the Tibetan guerrillas. Tibetan names in English are merely rough transliterations, often in different spellings. So we are not surprised to find the Sherpa "Nima Tenzing" on Slick's 1957 and 1958 expeditions, and the same individual "Nima Tshering" on Hillary's 1960 expedition. Was this person also the aforementioned "Nyma Tsering?" Were Peissel's connections woven into the espionage network?

This is the same Michel Peissel who wrote a yeti-debunking article for *Argosy* magazine in 1960 entitled "The Abominable Snow Job." Peissel mentioned that the subject of his 1966 book, Boris Lissanevitch, had been given a tranquilizer gun by the Tom Slick expedition. Peissel half-jokingly wrote that the "Indians thought Boris a Russian agent, the Russians thought him an American agent, and the Americans, a Russian agent" (Peissel, 1966). It is interesting that Peissel would show up in the Tibetan area to investigate the abominable snowman, during the critical time of the Dalai Lama's escape. Slowly, over the years, he revealed his deeper covert operations links.

Adrian Cowell, for his part, turned up in Burma in the mid-1960s filming guerrilla opium armies (McCoy, 1972) and recently has been involved in Brazilian projects. But Cowell's official biography in *Contemporary Authors* neglected to mention his Tibetan adventures with Patterson.

Something strange is going on here.

"Atomic Testing" In Colorado Anyone?

In 1959, after the Dalai Lama had been helped out of Tibet by the CIA, this same agency started sending Tibetans to America for covert instructions. The secret CIA training site for the Tibetans was Camp Hale, near Leadville, Colorado. (Coincidentally, Tom Slick's mother's family was from Leadville.) The Tibetans were silently flown out of Asia, had only one refueling stopover in Hawaii and, upon their arrival, did not even realize they were in the United States.

The intrigue surrounding this covert army is worthy of study by researchers who are looking for the techniques used in governmental coverups. Indeed, on July 16, 1959 (Prados, 1986) the CIA had:

"...planted a front page story in the Denver *Post* reporting that atomic testing-though not bomb detonation-was to be conducted at Camp Hale. The vast area of 14,000-foot peaks and valleys covered by the camp was henceforth strictly off bounds to the civilian population. People who were near Peterson Air Force Base, outside of Colorado Springs, when a subsequent group of Tibetans was flown out, found themselves detained. Up to forty-seven at a time were held at gunpoint behind army roadblocks until mysterious buses, their windows painted black, had passed by. When news of unidentified Orientals in Colorado reached the *New York Times,* Secretary of Defense Robert McNamara personally had the story suppressed. As a final resort, soldiers guarding the most sensitive areas of the base-as well as the Tibetans themselves-were given explicit instructions to shoot to kill anyone found within the perimeters" (Avedon, 1984).

Names of men involved in the training at Camp Hale are difficult to locate, but it is interesting to note the connection of the one person I *was* able to identify, to other parts of our examination. McCoy, writing in 1972 on the secret war in Laos, discussed only a handful of highly committed CIA men there. One was Anthony Poe. Agent Poe, before his Laos work, "recruited Khamba tribesmen in northeastern India, escorted them to Camp Hale in Colorado for training, and accompanied them into Tibet on long-range sabotage missions." And which hard-working CIA agent had Poe replaced in Laos? William Young, that's who, the gentleman we met earlier because of his probable link to Ivan Sanderson and the Burmese *Tok* stories (McCoy, 1972).

While Air America, Air Asia, and even a special Nepalese airline were all involved in the transport of the Tibetans to Camp Hale, was Slick Airways part of the picture? Henry Belk (1989) told me that he believes Slick Airways was responsible for taking agents to war theaters in Southeast Asia. Were Slick Airways' activities part of the deleted Tibetan material never released by the CIA?

Disinformation Chief Involved?

And what role might have Desmond FitzGerald played in all of this? A veteran of conflicts in Burma, FitzGerald was very much the Asian expert in the CIA. Assistant to the head of the Far Eastern Division of the CIA's "Directorate for Plans" in 1952, FitzGerald was described as "bright, amuent, cultured charming, and an avid bird watcher" who "undertook the deadly business of covert operations with a light-hearted, romantic activism...during the 1950s" (Leary, 1984). We now know that by the early 1960s, FitzGerald was named head of the Special Affairs staff and was responsible for at least one disinformation incident against the Chinese using UFO reports (Good, 1988). Shortly after that, on November 22, 1963, FitzGerald, posing as a senior United States senator in Europe, handed Rolando Cubela a weapon disguised as a fountain pen for use in an assassination attempt against Fidel Castro (Summers, 1980).

Deadly serious about his work, FitzGerald was a member of the CIA's so-called "Knights Templar," a group of original CIA officers and followers of Wild Bill Donovan. They seemed to have envisioned themselves like the ancient Catholic military order founded during the Crusades as a "mysterious and tightly knit group dedicated to a sacred cause" (Hougan, 1984). FitzGerald was very involved in the Tibet situation. "Despite the refusal [of President Eisenhower and the United States government] to associate with the Tibetans openly, secret plans continued. Before his NSC [National Security Council] meeting of February 4, 1960, the President met with a group including [former Psychological Strategy Board Staff Director and at that time special assistant to the President for national security affairs] Gordon Gray, [(Secretary of State) Christian] Herter, [CIA Director] Allen Dulles, [(CIA Deputy Director) Charles] Cabell, and Desmond FitzGerald" to discuss Tibet (Prados 1986). What kinds of disinformation was FitzGerald creating for the Tibetan operations? Did any of it refer to the yeti expeditions searching the border of Tibet for traces of the creatures?

Yeti Expeditions: Spy Missions?
Truth Stranger than Fiction?

Late in 1960, Sir Edmund Hillary, sponsored by the *World Book* encyclopedia company of Chicago, left on his famous expedition to Nepal in pursuit of the "Abominable Snowman." While Tom Slick's 1957-1959 expeditions may have been rumored to be espionage missions, what part did spying play in Hillary's trek? Driven by publicity and the media, most accounts of the yeti debunking affair mention only the high altitude medical testing as a subgoal of the fiasco. A few English and Italian press accounts exist confirming that one objective of the group was to spy on the Chinese in Tibet. Two rocket experts, Tom Nevison of the United States Air Force and Peter Mulgrew of the Royal New Zealand Navy, were closely watching and gathering data on the Chinese firing missiles from Tibet. Journalist Desmond Doig, Nevison and

Mulgrew were camped together at Tolum Bau glacier when they all witnessed just such a launching. Meanwhile, the Chinese were jamming the camp's radio (Coleman, 1989; Sanderson, 1961; Doig, 1960). All of the official chronicles of the Hillary-*World Book* expedition not too surprisingly fail to detail this aspect of the party's activities.

Strangely, in 1970 and 1971 two fictional accounts surfaced linking espionage activities with the abominable snowmen. The 1970 Billy Wilder movie, *The Private Life of Sherlock Holmes* is a story including large components of covert activities and the Loch Ness Monster. Interestingly, it also contains a segment set in the exclusive Diogenes Club where Holmes comments on the members' uncanny ability to turn up "here, there and everywhere." Then he later adds, "When there's trouble along the Indian frontier, some of your fellow members pop up in the Himalayas allegedly looking for the Abominable Snowman" (Haddon, 1987). *The Private Life of Sherlock Holmes* is not in distribution and difficult to locate today, aside from occasional television appearances.

Ronald Rosenblatt (1989) has informed me of another presently rare fictional work that connects intelligence agents and a search for a Tibetan mystery animal. In 1971, Jack Benton Scott's *Spargo: A Novel of Espionage* was published. The book details the activities of a renegade CIA agent who goes on a mission to Tibet and India, using a search for the so-called "Sun Bear," a supposedly extinct animal, as his cover.

Is truth stranger than fiction? During the hottest days of the secret war in Tibet in 1959 and 1960, eleven separate expeditions, including one led by the Chinese, were sent to the area on the track of the abominable snowmen of the Himalayas (Coleman, 1989, Sanderson, 1961, Dong, 1984). Were all of these merely cryptozoological investigations, or was something more covert taking place? Has the yeti been a cover story for spy missions? Until some future Freedom of Information request produces a document or an expedition member talks openly, thus giving us some hard evidence for now we are left with only a few linkages and some intellectual possibilities. Still, something seems to be afoot!

Coverup vs. Cover?

For the last few years, a great debate has raged in ufology regarding the role of the CIA and other similar organizations in the UFO field. For example, Timothy Good's *Above Top Secret,* a 1988 book, has already taken on near classic status. Its stance, taken in the first paragraph, can be summarized as indicating that a "wide-scale coverup" of the involvement of the intelligence community in the study of UFOs is occurring. Good and others feel the government is hiding proof of the existence of UFOs.

In my cryptozoology-espionage examination, however, the reasons behind the alleged coverups seem to have more to do with hiding covers than burying evidence and special knowledge of the reality of the arcane subjects which occupy our interests. Over and over again, as we delved deeper into the subject of the Tibetan yeti expeditions and the Himalayan spy missions, the characters involved revealed a pattern of covert psychological warfare operations in their backgrounds. While in North Africa, Carleton Coon, for example, invented a mine disguised as donkey dung in order to kill Nazis. Meanwhile, in Algiers, Peter Tompkins was a member of the Psychological Warfare Branch of General Eisenhower's headquarters, conducting all manner of propaganda and direct actions, and possibly assassinations.

Desmond FitzGerald used false UFO sightings, and perhaps yeti ones also, to disrupt the Chinese. In a meeting to discuss secret activities in Tibet, FitzGerald discussed plans with Gordon Gray, among others. Gray was the first staff Director of the Psychological Strategy Board. The background to the Psychological Strategy Board is illuminating. In February 1949, President Truman created a State Department psychological warfare office. In March 1950, Truman adopted special order NSC-59 for more foreign information gathering and psychological warfare, and then NSC-74 for "A Plan for National Psychological Warfare." The President then moved quickly to get Rear Admiral Sidney W. Souers for consultations. Souers supported a recommendation to create an interagency group for nonmilitary cold war activities, and Truman responded by setting up the Psychological Strategy Board (PSB) under the National Security Council in Spring, 1951.

Gordon Gray was picked as first staff Director of PSB; Gray knew Frank Wisner, Directorate of Plans, and CIA deputy director William H. Jackson and the PSB assistant Gray hired, Tracy Barnes, because they all worked for the same Wall Street law firm, Carter, Ledyard and Milburn, before WWII. At the time, the Director of Central Intelligence was Walter Bedell Smith, Gray was asked to head PSB by W.B. Smith and William Jackson. Earlier Gray had been involved in the whole setup of the Army staff's adoption of "psywar," i.e. psychological warfare, in January 1948. Although the prime mover in that area was General Robert McClure, Gray as Assistant Secretary of the Army encouraged the effort. The Army's interest in "psywar" eventually evolved into the Army's "Special Forces." PSB disbanded in 1954 for political

reasons, and Gray was exiled to the review board that sat in judgment of nuclear physicist J. Robert Oppenheimer. But Gray would be back. He served in the intelligence community for forty years (Prados, 1986).

What if the whole thrust of the intelligence community's interest in cryptozoology has more to do with covers and fronts than with a coverup of data? Diplomatic, ornithological, and archaeological covers have been used. Why not present an agent as some half-crazed cryptozoologist searching for such and such a creature in some sensitive section of a foreign country? What better "psywar" technique than to search for and then promote a variety of positions on strange and bizarre subjects, be they yetis, giant salamanders, or lake monsters?

Strange Deaths

Early in October 1962, Tom Slick had gone to a Canadian meeting of the Board of Directors of Dresser Industries. Then he had taken a hunting trip for pheasant and quail, also in Canada. Some speculate that he also checked up on his Sasquatch operations north of the border. He was scheduled to fly to Salt Lake City on the 6th. Then Slick was flying home to San Antonio to have dinner with his children. Telling me of that night only recently, those now adult children will never forget waiting for that meal.

Saturday night at about 6 P.M., October 6th, 1962, Tom Slick and pilot Shelly Sudderth of Dallas were killed in the crash of their Beechcraft Bonanza 35. This is the same kind of plane that Buddy Holly, Richie Valens and the Big Bopper were in when they died in a wreck on February 3, 1959.

No one knows exactly how or why Slick died. Residents near Dell, Montana, reported hearing a "noise like a crash." The plane's wreckage was found forty miles south of Dillon in extreme southwestern Montana, near the town of Dell. Harold Briggs, search and rescue coordinator for the Federal Aviation Administration (FAA) and the local sheriff's department, said the plane apparently disintegrated in flight. One wing was found intact and one engine was found a considerable distance from all other wreckage. Slick's bag of game birds was strewn over the area. Searchers reported that Slick's and Sudderth's bodies apparently fell free from the plane since they were not close to the wreckage. Briggs explained the backs of both seats were found together about three quarters of a mile from the bodies. The bodies, both badly burned, were found alongside a county road about three quarters of a mile from the center of the crash-site.

We do not know what caused the Slick plane to crash, and we may never discover the official verdict either. I attempted to learn exactly what the final FAA report had concluded. I filed a Freedom of Information Act request, badgered the FAA and the National Transportation Safety Board, ask the Slick family to search their files for a copy, got the able assistance of Ralph Nader's Aviation Consumer Project, General Aviation Aircraft Owners data center, and countless librarians throughout the country but to no avail. All avenues turned up empty.

Finally the FAA told me that such general aviation accident investigations are the "responsibility of the National Transportation Safety Board (NTSB)," (Stewart, 1988).

The NTSB sent me a form letter with the date of Slick's "accident" handwritten in blue pen in the appropriate blank spot, but noting they were "unable to fill my request." The report on Tom Slick's crash investigation was required to be kept for only seven years. The letter ended, in form-letter-coldness: "The report(s) requested by you fall under the statute of limitations category and have been destroyed. Sincerely, Susan Stevenson" (1988).

I searched the Library of Congress for a possible hardcopy. No luck. Perhaps someone does have a copy of the report, but I could not locate that individual. Was he transporting bombs, or merely remembering the insect repellant? Slick was a man who avoided publicity. Was he involved in some way with the intelligence network? What hints exist in the record that there may be something to this notion?

In my book, *Tom Slick and the Search for the Yeti* (1989), I have detailed some of the theories surrounding his death. One of them centered on the explosion being caused by a bomb.

Tom Slick, a murder victim? Did his plane not get hit by lightning, but instead disintegrated due to a bomb? Far-fetched, outlandish? Yes, but among some people who were close to Tom Slick, the bomb theory ranks very high on their list of possible causes of death. One observation that Harold Briggs made that was not picked up by most press accounts was the possibility the plane could have experienced, in his words, "an internal explosion." Two sources that wish to remain unnamed quote the local sheriff's office in Montana as saying that Slick's death was murder.

More Deaths

Some of the thinking runs to the notion that Slick was an embarrassment, that he was wasting his money on his Snowmen/Bigfoot pursuits, and the only way to stop him was to kill him. Around some stove fires in the Pacific Northwest, even today, such discussions are seriously held. Folks see how suddenly that the men that had "co-sponsored" the expeditions to the

Himalayas died. F. Kirk Johnson, Sr. died within a year and Jr. within six, at 40 years old, of Slick's death, and they speculate.

Others wonder if Slick's peace work was rubbing certain folks the wrong way. After all, President John F. Kennedy would be killed in Texas, Slick's home state, only fourteen months after Slick died. Maybe the conservative forces in America were trying to send someone a message with a special Texas flare?

One of the more interesting linkages Slick had was through his role as a member of the National Advisory Board of the United World Federalists (Coleman, 1989). Founded in 1947, the United World Federalists' first president was the intellectual Cord Meyer. Suddenly in 1950, around the time that China was advancing on Tibet, Meyer left the organization's head post in the hands of liberal Alan Cranston (presently the senior United States Senator from California), and joined the CIA's covert operations division. A close associate was quoted as saying: "It was a great surprise to his friends. He was not the CIA type. He was a world government man" (Smith, 1972). In 1954, Meyer was named Chief of the CIA's Covert Action operations. Hardened by political battles with Joseph McCarthy and by personal tragedies, years later a friend would say that Cord Meyer "got Cold Warized" (Smith, 1972).

Tragedies haunted Cord Meyer. One of Meyer's sons died in an automobile accident. Then there's the story of his former wife, Mary Pinchot Meyer, JFK's last lover. Mary Meyer was killed by an unknown assailant on October 12, 1964, on a C&O towpath in Washington D.C. Much darkness surrounds Mary Pinchot Meyer's death, but it appears dozens of people connected to the JFK inner and outer circles were killed.

JFK assassination researcher John Gooch III of New Orleans has wondered aloud if perhaps Tom Slick was in on some early planning meetings regarding the Kennedy killing, backed out and was killed for knowing too much. There's that mysterious meeting of 14 individuals and Tom Slick that the FBI was watching in 1962. There's the hints and informants claims that "everyone knew Slick was helping run guns to Cuba." A deeper level of involvement between Slick and several figures in the JFK drama keep cropping up.

Tom Slick was a mystery man but his past is slowing illuminating some insights into cryptozoological and cryptopolitical intrigue in this country. Tom Slick's memorial service was held at the giant secretive Southwest Research Institute that he had created. At the end of the ceremony Dr. James W. Laurie closing prayer uttered words that seem even more authentic today: "Truly we would thank Thee for Thy servant, Tom, who being dead yet speaks to us."

References:

Avedon, John F. *In Exile from the Land of Snows.* New York: Alfred A. Knopf, 1984.

Belk, Henry. Personal communication, 1989.

Business Week. "The Slicks: What Rich Men's Sons Can Do," November 17, 1951.

Byrne, Peter. Personal communication, 1989.

Chorvinsky, Mark. Personal communication, 1989.

Coleman, Loren. *Curious Encounters.* Boston and London: Faber and Faber, 1985.

-*Tom Slick and the Search for the Yeti.* Boston and London: Faber and Faber, 1989.

Coon, Carleton. *A North Africa Story: The Anthropologist as OSS Agent 1941-1943.* Ipswich, Massachusetts: Gambit, Inc., 1980.

-*Adventures and Discoveries: The Autobiography of Carleton S. Coon,* Prentice-Hall, Inc., Englewood Cliffs, New Jersey, 1981.

Davies, R.E.G. *Airlines of the United States Since 1914.* Washington, D.C.: Smithsonian Institution Press, 1972.

Doig, Desmond. "Chinese Jam Camp Radio." *Sunday Times,* London, Nov. 13, 1960.

Dong, Paul. *The Four Major Mysteries of Mainland China.* Englewood Cliffs, New Jersey: Prentice-Hall, 1984.

Good, Timothy. *Above Top Secret.* New York: William Morrow, 1988.

Ford, Corey. *Donovan of OSS.* Boston: Little, Brown and Company, 1970.

Haddon, Jonathon. "The Swan that Wasn't a Swan." *Strange Magazine,* No. 1, 1987.

Heuvelmans, Bernard. *On the Track of Unknown Animals.* New York: Hill and Wang, 1959.

-"The Birth and Early History of Cryptozoology." *Cryptozoology,* Vol. 3, 1984.

Hougan, Jim. *Secret Agenda.* New York: Ballantine, 1984.

Leary, William M. *Perilous Mission: Civil Air Transport and CIA Covert Operations in Asia.* University, Alabama: University of Alabama Press, 1984.

-Personal communication, 1989.

McCoy, Alfred W. with Cathleen B. Read and Leonard P. Adams II. *The Politics of Heroin in Southeast Asia.* New York: Harper & Row, 1972.

Marchetti, Victor and John D. Marks. *The CIA and the Cult of Intelligence.* New York: Alfred A. Knopf, 1974.

Morris, Ramona and Desmond. *Men and Pandas.* New York: McGraw Hill, 1966.

Peissel, Michel. "Abominable Snow Job." *Argosy,* December,1960.

-*Tiger for Breakfast: The Story of Boris of Kathmandu.* New York: E.P. Dutton, 1966.

-*The Secret War in Tibet.* Boston: Little, Brown & Co., 1973.

Perry, Richard. *The World of the Giant Panda.* New York: Taplinger, 1969.

Prados, John. *Presidents' Secret Wars: CIA and Pentagon Covert Operations from World War II through Iranscam.* New York: Quilt/William Morrow, 1986.

Prouty, L. Fletcher. *The Secret Team: The CIA and Its Allies in Control of the United States and the World.* Englewood Cliffs, New Jersey: Prentice-Hall, 1973.

Rosenblatt, Ronald. Personal communication, 1989.

Sanderson, Ivan T. *Abominable Snowmen: Legend Come to Life.* Philadelphia: Chilton, 1961.

-Personal communication, 1970.

Scott, Jack Denton. *Spargo: A Novel of Espionage.* New York: World Publishing Co., 1971.

Silver, Pat and Jesse Lasky, Jr. "Hell Fire Dashwood." In Colin Wilson's *Men of Mystery.* London: Star/W.H. Allen & Co., 1977.

Smith, R. Harris. *OSS: The Secret History of America's First Central Intelligence Agency.* Berkeley: University of California Press, 1972.

Summers, Anthony. *Conspiracy.* New York: McGraw Hill, 1980.

Loren Coleman is the author of several books on social problems, cryptozoology and unexplained phenomena. Coleman is employed as a research associate and associate professor at the University of Southern Maine in Portland. His 1989 book, published by Faber and Faber, Inc., Tom Slick and the Search for the Yeti, *serves as background to some of the material explored in this chapter. Readers with further information on connections between secret intelligence, Tom Slick and cryptozoology—in Tibet or elsewhere—are encouraged to write Loren Coleman at Post Box 360, Portland, Maine 04112.*

Steamshovel Debris: The November 22, 1993 edition of the *San Antonio Express-News* reported upon the increased publicity efforts of Southwest Research Institute, Southwest Foundation for Biomedical Research and the Mind Science Foundation, three San Antonio research facilities that "share in common the founding imprint of the late Tom Slick, Jr.", examined briefly in Loren Coleman's book, *Tom Slick and the Search For The Yeti.* The newspaper noted that

Mind Sciences Foundation developed from an interest in parapsychology Slick developed "after one of his worldwide trips brought him in contact with an old guru who supposedly had the ability to appear and reappear in different locations," and someone whose ability to levitate Slick felt he could apply to the construction trade according to Coleman.

Prior to 1993, the Mind Sciences Foundation studied a long list of unusual phenomena, including the effects of positive imagery and visualization; the functioning of the immune system on breast cancer patients; Alzheimer's disease; spiritual healing; biological psychokinesis; relaxation techniques to lower blood pressure; extrasensory perception; clairvoyance; creativity; motivation and self-esteem; asthma and allergies. Although mind control did not make the list, Slick's predilection for similar topics when he founded the group puts an interesting spin on his possible link to the Kennedy assassination and Mary Pinchot Meyer. Despite the date of this newspaper report, it had no connection to JFK.

Executive director Catherine Nixon remarked that with regard to all this research, the foundation had been "content to be ignored." It phased out its last "in-house" project in July 1993 but intended to continue to pursue its collaborative efforts with such allied institutions as the University of Texas Health Science Center and Ecumenical Center for Religion and Health in San Antonio.

The *Express-News* quoted foundation trustee Tom Slick III, founder Slick Jr.'s son and a businessman based in Atlanta, as saying, "I'm not sure how much of a philosophical change it is, but it's a methodological change. We're not denouncing parapsychology, but we're wanting to do other things too. My dad fostered the possibility of hitting a home run — making big, positive improvements in society...We settled on parapsychology in the early 1970s because the field had opportunity and suited the philosophy of the board. Now we want to refocus the (financial) resources we have." Mind Science Foundation has a permanent $3 million endowment; it plans to raise additional funds through this new pursuit of collaborative grants.

Black Cars at Night: The Men in Black Reanimated
by Scott Corrales

In a recent Spanish publication, an article on features of the worldwide UFO scene wistfully mentioned "the almost forgotten Men-In-Black" in passing. The absence of these black-garbed, sinister personages, variously described as agents from a supersecret government command, an Earth-based "silencing" arm belonging to an extraterrestrial power, or manifestations of negative paranormal forces had taken some of the spookiness out of the phenomenon. However, there is mounting evidence that the MIB have not only *not* retired from the scene, but have returned with renewed vigor force.

Men-in-Black reputedly harass eyewitnesses to UFO sightings and encounters, usually turning up at their homes (or places of business, as transpired in one Puerto Rican case) usually way before the witnesses have even thought about going public with their stories. Case histories have them dressing in black suits, white shirts and jaunty red ties (the fabrics, however, have often been described as being unusual or unearthly), travelling in threes, more often than not aboard spanking new models of large, outdated cars. With notable exceptions, they seem to deliver a boilerplate warning: do not discuss the particular sighting, if a witness, or cease and desist investigation, if a ufologist.

These sartorial agents of silence have acquired mythic proportions in the UFO community over a timespan as lengthy as the phenomenon itself. From the first appearance of a black suited, red-cravatted man in the wake of the infamous Maury Island "Hoax", threatening witness Harold Dahl to silence, to a growing number of appearances in the '90s, MIBs remain an enthralling facet of the supernatural.

Early UFO sightings always ended with the involvement of the Air Force as the best qualified source of investigating the precise nature of these things. Airmen routinely turned up at witnesses' homes to ask questions, and in many instances, to confiscate evidence—such as samples of elusive "angel hair" taken from the home of journalist R. DeWitt Miller (author of *You Do Take It With You*) in 1954. When Asiatic-looking men in black suits started showing up claiming an affiliation with the Air Force, no one thought to question them, but their strange behavior—and uncanny psychic abilities—soon arose suspicion.

After being pursued by a UFO over the Mediterranean in 1951, Col. Jim Doherty was visited by a spindly young man in an Air Force lieutenant's overcoat. The gaunt-looking fellow warned Doherty, in an oddly accented voice, to forget all about the UFO encounter. Doherty was to learn later on that there was no such officer working for AFOSI. Years after the incident, Doherty still has nightmares about his UFO encounter in which a spindly being, reminiscent of the false lieutenant, figured prominently. (1) The Air Force promptly denied any connection whatsoever to the Men in Black. A Pentagon colonel told author John Keel that they had looked into a number of Men in Black reports. The same Pentagon official stated that the UFO silencers, whoever they were, were committing a federal offense by impersonating a member of the armed forces. These trivialities did not seem to trouble the Men in Black: One such impostor, using the handle "Captain Munroe", turned up to threaten the teenage photographers of the Beaver Falls, PA UFO in 1968. The impostor told one of the young Pennsylvanians that something unpleasant might happen to him if he continued discussing his sighting. (2)

The Men in Black phenomenon soon took on a life of its own when Albert K. Bender, director of the International Flying Saucer Bureau, announced his retirement from "flying saucer investigation" and the IFSB's shutdown in 1953, as a result of harassment by three men in black. As rumors flew concerning the provenance of the trio, Bender himself would later state that they were not from the FBI, but "from another branch." (3) The Men in Black proved to have quite a long reach, as well: Edgar J. Jarrold, head of the Australian Flying Saucer Bureau, received a mysterious visitor who advised him that "the most fantastic situation it is possible to conceive by normal standards" (4). Jarrold would disappear mysteriously years later. Bender would try to expand on the reasons for his hasty departure from ufology in his *UFOs and the Three Men,* where he describes Kazik, the dismal homeworld of the Men in Black, and the experiences he endured at their hands (5). Bender could claim the distinction of being the first investigator to be molested by these unknown quantities, and his story would repeat itself in the lives of a number of investigators hence.

Warren Smith, a noted writer during the 1970s (under the name Eric Norman), had acquired a piece of metal allegedly recovered from a UFO in Madison, Wisconsin which had dumped "slag" (*á la* Maury Island) over an interstate highway. Aware that someone was tailing him during the investigation, Smith chose to conceal the fragment of slag within a television set in his motel room. Upon returning to his room one evening, he was faced by two men who demanded that he turn over the find, threatening harm to his family if he chose not to (6).

While never caught red-handed, the disappearances of UFO related documents, even copies stored in different locations, have been blamed on Men in Black. A NJ housewife who made a one-line entry about a UFO sighting in 1973 in her diary lost the entire book, which was in a locked desk. UFO researchers Ivan Sanderson and Capt. Edward Ruppelt both had files containing UFO data stolen from their homes in break-ins where objects of value to an authentic burglar were left untouched. (7)

Men in Black were also involved in the disappearances of children. In August 1969, an alarming number of children suddenly vanished from the Brazilian town of Vilha Verde, reappearing with equal abruptness weeks later. The children had no recollection of where they had been during their absence, but their last recollection seemed to be having taken a ride in an expensive automobile driven by a "gentleman all dressed in black." (8) One girl claimed that a man in black had led her to the outskirts of town to a strange machine, having asked her to take her a ride "in his airplane", but seeing her discomfiture, gave her a handful of candies and told her to go back home. Nor have they apparently shied away from involvement in the cattle mutilations scene. (9)

John Keel, whose delving into the subject would make him the unquestioned expert in these matters documented the uncanny powers of these beings: in 1960, William Dunn Jr., a UFO investigator, had his home burglarized, his files burned, and his photos stolen. (10) Men in Black were notably active during the West Virginia "Mothman" Sightings of 1966-67 as well as in Long Island, N.Y. Far from believing them to be extraterrestrial agents, Keel introduced the concept of the Men in Black as negative, paraphysical forces whose warnings were not to be taken lightly. His sentiments would be echoed by other writers and researchers. Some, like David Tansley, believe that they are a form of demonic psychic energy—a conjecture substantiated by records from past centuries. Others opine that they are thought-forms of some sort, although *whose* thought forms remains unclear. (11)

The late British paranormalist F.W. Holiday had a personal encounter with an unusual Man in Black in the aftermath of the exorcism of Loch Ness in 1978. The figure, which stood some 30 yards away from him, was six feet tall and clothed in black motorcycle leathers with a helmet covering its features. (12) Holiday could detect no eyes behind the visor and felt "a strong sensation of malevolence" issuing from it. He walked within a few feet of it and past it, but when he turned around to look at it again, the figure had vanished.

A more mundane origin for these elusive characters, in step with the "secret government agent" theory, is that they were in fact elements of the Air Force Special Activities Center (AFSAC), devoted to non-electronic intelligence gathering, in particular the 1127th Field Activities Group, comprising a varied array of shady types, ranging from lock-pickers and impersonators to ex-convicts, whose tasks were made even easier by the paranoia surrounding the UFO community. A corollary belief is that a great many Men in Black were Tibetan monks who followed the Dalai Lama and the Khamba riders into exile, placing their uncanny prowess at the service of the CIA. While fanciful, this would certainly account for the Asiatic physiognomy and unfamiliarity with certain customs.

Some Men in Black have upon occasion demonstrated non-stereotypical behavior: In November 1973 a young woman working for an employment agency in San Juan, Puerto Rico received an afternoon visit from a man clad in an immaculately black suit with a shirt that seemed to be woven of a texture unknown on Earth. The man had extremely long, tapering fingers (as reported in other Men in Black cases) and a mannequin-smooth complexion. The woman found herself mesmerized by his conversation, which ranged from the ecology to war, along with statements such as: "there were other worlds than this one." According to author Salvador Freixedo, the Men in Black often respond positively to courteous treatment. (13)

The Men in Black seemed to have taken an extended furlough sometime in the late '70s. One of their last major appearances was in the wake of the failed hijacking of a private plane by three small UFOs over Lake Tequesquitengo, Mexico. The pilot, Carlos de los Santos Montiel, was harassed by Men in Black on his way to an interview with the late Dr. J. Allen Hynek. Many believe that the increased willingness to discuss the phenomenon in the wake of 1978s *Close Encounters of the Third Kind* spiked the MIB's usefulness as tools of fear and intimidation.

But the Nineties have witnessed their disturbing return to the scene in a number of cases: Puerto Rican investigator Jorge Martín, editor of *Evidencia Ovni* magazine, unearthed an astonishing MIB story while interviewing the late Diego Segarra, a key witness to the Laguna Cartagena sightings. Segarra told Martín that a friend had had a chilling experience while exploring the vicinity of the lagoon, recording things on a small camcorder. The witness saw a bright flash that proved to emanate from a spherical UFO about to land. Hiding behind the dense tropical vegetation, Segarra's friend was able to see—and allegedly capture on video—jumpsuited Greys emerging from the craft, followed by a tall, albinoesque human figure clad in a black suit, white shirt, and red tie. The witness also added that the man in the black suit wore sunglasses and had silvery hair, and was whisked away by two soldiers riding a jeep—a notable step down from the ubiquitous black Cadillac.

This is by no means the first time that such an event has been recorded. A United Press International newswire circulated among the Caribbean basin's major newspapers reported an event in San Juan de los Morros, Venezuela, in which two physicians made a startling observation. On an open road near their clinic, a magenta-colored Mustang stopped to disgorge two passengers dressed exactly alike: black suits, sunglasses, and red neckties. The unusual pair immediately donned what appeared to be belts of some sort. Moments later, a UFO appeared out of the sky, coming close enough to the ground to allow them to enter via a ladder. After a 180 turn, the vehicle sped off into space. (14)

When Karl Brugger, author of the "Chronicles of Akakor" (a narration of "lost" underground cities in Brazil) was mysteriously murdered on the streets of Rio de Janeiro in January 1984, a number of South American investigators promptly placed responsibility for the crime on the HDN (*hombres de negro*, the Spanish acronym for MIB). Fabio Zerpa, editor of the now defunct *Cuarta Dimensión*, declared: "These deaths always have the appearance of being natural events, but curiously enough, every time someone has important information on a crucial subject, strange accidents seem to befall them." (15)

Pennsylvanian UFO investigator Lois Le Gros has studied a number of cases involving MIB activity in the 1990s: two witnesses, one of them an abductee, were cornered by a Man in Black in the aisle of a discount store near Pittsburgh. According to their testimony, the strange personage appeared intent on mesmerizing them with an unusual ring on one of the fingers of his hand. In a completely unrelated case, another young abductee from a Pittsburgh suburb would encounter a Man in Black every day—on her way to work.

Describing him as "intimidating", the witness told Le Gros that he would board the bus every day and gradually sit closer to her. The sinister figure wore a full-length black trenchcoat, even in unseasonable weather, and hat, shoes, gloves and shirt of the same color. On one occasion, the stranger sat next to her on the bus, causing her to cringe against the window. In spite of the confined space on the vehicle, the witness expressed a belief that she may well have been the only one to have noticed the sinister, outlandishly dressed character.

Another Pennsylvanian researcher, Mike Lonzo, interviewed the protagonist of a singular case: an elderly woman witnessed the fall of a strange black stone into her backyard, and almost immediately after, received the visit of two tuxedo-wearing MIBs who demanded—in no uncertain terms—the return of the black stone, claiming that its loss would "bring about the destruction of their universe." Frightened, the woman complied with their request, and there was an even more amazing turn of events: her tuxedoed visitors invited her out to dinner at a Pittsburgh restaurant, where they were joined by their female counterparts (it is unclear if they, too, were clad in ever-fashionable black). (15)

The strange "reanimation" of the Men in Black seems to have adapted itself to the belt-tightening Nineties: travelling in twos rather than threes, using public transport rather than the obligatory Cadillacs, and departing UFO landing sites in humvees or jeeps. This should not be surprising, given the phenomenon's propensity toward mimicry of the human condition. The fact that they have returned from their improbable reality to trouble our own, however, should be a cause for concern.

Notes:

1. Drake, Rufus. "Return of the Men in Black," *Saga UFO*, Oct. 76, p.39.

2. Steiger, Brad. "Three Tricksters in Black," *Saga UFO Report*, Winter 1974, p.42.

3. Barker, Grey. *They Knew Too Much About Flying Saucers*, University Books, NY, 1956. p.143.

4. Barker, p.156.

5. Bender, Albert K. *Flying Saucers And The Three Men*, New York: Paperback Library, 1968.

6. Randle, K. *UFO Casebook*, New York: Warner Books, p. 229.

7. Drake, Rufus. *Return of the Men in Black*, p. 154.

8. Freixedo, Salvador. *Ellos*, Mexico: Posada, 1989. p.179.

9. Howe, Linda. Conversation on paranet BBS 22 Jan 1988.

10. Keel, John. "Strange Riddle of the Men in Black," *Saga UFO Report*, Spring 74, p.76.

11. Gordon, Stuart. *The Paranormal*, p.438. London: Headline Books, 1992.

12. Holiday, F.W. *The Goblin Universe*. St. Paul:

Llewellyn Books.

13. Freixedo, S. *Visionaries, Mystics and Contactees.* Lilburn, GA: Illuminet Press, 1992.

14. Freixedo, S. *Parapsicología y Religión,* Madrid: Quintá, 1985, p. 201.

15. Conversation with Mike Lonzo, 8/27/94.

Undeclared War Exists
Faxed by Norman Olson

At this writing, police authorities report that Timothy McVeigh and another suspect, identified now only as John Doe #2, left the scene of Oklahoma City's Murrah Federal Building in separate cars. Moments later, of course, the terrible bomb mayhem occurred at the building, killing an as yet undetermined number of people, over 100, including many children. McVeigh and some comrades previously had been asked by the leaders of the Michigan Militia—a homegrown, Second Amendment, paramilitary outfit similar to many across the country—to leave the group apparently because their strident views about the use of violence became embarrassing.

After the bombing, police pulled McVeigh over for speeding in a car with missing license plates, arrested him for carrying a concealed weapon, and later charged him with the crime. It has not been determined if McVeigh did not know if the plates were already missing or if they had fallen off during the getaway. His partner, however, suffered no similar calamity and remains on the loose, perhaps with the license plates fastening screws sitting next to a screwdriver on the front passenger seat of his car. In any event, Timothy McVeigh has not come to be regarded as a criminal genius.

Shortly after McVeigh's arrest, the leader of the Michigan Militia issued the following as an explanation for the Oklahoma City bombing incident:

PLEASE FAX ACROSS AMERICA
OKLAHOMA CITY BOMBING EXPOSED
PLEASE REFAX ACROSS AMERICA

FROM: NORMAN OLSON, COMMANDER, MICHIGAN MILITIA CORPS
TO: THE AMERICAN PEOPLE
Attention, Citizens of America - Undeclared War Exists

The wrath of the country has been directed toward the brave men and women of the Michigan Militia Corps. Now the truth: On April 19, 1995 a day that will live in infamy, the government of Japan, in retaliation for the U.S. gas attack on the subway there, blew up the Federal Building in Oklahoma City.

The Japanese attack was reported to Sarah McLendon, McLendon News Agency on April 18, just hours before the destruction of that building.

FBI employee Robert Goetzman (operating out of the executive office of the Bush presidency, and having "dual agency" status with CIA), CIA employee Wes Thomas and U.S. Intelligence employee, James Cofield, were hired by the Japanese Embassy at the beginning of the Clinton presidency to bug the executive offices of the President. These men had lost lucrative programs assigned to them by Bush and although not out when Clinton became President, they were out of funds. (A great deal of money had been deferred while under Bush, to their own private accounts to the extent that they were setting up their own private companies.) Once bought by the Japanese, these men were paid through MCA/Universal (owned by the Japanese) to provide intelligence information gathered from the surveillance devices and bugs Goetzman has installed inside the surveillance devices and bugs Goetzman had installed inside electronic devices (computers, faxes, etc.) in order to win the Japanese trade war going on at that time. The U.S. and Japan had completely lost cooperation on the trade talks and threatened sanction deadline against Japan. Japan retaliated by devaluating the dollar against the yen, which was trading at its lowest amount ever recorded on the day of the subway attack.

Walter Mondale gained knowledge of the espionage activity on Jan 27, 1994, the day before sanction deadline and attempted to have the matter investigated. The source of this information contacted William Perry for protection and assistance after learning of Justice Department employee Paul Coffey's attempt to kill the investigation. CIA director, John Deutch, was in charge of the investigation into the matter.

In retaliation of the attack against the dollar, the U.S. government gassed citizens of Japan to discredit the government. The Japanese government, not willing to reveal their own espionage, blamed the act on a religious cult with a massive disinformation effort. In retaliation the Japanese destroyed the Federal Building in Oklahoma City. To further embarrass the President, a copycat bomb was used so that the Arab people would be blamed by U.S. citizens. With anger growing toward the Mideast the Feds had to find a quick scapegoat, so they triggered CNN and ABC.

They were visible, there were many of them, and a recent "non-incident" had occurred in Michigan involving "Rambo" talk about blowing up some junk Russian armor. It was the Fed's only card to play. Surely someone could be found inside Michigan to hang. But this is where they made their mistake. American patriots in Michigan don't kill patriots in

Oklahoma. Their suppressed sacrificial lamb climbed off the altar and became a Wolverine.

The actual target of the Japanese was in fact the senior Secret Service agent (whose widow and orphaned child sat behind Clinton and Hillary at the memorial service) who was "in the loop" with Goetzman, et. al. He had been transferred to OKC only months earlier. His death was a symbol that the President and the nation are "touchable."

The President knew, Janet Reno knew, William Perry knew, Mondale knew, Stephanopoulas knew, Panetta knew, CNN knew, ABC knew, the CIA knew, the FBI knew. And now the American people know the truth.

The top five conspirators are: Robert Goetzman, Dan Starkey, Wes Thomas, Paul Steel, and Jim Cofield. Peter Stanley and Walter Mondale did all they could to stop it, but no one listened and those who listened could not talk.

President Bush's CIA controls the presidency. To make that point clear to Clinton, the CIA hit Vince Foster as a reminder of who really runs the roost. The war between agencies has escalated into undeclared war between Japan and America. The American people are paying the price. Expect blackmail actions by Japan. The governments of both countries may soon collapse under the weight of their own corruption.

Signed, Brigadier General Norman E. Olson, Commander, Michigan Militia Corp

Esther 7:10: So they hanged Haman on the gallows that he had prepared for Mordecai. Then was the king's wrath pacified.

On April 28, after Olson released this fax and made similar comments to a television station in Chile, the Michigan Militia asked him to resign as its head— a second dismissal for reasons of acute embarrassment. The communications director for the militia, Ken Adams, remarked to the Chicago Tribune *that "Norm has been under tremendous stress and lack of sleep, which affects everyone's judgement." As it turns out, the rant was not even original: it actually originated with a woman named Debra Van Trapp, sans the vaguely anti-Semitic biblical reference to Haman, an enemy of the Jews. Sherman Skolnick (see chapter 8) explored the dimensions of this version of events in Oklahoma City at length in an interview with Ms. Von Trapp that appeared on Brian Redman's highly recommended electronic newsletter,* Conspiracy Nation, *available at bigxc@prairienet.org. Normam Olson reemerged during a June 1995 Senate hearing on the militia movement, provoking Senator Arlen Specter (R.-Pa.) into an angered insistence that Olson point to proof of his charges of government corruption. Olson missed the opportunity to mention the Magic Bullet Theory, the physics-defying explanation of the bullet trajectory that killed JFK, which Specter authored.*

Carlos Castenada; Criticism and Conspiracies
by Tom Lyttle

Carlos Castaneda is the popular writer whose autobiographical books on Yaqui sorcery have sold into the millions. It has been stated that after Margaret Mead, he is the most well-known American anthropologist. His books and lectures chronicle his initiations into shamanic secret societies and traditions, some written while studying to obtain his Ph.D. in anthropology from UCLA. After he earned his degree, more adventures were chronicled. His books are very compelling and original, very mystical in appearance, and very readable.

According to *Time* magazine, Castaneda wrote his first unpublished works centering around Don Juan in about 1956. This happened eleven years before his first book was published. He also had a co-author at the time named Alberta Greenfield. Castaneda titled his first unpublished manuscript about Don Juan and shamanic magic, *The Whole World Sounds Strange, Don't You Think...?* Response within Castaneda's circle of friends was so great regarding these unpublished works that he abandoned painting in favor of writing.

Eleven years later, in 1967, UCLA anthropology student Carlos Castaneda presented a copy of a manuscript he had written to a professor for comments, titled *The Teachings of Don Juan.* Very impressed, the professor encouraged Castaneda to submit the work to the University of California Press for consideration. In late 1967, three editors of UC Press read the work and recommended it for publication. Retitled *The Teachings of Don Juan: A Yaqui Way of Knowledge* (University of California Press, 1968), UC Press released it on June 27, 1968. At the time college students and a young America were becoming openly exposed to drug experimentation and alternative politics through the Vietnam war protests. Timothy Leary's LSD evangelism was in full bloom, and Castaneda's books were absorbed directly into the mainstream of sub-cultural America. At its peak, the second printing of *The Teachings Of Don Juan* sold over 16,000 copies a week!

Like Timothy Leary, Castaneda set the standard for what psychedelic drug use might be, or could be. It also started a sort of hero-worship or "celebrity cult" within consciousness studies, or psychedelic studies. Another celebrity-cult had started up about that time, around New York banker R. Gordon Wasson. Wasson published a *Life* magazine article regarding Mexican shaman Maria Sabina and the ritual uses of Mexican "magic mushrooms." Wasson was an amateur expert on psychedelic mushroom cults and had published many well received books.

These three men, Leary, Wasson, and Castaneda, more or less started psychedelic anthropology studies. Today this science calls this ethnopharmacology. Hundreds of books, magazines, science papers, movies and journals centered around serious looks at ritual, culture and the rare-plant or drugs used by magicians and shamans. My own journal, *Psychedelic Monographs and Essays,* focuses partly in these areas. As a gauge of the popularity of psychedelic studies and ethnopharmacology, my journal is sold in thirty countries. These three men started this popularity back in the 1950s.

All three gentlemen also battled each other alternatively for notoriety and celebrity status. Wasson and Leary openly despised each other's works and often said so in print. Castaneda often said Leary was his main competitor, although when the two met in person Castaneda tried to get Leary to initiate him into Leary's Mexican research group called IFIF (the International Federation for Internal Freedom). Wasson and Castaneda exchanged many letters, with Wasson being most skeptical to Castaneda's claims. These letters are on file at Harvard at the Botanical Museum.

By 1971 a Castaneda sequel was released entitled *A Separate Reality* (Pocket Books, 1971). This also was an extremely popular work, and further explored Castaneda's apprenticeship to the Yaqui sorcerer named Don Juan. At no time was a person named Don Juan ever photographed, interviewed (except by Castaneda) or established as real. However, Castaneda did provide detailed descriptions of Don Juan, and an assistant named Don Genero. Several other well-known and popular Castaneda books emerged in the next few years, with the latest entitled *The Art of Dreaming* (Harper-Collins, 1994).

All these books more or less center on the same theme, Yaqui Indian sorcery and a credentialed anthropologist's initiation into the alternative worlds of the Brujos and Curanderos. These are types of Meso-American shamans that heal or harm, talk to spirits and more or less act as local soothsayers. Castaneda originally presented all the material as matter-of-fact anthropology, real adventures with real people. Real descriptions of real hallucinogenic plant uses and ritual occur throughout his books and were—and are—often mimicked by the readers. Real magic and sorcery, brought back to us like the adventures of Indiana

Jones. Much interest in dream research, alternate dimensions, witchcraft, Indian lore, initiation, and psychedelics were instigated through Castaneda's works.

What Plants Were Used to Train Castaneda?

Castaneda described three main hallucinogens in his books used by Don Juan to train him in sorcery. The first is jimson Weed, or datura. The second is psilocybin mushrooms. The third is peyote, a cactus.

In his first books, Don Juan taught Castaneda to "fly" through uses of jimson weed, and to smoke a magical blend based in mixtures of psilocybin mushrooms and other herbs. Castaneda mostly focused on the visions of these trips, what he saw and who he encountered while intoxicated, strange physical effects and never gave actual locations or places where these plants were obtained.

Don Juan would tell Carlos what was actually going on. He translated the often bizarre places Carlos ended up in by biting off more than he could chew with these psychedelic plants. Castaneda often encountered a being called Mescalito, an Indian divinity. The word Mescalito is derived from the same root as mescaline, a psychedelic chemical or drug derived from the peyote cactus. Jimson weed was also called Devil's Weed by Castaneda. It is also called "locoweed" by Mexicans. This is a very common plant/drug used by Meso and American Indians like the Huichol and the Tepacano.

In medieval Europe, witches claimed to be able to fly, though uses of jimson weed. Datura is very deadly also, although there are healing applications. The most famous fatality is Abraham Lincoln's mother, who died after drinking cow's milk tainted with Datura. In those days this was called "milk sickness."

Castaneda gave such detailed and powerful descriptions that many readers actually traveled to Mexico to search for these magical plants. A July 1970 story in the *New York Times* spoke about "thousands of hippies...invading Mexico in search of the 'magic mushrooms'." Psilocybin mushrooms and peyote are also used for divination and healing purposes by shamans all over the world. Peyote is illegal in most of the US and Mexico but the Indian Native American Church uses it for religious purposes off and on, depending on the laws surrounding Indian religious uses, which seem to change every other year.

In the US and Mexico, types of psilocybin mushrooms are picked out of cow pastures by hippies, amateur mycologists and the curious. They often grow in cow manure. Psilocybin mushrooms are one of the most powerful hallucinogens known to man.

Unpublished Castaneda: What Is Really On His Mind?

I have just finished a new book manuscript titled *Psychedelics ReImagined*, four hundred pages of essays on hallucinogens and hallucinogenic drug culture. My agent, Bernard Shir-Cliff, represented Castaneda at one point, so I have had numerous conversations about the old days, his going to lunch with Castaneda and all the behind-the-scenes business.

One chapter of my new book contains new, unpublished material by Carlos Castaneda from the 1968 period, the time of his first book *The Teachings of Don Juan*. This material is based on original recordings, supplied by researcher David Christie.

Castaneda apparently tried to use his powers to find lost treasure and money. I quote from some of the questions and answers Castaneda gave before a private audience at that time. The following are never-before-published, verbatim quotes from Carlos Castaneda:

"I've been involved with hunting treasures lately...A Mexican came to me and told me there was a house that, uh, belonged to a man who apparently stored a lot of money and never used a bank...He figured and calculated that there was at least $100,000 dollars and he asked if I could discover where the money was. *Laughter*. So I, um, followed this ritual. It was a minor vision; not as clear as a divination procedure. But it was a vision that could be interpreted. A fire has to be made that attracts whatever it is that has to be attracted. So this bunch of about four people and I, they all did the ritual. we waited for a vision and nothing came at all. we dug up the whole house and the guy that was digging, he got bitten by a black-widow spider [author's note: Carlos Castaneda means 'Charly Spider' in Spanish].

"...So I have this dream. A dream in which the owner of the house points to the ceiling...So I was walking on the beams and this guy got very suspicious; he thought I was going to cheat him out of his money - we never did...He came up...He got hooked, you know, with his legs dangling in the upper part...

"...I went to see Don Juan, and I told him of this failure...and he said this was very natural...what is left of a man guards whatever he is hiding."

Further Castaneda Conspiracies

While Castaneda's books contain a lot of power, so do many of his critics. Most of these criticisms focus on inconsistencies in his storytelling, confused or false anthropology, inaccurate quotes, wrong geography, and unsubstantiated ethnography. Castaneda seems to have regularly "pasted together" various places and people. Indian tribes get combined and appear in wrong locations, or one character's activities get draped over another's. Actual anthropology field-notes about Yaqui or Huichol territory get combined or cut-up and remixed or exaggerated. Important things regarding authentic Yaqui ritual, for instance, are completely overlooked or left out of descriptions.

The first main series of criticisms appeared in 1976 by Richard deMille, titled *Castaneda's Journey: The Power and the Allegory* (Ross-Erickson, 1976). A follow-up book in 1980 by DeMille was titled *The Don Juan Papers: Further Castaneda Controversies* (Ross-Erickson, 1980). Both were very popular books. In them, experts in Yaqui and Huichol culture repeatedly contradict Castaneda's claims. Experts in ethno-pharmacology and hallucinogens also contradict many of Castaneda's claims regarding the effects of certain drugs or plants. These two books are explosive and disturbing, and still in print.

Authentic scholars like peyote expert Dr. Weston La Barre, author of *The Peyote Cult* (Schocken Books, 1969) lambasted Castaneda for faking data and misleading the public. A Yaqui Indian expert from UCLA—the original Castaneda publisher—Dr. Ralph Beals requested Castaneda's field notes several times. Castaneda never supplied anything, in fact, to four other anthropologists from UCLA. Many other critical publications have appeared, further fueling book sales, and controversy.

My just-released book, *Psychedelics: The Most Exciting New Materials On Psychedelic Drugs* (Lyle Stuart/Barricade, 1994) has a chapter called "The Breaching Of Don Juan's Teaching." This chapter, by author Ray Clare, attempts to determine where Castaneda originally got his shamanic ideas. One source seems to be a tribe of Yaqui shamans called the Pascolas. The Pascolas are clown shamans involved in tricksterism and burlesque. Part of the tradition of the Pascola involves taking actual ceremony or tradition and distorting it, lampooning it, much like Castaneda may have done with real Yaqui ceremony. My book contains photographs of an actual Pascola clown-shaman connected with a cult called the Trembling Instrument Tribe, a Yaqui cult possibly connected to ancient Toltec magic. The Toltecs preceded the Mayan and Aztecs, as well as the Yaqui Indians in Mexico. Little is known about the religious practices of the Toltecs. Ray Clare believes that Castaneda derived the Don Juan Matus character from the Spanish word *Matus,* short for *Methuselah,* or "old wise man." French poet Antonin Artaud also saw versions of the Pascola while in Mexico, and described them in detail in his 1950s book, *The Peyote Dance* (Farrar, Straus and Giroux, 1976 [1948, 1st ed.]).

Dr. Jay Fikes' has recently produced a new ground-breaking book, *Carlos Castaneda, Academic Opportunism In The Psychedelic Sixties* (Millennia Press, 1993). It attempts to implicate three UCLA anthropologists, Dr. Myerhoff, Dr. Furst and Dr. Delgado, in deliberately faking or distorting scholarly information supporting Castaneda's Ph.D. thesis and books. These three scholars helped Castaneda get his book contract through the University of California Press. Dr. Fikes reveals that several actual shamans were used to model the fictitious Don Juan Matus. These included an Indian named Ramon Medina and Mexican shamaness Marina Sabina.

Some of the more amazing claims described and then discredited in Fikes' book include:

1. Dr. Myerhoff claims to show an Indian sorcerer (later known to be the informant Medina) actually "flying." Furst called this photo "strikingly similar to...Don Juan's feats." This later proved to be a totally staged photo (with no field notes) taken well outside Chapalanga Huichol territory.

2. Dr. Furst and others repeatedly sold Medina to UCLA as a sacred Huichol "singer", trying to make him a saleable celebrity. In fact, a "singer" must make at least ten peyote hunts and serve as Huichol temple officer for five years or more. Medina never represented himself in this manner.

3. Dr. Myerhoff recounts the many sexual feats of Medina. It is well known experts that a *mara'acame* (shaman healer) must live a totally pristine monogamous life.

4. Several anthropological experts including the very respected Dr. Weigand, accused Dr. Furst and Dr. Myerhoff of "representing data derived from the artisans of Western Mexico as if it were a presentation of the life or world view of the indigenous [Huichol] shamans."

This book also includes important descriptions and color photos of *actual* Huatacame and Huichol ceremonies. Once you see the real thing, Castaneda's plastic versions of these rituals stand out more. This book is so provocative and accusing that at least one of the doctors in question, Dr. Furst, threatened a lawsuit for slander if the tone wasn't downplayed. Another storm cloud comes from the soon to be published book by authors David Christie and Margaret Castaneda, Carlos's ex-wife. The Castaneda marriage ended on a bad note, expect a tell-all.

Author Richard Alan Miller (*The Magical and Ritual Uses of Perfumes,* Destiny, 1989; *The Modern Alchemist,* Phanes Press, 1994) also makes unsubstantiated claims that he was under contract by Simon and Schuster to help ghost-write and provide new ideas and background for Castaneda. This surrounded the *Tales of Power* writing sessions. Miller also claims to have met Don Genero, although it is more likely he met Juan Medina. While I haven't seen the Simon and Schuster contract, Miller is a respected author and lecturer, with dozens of books in print.

In Conclusion

Carlos Castaneda started a revolution within consciousness and New Age circles. He took modern America into the world of the shaman like no one has ever done, before or since. He definitely helped start the psychedelic revolution and Americans' fascination with natural hallucinogens like peyote and psilocybin. He also popularized the new age celebrity, Indian and Shamanic market places, magazines like *Shaman's Drum, Woman of Power* and *Magical Blend*, and countless workshops. Fire-walking, sweat-lodges, sacred rattles, dream pillows, etc., got a huge boost through Castaneda's original works. Literally hundreds of books on Indian shamanism and New Age shamanic meditation, drumming or fortune-telling exist because Castaneda made these things popular and saleable. *Careers have been made writing books that dispute his books!* A whole market has developed originally rooted in Carlos Castaneda. In this sense, he was—or

is—a prophet. Whether his ideas and books represent truth, or a version of the truth, is still in dispute. His work has engendered a new network of seekers, both on the street, in the university and even "on-line" through the Internet and services like *America On-Line*. He certainly has created a well from which millions of people have drawn.

This communication and community is the important aspect. If anything, Castaneda has left this as his legacy. He built a network from which other important information and art will emerge. Getting people to talk about the earth, about traditional spirituality, about natural healing and real spirituality is important now more than ever. Whether Castaneda is trickster or prophet remains to be seen, and the end this may not be as important as the community he serves.

Thomas Lyttle has published over seventy articles and seven books on states of consciousness, shamanism and hallucinogenic drugs. His latest is titled Psychedelics: The Most Exciting New Materials On Psychedelic Drugs *(Barricade/Lyle Stuart, 1994).*

Caries, Cabals and Correspondence

To the *Barnes Review*:

I agree with Mark Lane and Fletcher Prouty that all forums for open debate about history should be encouraged, so I welcome *Barnes Review*. As you may know, such a debate regarding the Liberty Lobby has developed in the pages of *Steamshovel Press*.

Many *Steamshovel* readers regard the Lobby as "fascist." The view is only strengthened by your use of the racist term "pygmies" to describe anyone who finds something wrong with siding with the Nazis in World War II ("Leon DeGrelle Redux," *Barnes Review* #1). The suggestion that the history of the Jews, lesbians, blacks and American Indians is not a genuine interest of historians but rather the result of "political correctness" also does little to enhance the *Review* credibility as an open forum. In fact, it suggests that your journal is more mainstream than it pretends, in these days of white, male, Republican anger.

The Lobby, and I presume the *Review,* counters that its sympathies are populist, not fascist. One good way to pursue this line of historical inquiry would be for the Barnes review to publish a point-by-point revisionist analysis of Scott McLemee's recent article in *Covert Action* (Fall 1994) linking Willis Carto and the Lobby to groups like Gerald L. K. Smith's Christian Nationalists. Please accept this suggestion in the spirit of open inquiry the *Review* claims to defend.

No less a source than William S. Burroughs has pointed out that fascism generally includes an element of imperialism. With this in mind, Harry Barnes' philosophy, as expressed in "Revisionism And The Promotion of Peace," seems more grounded in xenophobia than fascism. In the days of California's Proposition 187, this again moves *Barnes Review* in the mainstream of American thinking. As ever,

Kenn Thomas

Thank you so much for your good letter of January 29. I'm sorry that I am ignorant of the debate in your publication regarding Liberty Lobby. Perhaps you will be kind enough to bring me up to date.

Liberals have a very uninformed knowledge of fascism, it seems. this term was developed by Mussolini to describe his system. Mussolini practiced imperialism and so attacked Ethiopia.

However, Hitler, the interpreter of national socialism, although described as a fascist and though his regime had many, many similarities to Mussolini's, was anti-imperialism, and he, in fact, offered to the British to assent to their continued control of their overseas dominions and colonies and stated that Germany had no designs on the African colonies taken away from it in the Versailles Treaty. Hitler was anti-communist and pro-Britain.

So you see, Mr. Burroughs doesn't know what he's talking about and I just wonder if possibly the reason that Harry Elmer Barnes as well as all the other "isolationists" and the non-interventionists were opposed to foreign meddling is because they felt—perfectly correctly as it turned out—that intervention in the affairs of other nations is not and was not in the interest of the United States. It is amazing to me to note that internationalists and liberals, who are always bellyaching about racial equality, feel that they are so superior to everyone else that they have the right to blunder around all over the world telling all other people how to run their own affairs—while the United States is going down the tube.

I think it is puzzling that you say the term "pygmies" is racist. Pygmies exist and they are small people. Sorry about that.

As for Scott McLemee's article in *Covert Action* I did not read it. Numerous copies were sent to me but there is so much of that crap I don't have time to read it. In addition, I wouldn't answer because: 1. it would take a book or more to deal with what McLemee covers; 2. my record speaks for itself to those who are concerned about the survival of the West, which I'm certain McLemee is not; 3. this is not a proper subject for the *Barnes Review* and 4. McLemee is a hack doing a job for the Stern interests who own and control that funny magazine. If *Covert Action* was anything other than a CIA operation, why doesn't it tell the truth about the CIA's assassination of John Kennedy, as our attorney, Mark Lane, has done for twenty years? Judge McLemee's sputterings by the source.

Thanks again for writing. Sincerely,

Willis A. Carto
Washington, DC

Book Reviews

The Cambridge Crank Tournament: Transformational Grammars Ride Out To Joust With Statistical Control or Demonization in the Service (?) of Truth
by Roy Lisker

Rethinking Camelot
by Noam Chomsky, South End Press, 1993

In Retrospect
by Robert S. McNamara, Times Books, 1995

"Blood lust has its merits, but money talks even louder."

—**Noam Chomsky in *Rethinking Camelot***

"Statistics," he smiled, "McNamara dotes on statistics, but I've never been able to make head nor tail of them."

—**Sam Adams in *War of Numbers***

I begin by invoking an image, utterly fantastic of course, no doubt scientifically impossible yet which, given the utterly incredible character of all things that we do know about the planning, execution and aftermath of the Kennedy assassination, is no more improbable:

In the days following the events of November 22, 1963, a team of doctors from some neurological research institute, secretly funded by the CIA, are dispatched to Bethesda Memorial Hospital and to Dealey Plaza. Mission: to sweep up, collect or confiscate as many fragments of the grey matter one sees on the Zapruder film, extruding from JFK's skull at the moment of impact. These bits of his brain are carried back to the institute, cleaned in chemical baths, reconstructed with the help of computer enhancements with meticulous care, and so forth. The ultimate purpose of this macabre paleontology? To determine, from the suggestions of the remaining thought traces, which of these two words is inscribed in the residual pulp: "WITHDRAWAL!" or "ESCALATION!"

Thirty years later we find this very question at the center of a storm of uniquely quaint academic irrelevance. Journalists, writers, politicians and scholars heatedly engage in the lists, swinging their maces, lances, chains, battle-axes at one another under the opposing banners, "withdrawal" versus "escalation", as if the very survival or demolition of the age-old Yankee dream pivoted on this single issue.

For Noam Chomsky the question is so serious that he has devoted an entire book to its resolution, although only a small portion of its pages really focus on the matter at hand. The rest of it is filled with hysterical shrieking, name-calling, accusation, rant, and other staples of Chomskian rhetoric. In addition, most of that part of the book which supposedly deals with this pressing concern is given over to snide attacks on John Newman's exhaustive research effort on the same issue (*JFK and Vietnam*, which at least sticks to the point).

Newman concludes that JFK would have pulled us out of Vietnam, and darkly suggests that his resisting to the pressures put upon him to commit group troops was one of the key factors in the decision to assassinate him.

Chomsky's thesis is that - but before I present his thesis I want to say a few words about his peculiar rhetorical style. Although Noam Chomsky has gambled (and won!) his scientific career on the dogmatic insistence that a sentence must have a clear, unambiguous meaning to be acceptable as true English, his own writing conjures up whirlwinds of irrelevancies, almost always in the accusative mode, from which it is often impossible to extract any coherent meaning.

To take one example out of many: in two short pages of *Rethinking Camelot* (28, 29), he rambles on, in series and in parallel with scarcely any discursive connection, about:

(1) Andrew Jackson's genocidal war against the Seminole Indians.

(2) The evil soul of the historian Tacitus, who made the mistake of communicating the very astute observation that *"Crime once exposed has no refuge but in audacity."* Chomsky labels this "The Tacitus Principle". In some places he calls it, *'The vile maxim of the masters of mankind".*

(3) The POW/MIA smoke screen

(4) The re-arming of the Khmer Rouge in 1980s

(5) The corruption of Thailand by the West

(6) France's insistence in the 19th century that Haiti pay a huge indemnity for the crime of winning its revolution.

(7) The suppressed accounts of brutal treatment of Italian and German POWs during WWII by the US and Britain. None of this has anything at all to do with the thesis of *Rethinking Camelot*. It takes a bit of work to discover what this thesis is, but by pasting together bits and pieces scattered through the book, it seems to go something like this:

(i) In 1492, Europe launched a 500 year long genocidal war against the human race.

(ii) The Vietnamese war was the most recent and the most horrible chapter of that war.

(iii) It really ought to be called "Kennedy's War", because JFK pursued it with an insane zeal second only to Hitler's hatred of the Jews.

(iv) JFK was a right-wing fanatic, which is why he enthusiastically supported a terror state in Vietnam up to 1961.

(v) The decisive escalation of the war from indirectly supported state terror to direct naked aggression was done by JFK in August of 1961.

In addition to these 5 points, there are several buzz-words, some of which we have already seen. They reiterate through the text like the Leitmotifs of Wagner's operas: the 500 year conquest; the Columbian era; Kennedy's war; Kennedy's escalation; the masters of mankind; the cultural managers; the merchant warriors; the Kennedy cult, etc.

It is easy to parody of this style, which I dub "academic neo-Maoism". Here is an example:

"Invoking the Tacitus Principle, the masters of mankind have instructed the cultural managers of the 'liberal' academy and the Free Press to delude the oppressed victims of the 500 year European war on mankind as to the well-laid conspiracies of the military-industrial complex and the Tri-Lateral Commission..."

You can say anything you want with this style of writing; it is neither literature, journalism or scholarship. It is more like a *"vile, nefarious, conspiratorial blood-bath, an infamous assault on language! and truth!!"*, which should not surprise anyone who knows how his linguistic theories achieve the same ends by other means.

Once in awhile, Chomsky does manage to state his thesis in a reasonable way. On page 33 he writes: "As Kennedy took office, the US position seemed to face imminent collapse. Kennedy therefore escalated the war in 1961-62."

We now look through the book to discover what this initial escalation consisted of. On page 23, he tells us: *"On October 11, 1961, Kennedy ordered [...] 12 planes especially equipped for counter-insurgency warfare."*

This, which Chomsky would have us believe is a massive escalation, did not occur in August, but in October. What then does he mean when he states in several places that this fundamental rupture of the threshold 'twixt peace and war occurred in August? Examining the record, available from many independent sources, we realize that what he's talking about wasn't devised by Kennedy at all. Instead he's alluding to the infamous Taylor-Rostow recommendations, prepared for and approved by the Joint Chiefs of Staff. These called for:

(1) Helicopters manned by American pilots
(2) Air Force units manned by Americans
(3) 10,000 combat troops

(4) Contingency planning for US air strikes, in both the South and the North.

From this amazing shopping list, Kennedy approved only (1) and (2). In fact, as Newman tells us, Kennedy stunned the Joint Chiefs of Staff in his memo of November 22, 1961 (NSAM#111) with his firm refusal to commit ground combat troops.

This doesn't sound like escalation: if anything one gets the picture of an embattled man trying to keep a hoard of rabid dogs at bay by throwing them a few airplanes!

When we speak of escalation, we want to use the word in a reasonable way: The extreme right wing of the anti-abortion movement tells us that *any* contraceptive device is a "murder weapon"! One of the very important features of the Vietnamese war is that, when seen from the inside, it appears like a series of blunders made by lots of people with a wide range of intentions through idealism, patriotism, fanaticism, greed, stupidity, incompetence, delusion, and so on.

Seen from the outside, that is to say in much the same way as the Vietnamese themselves saw it, it looks more like the explosion of a supernova, or the collapsing of a Black Hole: A natural phenomenon unfolding in a manner that clearly follows deterministic physical laws, although we may never be able to write them down or even know what they are.

This undeviating chain of events goes right from the withdrawal of the French in 1955 to the departure of the Americans in 1975, through Eisenhower, Kennedy, Johnson and Nixon.

I therefore propose that we, in order to determine what we mean by an "escalation", draw a graph representing the official figures for the numbers of American military personnel in Vietnam from 1960 to 1968.* This graph doesn't give us any information about the intensity of the bombings, the loss of life, the destruction of the countryside and so on, but it does provide a very rough index on which to pin the mounting intensity of the war:

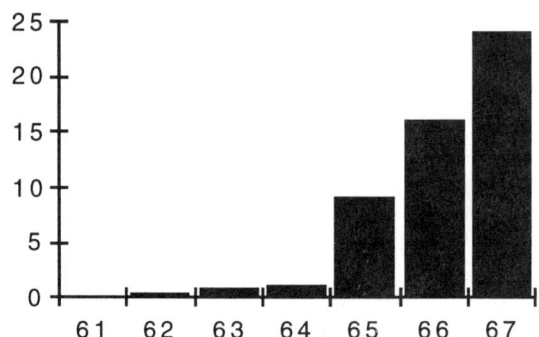

VIETNAM:
ESCALATION IN UNITS OF 20,000 TROOPS

* This chart has been put together from data supplied by *The Encyclopedia of the American Military,* Vol II, *Scribner's,* 1994, and "The Limits of Intervention," Townsend Hoopes, Murray 1970

Notice the regularity of the curve from 1960 to 1964: were Chomsky to content himself with the argument that JFK was something different from the peace-loving humanitarian that certain people like to imagine him as being, he would certainly have a case. It is true that the number of military advisors sent to Vietnam rose from less than 800 in 1960 to 16,000 by the time Kennedy was killed. This is an escalation of sorts, and it comes down to what one means by escalation. It also implies that we must be careful not to smudge the line of demarcation between "Kennedy" and the "Kennedy Administration", a nicety that never phases Chomsky. Although if these terms were freely interchangeable it is unlikely that Kennedy would have been assassinated. Nor do I think that JFK ought to be excused for his part in precipitating the eventual catastrophe.

However the number of troops in Vietnam jumps from about 40,000 at the beginning of 1965 to over 180,000 by the end of the year! The slope of the Kennedy engagement is 5,000 soldiers per year; that of the Johnson engagement after the Tonkin Bay resolution is 150,000 soldiers per year, a 30-fold increase.

Is abortion murder? Did Kennedy escalate? I've the impression that the abuse of language is at about the same level.

The most balanced view out of all those I've encountered in the literature seems to me to be that of Arthur Schlesinger, Jr. in his biography of Robert F. Kennedy, in which he writes:

"... Kennedy's Vietnam legacy was dual and contradictory. He had left on the public record the impression of a major national stake in the defense of South Vietnam against communism. He had left steadily enlarging programs of military and economic assistance. He had left national security advisors who for three years had been urging an American expeditionary force and a total commitment to the salvation of South Vietnam. On the other hand, he had consistently refused to send such a force or make such a commitment. He had left a formal plan, processed successfully through the Pentagon, for the withdrawal of advisors by the end of 1965. He had left a public campaign, belatedly begun, to instill the idea that American involvement must be limited in a war that only the South Vietnamese could win. And he had left private opposition, repeatedly and emphatically stated, to the dispatch of American ground forces." *(Robert Kennedy and His Times,* Arthur M. Schlesinger, 1978,

Vol II, pg. 758.

I can use my graph of the escalation as a lead into a discussion of the Robert S. McNamara memoir: for he too presents a graph. McNamara, as he tells us, minored in mathematics when he studied at Berkeley. That he did so appears to be one of our national tragedies. McNamara drew this picture for Kennedy as a kind of lesson to him on the wise use of power:

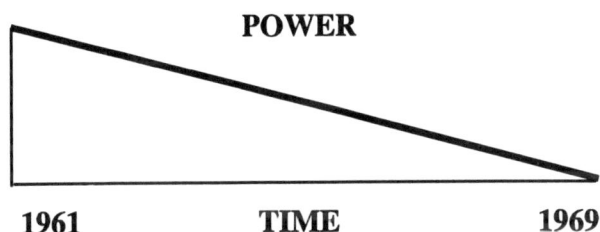

POWER

1961   **TIME**   1969

As in so many of McNamara's projections, this would only come to demonstrate once more his incompetence in the design and interpretation of mathematical images for the understanding of the real world. The historically accurate graph is this one:

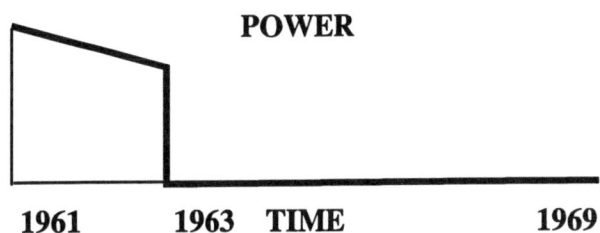

POWER

1961   1963 **TIME**   1969

Robert S. McNamara's major contribution (of which he is quite proud) to the advance of science and civilization lies in the application of a subject called "statistical control theory" to problems of higher management. It is a methodology which he and a team of like-minded geniuses at the Harvard School of Business Administration developed in 1945. They were then able to sell it and themselves to the Ford Motor Company where they became known as the "Whiz Kids". It is a mystery to me why Ford is still in business.

Statistical Control of an enterprise begins with drawing up a (finite) list of "vital signs", numerical variables that are judged to be reliable indicators of success or failure. Records on them are kept up to date and diligently monitored. Their increase is taken as evidence of success or health. If they begin to fall you see what has to be done to reverse the trend, so that they once again begin to rise (is it indelicate to use the word, "inflate"?)

Let us give McNamara the opportunity to explain

statistical control in his own words, (Page 237):

"Since my years at Harvard, I had gone by the rule that it is not enough to conceive of an objective and a plan to carry it out; you must monitor the plan to determine whether you are achieving the objective...I was convinced that...we could find variables that may indicate our success or failure. So we measured the targets destroyed in the North, the traffic down the Ho Chi Minh Trail, the weapons seized, the enemy body count, etc...Critics point to the use of the body count as an example of my obsession with numbers. 'This guy McNamara', they say, 'he tries to quantify everything'. Obviously there are things you cannot quantify: honor and beauty for example. But things you can count you ought to count. Loss of life is one when you are fighting a war of attrition."

One doesn't know where to begin in response to this astonishing confession. Clearly his degree from Berkeley in economics, with a minor in math, gave him a familiarity with statistics but no notion of how to use them correctly. If you chose a variable which you intend to monitor, you must try to determine if

(1) This variable is a reliable measure of progress or defeat:

A variable such as "body count" was in fact very effective in the context of Nazi Germany in which the objective was genocide. The Germans kept close tabs on the numbers of Jews being exterminated. But when the objective is "to thwart the morale of dedicated Communists", body counts are ridiculous.

(2) That the methods used in gathering data are giving you accurate numbers: Collecting accurate figures for the 'death toll of the enemies soldiers' under battle conditions, and in a situation in which one could not distinguish friend from foe, was simply impossible. The officers of the ARVN would then inflate these figures several times, because they knew that the Americans wanted high body counts. Another inflation would occur when the Americans transmitted what they had been given to the upper command, because they knew that McNamara was obsessed with statistics.

But the ugliest part of this farce came when, as anyone can discover through a little research, is that McNamara wasn't even honest with these figures, that he himself scorned his greatest discovery in the history of pseudo-mathematics!

There happens to be another book standing right now on the shelves of the bourgeois bookstores, which tells us a great deal about McNamara's contempt for the American people and for his own methods: "The War of Numbers: An Intelligence Memoir", by Sam Adams (Steerforth Press, 1994). Adams was (he died in 1988 of a mysterious heart attack) the ex-CIA agent who, on January 23, 1982, went public on CBS with detailed information on the extent to which the Pentagon was systematically falsifying the official figures on VC casualties and the Order of Battle (OB). This lead to General Westmoreland's libel suit against CBS and the long stream of public revelations that came out during the trial.

Here are the relevant passages from Adam's book (page 212):

"MACV [Military Assistance Command, Vietnam] discovered its vast underestimate of Vietcong numbers in late 1966....At this point, the main resistance against one came from the Pentagon, including the office of the secretary of defense, Robert S. McNamara. As McNamara explained to an aide in late January, he realized that the official OB was all wrong, but that he was not yet prepared to tell Congress. He meant what he said. On 6 March 1967, he briefed a Congressional committee using the official numbers, the same ones he knew to be low...

One morning, shortly before the start of the scheduled conference, a colonel from J-2 stopped by Lynn's desk with the suggestion that the strengths at which Lynn was carrying his six VC units were 'way too high'. Lynn denied it, at which the colonel simply picked up Lynn's strength sheet, crossed out the numbers by each regiment, and penciled in new ones, on the average one-third lower. To Lynn's amazement, a unit which he had carried with 3,100 men became 1,900 instead...Gorman remarked that by early September, 'You could march a VC regiment down the hall, and they wouldn't put it in the OB...'

"An order arrived (Sept 1967) from Secretary McNamara's office saying that McNamara wanted the newly agreed upon OB number of some 240,000 to be 'retroactively readjusted'..."

"The 'retroactive readjustment' took place in the third week of September...the readjustment was simple. A J-2 officer chalked a curve on a blackboard. On the right hand end of the curve he wrote the number agreed upon at the Saigon conference 241,000...He stepped back to look at the curve from a distance, then returned to the board to write 285,400 next to August 66 and 204,700 next to August 65."

It is possible to establish a connection between McNamara and Chomsky, in that their contributions to pseudo-science were both concocted and developed in that cradle of American crankiness, Cambridge, Massachusetts. It is my conviction that our future historians will come to recognize that the twin presence of Harvard and M.I.T. in the same place made Cambridge the most dangerous city in the whole United States, more than New York, Chicago, Miami or even Washington, D.C. It is ideas, ultimately, that restore or ruin the world, and in terms of the density of sinister thinking, much of which has been actualized in our own day, there are few places that compete with Cambridge : pragmatism, Skinner boxes, Behavioral Modification, Cybernetics, Artificial Intelligence, statistical control, transformational grammar, strategic hamlets, sociobiology, apologetics for nuclear power, electronic battlefields, Bean-Bayogian psychotherapies, etc., etc. Cambridge is decidedly not for the timid.

Quite apart from his theories and their "retroactive readjustment", the problem with all of McNamara's memoir is that he is one of those persons whose professional careers have so conditioned them to compulsive lying that they actually become incapable of formulating true statements. Were McNamara to be injected with a truth serum, sodium pentathol for example, nothing about him would change: his sincere state is one in which he is relentlessly speaking in falsehoods.

Despite all the apologetics and disclaimers in the memoir, McNamara was a ferocious, even demented, hawk, all through the Vietnamese war, and if he did express some reservations from time to time, it must only have been because he was afraid of the possible reckoning to come. It was certainly no accident that he was the person charged, on August 6th, 1964, by the Johnson administration to recount that monstrous fabrication of half-truths, fantasies and lies, the Vietnamese attack on the destroyer Maddox, that led to the Tonkin Bay resolution and the real escalation of the war.

On page 95, McNamara finds time to contribute his own opinions to the grey matter debate. He adds nothing new to what is already known and, as usual, is primarily concerned with covering his own ass:

"What would John F. Kennedy have done if he had lived? I have been asked that question countless times over the last thirty years. Thus far, I have refused to answer for two reasons: Apart from what I have related, the president did not tell me what he planned to do in the future....

"...But today I feel differently. Having reviewed the record in detail, and with the advantage of hindsight, I think it highly possible that, had President Kennedy lived, he would have pulled us out of Vietnam. He would have concluded that the South Vietnamese were incapable of defending themselves, and that Saigon's grave political weaknesses made it unwise to try to effect the limitation of South Vietnamese forces by sending U.S. combat troops on a large scale. I think that he would have come to that conclusion even if he reasoned, as I believe he would have, that South Vietnam and, ultimately, Southeast Asia, would then be lost to Communism.....

"...So I conclude that John Kennedy would have eventually gotten out of Vietnam rather than more deeply in. I express this judgment now because, in light of it, I must explain how and why we - including Lyndon Baines Johnson - who continued on in policy-making roles after President Kennedy's death made the decisions leading to the eventual deployment to Vietnam of half a million US combat troops."

It should come as no surprise to anyone that he finishes this passage by throwing the blame onto the shoulders of LBJ who, it could be argued, was only responding to the dubious statistics that McNamara was feeding him.

There is, in this entire book, only one passage that one can trust as being reasonably truthful. This is a transcription, on page 65, of a private memo sent by Kennedy to Henry Cabot Lodge in Saigon on September 17, 1963, the eve of the coup that ousted Diem and Nhu. I don't think that even McNamara would dare to tamper with the historical record, so we can assume that Kennedy really wrote the things that are presented here:

"CAP 63516

"EYES ONLY PERSONAL FOR AMBASSADOR LODGE. DEPT. PASS IMMEDIATELY. DELIVER ONLY COPY. NO OTHER DISTRIBUTION IN DEPT. WHATEVER, FROM THE PRESIDENT.

"*1. Highest level meeting today has approved broad outline of an action......program designed to obtain from GVN if possible, reforms and personnel necessary to maintain support of Vietnamese and US opinion in war against Viet Cong...*

"2. We see no good opportunity for action to remove present government in near future.

[...]

"4. (a). Diem should get everyone back to work and get them to focus on winning the war...A real spirit of reconciliation could work wonders on the people he leads; a punitive, harsh or autocratic attitude could only lead to further resistance.

"(b). Buddhists and students. Let them out and leave them unmolested. This more than anything else would demonstrate the return of a better day and the refocussing on the main object at hand - the war

[...]

"(d) Secret and combat police - Confine its role to operations against the VC - and abandon operations against non-Communist opposition groups thereby indicating clearly that a period of reconciliation and political stability has returned.

"5. Elections - These should be held, should be free, and should be widely observed.

"6. Specific reforms are apt to have little impact without dramatic, symbolic move which convinces Vietnamese that reforms are real...this we think would require Nhu's departure from Saigon and preferably Vietnam at least for extended vacation. We recognize the strong possibility that these and other pressures may not produce this result, but we are convinced that it is necessary to try.

"9. Meanwhile there is increasing concern here with strictly military aspects of the problem, both in terms of actual progress of operations and of need to make effective case with Congress for continued prosecution of the effort."

This memo is quite interesting, because it does lend some credence to Chomsky s view that Kennedy would not have pulled out the troops, but definitively refutes the notion that he supported the structure of a "terror state" and had no concern for human rights. The phrases highlighted in sections 5 and 6 are striking examples of black humor. They are a coded message for "dump the Diems," or it shows that Kennedy was living in a kind of cloud cuckoo land, quite typical of the American establishment which believes that, no matter what the realities of the situation, some naive application of "democracy" is a cure for all ills.

To conclude this comparative assessment of the views of Chomsky and McNamara as to what really happened in Vietnam, I should only state why I think that Chomsky's bitterness is to some degree understandable. This indeed gives his ideas some merit:

Chomsky is really angry at Kennedy because, being the ignorant preppy and self-styled liberal that he was, he didn't have the good sense to choose people like Chomsky for his Brain Trust, that group of intellectuals, largely associated with Boston and Cambridge who were given the privileged taste of real power for awhile as advisors to the president.

I agree with Chomsky in this matter. Who can seriously argue that an intelligent crank like Chomsky would not have been a better choice for Secretary of Defense than an utter dumbbell like McNamara? Or that a dedicated anarchist radical like Howard Zinn would not have forged a better foreign policy for us than a fatuous creep like McGeorge Bundy?

There exists in Boston and Cambridge (and in some other university circles), even today, a groaning, grumbling underground of embittered intellectuals, all mad as hell because the American government has never understood that they have to be mollified and ought to at least be listened to. Look at Mitterand's France, with its Pouvoir *Intellectuel*!

Among these we may count Chomsky, Zinn, Robert Coles, Seymour Mellman, Robert Jay Lifton, etc., etc...and, in the younger generation, myself; all of us so many guilt-ridden prophets of doom. You might call us the "Jercmiahs of the coffee table."

Shootings from the Hip and Shootings from the Lip But Jesse's Only Joking
by John Kimsey

It's Dec. 17th as I write this and the White House has just undergone its monthly dose of target practice. Yes, as of today, one more set of stray bullets has somehow found its way to within inches of the highest office in the land, this time while the first family slumbered inside the building, apparently undisturbed. According to CNN, the Secret Service is not sure whether this incident represents an act of aggression directed *against* the presidency per se; the latest bullets fired into the White House, they explain, may have been discharged in an unrelated—and unsolved—shooting which occurred nearby.

Yeah, right.

This is the third such incident in approximately three months: there was the plane crash/suicide incident of Sept. 12; the assault rifle attack of last month (recently confirmed as an actual assassination attempt) and now this. (*Steamshovel* Debris: On Dec. 20, yet another shooting occurred just outside the White House, this one by the police who shot and killed a homeless man. In the days following, another man with a gun was arrested trying to climb the White House fence and another, claiming wrongly to have a bomb in his car, also was arrested near the White House.)

Well, hey, what can you say? There is, after all, a "strong anti-Clinton sentiment" among the voters, chuckle some. Others observe that there are just a lot of lone nuts out there willing to take potshots at the president (a fact demonstrated, these folks sagely opine, by the history of the 1960s). Anyway, still others say, all these jokers *missed,* so what's the big deal?

Clearly though, a pattern is emerging, and it's a pattern worth looking at in context. Part of the context is the rhetoric that has been used, consistently, by prominent voices of the radical right. Three or so weeks ago, that underestimated wit Jesse Helms was quoted in a North Carolina newspaper as claiming that the anti-Clinton sentiment among military people of his close acquaintance was astonishingly high. (And by the way, *that's* a comforting democratic image, isn't it—an armed forces full of kissers-up to Jesse Helms?) This was a few days after Helms had stated, on network TV, that Clinton was unfit to be commander in chief. If, Helms told the newspaper, President Clinton comes down North Carolina way to inspect any goldang military bases, "He'd better bring a bodyguard."

Har de har. Beside being a US senator, Republican Helms is soon to be head of the Senate Foreign Relations Committee, one of the most powerful positions in government. Consequently, a few complaints were heard (from some pedantic nitpickers, one imagines) about the voicing of such sentiments by a person with so much power and responsibility. When the tiny squeaks of disapproval emerged in the press a few days later, Helms—and numerous prominent defenders—were quick to say that the Senator had only been joking, speaking off the cuff, etc. and anyway, who do these media types think they are, roasting a loud-mouthed racist cracker politician for just doing what comes naturally?

But in fact, most of what passed for "criticism" simply ascribed the remark to Helms' quaint, wacky way of expressing himself, to his abrasive, call-'em-like-he-sees-'em style, so offensive to snooty liberal types, but much beloved by his populist constituency. Here is journalist John Monk, in a widely circulated story from the Knight-Ridder news service:

Helms is known for standing his conservative ground
—ripping liberal targets with passionate. . .attacks that frequently offended. . . .

At the same time, he has pleased many Americans who felt he was voicing truths that other politicians were afraid to utter.

Such conduct, the commentators further suggested, was deplorable, but mostly because it was *declasse*—vulgar and embarrassing, like breaking wind in a confessional booth.

Of course, Helms does have a history of making bigoted, unfunny "jokes" and spewing ultra-rightist insults at liberal icons. This is the distinguished gentleman who, after a Senate debate about the use of the Confederate flag as a state symbol, stood in an elevator singing "Dixie" in the face of Sen. Carol Moseley Braun, saying he was going to keep doing so "until she cries." And this is the American statesman who argued against the establishment of a national holiday in honor of Dr. Martin Luther King because King was, he alleged, a communist sympathizer who had "hostility to and hatred for America."

Such are the "truths" that other politicians are, in journalist Monk's words, "afraid to utter." Of course,

David Duke, a politician—as well as ex-Nazi and ex-Klansman—utters such "truths" all the time, so perhaps, while we're at it, we should applaud him as well for fearlessly speaking the "truth." Why, veritable Ministers of Truth they are, Helms and Duke, worthy of the Ministry of Truth in George Orwell's *1984*. Its motto was "War is peace, freedom is slavery, ignorance is strength." Its stock in trade—shades of current talk radio—was a state-controlled exercise in demonization called the "Two-Minute Hate". A strained comparison? Not to worry; like other eminent truth-speakers, I'm only joking.

Yet Helms is a man who, in other contexts, has expressed grave fears about the power of words and images to harm or corrupt, and about the fragility of American institutions in the face of free speech irresponsibly wielded. This is, after all, the man who made an enormous national issue of the "degenerate art" of Robert Mapplethorpe and Andres Serrano, and who loudly questioned the right of such expressions to even exist. According to Helms, the utterances of Mapplethorpe and Serrano—even though made in complex images rather than words, in art galleries rather than the national press and before an audience a fraction of the size of the Senator's own—were dangerous threats to American values, assaults on our very way of life.

Unlike, say, a US senator making threats on the life of the president.

And this in a country where a Surgeon General can be hounded from office by a reactionary lobby because her sane, scientifically nuanced remarks (take a look at what she really said, as opposed to the caricature painted by right-wing propagandists) about AIDS and drug policy offended said lobby's twelfth-century sensibilities.

Had she just sung "Dixie," maybe Dr. Elders could have kept her job. It seems to have worked for Jesse.

But let us pause, for if we take up double standards here, we'll never see the end of it. Can you imagine the firestorm if a Democrat had said about a Republican president what Helms did about Clinton? Or consider the following: Early reports on last month's assault rifle assassination attempt by Francisco Duran noted that Duran's pickup truck was plastered with right-wing Limbaugh-oid bumper stickers and slogans, a detail that was quickly dropped from subsequent reports on the incident. Imagine what the coverage—or the treatment of the alleged assailant—would have been like had he been a leftist.

The past year has seen other such "incidents." Last January, Ronald Gene Barbour, an unemployed limousine driver from Orlando, FL, was arrested on a charge of threatening to kill Clinton. Armed with a .45 caliber automatic pistol, Barber was loitering suspiciously around Clinton's jogging routes, this after being overheard threatening to kill the president. And Barbour, it turns out, is a big Dittohead. In a story carried by both *New York Newsday* and the *Flush Rush Quarterly*, the jailed Barbour is quoted as telling Washington's WUSA-TV,

"I like Rush, I sure do. I love his polemics on Clinton. He's a disgrace to the country. He should be where I'm at. He's a criminal. He's a public enemy."

Of course, Limbaugh has run a nonstop campaign to demonize the Clintons, regularly referring to them as an alien occupational force and describing America as "held hostage by Clintonistas." Now this might seem like a call for some "patriot" to Stand Up and Do the Right Thing. But, lest you think Limbaugh is inciting violence, Rush assures us that, like Sen. Helms, he is only joking. He is, after all, merely an entertainer.

But make no mistake, such remarks, uttered widely and without cease by prominent people, help create the climate in which such incidents occur. Sure, these guys may be lone nuts, but even if they are, one has to wonder what it takes to tip them over the edge and in the direction of shooting at the president. Continual references to Clinton as an "enemy of the American people," endless smears, jokes about him needing bodyguards—these may well serve such a function. This is the purpose of all campaigns of demonization (consider the Nazi propaganda about Jews): to make violence against the targeted individual or group more conceivable, possible and, finally, permissible.

Consider the case of President Kennedy. When he arrived in Dallas on Nov. 22, 1963, he was greeted by a newspaper ad calling him a communist collaborator as well as by ubiquitous posters displaying his picture, mugshot style, under the heading, "Wanted For Treason." And at this point in Kennedy's controversial tenure, this sort of thing was nothing new. In April 1963, an anonymous flier had been circulated among Miami's Cuban exile community that read:

"Only through one development will you Cuban patriots ever live again in your homeland as free men.

"Only if an inspired Act of God should place in the White House within weeks a Texan known to be a friend of all Latin Americans."

The implied question: Who will rid us of this troublesome president? And no matter whether you think Kennedy was killed by a lone nut or a conspiracy, you have to wonder whether such a climate did not contribute to making the assassination conceivable, possible and, finally, permissible in the mind or minds of whoever was behind it.

With amusement that is almost palpable, the Knight-Ridder story describes Helms as a tough customer who "shoots from the lip." In a country that prizes free speech, even intolerant dogmatists like Helms, Limbaugh and Pat Robertson—no friends of certain kinds of speech—have the right to speak their tiny minds. They may indeed "shoot from the lip" with unsubstantiated smears and provocative remarks about Clinton's fitness, patriotism and personal safety. When others start shooting from assault rifles with bullets, we can comfort ourselves in the knowledge that Helms, Limbaugh and company were only joking.

Now: all rise for the Two-Minute Hate.

Contributor Notes

The information on the contributors to this volume appearing at the end of their contribution is current as of the time listed at the beginning of the chapter containing that contribution. The following contains current information from as many contributors as responded to a query sent out to all who have written for *Steamshovel Press* in preparation for *Popular Alienation*:

Len Bracken: Writer, Usefulness of Conspiracy Theory, POB 5585, Arlington, VA 22205.

Scott Corrales: Technical translation, Spanish to English; Scott Corrales Writing Consultants, POB 228, Derrick City, PA 16727-0228.

Jim Cregan: Can be reached at Jim Cregan Publications, c/o Overseas Book Service, Via Quadri 9, 40126, Bologna, Italy.

X. Sharks DeSpot: X. Sharks DeSpot has written articles about cattle mutilations, UFOs, and the late conspiratologist Mae Brussell for *Steamshovel Press*. He's also written about the mass media for *Crash Collusion*, and contributed to Jim Keith's *The Gemstone File*. He lives in Michigan.

Tom Flynn: Senior Editor of *Free Inquiry*, founding co-editor of *Secular Humanist Bulletin*, and director of Inquiry Media Productions. POB 664, Amherst, NY 14226-0664.

John Hayward: Would appreciate any materials on the Shroud to be forwarded in care of *Steamshovel Press*.

Dr. Wayne Henderson: Currently involved in several projects, including an in-depth historical analysis of the development of secret societies as an outgrowth of the early (paleo- & mesolithic) socioreligious structures of the marginal isolates and a novel (his first) based on the Green River Killings. Dr. Henderson's current business address is: c/o C.G. Hodges, 1268 Main Street, #176, Tewksbury, MA 01876.

Bob Heyer: Currently music teacher in St. Louis, MO; also performs rock and folk in clubs; composes songs for himself and other artists; performs with various musicians; appears on local cable as music/cultural historian.

Paul Kangas: Book: *The Role of George Bush and Richard Nixon in the Assassination of President John Kennedy and Dr. Martin Luther King*. POB 422644, San Francisco, CA 94142; 415-298-4882; fax: 415-864-3389.

Jim Keith: Multiple amputee fetishism; *business address:* a particularly run-down mobile in the world's largest trailer court.

John Kimsey: Writer, musician and teacher. He lives and works in Chicago, and he can be contacted c/o *Steamshovel Press*.

Roy Lisker: Well-qualified in his professional specialty in which he can, with justice, look upon himself as something of a pioneer: Applied Mathematics for the Arts. He entered the University of Pennsylvania at age 15, in an advanced program in mathematics especially created for him. He lived in France from 1968 to 1972, and again in 1988-89. In 1989 he translated two textbooks from French for the English scientific publishing house, Ellis Horwood: *Radiological Medicine* by Drs. Gambini and Garnier, and *Information Theory* by Jacques Oswald. His own research, in mathematics and mathematical physics, has been presented at conferences and colloquia in Sweden, France, Ireland, Puerto Rico and the U.S., and he has written extensively on the sciences for the educated public. His principal activity continues to be literary, and he has done work in every medium: fiction and non-fiction, poetry, theater, film, journalism and translations. He may be reached at 12 Frazier Ave., Middletown, CT 06457.

Tom Lyttle: Contact PM & E Publishing Group, POB 4465, Boynton Beach, FL 33424.

Jim Martin: Responsible for the graphic design of *Steamshovel Press* since issue #8, Jim Martin also publishes *Flatland Magazine* and runs the Flatland mail-order book service, POB 2420, Dept. PA, Fort Bragg, CA 95437.

William P. Meyers: The force behind III Publishing, bringing you books satirical, anti-authoritarian fiction and non-fiction. He also publishes *The Stake* magazine. III Publishing, POB 1581, Gualal, CA 95445.

Raliegh Muns: *Fugitive Pope*

Timothy J. O'Neill: Director, Athanor Institute, an educational organization devoted to the study of Gnosticism, Hermeticism, Alchemy, Rosicrucianism, Illuminism and Freemasonry. Current projects include: *Inside AMORC,* the true story of Modern Rosicrucianism; *UFOs and the Illuminati, The Way of the Circle*; *The Theory and Practice of Spiritual Alchemy*; and *A Flame in the Mountain: Collected Essays 1985-1995* (all book length). Athanor Institute, 236 West Portal Avenue, Suite 106, San Francisco, CA 94127.

Kenn Thomas: Edits and publishes *Steamshovel Press,* a journal that examines arcane historical and political topics, listed in *JFK-The Book of the Film* as a key source for information on the Kennedy assassination, also noted in such books as *Secret and Suppressed* and *The 50 Greatest Conspiracies of All Time,* and in the journals *Smithsonian, Puck, Midweek, The New York Times, The Chicago Tribune* and the *Washington Post.* Currently at work on a book about Danny Casolaro and INSLAW, Mr. Thomas has lectured on that subject, as well the life and career of psychologist Wilhelm Reich (the subject of a recent FOIPA request by Thomas), current in JFK research and UFOs at such venues as Atlanta's Phenomicon and the International UFO Congress in Las Vegas. He is available for future lectures through *Steamshovel,* POB 23715, St. Louis, MO 63121.

Timothy L. Wheeler: Editor, *People's Weekly World,* 235 W. 23rd Street, New York, NY 10011.

Jack White: Jack White's photoanalysis has proved beyond a doubt that the famous "backyard photos" of Lee Harvey Oswald are clever forgeries used to incriminate Oswald by the planners of President Kennedy's execution. White served as consultant to the HSCA because of his expertise in photography and photoanalysis, and testified regarding his research on these mysterious photos. He makes available two videos, *Fake* and *The Many Faces of Lee Harvey Oswald,* and a research poster, *The Evolution of Lee Harvey Oswald.* 704 Candlewood Road, Fort Worth, TX 76103.

Robert Anton Wilson: *Trajectories* newsletter, $20/4 issues; POB 700305, San Jose, CA 95170.

Appendix A

Please Note: This issue is not included with this volume. It is available at all good alternative book stores and news stands (if you can't find it, complain!), or order for $5 from *Steamshovel Press,* POB 23715, St. Louis, MO 63121. Subscriptions: Four issues, $22

Steamshovel Press #12, **1995**

A Day In The Life: Newly Declassified Document on Wilhelm Reich
The Persian Gulf Syndrome
    by Alan Cantwell
Robert Anton Wilson and Beyond, An Interview
    by Kenn Thomas
Off (With) The Top of My Head
    by Bob Harris

Saucer Section:
A New View of Bill Cooper
The Hoax On You: Before There Was The Crash At Roswell, There Was...Maury Island
    by Ron Halbritter
A Lineman For Lincoln County, Area 51's Glenn Campbell Interviewed

Response To Jim Keith
    by William Bramley
Whitewater and the Mysterious Fifty Million Dollars
    by Sherman Skolnick
"this is my last letter" Tarantula Returns
    by Jenny Ledeen
Mexico '94, A Pre-Election Analysis by Milvia Archilla
    As Translated by Scott Corrales

Book Reviews

Caries, Cabals and Correspondence

Things Are Gonna Slide

Steamshovel Press

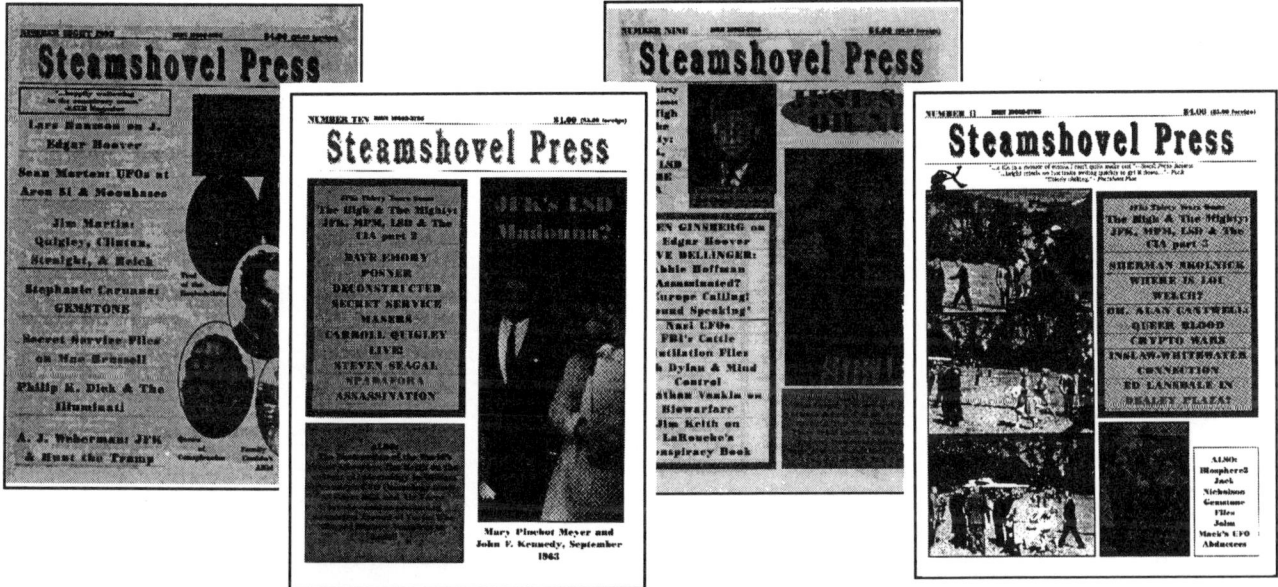

"...on the cutting edge - and a strange place that is..." **—New Yorker**

"...unbelievably important research that establishment magazines don't have the cojones to publish..." **—Adam Parfrey in** *Utne Reader*

Hopefully, *Popular Alienation* has demonstrated that *Steamshovel Press* explores theories that are farther out, with writing more comprehensive, and research better documented than virtually anything coming down the conspiracy pipeline. It is not available in bookstore where the conspiracy prevails, so to ensure that you do not miss an issue, order the latest one, or subscribe today!

Name:_____

Street:_____

City:_____ State: _____Zip:_____

Single Issue: $4.50 plus $1.00 postage and handling

Subscriptions: $22.00